Japanese Aircraft
of the Pacific War

Marine aircraft played a big part in the Pacific War. Japanese Navy Aichi E13A1a Navy Type 0 Reconnaissance Seaplane Model 11As are seen here in formation. (*US Navy Department.*)

CONTENTS

Preface	xi
Japanese Aircraft Industry—A Brief History	1
Japanese Army Air Force—A Brief History	29
Japanese Navy Air Force—A Brief History	37
Japanese Aircraft Designation Systems	46
Japanese Aircraft Camouflage and Markings	60

Imperial Japanese Army Aircraft

  Kawasaki

Ki-10	86
Ki-32	90
Ki-45 Toryu (Dragon Killer)	93
Ki-48	102
Ki-56	108
Ki-60	110
Ki-61 Hien (Swallow)	112
Ki-64	121
Ki-66	123
Ki-78	125
Ki-96	127
Ki-100	129
Ki-102	134
Ki-108	138
Ki-119	141

  Kayaba

Ka-1 and Ka-2	143

  Kokusai

Ki-59	145
Ki-76	147

  Mitsubishi

Ki-15 and C5M	149
Ki-21	155
Ki-30	164
Ki-46	168

Ki-51	178
Ki-57	182
Ki-67 Hiryu (Flying Dragon)	186
Ki-83	192
Ki-109	194

Nakajima
Ki-27	196
Ki-34	204
Ki-43 Hayabusa (Peregrine Falcon)	206
Ki-44 Shoki (Devil-Queller)	215
Ki-49 Donryu (Storm Dragon)	223
Ki-84 Hayate (Gale)	230
Ki-87	238
Ki-115 Tsurugi (Sabre)	241

Rikugun
Ki-93	244

Tachikawa
Ki-9	246
Ki-17	248
Ki-36 and Ki-55	250
Ki-54	254
Ki-70	257
Ki-74	259
Ki-77	262
Ki-94	265

Imperial Japanese Navy Aircraft

Aichi
D1A	268
D3A	271
E13A	277
H9A	281
E16A Zuiun (Auspicious Cloud)	284
B7A Ryusei (Shooting Star)	288
M6A Seiran (Mountain Haze)	291
S1A Denko (Bolt of Light)	295

Kawanishi
E7K	297
H6K	301
H8K	307
E15K Shiun (Violet Cloud)	314
N1K Kyofu (Mighty Wind)	317
N1K1-J Shiden (Violet Lightning) and N1K2-J Shiden Kai	320

Kyushu
- K11W Shiragiku (White Chrysanthemum) — 330
- Q1W Tokai (Eastern Sea) — 332
- J7W Shinden (Magnificent Lightning) — 335

Mitsubishi
- K3M — 339
- A5M — 342
- G3M — 350
- F1M — 358
- A6M Reisen (Zero Fighter) — 362
- G4M — 378
- J2M Raiden (Thunderbolt) — 388
- A6M2-K and A6M5-K — 397
- A7M Reppu (Hurricane) — 399
- J8M Shusui (Sword Stroke) — 404

Nakajima
- E8N — 408
- B5N — 411
- J1N Gekko (Moonlight) — 417
- G5N Shinzan (Mountain Recess) — 423
- A6M2-N — 426
- B6N Tenzan (Heavenly Mountain) — 429
- C6N Saiun (Painted Cloud) — 434
- G8N Renzan (Mountain Range) — 440
- Kikka (Orange Blossom) — 443

Yokosuka
- K5Y — 446
- B4Y — 449
- E14Y — 451
- D4Y Suisei (Comet) — 454
- P1Y Ginga (Milky Way) — 462
- D3Y Myojo (Venus) — 469
- R2Y Keiun (Beautiful Cloud) — 472
- MXY7 Ohka (Cherry Blossom) — 476

Appendix A—Lesser Types; Imperial Japanese Army

Kawasaki
- Ki-88 — 483
- Ki-91 — 484

Kokusai
- Ku-8 — 484
- Ku-7 Manazuru (Crane) — 485
- Ki-105 Ohtori (Phoenix) — 485

Mansyu	
Ki-79	486
Ki-98	486
Nakajima	
Ki-19	487
Ki-62	487
Ki-201 Karyu (Fire Dragon)	488
Tokyo Koku	
Ki-107	488

Appendix B—Lesser Types; Imperial Japanese Navy

Aichi	
E11A1	489
Kawanishi	
J3K1/J6K1 Jinpu (Squall)	490
Baika (Plum Blossom)	490
Mitsubishi	
B5M1	491
J4M1 Senden (Flashing Lightning)	491
Nakajima	
J5N1 Tenrai (Heavenly Thunder)	492
G10N1 Fugaku (Mount Fuji)	493
Yokosuka	
K2Y1/K2Y2	493
K4Y1	494
H5Y1	495

Appendix C—Foreign-designed Aircraft	496
Douglas DC-2	498
Douglas L2D	499
Kyushu K9W Momiji (Maple) and Kokusai Ki-86	503
Kyushu K10W1	506
Lockheed Type LO	507
Appendix D—Aircraft Carriers, Seaplane and Flying-boat Tenders, and Aircraft-carrying Submarines	510
Appendix E—Japanese Aero-engines	515
Appendix F—Japanese Aircraft Armament and Guided Missiles	526

Designation Index	534
Imperial Japanese Army	535
Kitai numbers	535
Guraida numbers	539
Kazaguruma numbers	540
Sundry designation numbers	540
Type numbers	540
Popular names	543
Imperial Japanese Navy	544
Shi numbers	544
Short designation system	549
Type numbers	557
Foreign aircraft	560
Popular names	561
Miscellaneous and Unofficial names	564
Service Aeroplane Development Programme numbers	565
Allied Code name system	566

PREFACE

During the 1930s, while their armed forces were involved in several fighting incidents on the Asiatic mainland, the Japanese, guided by the slogan 'Every foreigner is a spy', established a strong security system which successfully hid the qualitative and quantitative build-up of their air forces. So effective was this system that in 1941, shortly before the Japanese attacks against the Allies, it was commonly believed—even among military intelligence circles in the Western Hemisphere—that Japan possessed only a motley collection of obsolete aircraft copied from imported types.

It is true that Japan cannot claim a place among the leading nations contributing to the initial development of aviation but, by the late thirties, the country had created an efficient aircraft industry which designed and produced several formidable types which surprised the Allies when the Japanese forces overran the Southeast Asia and Southwest Pacific areas. Throughout the war, despite the introduction of the effective Allied code name system, identification of Japanese aircraft remained spotty at best. Non-existing types were reported while new aircraft were introduced by the Japanese without much advance data being available to Allied personnel. Now, some twenty-five years after the end of the Pacific War, little is remembered of the Japanese air forces and, with the exception of such legendary aircraft as the Zero (Mitsubishi A6M series) and the BETTY (Mitsubishi G4M series), their aircraft have once again faded into oblivion.

This book was conceived to provide, between the covers of a single volume, a compact history of all aircraft types operated by or designed for the Imperial Japanese Army and the Imperial Japanese Navy during the Pacific War. As little or no information regarding the Japanese aircraft industry is readily available separate sections have been included to provide a more complete historical analysis of Japanese military aviation during the second World War.

The first section is devoted to a brief history of the Japanese aircraft industry and includes a synopsis of major airframe and engine manufacturers in Japan. Two brief sections, respectively devoted to the history of the air arms of the Imperial Japanese Army and Navy, follow and provide a record of unit structure during the Pacific War. These three historical sections are followed by another dealing with the numerous Japanese military aircraft designation systems. Finally, the last introductory section deals with the fundamental camouflage and marking systems adopted by both Japanese Services during the war.

The main part of this work comprises descriptive text, technical data, photographs and multi-view drawings* of the most important operational aircraft and of the most significant experimental types. These descriptions are arranged in two main parts: Part I covering the aircraft designed for the Imperial Japanese Army and Part II the aircraft designed for the Imperial Japanese Navy. In each of these parts the manufacturers are listed alphabetically according to the best-known abbreviated names (e.g. aircraft designed by the Dai-Ichi Kaigun Koku Gijitsusho are found in Part II under the heading: Yokosuka) and the aircraft are listed chronologically under each manufacturer.

It has not been possible to give complete details of the units with which each type of aircraft served but representative units have been listed wherever possible.

Six appendices complete the book and respectively describe the less important types designed for the Imperial Japanese Army; the less important aircraft designed for the Imperial Japanese Navy; the types of foreign manufacture which contributed significantly to Japanese aircraft development immediately before World War II or which were built in Japan for use by Japanese military forces; the Japanese aero-engines; the Japanese aircraft weapons; and the Japanese aircraft carriers and tenders. Finally a very detailed Designation Index is provided for ease of reference.

The preparation of this book was only made possible by the understanding and help of my wife. Early in our marriage she realized the importance of this project in my life. Always I found her ready to help and advise and often, when the task appeared too heavy, she was ready to encourage me. Throughout these years I too often deprived her and our children of much needed vacation, but not once did she voice her disappointment.

Among those who helped materially in the preparation of this book I wish to single out my good friend Jim Roberts who prepared the line drawings and other illustrations found herein. Not once did I have to remind him of our schedule, and his work was an inspiration for my share of the task. Among the many other persons whose help I gratefully acknowledge are Mrs Tamaki Watanabe and Lee Yokota who helped me with the translation of countless documents. Data and photographs were generously contributed by Jiro Horikoshi, Syoichi Tanaka, Takeshi Hattori, Allan Bovelt, Richard Ward, Herbert Heckert, Francis Williams, William Green, Richard M. Bueschel and the staff of the Japanese magazines *Aireview*, *Koku Fan* and *Maru*.

I also wish to thank my many friends in Profile Publications, and in particular Francis K. Mason, Edward Shacklady and Martin C. Windrow. The encouragement of such noted writers helped me immensely throughout the years. Last but not least among individuals who stood behind me

* In certain of the general arrangement drawings some float attachment struts have, for the sake of simplicity, been omitted from the underside views. In the split plan views pitot heads have not always been shown in both views.

is my very good friend H. L. James; without Harry I would never have found the fortitude to write this book in a language other than my native French.

Finally I wish to express my deepest gratitude to the staff of the Magazine and Book Division of the Office of the Secretary of Defense, of the US National Archives and of the Library of Congress as well as to personnel from the United States Armed Forces who helped me so much in gathering material and photographs used throughout. At a time when it is fashionable to discredit military personnel and civil servants I want to express my most sincere admiration for their work and to thank each and every one of them for their kind co-operation.

R. J. F.

Mentone, California, 1969

Japanese Aircraft Industry
A Brief History

At the time of the Nipponese attacks against the Allies—even though Japan had been conducting extensive air operations over China for four and a half years—her aircraft industry was considerably underrated by the Western Powers. The prevailing opinion expressed by self-proclaimed experts was that the Japanese were mainly producing copies of obsolete foreign-designed aircraft. Indeed Japan had established its aircraft industry in this fashion and until shortly before the beginning of the war kept importing foreign aircraft to provide yardsticks by which to evaluate her own aircraft.

Following the swift Japanese advance in the first six months of the Pacific War, the Allies painfully had to reappraise the potential of their new enemy and the previously prevailing feeling of superiority gave place to a healthy respect for the capabilities of Japan's aircraft industry and airmen.

Still later, when the stupendous industrial power of the United States enabled the Allies to obtain complete numerical and qualitative superiority over the Japanese air forces, the feeling changed again to one of superiority and the Japanese aircraft and their manufacturers were once more belittled. To this day this attitude prevails and the Japanese aircraft industry is thought of by laymen as one with great ability to make poor copies of obsolete Western aircraft and to produce original designs characterized by their extreme flimsiness and propensity to catch fire and explode when hit.

The purpose of this brief history of the Japanese aircraft industry is to present an objective historical analysis of its achievements and problems and to provide details of the manufacturers which designed and built the aircraft described in the main body of the book.

Origin and Prewar Development

As early as April 1891 an enterprising Japanese, Chuhachi Ninomiya, succeeded in flying a rubber-powered model aeroplane. Later he designed a larger model powered by a watch spring driving a pusher propeller and successfully demonstrated the flying abilities of his aircraft. However, the Imperial Japanese Army showed little interest in these experiments and Ninomiya gave up his attempt to develop a Japanese flying machine.

In 1910 two Army officers were sent to Europe to learn to fly and, on 19 December, 1910, respectively demonstrated their ability in Japan by flying their imported Henri Farman and Grade aeroplanes. The era of heavier-than-air had begun in Japan. Less than a year later one of these officers, Captain Tokugawa, designed an improved variant of the imported Henri Farman biplane which, built by the Army balloon unit at Nakano, near Tokyo, became the first aircraft built in Japan.

Following the purchase of several types of foreign-built aircraft and the manufacture in Japan of modified versions of these aircraft, the first operational aircraft of Japanese design, the Type Yokosho float biplane, designed by First Lieutenant Chikuhei Nakajima and Second Lieutenant Kishichi Magoshi, was built in 1916.

The 'Big Three' of the Japanese aircraft industry, Mitsubishi, Nakajima and Kawasaki, began to operate in the late 1910s. The Mitsubishi and Kawasaki aircraft activities were started as departments of the heavy industries of the same name while Nakajima, independent of direct connection with other industry, was originally financed by the powerful Mitsui family.

For the next fifteen years these manufacturers depended essentially on foreign technology and French, English and German technicians helped to establish a domestic aircraft industry. At the same time young Japanese technicians were studying in American factories and top engineering schools. However, by the early 1930s Japanese Army and Navy officials were determined that the Japanese aircraft industry stand on its own feet, and they established a policy of self-sufficiency whereby only aircraft and engines of Japanese design would be considered. This, however, did not prevent Japanese technical missions from continuing to buy foreign aircraft and aircraft equipment which helped the Japanese industry to acquire new techniques.

By 1936 this policy was vindicated and the Japanese were independently

The Mitsubishi MC-21, a modified Ki-21-I, operated as a freight transport between Japan and China.

Kamikaze (*Divine Wind*), the second prototype of the Mitsubishi Ki-15 series, which made a record flight from Japan to London in April 1937. (*US Navy Department*.)

producing several types of military aircraft—among which were the Mitsubishi Ki-21 and G3M1 twin-engined bombers, Mitsubishi Ki-15 reconnaissance aircraft, Nakajima B5N1 carrier-based bomber and the Mitsubishi A5M1 carrier-based fighter—equal and often superior to contemporary foreign aircraft.

From 1937 onwards, following the outbreak of the second Sino-Japanese conflict, the Japanese aircraft industry was shrouded in purposeful secrecy and production began to increase sharply. In 1938 a new law went into effect requiring that all aircraft companies capitalized at three million yen or more be licensed by the government and controlled as to equipment, techniques and production plans. The law encouraged and protected such companies by exempting them from income and business taxes and export duties.

In March of 1941 the industry was given a last prewar expansion boost by the government, and the Imperial Japanese Army and Navy gave several companies definite orders to expand. The Japanese Government did not furnish the capital to cover the expense but did guarantee loans made through industrial banks. Furthermore, the Army and the Navy, which owned and controlled a pool of machine tools, leased or loaned this equipment to the different aircraft manufacturers in accordance with their needs. But Army machine tools could not be used for naval production and vice versa.

During that period the Army and the Navy set up inspection procedures and developed standards for acceptance of all classes of aeronautical material. Technical representatives and inspectors were stationed in the factories to see that standards of quality were maintained. These officers also acted as advisers to the plant managers. As a result of this system, the Services had a great deal of power and virtually controlled the management of the plants.

The effectiveness of these various measures can be judged from the fact that Japanese aircraft production experienced a three-fold increase between 1931 and 1936 and again a four-fold increase between 1936 and 1940 (*see Table I*).

TABLE I: JAPANESE AIRCRAFT PRODUCTION, 1930–45

Year	Number of Aircraft	Year	Number of Aircraft
1930	445	1938	3,201
1931	368	1939	4,467
1932	691	1940	4,768
1933	766	1941	5,088
1934	688	1942	8,861
1935	952	1943	16,693
1936	1,181	1944	28,180
1937	1,511	1945	11,066

Source: United States Strategic Bombing Survey.

FIGURE I: GROWTH OF JAPANESE AIRCRAFT PRODUCTION, 1930–45

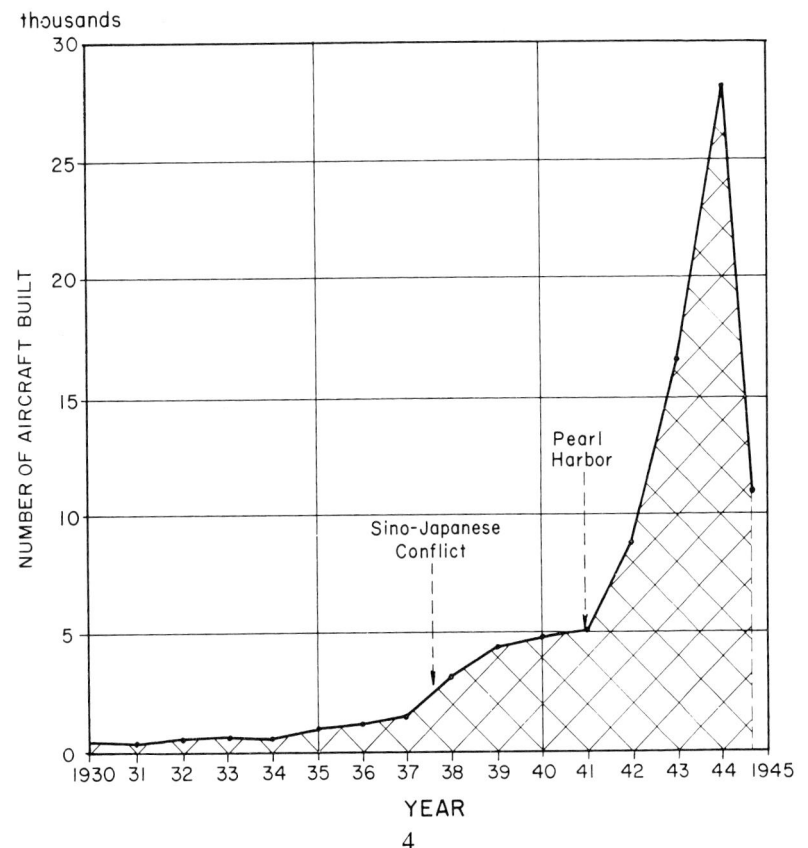

The Japanese Aircraft Industry during the Pacific War

With the outbreak of war the Services continued on the same general procurement programme but on an expanded scale. The Imperial Japanese Army and Navy headquarters independently contracted with the individual manufacturers, and most of the time the interest of each Service conflicted. What they lacked was effective liaison. As might have been expected, difficulties appeared.

Already in the latter part of 1941 certain materials became critical. Even at this early date problems resulting from control and allocation became increasingly difficult. As a result, the Army and Navy each organized their own control of raw material within their own sphere of influence and set up two general categories for material allocation, (1) materials for production and (2) materials for expansion. Based on the schedule of aircraft desired for the coming fiscal year, headquarters then allotted the material available to the manufacturers on the basis of their requirements. Orders for parts and components (for spares and for production) were issued from air headquarters direct to the manufacturers.

The material problem was further complicated by a persistent labour problem as neither the Army nor the Navy made any attempt to control or allocate labour. Manufacturers had to get along as well as they could in recruiting and training people for their plants. With notable lack of foresight, the armed Services complicated the labour problem tremendously by making continual drafts against the civilian labour forces without regard to skills or to industry requirements.

The Kawasaki Ki-32 light bomber resulted from a specification issued in May 1936. In 1942 Ki-32s were relegated to training duties. (*US Navy Department.*)

In an attempt to unify and simplify the production of military goods and military raw materials and to expedite the production of aircraft, the Japanese Government set up in November 1943 a Munitions Ministry designed to administer all matters dealing with production, including the control of labour and the allocation of raw materials.

In order to co-ordinate aircraft industrial capacity and needs, the Munitions Ministry set up a system for determining production requirements. The Imperial General Staff decided on the number of aircraft required for the tactical situation and sent a proposed programme to the Navy and War Ministers who in turn would approve and forward the plan to the Munitions Ministry and Army and Navy air headquarters for procurement. The Ministry then discussed the programme with the aircraft manufacturers with reference to expansion, materials, employees, machine tools and equipment. The manufacturers would then review their capacity and send an ability report to the Munitions Ministry. The Ministry and the Navy and Army air headquarters then decided together on monthly production programmes for each company which were forwarded to them by the Munitions Ministry.

The first low-wing monoplane fighter to enter service with the Japanese Navy was Mitsubishi's Navy Type 96 Carrier Fighter. The example illustrated is an A5M4 with under-fuselage fuel tank. (*US Navy Department.*)

For production purposes aircraft parts were broken down by the Munitions Ministry into three classes: (1) controlled parts, (2) government-co-ordinated parts and (3) government-supplied parts. Controlled parts (bolts, nuts, springs, etc) were made under government supervision but were distributed as required by the manufacturers. For government-co-ordinated parts (coolers, pumps, carburettors, etc) production orders were issued to certain accessories companies for delivery to aircraft or engine manufacturers for inclusion in final assemblies. Government-supplied parts (wheels, sparking plugs, guns, radios, etc) were ordered directly by the government and delivered to the government for distribution.

The Mitsubishi A6M Navy Type 0 Carrier Fighter Reisen (Zero Fighter) was built in greater numbers than any other Japanese type, and it served with front-line units throughout the war. Illustrated is a Model 21 aircraft. (*USAF.*)

At the time the Munitions Ministry was formed, an order was issued stopping any new expansion of aircraft plants. It was felt that there was plenty of plant space and that the big need was to increase efficiency in existing plants. In order to strengthen the control and administration of factories, various officials attached to the Commerce and Industry Ministry, the Welfare Ministry and the plant supervisors from the Imperial Japanese Army and Navy were combined and administered by district offices directly attached to the Munitions Ministry.

In spite of this elaborate system to control the industry by an impartial body, the Army and the Navy continued to exert undue influence, placing their own supervisors in the aircraft, engine and aircraft component factories and doing what they could to keep the more important factories under their control. Especially with respect to armament, parts and raw materials for aircraft production, the Imperial Japanese Army and the Imperial Japanese Navy set up their own plans and did not even give any details to the Munitions Ministry.

Despite the feud between the Army and the Navy and the tremendous odds under which the Munitions Ministry had to operate, the Japanese aircraft industry was able to increase its output steadily between 1941 and 1944 (*see Table II and Figures II and III*). In particular in 1944, the only

A radar-equipped Nakajima B5N2 undergoing evaluation tests at Anacostia Naval Air Station. (*US Navy Department.*)

TABLE II: JAPANESE AIRCRAFT, ENGINE AND PROPELLER PRODUCTION
JANUARY 1941–AUGUST 1945

	1941	1942	1943	1944	1945
Aircraft					
Fighters	1,080	2,935	7,147	13,811	5,474
Bombers	1,461	2,433	4,189	5,100	1,934
Reconnaissance	639	967	2,070	2,147	855
Trainers	1,489	2,171	2,871	6,147	2,523
Others*	419	355	416	975	280
Total	5,088	8,861	16,693	28,180	11,066
Engines	12,151	16,999	28,541	46,526	12,360
Propellers	12,621	22,362	31,703	54,452	19,922

Source: United States Strategic Bombing Survey.

* Including flying-boats, transports, gliders and suicide aircraft.

FIGURE II : JAPANESE AIRCRAFT PRODUCTION BY CLASS OF AIRCRAFT, 1941–45

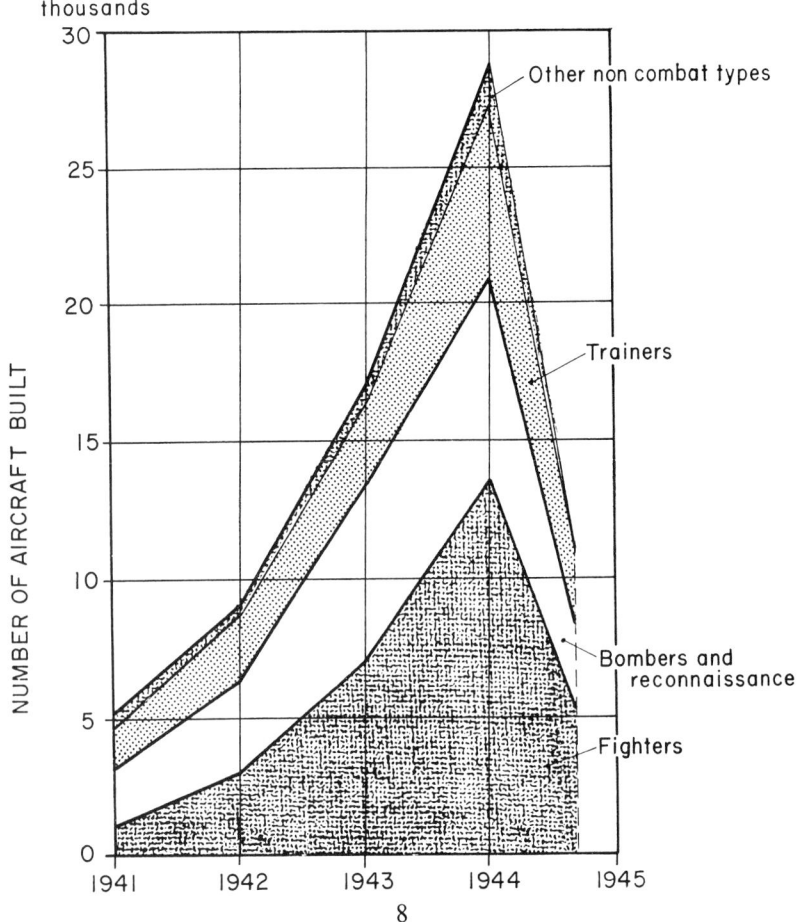

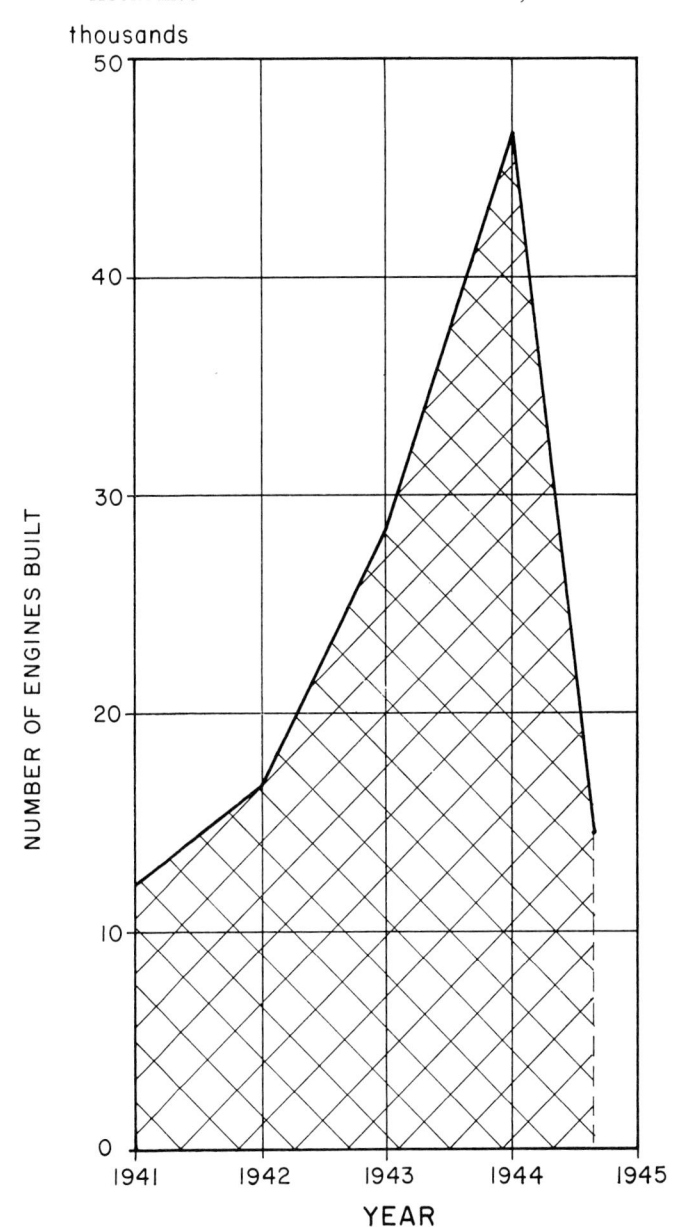

FIGURE III: JAPANESE AERO-ENGINE PRODUCTION, 1941–45

full year during which the Munitions Ministry was at least nominally in control of the industry, aircraft production registered an increase of 69 per cent over the previous year's figure, and the comparable increases in engine and propeller production were respectively 63 per cent and 70 per cent.

Even though these results were impressive they were far short of what was needed to keep up with the tremendous power of Japan's enemies. Between 1941 and 1945 the United States alone built more aircraft than Japan and Germany combined as shown in Table III.

TABLE III: COMPARATIVE PRODUCTION, JAPAN, GERMANY, UNITED STATES
TOTAL AIRCRAFT—1941-44

	1941	1942	1943	1944	Total
Japan	5,088	8,861	16,693	28,180	58,822
Germany	11,766	15,556	25,527	39,807	92,656
United States	19,433	49,445	92,196	100,752	261,826
USSR	15,735	25,430	34,900	40,300	116,365

Source: United States Strategic Bombing Survey.

Allied Bombing and Japanese Plant Dispersal Programme

The sixteen B-25 bombers which, launched from the carrier USS *Hornet* and led by Lieut-Colonel Doolittle, had made on 18 April, 1942, the first bombing attack on the Japanese homeland, had done little to perturb the Japanese aircraft industry. After this single raid Japan enjoyed a period of

Light anti-personnel bombs beneath the wings of a Mitsubishi A6M2 Reisen (Zero Fighter). (*US Navy Department.*)

more than two years during which no bomb fell on the homeland. However, on 15 June, 1944, the China-based B-29s made their historic raid on the Yawata steel plant. Still the Japanese aircraft industry, heavily concentrated in Tokyo, Nagoya and Osaka areas—out of reach of the China-based Superfortresses—escaped damage and enjoyed another four-month period of grace.

On 24 November, 1944, Marianas-based B-29s began pounding the industrial heartland of Japan, and aircraft and engine manufacturing plants ranked high on the list of priority targets for the 20th Air Force. From the standpoint of physical damage these attacks were extremely effective. With few exceptions the plants hit were made useless for continued production but, nevertheless, some departments escaped direct hits or fire damage, and certain well-protected heavy equipment was kept in operation by prodigious effort. Work, however, was generally disrupted and scattered,

Radar-equipped examples of the Yokosuka P1Y1 Ginga (Milky Way) on the final assembly lines at Nakajima's Koizumi factory. (*USAF*.)

and operating efficiency dropped well below average level. The United States estimated after the war that the loss in engine production from December 1944 to July 1945 amounted to 43 per cent of estimated production if dispersal and direct attacks had not taken place. The loss in airframe output was estimated at 18 per cent.

The bombing of populated areas also contributed to a decline in airframe and engine production. As food shortages became acute, workers stayed away from work to forage for supplies and absenteeism in the aircraft industry rose rapidly, direct attacks causing them to scatter into the countryside. As raids increased in frequency and severity, the first sound of any alert caused complete shutdowns. Attacks on urban areas wrecked many workers' homes, disrupted family life generally and kept people away from their jobs. All such factors combined to cause losses of productive man-hours of from 20 to 25 per cent in the aircraft industry by the spring of 1945. Furthermore, this situation was compounded by the fact that indiscriminate call-ups by the Army and the Navy had necessitated the use of large numbers of women, high-school children and soldiers to replace skilled labour (*Table IV and Figure IV*).

FIGURE IV: JAPANESE AIRCRAFT INDUSTRY AVERAGE MONTHLY EMPLOYMENT, 1941-45

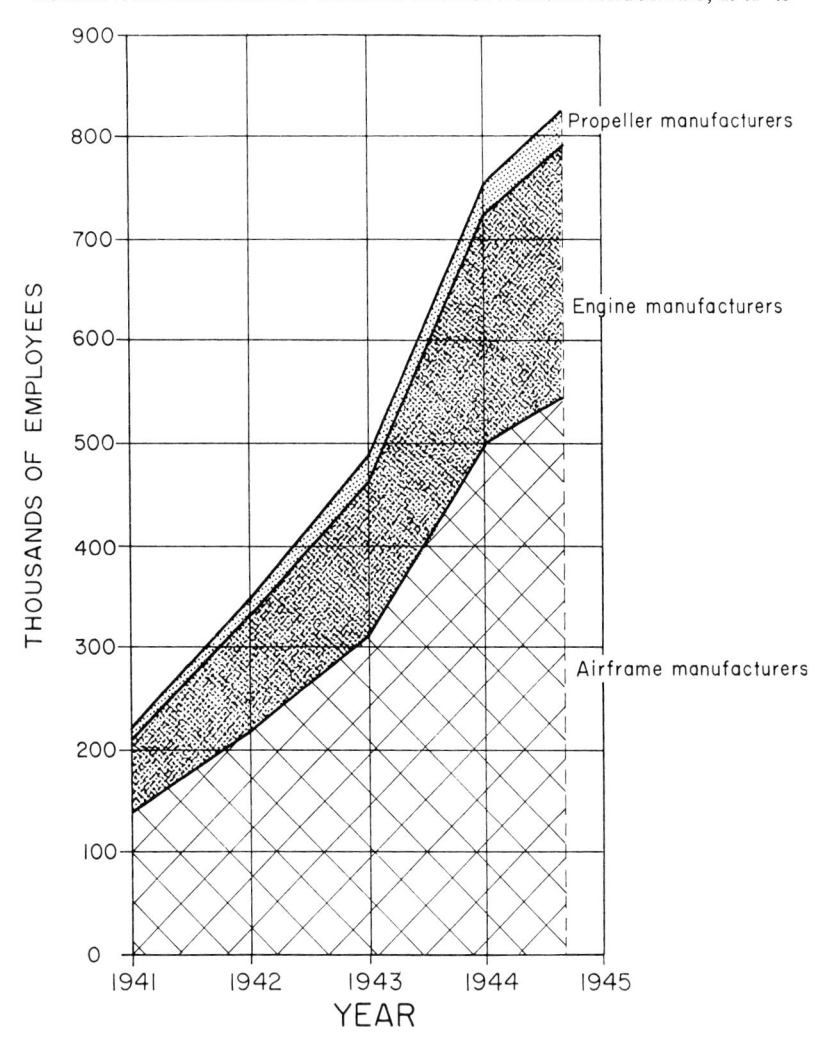

TABLE IV: JAPANESE AIRCRAFT INDUSTRY AVERAGE MONTHLY EMPLOYMENT
JANUARY 1941–AUGUST 1945

	1941	1942	1943	1944	1945
Airframe Manufacturers	140,081	216,179	309,655	499,344	545,578
Engine Manufacturers	70,468	112,871	152,960	228,014	247,058
Propeller Manufacturers	10,774	14,532	20,167	28,898	32,945
Total	221,323	343,582	482,782	756,256	825,581

Source: United States Strategic Bombing Survey.

Nakajima Ki-43 Hayabusa (Peregrine Falcon) Army fighters on the final assembly lines at Nakajima's Ota factory. (*US Navy Department.*)

The Allied navies also contributed heavily to the downfall of the Japanese aircraft industry. By mid-1944 the blockade and loss of shipping had created a critical situation, and the effect was felt first on aircraft engine production. Shortages of cobalt, nickel, chromium, molybdenum and tungsten—alloying materials necessary to make high-strength steel required in aircraft engines—posed serious problems for the manufacturers. Attempts to use substitute materials not only slowed down production but raised the rate of rejections at inspection and increased the number of failures on test stands and in flight. By October 1944 the supply of engines was scarcely adequate for installation in airframes and spares were disappearing rapidly. Engineless airframes began to pile up at factories, units in the field went without spares and production lines were slowed down.

By the summer of 1944 stocks of aluminium sheet were dwindling, but because of later dispersion and bomb damage, restricted aircraft production prevented complete drainage of available stocks. If the planned programmes for aircraft had been met, however, all available supplies of aluminium would have been exhausted long before the end of the war. As it was, the use of secondary metal was increasing rapidly at the war's end. Anticipating a progressively deteriorating situation, Japanese engineers were working on all-wood and all-steel designs for production late in 1945 and early 1946.

During the course of the war, emphasis shifted from bombers to fighters as operations became more and more of a defensive character. In anticipation of Allied bombing operations against their homeland and, later, in a futile attempt to ward off the Allied aircraft the Japanese accelerated even further the production of fighter aircraft. This trend is reflected by the share of total aircraft production devoted to fighter aircraft, which increased from 21 per cent in 1941 to 33 per cent in 1942, to 43 per cent in 1943, to 49 per cent in 1944 and to almost 50 per cent in 1945. However, the increasing emphasis on fighter aircraft production did not ease the manufacturers' problems since, during the war, the fighters had increased in airframe weight and engine horsepower and since many of the discontinued bomber types were of the single-engined variety.

Dispersal of aircraft plants was planned early in 1944, but the constant pressure for production caused the government to withhold permission to disperse to semi-underground and underground plants until production could be maintained or expanded in the process. Although many companies had anticipated a government order and had actually started to dismantle their plants in the autumn of 1944, it was not until November and December 1944, following the initial strikes by B-29s, that a panic dispersal of the industry took place.

Mitsubishi J2M3 Raiden (Thunderbolt) fighters on an underground assembly line at Atsugi in August 1945. The nearest aircraft bears the number 137 on its fin. (*USAF.*)

The initial haphazard dispersal was followed in February 1945 by an attempt to organize this activity under the mandatory 'Urgent Dispersal of Plants Act'. This act ordered the general underground, semi-underground and surface dispersal of industry, with aircraft having first priority in construction, transport, building material and finance. It was April or May, however, before the movement became general and by then it had become too late.

By the time of the surrender there was scarcely a village or town of any size that did not house some sort of aircraft manufacturing activity such as dispersed plants, subcontractors and supplies of parts and materials. Many such shops and sub-factories were housed in schools, textile mills, warehouses and even shrines, but they suffered heavily from area raids. Early in 1945 a large number were being moved underground as Japan's precipitous terrain was well suited for this type of construction. Abandoned mines, stone quarries, railway tunnels and viaducts, and department store basements were converted. New tunnels were dug in hills of sedimentary and volcanic rock which were comparatively easy to excavate and which required little or no shoring for overhead support.

At the time of the Japanese surrender 100 underground aircraft plants were in various stages of completion, but most of the machinery was only in the process of alignment and testing and not yet ready for use. Consequently not more than 30 engines, 10 aircraft and a few thousand parts were actually produced in underground plants. During the dismantling of plants and the moving and re-establishment of production lines, the loss in production was greater than that due to direct air attacks. Fear of air attacks drove many factories to scatter and store their tools and supplies until adequate dispersal sites were built. However, it was confidently forecast that the total underground plant programme would have been realized by December 1945.

Despite material shortage and labour problems, production kept increasing until September 1944 when the peak monthly production of 2,572 aircraft was reached. From then on bombing operations by the Allies, the plant dispersal programme and employee absenteeism disrupted production and the 1,131 aircraft produced in July 1945 represented the lowest monthly figure since February 1943. The combined effects of these disruptive problems can be further evaluated by comparing the production of aircraft during the first and second half-year of 1944 (respectively

TABLE V: JAPANESE AIRCRAFT PRODUCTION—SHARE BY MANUFACTURERS, 1941–45

	All Aircraft (1)	Percentage	Combat Aircraft (2)	Percentage
Nakajima	19,561	28·0	19,396	37·1
Mitsubishi	12,513	17·9	12,039	23·0
Kawasaki	8,243	11·8	7,770	14·9
Tachikawa	6,645	9·5	3,130	6·0
Aichi	3,627	5·2	3,611	6·9
Nippon Hikoki	2,882	4·1	59	0·1
Kyushu	2,620	3·7	1,507	2·9
Mansyu	2,196	3·1	798	1·5
Kokusai	2,134	3·1	14	*
Kawanishi	1,994	2·9	1,629	3·1
Hitachi	1,783	2·6	—	—
Tachiarai	1,220	1·7	—	—
Fuji	871	1·2	—	—
Showa	616	0·9	1	*
Tokyo	258	0·4	—	—
Mitsui	17	*	—	—
Matsushita	4	*	—	—
Sub-total	67,184		49,954	
Navy Air Arsenals	1,700	2·4	1,284	2·5
Rikugun	1,004	1·4	1,004	1·9
Total	69,888	100·0	52,242	100·0

Source: United States Strategic Bombing Survey.

* Less than one-tenth of 1 per cent.

(1) Including gliders.
(2) Including fighters, bombers and reconnaissance aircraft.

TABLE VI: JAPANESE AIRCRAFT ENGINE PRODUCTION—SHARE BY MANUFACTURERS, 1941-45

	Number of Engines	Percentage
Mitsubishi	41,534	35·6
Nakajima	36,440	31·3
Hitachi	13,571	11·6
Kawasaki	10,274	8·8
Ishikawajima	2,286	2·0
Mansyu	2,168	1·9
Aichi	1,783	1·5
Nissan	1,633	1·4
Kokusai	837	0·7
Toyoda	160	0·1
Sub-total	110,686	95·0
Navy Air Arsenals	4,452	3·8
Rikugun	1,439	1·2
Total	116,577	100·0

Source: United States Strategic Bombing Survey.

14,088 and 14,092 aircraft) to the production of aircraft during the first six months of 1945 (9,439 aircraft), this representing a 33 per cent decrease.

When asked after the war to explain the reason for this situation, General Saburo Endo, Chief of the Air Ordnance Bureau of the Munitions Ministry, said:

'Both the Army and the Navy had decisive battles to win. The Imperial Japanese Navy considered the decisive battle to be coming in June 1944 north of New Guinea; the Imperial Japanese Army thought their decisive battle would be in August 1944 in the Philippines. Until this was accomplished, dispersion was secondary. The Japanese disregarded all plans for the year and shoved everything towards production. After the peak was achieved (and battles not won), the employees required rest, the machinery was worn out and had to be repaired, parts and supplies were exhausted, and readjustments had to be made. The drop in production was due to these factors, as well as dispersion, earthquake

Built in Kawasaki's Kagamigahara factory, the Ki-61 Hien (Swallow) was the only Japanese Army wartime fighter to be powered by a liquid-cooled engine. (*Consiglio*.)

FIGURE V: JAPANESE COMBAT AIRCRAFT PRODUCTION—
SHARE BY MANUFACTURERS, 1941-45

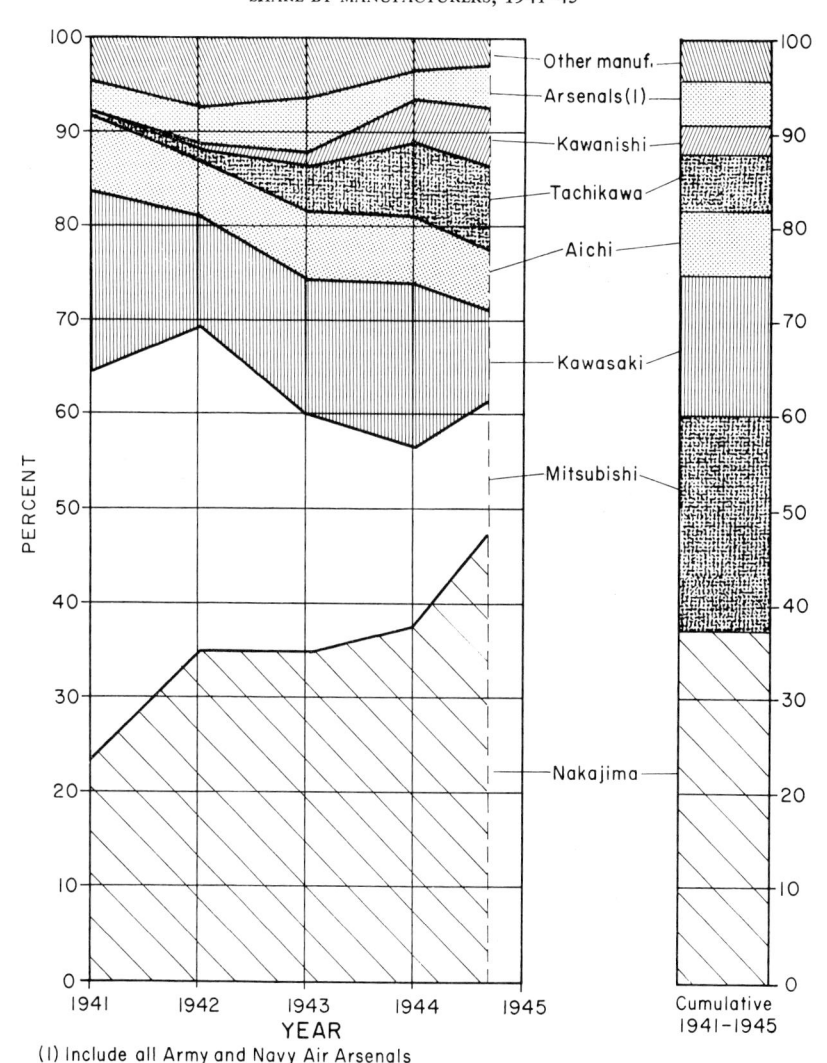

(1) Include all Army and Navy Air Arsenals

(on 7 December, 1944, a major earthquake rocked the Tokai District and badly damaged Aichi plants, Mitsubishi's Nagoya plants and Nakajima's Handa plant—*Author*), bombing and the low morale of the people.'

Synopsis of Major Airframe and Engine Manufacturers

The Japanese aircraft industries were dominated by four companies, Nakajima, Mitsubishi, Kawasaki and Tachikawa, which turned out two-thirds of all aircraft built between 1941 and 1945, and three companies, Nakajima, Mitsubishi and Kawasaki, produced three-fourths of all combat types and almost 80 per cent of all aircraft engines during the same period.

A brief history of these and other important Japanese airframe and engine manufacturers follows, arranged alphabetically.

AICHI KOKUKI K.K. (Aichi Aircraft Co Ltd)

This company, the name of which was usually abbreviated to Aichi, ranked fourth in the industry. The Aichi Tokei Denki K.K. (Aichi Clock and Electric Co Ltd), forerunner of Aichi Kokuki K.K., entered the aircraft industry in 1920 when it began production of airframes at the Funakata plant in Nagoya. Production of engines was commenced there in 1927. In 1938, engine production was transferred to the newly completed Atsuta plant in south central Nagoya while a new airframe plant, the Eitoku plant, also in Nagoya, was added in 1941.

In March 1943 a separate firm, Aichi Kokuki K.K., was formed and took over the aircraft and aero-engine production from Aichi Tokei Denki K.K. In late 1944, Aichi began dispersing its airframe production to Ogaki in Gifu Prefecture and an underground plant in Seto, ten miles east of Nagoya. The engine production was moved to the Tsu Naval Air Station and underground facilities southwest of Tsu.

Principal aircraft built by Aichi included the D3A, D4Y, E16A and B7A series, but the only type of engine produced during the war was the Atsuta inline series (licence-built Daimler-Benz DB 601).

Navy Experimental 16-Shi Reconnaissance Seaplane (Aichi E16A1). The light patches in the background are the work of the Japanese wartime censor. (*Courtesy USAF.*)

The Aichi B7A1 Ryusei (Shooting Star) was designed as a torpedo-bomber, but could also be used as a dive-bomber.

FUJI HIKOKI K.K. (Fuji Aeroplane Co Ltd)

Fuji, as the company was best known, with plants in Tokyo, Osaka and Taira, was one of the smaller producers in the Japanese industry. Its only complete aircraft was the Navy Type 93 Intermediate Trainer (K5Y, WILLOW). In addition, the company engaged in fabrication of sub-assemblies for Nakajima Hikoki K.K. and made the main wing and tail assemblies for the Navy Suicide Attacker Ohka Model 11 (BAKA).

HITACHI KOKUKI K.K. (Hitachi Aircraft Co Ltd)

Hitachi ranked third and eleventh respectively among Japanese engine and airframe producers. Most of the airframes and engines produced were for small training aircraft.

Hitachi Kokuki K.K. was formed in May 1939 when it began operation of three plants purchased from Hitachi Seisakusho K.K. (Hitachi Manufacturing Co Ltd). Hitachi Seisakusho K.K. had acquired the three plants —Omori, Tachikawa and Haneda—through a merger previously made with Tokyo Gasu Denki Kogyo K.K. (Tokyo Gas and Electric Co Ltd). In 1939 a new engine casting plant was built in Kawasaki and a new airframe plant—initially intended for the licence-manufacture of fighters and bombers designed by Ernst Heinkel Flugzeugwerke A.G.—was built in Chiba. This latter plant took over most final assembly work in 1944.

Aircraft built by Hitachi during the war included the K2Y2, K5Y1, K9W1 and A6M2-K trainers, and engine production included the Ha-11, Ha-12, Ha-13, Ha-26, Ha-42, Ha-112 and Tempu series.

ISHIKAWAJIMA KOKU KOGYO K.K.
(Ishikawajima Aircraft Industries Co Ltd)

Ishikawajima was a small engine manufacturer producing the Ha-35 radial in their Tomioka plant. The company was founded in 1937 as a branch of the Ishikawajima Zosensho K.K. (Ishikawajima Shipbuilding Co Ltd).

Kawanishi H8K2 Navy Type 2 Flying-Boat Model 12. (*Eckert.*)

KAWANISHI KOKUKI K.K. (Kawanishi Aircraft Co Ltd)

Kawanishi Kokuki K.K. was founded in 1928 and assumed all assets and activities of the Kawanishi Engineering Works which had started producing seaplanes in 1921. During the war Kawanishi was the sixth largest combat aircraft producer in the Japanese aircraft industry. The company manufactured only airframes and was exclusively a Navy contractor.

The company had four primary plants, all of modern construction, three aircraft assembly plants and one aircraft components plant. Of the three airframe assembly plants, the Naruo plant near Osaka was the largest, the Konan plant between Osaka and Kobe was the next largest and the Himeji plant forty miles northwest of Kobe was the smallest. The Takarazuka plant, the aircraft parts plant, was six miles north of the Naruo plant.

During the war Kawanishi manufactured float seaplanes, flying-boats and fighters of their own design as well as the Yokosuka P1Y2 bomber.

The Kawanishi N1K1 Kyofu (Mighty Wind) floatplane fighter had such a remarkable performance that Kawanishi developed from it the land-based N1K1-J Shiden (Violet Lightning).

When its Nakajima Homare engine developed its full rated power the Kawanishi N1K1-J Shiden (Violet Lightning) was a dangerous adversary. (*US Navy Department.*)

KAWASAKI KOKUKI KOGYO K.K. (Kawasaki Aircraft Engineering Co Ltd)
Kawasaki Kokuki Kogyo K.K. was a wholly-owned subsidiary of Kawasaki Jukogyo K.K. (Kawasaki Heavy Industries Co Ltd). The aircraft division of the parent company was organized in 1918 but in 1937 and 1939 respectively the airframe and engine manufacturing activities were removed from the parent corporation. During the war Kawasaki occupied the third place in Japan's airframe industry and the fourth place in Japan's engine industry.

By far the greatest proportion of the company's facilities was concentrated in two large plants, one manufacturing aircraft and engines at Akashi, near Kobe, and the other aircraft only at Kagamigahara (Gifu) near Nagoya. Smaller plants producing complete airframes were at Ichinomiya, also near Nagoya, and at Miyakonojo on Kyushu. Additional engine plants were at Futami and Takatsuki, both in the Osaka–Kobe area.

During the war Kawasaki produced the Ki-61 and Ki-100 fighters, the Ki-45, Ki-102 and Ki-108 twin-engined fighters, the Ki-48 bomber, the Ki-36 and Ki-55 direct co-operation and training aircraft, and the Ki-56 transport. Engine production included the Ha-13, 25, 40 and 115.

Damaged Kawasaki Ki-45 KAIc Toryu (Dragon Killer) of the 27th Sentai. (*US Navy Department.*)

KYUSHU HIKOKI K.K. (Kyushu Aeroplane Co Ltd)
  Kyushu Hikoki K.K. was founded in 1943 to succeed K.K. Watanabe Tekkosho (Watanabe Ironworks Co Ltd). Watanabe began manufacturing aircraft parts in the twenties and in 1931 began the manufacture of trainers. The company was located on the island of Kyushu, with three small plants, of which the Zasshonokuma works was the largest, centred around the city of Fukuoka, a further three being added in 1944–45.
  During the war the company produced the E13A and E14Y seaplanes, the A5M and J7W fighters, the Q1W anti-submarine patrol bomber and the K9W, K10W and K11W trainers. In addition the company built outer-wing panels for the Mitsubishi G4M series and was the second largest aircraft wheels manufacturer in Japan.

Kyushu K11W1 Navy Operations Trainer Shiragiku (White Chrysanthemum) in surrender markings. An anti-submarine patrol version was developed as the Q3W1 Nankai (South Sea).

MANSYU HIKOKI SEIZO K.K. (Manchurian Aeroplane Manufacturing Co Ltd)
  Mansyu was established in late 1938 under the supervision of the Japanese Government. The company had its plant in Harbin, Manchukuo. During the war the company built under licence from other Japanese manufacturers some fighter, ground support and training aircraft and was responsible for a number of original designs. The Ki-79 trainer was the only Mansyu-designed aircraft to reach production status. The company ranked eighth and sixth respectively among Japanese airframe and aero-engine manufacturers.

MITSUBISHI JUKOGYO K.K. (Mitsubishi Heavy Industries Co Ltd)
  Mitsubishi ranked first among Japanese industries in weight of aeroplanes produced, because of the large number of relatively heavy bombers it assembled, but ranked second in number of aircraft produced. Mitsubishi was also the largest engine producer, manufacturing 38 per cent of all Japanese combat engines during the war.

A Mitsubishi Ki-46-II Army Type 100 Command Reconnaissance Plane Model 2 of the 76th Dokuritsu Dai Shijugo Chutai at Gasmata in New Britain. (*Australian War Memorial*.)

Mitsubishi's interest in aircraft originated in 1918 when Dr Kumezo Ito was sent to France to study the role aircraft played in the first World War. In 1920 Mitsubishi Nainenki Seizo K.K. (Mitsubishi Internal Combustion Engine Co Ltd) was registered as an aircraft manufacturing company, with its plant in Kobe. The nucleus for this company was separated from the shipbuilding and other engineering activities of the Mitsubishi holding company.

In 1922, aircraft activites were shifted to Oe-machi on the southern outskirts of Nagoya. These activities grew, and in 1928 the company changed its name to the Mitsubishi Kokuki K.K. (Mitsubishi Aircraft Co Ltd). In 1934 a change in policy regrouped and amalgamated all Mitsubishi

The rocket-powered Mitsubishi J8M1 Shusui (Sword Stroke) inspired by the Messerschmitt Me 163.

23

industrial activities under a single company, the Mitsubishi Jukogyo K.K. (Mitsubishi Heavy Industries Co Ltd).

During the war the centre of Mitsubishi's activities was Nagoya where airframe and engine plants were located. Other airframe assembly plants were at Naguno, Takaoka, Suzuka, Kagamigahara, Inami, Obu, Tsu, Okayama, Yawata, Yokkaichi, Naruo, Mizushima and Kumamoto; other engine plants were at Kyoto, Shizuoka, Nagano, Hiroshima, Ogaki, Fukui, Koromo and Niigata. These various plants were organized in six airframe and eleven engine works.

TABLE VII: MITSUBISHI'S AIRFRAME AND ENGINE PLANTS

Plants	Major Products
Airframes	
No. 1 Plant (Dai-Ichi Kokuki Seisakusho)	Experimental Aircraft; Ki-21, Ki-83, A7M, J8M
No. 3 Plant (Dai-San Kokuki Seisakusho)	G4M, J2M, A6M
No. 5 Plant (Dai-Go Kokuki Seisakusho)	Ki-67, Ki-83
No. 7 Plant (Dai-Nana Kokuki Seisakusho)	G4M, N1K2-J
No. 9 Plant (Dai-Ku Kokuki Seisakusho)	Ki-67
No. 11 Plant (Dai-Juichi Kokuki Seisakusho)	Ki-46
Engines	
No. 2 Plant (Dai-Ni Hatsudoki Seisakusho)	Ha-104, Ha-43, Ne 230
No. 4 Plant (Dai-Yon Hatsudoki Seisakusho)	Ha-102, Ha-43
No. 6 Plant (Dai-Roku Hatsudoki Seisakusho)	Ha-112, Kinsei
No. 8 Plant (Dai-Hachi Hatsudoki Seisakusho)	Kasei
No. 10 Plant (Dai-Ju Hatsudoki Seisakusho)	Components
No. 12 Plant (Dai-Juni Hatsudoki Seisakusho)	Components
No. 14 Plant (Dai-Juyon Hatsudoki Seisakusho)	Components
No. 16 Plant (Dai-Juroku Hatsudoki Seisakusho)	Ha-104, Ha-214 Ru
No. 18 Plant (Dai-Juhachi Hatsudoki Seisakusho)	Ha-43
No. 20 Plant (Dai-Niju Hatsudoki Seisakusho)	Ha-102
No. 22 Plant (Dai-Nijuni Hatsudoki Seisakusho)	Components

Source: United States Strategic Bombing Survey.

In terms of productive floor area, Mitsubishi tripled the size of its airframe assembly works between 1941 and 1944. There was a slightly more efficient use of productive floor area in 1944 than in 1941 in that airframe production increased almost four-fold while productive floor area only tripled. Engine production tripled in the same year while productive floor area increased only 2·5 times. In 1945 bombing and dispersal caused the abandonment of some factory areas and a reduction in productive floor area of about 20 per cent.

NAKAJIMA HIKOKI K.K. (Nakajima Aeroplane Co Ltd)

Nakajima was Japan's oldest aircraft company and the largest producer of both airframes and engines in the last year of the war. In 1945 Nakajima produced 36 per cent of all Japanese aircraft, 47 per cent of all combat aircraft and 32 per cent of all engines. Over the five-year period from 1941 to 1945 it was the leading producer of airframes but was second by a narrow margin to Mitsubishi in the production of engines.

A Nakajima Ki-44-Ib Shoki (Devil-Queller) of the Akeno Fighter Training School.

Nakajima Ki-84-Ia Hayate (Gale) Army Type 4 Fighter Model 1A with attachments for underwing drop tanks.

A late production Nakajima J1N1-Sa Gekko Model 11A with nose-mounted radar antennae.

25

The company was founded on 6 December, 1917, by Lieutenant Chikuhei Nakajima, a young retired Navy engineer, and Seibei Kawanishi, as the Nihon Hikoki Seisakusho K.K. (Japan Aeroplane Manufacturing Work Co Ltd). In December 1919, following differences of opinion between Nakajima and Kawanishi, the company was dissolved and Nakajima obtained the financial backing of the powerful Mitsui Bussan K.K. (Mitsui Trading Co Ltd) to start the Nakajima Hikoki K.K. (Nakajima Aeroplane Co Ltd). The company operated as such until 1 April, 1945, when it was nominally transferred to state management and called the First Munitions Arsenal.

Nakajima was a highly integrated engine and airframe production complex. Together with its wholly-owned subsidiary, the Nakajima Koku Kinzoku K.K. (Nakajima Aero-Metals Co Ltd), it produced almost every part required in the assembly of engines and airframes. It included an aircraft ordnance division and even a pig-iron plant. The complex did not, however, extend its operations to the manufacture of its own machine tools and propellers.

TABLE VIII: NAKAJIMA'S AIRFRAME AND ENGINE PLANTS

Plants	Location	Major Products
Airframes		
No. 1 Ota	Ota, Gumma Pref.	Ki-21, Ki-27, Ki-43, Ki-44, Ki-84, Ki-115, B5N, E8N, K2Y, L2D
No. 2 Koizumi	Okawa, Gumma Pref.	B5N, G3M, L2D, A6M, A6M2-N, B6N, C6N, P1Y
No. 3 Handa	Handa, Aichi Pref.	B6N, C6N
No. 4 Utsonomiya	Utsonomiya, Tochigi Pref.	Ki-84
Engines		
No. 11 Musashi	Musashi, Tokyo Pref.	Ha-1B, Ha-5, Ha-25, Ha-41, Ha-45, Ha-109, Ha-115, Ha-117, Kotobuki, Hikari, Sakae, Mamoru, Homare
No. 12 Omiya	Omiya, Saitama Pref.	Components and Homare
No. 13 Hamamatsu	Hamamatsu, Shizuoka Pref.	Components and Ha-45
No. 14 Oya	Shiroyama, Tochigi Pref.	Components

Source: United States Strategic Bombing Survey.

NIPPON HIKOKI K.K. (Japan Aeroplane Co Ltd)

Nippon Hikoki K.K. was founded in October 1934 and consisted of two plants, located at Tomioka in Yokohama and at Yamagata in Yamagata Prefecture. The dispersal programme led to the partial completion of an underground plant at Yamagata.

The company was principally concerned in the manufacture of primary and intermediate trainers including the K4Y1, K2Y2 and K10W1. The main type built was the Navy Type 93 Intermediate Trainer (K5Y1 and K5Y2). In 1943 and 1944 the company produced approximately 20 per cent of the trainers manufactured in Japan; in 1945 its share had declined to 12 per cent. The only combat type produced during the war was the Aichi-designed E16A1 Zuiun reconnaissance seaplane.

NIPPON KOKUSAI KOKU KOGYO K.K. (Japan International Air Industries Co Ltd)

Formed in June 1941 by the amalgamation of Nippon Koku Kogyo K.K. (Japan Air Industries Co Ltd) and Kokusai Kokuki K.K. (International Aircraft Co Ltd). Kokusai (to use the name by which the merged company was best known) was one of the smallest Japanese aircraft manufacturers. The company had two main plants—one at Okubo in Kyoto Prefecture and one at Hiratsuka in Kanagawa Prefecture—as well as six smaller component-manufacturing plants. The main aircraft type produced was the Ki-86 primary trainer.

NISSAN JIDOSHA K.K. (Nissan Automobile Co Ltd)

The company manufactured the 100 hp Ha-11 engine in its Yokohama and Yoshiwara plants beginning in August 1943. In 1944 and 1945 it ranked sixth in unit engine production.

SHOWA HIKOKI K.K. (Showa Aeroplane Co Ltd)

The company started producing naval aircraft in 1939 in a plant at Showa near Tokyo. During the war three feeder plants were added, one at Matsumoto built in 1943, one at Oine built in 1944 and one at Shinonoi built in 1945. The chief products were the L2D transport and the D3A2 dive-bomber.

An L2D3a, Showa-built Douglas DC-3, powered by Mitsubishi Kinsei 53 engines. The L2Ds had additional flight deck windows. This example is seen with United States markings and was photographed in May 1945. (*US Navy Department.*)

TACHIKAWA HIKOKI K.K. (Tachikawa Aeroplane Co Ltd)

The company was founded in 1924 and delivered its first complete aircraft but remained comparatively small until 1941 when the area of the Tachikawa plant increased almost thirteen-fold. New plants at Okayama, in southern Honshu, and Kofu were added in 1942 and 1944 respectively.

Tachikawa produced approximately 9 per cent of all Japanese aircraft during the war. Major combat types included the Ki-43 fighter and Ki-36 direct co-operation aircraft but Tachikawa was also a major producer of trainers (Ki-9, Ki-17, Ki-54 and Ki-55) and transports (Ki-34 and Lockheed-designed Type LO).

ARMY AND NAVY AIR DEPOTS

The Imperial Japanese Army and Navy Air depots were similar to those of other countries in that they handled repair, modification and distribution of aircraft. One Japanese Army air arsenal and four naval air depots were themselves producers of aircraft and accounted for 4·4 per cent of the total Japanese combat aircraft production and 5 per cent of the total engine production from 1941 to 1945. These arsenals and their major products are listed in Table IX.

TABLE IX: ARMY AND NAVY AIR ARSENALS

Name	Major Products
Tachikawa Dai-Ichi Rikugun Kokusho (First Army Air Arsenal) at Tachikawa	Aircraft: Ki-30, Ki-43, Ki-51 Engines: Ha-23, Ha-31, Ha-45
Dai-Ichi Kaigun Kokusho (1st Naval Air Arsenal) at Kasumigaura	Aircraft: L3Y, Ohka Model 11
Dai-Juichi Kaigun Kokusho (11th Naval Air Arsenal) at Hiro	Aircraft: B5N, D4Y, K5Y, E13A Engines: Hikari, Kinsei, Homare
Dai-Nijuichi Kaigun Kokusho (21st Naval Air Arsenal) at Sasebo	Aircraft: F1M2, A5M4-K, A6M2-K, B7A2 Engines: Kotobuki
Koza Kaigun Kokusho (Koza Naval Air Arsenal) at Koza	Aircraft: J2M3

Research work and design were also done for the Imperial Japanese Army by the Rikugun Kokugijutsu Kenkyujo (Army Aerotechnical Research Institute) at Tachikawa and for the Imperial Japanese Navy by the Dai-Ichi Kaigun Koku Gijitsusho (First Naval Air Technical Arsenal) at Yokosuka.

Japanese Army Air Force
A Brief History

The Imperial Japanese Army's first flying experience began, as early as 1877, with the use of balloons. Those early experiences were followed in 1904, during the Russo-Japanese War, by the use of two balloons which made fourteen successful flights in support of the Japanese forces besieging Port Arthur. In the field of heavier-than-air machines, since 1789 attempts had been made by private citizens to test ornithopter-type gliders but none of the military Services paid much attention to these efforts. Yet, during the first decade of the twentieth century, the development abroad of flying machines caught the attention of the Japanese and, on 30 July, 1909, the Provisional Military Balloon Research Society was formed with members selected from the Imperial Japanese Army and Navy and from the staff of the Tokyo Imperial University.

In 1910 the Society sent Captain Yoshitoshi Tokugawa to France and Captain Kumazo Hino to Germany to receive pilot training and to purchase aircraft. Upon returning to Japan these officers brought back an Henri Farman biplane and a Grade monoplane and, on 19 December, 1910, made their first flight in Japan. During 1911 several types of aircraft were imported and Captain Tokugawa designed an improved version of the Henri Farman which was built by an Army balloon unit. Other Japanese officers were trained abroad but, finally, an initial group of officers completed their training in Japan.

A line-up of Nakajima Ki-27b Army Type 97 Model B Fighters of the 59th Sentai, 1st Chutai. (*US National Archives.*)

Still using imported aircraft and Japanese-built machines modified from foreign designs, the Imperial Japanese Army continued to train flying personnel but, with the exception of a token number of officers who in 1918 served with the French Aviation Militaire, this Service did not take part in the air operations of World War I. During this period the air unit of the Imperial Japanese Army gained some degree of independence when in December 1915 it was organized as the Air Battalion of the Army Transport Command. Further gain in status was achieved in April 1919 when the Army Air Division was established under the command of Maj-Gen Ikutaro Inouye.

Mitsubishi Ki-21-Ia being prepared for a bombing raid. This scene was photographed in northern China.

The activation of the Army Air Service was the result of the visit of a French mission which, led by Colonel Faure and comprising 63 instructors, brought to Japan several types of French aircraft which had acquired fame during World War I. Thus the SPAD S.13C-1 was adopted as the standard fighter of the Imperial Japanese Army while the Nieuport 24C-1 was placed in production by Nakajima Hikoki K.K. as a fighter trainer and the Salmson 2A-2 was built by Kawasaki Kokuki Kogyo K.K. as the Type Otsu 1 reconnaissance aircraft. Other types of aircraft were obtained from the United Kingdom and included the Sopwith Pup and Avro 504K.

On 1 May, 1925, the Army Air Corps was established and, with status equal to that of the Artillery, Cavalry and Infantry, was placed under the command of Lieut-Gen Kinichi Yasumitsu's Koku Hombu (Air Headquarters). Upon its inception the Army Air Corps had a personnel strength of 3,700 officers and men and could muster a strength of some 500 aircraft. Shortly thereafter the Army Air Corps began to take delivery of various aircraft of Japanese design.

During its first ten years of existence the Army Air Division/Corps had seen action on a small scale at Vladivostok in 1920 and in China during the 1928 Tsinan Incident. However, the next decade was to see greatly expanded air activities on the part of units of the Imperial Japanese Army.

The Mitsubishi Ki-57-II was the standard personnel transport operated throughout the war by the Japanese Army and Dai Nippon Koku K.K. (*US Navy Department.*)

The first of these actions was the Manchurian Incident, which broke out in September 1931 and was followed in January 1932 by the Shanghai Incident. By then the air units of the Imperial Japanese Army were equipped with a number of Japanese-built aircraft including the Mitsubishi Type 87 light bomber, the Kawasaki Type 88 reconnaissance type and the Nakajima Type 91 fighter and they had little difficulty in achieving superiority over the Chinese forces. As a result the Japanese puppet state of Manchukuo was established in Manchuria. Soon thereafter the Imperial Japanese Army undertook a major modernization and expansion programme and instigated at that time the development of many aircraft which were still operated by that Service during the Pacific War.

While this re-equipment programme was being pushed forward, fighting flared up anew in China on 7 July, 1937. The second Sino-Japanese conflict had begun. During the initial phase of operations the Imperial Japanese Army left the brunt of offensive air operations to the rival Japanese Navy and limited their activities to air support of ground operations along the Manchukuo border in order to concentrate on forming new units.

The Nakajima Ki-43-I Hayabusa (Peregrine Falcon) which entered service just in time to take part in the initial operations in Malaya. (*US Navy Department.*)

The Kawasaki Ki-45 KAIc Toryu (Dragon Killer) was the Japanese Army's standard heavy fighter and only operational night fighter.

Up to that time the basic air units of the Imperial Japanese Army had been the Hiko Rentais (Air Regiments) made up of fighter, bomber, reconnaissance and/or transport Chutais (Squadrons or Companies). However, early combat experience in China dictated a complete reorganization, and the Hiko Rentais gave place to smaller, more flexible, specialized units: the Sentais (Groups). The unit structure then implemented formed the basic organization used during the Pacific War.

Under this system the basic unit was the Sentai (Group) which normally comprised three Chutais (Squadrons or Companies) of nine to twelve aircraft and a Sentai Hombu (HQ Section) and was commanded by a Lieut-Colonel or a Major. The next units in the command chain were the Hikodans (Wings or Air Brigades), normally commanded by a Major-General or Colonel. They consisted of a Shireibu Hikodan (Command Section), a reconnaissance unit of varying size up to full Sentai level and usually any combination of three Sentoki (Fighter) Sentais, Keibaku (Light Bomber) Sentais and/or Jubaku (Heavy Bomber) Sentais. Two or

A Kawasaki Ki-48-II Army Type 99 Twin-engined Light Bomber Model 2 at Clark Field, Manila.

three Hikodans formed a Hikoshidan (Air Division) and a Kokugun (Air Army) grouped two or three Hikoshidans. In addition, independent units smaller than a Sentai were formed whenever the tactical situation required it, e.g. Dokuritsu Dai Shijugo Chutais (Independent Squadrons or Companies) and Dokuritsu Hikotais (Independent Wings).

Supreme command of the Imperial Japanese Army was lodged in the Daihonei (Imperial General Headquarters) to which reported the Sanbo Shocho (Chief of Army General Staff). Reporting directly to the Chief of Army General Staff were the Koku Sokambu (Inspectorate General of Aviation), which planned and supervised the training of flying and maintenance personnel, and the Koku Hombu (Air Headquarters), which among other duties was responsible for aircraft, aero-engine and aircraft-equipment design and research.

The Nakajima Ki-49-II Donryu (Storm Dragon), seen here, was intended to supplant the Mitsubishi Ki-21-II but was in fact outlived by its predecessor. (*US Navy Department.*)

As their organization was consolidated and training accelerated and as new aircraft of Japanese design and manufacture were becoming available in increasing numbers, the Imperial Japanese Army stepped up their air operations over the Chinese mainland. Concurrently with operations against Chinese forces the Army found themselves involved in two brief but costly border incidents at Changkufeng and Nomonhan during which they bitterly fought the Soviet Air Force. Although the losses incurred during these incidents, partially offset by the valuable experience acquired, only temporarily set back the realization of their modernization programme, the Imperial Japanese Army were strongly influenced by their encounter with the Soviet Air Force. In the eyes of the Army Headquarters the USSR became the prime potential enemy, and equipment planning, especially in the field of aircraft, was influenced by the desire to be prepared for a conflict along the Manchukuo–Siberia border. Thus the Koku Hombu concentrated on the development of aircraft suited to short tactical land sorties in cold weather and consequently their aircraft were ill-suited to long overwater missions among the islands of the Pacific.

During the planning for war operations in Southeast Asia and the Pacific the Imperial Japanese Army—due to the technical constraints indicated above—were primarily assigned the responsibility for air operations over extensive land areas, e.g. China, Malaya, Burma, the Netherlands East Indies and the Philippines. When the war broke out this Service had some 1,500 aircraft available of which some 650 were assigned to the 3rd Hikoshidan (operations against Malaya) and the 5th Hikoshidan (operations against the Philippines) as follows:

3rd Hikoshidan

3rd Hikodan	
27th Sentai	(23 Ki-51s)
59th Sentai	(24 Ki-43s)
75th Sentai	(25 Ki-48s)
90th Sentai	(30 Ki-48s and Ki-30s)
7th Hikodan	
12th Sentai	(21 Ki-21s)
60th Sentai	(39 Ki-21s)
64th Sentai	(35 Ki-43s and 6 Ki-27s)
98th Sentai	(42 Ki-21s)
10th Hikodan	
31st Sentai	(24 Ki-30s)
62nd Sentai	(22 Ki-21s)
77th Sentai	(27 Ki-27s)
70th Dokuritsu Dai Shijugo Chutai	(8 Ki-15s)
12th Hikodan	
1st Sentai	(42 Ki-27s)
11th Sentai	(39 Ki-27s)
15th Dokuritsu Hikotai	
50th Dokuritsu Dai Shijugo Chutai	(5 Ki-15s and Ki-46s)
51st Dokuritsu Dai Shijugo Chutai	(6 Ki-15s and Ki-46s)
83rd Dokuritsu Hikotai	
71st Dokuritsu Dai Shijugo Chutai	(10 Ki-51s)
73rd Dokuritsu Dai Shijugo Chutai	(9 Ki-51s)
89th Dokuritsu Dai Shijugo Chutai	(12 Ki-36s)
81st Sentai	(9 Ki-15s and 7 Ki-46s)
12th Hiko Chutai	(Ki-57s)

5th Hikoshidan

4th Hikodan	
8th Sentai	(27 Ki-48s, 9 Ki-15s and 2 Ki-46s)
14th Sentai	(18 Ki-21s)
16th Sentai	(27 Ki-30s)
50th Sentai	(36 Ki-27s)
10th Dokuritsu Hikotai	
52nd Dokuritsu Dai Shijugo Chutai	(13 Ki-51s)
74th Dokuritsu Dai Shijugo Chutai	(10 Ki-36s)
76th Dokuritsu Dai Shijugo Chutai	(9 Ki-15s and 2 Ki-46s)
24th Sentai	(36 Ki-27s)
11th Hiko Chutai	(Ki-57s)

In the first nine months of the war the air units of the Imperial Japanese Army met with considerable success, the only serious opposition being encountered over Burma where the Royal Air Force and the American Volunteer Group inflicted severe losses to the Nipponese units. With the exception of the further offensive on the western front towards India, the Japanese advance had reached its limits by July 1942. During this period the aircraft and crews of the JAAF gave a good account of themselves and proved equal and often superior to the motley collection of aircraft, albeit gallantly manned, which the Allies then had available.

From the autumn of 1942 until October 1944 the Imperial Japanese Army fought a war of attrition while suffering steadily increasing air losses particularly in New Guinea and China. Despite the priority assigned to the European Theatre of Operations the Allies were, during these two years, able to obtain an ever more apparent numerical superiority in their war against Japan. Facing such odds the JAAF's aircraft, developed before the war, started to show their age and, with few exceptions, the Army were unable to introduce more modern aircraft in sufficient numbers. This situation particularly affected the bomber aircraft class where the Mitsubishi Ki-21 heavy bombers and the Kawasaki Ki-48 light bombers—with insufficient offensive load, defensive armament, armour protection and speed—had to bear the brunt of the operations. The fighter units of the Imperial Japanese Army fared somewhat better with the introduction of the Kawasaki Ki-61, but most units retained their lightly armed, unprotected Nakajima Ki-43s. Only reconnaissance units had at their disposal in the Mitsubishi Ki-46 an aircraft comparing favourably with Allied machines.

A Kawasaki Ki-61-I KAIc Hien (Swallow) of the 244th Sentai, one of the units assigned to Japanese home defence in 1944. (*Consiglio*.)

In October 1944, as the Imperial Japanese Army was beginning to take delivery of modern bombers (Mitsubishi Ki-67) and fighters (Nakajima Ki-84) the Allies landed in the Philippines, thus starting the third phase of the Pacific War. Hopelessly outnumbered, the Japanese Army bitterly fought to slow down the Allied thrust towards the homeland. The Mari-

The Nakajima Ki-84-Ia Hayate (Gale) made its début in China in August 1944. It was an outstanding fighter, but went into battle hopelessly outnumbered.

anas, the Philippines, Iwo Jima and Okinawa having fallen, Japan lay at the mercy of the Allies.

Bombing of the homeland on a regular basis had begun on 15 June, 1944, with the first raid by China-based B-29s. In an attempt to disrupt Allied bombing operations, the Imperial Japanese Army committed an ever increasing number of fighter units to the defence of the homeland, but their Nakajima Ki-43s, Ki-44s and Ki-84s, and their Kawasaki Ki-61s and Ki-100s lacked the high-altitude performance and heavy armament required to blunt daylight operations by the formidable Superfortresses. This Service was even less prepared for night operations, as the only aircraft type available, the Kawasaki Ki-45 KAI, had no A.I. radar and its performance was only marginal against the B-29s. Concurrently with these operations the Imperial Japanese Army prepared themselves for the expected invasion of Japan. To that effect air operations were curtailed to a minimum to conserve aircraft and dwindling fuel supplies, and plans were on hand for the mass use of obsolete aircraft, specially built types and trainers in taiatari (suicide) sorties such as those first used on a large scale during the Philippines campaign. The atomic bombs and the subsequent Japanese surrender made this contingency plan unnecessary.

Japanese Navy Air Force
A Brief History

Quantitatively and qualitatively the most important Japanese air force during the Pacific War was that operated by the Imperial Japanese Navy and this Service bore the brunt of the fighting against the Allies from the early hours of 8 December, 1941, (Japanese time), to the dawn of the atomic age.

The first step towards creating a naval air arm was taken in June 1912 by the Imperial Japanese Navy with the establishment of the Naval Aeronautical Research Committee. Soon thereafter six officers were sent to France and to the United States with instructions to purchase a number of seaplanes and to learn to fly and maintain these machines, and on 2 November, 1912, two of these officers flew their Farman and Curtiss seaplanes from the newly created naval air station on the Oppama Coast near Yokosuka. Domestic training of naval pilots was then undertaken on a limited scale and, within a year, the Imperial Japanese Navy commissioned their first seaplane tender, the *Wakamiya Maru*.

An Aichi D1A2. This type took an active part in combat operations during the second Sino-Japanese conflict. (*US Navy Department*.)

During the first World War the Imperial Japanese Navy made one of the first successful uses of aircraft when in September and October 1914 they operated four seaplanes from the *Wakamiya Maru* against the German fortress at Tsingtao. Making bombing as well as reconnaissance sorties these aircraft succeeded in sinking a small German mine-layer. However, not being actively engaged in the war on the European continent, the Imperial Japanese Navy had no further opportunity to test their fledgling air arm in action. Nevertheless the World War I period was

Mitsubishi A6M2 Reisen (Zero Fighter) of the 3rd Kokutai during operations in the Netherlands East Indies early in 1942.

marked by two significant events affecting the development of Japanese naval aviation: the first two Naval Air Corps, the Yokosuka and Sasebo Kokutais, were respectively activated in April 1916 and March 1918 and, in 1917, the first operational naval aircraft designed in Japan was manufactured at the Yokosuka Naval Arsenal.

Following the end of the war Japanese naval air activities were reduced and the only significant event of this period was the first successful take-off from a deck mounted on the *Wakamiya Maru* made in June 1920 by an imported Sopwith Pup flown by Lieutenant Kuwabara. The year 1921 was, however, to see a reversal in the trend as the Imperial Japanese Navy began the second phase in the development of their air arm following the arrival in Japan of the British Aviation Mission, led by the Master of Sempill, which brought with it instructors and modern aircraft. Late during the same year the *Hosho*, the world's first aircraft carrier built as such, was launched, and development of a series of aircraft—designed in Japan by Herbert Smith, the former chief designer of Sopwith Aviation Co —was undertaken.

During the twenties and early thirties the air units of the Imperial

A Nakajima C6N1 Navy Carrier Reconnaissance Plane. Named Saiun (Painted Cloud), it was an aircraft of this type which discovered the United States fleet at the start of the battle of the Marianas in June 1944.

Japanese Navy were involved in a series of incidents against Chinese forces, but it was not until 7 July, 1937, that this Service participated in a major action. Meanwhile, in 1932, the Naval Aircraft Establishment was organized and the Imperial Japanese Navy initiated their ambitious 7-Shi programme calling for the design of a series of aircraft including carrier fighters, carrier attack bombers, carrier bombers, reconnaissance seaplanes and land-based attack bombers. This programme was, however, a failure as, from all the aircraft submitted, only the Kawanishi E7K1 reconnaissance seaplane was placed in quantity production, the Hiro G2H1 attack bomber was procured in limited numbers and all other types remained in prototype form. Despite these discouraging results a new impetus had been given to the Japanese aircraft industry and, two years later, a 9-Shi

An Aichi E13A1—numerically the most important Japanese Navy wartime reconnaissance seaplane. (*US Navy Department.*)

programme was to result in the production of several famous Japanese aircraft among which were the Mitsubishi A5M series of carrier fighters, the Mitsubishi G3M attack bombers, the Yokosuka B4Y carrier attack bombers and the Kawanishi H6K flying-boats. With the availability of these aircraft the Imperial Japanese Navy were able to pursue vigorously their expansion programme and were ready for combat operations when the second Sino-Japanese conflict flared up in July 1937.

Operating from carriers as well as from land bases—the world's first transoceanic raids were made by Mitsubishi G3M bombers of the Kanoya and Kisarazu Kokutais within one week of the beginning of hostilities—

the aircraft of the Imperial Japanese Navy immediately gave a good account of themselves. As Japanese air superiority forced the Chinese to withdraw their aircraft far from the battlefields, the Japanese Navy had a good opportunity to demonstrate the long range of their bombers by flying deep into Chinese territory while, in the latter phase of the war, they began to use most of the aircraft which were to bear the brunt of the fighting against the Allies during the Pacific War.

During the second Sino-Japanese conflict the Imperial Japanese Navy were able to perfect their tactics and to strengthen their air unit organization. Like the Japanese Army this Service was placed under the supreme command of the Daihonei (Imperial General Headquarters) to which reported the Gunreibu Socho (Chief of Navy General Staff). One of the sections reporting to this officer was the Kaigun Koku Hombu (Navy Air Headquarters) which were responsible for aircraft, engines and equipment selection and testing as well as for supervision of training of flight and maintenance personnel. Operational control of air units was vested with the individual Kantais (Fleets), Koku Kantais (Air Fleets) and Homen Kantais (Area Fleets). Carrier-based aircraft were assigned to specific Koku Sentais (Carrier Divisions), usually comprising two aircraft carriers, and a varying number of Koku Sentais were assigned to Koku Kantais. Later during the Pacific War the carrier-based aircraft were reorganized into Kokutais (Naval Air Corps) with one or more Kokutais being assigned either to land bases or to carrier units grouped into Koku Kantais. Land-based aircraft were normally assigned to Koku Kantais which included one or more Koku Sentais (Air Flotillas), these units being in turn subdivided into Kokutais (Naval Air Corps). The Kokutais were the basic air units of the Imperial Japanese Navy and they had a strength of up to 150 aircraft of one or more types, although smaller aircraft complements were the rule rather than the exception. Other land-based units,

Abandoned Japanese Navy aircraft at Atsugi at the end of the war. In the foreground are a number of Mitsubishi A6M Reisen (Zero Fighters), one with wingtips folded and arrester hook lowered, and in the background a Mitsubishi G3M bomber. (*USAF.*)

A battle-damaged Nakajima B6N2 Tenzan (Heavenly Mountain) at Clark Field, Manila, in March 1945. (*US Navy Department.*)

often smaller than Kokutais, were directly assigned to local Homen Kantais (Area Fleets) as the tactical situation required.

On the eve of the Pacific War the Japanese Navy had some 3,000 combat aircraft on strength of which almost 1,400 aircraft were assigned to first line units as follows:

Rengo Kantai (Combined Fleet)

First Kantai
    Third Koku Sentai
        Hosho   (11 A5M4s and 8 B4Y1s)
        Zuiho   (16 A5M4s and 12 B5N2s)
    Surface units (battleships
        and cruisers)   (34 seaplanes)

Second Kantai
    Surface units (cruisers)   (39 seaplanes)

Third Kantai
    Surface units (cruisers and
        seaplane tender *Sanuki
        Maru*)   (15 seaplanes)
    Twelfth Koku Sentai
        Kamikawa Maru   (12 seaplanes)
        Sanyo Maru   (8 seaplanes)

Fourth Kantai
    Surface vessels (cruiser
        and mine-layer)   (2 seaplanes)
    24th Koku Sentai
        Chitose Kokutai   (36 G3Ms)
        Yokohama Kokutai   (24 H6Ks)
    16th, 17th, 18th and 19th
        Kokutais   (42 seaplanes)
    Kiyokawa Maru   (12 seaplanes)

Fifth Kantai
  Chichijima Maru   (6 seaplanes)
  Kimikawa Maru   (8 seaplanes)

Nanha Homen Kantai (Southern Area Fleet)
  Sagara Maru and *Kashii*   (9 seaplanes)

First Koku Kantai
  First Koku Sentai
    Akagi   (27 A6M2s, 18 D3A1s and 27 B5N2s)
    Kaga   (27 A6M2s, 27 D3A1s and 27 B5B2s)
  Second Koku Sentai
    Soryu   (27 A6M2s, 18 D3A1s and 18 B5N2s)
    Hiryu   (24 A6M2s, 18 D3A1s and 18 B5N2s)
  Fourth Koku Sentai
    Ryujo   (22 A5M4s and 18 B5N2s)
  Fifth Koku Sentai
    Zuikaku   (15 A6M2s, 27 D3A1s and 27 B5N2s)
    Shokaku   (15 A6M2s, 27 D3A1s and 27 B5N2s)

Eleventh Koku Kantai
  21st Koku Sentai
    Kanoya Kokutai   (27 G4M1s)
    First Kokutai   (36 G3M2s)
    Toko Kokutai   (24 H6ks)
  22nd Koku Sentai
    Mihoro Kokutai   (36 G3M2s)
    Genzan Kokutai   (36 G3M2s)
    Kanoya Kokutai   (27 G4M1s)
    Special Detachment   (6 C5M2s, 25 A6M2s and 12 A5M4s)
  23rd Koku Sentai
    Takao Kokutai   (54 G4M1s)
    Tainan Kokutai   (92 A6M2s, 6 C5M2s and 12 A5M4s)
    Third Kokutai   (92 A6M2s, 6 C5M2s and 12 A5M4s)
  Special seaplane tender detachment
    Mizuho   (20 seaplanes)
    Chitose   (20 seaplanes)

Shina Homen Kantai (China Area Fleet)
  Special Detachment   (12 B5N2s and 8 seaplanes)

Possessing the necessary combination of long-range aircraft and flight crews experienced in lengthy overwater flights, which the Japanese Army lacked, the land-based units of the Japanese Navy were assigned the prime responsibility for the campaign in the islands of the Pacific while the carrier-based aircraft of the First Koku Kantai were assigned the task of neutralizing the US Fleet by first striking at the Pacific Fleet's home base of Pearl Harbor.

Whether land- or carrier-based, the units of the Japanese Navy obtained a great series of victories during the first six months of the Pacific War but none did better than the First Koku Kantai. This air fleet, carrying the élite of the Imperial Japanese Navy, achieved successes from Pearl Harbor to Wake Island, Rabaul, Ambon (Amboina), the Marshall Islands, Darwin, Ceylon and the Coral Sea. However, on 4–6 June, 1942, the crushing defeat off Midway—the result of effective intelligence work by US forces and Japanese tactical errors and not consequent on poor equipment or lack of valour on the part of Japanese crews—effectively stopped the Japanese advance. In a final offensive gasp the Imperial Japanese Navy occupied Guadalcanal and Tulagi in the Solomons from where they prepared to contain the Allied counter-offensive in the hope that the Allies would finally settle the conflict at the conference table.

Two nearly completed Mitsubishi J2M3 Raiden (Thunderbolt) fighters at Atsugi in September 1945. The engine-cooling fan blades can be clearly seen on the nearest aircraft. (*USAF*.)

Unfortunately for the Japanese, this hope never materialized, and losses —which had been comparatively small until the battle of Midway—began to rise steadily during the air, land and sea battles in the Solomons. Following the inconclusive Battle of Santa Cruz in October 1942, during which the carrier-based units of the Japanese Navy almost regained the initiative, Guadalcanal had finally to be evacuated by Japan in February 1943. A comparative lull followed during which none of the opponents was able to mount major offensives, but the air arm of the Japanese Navy had their strength slowly drained during the war of attrition in the Solomons/Rabaul/New Guinea area.

When finally in June 1944 the Americans had been able to build up their carrier fleet to mount a major offensive against the Japanese-held Marianas, the Japanese Navy assembled nine aircraft carriers embarking some 450 aircraft as well as some 200 land-based aircraft. During the infamous 'Marianas Turkey Shoot' the Japanese Navy suffered a major defeat. To a large extent this defeat was due to their neglecting to develop in time a new carrier fighter to supplement the ageing Mitsubishi A6M series. Whereas the JAAF kept introducing new aircraft types, often too soon to correct their teething troubles, the JNAF relied mainly on a continuous upgrading of existing types, e.g. Mitsubishi A6M fighters and Mitsubishi G4M bombers which formed the mainstay of that Service throughout the war.

In the early autumn of 1944 a new Allied offensive led to major air battles around the Philippines and Formosa during which the Japanese Navy suffered alarming losses. The situation became worse following the American landing at Leyte Gulf, and Japan was severely defeated during the second Battle of the Philippine Sea. From then on the Japanese Navy were left without an effective carrier fleet. In the Philippines, the First and Second Koku Kantais fought a desperate battle and, despite the increasing use of kamikaze attacks—first attempted on 25 October, 1944—finally all Japanese air activities in the Philippines ceased in early January 1945. Little respite was given to the aircrews of the JNAF as a month later the Allies landed at Iwo Jima and in April 1945 it was the turn of Okinawa where kamikaze operations increased sharply. Fighting against tremendous numerical odds the air units of the Japanese Navy, despite the increasing use of better aircraft such as the Kawanishi N1K1-J and N1K2-J fighters

Kyushu Q1W1 Tokai (Eastern Sea) anti-submarine patrol aircraft at Mizutani, Hokkaido. This was the only type specially designed for this duty with the Japanese Navy. (*USAF.*)

The experimental hangar at the Dai-Ichi Kaigun Koku Gijitsusho (First Naval Air Technical Arsenal). In the foreground are Yokosuka MXY7 Ohka (Cherry Blossom) piloted bombs, beyond are components of the Yokosuka R2Y1 Keiun (Beautiful Cloud). (*US Navy Department.*)

and Yokosuka P1Y1 bombers, could not contain the Allied advance. Meanwhile, in Japan itself, other units fought an equally desperate battle against the Superfortresses and the carrier-based aircraft of the US Navy until 21 August, 1945, when the Imperial Japanese Navy ceased all hostilities in accordance with an Imperial Rescript of 14 August. The Rising Sun had finally set.

Army Type 1 Transport Model C (Ki-54c), the third version of the versatile Tachikawa twin-engined light transport. (*US Navy Department.*)

Japanese Aircraft Designation Systems

Throughout the Pacific War the Japanese military forces used a variety of aircraft designation systems which proved highly confusing for Allied intelligence personnel. For example, a typical aircraft operated by the Japanese Army carried a Kitai number (e.g. Ki-61), a type number (Army Type 3 Fighter) and a name (Hien). To simplify and expedite aircraft identification the Allies added to most aircraft a code name (e.g. TONY).

Today it is the code names that are still remembered, and this section has been conceived to give an insight into the various Japanese aircraft designation systems while also giving some historical background on the introduction and use of Allied code names.

To provide a complete listing of designations given within each system, all are listed in the Designation Index found at the end of this book whether or not the aircraft which bore such designations were still in service during the Pacific War.

I — JAPANESE ARMY AIR FORCE DESIGNATION SYSTEMS

During the first fifteen years of their existence the JAAF designated their aircraft under various systems although mostly adopting manufacturers' designations; but as none of these designations remained in use at the beginning of World War II they are not listed here.

In 1927 the type number system was adopted and remained in use until the final collapse; so also was the Kitai number system, first introduced in 1932. In addition, some aircraft received a popular name while research aeroplanes, gliders and rotary wing aircraft were given special designations.

The first Kitai designation, Ki-1, was given in 1932 to the Mitsubishi-built Army Type 93 Heavy Bomber. (*J. C. Caler.*)

The Tachikawa A-26, designed as a civil aircraft, became the Ki-77 when the project was taken over by the Imperial Japanese Army.

Guraida designations were given to gliders used by the Japanese Army, in this case the Kokusai Ku-8. (*Courtesy Heinz J. Nowarra.*)

Section 1 — Kitai numbers

In 1932 the Koku Hombu began assigning Kitai (Ki) or airframe numbers to all aircraft projected for the Imperial Japanese Army. Aircraft built prior to this date but still in service or undergoing tests received a Kitai number retrospectively. The Ki numbers were assigned in numerical sequence until 1944 when the Japanese felt the need to confuse Allied intelligence further.

Models of a basic type kept the same Ki number but received an additional Roman numeral to differentiate one model from another. Versions of the same model received an additional Japanese character such as 甲 (Ko), 乙 (Otsu), 丙 (Hei), etc. (commonly replaced by an equivalent letter to facilitate printing) following the Roman numeral. In some cases the Roman numerals and letters were supplemented by a Kaizo (Kai) or modification symbol. These systems are best explained by an example, the famous Kawasaki Hien (TONY):

Ki-61	Designation of the project and prototypes.
Ki-61-Ia	First production version of the first model.
Ki-61-Ib	Second production version of the first model.
Ki-61-I KAIc	Third production version of the first model.
Ki-61-I KAId	Fourth production version of the first model.
Ki-61-II	Prototypes of the second model.
Ki-61-II KAI	Modified prototypes of the second model.
Ki-61-II KAIa	First production version of the second model.
Ki-61-II KAIb	Second production version of the second model.
Ki-61-III	Projected third model.

To complicate the matter further, gliders, which initially received a Kitai number (e.g. Fukuda Ki-23), later received a Ku (Guraida) or glider number (e.g. Kokusai Ku-7).

In addition, aircraft which did not originate at the Koku Hombu received a designation based on their manufacturer's name or designation (e.g. Kayaba Ka-1, Kobe Te-Go, Tachikawa SS-1). Missiles received a special designation, although the Kawasaki Igo-1-B was also known as the Ki-148 to confuse Allied intelligence.

Section 2 — Type numbers

Beginning in 1927, aircraft accepted for quantity production and operational service were known by a designation combining a brief description of their function and a type number. The type number was based on the last digits of the Japanese year during which a particular aircraft was accepted. Prior to the year 2599 (1939 A.D.) the last two digits were used; in 2600 (1940 A.D.) the type number became 100, and on and after 2601 (1941 A.D.) only the last digit was used.

Aeroplanes accepted during 2597 (1937 A.D.) had the type number 97 and included the Army Type 97 Fighter (Nakajima Ki-27), Army Type 97 Light Bomber (Mitsubishi Ki-30), Army Type 97 Heavy Bomber (Mitsubishi Ki-21) and Army Type 97 Command Reconnaissance Plane (Mitsu-

Army Type 100 Command Reconnaissance Plane Model 4A (Mitsubishi Ki-46-IVa), final experimental version of one of the best Japanese wartime aircraft.

bishi Ki-15). The exact description of the function of each aircraft was of great importance to avoid confusion between two or more aircraft, as can be seen in the case of the Mitsubishi Type 97 Bomber, which could either be the single-engined Light Bomber (Ki-30) or the twin-engined Heavy Bomber (Ki-21).

As with the Kitai designations it was necessary to distinguish between the models and versions of a basic type. Models of the same aircraft were listed in numerical sequence using the Arabic numerals corresponding to the Roman numerals used in its Kitai designation. Similarly, each version received an additional letter or Kaizo designation following the type and model numbers. Once again the Kawasaki Hien (TONY) is chosen as the example:

Ki-61	No type number as this was the Kitai designation of the project and prototypes.
Ki-61-Ia	Army Type 3 Fighter Model 1A (Type 3 as this aircraft was accepted for quantity production during the Japanese fiscal year 2603).
Ki-61-Ib	Army Type 3 Fighter Model 1B.
Ki-61-I KAIc	Army Type 3 Fighter Model 1C.
Ki-61-I KAId	Army Type 3 Fighter Model 1D.
Ki-61-II	Prototypes of the second model, no type number.
Ki-61-II KAI	Modified prototypes of the second model, no type number.
Ki-61-II KAIa	Army Type 3 Fighter Model 2A.
Ki-61-II KAIb	Army Type 3 Fighter Model 2B.
Ki-61-III	Projected third model, no type number.

In the case of foreign-built aircraft, instead of using the last digits of the Japanese year, the Koku Hombu assigned to them a type letter based either on the country of manufacture (e.g. Type I Heavy Bomber for the Italian Fiat B.R.20) or the manufacturers' initials (e.g. Type LO Transport for the Lockheed 14).

Section 3 — Popular names

Soon after the opening of hostilities in the Pacific area it became evident to the Japanese High Command that the use of the Kitai and Type number systems in battle communiqués had two shortcomings: they revealed too much to the enemy and were too complex for any particular aircraft to appeal to the Japanese populace. Therefore popular names were given to the principal aircraft likely to attract the enthusiasm of the public. Whereas the Navy gave popular names to their aircraft according to a set pattern, the Army chose their names haphazardly.

In addition to these popular names, abbreviated designations, such as Shin-Shitei (Army Type 100 Command Reconnaissance Plane) and Guntei (Army Type 99 Assault Plane), became quite famous in Japan. However, they were never popular names.

II — JAPANESE NAVY AIR FORCE DESIGNATION SYSTEMS

On the eve of the Pacific War the aircraft of the Japanese Navy were designated according to three distinct systems: the Shi numbers, the type numbers and the short designations. Later in the war the JNAF adopted two new designation systems, the popular names and the SADP designations.

Section 1 — Experimental Shi numbers

From 1931 onward a Shi or experimental number based on the current Japanese imperial year of reign was assigned to every new aircraft projected for the Navy. Thus all aircraft projects initiated during 1932, the seventh year of Showa as the reign of His Majesty Hirohito is called, were known as Experimental 7-Shi, whereas those designed in 1940 became known as Experimental 15-Shi. To differentiate between the different projects bearing the same Experimental Shi number each aircraft was briefly described as to its main purpose (e.g. carrier fighter, reconnaissance seaplane, etc). Thus the full Shi number of a reconnaissance seaplane de-

Navy Experimental 16-Shi Carrier Attack Bomber (Aichi B7A1 Ryusei).

veloped in 1932 by Kawanishi was Navy Experimental 7-Shi Reconnaissance Seaplane.

This system of designations, quite similar in principle to the British specification system, was in constant use up to the end of the war and aircraft projected in 1945 came under the Navy Experimental 20-Shi group.

Navy Type 0 Carrier Fighter Model 52C (Mitsubishi A6M5c). This example of Reisen (Zero Fighter) has underwing rocket launching rails.

Section 2 — Short designation system

During the late twenties the Japanese Navy introduced an aircraft designation system similar in its basic concept to the one used until 1962 by the US Navy. When the detailed design of a new aircraft was initiated it was designated by a group of letters and numbers known as the 'short designation' (e.g. A6M1).

The first capital letter, or type symbol, indicated the primary function of the aircraft, i.e. A for carrier fighter, B for carrier attack bomber (torpedo bomber), etc. (*Refer to Designation Index for complete listing of type symbols.*) The first number, or type number, indicated the number of different aircraft that had been ordered under each type designation while the second capital letter indicated the company responsible for the design of the aircraft. The two letters and the first number remained unchanged during the life of the aircraft while the second number, indicating the particular model of the aircraft, changed with each new model. Minor modifications, not justifying a change in model number, were identified by a lower case letter following the second number (e.g. A6M5c).

When an aircraft was modified to perform some other duty, the new duty was indicated by the appropriate type symbol following the second number and separated from it by a hyphen (e.g. A6M2-K).

Foreign aircraft adopted for service use by the JNAF followed the regular pattern (e.g. A7He1) while foreign aircraft bought for experimental purpose only received a similar short designation in which the first number was replaced by the capital letter X (e.g. AXHe1).

The following letters were assigned to the Japanese and foreign manufacturers supplying aircraft to the Japanese Navy:

A	Aichi (Aichi Tokei Denki K.K. and Aichi Kokuki K.K.).
	North American (North American Aviation Inc).
B	Boeing (The Boeing Aircraft Company).
C	Consolidated (Consolidated Aircraft Corp).
D	Douglas (Douglas Aircraft Company Inc).
G	Hitachi (Hitachi Kokuki K.K.).
	Grumman (The Grumman Aircraft Engineering Corp).
H	Hiro (Dai-Juichi Kaigun Kokusho).
	Hawker (Hawker Aircraft Ltd).
He	Heinkel (Ernst Heinkel Flugzeugwerke A.G.).
J	Nihon Kogata (Nihon Kogata Hikoki K.K.).
	Junkers (Junkers Flugzeug und Motorenwerke A.G.).
K	Kawanishi (Kawanishi Kokuki K.K.).
	Kinner (Kinner Airplane & Motor Corp).
M	Mitsubishi (Mitsubishi Jukogyo K.K.).
N	Nakajima (Nakajima Hikoki K.K.).
P	Nihon (Nihon Hikoki K.K.).
S	Sasebo (Dai-Nijuichi Kaigun Kokusho).
Si	Showa (Showa Hikoki K.K.).
V	Vought-Sikorsky (Vought-Sikorsky Division of United Aircraft Corp).
W	Watanabe (K.K. Watanabe Tekkosho).
	Kyushu (Kyushu Hikoki K.K.).
Y	Yokosuka (Dai-Ichi Kaigun Koku Gijitsusho).
Z	Mizuno (Mizuno Guraida Seisakusho).

Section 3 — Type number system

From 1921 onwards, as a substantial number of Japanese-built aircraft entered service, the Navy assigned to each type of aircraft going into production a designation combining a brief description of their function with a type number. From 1921 to 1928 the type numbers were based on the current Japanese year of reign during which a particular type of aircraft was accepted for production, e.g. 1921–26 = Taisho 10 to Taisho 15 and 1927 and 1928 = Showa 2 and 3. However, commencing in 1929 the type numbers were based on the last digits of the Japanese calendar year. The JNAF system of type numbers was then similar to the one initiated in 1927 by the JAAF with the exception of the type number for aircraft accepted for production during the year 2600 (1940 A.D.) which were Type 0 under the Naval nomenclature and Type 100 under the Army's nomenclature.

To distinguish between models and versions of a basic type of aircraft the Navy used a system of model numbers. Initially a single digit was used for each version, the first one being designated Model 1, and a sub-version of that Model 1 being known as the Model 1-1. In the late thirties the

Best flying-boat of the war was the Navy Type 2 Flying-Boat Model 12 (Kawanishi H8K2). (*US Navy Department.*)

model number system was modified, each model number comprising two digits. The first digit was changed each time the airframe was modified and the second digit was changed each time a different engine model was adapted to the airframe. Thus, the first model of a basic type of aircraft was designated Model 11, the second model became Model 21 if there was only an airframe modification, Model 12 if only the type of engine had changed, or Model 22 if both airframe and engine were different to those of the first model. Minor modifications, not justifying a change in model number, were identified by a Japanese character such as 甲 (Ko), 乙 (Otsu), 丙 (Hei), etc., following the appropriate Model number. For practical purposes, in the Western World these characters are usually replaced by Roman letters (e.g. the Type and Model numbers for the Mitsubishi A6M5c were Navy Type 0 Carrier Fighter Model 52丙—or 52C).

Foreign aircraft in JNAF service were known by a similar system in which the type number was replaced by a type letter, the letter corresponding to that assigned to the manufacturers under the short designation system (e.g. the Heinkel A7He1 was known as the Navy Type He Air Defence Fighter).

Navy Bomber Ginga (Milky Way)—the Yokosuka P1Y1—was the only aircraft in the Bomber class to come under the Type Number system.

The full designation of the Aichi E16A1 under the Type Number system was Navy Reconnaissance Seaplane Zuiun (Auspicious Cloud) Model 11.

In late 1942, the type number system was modified for security reasons. The type number gave place to a popular/code name as detailed in *Section 4* while the brief description of the aircraft's function and the model number continued in use as before (e.g. Navy Suisei Carrier Bomber Model 33 for the Yokosuka D4Y3).

Section 4 — Popular names

For a long time the Japanese Navy discouraged the use of popular names and only a few aircraft, such as the Mitsubishi G4M1 which was known to its crews as the Hamaki (Cigar) due to the shape of its fuselage, did receive a popular name. However, in July 1943, the Navy reversed their long-standing aversion towards popular names and officially assigned names to their aircraft in lieu of type numbers. These popular names were chosen according to the following code:

Fighters:	Named after meteorological phenomena.
Carrier and seaplane fighters:	Names ending in pu or fu (wind).
Interceptor fighters:	Names ending in den (lightning).
Night fighters:	Names ending in ko (light).
Attack aircraft:	Named after mountains.
Reconnaissance aircraft:	Named after clouds.
Bombers:	Named after stars (sei) or constellations (zan).
Patrol planes:	Named after seas and oceans.
Transports:	Named after skies.
Trainers:	Named after trees, plants and flowers.
Miscellaneous aircraft:	Named after landscape effects.

A Navy Interceptor Fighter Raiden (Thunderbolt) Model 21 (Mitsubishi J2M3) abandoned in the Philippines by retreating Japanese forces. (*US Navy Department*.)

Section 5 — Service Aeroplane Development Programme (SADP) systems

In 1939 the Bureau of Aeronautics of the Imperial Japanese Navy instituted the Service Aeroplane Development Programme under which the design teams in charge of new aircraft projects could study the requirements and problems of new aircraft for submission to the JNAF prior to undertaking detailed design. An aircraft coming under this programme received a special project designation consisting of its manufacturer's letter under the short designation system and a two-digit number (10, 20, 30, etc). However, records of most of these SADP numbers were destroyed prior to the Allied occupation of Japan.

Navy Special Attack Bomber Seiran (Mountain Haze). This was the Aichi M6A1 which was about to enter service when the war ended. (*Eckert*.)

Allied intelligence believed, wrongly, that the obsolete Mitsubishi Ki-2-I was still operational and gave it the code name LOUISE. (*Eckert*.)

III — PACIFIC CODE NAME SYSTEM

The development of the use of the colourful code names given to the Japanese aircraft during World War II began in the Southwest Pacific Theatre in the second half of 1942. Initially, Japanese aircraft were 'identified' as Zeros if they were fighters and as Mitsubishis if they dropped bombs. The result was unavoidable confusion and the problem of labelling Japanese aeroplanes was delegated to the theatre's Air Technical Intelligence Unit (ATIU) of the Allied Air Forces.

Discovery of Japanese official names helped little. They were unwieldy and the list was incomplete. Cumbersome though such designations were, some agencies started to use them for lack of something better. Others attempted to describe the types by manufacturers but this only added to confusion inasmuch as more than one manufacturer was sometimes involved.

Early in 1942, Captain Frank T. McCoy Jr, of Nashville, Tennessee, was sent to Australia as the Intelligence Officer of the 38th Bombardment Group. In June 1942 he became the founder and head of the Materiel

CLAUDE, the predecessor of ZEKE, was the Mitsubishi A5M Type 96 Carrier-Based Fighter and it is seen here in the markings of the 13th Kokutai during the second Sino-Japanese conflict. (*US Navy Department*.)

Section of the Directorate of Intelligence, Allied Air Forces, Southwest Pacific Area, in Melbourne. Captain McCoy's staff numbered two: Technical Sergeant Francis Williams and Corporal Joseph Grattan. These three men were assigned the task of identifying Japanese aircraft.

The early activities of the Directorate of Intelligence, which became the Technical Air Intelligence Unit in October 1944, are well described by Colonel (then Captain) McCoy himself: 'The need for classification was urgent so we decided to start out fresh, with our own system of code names for enemy aircraft. I am from Tennessee, and the first selections we made

The Directorate of Intelligence, Allied Air Forces, SWPA, gave the code name PETE to the Navy Type 0 Observation Seaplane (Mitsubishi F1M2). (*US Navy Department*.)

were hillbilly names such as ZEKE, NATE, RUFE, JAKE, PETE—short, simple and unusual and easy to remember.

'Sergeant Williams and I selected most of the names in our numerous bull sessions, and we started assigning them in July 1942 while we were still in Melbourne. Air Commodore J. E. Hewitt, RAAF, the Director of Intelligence, and his executive and deputy, Major Ben B. Cain, USAAF, gave 100 per cent approval on the code names and helped us in the fight from then on. I say fight unqualifiedly, because everyone thought we were crazy. We assigned 75 code names in the first month.'

Thus were born most of the code names which were to come into common usage throughout the Allied air forces. By September 1942, the Southwest Pacific Area's intelligence information sheets were using the code names exclusively. Shortly thereafter, the South Pacific and China–India–Burma theatres were employing the TAIU code names and silhouette sheets. McCoy began a series of cables to Washington and to the Air

MYRT was the code name given to the fast reconnaissance carrier-based Nakajima C6N1 Saiun (Painted Cloud).

Ministry in London, requesting the adoption of the same or similar system of standardized identification. His involved, strange-sounding messages aroused suspicion on one occasion (one of his code names was HAP, the nickname of General Henry H. (Hap) Arnold, USAAF Chief of Staff) and he was summoned before General MacArthur's chief of operations to explain them. Late in 1942, the code name system was adopted by all United States Air Forces and by the United States Navy, and several months later the British Air Ministry gave it their approval.

Thereafter, when the Materiel Section of the Directorate of Intelligence identified a new Japanese aircraft it would assign a tentative label, check

DINAH (Mitsubishi Ki-46-II) undergoing flight evaluation in the United States. (*USAF.*)

with Washington, London and India headquarters for any available confirmation and then announce the designated code name. No classification was given to these names. In the summer of 1944 a joint Army–Navy Air Technical Center at Anacostia, DC, took over the responsibility for assigning the names.

The code names were allotted on the following basis:

Male first names:	Fighters (Army and Navy, single- and twin-engined).
	Reconnaissance seaplanes.
Female first names:	Bombers, attack bombers and dive-bombers.
	Reconnaissance aircraft (land- or carrier-based).
	Flying-boats.
	Transports (names beginning with the letter T).
Tree names:	Trainers.
Bird names:	Gliders.

Two famous Nakajima fighters. TOJO, Ki-44-II Shoki (Devil-Queller), in the foreground and FRANK, Ki-84-I Hayate (Gale). (*US Navy Department.*)

Several exceptions to the above pattern may be noted. The Nakajima Ki-44, TOJO, was first spotted in China and dubbed there. A request was made for the name to stick and all co-ordinating parties agreed.

Japanese Aircraft Camouflage and Markings

The purpose of this section is not to provide a complete history of aircraft camouflage and markings as this subject, adequately covered in specialized volumes, is beyond the scope of this book, but rather to provide a survey of the basic schemes used by the Japanese forces to camouflage and identify their aircraft. No attempt has therefore been made to cover the often unusual schemes resulting from field contingencies when the ground personnel had to adopt expedient methods using whatever paints were available to them. Like the main body of the book this section is divided into two parts respectively covering the camouflage and markings used by the Imperial Japanese Army and the Imperial Japanese Navy.

An early production Mitsubishi Ki-21-Ia in segmented camouflage. (*USAF*.)

AIRCRAFT OF THE IMPERIAL JAPANESE ARMY

At the start of the Pacific War most combat aircraft of the Japanese Army were either left in natural metal finish or were painted light grey-green overall (*see page 68*). However, during the second Sino-Japanese conflict some aircraft types—in particular the Mitsubishi Ki-21 and Kawasaki Ki-32 bombers—displayed an early form of camouflage. The most common camouflage scheme then used consisted of irregular olive green (A3) and brown (A/N14) areas separated by thin white or light blue wavy lines on the upper surfaces while under surfaces were finished in light grey (A/N2) (*see page 69*).

As the war went on the need for camouflage became more pressing and field units began to apply a series of varied schemes. Most of these took the form of either olive green (A3) blotches or snake-weave stripes over the factory finish or natural metal finish (*see page 66*). Meanwhile, camouflage schemes began to be applied at the factory and commonly consisted of either olive green (A3) over all upper surfaces with light grey

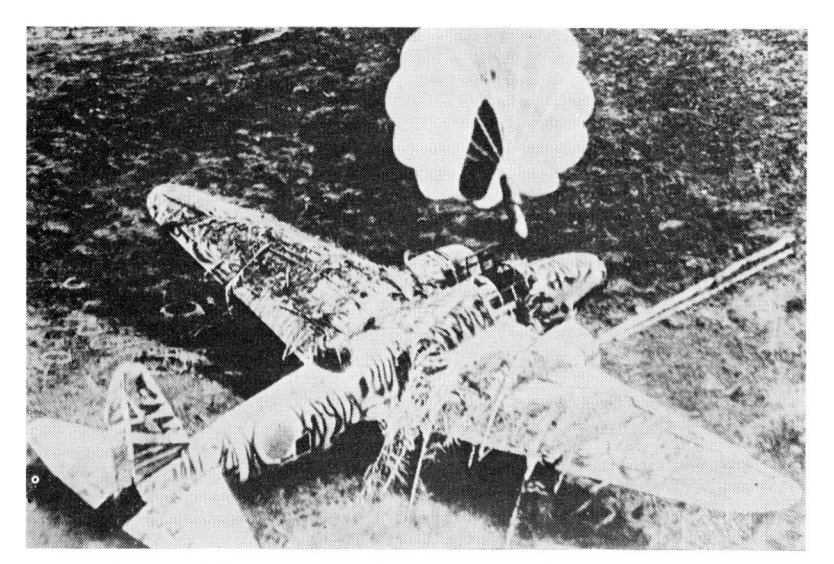

A Mitsubishi Ki-21-IIb of the 14th Sentai under attack by parachute mines. The aircraft has typical snake-weave camouflage and palm fronds have been laid on the wings as additional camouflage.

(A/N2) or natural metal finish on under surfaces (*see pages 68 and 70*) or olive green (A3) blotches spray-painted over the base finish (*see pages 67 and 71*). In either case a flat black or dark blue anti-glare panel was frequently applied on the nose of fighter aircraft.

Other frequently-used schemes included the colours applied to many experimental or training aeroplanes. However, in this instance the purpose was not camouflage but rather the opposite, such aircraft being painted in bright training orange (E18) overall (*see pages 73 and 74*).

Identification markings consisted of a 'combat identification stripe' in white around the rear fuselage forward of the tail surfaces and, during the last two years of the war, yellow (A/N20 or A/N4) wing leading edge panels extending from the root to a position about level with the flaps/ailerons divide. As with the camouflage schemes exceptions were rather frequent.

National markings consisted of solid red circles (Hinomarus) normally

Mitsubishi Ki-21s bearing abstract representations of three Kanji characters spelling Hamamatsu, home base of the Hamamatsu Army Bomber Training School.

A Nakajima Ki-43-I Hayabusa (Peregrine Falcon) of the 50th Sentai, showing the infrequently used unit markings on the fuselage. The Ki-43 is seen after being shot down near Chittagong. (*British Official*.)

painted on both sides of the fuselage and above and below the wings. On biplanes the Hinomarus were painted on both upper wings and under both lower wings. On camouflaged aircraft the Hinomarus were normally outlined in white on dark surfaces but many aircraft operating in defence of the homeland had their Hinomarus applied on white bands circling the fuselage and wings (*see page 66*) while at least one unit applied an additional narrow red circle around the white-ringed Hinomarus.

Unit markings, first introduced during the latter phase of the second Sino-Japanese conflict, consisted of brightly coloured designs. These markings often took the form of abstract symbols of either the Sentai number (*see page 70 showing the markings of the 74th Sentai*) or the Kanji characters spelling the name of the unit's home base (e.g. Akeno for the Akeno Fighter Training School). Other markings were geometric designs (*see arrow on Ki-43 of the 64th Sentai on page 66*) or, less frequently, were more conventional (e.g. *rampant tiger on Ki-46 of the 82nd Sentai*).

The red and blue tail markings indicated that this Nakajima Ki-44-II Shoki (Devil-Queller) belonged to the 246th Sentai. (*USAF.*)

These markings were initially applied on the rear fuselage or on the vertical tail surfaces but during the war were confined to the fin and rudder. The colour of these markings served to identify the Chutais within a given Sentai: cobalt blue was used for the Sentai Hombu and white, red, yellow and green were normally used by the 1st, 2nd, 3rd and 4th Chutais. A white outline was often used on camouflaged aircraft.

Representative camouflage and markings are illustrated on the following pages and are keyed to the colour chart (*see jacket flap*). The IPMS colour code numbers, well-known to modellers and used by hobby paint manufacturers, are used as an aid to the reader.

AIRCRAFT OF THE IMPERIAL JAPANESE NAVY

During the early part of the second Sino-Japanese conflict most aircraft of the Japanese Navy were left in natural metal finish or were aluminium doped. Later on, however, most aircraft were painted sky grey (N8) or were camouflaged in dark green (N1) and tan (N17) on their upper surfaces, and light grey (A/N2) on their lower surfaces. On the eve of the Pacific War these two schemes were the most prevalent among naval combat aircraft (*see pages 76 and 81*) but many aircraft were still left in natural metal finish (*see pages 78 and 85*).

Navy Aichi D1A1 in typical prewar overall aluminium finish with red fin and rudder. Wheel-spats have been removed.

During the early part of the Pacific War a new scheme was introduced and first applied to land-based attack bombers, floatplanes and flying-boats. This scheme consisted of dark green (N1) upper surfaces with either light grey (A/N2), light blue (N10) or natural metal finish (A6) lower surfaces (*see pages 81, 85 and 78 respectively*). For a while carrier-based aircraft retained their sky grey (N8) finish but with their assignment to land bases becoming increasingly frequent the ground crews began to apply dark green (N1) blotches on their upper surfaces and fuselage sides (*see page 76*). The extent of blotching varied from widely spaced spots

Mitsubishi A6M2 Reisen (Zero Fighter) of the Tainan Kokutai, seen with sky grey (N8) finish. Engine cowling and tail number were black. (*USAF*.)

to an almost uniform application of dark green. However, in July 1943 solid dark green (N1) was adopted as the standard camouflage colour for the upper surfaces of all naval combat aircraft.

Experimental and training aircraft were initially painted training orange (E18) all over (*see pages 82 and 84*) but, as their bases became the frequent targets of Allied aircraft, their upper surfaces were finished in dark green, training orange being retained on their lower surfaces. Finally, late in the war, these aircraft were camouflaged in the same way as the combat aircraft (dark green upper surfaces and light grey or natural metal finish lower surfaces).

A common feature on radial-engined aircraft of the Japanese Navy was the painting of the engine cowling(s) in matt black (A/N22); however, several aircraft types (e.g. Mitsubishi G4M and J2M series) did not comply with this rule.

Early during the war the white combat stripe on the rear fuselage was discarded on Navy aircraft, but yellow (A/N4 or A/N20) wing leading edge

Mitsubishi G4M2 finished in overall training orange (E18). The first character on the fin identifies the aircraft as belonging to the Koku Gijutsu Sho (Air Technical Arsenal).

identification panels—similar to those applied on Army aircraft—were normally applied.

National markings used on JNAF aircraft were similar to those applied to JAAF aircraft but the home defence bands circling the fuselage and wings were not used by the Navy. Some Navy aircraft had their Hinomarus painted over white or yellow squares (*see page 83*).

Unit markings, painted across both sides of fin and rudder, underwent a series of changes during the Pacific War. At the start of the war Navy aircraft used a unit marking system consisting of either one or two Kana characters referring to the aircraft's home base (*e.g. page 84 where the character Ka stands for Kasumigaura*) if the aircraft was based in Japan or Korea, of a Roman letter (*e.g. page 85 where W identifies the 14th Kokutai*) for land-based aircraft in a combat zone or of a Roman letter and Roman numeral (*e.g. page 79 where BI identifies the first aircraft carrier -I- of the Second Koku Sentai -B-*) for carrier-based aircraft. The

Overall matt black finish and Hinomarus without borders were applied to Japanese Navy night fighters. This colour scheme is seen on a Nakajima J1N1-S Gekko (Moonlight). (*Copyright 'Maru'*.)

unit marking was followed by a hyphen and a series of digits—usually three—which identified the individual aircraft in the unit.

In the mid-war years these systems of unit markings were replaced by an all-digit system whereby each unit received a call number of two to four digits (three digits were the rule but many exceptions existed). The first digit was intended to identify the unit's role, but this principle was not consistently followed. The use of individual aircraft numbers, separated from the unit call number by a hyphen, remained identical. Finally, at the war's end, as units were once again stationed in Japan, some of them chose again to paint the Kana character identifying their home base in place of their call number (e.g. Tainan Kokutai).

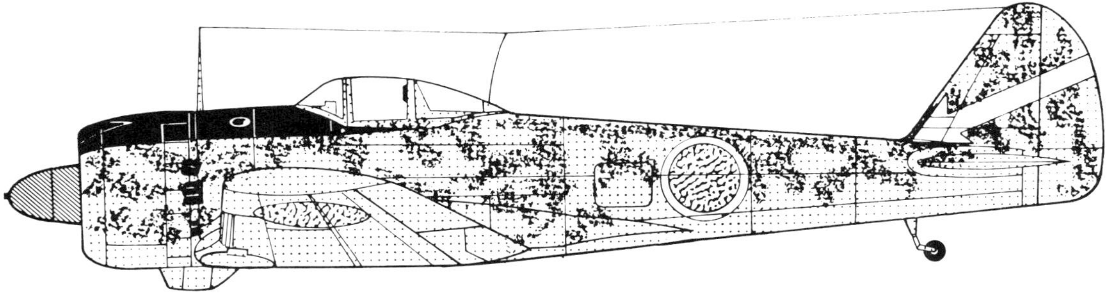

Nakajima Ki-43-II of the 64th Sentai, 1st Chutai. Natural metal finish (A6) overall with olive green (A3) blotches over upper wing surfaces and fuselage sides. Black anti-glare panel. Brown (A/N14) spinner and white tail markings. Deep yellow (A/N20) wing leading edge panels. Red (A/N16) Hinomarus with white outline on fuselage sides and wing upper surfaces.

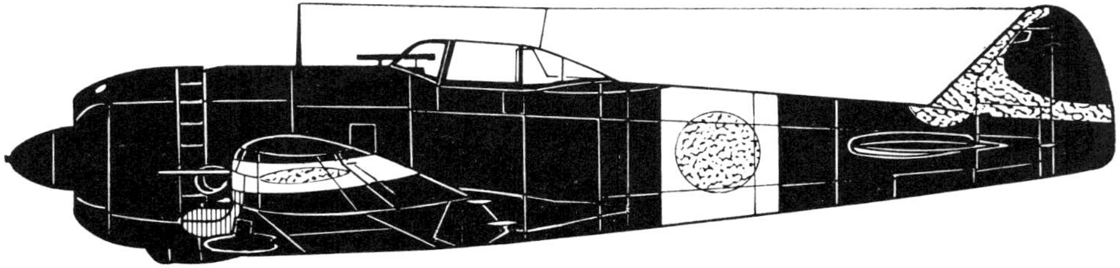

Nakajima Ki-44-II of the 87th Sentai, 2nd Chutai. Aircraft serving in the defence of Japan and finished matt black (A/N22) overall. Deep yellow (A/N20) wing leading edge panels. White fuselage and wing bands enclosing Hinomarus.

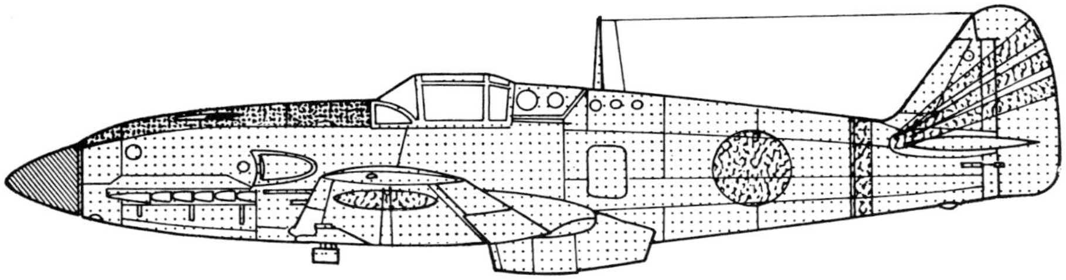

Kawasaki Ki-61-Ib of the 18th Sentai. Overall natural metal finish (A6) with olive green (A3) anti-glare panel. Red (A/N16) Hinomarus, rear fuselage stripe and tail markings. Brown (A/N14) spinner.

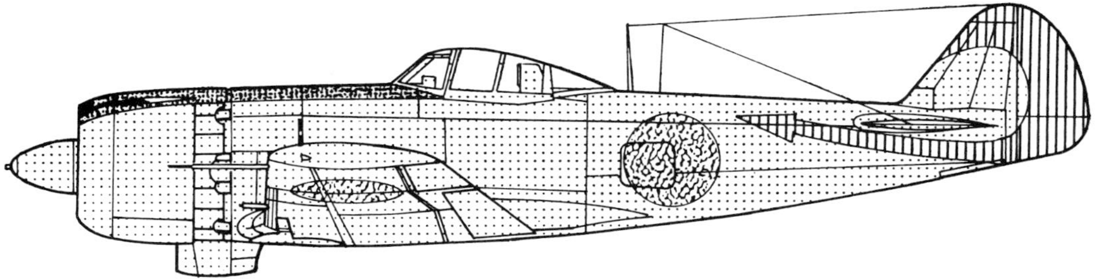

Nakajima Ki-84-Ia of the 29th Sentai, Sentai Hombu. Overall natural metal finish (A6) with olive green (A3) anti-glare panel. Deep yellow (A/N20) wing leading edge panels. Cobalt blue (A21) tail markings. Red (A/N16) Hinomarus.

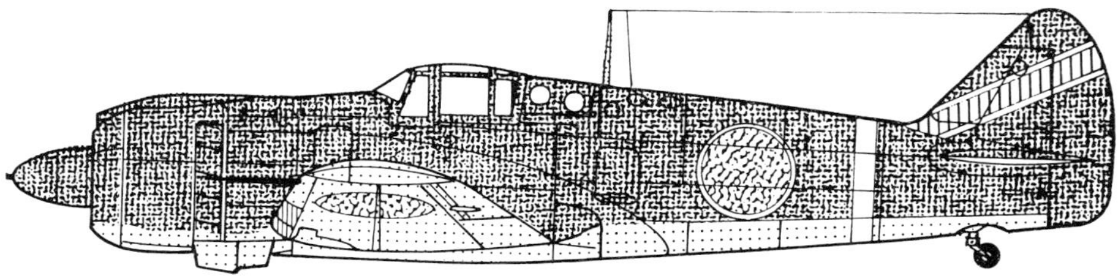

Kawasaki Ki-100-Ia of the 59th Sentai, Sentai Hombu. Olive green (A3) upper surfaces and natural metal finish (A6) lower surfaces. White fuselage combat stripe. Cobalt blue (A21) tail markings with white outline. Red (A/N16) Hinomarus with white outline on fuselage sides and wing upper surfaces.

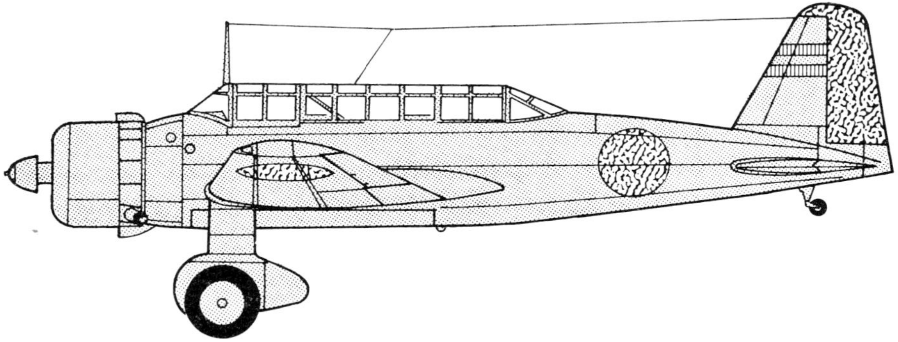

Mitsubishi Ki-30 of 90th Sentai, 1st Chutai. Light grey (A/N2) overall. Deep yellow (A/N20) fin strips. Red (A/N16) rudder and Hinomarus.

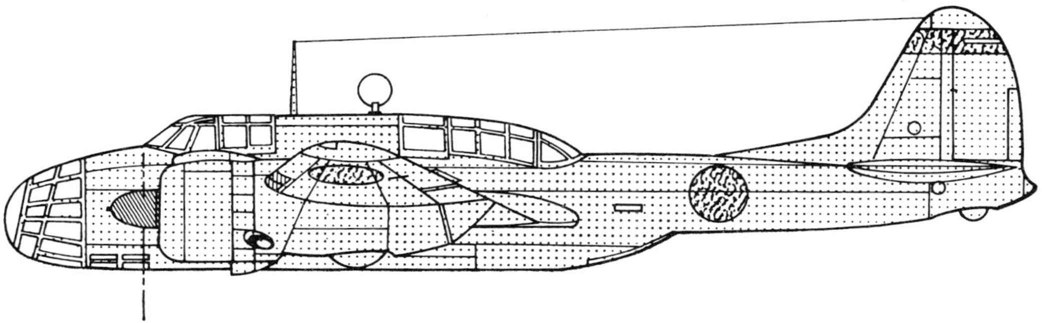

Kawasaki Ki-48-II of 3rd Sentai. Natural metal finish (A6) overall. Brown (A/N14) spinners. Deep yellow (A/N20) wing leading edge panels. Red (A/N16) Hinomarus and tail markings.

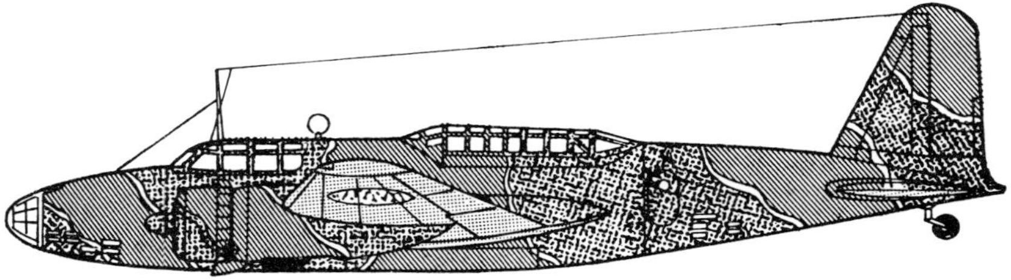

Mitsubishi Ki-21-I. Overall olive green (A3) and brown (A/N14) with thin white lines separating dark colours except for under surfaces of wings and horizontal stabilizer which were light grey (A/N2). Red (A/N16) Hinomarus on four wing positions only.

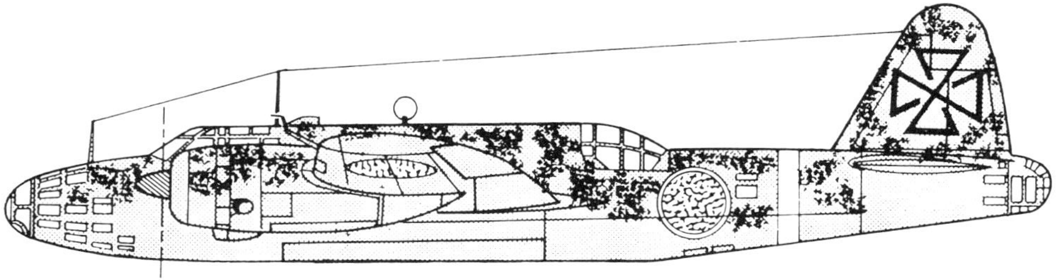

Nakajima Ki-49-II of 74th Sentai, 2nd Chutai. Overall light grey (A/N2) with olive green (A3) blotches on upper surfaces and vertical tail surfaces. White fuselage combat stripe. Brown (A/N14) spinners. Red (A/N16) tail markings and Hinomarus with white outline on fuselage sides and wing upper surfaces.

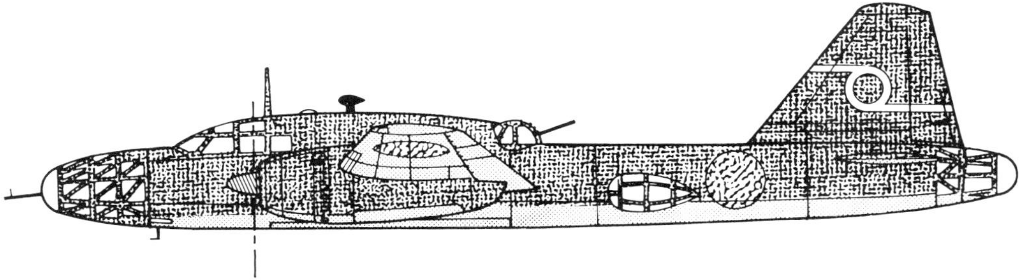

Mitsubishi Ki-67-I of 110th Sentai. Olive green (A3) upper surfaces and light grey (A/N2) lower surfaces. White tail markings. Deep yellow (A/N20) wing leading edge panels. Brown (A/N14) spinners. Red (A/N16) Hinomarus.

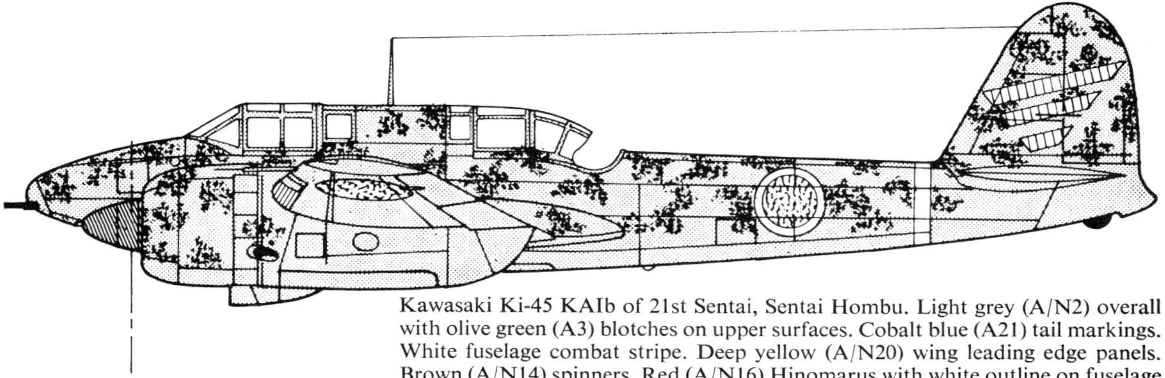

Kawasaki Ki-45 KAIb of 21st Sentai, Sentai Hombu. Light grey (A/N2) overall with olive green (A3) blotches on upper surfaces. Cobalt blue (A21) tail markings. White fuselage combat stripe. Deep yellow (A/N20) wing leading edge panels. Brown (A/N14) spinners. Red (A/N16) Hinomarus with white outline on fuselage sides and wing upper surfaces.

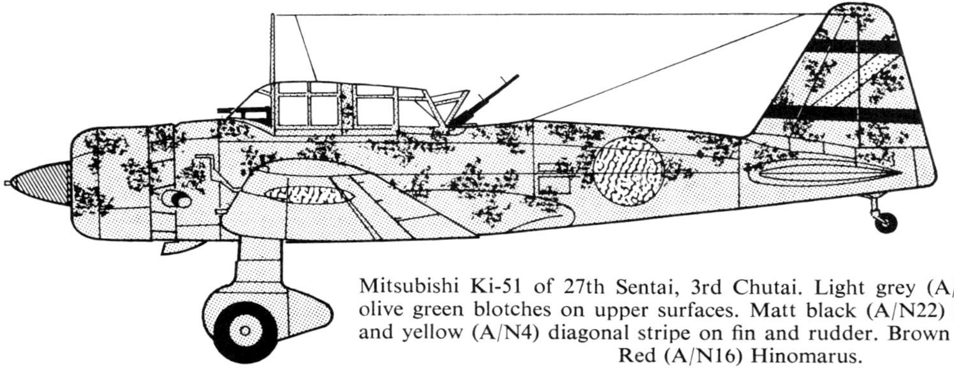

Mitsubishi Ki-51 of 27th Sentai, 3rd Chutai. Light grey (A/N2) overall with olive green blotches on upper surfaces. Matt black (A/N22) horizontal stripes and yellow (A/N4) diagonal stripe on fin and rudder. Brown (A/N14) spinner. Red (A/N16) Hinomarus.

71

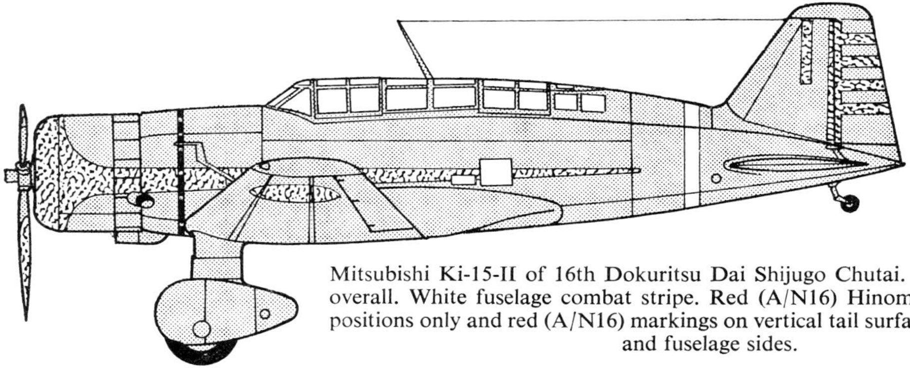

Mitsubishi Ki-15-II of 16th Dokuritsu Dai Shijugo Chutai. Light grey (A/N2) overall. White fuselage combat stripe. Red (A/N16) Hinomarus on four wing positions only and red (A/N16) markings on vertical tail surfaces, engine cowling and fuselage sides.

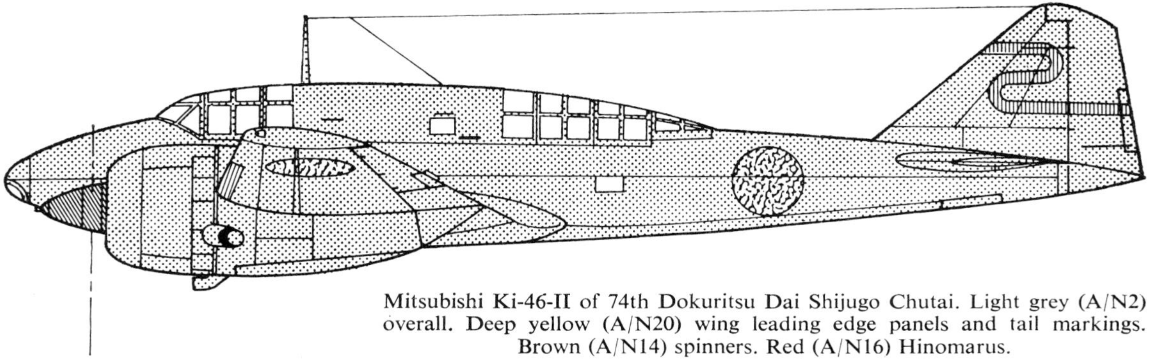

Mitsubishi Ki-46-II of 74th Dokuritsu Dai Shijugo Chutai. Light grey (A/N2) overall. Deep yellow (A/N20) wing leading edge panels and tail markings. Brown (A/N14) spinners. Red (A/N16) Hinomarus.

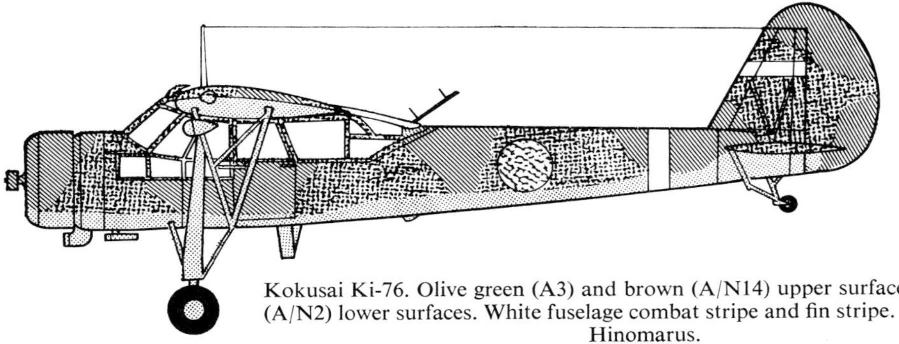

Kokusai Ki-76. Olive green (A3) and brown (A/N14) upper surfaces. Light grey (A/N2) lower surfaces. White fuselage combat stripe and fin stripe. Red (A/N16) Hinomarus.

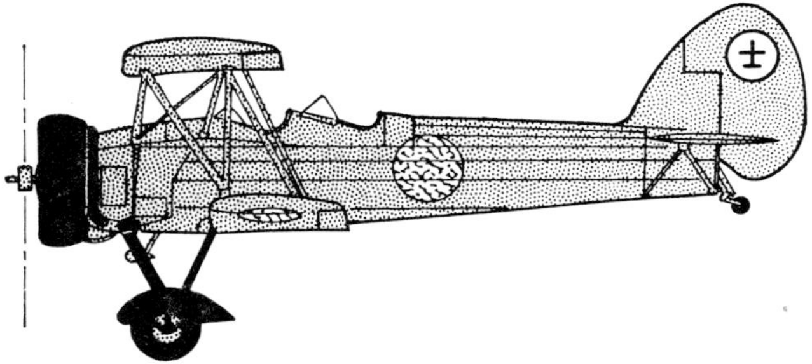

Tachikawa Ki-9 of Koku Shikan Gakko (Air Academy). Training orange (E18) overall. Matt black (A/N22) engine cowling and undercarriage. Red (A/N16) Hinomarus. Tail markings in black over white circle outlined in black.

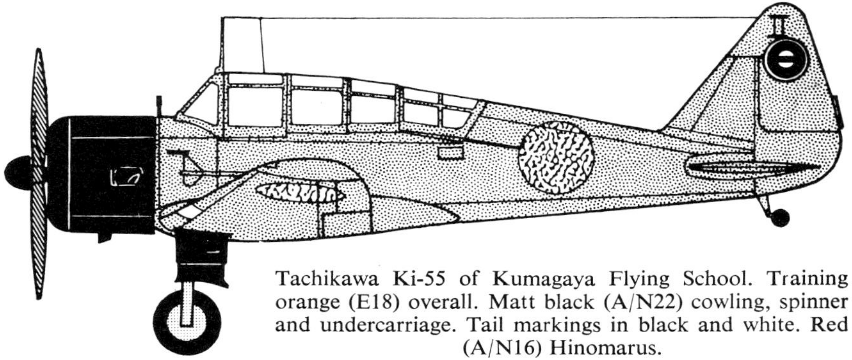

Tachikawa Ki-55 of Kumagaya Flying School. Training orange (E18) overall. Matt black (A/N22) cowling, spinner and undercarriage. Tail markings in black and white. Red (A/N16) Hinomarus.

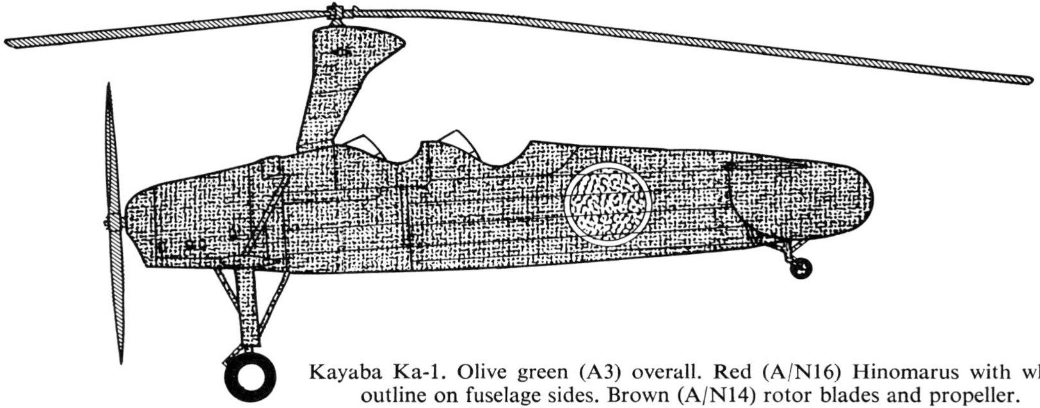

Kayaba Ka-1. Olive green (A3) overall. Red (A/N16) Hinomarus with white outline on fuselage sides. Brown (A/N14) rotor blades and propeller.

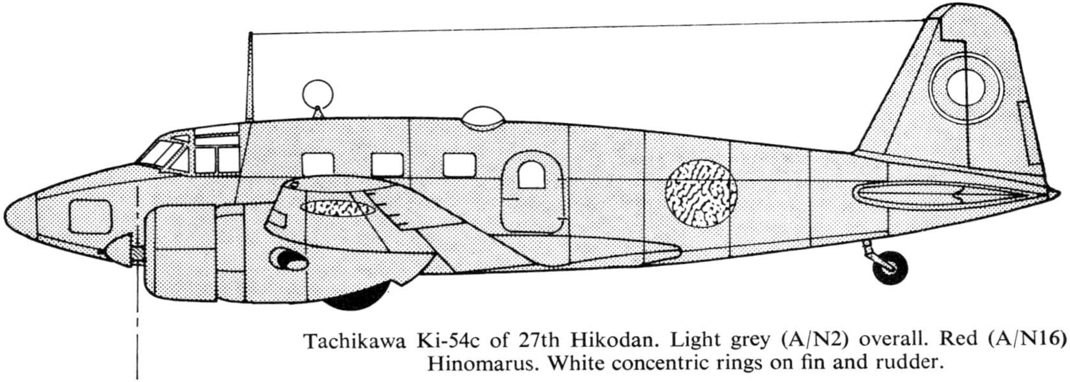

Tachikawa Ki-54c of 27th Hikodan. Light grey (A/N2) overall. Red (A/N16) Hinomarus. White concentric rings on fin and rudder.

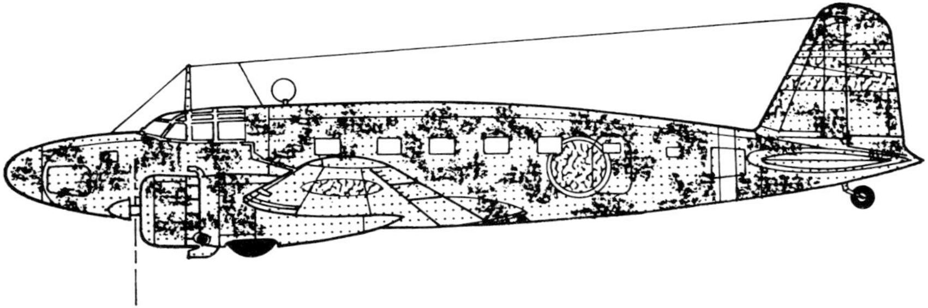

Mitsubishi Ki-57-I of 7th Hikodan. Natural metal finish (A6) overall with olive green (A3) blotches over upper surfaces. White fuselage combat stripe. Red (A/N16) tail markings and Hinomarus with white outline on fuselage sides and wing upper surfaces.

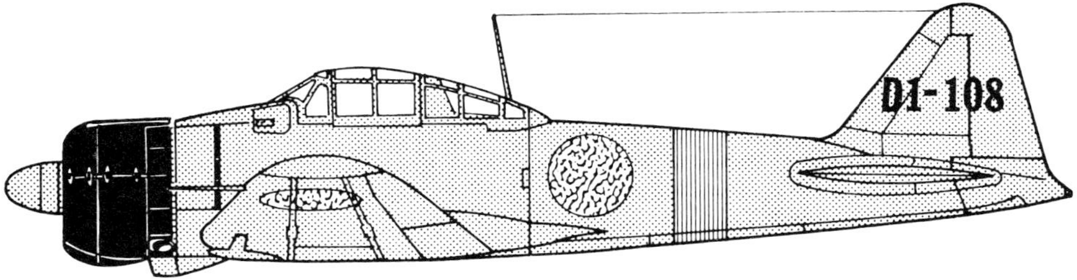

Mitsubishi A6M2 Model 21 of the first carrier (*Ryujo*) of the Fourth Koku Sentai. Sky grey (N8) overall. Matt black (A/N22) cowling and tail number. Deep yellow (A/N20) rear fuselage stripe. Red (A/N16) Hinomarus.

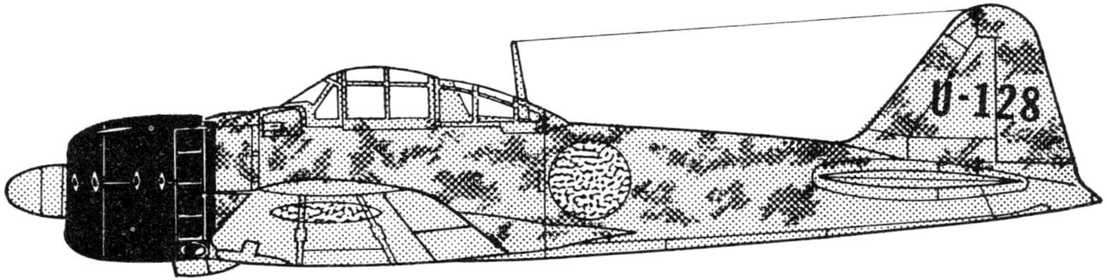

Mitsubishi A6M3 Model 32 of 6th Kokutai. Sky grey (N8) overall with dark green (N1) blotches on upper surfaces. Matt black (A/N22) cowling. Red (A/N16) Hinomarus and tail number.

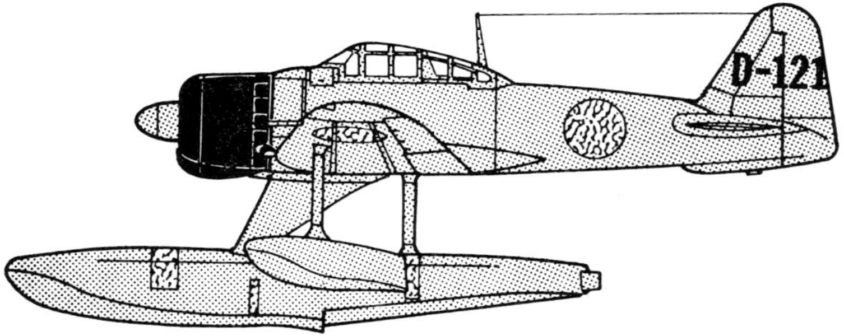

Nakajima A6M2-N of 5th Kokutai. Sky grey (N8) overall. Matt black (A/N22) cowling. Red (A/N16) Hinomarus and tail number.

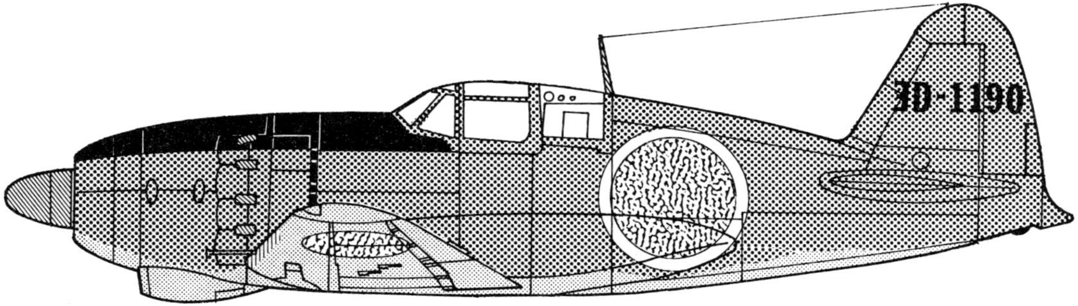

Mitsubishi J2M3 of 302nd Kokutai. Dark green (N1) upper surfaces and light grey (A/N2) lower surfaces. Brown (A/N14) spinner. Deep yellow (A/N20) wing leading edge panels. Off-white tail number. Red (A/N16) Hinomarus with white outline on fuselage sides and wing upper surfaces.

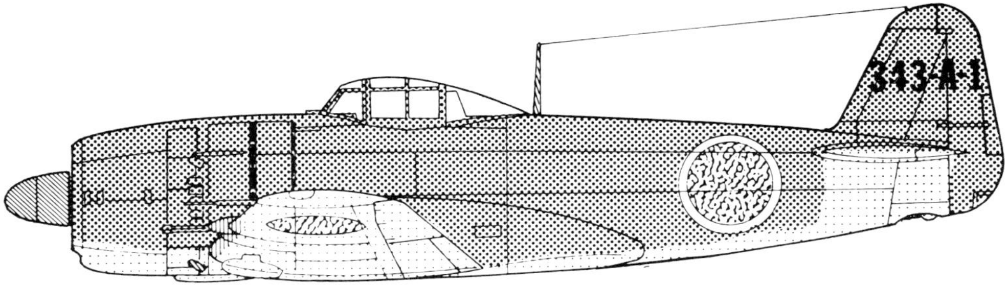

Kawanishi N1K2-J of 343rd Kokutai. Dark green (N1) upper surfaces and natural metal finish (A6) lower surfaces. Brown (A/N14) spinner. Deep yellow (A/N20) wing leading edge panels. Off-white tail number. Red (A/N16) Hinomarus with white outline on fuselage sides and wing upper surfaces.

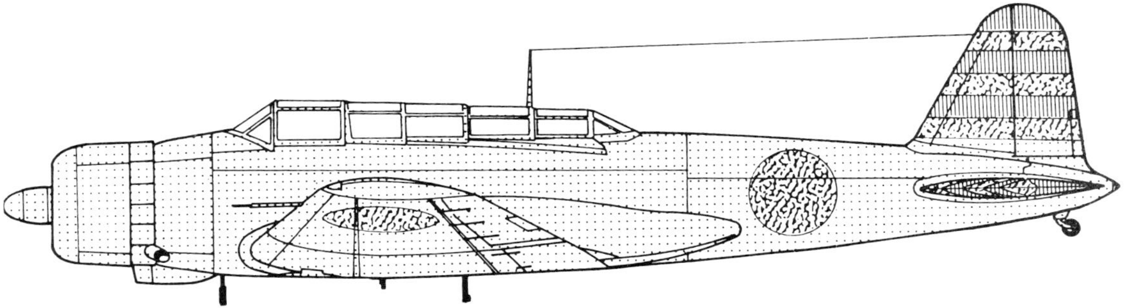

Nakajima B5N2 flown by Commander Mitsuo Fuchida at Pearl Harbor. Natural metal finish (A6) overall. Red (A/N16) Hinomarus. Deep yellow (A/N20) and red (A/N16) stripes on fin and rudder.

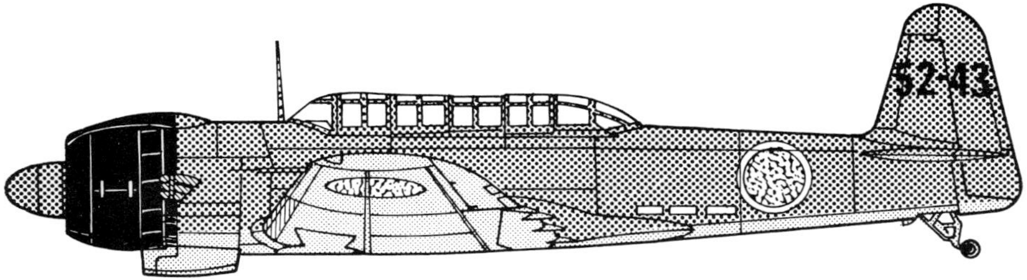

Nakajima B6N2 of Southern Islands Kokutai. Dark green (N1) upper surfaces and light grey (A/N2) lower surfaces. Matt black (A/N22) cowling. Deep yellow (A/N20) wing leading edge panels. Off-white tail number. Red (A/N16) Hinomarus with white outline on fuselage sides and wing upper surfaces.

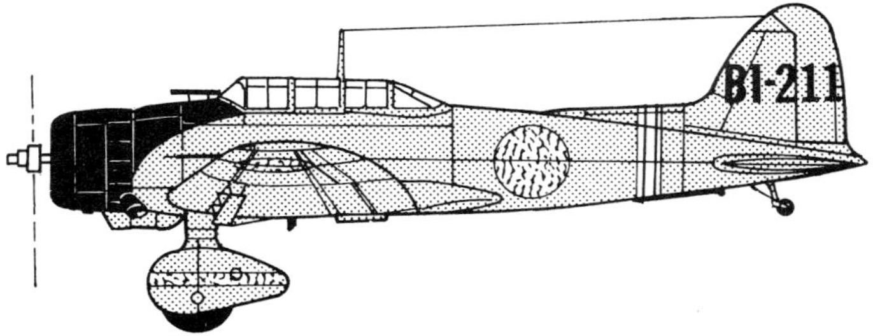

Aichi D3A1 of first carrier (*Soryu*) of the Second Koku Sentai. Sky grey (N8) overall. Matt black (A/N22) cowling and tail number. Red (A/N16) Hinomarus and wheel cover stripe.

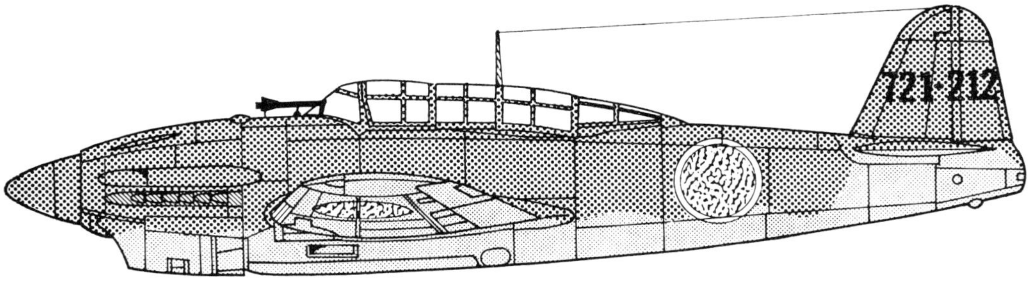

Yokosuka D4Y2 of 721st Kokutai. Dark green (N1) upper surfaces and light grey (A/N2) lower surfaces. Deep yellow (A/N20) wing leading edge panels. Off-white tail number. Red (A/N16) Hinomarus with white outline on fuselage sides and wing upper surfaces.

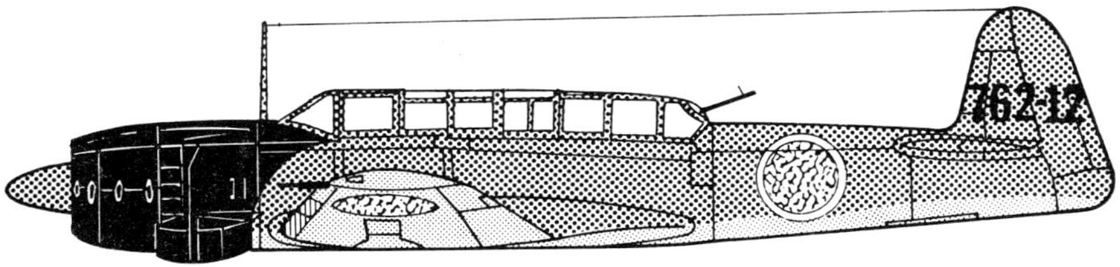

Nakajima C6N1 of 762nd Kokutai. Dark green (N1) upper surfaces and light grey (A/N2) lower surfaces. Matt black (A/N22) cowling. Deep yellow (A/N20) wing leading edge panels. Off-white tail number. Red (A/N16) Hinomarus with white outline on fuselage sides and wing upper surfaces.

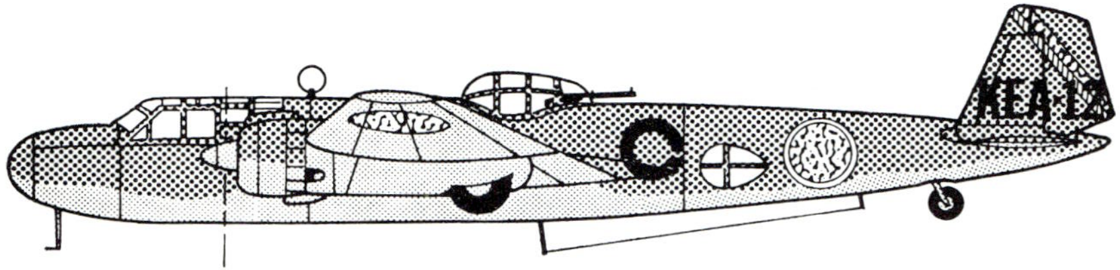

Mitsubishi G3M3. Dark green (N1) upper surfaces and light grey (A/N2) lower surfaces. Off-white tail number and 'closed C' on fuselage sides. Red (A/N16) and deep yellow (A/N20) diagonal stripes on fin and rudder. Red (A/N16) Hinomarus with white outline on fuselage sides and wing upper surfaces.

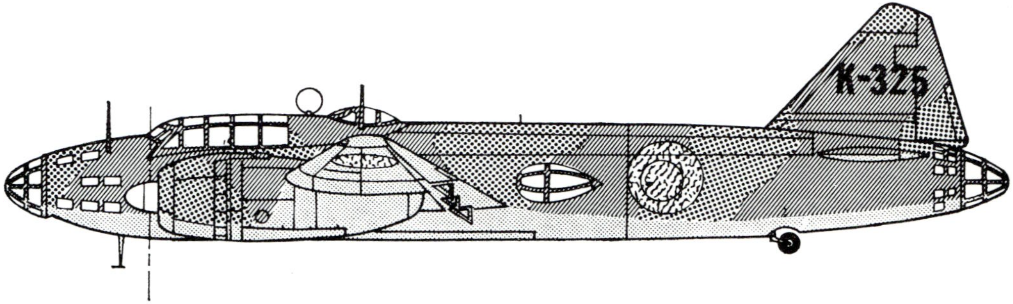

Mitsubishi G4M1 of Kanoya Kokutai. Dark green (N1) and tan (N17) upper surfaces and light grey (A/N2) lower surfaces. Off-white tail number and spinners. Red (A/N16) Hinomarus.

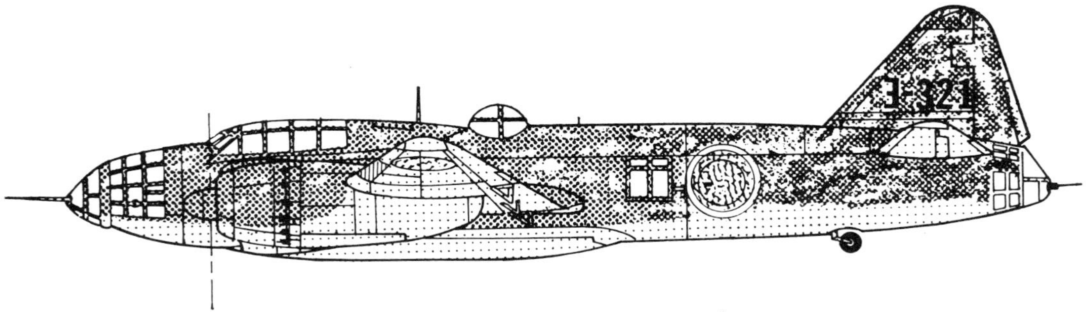

Mitsubishi G4M3 of Yokosuka Kokutai. Dark green (N1) upper surfaces, peeling off, and natural metal finish (A6) lower surfaces. Deep yellow (A/N20) wing leading edge panels. Off-white tail number. Red (A/N16) Hinomarus with white outline on fuselage sides and wing upper surfaces.

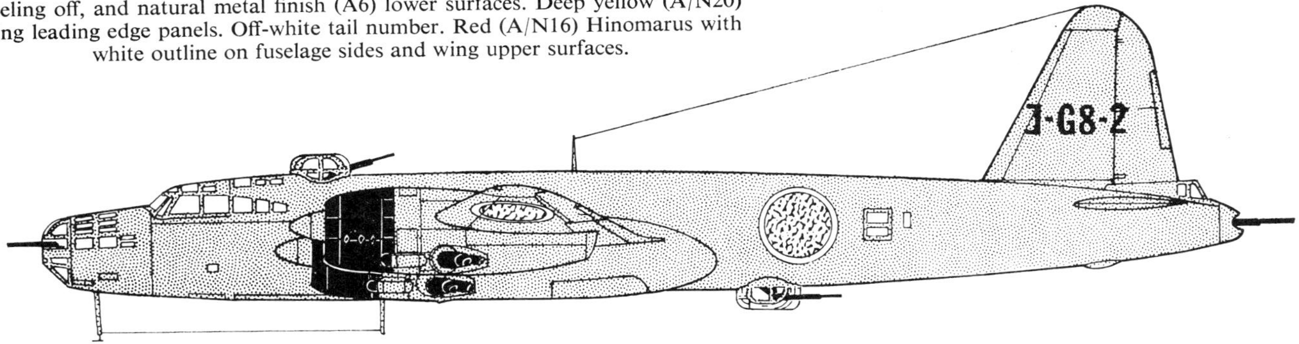

Nakajima G8N1 in prototype markings. Training orange (E18) overall. Matt black (A/N22) cowlings and tail number. Red (A/N16) Hinomarus with white outline on all six positions.

82

Douglas L2D2 of 4th Kantai's Transport Unit. Dark green (N1) upper surfaces and light grey (A/N2) lower surfaces. Off-white tail number. Red (A/N16) Hinomarus with white outline on fuselage sides and wing upper surfaces.

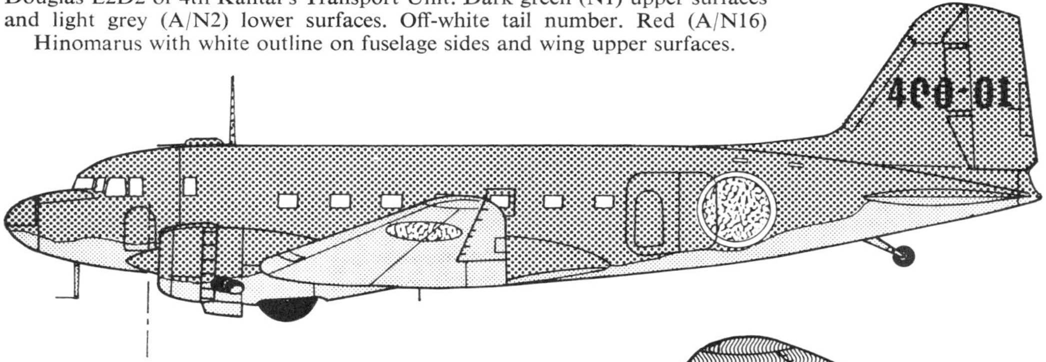

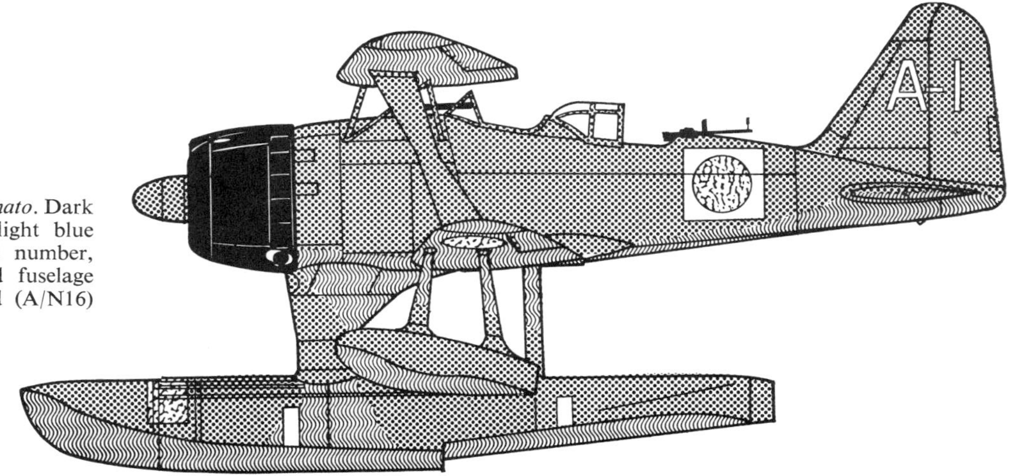

Mitsubishi F1M2 of battleship *Yamato*. Dark green (N1) upper surfaces and light blue (N10) lower surfaces. White tail number, float stripes and squares around fuselage and upper wing Hinomarus. Red (A/N16) Hinomarus.

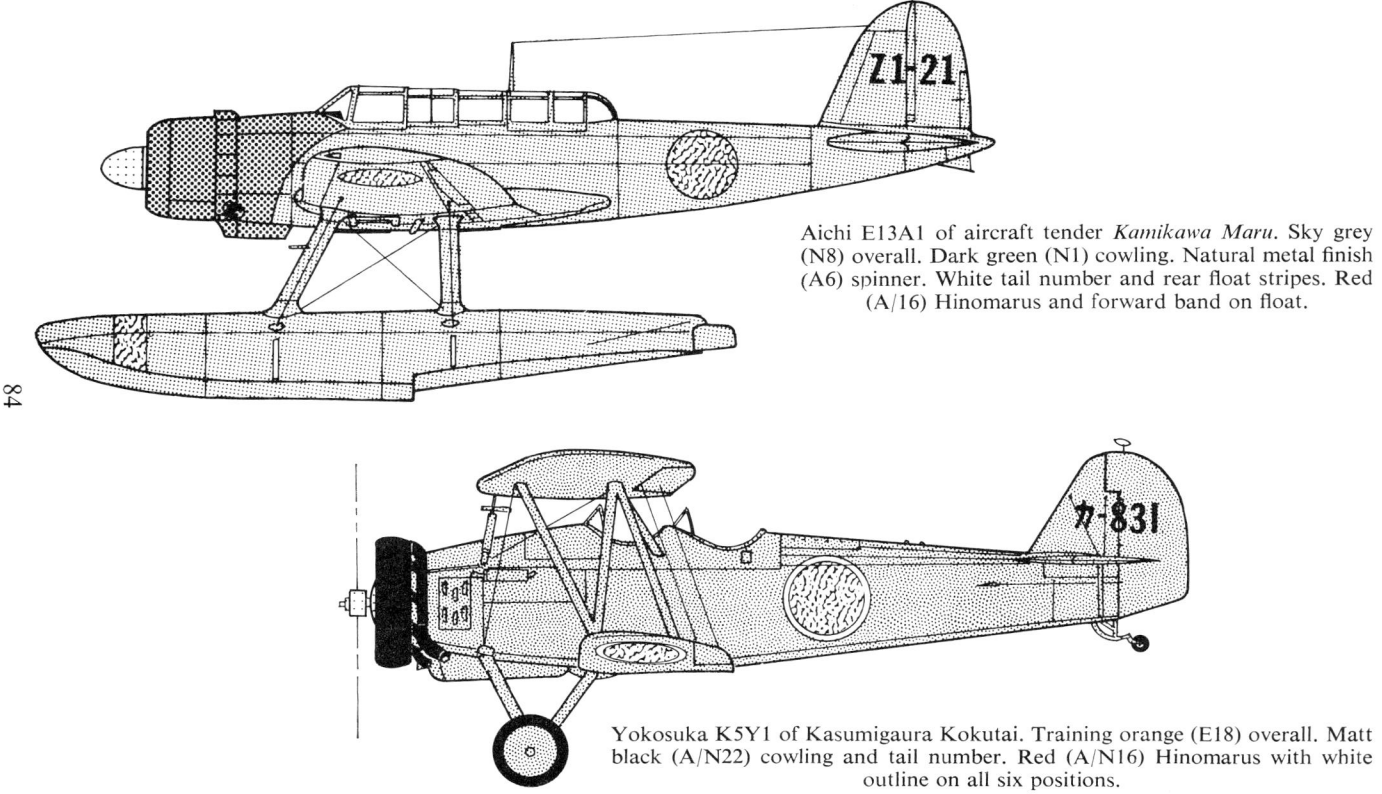

Aichi E13A1 of aircraft tender *Kamikawa Maru*. Sky grey (N8) overall. Dark green (N1) cowling. Natural metal finish (A6) spinner. White tail number and rear float stripes. Red (A/16) Hinomarus and forward band on float.

Yokosuka K5Y1 of Kasumigaura Kokutai. Training orange (E18) overall. Matt black (A/N22) cowling and tail number. Red (A/N16) Hinomarus with white outline on all six positions.

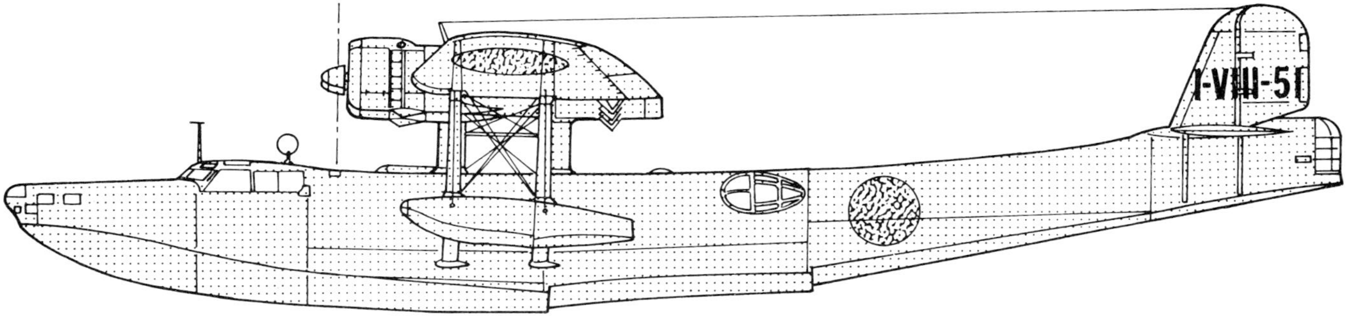

Kawanishi H6K5 of 8th Kokutai. Natural metal finish (A6) overall. Red (A/N16) Hinomarus and tail number.

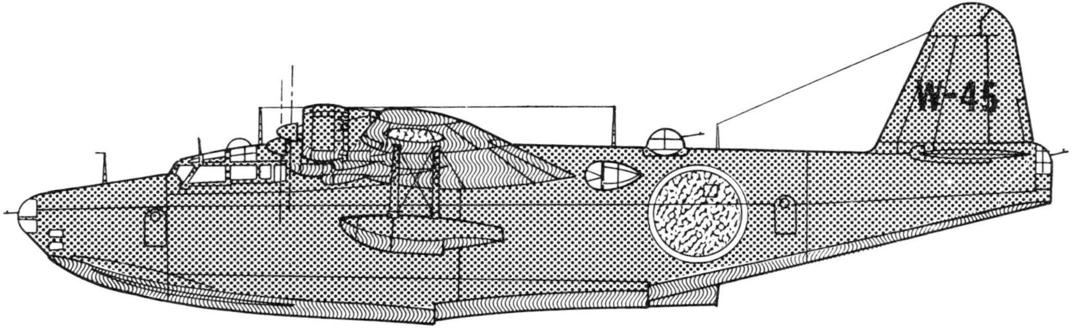

Kawanishi H8K2 of 14th Kokutai. Dark green (N1) upper surfaces and light blue (N10) lower surfaces. Off-white tail number. Red (A/N16) Hinomarus with white outline on hull sides and wing upper surfaces.

IMPERIAL JAPANESE ARMY AIRCRAFT
Kawasaki Ki-10

With the appearance of the Ki-10 the classic biplane fighter design reached its peak in Japan and the aircraft marked the end of an era. However, its superior manoeuvrability and supreme dog-fight agility were to influence the thinking of Japanese fighter pilots who, for many years after the introduction of the monoplane fighter, kept insisting that these aircraft be equally manoeuvrable.

In the early thirties the fighter units of the Imperial Japanese Army were equipped with Army Type 91 Fighter parasol monoplanes built by Nakajima and with Army Type 92 Fighter biplanes built by Kawasaki, but both types of aircraft were markedly slower than the Hawker Fury then used by the Royal Air Force and the Boeing P-26A then being delivered to the US Army Air Corps. In an attempt to produce in Japan a fighter aircraft equal or superior to contemporary foreign types, in 1933 Kawasaki had designed the Ki-5, a clean inverted gull-winged cantilever monoplane, but in 1934 it was rejected by the Army as tests revealed that its manoeuvrability was unsatisfactory. In September 1934, shortly after the Ki-5's development had been discontinued, the Koku Hombu instructed Kawasaki to design a high-performance fighter biplane while Nakajima were asked to develop a competitive fighter monoplane.

Designed by Takeo Doi with the assistance of Engineers Imachi and Tojo, the Kawasaki Ki-10 was a clean-contoured biplane of unequal span with ailerons fitted to the upper wing only. Powered by an 850 hp Kawasaki Ha-9-IIa twelve-cylinder vee liquid-cooled engine driving a two-blade fixed-pitch propeller, the first Ki-10 prototype was completed in March 1935 and was followed a month later by a second, identical, aircraft. Early flight test results confirmed that the aircraft was markedly superior to the

Fourth prototype of the Kawasaki Ki-10 Army Type 95 Fighter.

The Kawasaki Ki-10 Army Type 95 Fighter Model 1 was the Japanese Army's last operational fighter biplane.

unsuccessful Ki-5 in speed as well as in manoeuvrability. However, the competitive Nakajima Ki-11 with its low-wing monoplane configuration was still faster and Kawasaki feared that the production contract would go to Nakajima. Every effort was made to improve speed and the third prototype was fitted with a three-blade metal propeller in place of the two-blade wooden airscrew used on the first two aircraft, and flush-head rivets were adopted. The fourth prototype was identical with the exception of the upper wing which featured increased dihedral to improve stability. Even so modified the Ki-10 was still slower than the Ki-11, but the gap had been sufficiently reduced for the Ki-10 to win a large production contract on account of its exceptional manoeuvrability. The production Ki-10-I, designated officially Army Type 95 Fighter Model 1, was identical to the third prototype and 300 were built by Kawasaki between December 1935 and October 1937.

When placing a production contract for the Ki-10-I, the Army had instructed Kawasaki to initiate a development programme aimed at improving the aircraft's stability. For this purpose the 185th Ki-10 was fitted with wings of increased span and area, and with a lengthened fuselage. Flight test results showed a marked improvement and the aircraft served as a prototype for the Ki-10-II series which went into production as the Army Type 95 Fighter Model 2 beginning in June 1937.

In April 1936, design of a cleaned-up version began and the 200th Ki-10 airframe was completed in October 1936 as the Ki-10-I KAI. The large radiator was moved back from under the engine cowling to between the redesigned low-drag cantilever undercarriage with internally sprung wheels covered by drag-reducing wheel covers. At the same time the engine cowling, still housing an Ha-9-IIa, was cleaned-up. During tests a maximum speed of 420 km/h (261 mph) was reached, this speed exceeding that of the standard Ki-10-I by some 20 km/h (12·5 mph). Two generally similar Ki-10-II KAI were produced by incorporating the aerodynamic

KAWASAKI Ki-10

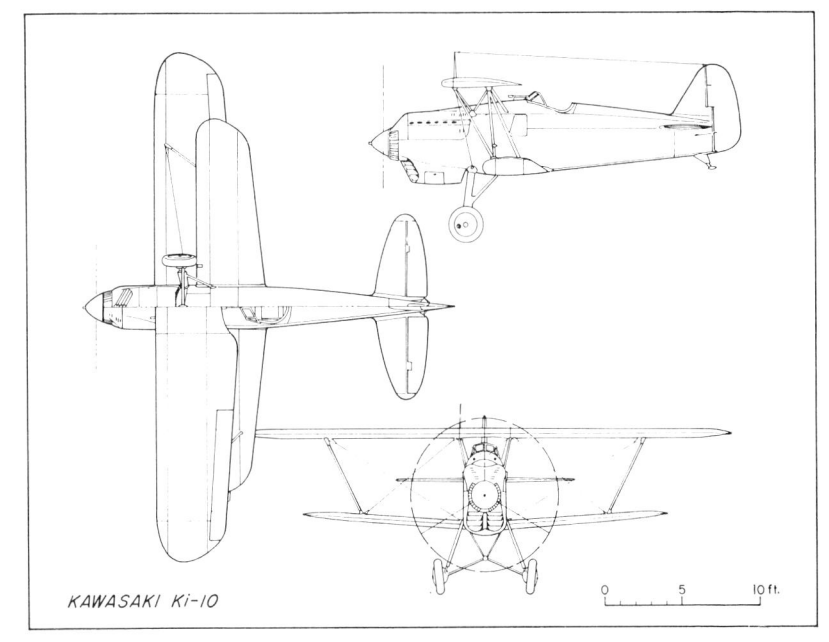

improvements of the Ki-10-I KAI into Ki-10-II airframes and, powered by the Ha-9-IIb with a maximum rating of 950 hp at 3,800 m (12,470 ft) for short periods, they reached a top speed of 445 km/h (276·5 mph). Despite a maximum speed almost equal to that of the Nakajima Ki-27 fighter monoplane, the Ki-10-II KAI remained in prototype form as it was obvious that the heyday of the biplane combat aircraft was over.

The Ki-10-I and Ki-10-II saw service with units of the Japanese Army in Japan, Formosa, Korea and Manchukuo and participated in combat

The experimental Kawasaki Ki-10-II KAIs had a maximum speed of 276·5 mph and were the fastest of the Ki-10 series.

operations in China and Manchuria during the second Sino-Japanese conflict and the Nomonhan Incident. However, when the Pacific War began the Ki-10 had been relegated to training and other ancillary duties. Allied intelligence officers, who early in the war still believed the aircraft to be in first-line service, assigned to it the code name PERRY but aircraft of this type were only occasionally encountered over China.

UNITS ALLOCATED

1st, 4th, 5th, 6th, 8th, 11th and 13th Rentais. 4th, 9th, 33rd, 59th, 64th and 77th Sentais. Akeno Fighter Training School.

TECHNICAL DATA

Description: Single-engined fighter biplane. All-metal structure with light alloy and fabric covering.
Accommodation: Pilot in open cockpit.
Powerplant: One Kawasaki Ha-9-IIa twelve-cylinder vee liquid-cooled engine, rated at 850 hp for take-off, 720 hp at sea level and 800 hp at 3,500 m (11,485 ft), driving a two-blade wooden propeller (first and second Ki-10 prototypes) or three-blade metal propeller (third and fourth Ki-10 prototypes, Ki-10-I, Ki-10-I KAI and Ki-10-II).

One Kawasaki Ha-9-IIb twelve-cylinder vee liquid-cooled engine, rated at 850 hp for take-off, 700 hp at sea level and 950 hp at 3,800 m (12,470 ft), driving a three-blade metal propeller (Ki-10-II KAI).
Armament: Two 7·7 mm Type 89 machine-guns mounted in the upper decking of the engine cowling.

	Ki-10-I	Ki-10-II	Ki-10-I KAI	Ki-10-II KAI
Dimensions:				
Span	9·55 m (31 ft 3$\frac{31}{32}$ in)	10·02 m (32 ft 10$\frac{1}{2}$ in)	9·55 m (31 ft 3$\frac{31}{32}$ in)	10·02 m (32 ft 10$\frac{1}{2}$ in)
Length	7·2 m (23 ft 7$\frac{15}{32}$ in)	7·55 m (24 ft 9$\frac{1}{4}$ in)	7·2 m (23 ft 7$\frac{15}{32}$ in)	7·55 m (24 ft 9$\frac{1}{4}$ in)
Height	3 m (9 ft 10$\frac{1}{8}$ in)	3 m (9 ft 10$\frac{1}{8}$ in)	3 m (9 ft 10$\frac{1}{8}$ in)	3 m (9 ft 10$\frac{1}{8}$ in)
Wing area	20 sq m (215·277 sq ft)	23 sq m (247·569 sq ft)	20 sq m (215·277 sq ft)	23 sq m (247·569 sq ft)
Weights:				
Empty	1,300 kg (2,866 lb)	1,360 kg (2,998 lb)	1,300 kg (2,866 lb)	1,400 kg (3,086 lb)
Loaded	1,650 kg (3,638 lb)	1,740 kg (3,836 lb)	1,650 kg (3,638 lb)	1,780 kg (3,924 lb)
Wing loading	82·5 kg/sq m (16·9 lb/sq ft)	75·7 kg/sq m (15·5 lb/sq ft)	82·5 kg/sq m (16·9 lb/sq ft)	77·4 kg/sq m (15·9 lb/sq ft)
Power loading	1·9 kg/hp (4·3 lb/hp)	2 kg/hp (4·5 lb/hp)	1·9 kg/hp (4·3 lb/hp)	2·1 kg/hp (4·6 lb/hp)
Performance:				
Max speed	400 km/h at 3,000 m (248·5 mph at 9,845 ft)	400 km/h at 3,000 m (248·5 mph at 9,845 ft)	420 km/h at 3,000 m (261 mph at 9,845 ft)	445 km/h at 3,800 m (276·5 mph at 12,470 ft)
Climb to	5,000 m (16,405 ft)	5,000 m (16,405 ft)	5,000 m (16,405 ft)	5,000 m (16,405 ft)
in	5 min	5 min	5 min	5 min
Service ceiling	10,000 m (32,810 ft)	11,500 m (37,730 ft)	10,000 m (32,810 ft)	11,500 m (37,730 ft)
Range	1,100 km (684 miles)	1,100 km (684 miles)	1,000 km (621 miles)	1,000 km (621 miles)

Production: A total of 588 Ki-10s were built by Kawasaki Kokuki Kogyo K.K. at Gifu as follows:

4 Ki-10 prototypes (spring of 1935)
300 Ki-10-I production aircraft (Dec 1935–Oct 1937)
1 Ki-10-II prototype (May 1936)
280 Ki-10-II production aircraft (June 1937–Dec 1938)
1 Ki-10-I KAI prototype (Oct 1936)
2 Ki-10-II KAI prototypes (Nov 1937)

Kawasaki Ki-32s of the 75th Sentai, 2nd Chutai. Rudder markings were red.

Kawasaki Ki-32

The Kawasaki Ki-32, which was the last type of bomber aircraft powered by a liquid-cooled engine to be used by the Japanese Army, had more than the average share of teething troubles and, although as technically remarkable as the contemporary Mitsubishi Ki-30 designed to meet the same military requirements, it never achieved the fame of its Mitsubishi rival.

In May 1936, the Army instructed Mitsubishi and Kawasaki to design a single-engined light bomber to replace the obsolete Army Type 93 Single-engined Light Bomber (Kawasaki Ki-3). Possessing a maximum speed of 400 km/h at 3,000 m (248·5 mph at 9,845 ft), the aircraft was required to carry a bomb-load of 300 to 450 kg (661 to 992 lb) at a cruising speed of 300 km/h (186 mph) between 2,000 m and 4,000 m (6,560 ft to 13,125 ft) and was to carry a defensive armament comprising a fixed forward-firing 7·7 mm machine-gun and a flexible rear-firing 7·7 mm machine-gun. Like their rivals at Mitsubishi, the Kawasaki design team, led by Engineers Isamu Imashi and Shiro Ota, adopted for the Ki-32 a mid-wing cantilever monoplane configuration with a fixed spatted undercarriage and an internal fuselage bomb-bay but, whereas the Mitsubishi engineers had selected an air-cooled engine, Kawasaki decided to use an Ha-9-II engine of their own design, the choice of this twelve-cylinder liquid-cooled engine later proving to be the source of considerable difficulties.

The first of eight Ki-32 prototypes was completed and flown in March 1937 but flight trials were marred by protracted engine teething troubles necessitating several redesigns of the engine nacelle and a strengthening

The Kawasaki Ki-32 Army Type 98 Single-engined Light Bomber. (*USAF.*)

of the crankshaft. During competitive trials against the Mitsubishi Ki-30, the Ki-32 was found to possess better flying characteristics. However, the Japanese Army, which by now had a full-fledged war on their hands, decided first to order the Mitsubishi aircraft with its more reliable powerplant. Finally, in July 1938, the Ki-32 was also placed in production as the Army Type 98 Single-engined Light Bomber and, ultimately, more Ki-32s than Ki-30s were built.

In service the Ki-32 was liked by its crews for its manoeuvrability, superior to that of the Ki-30, and it took an active part in the second Sino-Japanese conflict despite the fact that its liquid-cooled engine proved susceptible to battle damage. Although the Ki-32 was fitted with a fixed undercarriage it was slightly faster than the contemporary British Fairey Battle with its retractable undercarriage and it should be remembered as one of the types which brought Japanese military aviation on a par with the air forces of the Western nations. In December 1941 the Ki-32 was still in front-line service and the type took part in the bombing operations

Kawasaki Ki-32s with segmented camouflage. (*USAF.*)

leading to the surrender of the Commonwealth forces defending Hong Kong. Soon thereafter, the Ki-32 (code name MARY) was assigned to training units.

UNITS ALLOCATED
3rd, 6th, 10th, 35th, 45th, 65th and 75th Sentais.

TECHNICAL DATA
Description: Single-engined light bomber. All-metal construction with fabric-covered control surfaces.
Accommodation: Pilot and radio-operator/bombardier in enclosed cockpit.
Powerplant: One Army Type 98 (Ha-9-IIb) twelve-cylinder vee liquid-cooled engine, rated at 850 hp for take-off, 775 hp at sea level and 950 hp at 3,800 m (12,470 ft), driving a three-blade variable-pitch metal propeller.
Armament: One forward-firing 7·7 mm Type 89 machine-gun in the engine cowling and one flexible rear-firing 7·7 mm Type 89 machine-gun.
   Bomb-load—normal, 300 kg (661 lb)
      —maximum, 450 kg (992 lb)
Dimensions: Span 15 m (49 ft 2 9/16 in); length 11·64 m (38 ft 2 9/32 in); height 2·9 m (9 ft 6 3/8 in); wing area 34 sq m (365·972 sq ft).
Weights: Empty 2,349 kg (5,179 lb); loaded 3,539 kg (7,802 lb); maximum 3,762 kg (8,294 lb); wing loading 104·1 kg/sq m (21·3 lb/sq ft); power loading 4·2 kg/hp (9·2 lb/hp).
Performance: Maximum speed 423 km/h at 3,940 m (263 mph at 12,925 ft); cruising speed 300 km/h (186 mph); climb to 5,000 m (16,405 ft) in 10 min 55 sec; service ceiling 8,920 m (29,265 ft); range: normal 1,300 km (826 miles), maximum 1,960 km (1,218 miles).
Production: A total of 854 Ki-32s were built by Kawasaki Kokuki Kogyo K.K. as follows:
   8 Ki-32 prototypes (1937)
   846 Ki-32 production aircraft (July 1938–May 1940)

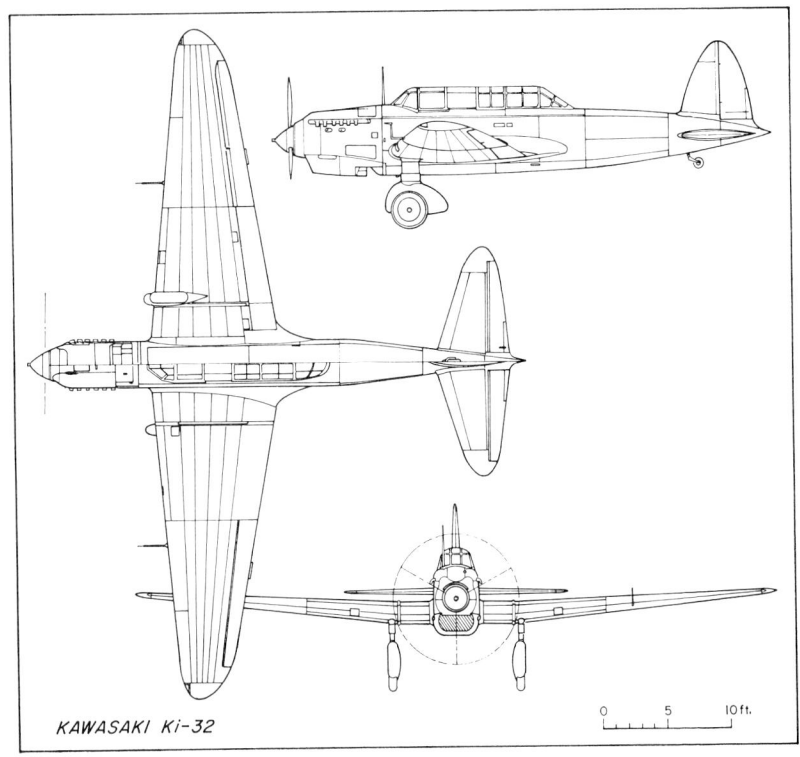

KAWASAKI Ki-32

A captured Kawasaki Ki-45 Toryu. (*USAF.*)

Kawasaki Ki-45 Toryu (Dragon Killer)

The Kawasaki Ki-45 had one of the longest and most frustrating preproduction development periods of any Nipponese aircraft seeing active duty during the second World War but, during the last months of the war when the Japanese were vainly trying to defend their country from the devastating night bombing raids by the B-29s, it was the Army's only operational night fighter, a task for which it had not been originally designed.

The appearance in Europe and America of twin-engined long-range fighters had not escaped the attention of the Japanese military staff which saw in this type of aircraft an answer to the limited range of contemporary single-engined fighters. However, when in March 1937 an official specification for a twin-engined heavy fighter was issued to the Japanese aircraft manufacturers, no stringent requirements were imposed as factions within the Army were unable to agree on the relative importance to be given to armament, speed and handling characteristics. In answer to this specification three projects were submitted to the Koku Hombu, the Nakajima Ki-37, the Kawasaki Ki-38 and the Mitsubishi Ki-39. As they had more pressing projects, Nakajima and Mitsubishi were allowed to abandon the Ki-37 and the Ki-39 fairly rapidly, but the Ki-38 design studies progressed smoothly at Kawasaki under the leadership of Isamu Imashi. A detailed mock-up of the Ki-38, a clean monoplane powered by two twelve-cylinder liquid-cooled engines and characterized by a wing of elliptical planform, was completed in October 1937 but the project was then shelved to give the JAAF time to formalize their performance and handling requirements.

In December 1937 Kawasaki were instructed to initiate work on the Ki-45, a development of the Ki-38, to meet a new specification for a twin-engined two-seat fighter calling for: (1) maximum speed, 540 km/h at

The first prototype of the Kawasaki Ki-45 series. This aircraft bore c/n 4501 and the type went into service as the Toryu (Dragon Killer).

3,500 m (335·5 mph at 11,480 ft); (2) operating altitude, 2,000 m to 5,000 m (6,560 ft to 16,405 ft); (3) endurance, 4 hr and 40 min at 350 km/h (217 mph) plus 30 min at combat rating; (4) armament, two forward-firing guns and one flexible rear-firing machine-gun; and (5) engines, two Nakajima Ha-20b nine-cylinder radials, a licence-built version of the Bristol Mercury. With Takeo Doi as chief project engineer, work began in January 1938 and twelve months later the first prototype (c/n 4501) Army Experimental Ki-45 was rolled out at the Gifu plant. The aircraft was powered by a pair of Nakajima Ha-20b, rated at 820 hp at 3,900 m (12,795 ft) and housed in large nacelles with an exhaust collector ring in front of the engine, and was armed with two 7·7 mm Type 89 machine-guns mounted in the upper fuselage nose, a 20 mm Ho-3 cannon mounted in a ventral tunnel on the starboard underside of the fuselage and one flexible rear-firing 7·7 mm Type 89 machine-gun.

Flight trials were immediately disappointing due to excessive nacelle drag, to difficulties with the manually retracted undercarriage and to teething troubles with the engines failing to deliver their rated power. In an effort to reduce drag, the second prototype (c/n 4502) had its engines mounted in closer-fitting cowlings and propeller spinners were added; the third prototype (c/n 4503) had ducted spinners, cooling air being forced

Second prototype of the Kawasaki Ki-45 Toryu (Dragon Killer) series. This aircraft, c/n 4502, was powered by Nakajima Ha-20b engines.

through their centres and exhausting through slots in the wings. On this third prototype use of an electrically-operated retraction mechanism improved undercarriage reliability. Despite drag reduction, the maximum speed was only 480 km/h at 4,000 m (298 mph at 13,125 ft), a figure well below requirements, and the Ki-45 in its present form was obviously a failure. In particular, nacelle stall persisted and Kawasaki suggested modifying the engines to use handed propellers instead of the right-hand rotating airscrews fitted to c/n 4501 to 4503. However, late in 1939, the Army decided to curtail flight trials pending review of the project and six additional aircraft, c/n 4504 to 4509, were left in various stages of manufacture.

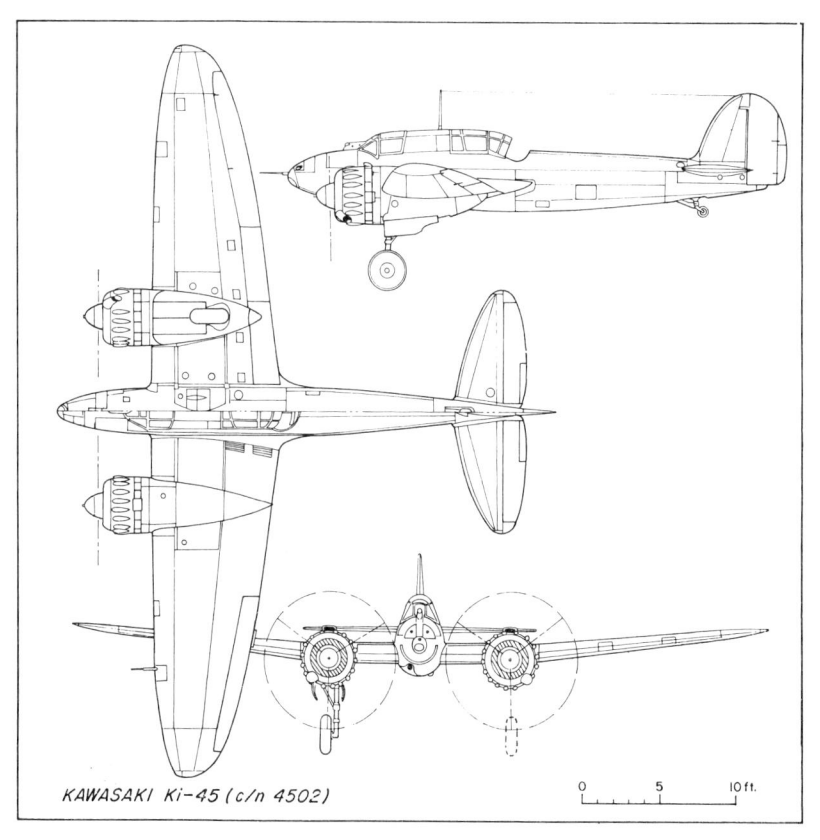

KAWASAKI Ki-45 (c/n 4502)

In April 1940, Kawasaki were instructed to fit two 1,000 hp Nakajima Ha-25 fourteen-cylinder double-row radials with single-stage superchargers on one of the uncompleted airframes (c/n 4507). As the Nakajima Ha-25 had a smaller diameter than the Ha-20b, new NACA-type nacelles with small propeller spinners were adopted and, thus fitted, the new prototype, designated Experimental Improved Type 1 Ki-45, was

Kawasaki Ki-45 Improved Type 1 prototype with Ha-25 engines.
(*R. J. Francillon collection.*)

completed in July 1940. Despite the loss of a cowling flap which resulted in a forced landing at the end of the first flight, the modification was judged successful and five additional airframes (c/n 4504, 4505, 4506, 4508 and 4509) were similarly completed, these aircraft later reaching a top speed of 520 km/h at 3,500 m (323 mph at 11,480 ft). Two additional aircraft (c/n 4510 and 4511) were also built to this standard.

While the Army had the Ki-45 project under review, Takeo Doi had been studying the possibility of redesigning the aircraft to simplify its manufacture and improve its performance and handling characteristics. Based on the Ha-25 powered prototypes, the Ki-45 KAI incorporated the following design changes: (1) slimmer fuselage with straight contours and redesigned tail surfaces; (2) straight tapered wing of increased span and area; (3) new engine nacelles of smaller diameter mounted lower on the wings; (4) replacement of the 7·7 mm Type 89 machine-guns by two 12·7 mm Type 1 (Ho-103) machine-guns in the nose and one flexible rear-firing 7·9 mm Type 98 machine-gun; and (5) replacement of the telescopic gunsight by a reflector gunsight. The Koku Hombu agreed to these changes in October 1940 and the first Ki-45 KAI prototype was completed in May 1941. Flight tests conducted with this aircraft, two additional prototypes

A Kawasaki Ki-45 KAIa, the first production version of the Toryu series.
(*US Navy Department.*)

and twelve pre-production machines, were conclusive and, late in 1941, Kawasaki were instructed to commence production in their Akashi and Gifu plants under the designation Army Type 2 Two-seat Fighter Model A Toryu (Dragon Killer), Ki-45 KAIa.

The first unit taking delivery of the Toryu was the 5th Sentai at Kashiwa, Chiba Prefecture, which received its Ki-45 KAIas in August 1942, but the 21st Sentai in Burma and the 16th Sentai in China were the first Ki-45 KAI groups to reach the combat area, in October and November 1942 respectively. Heavy armament and petrol tank protection made the aircraft popular with its crews and it enjoyed a good reputation in the ground

Kawasaki Ki-45 KAIa Army Type 2 Two-seat Fighter Model A.

attack and anti-shipping roles. A new version, the Ki-45 KAIb or Army Type 2 Two-seat Fighter Model B, was specially built to fulfil these tasks and its forward-firing armament was revised to include one 20 mm Ho-3 cannon mounted centrally in the nose and one hand-loaded 37 mm Type 98 cannon in the ventral tunnel. Late production Ki-45 KAIbs were powered by a pair of 1,050 hp Army Type 101 fourteen-cylinder radials (Mitsubishi Ha-102) rated at 1,080 hp for take-off. The nacelles housing these more reliable engines had slightly smaller diameter and were longer. Known to the Allies as NICK, the Toryu was frequently met in the New Guinea theatre where it was actively used against the US Navy P.T. boats. Its potent armament also made it one of the most effective fighters used against the far-ranging B-24 bombers of the US 5th Air Force and, when the B-24s were increasingly used for night operations, the Ki-45 KAIa—with the added safety of its twin-engined configuration— proved easily adaptable to this new task. Some of these aircraft were modified in the field by replacing the upper fuselage petrol tank with a pair of 12·7 mm Type 1 (Ho-103) machine-guns mounted obliquely to fire upward.

As this modification proved effective, the Koku Hombu instructed Kawasaki to manufacture a new model specially intended for night fighting. This version, the Ki-45 KAIc, retained the Ha-102 engines of the late production Ki-45 KAIb but was armed with a semi-automatic 37 mm Ho-203 cannon in the ventral tunnel and two obliquely-mounted upward-

KAWASAKI Ki-45 KAIb

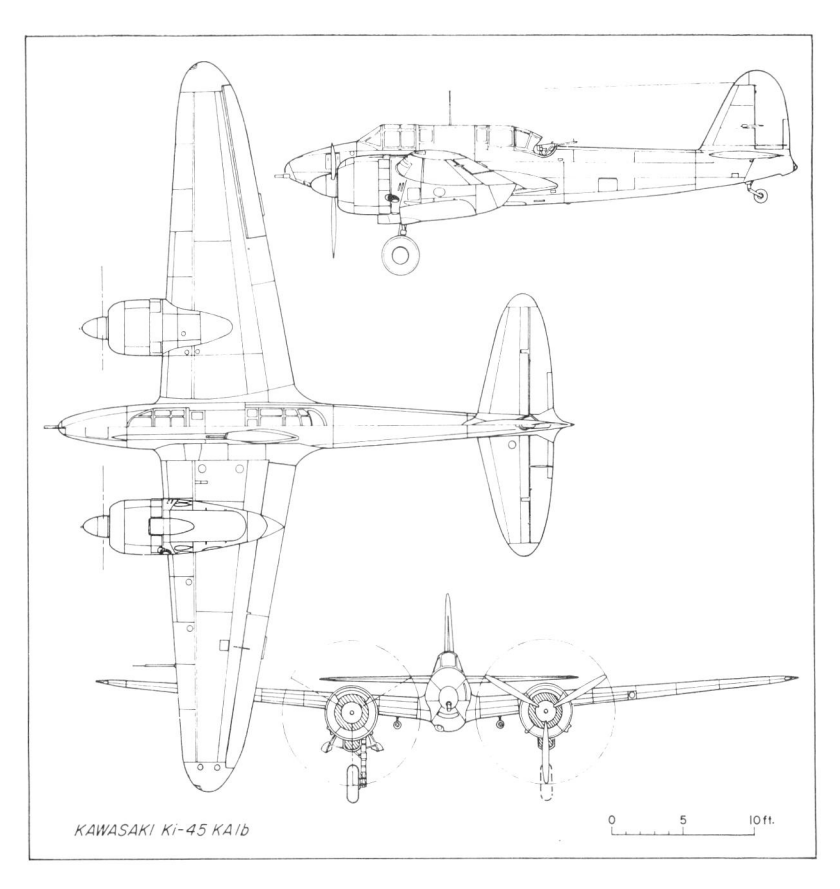

Kawasaki Ki-45 KAIc with 20 mm cannon mounted obliquely behind the pilot's cockpit. (*R. J. Francillon collection.*)

Kawasaki Ki-45 KAIc Army Type 2 Two-seat Fighter Model C of the 53rd Sentai.

firing 20 mm Ho-5 cannon in the centre fuselage, but its more pointed nose carried no armament because it was to be fitted with radar. Technical and production delays prevented the realization of this project, only one aircraft being tested with a centimetric radar mounted under a plexiglass nose cover. A total of 477 Ki-45 KAIcs without radar were built in the Akashi plant which, after September 1943, was solely responsible for the Toryu's production. When the B-29s commenced their bombing operations over Japan, the Ki-45 KAIc took an active part in the defence of the homeland, claiming at least eight Superfortresses on their first mission. The switch to low-level night raids by the B-29s resulted in increased activity for the Toryu Sentais and during the closing months of the war the 4th, 5th and 53rd Sentais were assigned to night operations in the Eastern Defence Sector and the 5th (after transfer), 45th and 70th Sentais were assigned similar duties in the Middle Defence Sector.

The Ki-45-II was a projected development of the Toryu with two 1,500 hp Mitsubishi Ha-112-II, but the aircraft was redesignated Ki-96 when the Koku Hombu decided to have the aircraft completed as a single-seat heavy fighter. Other developments of the Ki-45 KAI were mainly the result of armament modifications in the field and the only other version of the aircraft was the Ki-45 KAId, a specialized anti-shipping version built at Akashi and mounting an armament of two 20 mm Ho-5 cannon in the nose, one 37 mm Ho-203 cannon in the ventral tunnel and one flexible 7·9 mm Type 98 machine-gun in the rear cockpit on a Ki-45 KAIc airframe. One aircraft was experimentally armed with a 75 mm anti-tank cannon but the heavy calibre gun proved too much for the fairly light structure of the Toryu.

Captured Kawasaki Ki-45 KAIc. The starboard ventral tunnel houses a 37 mm Ho-203 cannon. (*US Navy Department.*)

UNITS ALLOCATED
4th, 5th, 13th, 16th, 21st, 27th, 45th, 53rd, 65th and 70th Sentais. 25th and 71st Dokuritsu Hiko Chutais. Akeno Fighter Training School.

TECHNICAL DATA
Description: Twin-engined heavy fighter, ground attack aircraft and night fighter. All-metal construction with fabric-covered control surfaces.

Accommodation: Pilot and radio-operator/gunner in separate enclosed cockpits.

Powerplant: Two Nakajima Ha-20b nine-cylinder air-cooled radials, rated at 730 hp for take-off and 820 hp at 3,900 m (12,795 ft), driving variable-pitch three-blade propellers (first, second and third prototypes).

Two 950 hp Army Type 99 (Nakajima Ha-25) fourteen-cylinder air-cooled radials, rated at 1,050 hp for take-off and 970 hp at 3,400 m (11,155 ft), driving constant-speed three-blade metal propellers (Improved Type 1 Ki-45, Ki-45 KAIa and early production Ki-45 KAIb).

Two 1,050 hp Army Type 1 (Mitsubishi Ha-102) fourteen-cylinder air-cooled radials, rated at 1,080 hp for take-off, 1,050 hp at 2,800 m (9,185 ft) and 950 hp at 5,800 m (19,030 ft), driving constant-speed three-blade metal propellers (late production Ki-45 KAIb, Ki-45 KAIc and Ki-45 KAId).

The Kawasaki Ki-45 KAId was the last production version of the Army Type 2 Two-seat Fighter.

Armament:	Nose	Ventral Tunnel (Starboard Side)	Dorsal Fixed (Obliquely Mounted)	Rear Firing Flexible
Ki-45 prototypes	7·7 mm × 2 (Type 89)	20 mm × 1 (Ho-3)	—	7·7 mm × 1 (Type 89)
Ki-45 KAIa	12·7 mm × 2 (Type 1)	20 mm × 1 (Ho-3)	—	7·92 mm × 1 (Type 98)
Ki-45 KAIa (experimental night fighter)	12·7 mm × 2 (Type 1)	20 mm × 1 (Ho-3)	12·7 mm × 2 (Type 1) or 20 mm × 2 (Ho-5)	—
Ki-45 KAIb	20 mm × 1 (Ho-3)	37 mm × 1 (Type 98)	—	7·92 mm × 1 (Type 98)
Ki-45 KAIc	—	37 mm × 1 (Ho-203)	20 mm × 2 (Ho-5)	7·92 mm × 1 (Type 98)*
Ki-45 KAId	20 mm × 2 (Ho-5)	37 mm × 1 (Ho-203)	—	7·92 mm × 1 (Type 98)
Ki-45 KAI	—	75 mm × 1	—	—
Ki-45 KAI	37 mm × 1 (Ho-203)	20 mm × 1 (Ho-3)	20 mm × 2 (Ho-5)	—
Ki-45 KAI	12·7 mm × 2 (Type 1)	—	20 mm × 2 (Ho-5)	7·92 mm × 1 (Type 98)
Ki-45 KAI	37 mm × 2 (Ho-203)	—	12·7 mm × 2 (Type 1)	—
Ki-45 KAI	37 mm × 1 (Ho-203)	—	20 mm × 2 (Ho-5)	7·92 mm × 1 (Type 98)

Many other field modifications. External stores: (All Ki-45 KAI) two 200 litre (44 Imp gal) drop tanks, or two 250 kg (551 lb) bombs.

* Not retained on late production aircraft.

	Ki-45 (c/n 4502)	Ki-45 (c/n 4507)	Ki-45 KAIa	Ki-45 KAIc
Dimensions:				
Span	14·5 m (47 ft 6⅞ in)	14·5 m (47 ft 6⅞ in)	15·02 m (49 ft 3⅝ in)	15·02 m (49 ft 3⅝ in)
Length	10·26 m (33 ft 7 13/16 in)	10·26 m (33 ft 7 13/16 in)	10·6 m (34 ft 9⅜ in)	11 m (36 ft 1 1/16 in)
Height	3·57 m (11 ft 8 9/16 in)	3·57 m (11 ft 8 9/16 in)	3·7 m (12 ft 1 11/16 in)	3·7 m (12 ft 1 11/16 in)
Wing area	29 sq m (312·152 sq ft)	29 sq m (312·152 sq ft)	32 sq m (344·444 sq ft)	32 sq m (344·444 sq ft)
Weight:				
Empty	2,500 kg (5,512 lb)	3,150 kg (6,945 lb)	3,695 kg (8,146 lb)	4,000 kg (8,818 lb)
Loaded	3,750 kg (8,267 lb)	4,400 kg (9,700 lb)	5,276 kg (11,632 lb)	5,500 kg (12,125 lb)
Wing loading	129·3 kg/sq m (26·5 lb/sq ft)	151·7 kg/sq m (31·1 lb/sq ft)	164·9 kg/sq m (33·8 lb/sq ft)	171·9 kg/sq m (35·2 lb/sq ft)
Power loading	2·6 kg/hp (5·7 lb/hp)	2·1 kg/hp (4·6 lb/hp)	2·5 kg/hp (5·5 lb/hp)	2·55 kg/hp (5·6 lb/hp)
Performance:				
Max speed	480 km/h at 4,000 m (298 mph at 13,125 ft)	520 km/h at 3,500 m (323 mph at 11,485 ft)	547 km/h at 7,000 m (340 mph at 22,965 ft)	540 km/h at 6,000 m (335·5 mph at 19,685 ft)
Climb to	5,000 m (16,405 ft) in 10 min 12 sec	—	5,000 m (16,405 ft) 6 min 17 sec	5,000 m (16,405 ft) 7 min
Service ceiling	—	—	10,730 m (35,200 ft)	10,000 m (32,810 ft)
Range	1,750 km (1,087 miles)	—	2,260 km (1,404 miles)	2,000 km (1,243 miles)

Production: A total of 1,701 Ki-45s were built by Kawasaki Kokuki Kogyo K.K. in their Gifu and Akashi plants as follows:

Gifu plant:
- 3 Ki-45 prototypes (Jan–May 1939)
- 8 Improved Type 1 Ki-45 prototypes (July 1940–Feb 1941)
- 3 Ki-45 KAI prototypes (Aug–Oct 1941)
- 12 Ki-45 KAI pre-production aircraft (Oct–Dec 1941)
- 305 Ki-45 KAIa and KAIb production aircraft (Jan 1942–Sept 1943)

331

Akashi plant:
- 893 Ki-45 KAIa, b and d production aircraft (Sept 1942–July 1945)
- 477 Ki-45 KAIc production aircraft (Apr–Dec 1944)

1,370

Kawasaki Ki-48

Early in the second Sino-Japanese conflict the appearance of the Russian-built Tupolev SB-2 in Chinese skies took the Japanese Army completely by surprise. Initially at least, the SB-2 appeared virtually immune from fighter interception as it was almost as fast at altitude as the Nakajima Ki-27, then just entering service with fighter units of the JAAF. The performance of the Russian aircraft so impressed Japanese staff officers that they obtained authorization from the Koku Hombu to begin development of a similar aircraft in Japan. Accordingly in December 1937 Kawasaki Kokuki Kogyo K.K. were instructed to design a twin-engined light bomber to meet the following requirements: (1) maximum speed, 480 km/h at 3,000 m (298 mph at 9,845 ft); (2) cruising speed, 350 km/h at 3,000 m

Formation of Kawasaki Ki-48 Army Type 99 Twin-engined Light Bomber Model 1s.

A captured Kawasaki Ki-48-IIa of an unidentified sentai. The aircraft is seen at Noshiro in the northern part of Honshu and has one propeller removed to comply with the surrender agreement. (*USAF.*)

(217 mph at 9,845 ft); (3) climb to 5,000 m (16,405 ft) in 10 min; (4) bomb-load, 400 kg (882 lb); (5) defensive armament, including three or four flexible 7·7 mm machine-guns; (6) powerplant: two Nakajima Ha-25 radials; and (7) ability to operate under extreme cold weather conditions such as those prevailing during the winter months on the Manchukuo–Siberia border.

Actual design work on the Ki-48 began in January 1938 with Takeo Doi acting as chief engineer. Experiences gained in the design of the Ki-45 were incorporated in the bomber project and a mid-wing cantilever configuration was selected to allow the use of an internal bomb-bay. The crew of four consisted of a pilot, a bombardier/gunner manning the flexible 7·7 mm Type 89 machine-gun mounted in the nose, a radio-operator/gunner manning the flexible dorsal gun and a navigator/gunner manning the flexible Type 89 machine-gun in the ventral position. Normal bomb-load consisted of either twenty-four 15 kg (33 lb) bombs or six 50 kg (110 lb) bombs. The aircraft was powered by two 950 hp Nakajima Ha-25 engines driving variable-pitch propellers. Completion of design work on the Ki-48 was delayed because difficulties encountered with the Ki-45 programme required Takeo Doi's constant attention and the first of four Ki-48 prototypes was not completed until July 1939.

A Kawasaki Ki-48-IIa somewhere in the Philippines. (*US Navy Department.*)

During flight trials the Ki-48 easily met all performance requirements and the manoeuvrability and handling characteristics of the aircraft were praised by the Service test pilots who submitted the aircraft to intensive testing at Tachikawa. However, the prototypes suffered from severe tail flutter, and five pre-production Ki-48s, built between September and November 1939, were used to test various tail surface modifications. By raising the horizontal tail surfaces 400 mm (13$\frac{3}{4}$ in) and strengthening the rear fuselage the tail flutter problem was eradicated, and in late 1939 quantity production of the aircraft was initiated under the designation Army Type 99 Twin-engined Light Bomber Model 1A (Ki-48-Ia).

The first production Ki-48-Ia was completed in July 1940 and as soon as sufficient aircraft were available the 45th Sentai, previously flying the Kawasaki Ki-32, converted to the Army Type 99 Twin-engined Light Bomber. In the autumn of 1940, this unit was transferred to the Northern China front where the Ki-48 distinguished itself in combat. Facing virtually no opposition from the Chinese Air Force, the Ki-48-Is performed satisfactorily and the aircraft's speed was praised by its crews. In addition to

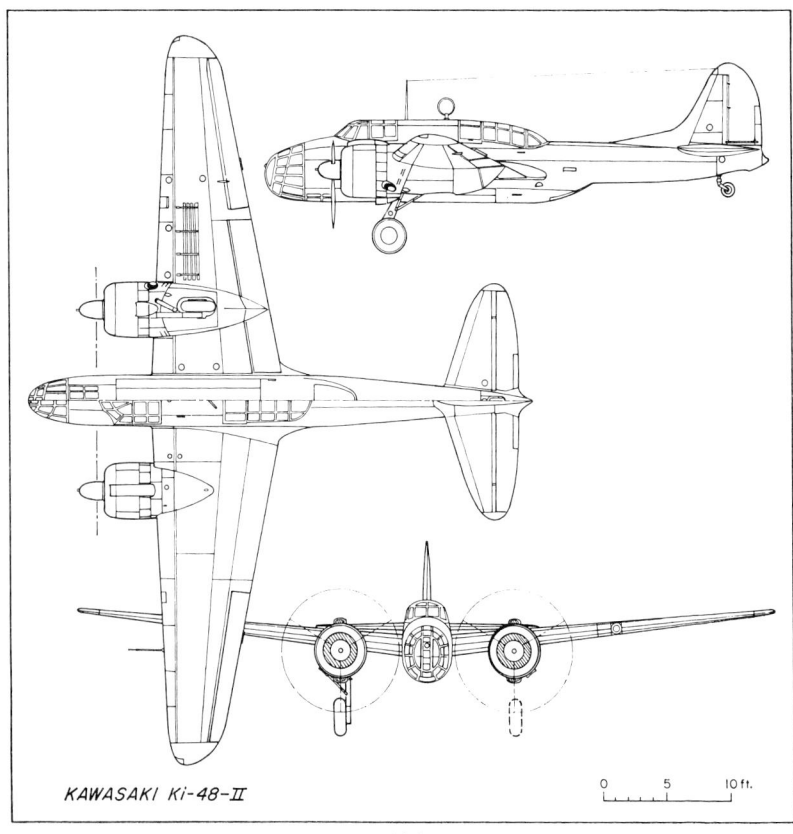

KAWASAKI Ki-48-II

Two views of a Kawasaki Ki-48-IIa Army Type 99 Twin-engined Light Bomber Model 2A with Ha-115 engines. (*US Navy Department*.)

purely tactical sorties the Ki-48s were also used for strategic operations at night in preparation for forthcoming deployment against British and American forces. Late production aircraft were designated Ki-48-Ib or Model 1B and incorporated various minor equipment changes and improved gun mountings, and a total of 557 Ki-48-Ias and -Ibs were built until June 1942. When the war began the Ki-48-Is were the Army's most important light bomber outside the Chinese front, and the aircraft of the 8th, 27th, 75th and 90th Sentais initially operated against Commonwealth forces in Malaya and Burma and against American forces in the Philippines prior to being deployed to the Netherlands East Indies/New Guinea area. Against Allied aircraft the Ki-48-I did not fare too well as its speed was too low to avoid interception, its defensive armament was ineffective, its bomb-load was insufficient and it lacked crew and petrol tank protection. To limit combat losses the aircraft were operated at night whenever possible thus reducing their effectiveness. However, an improved model of the aircraft was already under development when the Pacific War began.

Powered by two Nakajima Ha-115 engines, an advanced version of the Ha-25 with two-stage blower, three Ki-48-II prototypes were completed in February 1942. With the exception of a small increase in fuselage length introduced to improve stability, the Ki-48-II was externally identical to the Ki-48-I but as well as fuel tank protection there was armour plating for the crew in the form of a 12·5 mm plate behind the bombardier's seat, a 6·5 mm plate under the pilot's seat, a 16·5 mm plate behind the pilot's seat and 16·5 mm plates behind the ammunition boxes of the dorsal and ventral machine-guns. Within two months of its first flight the Ki-48-II was placed in production as the Army Type 99 Twin-engined Light Bomber Model 2A. The Ki-48-IIa production aircraft differed from the Ki-48-II prototypes in minor details such as local strengthening of the fuselage. The Ki-48-IIb or Model 2B was a dive-bomber version incorporating retractable snow-fence type dive-brakes under the outboard wing panels, and late production Ki-48-IIas and -IIbs were fitted with a dorsal fin extension to improve stability further. Although the maximum bomb-load of the Army Type 99 Twin-engined Light Bomber Model 2 was double that of the Model 1 it was still insufficient, and in this respect the Ki-48-II compared poorly with contemporary Allied aircraft. Likewise its maximum speed was too low to avoid interception and LILY (the Allied code name) was an easy target for Allied fighter aircraft. Also, a large number of Ki-48s were destroyed on the ground in New Guinea despite strenuous efforts by the Japanese to camouflage and disperse their aircraft on the jungle airfields. However, the main deficiency of the aircraft was its wholly inadequate defensive armament.

Attempts to increase the aircraft defensive armament proved generally unsatisfactory and the experimental use of a dorsal turret housing a 20 mm cannon was not adopted for production. However, in 1943, the Ki-48-IIc or Model 2C was armed with a flexible 12·7 mm Type 1 machine-gun replacing the previously used dorsal 7·7 mm Type 89 machine-gun. The 7·7 mm machine-guns in the nose and ventral positions were retained while an additional flexible weapon of the same calibre was mounted in the nose and could be fired from windows on the port and starboard sides of the bombardier's position. Despite these changes, the Ki-48-II had become obsolescent and in October 1944 production ended with the 1,408th. The Ki-48-II was still active in the Philippines campaign and was also met at night over Okinawa. However, most surviving Ki-48-IIs were expended around Okinawa in taiatari suicide attacks. Some of these aircraft, designated Army Type 99 Special Attack Plane (Ki-48-II KAI), were specially modified by the Dai-Ichi Rikugun Kokusho (First Army Air Arsenal) and carried an 800 kg (1,764 lb) bomb-load triggered by contact with the target by means of a long rod protruding from the nose.

In 1944 four Ki-48-IIbs were modified to test the air-to-ground Kawasaki I-Go-1-B guided missile and another Ki-48-II was used in the flight test programme of the experimental Ne-0 turbojet. For this purpose the bomb-bay doors were removed and the jet engine was hung under the fuselage. Uncompleted versions of the Ki-48 included the heavily armed and armoured Ki-81 for use by formation commanders and the single-seat Ki-174 special attack aircraft.

UNITS ALLOCATED

3rd, 6th, 16th, 27th, 31st, 32nd, 34th, 45th, 65th, 75th, 90th, 95th and 208th Sentais. 82nd Dokuritsu Dai Shijugo Chutai. Hokota Army Light Bomber Flying School.

TECHNICAL DATA

Description: Twin-engined light bomber. All-metal construction with fabric-covered control surfaces.
Accommodation: Crew of four in enclosed cockpits.
Powerplant: Two 950 hp Army Type 99 (Nakajima Ha-25) fourteen-cylinder air-cooled radials, rated at 1,000 hp for take-off and 980 hp at 3,000 m (9,845 ft), and driving three-blade metal propellers (Ki-48-I).
Two 1,150 hp Army Type 1 (Nakajima Ha-115) fourteen-cylinder air-cooled radials, rated at 1,130 hp for take-off, 1,070 hp at 2,800 m (9,185 ft) and 950 hp at 5,600 m (18,375 ft), and driving three-blade metal propellers (Ki-48-II).
Armament: Three flexible 7·7 mm Type 89 machine-guns (one each in the nose, dorsal and ventral positions) (Ki-48-Ia, -Ib, -IIa and -IIc).
Three flexible 7·7 mm Type 89 machine-guns (two in the nose and one in the ventral positions) and one flexible 12·7 mm Type 1 machine-gun in the dorsal position (Ki-48-IIc).
Bomb-load—normal, 300 kg (661 lb) (Ki-48-I)
400 kg (882 lb) (Ki-48-II)
—maximum, 400 kg (882 lb) (Ki-48-I)
800 kg (1,764 lb) (Ki-48-II)

	Ki-48-I	Ki-48-IIb
Dimensions:		
Span	17·47 m	17·45 m
	(57 ft 3 $\frac{23}{32}$ in)	(57 ft 3 in)
Length	12·6 m	12·75 m
	(41 ft 4 $\frac{1}{16}$ in)	(41 ft 9 $\frac{31}{32}$ in)
Height	3·8 m	3·8 m
	(12 ft 5 $\frac{19}{32}$ in)	(12 ft 5 $\frac{19}{32}$ in)
Wing area	40 sq m	40 sq m
	(430·555 sq ft)	(430·555 sq ft)
Weights:		
Empty	4,050 kg	4,550 kg
	(8,929 lb)	(10,031 lb)
Loaded	5,900 kg	6,500 kg
	(13,007 lb)	(14,330 lb)
Maximum	6,050 kg	6,750 kg
	(13,338 lb)	(14,881 lb)
Wing loading	147·5 kg/sq m	162·5 kg/sq m
	(30·2 lb/sq ft)	(33·3 lb/sq ft)
Power loading	2·95 kg/hp	2·9 kg/hp
	(6·5 lb/hp)	(6·3 lb/hp)
Performance:		
Maximum speed	480 km/h at 3,500 m	505 km/h at 5,600 m
	(298 mph at 11,485 ft)	(314 mph at 18,375 ft)
Cruising speed	350 km/h at 3,500 m	—
	(217 mph at 11,485 ft)	—
Climb to	5,000 m	5,000 m
	(16,405 ft)	(16,405 ft)
in	9 min	8 min 30 sec
Service ceiling	9,500 m	10,100 m
	(31,170 ft)	(33,135 ft)
Range: normal	1,980 km	2,050 km
	(1,230 miles)	(1,274 miles)
maximum	2,400 km	2,400 km
	(1,491 miles)	(1,491 miles)

Production: A total of 1,977 Ki-48s were built at the Gifu plant of Kawasaki Kokuki Kogyo K.K. as follows:

4 Ki-48 prototypes (1939)
5 Ki-48 pre-production aircraft (1940)
557 Ki-48-I production aircraft (July 1940–June 1942)
3 Ki-48-II prototypes (Feb 1942)
1,408 Ki-48-II production aircraft (Apr 1942–Oct 1944)

The only known photograph of the Kawasaki Ki-56.
(*Courtesy Richard M. Bueschel.*)

Kawasaki Ki-56

In September 1939, while tooling up for the licence production of the Lockheed 14-WG3 twin-engined transport aircraft, Kawasaki were told by the Koku Hombu to design an improved version of the aircraft, as the Ki-56. Emphasis was placed on improving take-off characteristics and increasing the volume of the cabin.

Under the guidance of Takeo Doi, and without assistance from Lockheed who had incorporated similar modifications to produce the Lockheed 18, Kawasaki engineers increased the fuselage length by 1·5 m (4 ft 11 in) and redesigned the Fowler flaps to improve their efficiency. At the same time careful attention was paid to reducing the weight of the wing structure and the two 900 hp Army Type 99 Model 2 radials (Mitsubishi Ha-26-II) powering the licence-built Lockheed 14-WG3 were replaced by two lighter 950 hp Army Type 99 radials (Nakajima Ha-25). To facilitate cargo loading a large door, incorporating a smaller personnel door, was cut in the port rear fuselage side and a loading beam was mounted in the top of the cabin. So fitted, the Ki-56 could carry two liquid-cooled or three air-cooled engines in its cabin. Despite its increased size and the incorporation of cargo loading equipment the Ki-56 was some 52 kg (115 lb) lighter than the licence-built Lockheed 14-WG3 from which it had been modified.

Following the completion in November 1940 of the first of two prototypes, the Ki-56 underwent accelerated flight trials at Tachikawa during which the aircraft demonstrated considerably improved take-off and inflight handling characteristics. Accordingly, the Ki-56 was ordered into production as the Army Type 1 Freight Transport and initially production models were built on the same line as the Type LO Transport (Lockheed 14-WG3). However, in December 1941 Kawasaki ended their production of the Type LO Transport while the Ki-56 remained in production until September 1943 when the 121st aircraft was delivered.

Widely used throughout the Pacific War, the Ki-56 first saw action during the invasion of Sumatra. Later the aircraft was found in all theatres of operation where it was coded THALIA by the Allies.

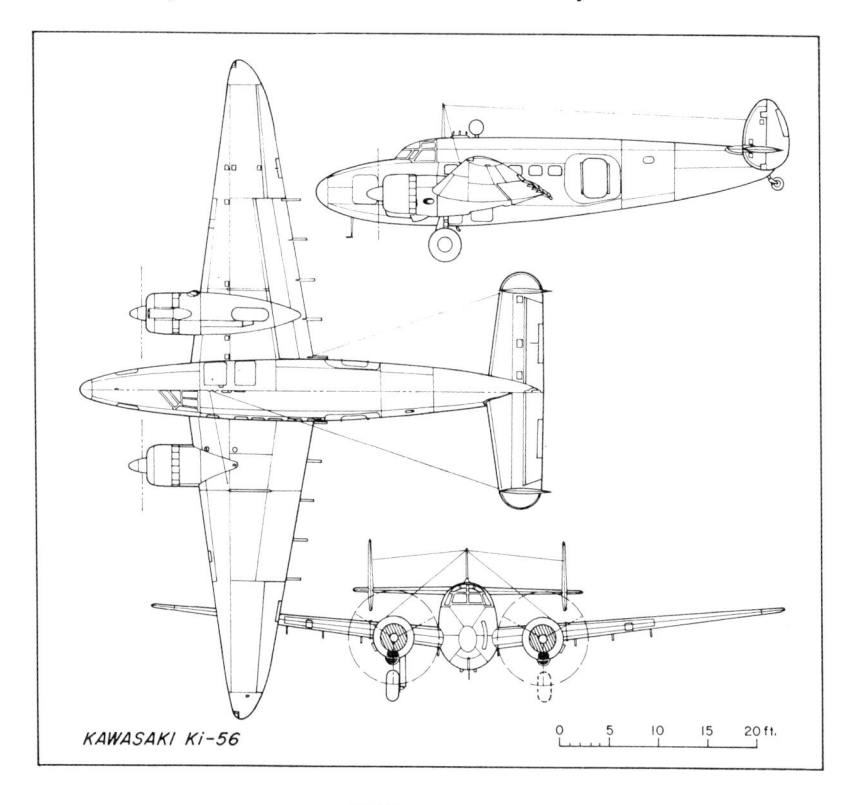

KAWASAKI Ki-56

TECHNICAL DATA

Description: Twin-engined transport. All-metal construction with fabric-covered control surfaces.
Accommodation: Crew of four and 2,400 kg (5,291 lb) of freight.
Powerplant: Two 950 hp Army Type 99 (Nakajima Ha-25) fourteen-cylinder air-cooled radials, rated at 990 hp for take-off and 970 hp at 3,400 m (11,155 ft), driving constant-speed three-blade metal propellers.
Dimensions: Span 19·964 m (65 ft 6 in); length 14·9 m (48 ft 10⅝ in); height 3·6 m (11 ft 9¾ in); wing area 51·2 sq m (551·117 sq ft).
Weights: Empty 4,895 kg (10,791 lb); loaded 8,025 kg (17,692 lb); wing loading 156·7 kg/sq m (32·1 lb/sq ft); power loading 4·05 kg/hp (8·9 lb/hp).
Performance: Maximum speed 400 km/h at 3,500 m (248·5 mph at 11,480 ft); climb to 3,000 m (9,845 ft) in 12 min 38 sec; service ceiling 8,000 m (26,250 ft).
Production: A total of 121 Ki-56s were built by Kawasaki Kokuki Kogyo K.K. as follows:
    2 prototypes (Nov 1940)
    119 production aircraft (Aug 1941–Sept 1943)

This Kawasaki Ki-60 line-up shows, from left to right, the third, first and second prototypes. (*Aireview*.)

Kawasaki Ki-60

While negotiating with Daimler-Benz A.G. for the manufacturing rights for the German DB 601A inverted-vee liquid-cooled engine, Kawasaki were successful in impressing upon members of the Koku Hombu that most contemporary foreign high-performance fighters were powered by liquid-cooled engines. Consequently, in February 1940, Kawasaki were instructed to design around the German engine, or its Japanese version, two fighter aircraft: the Ki-60 heavy interceptor and the Ki-61, a lighter all-purpose fighter. Priority was given to the Ki-60 and, in a complete reversal from previous Japanese Army requirements, speed, rate of climb and cannon armament were stressed at the expense of range and manoeuvrability.

Enlargement of the top photograph to show the first Kawasaki Ki-60 experimental heavy fighter. Pilots preferred the lighter and more manoeuvrable Ki-61 and it was selected for production. (*Aireview*.)

Designed by Takeo Doi and Shin Owada, the Ki-60 was a clean low-wing fighter powered by one 1,100 hp Daimler-Benz DB 601A liquid-cooled engine and was armed with two fuselage-mounted 12·7 mm Ho-103 machine-guns and two wing-mounted 20 mm Mauser MG 151 cannon imported from Germany. The first prototype was completed and flown in March 1941. Although basically successful, the Ki-60 was not liked by Service test pilots who reported negatively on the aircraft's high wing loading and resultant high landing speed and noted that the aircraft reached a maximum speed of only 550 km/h (342 mph) compared to 600 km/h (373 mph) as calculated by the manufacturers. Consequently, the second Ki-60 prototype was fitted with a wing of increased area—16·2 sq m (174·375 sq ft) against 15·9 sq m (171·146 sq ft)—featured a redesigned and cleaner engine cowling offering reduced drag and was

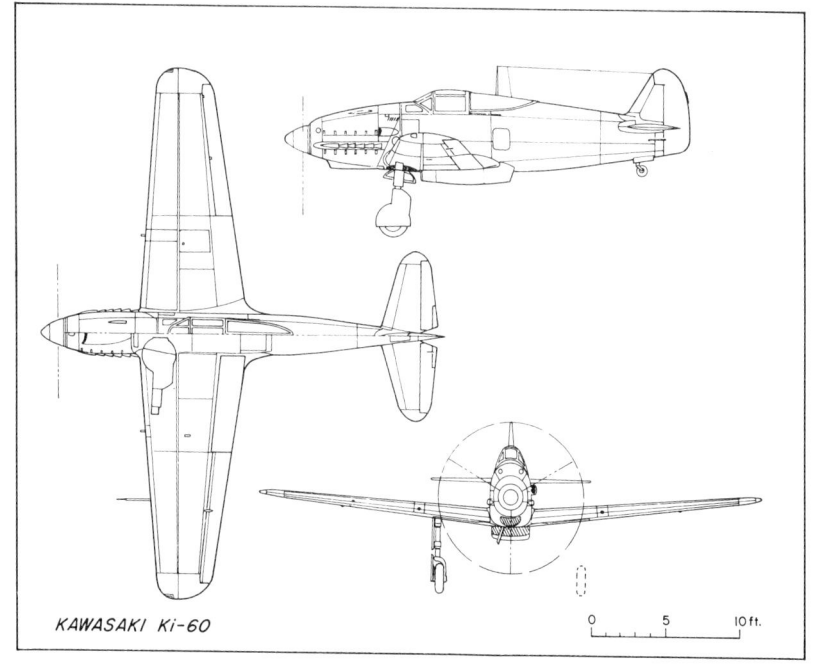

KAWASAKI Ki-60

slightly lighter. Maximum speed increased to 560 km/h (348 mph) and manoeuvrability improved somewhat. Further improvements were obtained with the third and last prototype which, retaining the larger wing of the second prototype, had an even smoother cowling. Weight was reduced by careful attention to detail fittings and replacement of the wing-mounted Mauser MG 151 by a pair of Ho-103 machine-guns. Despite these modifications maximum speed was still only 570 km/h (354 mph) and the Ki-60 was finally abandoned in favour of the lighter and faster Ki-61.

TECHNICAL DATA

Description: Single-seat interceptor fighter. All-metal construction with fabric-covered control surfaces.
Accommodation: Pilot in enclosed cockpit.
Powerplant: One 1,100 hp Daimler-Benz DB 601A twelve-cylinder inverted-vee liquid-cooled engine, rated at 1,150 hp for take-off and 1,100 hp at 4,000 m (13,125 ft), and driving a constant-speed three-blade metal propeller.
Armament: Two fuselage-mounted 12·7 mm Ho-103 machine-guns and two wing-mounted 20 mm Mauser MG 151 cannon (first and second prototypes).
Two fuselage-mounted 12·7 mm Ho-103 machine-guns and two wing-mounted 12·7 mm Ho-103 machine-guns (third prototype).
Dimensions: Span 10·5 m (34 ft 5⅜ in); length 8·47 m (27 ft 9½ in); height 3·7 m (12 ft 1 $\frac{21}{32}$ in); wing area 16·2 sq m (174·375 sq ft).
Weights: Empty 2,150 kg (4,740 lb); loaded 2,750 kg (6,063 lb); wing loading 169·8 kg/sq m (34·8 lb/sq ft); power loading 2·4 kg/hp (5·3 lb/hp).
Performance: Maximum speed 560 km/h at 4,500 m (348 mph at 14,765 ft); climb to 5,000 m (16,405 ft) in 8 min; service ceiling 10,000 m (32,810 ft).
Production: Three prototypes built in 1941.

Kawasaki Ki-61 Hien (Swallow)

With its liquid-cooled engine, long tapered nose and wings of high aspect-ratio, the Ki-61 was unique among Nipponese fighter aircraft of World War II and it marked the first attempt by the JAAF to incorporate in a fighter design the armour protection and self-sealing fuel tank which had been shown to be indispensable by early war reports received from Europe. The Hien (Swallow) was so un-Japanese in its appearance that it was initially reported as being a licence-built version of either the Messerschmitt Bf 109 or of an unspecified Italian aircraft, the latter report earning for it the code name TONY.

During the twenties and thirties, initially under the guidance of Dr Richard Vogt, the German engineer who later became the chief designer of Blohm und Voss, Kawasaki Kokuki Kogyo K.K. were the leading exponents in Japan of liquid-cooled engines and held manufacturing rights for the German BMW VI, a V-12 engine, which powered most of their aircraft during that period. Following the Army's selection of the Nakajima Ki-27 over their own Ki-28, Kawasaki decided to negotiate with Daimler-Benz for a licence for the new series of twelve-cylinder inverted-vee engines which the German company had developed. Negotiations were successfully concluded in April 1940 when a Japanese technical team brought back from Stuttgart the blueprints for the DB 601A as well as a number of assembled engines to serve as production patterns. Adaptation to Japanese production techniques began immediately at Kawasaki's Akashi plant and the first Japanese-built DB 601A, designated Ha-40, was completed in July 1941. Four months later the Ha-40 had successfully passed all ground

Second prototype of the Kawasaki Ki-61 Army Type 3 Fighter. The c/n was 6102.

tests and production started under the designation 1,100 hp Army Type 2 engine (Kawasaki Ha-40).

While negotiating with Daimler-Benz, Kawasaki had approached the Army with initial design studies for various fighter aircraft making use of this engine. As reports from the air war in Europe were showing the apparent superiority of aircraft powered by liquid-cooled engines, the Koku Hombu instructed Kawasaki in February 1940 to proceed with two aircraft of this type: the Ki-60, a heavy interceptor, and the Ki-61, a lighter all-purpose fighter, priority being given to the heavier aircraft. In December 1940, however, the emphasis shifted to the Ki-61 for which Takeo Doi and Shin Owada were responsible. The aircraft, powered by a Kawasaki Ha-40, showed in its design the strong influence left by Dr Vogt on his Japanese pupils. To provide good manoeuvrability and to obtain long endurance a wing of high aspect-ratio and large area was selected by Takeo Doi, considerable attention being given to weight and drag reduction. An armament

Kawasaki Ki-61-I armed with two wing-mounted 20 mm Mauser MG 151/20 cannon. (*Copyright 'Maru'*.)

A captured Kawasaki Ki-61-Ia Hien (Swallow) on a test flight.

of two 12·7 mm Type 1 (Ho-103) machine-guns mounted in the upper fuselage decking and either two 7·7 mm Type 89 or two 12·7 mm Type 1 wing-mounted machine-guns was selected, this armament representing a one hundred per cent increase over that carried by the Ki-43-I then just entering service.

One year after receiving authorization from the Koku Hombu to proceed with the design, the first aircraft was completed at the Kagamigahara plant where flight tests began in December 1941. Prior to this event, Kawasaki had been authorized to prepare for production and to purchase the necessary tooling and material. Fortunately the wisdom of this decision was vindicated when the prototype met the most sanguine hopes of its designers and the Army staff. Eleven additional prototypes and pre-production machines were built in the early part of 1942 and, following handling and performance tests during which a maximum speed of 591 km/h at 6,000 m (367 mph at 19,685 ft) was reached, Service trials began. The wing loading of 146 kg/sq m (29·9 lb/sq ft), high by Japanese standards of the time, was criticized by military pilots, but the majority of those who flew the aircraft were impressed by its high diving speed, and its armour protection, self-sealing fuel tanks and armament were also commented upon favourably.

The thirteenth Ki-61, the first machine built with production tooling, was completed in August 1942 and differed from the prototypes only in minor equipment details, the deletion of a small window on each side of the fuselage ahead of the windshield providing the only recognition feature. During competitive trials against prototypes of the Nakajima Ki-43-II and Ki-44-I, an imported Messerschmitt Bf 109E and a captured Curtiss P-40E, the Ki-61 was judged to have the best overall performance and to be an effective weapon against enemy aircraft.

Consequently, late in 1942, the aircraft was accepted for Service use under the designation Army Type 3 Fighter Model 1A when armed with two fuselage-mounted 12·7 mm machine-guns and two wing-mounted 7·7 mm machine-guns and Model 1B when the wing guns were the 12·7 mm Type 1. Initial deliveries of the aircraft were made in February 1943 to the 23rd Dokuritsu Dai Shijugo Chutai at Ota, which acted as a pilot conversion and training unit. Combat operations began two months later when the 68th and 78th Sentais were deployed to the north coast of New Guinea. Immediately these units proved that the Ki-61s, then named Hien, were better suited to combat the US and Australian aircraft than the Ki-43s, which they supplemented in this theatre, due to their heavier armament, good protection and high diving speed—a performance required to overcome the enemy fighters which favoured hit and run attacks from higher altitude against the nimbler Nipponese fighter aircraft. The idiosyncrasies of the liquid-cooled Ha-40 which powered the Hien caused the aircraft to be difficult to handle on the ground because of the prevailing hot and damp weather but in the air the Ki-61-I was an outstanding aircraft liked by its pilots and respected by its foes.

At an early stage in the design of the Ki-61 replacement of the fuselage-mounted machine-guns by a pair of 20 mm cannon had been contemplated. However, as cannon of domestic design were not yet available, 388 Ki-61-Ias and Ki-61-Ibs were modified on the assembly line to carry one 20 mm Mauser MG 151 in each wing. As space in the wing was limited, the cannon had to be mounted on its side, a small underwing fairing covering the breech, while some local strengthening was required because of the increased recoil force. One other aircraft was modified to test the surface evaporation cooling system which Takeo Doi proposed to use on the Ki-64. This experimental Hien had its large ventral radiator replaced by a smaller retractable unit, for use on the ground, mounted further forward, while in flight cooling was provided by steam evaporation through wing condensers with a total area of 14 sq m (150·694 sq ft). Tests began in October 1942 and thirty-five flights—during which a maximum speed of 630 km/h (391 mph) was attained—were made until the end of 1943 when the purpose of the tests was sufficiently achieved.

Operations in New Guinea, New Ireland and New Britain had shown that ease of maintenance had to be improved and Takeo Doi decided to simplify and strengthen the Hien's structure in the next version of the aircraft. With the availability of the indigenous 20 mm Ho-5 cannon the

The Kawasaki Ki-61-Ib Army Type 3 Fighter Model 1B.

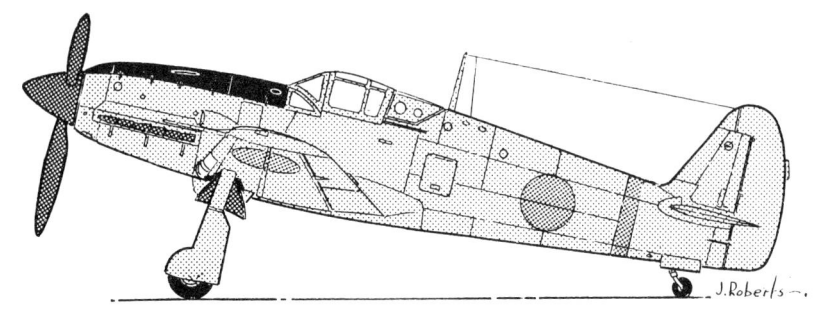

A Kawasaki Ki-61-I experimentally fitted with surface evaporation cooling system.

Ki-61-I KAIc was produced with a pair of these replacing the two fuselage-mounted 12·7 mm Type 1 machine-guns. Stronger wings, allowing an increase in diving speed and featuring provision for fixed pylons for external stores outboard of the wheel wells, were mated to a slightly longer fuselage with detachable rear section. On this version the retractable tailwheel was replaced by a fixed unit while minor control modifications were incorporated. Production of the Ki-61-I KAIc began in January 1944, and the type had completely supplanted the earlier versions on the Kagamigahara assembly line in August of the same year. Following the introduction of this version the Hien's production, which so far had been somewhat slow, quickly gained tempo and the monthly rate reached a peak of 254 aircraft in July 1944. Including a few Ki-61-I KAIds, which were armed with a pair of 30 mm Ho-105 cannon in the wings and two fuselage-mounted 12·7 mm Type 1 machine-guns, a total of 2,654 Ki-61-Is and Ki-61-I KAIs—of which the former type accounted for over half of the total—were built until January 1945 when production was terminated. Many of the Ki-61-Is and Ki-61-I KAIs saw operation in the New Guinea/Rabaul area with the two previously mentioned Sentais, but they were mostly active in the Philippines campaign of 1944–45 (17th, 18th and 19th Sentais) and over Formosa and Okinawa (19th, 37th, 59th and 105th Sentais, and 23rd Dokuritsu Dai Shijugo Chutai). Finally the type played an important role in the defence of the Japanese homeland where the Hien-equipped 18th, 23rd, 28th and 244th Sentais were assigned to the Tokyo Defence Area, the 59th Sentai to the Western Defence Area and the 55th and 56th Sentais to the Central Defence Area. Over Japan the Hiens were engaged against the B-29s, US Navy carrier aircraft and, later, against Iwo Jima based P-51 Mustangs. Against the high-flying B-29s the Ki-61-I lacked the necessary altitude performance, but the type was not really outclassed until the arrival of the superb Mustang.

Soon after commencing production of the Ha-40 at the Akashi plant, the Kawasaki engineering team began developing a more powerful version of this engine, the Ha-140. Primary emphasis was placed on altitude rating, and Takeo Doi, urged by the Army Staff to develop an advanced version of the Hien, decided to mount the 1,500 hp Ha-140 in a specially redesigned version of the Ki-61. Completed in December 1943, the first prototype Ki-61-II had a wing area increased by 10 per cent to 22 sq m (236·806 sq ft) and a redesigned aft canopy providing improved pilot visibility. However, flight trials were disappointing as the Ha-140 had more than its fair share of teething troubles, the crankshaft proving particularly weak. Even the airframe was not without its problems, and the enlarged wings, which had been designed to enhance the aircraft's manoeuvrability and performance at high altitude, suffered from several failures. The handling characteristics, too, left much to be desired. Consequently, only eight of the eleven Ki-61-IIs built were tested and the ninth airframe was modified as the Ki-61-II KAI before completion in April 1944. The fuselage length was increased from 8·94 m (29 ft 4 in) to 9·16 m (30 ft $0\frac{5}{8}$ in), the rudder area was enlarged to offset the increased wetted area and the larger wings were replaced by standard Ki-61-I KAI wings. The airframe problems were thus eradicated and, when the engine performed smoothly, the Ki-61-II KAI was an outstanding interceptor with a maximum speed of 610 km/h at 6,000 m (379 mph at 19,685 ft) and a climb rate of 5,000 m (16,405 ft) in six minutes. Still confident that the persistent engine teething troubles would be eradicated, the Ministry of Munitions, acting on behalf of the Army, instructed Kawasaki to proceed with the mass production of the aircraft under the designation Army Type 3 Fighter Model 2.

Starting in September 1944 the Ki-61-II KAI was built in two versions, the Model 2A with an armament of two fuselage-mounted 20 mm Ho-5 cannon and two wing-mounted 12·7 mm Type 1 machine-guns and the Model 2B with an armament of four 20 mm Ho-5 cannon, two in the fuselage and two in the wings. The Ki-61-II KAI never supplanted the Ki-61-I KAI in operational units as its engine was still suffering from chronic weaknesses, and comparatively few Hiens of this model saw limited operations in Japan. When the engine was operating smoothly the Ki-61-II KAI was an effective interceptor and was the only Army fighter able to maintain combat formation at the operating altitude of the B-29s. However, the lack of skilled workers was by then being badly felt and seldom did the Ha-140 give its full rated power. Finally, production of the Army Type 3

Kawasaki Ki-61-I KAIc of the 244th Sentai. (*Consiglio.*)

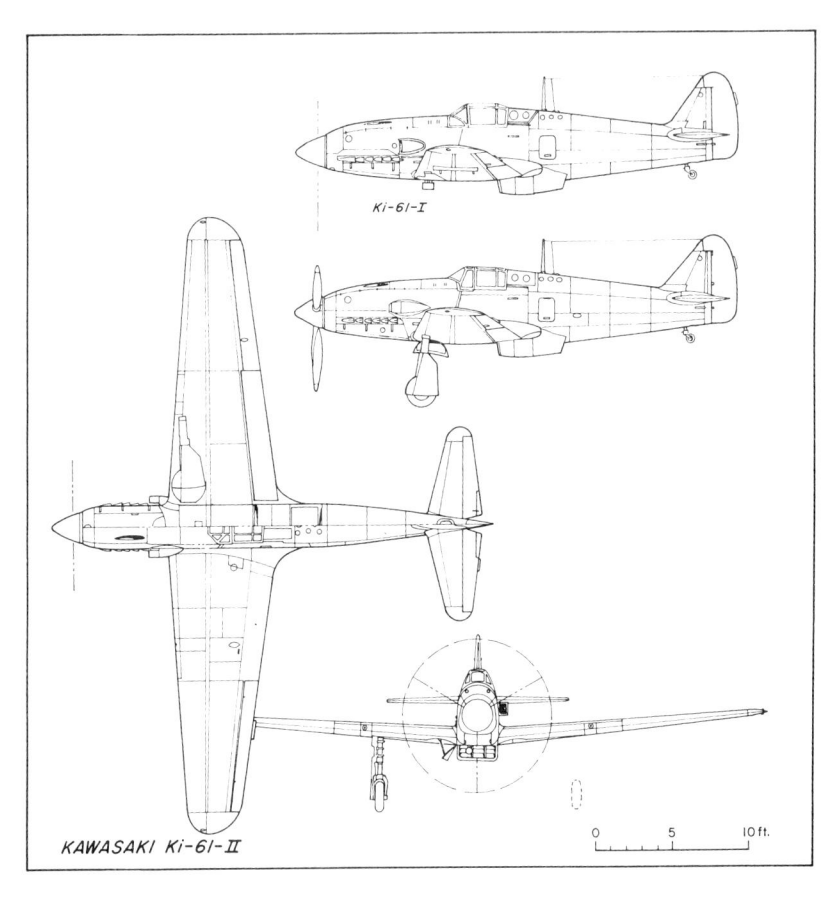

Fighter Model 2 was dealt a crippling blow when, on 19 January, 1945, the US Air Force destroyed the Akashi engine plant. Only 374 Ki-61-II KAI airframes were built in slightly less than a year but some thirty were destroyed on the ground prior to delivery to Service units and 275 were left without engines until the successful adoption of the fourteen-cylinder Mitsubishi Ha-112-II radial engine which gave birth to the Ki-100. Prior to this conversion it had been proposed to incorporate various modifications in a new version, the Ki-61-III, but only one aerodynamic prototype was built, this aircraft being characterized by the fitting of an all-round-vision canopy to a modified Ki-61-II KAI.

Plagued with engine troubles and production difficulties, the Hien never saw as extensive a Service use as the more numerous Nakajima fighters, but during the mid-war years it was the only Japanese aircraft which could successfully engage the fast Allied fighters by combining some of the Nipponese machines' traditional manoeuvrability with a strong and well protected structure.

Kawasaki Ki-61-I KAIc of the 19th Sentai. (*US Navy Department.*)

UNITS ALLOCATED

17th, 18th, 19th, 23rd, 26th, 28th, 37th, 55th, 56th, 59th, 65th, 68th, 78th, 105th and 244th Sentais. 23rd and 28th Dokuritsu Dai Shijugo Chutais. 8th Kyo-iku Hikotai. 5th, 11th, 16th and 18th Lensei Hikotais. Akeno Fighter Training School.

TECHNICAL DATA

Description: Single-seat fighter. All-metal construction with fabric-covered control surfaces.

Accommodation: Pilot in enclosed cockpit.

Powerplant: One Kawasaki Ha-40 twelve-cylinder inverted-vee liquid-cooled engine, rated at 1,175 hp for take-off and 1,100 hp at 4,200 m (13,780 ft), driving a constant-speed three-blade metal propeller (Ki-61 prototypes).

One 1,100 hp Army Type 2 twelve-cylinder liquid-cooled engine (Kawasaki Ha-40), rated at 1,175 hp for take-off and 1,080 hp at 3,500 m (11,480 ft), driving a constant-speed three-blade metal propeller (Ki-61-Ia and Ki-61-Ib).

One 1,100 hp Army Type 2 twelve-cylinder liquid-cooled engine (Kawasaki Ha-40), rated at 1,180 hp for take-off and 1,100 hp at 3,900 m (12,795 ft), driving a constant-speed three-blade metal propeller (Ki-61-I KAIc and Ki-61-I KAId).

One Kawasaki Ha-140 twelve-cylinder liquid-cooled engine, rated at 1,500 hp for take-off and 1,250 hp at 5,700 m (18,700 ft), driving a constant-speed three-blade metal propeller (Ki-61-II and Ki-61-II KAI).

Armament: Two fuselage-mounted 12·7 mm Type 1 (Ho-103) machine-guns and two wing-mounted 7·7 mm Type 89 machine-guns (Ki-61-Ia).

Two fuselage-mounted 12·7 mm Type 1 (Ho-103) machine-guns and two wing-mounted 12·7 mm Type 1 (Ho-103) machine-guns (Ki-61-Ib).

Two fuselage-mounted 12·7 mm Type 1 (Ho-103) machine-guns and two wing-mounted 20 mm Mauser MG 151/20 cannon (modified Ki-61-Ia and -Ib).

Two fuselage-mounted 20 mm Ho-5 cannon and two wing-mounted 12·7 mm Type 1 (Ho-103) machine-guns (Ki-61-I KAIc, Ki-61-II and Ki-61-II KAIa).

Two fuselage-mounted 12·7 mm Type 1 (Ho-103) machine-guns and two wing-mounted 30 mm Ho-105 cannon (Ki-61-I KAId).

Two fuselage-mounted 20 mm Ho-5 cannon and two wing-mounted 20 mm Ho-5 cannon (Ki-61-II KAIb).

External stores: two 200 litre (44 Imp gal) drop tanks, or (Ki-61-I KAI and -II KAI) two 250 kg (551 lb) bombs.

A Kawasaki Ki-61-II KAI Army Type 3 Fighter Model 2A—one of the versions powered by the unreliable Kawasaki Ha-140 engine.

	Ki-61-Ib	Ki-61-I KAIc	Ki-61-II KAIa
Dimensions:			
Span	12 m	12 m	12 m
	(39 ft 4 $\frac{7}{16}$ in)	(39 ft 4 $\frac{7}{16}$ in)	(39 ft 4 $\frac{7}{16}$ in)
Length	8·75 m	8·94 m	9·16 m
	(28 ft 8½ in)	(29 ft 4 in)	(30 ft 0⅝ in)
Height	3·7 m	3·7 m	3·7 m
	(12 ft 1 $\frac{11}{16}$ in)	(12 ft 1 $\frac{11}{16}$ in)	(12 ft 1 $\frac{11}{16}$ in)
Wing area	20 sq m	20 sq m	20 sq m
	(215·278 sq ft)	(215·278 sq ft)	(215·278 sq ft)
Weights:			
Empty	2,210 kg	2,630 kg	2,840 kg
	(4,872 lb)	(5,798 lb)	(6,261 lb)
Loaded	2,950 kg	3,470 kg	3,780 kg
	(6,504 lb)	(7,650 lb)	8,333 lb)
Maximum	3,250 kg	—	3,825 kg
	(7,165 lb)		(8,433 lb)
Wing loading	147·5 kg/sq m	173·5 kg/sq m	189 kg/sq m
	(30·2 lb/sq ft)	(35·1 lb/sq ft)	(38·8 lb/sq ft)
Power loading	2·51 kg/hp	2·94 kg/hp	2·52 kg/hp
	(5·53 lb/hp)	(6·48 lb/hp)	(5·56 lb/hp)
Performance:			
Maximum speed	592 km/h at 4,860 m	590 km/h at 4,260 m	610 km/h at 6,000 m
	(368 mph at 15,945 ft)	(366 mph at 13,980 ft)	(379 mph at 19,685 ft)
Cruising speed	400 km/h at 4,000 m	—	—
	(249 mph at 13,125 ft)	—	—
Climb to	5,000 m (16,405 ft)	5,000 m (16,405 ft)	5,000 m (16,405 ft)
in	5 min 31 sec	7 min	6 min
Service ceiling	11,600 m	10,000 m	11,000 m
	(37,730 ft)	(32,810 ft)	(36,090 ft)
Range—normal	600 km	—	1,100 km
	(373 miles)	—	(684 miles)
—maximum	1,100 km	1,800 km	1,600 km
	(684 miles)	(1,120 miles)	(995 miles)

Production: A total of 3,078 Ki-61s were built by Kawasaki Kokuki Kogyo K.K. in their Kagamigahara plant as follows:

    12 Ki-61 prototypes (1941–42)
    1,380 Ki-61-I production aircraft (Aug 1942–July 1944)
    1,274 Ki-61-I KAI production aircraft (Jan 1944–Jan 1945)
    8 Ki-61-II prototypes (Aug 1943–Jan 1944)
    30 Ki-61-II KAI prototypes and pre-production aircraft (Apr–Sept 1944)
    374 Ki-61-II KAI production aircraft (Sept 1944–Aug 1945)
However, out of 374 Ki-61-II KAI airframes built 275 were completed as Ki-100-Ia.

Kawasaki Ki-64

Despite active efforts to cure the early difficulties with the Ki-45 and to commence preliminary design studies for what were to become the Ki-60 and Ki-61, Takeo Doi found time in 1939 to conceive a highly unorthodox high-speed fighter. However, as a pressing need existed for the more conventional aircraft the Japanese Army did not authorize Kawasaki to proceed with the design until October 1940 when the project was revived under the Ki-64 designation to meet a specially drafted specification calling for a maximum speed of 700 km/h at 5,000 m (435 mph at 16,405 ft) and a climb to 5,000 m (16,405 ft) in 5 min.

Takeo Doi, co-operating with his colleagues of the Akashi engine plant, decided to use the 2,350 hp Kawasaki Ha-201 which actually comprised two Ha-40 twelve-cylinder liquid-cooled engines mounted in tandem fore and aft of the pilot's cockpit and drove two contra-rotating three-blade propellers. The forward propeller, driven by the rear engine, was of the controllable-pitch type and the rear propeller, driven by the front engine, was of fixed-pitch. Perhaps the most unusual feature of the powerplant was the steam vapour cooling system which utilized the wing and flap surfaces for cooling area. The coolant used was water, carried in a 70 litre (15·4 Imp gal) tank in each wing, and the total cooling area was 24 sq m (258·333 sq ft). The front engine used the cooling elements in the port wing while the rear engine used those in the starboard wing. The wings themselves were of modified laminar flow section and contained the fuel tanks and two 20 mm Ho-5 cannon. The entire powerplant installation was tested during extensive wind-tunnel experiments and a Ki-61 was specially modified to test the surface evaporation cooling system. These various tests, although delaying completion of the prototype until December 1943, proved conclusively that the cooling system performed satisfactorily. It permitted an increase in speed of some 25 mph and combat damage to it was not believed to create special problems, but it had the disadvantage of limiting the space available for fuel tanks thus reducing range.

Starting in December 1943, only five test flights were made as during the fifth fire developed in the rear engine, necessitating an emergency landing.

The only completed Kawasaki Ki-64 prototype. (*Aireview.*)

KAWASAKI Ki-64

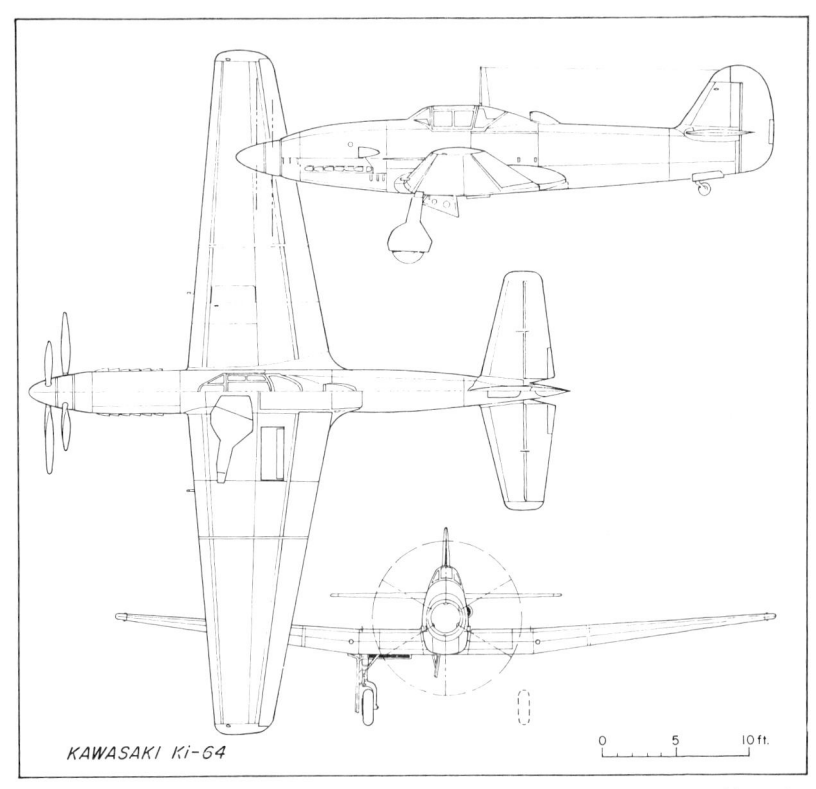

The engine was sent to Akashi for repair and the airframe to Gifu. The engine repair was not completed, and the airframe was captured at the end of the war and elements of the cooling system sent to Wright Field for evaluation.

The Ki-64 KAI was a proposed production version with a more powerful Ha-201 engine, rated at 2,800 hp at altitude, and driving electrically-operated constant-speed contra-rotating propellers. A maximum speed of 800 km/h (497 mph) was anticipated, but the project was cancelled in favour of more conventional aircraft already in production.

TECHNICAL DATA

Description: Single-seat fighter with tandem-mounted engines. All-metal construction.
Accommodation: Pilot in enclosed cockpit.
Powerplant: One Kawasaki Ha-201 ([Ha-72] 11) twenty-four cylinder inverted-vee liquid-cooled engine, rated at 2,350 hp for take-off and 2,200 hp at 3,900 m (12,795 ft), driving three-blade contra-rotating propellers.
Armament: Two 20 mm Ho-5 cannon in the fuselage decking and two 20 mm Ho-5 cannon in the wings.
Dimensions: Span 13·5 m (44 ft 3½ in); length 11·03 m (36 ft 2¼ in); height 4·25 m (13 ft 11 $\frac{5}{16}$ in); wing area 28 sq m (301·388 sq ft).
Weights: Empty 4,050 kg (8,929 lb); loaded 5,100 kg (11,244 lb); wing loading 182·1 kg/sq m (37·3 lb/sq ft); power loading 2·17 kg/hp (4·78 lb/hp).
Performance: Maximum speed 690 km/h at 5,000 m (429 mph at 16,405 ft); climb to 5,000 m (16,405 ft) in 5 min 30 sec; service ceiling 12,000 m (39,370 ft); range 1,000 km (621 miles).
Production: One prototype completed in December 1943.

The first prototype Kawasaki Ki-66. (*Eckert.*)

Kawasaki Ki-66

The achievements of the German dive-bombers during the Spanish Civil War and the campaigns of Poland and France—magnified by Nazi propaganda—had attracted the attention of the Koku Hombu which, in September 1941, instructed Kawasaki Kokuki Kogyo K.K. to initiate the design of an aircraft specially intended for dive-bombing attacks in support of land forces. The Japanese Army specified that the aircraft was to be of twin-engined design and that armament was to consist of two forward-firing 12·7 mm machine-guns and one flexible rear-firing 7·7 mm machine-gun. Normal and maximum bomb-load were respectively specified at 300 kg (661 lb) and 500 kg (1,102 lb).

Drawing heavily on the experience acquired in designing the twin-engined Ki-45 heavy fighter and Ki-48 light bomber, Takeo Doi began in October 1941 to design the Ki-66 to meet this new Army requirement. Bearing a strong resemblance to its two predecessors, the aircraft had mid-mounted wings and was powered by a pair of 1,130 hp Nakajima Ha-115 engines. Snow-fence dive-brakes were flush-mounted under the wings outboard of the engine nacelles and were hinged clear of the undersurface when opened. Armament consisted of two 12·7 mm Type 1 machine-guns mounted in the nose, one flexible rear-firing 7·7 mm Type 89 machine-gun and one flexible 7·7 mm Type 89 machine-gun firing through a ventral hatch. The crew consisted of a pilot and a radio-operator/gunner.

Six prototypes were completed between October 1942 and April 1943 but, despite successfully completing its flight test programme, the Ki-66-Ia was not placed in production as its performance was only marginally superior to that of the Ki-48-II already in production. However, the aircraft contributed to the development of a dive-bomber version of the Ki-48-II which used dive-brakes similar to those fitted to the Ki-66.

Several versions of the aircraft including the Ki-66-Ib powered by two 1,360 hp Nakajima Ha-315-I radials—of which one prototype was built

123

KAWASAKI Ki-66

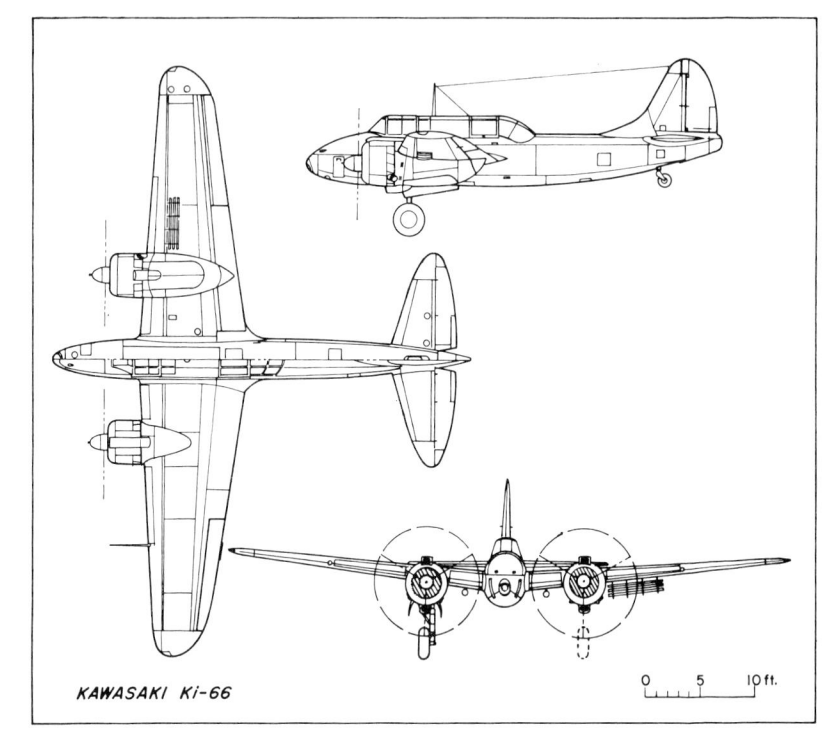

by modifying one of the six Ki-66-Ias, the Ki-66-Ic with two 2,100 hp Nakajima Ha-39, the Ki-66-Id with two 1,900 hp Nakajima Ha-45 and the heavy fighter Ki-66-II powered by two 1,360 hp Nakajima Ha-315-II were projected but all development work was suspended in October 1943.

TECHNICAL DATA

Description: Twin-engined dive-bomber. All-metal construction with fabric-covered control surfaces.
Accommodation: Crew of two in enclosed cockpits.
Powerplant: Two 1,150 hp Army Type 1 (Nakajima Ha-115) fourteen-cylinder air-cooled radials, rated at 1,130 hp for take-off, 1,100 hp at 2,850 m (9,350 ft) and 940 hp at 5,600 m (18,370 ft), driving three-blade metal propellers (Ki-66-Ia).

Two 1,360 hp Nakajima Ha-315-I fourteen-cylinder air-cooled radials, rated at 1,350 hp for take-off and 1,210 hp at 4,200 m (13,780 ft), driving three-blade metal propellers (Ki-66-Ib).

Armament: Two forward-firing 12·7 mm Type 1 (Ho-103) machine-guns mounted in the nose, one flexible 7·7 mm Type 89 in the ventral position and one flexible rear-firing 7·7 mm Type 89 machine-gun in the dorsal position.
  Bomb-load—normal, 300 kg (661 lb)
        —maximum, 500 kg (1,102 lb)
Dimensions: Span 15·5 m (50 ft 10¼ in); length 11·2 m (36 ft 8 ⅝ in); height 3·7 m (12 ft 1 ³¹⁄₃₂ in); wing area 34 sq m (365·972 sq ft).
Weights: Empty 4,100 kg (9,039 lb); loaded 5,750 kg (12,677 lb); wing loading 169·1 kg/sq m (34·6 lb/sq ft); power loading 2·5 kg/hp (5·6 lb/hp).
Performance: Maximum speed 535 km/h at 5,600 m (332 mph at 18,370 ft); climb to 5,000 m (16,405 ft) in 7 min 30 sec; service ceiling 10,000 m (32,810 ft); range 2,000 km (1,243 miles).
Production: A total of six Ki-66 prototypes were built by Kawasaki Kokuki Kogyo K.K. between October 1942 and April 1943.

Kawasaki Ki-78 high-speed research aircraft.

Kawasaki Ki-78

Begun in 1938 as a civil project for use in a high-speed research programme and for a contemplated attempt to break the world air speed record, the KEN III (indicating Kensan III or Research III) project was taken over by the Imperial Japanese Army under the Ki-78 designation upon Japan's entry into the war.

    Designed by a team of the Aeronautical Research Institute of the University of Tokyo, led by Shoroku Wada and comprising Mineo Yamamoto (fuselage design), Eichiro Tani (wing design) and Seichi Kurino and Shojiro Nomura (engine installation), the Ki-78 introduced several advanced design features not previously used by the Japanese aircraft industry. To minimize drag a fuselage of minimum cross section was designed and a laminar flow section was adopted for the wings. As the wing area was remarkably small, 11 sq m (118·403 sq ft), a combination of Fowler and split flaps and drooping ailerons was selected to reduce landing speed. An imported 1,175 hp Daimler-Benz DB 601A twelve-cylinder inverted-vee liquid-cooled engine was selected to power the aircraft and was modified to incorporate a system of water-methanol injection —the first such device used in Japan—to momentarily boost its power to 1,550 hp. Radiators of small frontal area were mounted on each side of the rear fuselage, and a fan, driven by a 60 hp turbine, was used to improve cooling.

    A wooden mock-up of the KEN III was completed in May 1941 and production of two prototypes was entrusted to Kawasaki, where Isamu Imashi took charge of the project. Eventually only the first prototype, construction of which had begun at Gifu in September 1941, was completed and this aircraft first flew on 26 December, 1942. It was found extremely difficult to fly at low speeds, and take-off and landing speeds were respectively 205 km/h (127 mph) and 170 km/h (106 mph). Furthermore, loaded weight and wing loading exceeded calculated values and elevator flutter was experienced at 635 km/h (395 mph). On 27 December, 1943, during its 31st flight, the Ki-78 reached a maximum speed of 699·6 km/h at 3,527 m (434·9 mph at 11,539 ft). This was considerably less than the speed of 850 km/h (528 mph) which had been set as the ultimate goal for the programme. To achieve the calculated performance too many airframe and engine modifications were required and the flight trials of the Ki-78 were suspended after the 32nd flight, on 11 January, 1944.

TECHNICAL DATA

Description: Single-engined high-speed research aircraft. All-metal construction.
Accommodation: Pilot in enclosed cockpit.
Powerplant: One 1,175 hp Daimler-Benz DB 601A twelve-cylinder inverted-vee liquid-cooled engine, rated at 1,550 hp for short duration, driving a three-blade metal propeller.
Dimensions: Span 8 m (26 ft 2 11/32 in); length 8·1 m (26 ft 6 29/32 in); height 3·07 m (10 ft 0 7/8 in); wing area 11 sq m (118·403 sq ft).
Weights: Empty 1,930 kg (4,255 lb); loaded 2,300 kg (5,071 lb); wing loading 209 kg/sq m (42·8 lb/sq ft); power loading 2 kg/hp (4·4 lb/hp).
Performance: Maximum speed 700 km/h at 3,500 m (435 mph at 11,485 ft); ceiling 8,000 m (26,245 ft); range 600 km (373 miles).
Production: One Ki-78 was completed in December 1942 at the Gifu plant of Kawasaki Kokuki Kogyo K.K.

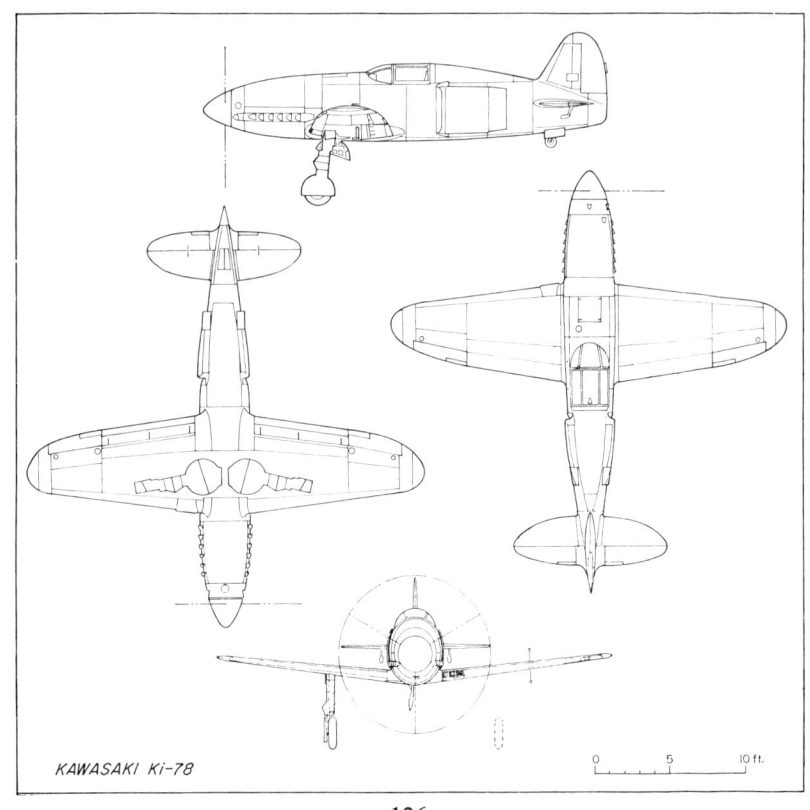

KAWASAKI Ki-78

Third prototype of the Kawasaki Ki-96 single-seat twin-engined heavy fighter. (*Aireview*.)

Kawasaki Ki-96

In August 1942, as the Ki-45 KAIa was entering service with the 5th Sentai, Takeo Doi and his team started working on the Ki-45-II, an improved version of the Toryu designed around a pair of 1,500 hp Mitsubishi Ha-112-II engines. Compared with its forerunner, the Ki-45-II had a refined airframe of larger dimensions—span being increased from 15·02 m (49 ft $3\frac{5}{16}$ in) to 15·57 m (51 ft 1 in)—and larger square-tipped vertical tail surfaces were adopted to improve handling characteristics with one engine out. Detailed design studies progressed slowly as the Army did not show much interest in a new two-seat fighter and Kawasaki had several projects under development, but the construction of three prototypes was authorized. However, in December 1942 the Koku Hombu revised their requirements and instructed Kawasaki to complete the aircraft as a single-seat fighter since the addition of a second crew member to handle a single manually-operated machine-gun did not then appear to justify the extra weight. Thus revised the project received the Ki-96 designation, a change justified by the fact that only few components were common to the Ki-45 KAI and the new aircraft.

In 1943 work on the Ki-96 gained tempo and in September of that year the first prototype was completed. As the decision to adopt a single-seat configuration had been taken after the construction of the fuselage of the first Ki-45-II was already well in hand, the first Ki-96 made use of this fuselage and was characterized by a larger canopy than the one used on subsequent machines, the second cockpit being faired over. Two additional prototypes, built from the outset as single-seaters, with all-round-vision canopy, also took part in the flight trials. Results of these tests were most satisfactory, the Ki-96 combining good handling characteristics with performance exceeding design estimates but, even before the first flight of the

KAWASAKI Ki-96

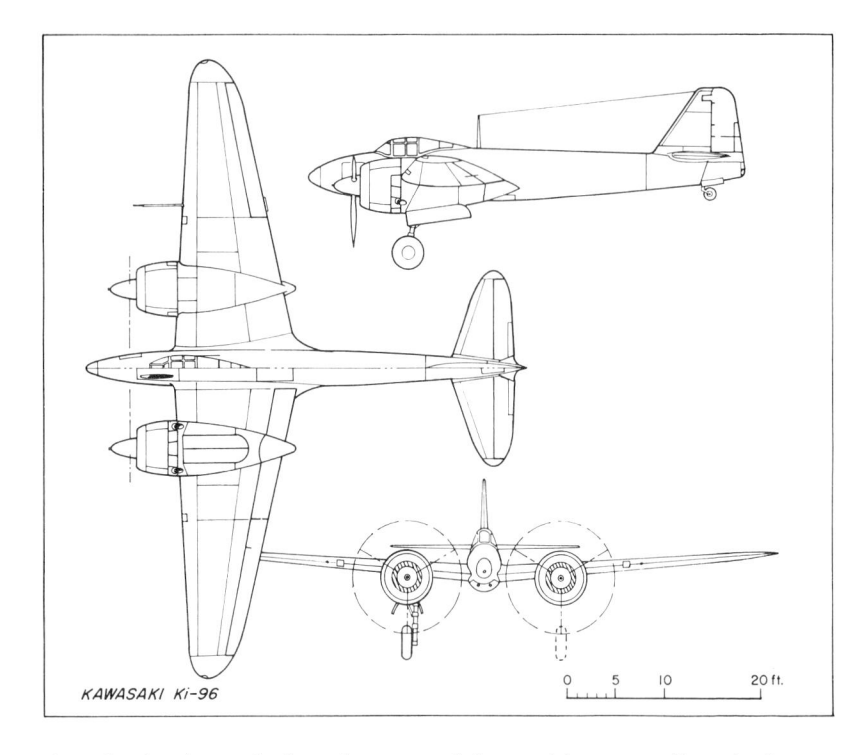

aircraft, the Army had again reversed its position regarding single-seat twin-engined heavy fighters and consequently the Ki-96 had only a brief life as an aerodynamic prototype for the two-seat Ki-102 which supplanted it.

TECHNICAL DATA

Description: Twin-engined experimental heavy fighter. All-metal construction with fabric-covered control surfaces.
Accommodation: Pilot in enclosed cockpit.
Powerplant: Two Mitsubishi Ha-112-II fourteen-cylinder air-cooled radials, rated at 1,500 hp for take-off, 1,350 hp at 2,000 m (6,560 ft) and 1,250 hp at 5,800 m (19,030 ft), driving constant-speed three-blade metal propellers.
Armament: One 37 mm Ho-203 cannon in the nose and two 20 mm Ho-5 cannon under the fuselage. External stores: two 200 litre (44 Imp gal) drop tanks, or two 250 kg (551 lb) bombs.
Dimensions: Span 15·57 m (51 ft 1 in); length 11·45 m (37 ft 6¾ in); height 3·7 m (12 ft 1¾ in); wing area 34 sq m (365·972 sq ft).
Weights: Empty 4,550 kg (10,031 lb); loaded 6,000 kg (13,228 lb); wing loading 176·5 kg/sq m (36·1 lb/sq ft); power loading 2 kg/hp (4·4 lb/hp).
Performance: Maximum speed 600 km/h at 6,000 m (373 mph at 19,685 ft); climb to 5,000 m (16,405 ft) in 6 min; service ceiling 11,500 m (37,730 ft); range 1,600 km (994 miles).
Production: Three prototypes built in 1943 by Kawasaki Kokuki Kogyo K.K.

Kawasaki Ki-100-Ia Army Type 5 Fighter Model 1A of the 59th Sentai, 1st Chutai.

Kawasaki Ki-100

When in June 1944 the USAAF began daylight bombing operations against Japan, the Japanese Army found themselves without an adequate high-altitude interceptor capable of successfully engaging the B-29s at their cruising altitude of 30,000 ft. This situation had been foreseen but, even in their most confident estimates, the Koku Hombu could not hope to have the specialized interceptor aircraft then under development in service much before the late summer of 1945. As a stopgap the Army had planned to use the Ki-61-II KAI which had begun flight trials two months before. However, teething troubles with the aircraft's Ha-140 engine frustrated this plan, and proven and reliable Ki-61-II KAI airframes were left unused at the Kagamigahara plant while the fighter Sentais had to defend the homeland with older aircraft. Time was of the essence and a solution had to be found to provide an alternate powerplant for the Ki-61-II KAI and for the rapid supply of a new type of interceptor fighter to the Army. Consequently, in November 1944, the Ministry of Munitions instructed Kawasaki to install a different engine in the Ki-61-II KAI.

By the end of 1944 the factories producing engines with sufficiently small diameter to be mounted in a fighter aircraft already had their production facilities overtaxed by the pressing demands resulting from the war situation, and Kawasaki engineers had to find a suitable type of engine among those then manufactured for bomber aircraft. It soon appeared that the only powerplant combining availability and reliability with a suitable output was the 1,500 hp Mitsubishi Ha-112-II fourteen-cylinder double-row radial. As this engine had a diameter of 1·22 m (4 ft) it appeared at first difficult to install it in the Ki-61-II KAI airframe with its fuselage width of only 0·84 m (2 ft 9$\frac{1}{16}$ in). However, the Kawasaki engineers were able to study the engine mounting of an imported Focke-Wulf Fw 190A, an aircraft in which a radial engine had been successfully fitted to a slim fuselage, and to call on the experience of the Imperial Japanese Navy which had fitted the same Mitsubishi Ha-112-II to the Aichi-built D4Y3, earlier versions of this aircraft also being powered by an inverted-vee liquid-cooled engine. Work began immediately on the experimental modification of three Ki-61-II KAIs and the first aircraft, designated Ki-100, made its first flight on 1 February, 1945.

Compared with its forerunner the Ki-100 was lighter—empty and loaded weight being respectively reduced by 315 kg and 285 kg to 2,525 kg and 3,495 kg (694 lb and 628 lb to 5,567 lb and 7,705 lb)—and manoeuvrability and handling characteristics were markedly improved due to the lower wing and power loadings. Even though the engines of the Ki-61-II KAI and the Ki-100 had nominally the same power, the Ki-100 had slightly lower maximum speed due to its engine's larger frontal drag, but other performance figures were comparable. However, whereas the Ki-61-II KAI reached its calculated performance only now and then as its engine was temperamental, the Ki-100 benefited from the high reliability of its engine. Accelerated flight tests taking place in February 1945 revealed that the aircraft performed even better than anticipated and a fourth Ki-61-II KAI was modified the same month to full production standard as Army Type 5 Fighter Model 1A (Ki-100-Ia). Two hundred and seventy-one Ki-61-II

Kawasaki Ki-100-Ib Army Type 5 Fighter Model 1B of the 5th Sentai. (*Eckert.*)

KAI airframes were similarly converted at the Kagamigahara plant between March and June 1945 and were immediately delivered to Service units in Japan. Under combat conditions the Ki-100-Ia proved itself to be an outstanding fighter, equally suited to intercepting high-flying B-29s and to engaging the Grumman F6F Hellcats of the US Navy which were now frequently operating in the Japanese sky. To the Allies the aircraft was a complete and unpleasant surprise, and its Nipponese pilots joined their ground crews in hailing the Ki-100 as the best and most reliable operational fighter of the Imperial Japanese Army. The aircraft was easy to handle and gave a fighting chance even to the youngest pilots who often had less than 100 hours of flight training prior to joining their operational units.

As soon as flight trials had shown that the development of the Ki-100-Ia was a success, Kawasaki began preparations to produce two new versions. Characterized by an all-round-vision canopy similar to that planned for the Ki-61-III and tested on a Ki-61-II KAI, the Ki-100-Ib was no longer a

The Kawasaki Ki-100-Ib was the last type of single-seat fighter to enter service with the Japanese Army.

conversion from existing airframes but was built to the new standard from the start. The first Ki-100-Ibs were built at the Kagamigahara and Ichinomiya factories in May 1945 but production was hampered by Allied bombings, the Ichinomiya plant being forced to cease production in July 1945 and the Kagamigahara production being considerably slowed down. When Japan surrendered only 106 Ki-100-Ibs had been built at Kagamigahara and the Ichinomiya plant had delivered only twelve aircraft of this version.

In an attempt to further improve the performance of the aircraft at altitude, in March 1945 Kawasaki began the development of the Ki-100-II powered by a 1,500 hp Mitsubishi Ha-112-II Ru with Ru-102 turbosupercharger and water-methanol injection. Due to the lack of internal space the turbosupercharger was fitted beneath the fuselage without provision for an intercooler and air was ducted directly from the compressor to the carburettor. The installation of the turbosupercharger necessitated the relocation of some of the fuel lines and the ventral air scoop was offset to starboard while an additional intake was mounted in the port wing root. The first Ki-100-II flew in May 1945 and within a month was joined on the flight trials by two additional prototypes. Compared with the Ki-100-I, the Ki-100-II was slightly heavier and consequently suffered a performance penalty below 8,000 m (26,250 ft). Despite the lack of intercooler preventing full advantage being gained from the installation of a turbosupercharger, the Ki-100-II had better performance than the Ki-100-I above 8,000 m (26,250 ft) and its maximum speed of 590 km/h (367 mph) was reached at 10,000 m (32,810 ft), the cruising altitude of the B-29s during daylight operations. It was planned to begin production of the Ki-100-II in September 1945 but the war ended before implementation of this schedule.

It was fitting that the last operational fighter of the Imperial Japanese Army made the last flight for that Service when two Ki-100-Ibs of the 111th Sentai were ferried between Komachi and Yokosuka where they were shipped to the USA for evaluation.

UNITS ALLOCATED

5th, 17th, 18th, 59th, 111th and 244th Sentais.

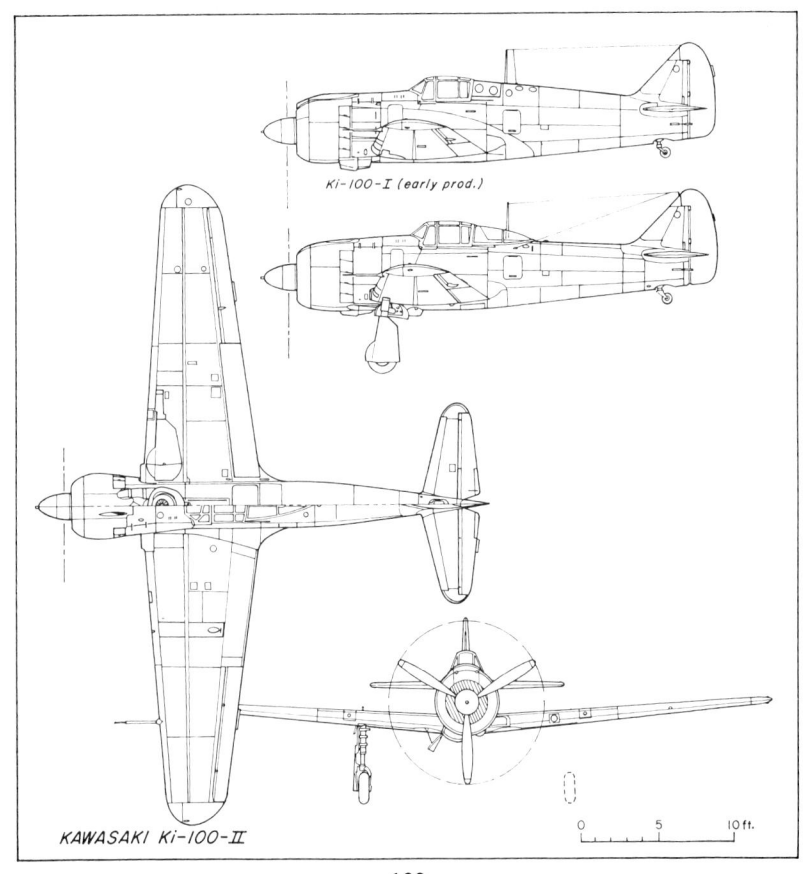

The third Ki-100-II as it was found at the end of the war in the Gifu plant. Note characteristic airscoop on wing root and turbo-supercharger installation beneath the fuselage. (*USAF.*)

TECHNICAL DATA

Description: Single-seat fighter and fighter-bomber. All-metal construction with fabric-covered control surfaces.

Accommodation: Pilot in enclosed cockpit.

Powerplant: One Army Type 4 fourteen-cylinder air-cooled radial (Mitsubishi [Ha-33] 62 or Ha-112-II), rated at 1,500 hp for take-off, 1,350 hp at 2,000 m (6,560 ft) and 1,250 hp at 5,800 m (19,030 ft), driving a constant-speed three-blade metal propeller (Ki-100-I).

One 1,500 hp Mitsubishi Ha-112-II Ru fourteen-cylinder air-cooled radial, rated at 1,500 hp for take-off, 1,370 hp at 7,000 m (22,965 ft) and 1,240 hp at 10,000 m (32,810 ft), driving a constant-speed three-blade metal propeller (Ki-100-II).

Armament: Two fuselage-mounted 20 mm Ho-5 cannon and two wing-mounted 12·7 mm Type 1 (Ho-103) machine-guns.

External stores: two 200 litre (44 Imp gal) drop tanks, or two 250 kg (551 lb) bombs.

	Ki-100-I	Ki-100-II
Dimensions:		
Span	12 m	12 m
	(39 ft 4 $\frac{7}{16}$ in)	(39 ft 4 $\frac{7}{16}$ in)
Length	8·82 m	8·82 m
	(28 ft 11¼ in)	(28 ft 11¼ in)
Height	3·75 m	3·75 m
	(12 ft 3⅝ in)	(12 ft 3⅝ in)
Wing area	20 sq m	20 sq m
	(215·278 sq ft)	(215·278 sq ft)
Weights:		
Empty	2,525 kg	2,700 kg
	(5,567 lb)	(5,952 lb)
Loaded	3,495 kg	3,670 kg
	(7,705 lb)	(8,091 lb)
Wing loading	174·8 kg/sq m	183·5 kg/sq m
	(35·8 lb/sq ft)	(37·6 lb/sq ft)
Power loading	2·33 kg/hp	2·44 kg/hp
	(5·1 lb/hp)	(5·4 lb/hp)

Performance:

	Ki-100-I	Ki-100-II
Maximum speed	580 km/h at 6,000 m	570 km/h at 6,000 m
	(360 mph at 19,685 ft)	(354 mph at 19,685 ft)
	535 km/h at 10,000 m	590 km/h at 10,000 m
	(332 mph at 32,810 ft)	(367 mph at 32,810 ft)
Cruising speed	400 km/h at 4,000 m	400 km/h at 4,000 m
	(249 mph at 13,125 ft)	(249 mph at 13,125 ft)
Climb to	5,000 m (16,405 ft)	5,000 m (16,405 ft)
in	6 min	6 min 40 sec
to	10,000 m (32,810 ft)	10,000 m (32,810 ft)
in	20 min	18 min
Service ceiling	11,000 m	11,000 m
	(36,090 ft)	(36,090 ft)
Range—normal	1,400 km	—
	(870 miles)	—
—maximum	2,200 km	1,800 km
	(1,367 miles)	(1,118 miles)

Production: A total of 396 Ki-100s, including 275 Ki-61-II KAI conversions, were built by Kawasaki Kokuki Kogyo K.K. as follows:

Kagamigahara plant:
   3 Ki-100 prototypes (Feb 1945)
   272 Ki-100-Ia production aircraft (Feb–June 1945)
   106 Ki-100-Ib production aircraft (May–Aug 1945)
   3 Ki-100-II prototypes (May–June 1945)
   ———
   384

Ichinomiya plant:
   12 Ki-100-Ib production aircraft (May–July 1945)

Kawasaki Ki-102

While the first prototype of their Ki-96 twin-engined heavy fighter was nearing completion the Kawasaki design team led by Takeo Doi suggested to the Imperial Japanese Army that a version of the aircraft be built as a replacement for the Toryu used in the ground attack role. In August 1943, the Koku Hombu gave their approval to the project and instructed Kawasaki to begin construction of prototypes under the Ki-102 designation. To gain time Takeo Doi decided to retain the basic structure and powerplants of the Ki-96 in its original two-seat configuration. However, additional armour and petrol tank protection were designed into the Ki-102, and heavier armament was fitted comprising one nose-mounted 57 mm Ho-401 cannon, two fuselage-mounted 20 mm Ho-5 cannon and one flexible rear-firing 12·7 mm Ho-103 machine-gun. Powered by two 1,500 hp Mitsubishi Ha-112-II fourteen-cylinder air-cooled radials, the first of three Ki-102 prototypes was completed and flown in March 1944.

A captured Kawasaki Ki-102b. The word fumigated appears in capital letters on the rear fuselage.

Twenty pre-production aircraft were also built and, together with the three prototypes, initially served in the development of the original ground attack version of the Ki-102. Inflight handling characteristics and performance gave entire satisfaction, but during the landing approach the aircraft suffered from marked directional instability. To correct this the three-point attitude of the aircraft on the ground was reduced by fitting a tailwheel strut of increased length and, so modified, in October 1944 the aircraft was placed in production as the Army Type 4 Assault Plane (Ki-102b). Most of the production aircraft were kept in reserve in Japan, but a few saw limited action during the Okinawa campaign where the Ki-102b became known as RANDY to the Allied forces. In Japan, the Ki-102b was used in the development programme of the Igo-1-B air-to-ground guided missile with which it was hoped to equip the aircraft prior to the anticipated Allied invasion of the Japanese homeland.

A month before the maiden flight of the first Ki-102 prototype, the Koku Hombu once again indicated their desire to obtain a heavy high-altitude version of the Kawasaki series of twin-engined aircraft. To meet this requirement, Kawasaki already had under development the Ki-108 but, as its intended pressure cabin required considerable time to be fully

Kawasaki Ki-102b Army Type 4 Assault Plane Model B. (*Aireview*.)

KAWASAKI Ki-102

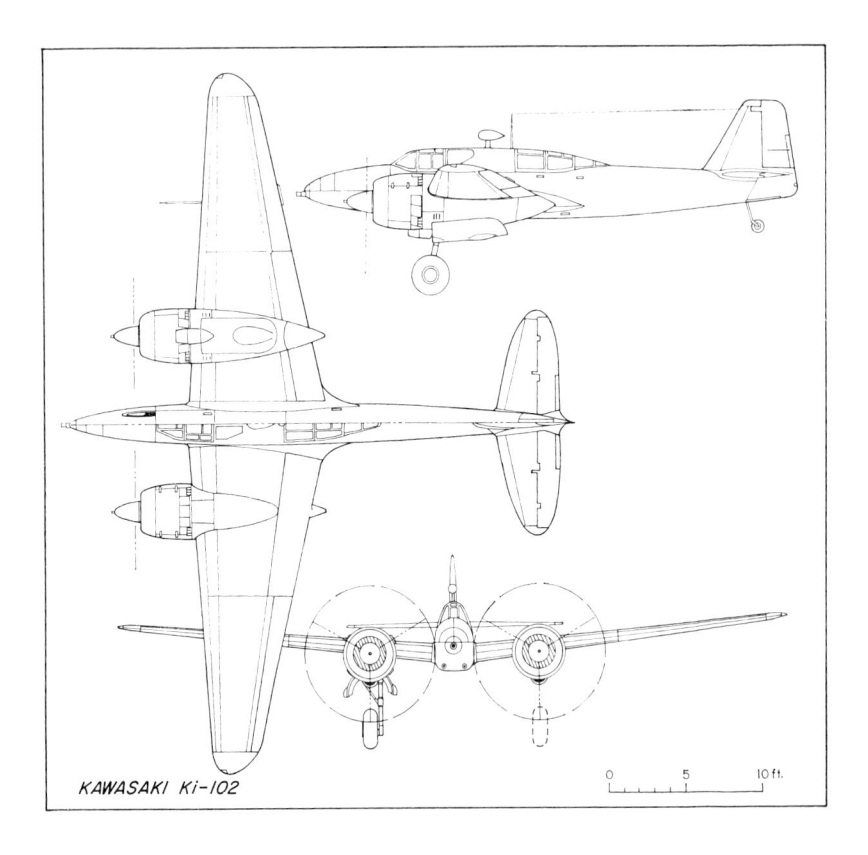

developed, the manufacturers were instructed by the Koku Hombu to design a straightforward version of the Ki-102 capable of operating as a high-altitude fighter. Six pre-production Ki-102s were modified as prototypes for the Ki-102a high-altitude fighter, the first aircraft being completed in June 1944. Externally the Ki-102a was identical to the Ki-102b but was powered by two 1,500 hp Mitsubishi Ha-112-II Ru engines fitted with Ru-102 turbosuperchargers which maintained their rated power of 1,250 hp up to 8,200 m (26,900 ft), the standard Ha-112-II giving this power at 5,800 m (19,030 ft). The Ki-102a had revised armament comprising a 37 mm Ho-203 cannon and two fuselage-mounted 20 mm Ho-5 cannon, the flexible rear-firing machine-gun being omitted. Following satisfactory completion of flight trials with the six prototypes, an additional series of twenty Ki-102as was built by modifying a similar number of production Ki-102b airframes. However, only fifteen of these aircraft could be delivered to the Army before the end of the war, and the Ki-102a was never placed in quantity production.

By the end of 1944, when the B-29 operations against Japan were intensified, the Army had so far failed to develop a specialized night fighter.

As the Toryu was proving to be a satisfactory stopgap aircraft, the Koku Hombu instructed Kawasaki to produce a night fighter version of their Ki-102a, itself a development of the Toryu. This variant, designated Ki-102c, was fitted with a lengthened fuselage, a new cockpit and redesigned tail surfaces, and wing area and span were increased to improve landing characteristics for night operations. Interception radar with revolving antenna dish under a plexiglass radome above the fuselage was installed and armament was completely revised to include two 30 mm Ho-105 cannon in the fuselage belly and two 20 mm Ho-5 cannon installed obliquely in the fuselage behind the cockpit. Powered by a pair of turbosupercharged Ha-112-II Ru engines the first Ki-102c prototype—modified from a Ki-102b airframe—was completed in July 1945 and followed within a month by a similar machine. Flight trials of the Ki-102c were interrupted by the end of the war and production was never initiated.

A smaller and lighter version of the Ki-102 to be powered by a pair of 1,900 hp Mitsubishi Ha-104 radials was designed to improve maximum speed at the expense of flight duration. Bearing the project designation Special Fighter 2 (2 meaning twin-engined design) the aircraft remained on the drawing board.

UNITS ALLOCATED
28th and 45th Sentais. 27th Dokuritsu Dai Shijugo Chutai.

TECHNICAL DATA

Description: Twin-engined high-altitude fighter (Ki-102a), ground attack aircraft (Ki-102b) or night fighter (Ki-102c). All-metal construction.

Accommodation: Pilot and radio-operator (Ki-102a and Ki-102b), or pilot and radar operator (Ki-102c) in enclosed cockpit.

Powerplant: Two Army Type 4 fourteen-cylinder air-cooled radials (Mitsubishi Ha-112-II or [Ha-33] 62), rated at 1,500 hp for take-off, 1,350 hp at 2,000 m (6,560 ft) and 1,250 hp at 5,800 m (19,030 ft), driving constant-speed three-blade metal propellers (Ki-102b).

Two 1,500 hp Mitsubishi Ha-112-II Ru fourteen-cylinder air-cooled radials, rated at 1,500 hp for take-off, 1,250 hp at 8,200 m (26,900 ft) and 1,000 hp at 10,000 m (32,810 ft), driving constant-speed three-blade metal propellers (Ki-102a and Ki-102c).

Armament: One 57 mm Ho-401 cannon in the nose, two 20 mm Ho-5 cannon in the fuselage belly and one flexible rear-firing 12·7 mm Type 1 (Ho-103) machine-gun (Ki-102b).

One 37 mm Ho-203 cannon in the nose and two 20 mm Ho-5 cannon in the fuselage belly (Ki-102a).

Two 30 mm Ho-105 cannon in the fuselage belly and two 20 mm Ho-5 cannon mounted obliquely in the fuselage (Ki-102c).

External stores: two 200 litre (44 Imp gal) drop tanks (all versions of the Ki-102), or two 250 kg (551 lb) bombs (Ki-102b only).

	Ki-102b	Ki-102c
Dimensions:		
Span	15·57 m	17·25 m
	(51 ft 1 in)	(56 ft 7⅛ in)
Length	11·45 m	13·05 m
	(37 ft 6³³⁄₆₄ in)	(42 ft 9³³⁄₆₄ in)
Height	3·7 m	3·7 m
	(12 ft 1³¹⁄₆₄ in)	(12 ft 1³¹⁄₆₄ in)
Wing area	34 sq m	40 sq m
	(365·972 sq ft)	(430·555 sq ft)

	Ki-102b	Ki-102c
Weights:		
Empty	4,950 kg	5,200 kg
	(10,913 lb)	(11,464 lb)
Loaded	7,300 kg	7,600 kg
	(16,094 lb)	(16,755 lb)
Wing loading	214·7 kg/sq m	190 kg/sq m
	(44 lb/sq ft)	(38·9 lb/sq ft)
Power loading	2·4 kg/hp	2·5 kg/hp
	(5·4 lb/hp)	(5·6 lb/hp)
Performance:		
Maximum speed	580 km/h at 6,000 m	600 km/h at 10,000 m
	(360 mph at 19,685 ft)	(373 mph at 32,810 ft)
Climb to	5,000 m (16,405 ft)	10,000 m (32,810 ft)
in	6 min 54 sec	18 min
Service ceiling	10,000 m	13,500 m
	(32,810 ft)	(44,290 ft)
Range	2,000 km	2,200 km
	(1,243 miles)	(1 367 miles)

Production: A total of 238 Ki-102s were built by Kawasaki Kokuki Kogyo K.K. as follows:
- 3 Ki-102 prototypes (Feb–Mar 1944)
- 20 Ki-102 pre-production aircraft (Apr–Oct 1944)
- 215 Ki-102b production aircraft (Oct 1944–July 1945)
- (26) Ki-102a pre-production aircraft (6 pre-production Ki-102 and 20 production Ki-102b modified) (June 1944–Mar 1945)
- (2) Ki-102c prototypes (2 Ki-102b modified) (July–Aug 1945)

Kawasaki Ki-108

Development of the Ki-108 began in April 1943 to meet an operational requirement for a single-seat high-altitude fighter. As the Kawasaki engineering team was already committed to several new projects, Takeo Doi suggested that to save time the new aircraft be developed along the lines of the Ki-96. The proposal was accepted by the Koku Hombu and design of the pressure cabin for installation in the Ki-108 began at once. Benefitting from the experience acquired with the Tachikawa SS-1 research aircraft, Kawasaki's engineers strove to obtain a hermetically sealed cabin to avoid boosting the capacity of the cabin blowers. Accordingly the pressure cabin of the Ki-108 was fitted with an airtight entrance door and a double-glazed canopy, and it was hoped that an equivalent pressure of 3,000 m (9,845 ft) could be maintained up to 10,000 m (32,810 ft).

In the spring of 1944 the seventh and eighth Ki-102b airframes were fitted with the pressure cabin and modified tail surfaces to serve as Ki-108 prototypes. Completed respectively in July and August 1944, these two aircraft were powered by two turbosupercharged Mitsubishi Ha-112-II Ru fourteen-cylinder radials and armament comprised one 37 mm Ho-203 and two 20 mm Ho-5 cannon. Flight trials, hampered by many air raid

View of the Ki-108 showing the unusual entrance hatch to the pressure cabin.

alerts and minor technical difficulties with the superchargers, progressed slowly. During an early test flight, while the Ki-108 was flying at 10,000 m (32,810 ft), the entrance door was blown away and the pressure in the cabin dropped suddenly. Following a steep dive to safer altitude the pilot managed to land his crippled Ki-108, thus proving that battle damage to the pressure cabin would not be catastrophic.

While the two Ki-108 prototypes were undergoing flight trials, production of two modified aircraft began. To improve performance and manoeuvrability at high altitudes the Ki-108 KAI featured a lengthened fuselage and wings of increased span and area similar to those used on the Ki-102c night fighter. The two prototypes, completed in March and May 1945, were still being tested at the end of the war.

TECHNICAL DATA

Description: Twin-engined high-altitude fighter. All-metal construction.
Accommodation: Pilot in pressure cabin.
Powerplant: Two Mitsubishi Ha-112-II Ru fourteen-cylinder air-cooled radials, rated at 1,500 hp for take-off, 1,250 hp at 8,200 m (26,900 ft) and 1,000 hp at 10,000 m (32,810 ft), driving constant-speed three-blade metal propellers.
Armament: One 37 mm Ho-203 cannon in the nose and two 20 mm Ho-5 cannon in the fuselage belly.

KAWASAKI Ki-108 KAI

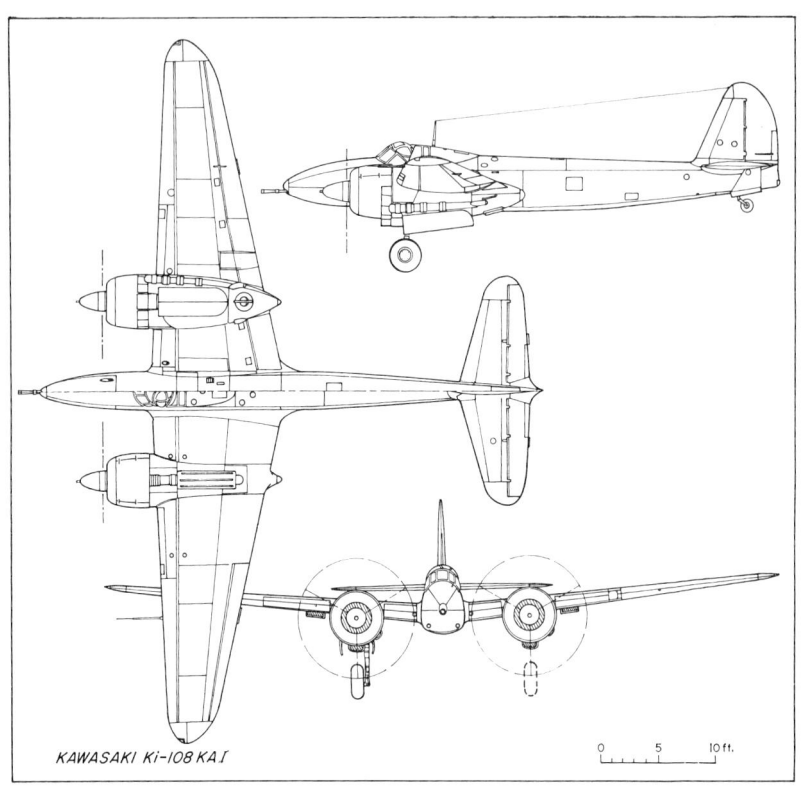

	Ki-108	Ki-108 KAI
Dimensions:		
Span	15·67 m	17·35 m
	(51 ft 4 13/16 in)	(56 ft 11 1/16 in)
Length	11·71 m	13·05 m
	(38 ft 5 in)	(42 ft 9 29/32 in)
Height	3·7 m	3·7 m
	(12 ft 1 21/32 in)	(12ft 1 21/32 in)
Wing area	34 sq m	40 sq m
	(365·972 sq ft)	(430·555 sq ft)
Weights:		
Empty	5,300 kg	5,200 kg
	(11,684 lb)	(11,464 lb)
Loaded	7,200 kg	7,600 kg
	(15,873 lb)	(16,755 lb)
Wing loading	211·8 kg/sq m	190 kg/sq m
	(43·4 lb/sq ft)	(38·9 lb/sq ft)
Power loading	2·4 kg/hp	2·5 kg/hp
	(5·3 lb/hp)	(5·6 lb/hp)
Performance:		
Maximum speed	580 km/h at 10,000 m	600 km/h at 10,000 m
	(360 mph at 32,810 ft)	(373 mph at 32,810 ft)
Service ceiling	13,500 m	13,500 m
	(44,290 ft)	(44,290 ft)
Range	1,800 km (1,118 miles)	2,200 km (1,367 miles)

Production: Two Ki-108s, modified from Ki-102b airframes, and two Ki-108 KAIs were built between July 1944 and May 1945 at the Gifu plant of Kawasaki Kokuki Kogyo K.K.

Kawasaki Ki-119

In early 1945, as the Allies were fast closing their ring around Japan, the Koku Hombu foresaw an urgent need for a new type of light bomber to supplement the suicide forces in the defence of the homeland. The aircraft had to be easy to manufacture, to maintain and to fly, had to have good performance and load-carrying capability and had to make only minimal demands on the already overtaxed engine manufacturing facilities. As range requirement was less than for previous bombers, choice of a single-seat, single-engined configuration became attractive. Accordingly the JAAF instructed Kawasaki in March 1945 to proceed immediately with the design of a single-seat aircraft to meet the following requirements: (1) normal radius of action, 600 km (373 miles) with an 800 kg (1,764 lb) bomb-load; (2) built-in armament, two 20 mm Ho-5 cannon; (3) powerplant, one 1,900 hp Army Type 4 eighteen-cylinder radial; (4) good take-off and landing performance; and (5) ease of manufacture in dispersed underground factories.

An artist's impression of the Kawasaki Ki-119. (*L. Hefley by courtesy J. Justin.*)

KAWASAKI Ki-119

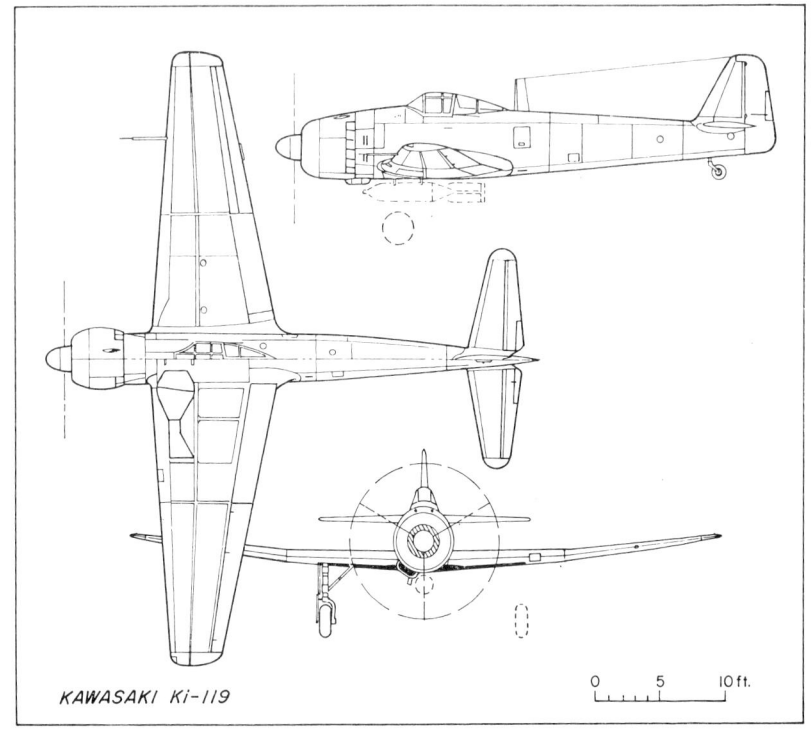

In less than three months a team led by Takeo Doi and Jun Kitano completed the basic design of the aircraft and a mock-up was readied for inspection. A wing of high aspect-ratio and large area was selected to obtain good airfield performance and flying characteristics, and a wide-track undercarriage, utilizing the same shock absorbers as the Ki-102, was adopted as the aircraft was to be flown by pilots of limited experience. The design of the fuselage was influenced by that of the Ki-100, this aircraft also providing most of the equipment. The airframe was designed to be built in several sub-assemblies manufactured in shadow factories, with final assembly at Misunami in a converted tunnel.

The Ki-119 had been conceived as a light bomber armed with two fuselage-mounted cannon and carrying one 800 kg (1,764 lb) bomb under the fuselage; but alternative missions included dive-bombing with two 250 kg (551 lb) bombs, and fighter escort, without bomb, but with two additional 20 mm Ho-5 cannon in the wings.

It was initially planned that the first flight would take place in September 1945, but most of the drawings were destroyed during air attacks on the Kagamigahara plant in June 1945. Despite this setback, Kawasaki strove to complete a new set of drawings and it was hoped that the first prototype would be ready in November 1945 but the Japanese surrender halted further work.

TECHNICAL DATA

Description: Single-engined light bomber, dive-bomber and escort fighter. All-metal construction.
Accommodation: Pilot in enclosed cockpit.
Powerplant: One 1,900 hp Army Type 4 eighteen-cylinder air-cooled radial (Mitsubishi Ha-104), rated at 2,000 hp for take-off, 1,870 hp at 1,700 m (5,580 ft) and 1,720 hp at 5,400 m (17,715 ft), driving a constant-speed three-blade metal propeller (production aircraft) or four-blade propeller (prototype).
Armament: Two synchronized 20 mm Ho-5 cannon and (fighter escort) two wing-mounted 20 mm Ho-5 cannon.
External stores: one 800 kg (1,764 lb) bomb, or two 250 kg (551 lb) bombs, or two 600 litre (132 Imp gal) drop tanks.
Dimensions: Span 14 m (45 ft 11 $\frac{3}{16}$ in); length 11·85 m (38 ft 10 $\frac{11}{32}$ in); height 4·5 m (14 ft 9 $\frac{5}{32}$ in); wing area 31·9 sq m (343·367 sq ft).
Weights: Empty 3,670 kg (8,289 lb); loaded 5,980 kg (13,184 lb); wing loading 187·4 kg/sq m (38·4 lb/sq ft); power loading 3 kg/hp (6·6 lb/hp).
Performance: Maximum speed 475 km/h (295 mph) at sea level and 580 km/h at 6,000 m (360 mph at 19,685 ft); climb to 6,000 m (19,685 ft) in 6 min 6 sec; service ceiling 10,500 m (34,450 ft); radius of action—normal, 600 km (373 miles), maximum, 1,200 km (746 miles).

Kayaba Ka-1 and Ka-2

Although relatively unknown the Kayaba Ka-1 autogyro deserves a special place in aviation history since it was the first armed machine of the autogyro/helicopter family to have been used operationally.

In the late thirties the Imperial Japanese Army began to show considerable interest in the use of the autogyro as an artillery spotter and in 1939 a Kellet KD-1A single-engined two-seat autogyro was imported from the United States. Powered by a 225 hp Jacobs L-4M4 seven-cylinder air-cooled radial, the KD-1A featured an advanced version of the Kellet direct control rotor system. Unfortunately, shortly after its arrival in Japan, the aircraft was seriously damaged during flight trials at low speeds. The Kellet KD-1A had been damaged beyond repair, but the Japanese Army delivered the wreck to K.K. Kayaba Seisakusho (Kayaba Industrial Co Ltd), a small company doing autogyro research, with instructions to develop a similar machine.

A Kayaba Ka-1 autogyro with its rotor blades being unfolded. (*Aireview*.)

At the request of the Koku Hombu the Kayaba engineering team developed a two-seat observation autogyro based on the Kellet KD-1A but modified to Japanese production standards. Designated Ka-1, this autogyro was powered by a 240 hp Argus As 10c eight-cylinder inverted-vee air-cooled engine driving a two-blade propeller, and had a three-blade rotor. Completed in May 1941 at the Sendai (Miyagi Prefecture) plant of Kayaba, the first Ka-1 made its maiden flight at Tamagawa on 26 May, 1941. During its flight test programme the Ka-1 performed remarkably well, demonstrating its ability to take-off after running only 30 m (98 ft) in still air. By running the engine at full power and holding the nose 15 degrees up, the Ka-1 could hover and could also execute a full 360 degree turn while hovering. As maintenance in the field appeared to present less difficulty than anticipated the aircraft was placed in production for service with artillery units.

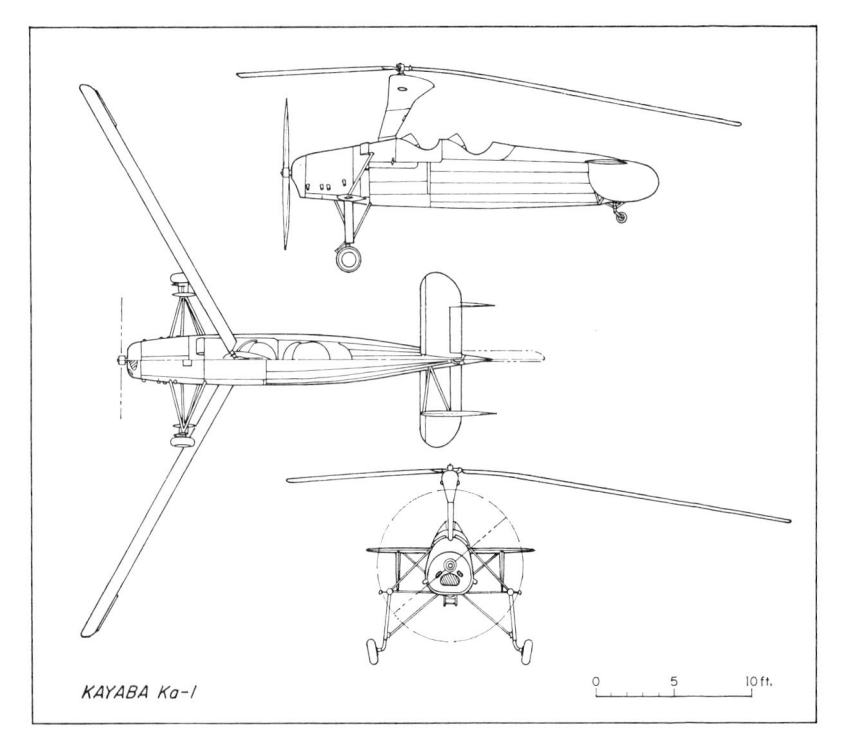

KAYABA Ka-1

When shipping losses began to rise alarmingly the Japanese Army commissioned the light escort carrier *Akitsu Maru*, a converted merchant ship. The short take-off characteristics of the Ka-1 rendered it suitable for operation from this small vessel and accordingly a small number of Ka-1s were modified as anti-submarine patrol aircraft. As the load-carrying capability of the standard two-seat Ka-1 was too limited, the carrier-borne

Ka-1s were operated as single-seaters and carried two 60 kg (132 lb) depth-charges. In this role the Ka-1s operated over Japanese coastal waters and particularly over the Tsugara and Korean channels. At least one of these aircraft, the Ka-1 KAI, was tested with powder rockets on the rotor tips in an attempt to improve its load-carrying capability while another aircraft was fitted with a 240 hp Jacobs L-4MA-7 seven-cylinder air-cooled radial. With Jacobs engine the type became the Ka-2.

TECHNICAL DATA

Description: Single-engined autogyro. Mixed construction.
Accommodation: Pilot and observer in tandem open cockpits.
Powerplant: One 240 hp Kobe-built Argus As 10c eight-cylinder inverted-vee air-cooled engine, driving a two-blade propeller (Ka-1).
  One 240 hp Jacobs L-4MA-7 seven-cylinder air-cooled radial, driving a two-blade propeller (Ka-2).
Armament: Two 60 kg (132 lb) depth-charges.
Dimensions: Length 9·2 m (30 ft 2$\frac{5}{32}$ in); rotor diameter 12·2 m (40 ft 0$\frac{5}{16}$ in).
Weights: Empty 775 kg (1,709 lb); loaded 1,170 kg (2,579 lb); power loading 4·9 kg/hp (10·7 lb/hp).
Performance: Maximum speed 165 km/h (102·5 mph); cruising speed 115 km/h (71·5 mph); climb to 1,000 m (3,280 ft) in 3 min 20 sec and to 2,000 m (6,560 ft) in 7 min 30 sec; service ceiling 3,500 m (11,485 ft); range 280 km (174 miles).
Production: Approximately 240 Ka-1s, including one Ka-1 KAI and one Ka-2, were built by K.K. Kayaba Seisakusho in their Sendai plant.

A Kokusai Ki-59 light personnel transport.

Kokusai Ki-59

In 1937, at the request of the Air Division of the Communications Ministry, Nippon Koku Kogyo K.K. (Japan International Air Industries Co Ltd) undertook to design an eight- to ten-seat commercial light transport for use on medium-range local services. Designated Teradakoken TK-3 and powered by a pair of 640 hp Nakajima Kotobuki 3 nine-cylinder air-cooled radials, the aircraft was of high-wing design with long faired under-

KOKUSAI Ki-59

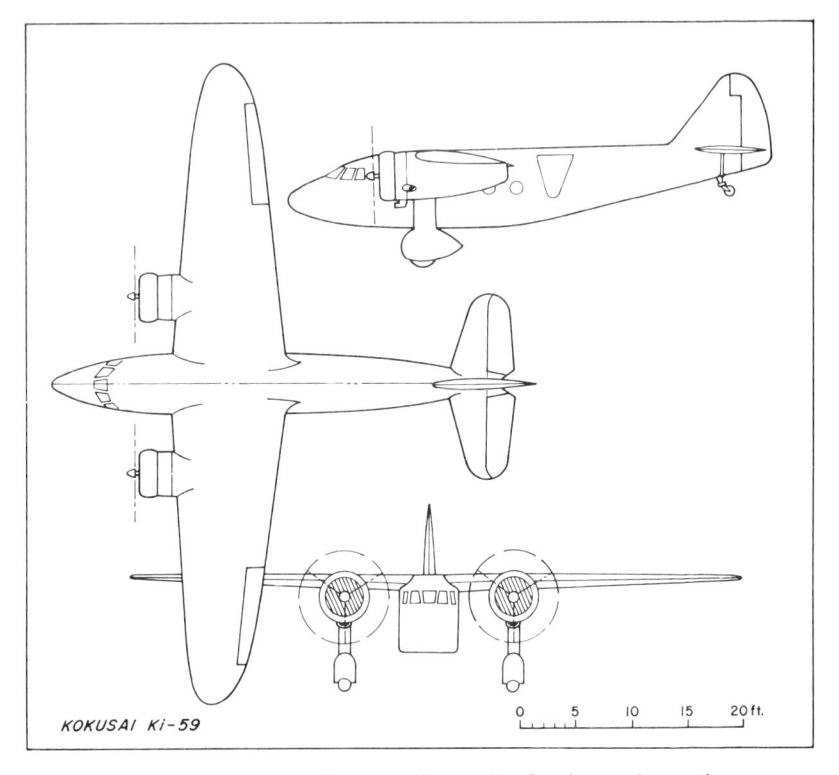

carriage attached to the engine nacelles and a fuselage of tapering square section. First flown in June 1938, the aircraft possessed some poor flying characteristics and rate of climb was disappointing; consequently, only two prototypes were built.

The aircraft's performance, however, closely matched the requirements of the Japanese Army's pressing need for light transport and communications aircraft. Military interest materialized in 1939 with the Koku Hombu's placing of an order for prototypes designated Ki-59. In their initial form these aircraft differed little from their commercial forerunner with the exception of the installation of military interior fittings and equipment and the replacement of the Nakajima Kotobuki 3 engines by a pair of 450 hp Hitachi Ha-13a nine-cylinder air-cooled radials. Flight tests, which began in June 1939, revealed the need to modify the shape of the nose to improve pilot visibility and to alter the shape of the undercarriage fairings, and redesigned vertical tail surfaces of greatly increased area had to be fitted. With the incorporation of these modifications the flying characteristics of the aircraft improved markedly and the Ki-59 was placed in production in 1941 as the Army Type 1 Transport. Dubbed THERESA by the Allies the aircraft remained in production for a short period only, as it was replaced by the Tachikawa Ki-54c.

In December 1941 a Ki-59 was modified to become a glider by removing the engines and undercarriage and by fitting skids to the bottom of the fuselage. Designated Army Experimental Glider (Ku-8-I) it led to the development of the Ku-8-II Army Type 4 Large-size Transport Glider.

TECHNICAL DATA

Description: Twin-engined light personnel transport. Mixed wood and metal construction with fabric-covered control surfaces.
Accommodation: Crew of two or three and eight passengers.
Powerplant: Two 450 hp Army Type 98 nine-cylinder air-cooled radials (Hitachi Ha-13a), rated at 510 hp for take-off and 470 hp at 1,700 m (5,580 ft), driving three-blade propellers.
Dimensions: Span 17 m (55 ft 9$\frac{9}{32}$ in); length 12·5 m (41 ft 0$\frac{1}{8}$ in); height 3·05 m (10 ft 0$\frac{1}{16}$ in); wing area 38·4 sq m (413·333 sq ft).
Weights: Empty 2,880 kg (6,349 lb); loaded 4,120 kg (9,083 lb); maximum 4,240 kg (9,348 lb); wing loading 107·3 kg/sq m (22 lb/sq ft); power loading 4 kg/hp (8·9 lb/hp).
Performance: Cruising speed 300 km/h at 2,000 m (186 mph at 6,560 ft).
Production: A total of 59 Ki-59s were built by Nippon Kokusai Koku Kogyo K.K. in their Hiratsuka plant.

A Kokusai Ki-76 Army Type 3 Command Liaison Plane. This type also served as an anti-submarine patrol aircraft aboard the Japanese Army's aircraft carrier *Akitsu Maru*.

Kokusai Ki-76

There is no denying that the Ki-76's concept and general appearance owed much to the Fieseler Fi 156 Storch; however, the aircraft was not simply a copy of the German machine since its design began ten months before the Japanese received an example of the Fi 156. In 1940 the apparent success obtained by the Germans with their Fi 156s prompted the Japanese Army to instruct Nippon Kokusai Koku Kogyo to build a similar machine for artillery spotting and liaison duties. Designated Ki-76 the aircraft owed its existence to a team led by Kozo Masuhara who patterned its design around that of the German aircraft. The external appearance of both aeroplanes was very much alike, but whereas the Storch was powered by a 240 hp Argus As 10c eight-cylinder inverted-vee air-cooled engine the Ki-76 was powered by a 310 hp Hitachi Ha-42 nine-cylinder air-cooled radial. Furthermore Masuhara decided to use Fowler flaps instead of the slotted flaps used on the Fieseler Storch. These Fowler flaps were synchronized with the variable-incidence horizontal tail surfaces and offered a higher lift coefficient.

First flown in May 1941, the Ki-76 proved somewhat unstable but, generally speaking, the aircraft was easy to fly and could be handled by pilots of only limited flight experience. In competitive tests against the Fi 156, one example of which was received in Japan in June 1941, the Ki-76 demonstrated superior performance on every count with the exception of landing distance which was somewhat longer than that of the German machine. Flight trials were completed in November 1942 and the aircraft was put into production at the Hiratsuka plant as the Army Type 3 Command Liaison Plane. The Ki-76, known as STELLA by the Allies, saw considerable service with artillery units until the end of the war.

Late in 1943 the Ki-76 was modified for service aboard the Japanese

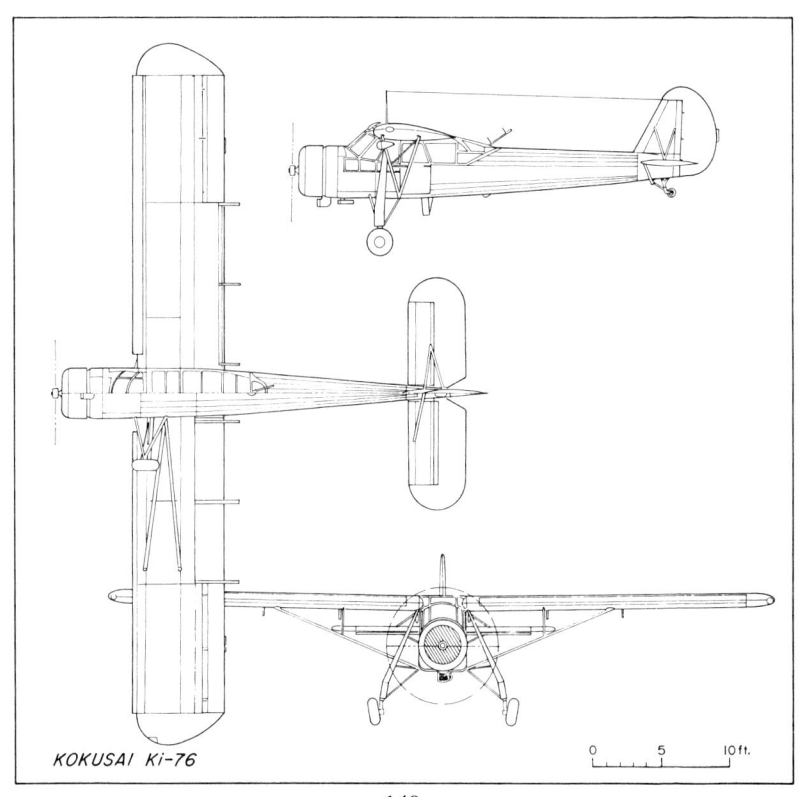

Army aircraft carrier *Akitsu Maru* as an anti-submarine patrol aircraft. For this duty the aircraft was fitted with a deck arrester hook and carried two 60 kg (132 lb) depth-charges. Normally seven Ki-76s were embarked aboard the *Akitsu Maru* but the aircraft was not too successful on this type of operation.

TECHNICAL DATA

Description: Single-engined liaison, artillery spotting and light anti-submarine patrol aircraft.
Accommodation: Pilot and observer in tandem in enclosed cabin.
Powerplant: One Hitachi Ha-42 nine-cylinder air-cooled radial, rated at 310 hp for take-off and 280 hp at 2,000 m (6,560 ft), driving a two-blade wooden propeller.
Armament: One flexible rear-firing 7·7 mm Type 89 machine-gun in the observer's position.
Two 60 kg (132 lb) depth-charges.
Dimensions: Span 15 m (49 ft 2⅝ in); length 9·56 m (31 ft 4⅜ in); height 2·9 m (9 ft 6¾ in); wing area 29·4 sq m (316·458 sq ft).
Weights: Empty 1,110 kg (2,447 lb); loaded 1,530 kg (3,373 lb); maximum 1,620 kg (3,571 lb); wing loading 52 kg/sq m (10·7 lb/sq ft); power loading 4·9 kg/hp (10·9 lb/hp).
Performance: Maximum speed 178 km/h (111 mph); service ceiling 5,630 m (18,470 ft); range 750 km (466 miles).
Production: An undetermined number of Ki-76s were built by Nippon Kokusai Koku Kogyo K.K. between 1941 and 1944.

Mitsubishi Ki-15 and C5M

When war broke out in the Pacific the Mitsubishi Ki-15 reconnaissance aircraft, later named BABS by the Allies, was one of the few well-known Japanese aircraft since in April 1937 a civil-registered aeroplane of this type had been flown in record time between Japan and England. Development of the Ki-15 had begun on 11 July, 1935, when the Koku Hombu instructed Mitsubishi Jukogyo K.K. to design a fast reconnaissance aircraft. Drafted by Captain Yuzo Fujita and Engineer Masao Ando of the Technical Department of the Koku Hombu, the specification called for a

A Mitsubishi Karigane I (Wild Goose) civil version of the Japanese Army Mitsubishi Ki-15-I. (*USAF.*)

two-seat reconnaissance aircraft with a top speed of 450 km/h at 3,000 m (280 mph at 9,845 ft); an operating altitude of 2,000 m to 4,000 m (6,560 ft to 13,125 ft); an endurance of one hour at combat rating at 400 km (250 miles) from base; a loaded weight of less than 2,400 kg (5,291 lb); and armament comprising a single flexible 7·7 mm machine-gun in the rear cockpit. The aircraft was to be powered by a single engine in the 700–800 hp class and be fitted with Hi-4 radio-equipment and light aerial cameras.

To meet the performance requirements Fumihiko Kono, assisted by Tomio Kubo and Shokichi Mizumo, designed a clean low-wing cantilever monoplane with spatted undercarriage and selected the Nakajima Ha-8 nine-cylinder air-cooled radial developing 750 hp at 4,000 m (13,125 ft) to power the aircraft. Construction of the prototype began in December 1935 and the machine was completed within five months, flying for the first time

The Mitsubishi Karigane I *Asakaze* (*Morning Breeze*) owned by Asahi Shimbun.

in May 1936. During the flight test programme the aircraft demonstrated pleasant flying characteristics and easily exceeded all performance requirements, achieving a top speed of 481 km/h at 4,050 m (299 mph at 13,290 ft). The Ki-15, however, offered poor forward visibility particularly on the ground, take-off and landing runs were somewhat disappointing, and speed fell sharply during prolonged wide turns. Despite these minor shortcomings the Ki-15 was enthusiastically received by the Army, and Mitsubishi were instructed to put the aircraft into production as the Army Type 97 Command Reconnaissance Plane Model 1 (Ki-15-I), the first production aircraft being delivered in May 1937.

While the first Ki-15 was undergoing flight trials, the *Asahi Shimbun*, one of Japan's leading newspapers, had obtained authorization from the Army to purchase from Mitsubishi the second prototype for use in an attempt to make a record flight between Japan and England on the occasion of the Coronation of HM King George VI. Built under the civil designation of Karigane I (Wild Goose I) Communication Plane, the aircraft was completed on 19 March, 1937, and, registered J-BAAI and

A Mitsubishi Ki-15-I of the Kumagaya Flying School.
(*Mitsubishi Jukogyo K.K.*)

named *Kamikaze* (*Divine Wind*), the aircraft was delivered to *Asahi Shimbun* on 25 March. The aircraft was identical to the military prototype except that all military equipment including cameras and armament was removed. The outstanding performance of this aircraft was revealed to the Western World when, between 6 and 9 April, 1937, Masaaki Iinuma, pilot, and Kenji Tsukagoshi, flight mechanic and navigator, flew J-BAAI from Tachikawa to London covering 9,542 miles in 94 hr 17 min 56 sec, the actual flying time being 51 hr 17 min 23 sec and the average speed 101·2 mph (according to the Fédération Aéronautique Internationale which homologated the record). Later a small number of Ki-15-Is were transferred to civilian operators and these included J-BAAL *Asakaze* (*Morning Breeze*) and J-BAAM *Sochikaze* (*Providential Wind*).

At the start of the second Sino-Japanese conflict the Army Type 97 Command Reconnaissance Planes were among the first aircraft to be committed to combat operations. Faced by a motley collection of Chinese

Mitsubishi Ki-15-II Army Type 97 Command Reconnaissance Model 2.

Civil registered Mitsubishi Karigane II.

fighters including the Curtiss Hawk, Gloster Gladiator and Polikarpov I-15bis and I-16, the Ki-15-Is were able to fly deep into China from their bases in Manchuria, as their top speed of 298 mph exceeded that of all Chinese-operated fighters with the exception of the Polikarpov I-16. Almost immune from interception, the Ki-15s and their crews could keep the Japanese Army informed well ahead of time of all Chinese ground movements. Under combat conditions the aircraft performed with great reliability and the only complaint against it stemmed from its pilots who deplored its lack of forward visibility. Even though the Ki-15-I proved to be far more successful than the most sanguine expectations could have foreseen, development of a model with higher performance was initiated within a year of the Service début of the Army Type 97 Command Reconnaissance Plane Model 1.

The engine selected to power the Ki-15-II was the Mitsubishi Ha-26-I fourteen-cylinder radial which had a smaller diameter than the Ha-8 nine-cylinder radial powering the Ki-15-I and thus improved forward visibility. The first Ha-26-I powered Ki-15-II was completed in June 1938 and during its flight trials reached a maximum speed of 510 km/h (317 mph), an increase of 30 km/h (19 mph) over the speed of the Ki-15-I. Despite this gain in performance the Ki-15-II was not placed in production until September 1939 when the aircraft was introduced as the Army Type 97 Command Reconnaissance Plane Model 2. At least two of these aircraft were completed as Karigane II (Wild Goose II) Communication Planes and, registered J-BAAO *Amakaze* (*Heavenly Wind*) and J-BACL, were operated by *Asahi Shimbun*.

The ability of the Ki-15 to penetrate deep into Chinese territory attracted the attention of the Imperial Japanese Navy which at that time, for lack of high-performance reconnaissance aircraft, had to rely on visual reconnaissance by Navy Type 96 Fighters wherever Chinese air opposition was anticipated. Accordingly in 1938 the Navy placed an order for twenty aircraft similar to the Ki-15-II but fitted with naval radio and camera equipment. Designated Navy Type 98 Reconnaissance Plane Model 1 or C5M1, these aircraft were powered by an 875 hp Mitsubishi Zuisei 12, a naval version of the Ha-26-I. Thirty externally similar C5M2s, specially designed for the Navy and powered by the 950 hp Nakajima Sakae 12 fourteen-cylinder radial driving a three-blade propeller, were acquired in 1940 under the designation Navy Type 98 Reconnaissance Plane Model 2. Despite its more powerful engine the C5M2 was slower than the Ki-15-II as loaded weight had been increased by the addition of extra equipment.

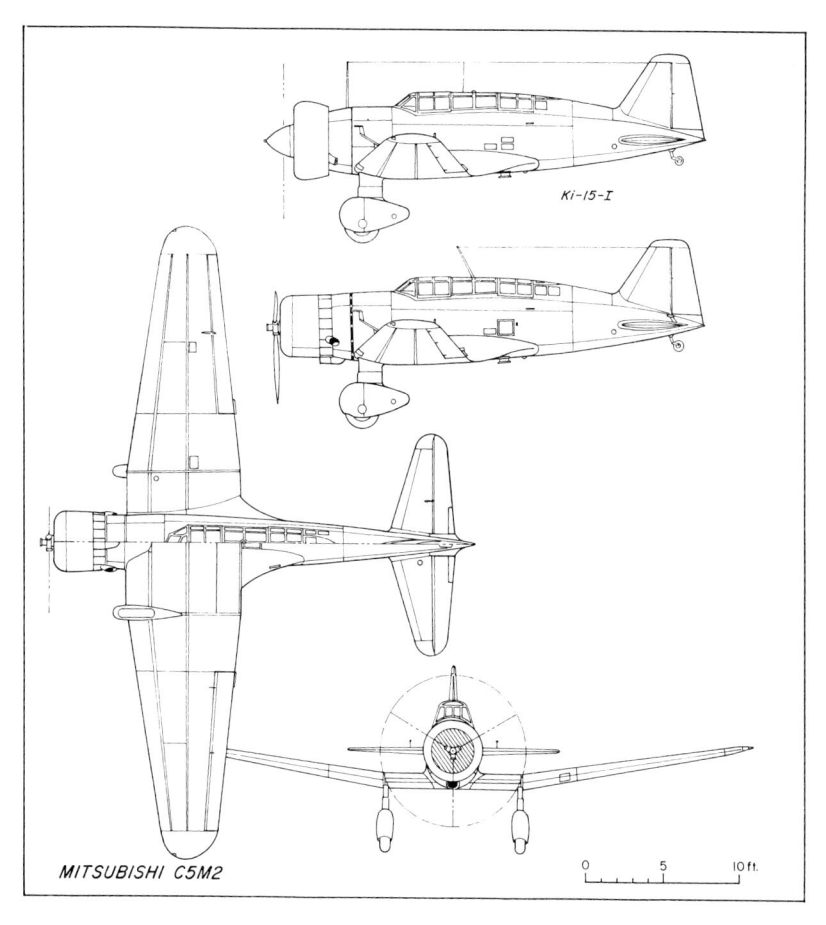

MITSUBISHI C5M2

The fastest version of the aircraft was the Ki-15-III which had been designed for the Japanese Army in 1939. Two prototypes of this aircraft, each powered by a 1,050 hp Mitsubishi Ha-102 driving a three-blade propeller, were built and reached a top speed of 530 km/h (329 mph). However, by that time the Mitsubishi Ki-46, the intended successor to the Ki-15, was about to commence flight trials and, as its performance was anticipated to substantially exceed that of the Ki-15-III, the latter was not placed in production.

When the war started the Japanese Army and Navy were still operating the Ki-15-II and C5M2, and these types were deployed for operations in the south. One of the Navy C5M2s belonging to the 22nd Koku Sentai spotted at sea on 10 December, 1941, the British battleships HMS *Prince of Wales* and HMS *Repulse*, thus leading to the sinking of these gallant ships. Others performed valuable duties during the first year of the war but, faced by faster Allied fighters and lacking pilot and fuel tank protection, suffered mounting losses. They were then withdrawn from first-line operation by both Services but continued to operate as advanced trainers and communication aircraft, some being finally expended in kamikaze sorties in the closing months of the war.

UNITS ALLOCATED

Ki-15: 8th, 10th, 15th, 28th, 29th, 81st and 82nd Sentais. 16th, 18th, 50th, 51st, 74th, 76th and 81st Dokuritsu Dai Shijugo Chutais. 17th and 18th Hikodans.

C5M2: 22nd and 23rd Koku Sentais.

TECHNICAL DATA

Description: Single-engined reconnaissance aircraft. All-metal structure with light alloy and fabric covering.
Accommodation: Pilot and radio-operator/observer in enclosed cockpit.
Powerplant: One 550 hp Army Type 94 nine-cylinder air-cooled radial (Nakajima Ha-8), rated at 640 hp for take-off and 750 hp at 4,000 m (13,125 ft), driving a two-blade metal propeller (Ki-15-I).

One 900 hp Army Type 99 Model 1 fourteen-cylinder air-cooled radial (Mitsubishi Ha-26-I), rated at 850 hp for take-off and 900 hp at 3,600 m (11,810 ft), driving a two-blade metal propeller (Ki-15-II).

One 1,050 hp Mitsubishi Ha-102 fourteen-cylinder air-cooled radial, rated at 1,080 hp for take-off, 1,055 hp at 2,800 m (9,185 ft) and 950 hp at 5,800 m (19,030 ft), driving a three-blade metal propeller (Ki-15-III).

One 875 hp Mitsubishi Zuisei 12 fourteen-cylinder air-cooled radial, rated at 780 hp for take-off and 875 hp at 3,600 m (11,810 ft), driving a two-blade metal propeller (C5M1).

One 950 hp Nakajima Sakae 12 fourteen-cylinder air-cooled radial, rated at 940 hp for take-off and 950 hp at 4,200 m (13,780 ft), driving a three-blade metal propeller (C5M2).

Armament: One flexible rear-firing 7·7 mm Type 89 machine-gun (Ki-15-I and Ki-15-II).

One flexible rear-firing 7·7 mm Type 92 machine-gun (C5M1 and C5M2).

	Ki-15-I	Ki-15-II	C5M1	C5M2
Dimensions:				
Span	12 m	12 m	12 m	12 m
	(39 ft 4 $\frac{7}{16}$ in)	(39 ft 4 $\frac{7}{16}$ in)	(39 ft 4 $\frac{7}{16}$ in)	(39 ft 4 $\frac{7}{16}$ in)
Length	8·49 m	8·7 m	8·7 m	8·7 m
	(27 ft 10$\frac{1}{4}$ in)	(28 ft 6$\frac{17}{32}$ in)	(28 ft 6$\frac{17}{32}$ in)	(28 ft 6$\frac{17}{32}$ in)
Height	3·34 m	3·34 m	3·465 m	3·465 m
	(10 ft 11$\frac{1}{2}$ in)	(10 ft 11$\frac{1}{2}$ in)	(11 ft 4$\frac{13}{32}$ in)	(11 ft 4$\frac{13}{32}$ in)
Wing area	20·36 sq m	20·36 sq m	20·36 sq m	20·36 sq m
	(219·152 sq ft)	(219·152 sq ft)	(219·152 sq ft)	(219·152 sq ft)
Weights:				
Empty	1,399 kg	1,592 kg	1,605 kg	1,715 kg
	(3,084 lb)	(3,510 lb)	(3,538 lb)	(3,781 lb)
Loaded	2,033 kg	2,189 kg	2,197 kg	2,345 kg
	(4,482 lb)	(4,826 lb)	(4,844 lb)	(5,170 lb)
Maximum	2,300 kg	2,481 kg	—	—
	(5,071 lb)	(5,470 lb)		
Wing loading	99·9 kg/sq m	107·5 kg/sq m	107·9 kg/sq m	115·2 kg/sq m
	(20·5 lb/sq ft)	(22 lb/sq ft)	(22·1 lb/sq ft)	(23·6 lb/sq ft)
Power loading	3·2 kg/hp	2·6 kg/hp	2·8 kg/hp	2·5 kg/hp
	(7 lb/hp)	(5·7 lb/hp)	(6·2 lb/hp)	(5·5 lb/hp)

	Ki-15-I	Ki-15-II	C5M1	C5M2
Performance:				
Max speed	480 km/h at 4,000 m (298 mph at 13,125 ft)	510 km/h at 4,330 m (317 mph at 14,205 ft)	253 kt at 4,280 m (291 mph at 14,040 ft)	263 kt at 4,550 m (303 mph at 14,930 ft)
Cruising speed	320 km/h (199 mph)	—	—	—
Climb to in	5,000 m (16,405 ft) 8 min 27 sec	5,000 m (16,405 ft) 6 min 49 sec	3,000 m (9,845 ft) 4 min 51 sec	3,000 m (9,845 ft) 3 min 58 sec
Service ceiling	11,400 m (37,400 ft)	—	8,230 m (27,000 ft)	9,580 m (31,430 ft)
Range	2,400 km (1,491 miles)	—	630 naut miles (725 miles)	600, naut miles (691 miles)

Production: A total of 489 Ki-15s and C5Ms were built by Mitsubishi Jukogyo K.K. at Nagoya as follows:
439 Ki-15-Is, Ki-15-IIs and Ki-15-IIIs (May 1936–1940)
20 C5M1s (1938)
30 C5M2s (1940)

A Mitsubishi Ki-21-Ia Army Type 97 Heavy Bomber Model 1A. (*Mitsubishi Jukogyo K.K.*)

Mitsubishi Ki-21

A major stage in the modernization programme initiated in the mid-thirties by the Imperial Japanese Army was reached in August 1938 when the 60th Sentai took delivery of the first Ki-21 heavy bomber, an aircraft equal to the best contemporary foreign twin-engined bombers. After 7 December, 1941, the Ki-21 led the Japanese bombing offensive in Southeast Asia and, although proven obsolescent when faced by Allied fighter aircraft, the type remained in first-line service until the Japanese surrender.

The Ki-21 was designed by Mitsubishi in answer to a specification asking for a twin-engined heavy bomber to replace the Army Type 92 Heavy Bomber (Mitsubishi Ki-20) and the Army Type 93 Heavy Bomber

Mitsubishi Ki-21-Ia formation over northern China.

(Mitsubishi Ki-1) which had been issued on 15 February, 1936, by the Koku Hombu. Requirements included : (1) operating altitude, 2,000 m to 4,000 m (6,560 ft to 13,125 ft); (2) endurance, over five hours at 300 km/h (186 mph); (3) maximum speed, 400 km/h at 3,000 m (248·5 mph at 9,845 ft); (4) climb to 3,000 m (9,845 ft) in 8 min; (5) take-off run, less than 300 m (985 ft); and (6) engines, two 850 hp Nakajima Ha-5 or two 825 hp Mitsubishi Ha-6 radials. The aircraft was required to be operated by a normal crew of four, with two extra seats made available for additional gunners as required. Defensive armament was to consist of no less than three flexible machine-guns in nose, dorsal and ventral positions and, with full fuel load, bomb-load was to equal 750 kg (1,653 lb) while maximum bomb-load for short range missions was to be 1,000 kg (2,205 lb).

Credited to a team led by Engineers Nakata and Ozawa, the two Ki-21 prototypes were completed at Mitsubishi's 5th Airframe Works in Nagoya in December 1936. Powered by two Mitsubishi Ha-6 radials driving variable-pitch propellers, the two aircraft were all-metal cantilever monoplanes with wings set at mid-fuselage above the ventral bomb-bay and were characterized by an angular glazed nose housing the bomb-aimer's position and a 7·7 mm Type 89 machine-gun movable only in the vertical axis. The second Ki-21 prototype differed from the first in the design of its dorsal turret, a long greenhouse replacing the semi-hemispherical turret which generated excessive drag. A third flexible 7·7 mm Type 89 machine-gun firing towards the rear was mounted in the ventral step. Commencing on 18 December, 1936, when the first Ki-21 made its maiden flight, the two aircraft were used in the manufacturer's flight test programme until March 1937 when both aircraft were pitted against the first two Ha-5 powered Nakajima Ki-19s. A third competitive design, the Kawasaki Ki-22, had been submitted in answer to the specification of 15 February, 1936, but had not been approved for prototype construction. The competitive evaluation of the Ki-21 and Ki-19 culminated in June 1937 with bombing trials held at Hamamatsu. The Ki-21 was credited with superior performance and lighter wing loading but the Ki-19 had more reliable engines, better flight characteristics and offered a more stable bombing platform. Consequently, the Koku Hombu ordered additional prototypes of both types and Mitsubishi were instructed to use the Nakajima Ha-5 engines and to improve the flight handling characteristics of their Ki-21.

The third Ki-21, the first to be powered by a pair of 850 hp Nakajima Ha-5s, featured a hemispherical nose housing a 7·7 mm Type 89 machine-gun on a ball-and-socket mounting and had a redesigned rear fuselage without ventral step. Directional stability, particularly important during the bombing run, was improved with the fitting of redesigned vertical tail surfaces. When a new series of competitive trials against the Ki-19 were held at Tachikawa, the Ki-21 so modified easily won a production order, and the last five Ki-21 prototypes actually became Service trials aircraft and were used for testing operational equipment. The initial production model, the Ki-21-Ia, ordered in November 1937 as the Army Type 97 Heavy Bomber Model 1A was externally identical to the Ha-5 powered prototypes but featured an increase in fuel tank capacity from 1,840 litres (405 Imp gal) to 2,635 litres (580 Imp gal). Beginning in the spring of 1938 Mitsubishi built 143 aircraft of this type (Ki-21 c/ns 9 to 151). A production order for the Ki-21 had also been awarded to Nakajima Hikoki K.K.

Formation of Mitsubishi Ki-21-Ia bombers during a raid on Chungking. A bomb can be seen just after leaving the nearest aircraft.

which, between August 1938 and February 1941, built a total of 351 Ki-21-Ia, Ki-21-Ib and Ki-21-Ic aircraft. These last two versions of the Ki-21 were developed by Mitsubishi to overcome the weakness of the aircraft's defensive armament and lack of fuel tank protection which had become painfully clear when the 60th and 61st Sentais had been sent to China with their Ki-21-Ias in the autumn of 1938.

The Ki-21-Ib retained the three flexible Type 89 machine-guns in the nose, dorsal and ventral positions and was also armed with a similar machine-gun firing through lateral openings on either side of the rear fuselage. A fifth 7·7 mm Type 89 machine-gun was mounted as a 'stinger' in the extreme tail of the aircraft, this remotely-controlled gun installation having previously been tested on the fifth prototype. The 120 Mitsubishi-built (Ki-21 c/ns 152 to 271) Army Type 97 Heavy Bomber Model 1B, like the Nakajima-built Ki-21-Ibs, had their fuel tanks partially protected by laminated rubber sheets. Other modifications incorporated in the Ki-21-Ib included an enlarged bomb-bay, larger landing flaps and new horizontal tail surfaces with a total area increased from 10·82 sq m (116·465 sq ft) to 11·32 sq m (121·847 sq ft). The Ki-21-Ic, of which Mitsubishi built 160 (Ki-21 c/ns 272 to 431), received an additional lateral machine-gun, and an auxiliary fuel tank with a capacity of 500 litres (110 Imp gal) could be fitted in the rear bomb-bay. When this tank was installed four 50 kg (110 lb) bombs were carried externally. Since the Ki-21 had been designed its weight had steadily increased and larger main wheels had to be installed on the Ki-21-Ic. In service the Ki-21-Ib and -Ic replaced the earlier version in front-line units operating in Northern China and Manchuria and the Ki-21-Ias were assigned to training units and bomber sentais retained in Japan.

Fighting a war in China, the Japanese Army found themselves critically short of transport aircraft and, pending delivery of the Ki-57, it was decided to modify some of the Ki-21-Ias taken out of front-line bomber units as freight transports for service with Dai Nippon Koku K.K. (Greater Japan Air Lines Co Ltd) on their military contract routes between Japan, Manchuria and China. Designated MC-21, these aircraft had all armament and military equipment removed but, initially at least, retained the bomber's glazed nose and dorsal greenhouse. Although primarily used as a freighter the MC-21 could be fitted if necessary with nine troop seats in a primitive cabin. Starting in February 1940 with J-BFOA *Hiei*, a small number of MC-21s were delivered to Dai Nippon Koku K.K. Later these aircraft were further modified by replacing the glazed nose with a metal fairing. Other Ki-21-Is were similarly modified in the field to serve as communication and hack aircraft with various Army commands.

In the light of negligible Chinese Air Force opposition, the Ki-21-Ib and -Ic were quite effective but, preparing themselves for a bigger conflict, in November 1939 the Japanese Army instructed Mitsubishi to increase the aircraft's speed and ceiling. The first Ki-21-Ic (Ki-21 c/n 272) was chosen as development aircraft for the advanced version of the Army Type

Mitsubishi MC-21 freight transport modified from a Ki-21-I and operated by Dai Nippon Koku K.K. on cargo services between Japan, Manchuria and China. The airline's insignia appears on the nose. (*Courtesy John Stroud.*)

97 Heavy Bomber and was powered by two 1,500 hp Mitsubishi Ha-101 fourteen-cylinder air-cooled radials. A complete redesign of the engine nacelles was necessary to house the Ha-101, which had larger diameter than the Ha-5, and fully enclose the undercarriage. The armament, fuel tank arrangement and other systems remained unchanged but the area of the horizontal tail surfaces was further increased from 11·32 sq m (121·847 sq ft) to 13·16 sq m (141·653 sq ft). Flight trials of the modified aircraft, the Ki-21-II, began in March 1940 and led to a production order as the Army Type 97 Heavy Bomber Model 2A (Ki-21-IIa). Commencing in December 1940 with the delivery of four Service trials machines, the Ki-21-IIa supplemented the earlier versions in front-line units and at the start of the Pacific War most Army jubaku sentais (heavy bomber groups) had converted to this variant.

When the war against the Allies started, the Japanese Army air units were assigned the primary task of supporting the invasion of Thailand,

Mitsubishi Ki-21-Ib aircraft of the 60th Sentai, 3rd Chutai. (*Courtesy Aeroplane Photo Supply.*)

Ki-21-IIa at Laverton, Victoria, in 1946. The tail markings on this captured aircraft indicate that it had belonged to the Headquarters Flight of the 3rd Kokugun. (*Frank Smith.*)

Burma and Malaya while maintaining constant pressure against the Chinese. On the first day of the war the 3rd Hikoshidan (Air Division) operating from bases in French Indo-China had three Jubaku Sentais with 87 of the Army Type 97 Heavy Bombers on strength and some of these aircraft were first deployed in support of the landing at Kota Bharu. During the following seven months the Ki-21-IIs supported Army ground operations in Southeast Asia and the Netherlands East Indies and played an important part in the fall of Hong Kong and Rangoon. Initially facing obsolete Allied aircraft the Ki-21-IIs proved quite successful but, when pitted against RAF Hurricanes and P-40s of the American Volunteer Group over Burma and China, losses increased sharply.

To remedy the chronic weakness of the defensive armament, the long dorsal greenhouse, offering only a limited field of fire to the dorsal light machine-gun, was eliminated starting with the Ki-21 c/n 1026. To replace this hand-held machine-gun Mitsubishi designed a large conical turret housing a 12·7 mm Type 1 machine-gun. With the installation of this turret —operated by bicycle pedals with chain-drive for gun traverse—the aircraft was redesignated Army Type 97 Heavy Bomber Model 2B or Ki-21-IIb, and late production aircraft of this variant were characterized by the replacement of the exhaust collector ring with individual exhaust stacks offering some thrust augmentation. Mitsubishi delivered 688 Ki-21-IIbs bringing total production of all Ki-21s, including prototypes and Nakajima-built aircraft, to 2,064.

During the early war years the Ki-21 was one of the best-known Japanese aircraft and it received one of the original code names: JANE after General MacArthur's wife. As the famous General did not appreciate this form of compliment the code name was quickly changed to SALLY. Later, the absence of the long dorsal greenhouse—one of SALLY's main recognition features—led Allied intelligence to identify the Ki-21-IIb as a new type of Japanese bomber which accordingly received the code name GWEN. When the aircraft was properly identified as being merely a version of the Ki-21 it was renamed SALLY 3, SALLY 1 referring to the Ha-5 powered models and SALLY 2 to the Ha-101 powered Ki-21-IIa. Whether known as GWEN or SALLY 3, the Ki-21-IIb was met by Allied forces from New Guinea to India and China. By 1943, the Ki-21-II equipped jubaku sentais outnumbered two-to-one the Ki-49 equipped units and the Army Type 97 Heavy Bomber carried the brunt of the Japanese offensive air actions against Calcutta. Other Ki-21-II Sentais fought gallantly to slow down the Allied advance from New Guinea to the Philippines but, with their fighter escort being outnumbered and being hunted on the ground by Allied fighter sweeps, their losses were very high. Fortunately for the Army, at long last a replacement for the Ki-21 was becoming available and the Army Type 97 Heavy Bombers began to be phased out of operations during the last year of the war. At the time of the Japanese surrender only the 58th Sentai still operated the Ki-21 in its original role and most remaining aircraft were being used as communication or headquarters aircraft or for special missions. One such mission was the commando attack on Yontan airfield, Okinawa, on which one out of nine Ki-21-IIbs despatched by the 3rd Dokuritsu Hikotai (Independent Wing) managed to crash-land near parked US aircraft and supply dumps, considerable damage being inflicted by the fanatical commandos.

The Mitsubishi Ki-21 had contributed more than any other aircraft to bringing the air branch of the Army to parity of equipment with other air forces. However, the inability of the Japanese aircraft industry to provide in time an adequate successor to the Ki-21 forced the use of the aircraft beyond its planned operational career. During the latter part of the war, despite its obsolescence, the Ki-21 was still liked by its crews for its pleasant handling characteristics and ease of maintenance and was preferred to the more modern Nakajima Ki-49.

UNITS ALLOCATED

7th, 12th, 14th, 58th, 60th, 61st, 62nd, 92nd, 94th, 95th and 98th Sentais. 3rd Dokuritsu Hikotai. 22nd Hikodan. 1st, 5th and 8th Hikoshidan Shireibu Hikodan. Hamamatsu Army Bomber Flying School.

Mitsubishi Ki-21-IIa formation from the Hamamatsu Army Bomber School.

MITSUBISHI Ki-21-IIb

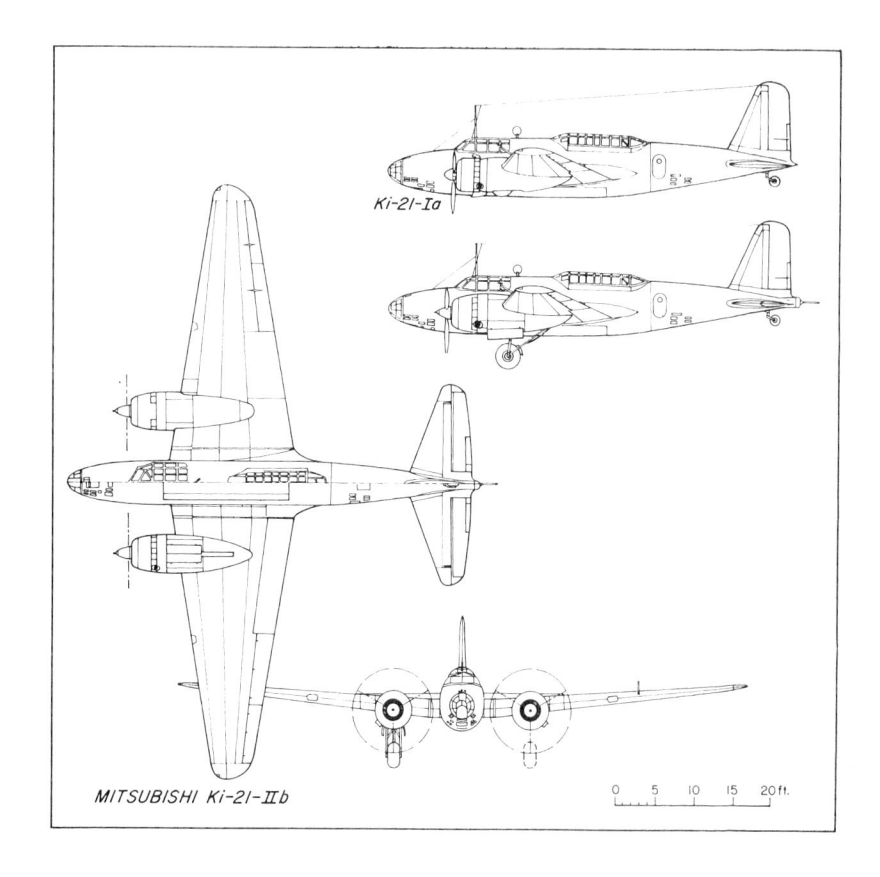

TECHNICAL DATA

Description: Twin-engined heavy bomber (Ki-21 series) and transport (MC-21 series). All-metal construction with fabric-covered control surfaces.

Accommodation: Normal crew of five consisting of pilot, co-pilot, navigator/bombardier, radio-operator/gunner and gunner. Two additional gunners could be carried when required (Ki-21).

Crew of four and nine passengers or cargo (MC-21).

Powerplant: Two 825 hp Mitsubishi Ha-6 fourteen-cylinder air-cooled radials, driving three-blade variable-pitch metal propellers (1st and 2nd Ki-21 prototypes).

Two 850 hp Army Type 97 fourteen-cylinder air-cooled radials (Nakajima Ha-5 KAI), rated at 950 hp for take-off and 1,080 hp at 4,000 m (13,125 ft), driving variable-pitch three-blade metal propellers (3rd through 8th Ki-21 prototypes, Ki-21-I and MC-21).

Two 1,450 hp Army Type 100 fourteen-cylinder air-cooled radials (Mitsubishi Ha-101), rated at 1,500 hp for take-off and 1,340 hp at 4,600 m (15,090 ft), driving constant-speed three-blade metal propellers (Ki-21-II).

Armament: One flexible 7·7 mm Type 89 machine-gun in each of the nose, ventral and dorsal positions (prototypes and Ki-21-Ia).

One flexible 7·7 mm Type 89 machine-gun in each of the nose, ventral and dorsal positions. One flexible 7·7 mm Type 89 machine-gun in a tail stinger and one flexible 7·7 mm Type 89 machine-gun firing from either side of the fuselage (Ki-21-Ib).

One flexible 7·7 mm Type 89 machine-gun in each of the nose, ventral, dorsal, tail, and port and starboard beam positions (Ki-21-Ic and Ki-21-IIa).

162

One flexible 7·7 mm Type 89 machine-gun in each of the nose, ventral, tail, and port and starboard beam positions and one 12·7 mm Type 1 machine-gun in the dorsal turret (Ki-21-IIb).
Bomb-load—normal, 750 kg (1,653 lb)
　　　　　—maximum, 1,000 kg (2,205 lb)

	Ki-21-Ia	Ki-21-IIb
Dimensions:		
Span	22·5 m	22·5 m
	(73 ft 9 13/16 in)	(73 ft 9 13/16 in)
Length	16 m	16 m
	(52 ft 5 29/32 in)	(52 ft 5 29/32 in)
Height	4·35 m	4·85 m
	(14 ft 3 13/32 in)	(15 ft 10 18/32 in)
Wing area	69·6 sq m	69·6 sq m
	(749·165 sq ft)	(749·165 sq ft)
Weights:		
Empty	4,691 kg	6,070 kg
	(10,342 lb)	(13,382 lb)
Loaded	7,492 kg	9,710 kg
	(16,517 lb)	(21,407 lb)
Maximum	7,916 kg	10,610 kg
	(17,452 lb)	(23,391 lb)
Wing loading	107·6 kg/sq m	139·5 kg/sq m
	(22 lb/sq ft)	(28·6 lb/sq ft)
Power loading	3·9 kg/hp	3·2 kg/hp
	(8·7 lb/hp)	(7·1 lb/hp)
Performance:		
Maximum speed	432 km/h at 4,000 m	486 km/h at 4,720 m
	(268 mph at 13,125 ft)	(302 mph at 15,485 ft)
Cruising speed	—	380 km/h at 5,000 m
	—	(236 mph at 16,405 ft)
Climb to	5,000 m (16,405 ft)	6,000 m (19,685 ft)
in	13 min 55 sec	13 min 13 sec
Service ceiling	8,600 m	10,000 m
	(28,215 ft)	(32,810 ft)
Range—normal	1,500 km	—
	(932 miles)	—
—maximum	2,700 km	2,700 km
	(1,680 miles)	(1,680 miles)

Mitsubishi Ki-21-IIb Army Type 97 Heavy Bomber Model 2B just before being shot down.

Production: A total of 2,064 Ki-21s were built by Mitsubishi Jukogyo K.K. at Nagoya and Nakajima Hikoki K.K. at Ota as follows:
Mitsubishi Jukogyo K.K.:
    8 prototypes and Service trials aircraft (Nov 1936–Feb 1938)
  143 Ki-21-Ia production aircraft (Mar 1938–1939)
  120 Ki-21-Ib production aircraft (1939–1940)
  160 Ki-21-Ic production aircraft (1940)
    4 Ki-21-II Service trials aircraft (Dec 1940)
  590 Ki-21-IIa production aircraft (Dec 1940–1942)
  688 Ki-21-IIb production aircraft (1942–Sept 1944)

1,713
Nakajima Hikoki K.K.:
  351 Ki-21-Ia, -Ib and -Ic production aircraft (Aug 1938–Feb 1941)
An unknown number of Ki-21-Is were modified as transport aircraft under the designation MC-21.

Mitsubishi Ki-30

Although remembered as the first Japanese light bomber fitted with double-row air-cooled radial engine, variable-pitch propeller, internal bomb-bay and split flaps, the Ki-30 cannot boast any claim to fame. Its operational career was inconspicuous as it served mainly in China at a time when little or no enemy opposition faced the Imperial Japanese Army, but, being a remarkably easy aircraft to fly and maintain and possessing few or no vices, the Ki-30 was long remembered by its crews.

    In the mid-thirties the Army began an ambitious expansion and modernization programme based on a new series of aircraft designed and built in Japan. By the spring of 1936 prototypes of fighter, heavy bomber and reconnaissance aircraft—leading to the production of the Nakajima Ki-27,

A Mitsubishi Ki-30 in factory finish.

Mitsubishi Ki-21 and Mitsubishi Ki-15—had been ordered and it only remained to provide a suitable replacement for the Kawasaki Ki-3 and Mitsubishi Ki-2 then serving in the Army's light bomber units. This gap in their re-equipment programme was filled in May 1936 when the Koku Hombu instructed Mitsubishi and Kawasaki each to build before December 1936 two prototypes of light bombers. Requirements included: (1) maximum speed, 400 km/h at 3,000 m (248·5 mph at 9,845 ft); (2) operating altitude, 2,000 m to 4,000 m (6,560 ft to 13,125 ft); (3) climb to 3,000 m (9,845 ft) in 8 min; (4) powerplant, one 825 hp Mitsubishi Ha-6 radial, or one 850 hp Nakajima Ha-5 radial, or one 850 hp Kawasaki Ha-9-IIb liquid-cooled engine; (5) normal bomb-load, 300 kg (661 lb) and maximum

A Mitsubishi Ki-30 Army Type 97 Light Bomber.

bomb-load, 450 kg (992 lb); (6) armament, one forward-firing machine-gun and one flexible rear-firing machine-gun; (7) ability to perform 60 deg dives; (8) crew of two; and (9) loaded weight not to exceed 3,200 kg (7,275 lb).

Designed by Engineers Kawano, Ohki and Mizuno working under the supervision of Colonel Komamura, the Mitsubishi Ki-30 was originally conceived with a retractable main undercarriage. However, when wind-tunnel tests indicated that the gain in speed would be more than offset by the added weight and complexity of the retractable undercarriage, a fixed gear with spatted main wheels was adopted. The design team also selected a mid-mounted wing fitted with landing flaps to allow the installation of a fuselage bomb-bay. So fitted, and powered by a Mitsubishi Ha-6 radial driving a variable-pitch three-blade propeller, the first prototype made its maiden flight at Kagamigahara on 28 February, 1937, with test pilot Yamaguchi at the controls. A second prototype, powered by a Nakajima Ha-5 radial, was completed the same month. Although these aeroplanes were completed two months behind schedule and were slightly overweight, their handling characteristics and performance exceeded requirements. A maximum speed of 423 km/h at 4,000 m (263 mph at 13,125 ft) was achieved and satisfied the Army's most sanguine hopes.

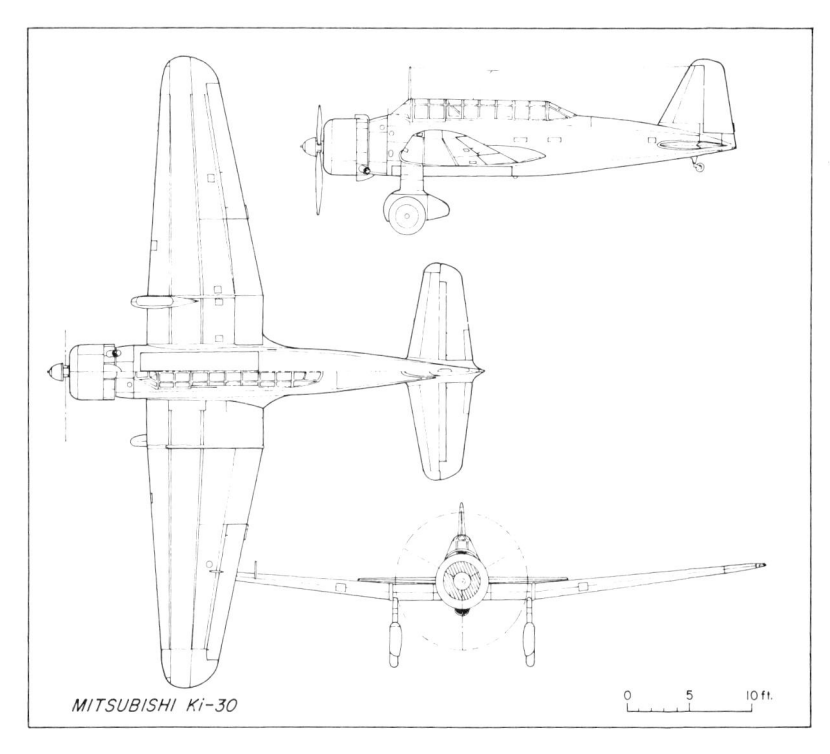

MITSUBISHI Ki-30

Sixteen Service trials aircraft, each powered by a Nakajima Ha-5 KAI radial, were built by January 1938 and differed from the prototypes by the relocation in the left wing of the forward-firing 7·7 mm Type 89 machine-gun previously mounted in the left main undercarriage and by the removal of the outboard wheel covers to facilitate operations from muddy fields, a modification dictated by the results of special tests conducted in October 1937 with one of the prototypes. Ski-operations were also tested in May 1939. Mass production of the Ki-30 as the Army Type 97 Light Bomber began at Mitsubishi's Nagoya plant in March 1938 where 618 production aircraft were built up to April 1940, and a further 68 aircraft were built at Tachikawa by the Tachikawa Dai-Ichi Rikugun Kokusho (First Army Air Arsenal).

Mitsubishi Ki-30s of the 90th Sentai. (*US Navy Department.*)

The Ki-30 began its operational career on the Chinese mainland in 1938 where it proved to be one of the Japanese Army's most reliable aircraft, and losses caused by enemy aircraft were low as it operated within the range of the Ki-27 fighter. When the war started Ki-30 units were also committed to operations in the Philippines after Allied aircraft had been driven off, but the type was already reaching the end of its operational life as losses increased sharply as soon as it was committed to theatres where Allied aircraft were operating. The Ki-30s were then retained for crew training while others were delivered to the Royal Thai Air Force which first deployed their Ki-30s in January 1941 against French forces in Indo-China. Finally the Ki-30, or ANN according to the Allied code name system, joined other obsolete aircraft allocated to suicide operations towards the end of the war.

UNITS ALLOCATED
6th, 16th, 31st, 32nd, 35th and 90th Sentais. 82nd and 87th Dokuritsu Hiko Chutais.

TECHNICAL DATA
Description: Single-engined light bomber. All-metal construction with fabric-covered control surfaces.
Accommodation: Crew of two seated in tandem enclosed cockpits.
Powerplant: One 825 hp Mitsubishi Ha-6 fourteen-cylinder air-cooled radial driving a variable-pitch three-blade metal propeller (first prototype).
   One 850 hp Army Type 97 fourteen-cylinder air-cooled radial (Nakajima Ha-5 KAI), rated at 950 hp for take-off and 960 hp at 3,600 m (11,810 ft), driving a variable-pitch three-blade metal propeller (all Ki-30s except first prototype).
Armament: One wing-mounted 7·7 mm Type 89 machine-gun and one flexible rear-firing 7·7 mm Type 89 machine-gun.
      Bomb-load—normal, 300 kg (661 lb)
         —maximum, 400 kg (882 lb)

Dimensions: Span 14·55 m (47 ft 8¾ in); length 10·34 m (33 ft 11⅜ in); height 3·645 m (11 ft 11¼ in); wing area 30·58 sq m (329·159 sq ft).
Weights: Empty 2,230 kg (4,916 lb); loaded 3,322 kg (7,324 lb); wing loading 108·6 kg/sq m (22·3 lb/sq ft); power loading 3·5 kg/hp (7·7 lb/hp).
Performance: Maximum speed 432 km/h at 4,000 m (263 mph at 13,125 ft); cruising speed 380 km/h (236 mph); climb to 5,000 m (16,405 ft) in 10 min 36 sec; service ceiling 8,570 m (28,120 ft); range 1,700 km (1,056 miles).
Production: A total of 704 Ki-30s were built by Mitsubishi Jukogyo K.K. at Nagoya and Tachikawa Dai-Ichi Rikugun Kokusho at Tachikawa as follows:
Mitsubishi Jukogyo K.K.:
    2 prototypes (Feb 1937)
    16 Service trials aircraft (Sept 1937–Jan 1938)
    618 production aircraft (Mar 1938–Apr 1940)
Tachikawa Dai-Ichi Rikugun Kokusho:
    68 production aircraft (1939–Sept 1941)

A captured Mitsubishi Ki-46-II with under-fuselage camera ports. (*USAF.*)

Mitsubishi Ki-46

To the Allied aircrews DINAH was known as the aircraft with the nice 'linah'. Indeed the Ki-46 had probably the most graceful lines of any fighting aircraft of the second World War. Cleanly designed, reliable and fast, this aeroplane performed its unspectacular tasks of high-altitude reconnaissance with considerable success from the first unauthorized overflight of Malaya before the Japanese invasion of that country to the surveillance flights over the US 20th Air Force's bases in the Marianas during the closing stage of the war. Respected by its foes and trusted by its crews, the Ki-46 also captured the attention of the Luftwaffe which fruitlessly negotiated the acquisition of a manufacturing licence under the Japanese–German Technical Exchange Programme.

A Mitsubishi Ki-46-II of the 81st Sentai, 2nd Chutai. (*Aireview*.)

Because of the geographical location of Japan and the vastness of the area in which a potential conflict requiring their participation would be fought, the Imperial Japanese Army had a constant requirement for reconnaissance aircraft combining high speed with substantial range performance. In 1937, while it appeared that the immediate requirements were going to be met by the Mitsubishi Ki-15, Major Fujita and Engineers Tanaka and Ando of the Technical Branch of the Koku Hombu set out to draw the preliminary specifications for its successor. On 12 December, 1937, the Koku Hombu issued to Mitsubishi a specification calling for a long-range photographic and visual reconnaissance aircraft which would possess a performance sufficient to complete its missions without being intercepted. Required endurance was six hours at a speed of 400 km/h (249 mph) between 4,000 m and 6,000 m (13,125 ft and 19,685 ft) and maximum speed was to be 600 km/h at 4,000 m (373 mph at 13,125 ft). One flexible rear-firing 7·7 mm Type 89 machine-gun had to be provided but Mitsubishi had the choice of single- or twin-engined configuration using either the 790 hp Nakajima Ha-20b, the 950 hp Nakajima Ha-25 or the 850 hp Mitsubishi Ha-26, and to meet the stringent range and speed specifications the design team was freed from all other usual requirements.

When Tomio Kubo began preliminary design studies for the Ki-46 he

A Mitsubishi Ki-46-II of the 55th Dokuritsu Dai Shijugo Chutai in the Philippines. (*US Navy Department*.)

was able to call on the experience recently acquired by Mitsubishi in designing the Ki-39, a twin-engined two-seat long-range fighter competing with the Kawasaki Ki-38, and the Ki-40, a projected reconnaissance aircraft derived from the Ki-39. Furthermore he obtained the co-operation of the Aeronautical Research Institute of the University of Tokyo which developed close-fitting cowlings for the two Mitsubishi Ha-26 fourteen-cylinder radials, with resultant improvement in pilot's sideways vision and a reduction in drag, and which also contributed to the design of the fully retractable landing gear selected for the aircraft. To meet the stringent performance requirements Tomio Kubo adopted a thin wing section and a fuselage of small diameter in which a large fuel tank was mounted close to the aircraft's centre of gravity. The pilot and radio-operator/gunner were seated in two cockpits separated by the fuselage fuel tank. Design and construction of the first prototype progressed slowly as it was found necessary to conduct extensive wind-tunnel tests in the facilities of the Aeronautical Research Institute of the University of Tokyo, and the aircraft was not completed at Mitsubishi's Nagoya plant until early November 1939.

With Major Fujita—whose efforts had resulted in the issuance of the Ki-46 specification—at the controls, the first flight took place in late November at Kagamigahara in Gifu Prefecture, north of Nagoya. Powered by two Mitsubishi Ha-26-I engines with a military rating of 900 hp at 3,600 m (11,810 ft) and driving constant-speed three-blade propellers, the prototype performed satisfactorily. However, when performance trials began, it soon became evident that the Ki-46 failed by some 40 mph to reach its design speed, a maximum of 540 km/h at 4,000 m (335·5 mph at 13,125 ft) being registered. Despite this failure to meet the speed requirement, the Ki-46 was received enthusiastically by the Army as it was still faster than the Ki-43-I, their newest fighter then about to be delivered, as well as faster than the A6M2 fighter of their rival, the Navy, and production of an initial batch of identical aircraft was authorized under the designation Army Type 100 Command Reconnaissance Plane Model 1 (Ki-46-I).

While testing of the Ki-46 was going on, the engine plant of Mitsubishi had under development an advanced version of the Ha-26-I engine, the Ha-102, with two-speed supercharger which was expected to boost take-off rating to 1,080 hp and military rating to 1,055 hp at 2,800 m (9,185 ft) without an increase in overall diameter. With this powerplant it was anticipated that the Ki-46 could easily meet its speed requirement and consequently Mitsubishi were instructed to proceed with the design of the Ki-46-II to be powered by a pair of Ha-102s. Pending availability of this version, the pre-production Ki-46-Is were issued to the Shimoshizu Rikugun Hikogakuko (Shimoshizu Army Flying School) for pilot training and to an experimental unit for intensive Service evaluation. During the following months minor problems arose and ground crews complained that the aircraft, considerably more complex than the Ki-15 it replaced,

Captured Mitsubishi Ki-46-II Army Type 100 Command Reconnaissance Plane Model 2. (*USAF.*)

was difficult to maintain in the field. Vapour locks occurred frequently under hot and humid weather conditions and special tests had to be conducted in Formosa during June 1940, using a Ki-46-I, and in June 1941 with a Ki-46-II, to locate the cause. Change from 87-octane to 92-octane fuel and relocation of the fuel lines around the engines corrected the condition. Pilots complained that oil was overheating during the long climb to cruising altitude, necessitating a slower rate of climb, that ailerons responded slowly and rudder was ineffective, and also that the oxygen system was unreliable during long flights. But the most serious problem was that affecting the undercarriage which, due to the aircraft's high rate of sink, often collapsed on landing. Despite the use of a stronger auxiliary rear strut, the landing gear suffered from chronic weakness throughout the operational life of the aircraft. However, as these difficulties rendered the Ki-46 neither difficult nor unsafe to fly, its production was accelerated and constant modifications finally overcame the major difficulties.

The first Ha-102 powered Ki-46-II was completed in March 1941 and early in its flight trials reached the speed of 604 km/h at 5,800 m (375 mph at 19,030 ft), thus slightly exceeding the maximum speed initially specified. As the Ki-46-II had an identical airframe to that of the earlier Ki-46-I, flight tests progressed smoothly and, as fast as the production rate allowed, the aircraft were delivered, starting in July 1941, to the 18th, 50th, 51st, 70th, 74th, 76th and 81st Dokuritsu Dai Shijugo Chutais in Manchuria and China. Its high speed enabled the Ki-46-II to avoid interception by the few fighters then available to the Chinese Air Force, and the Japanese crews took advantage of the situation to familiarize themselves with their new mount. With the war against the Allies about to begin, a unit of Ki-46-IIs was moved to French Indo-China and, on 20 and 22 October, 1941, its commanding officer, Captain Ikeda, reconnoitred the area selected by the Japanese High Command for the planned amphibious landings in Malaya. When hostilities finally broke out, the Ki-46 units were deployed in small detachments to cover the entire Southeast Asia area. The Army Type 100 Command Reconnaissance Planes were able to perform their missions with almost complete freedom from interception as, without the benefit of ground control radar to guide them, the Allied squadrons' obsolescent fighters failed to reach the elusive Nipponese aircraft in time. This ability attracted the attention of the Japanese Navy which negotiated the acquisition of a small number of the type. Some of the Ki-46s operated by that Service flew regular missions over Northern

A Mitsubishi Ki-46-III with flaps lowered and part of the wing leading edge removed.

Australia from their bases on Timor, while the aircraft of the Japanese Army operated as far west as the Bay of Bengal.

When the USAAF deployed P-38Fs to the Pacific and the RAAF received some Spitfire Vs for the defence of Darwin, the losses suffered by Ki-46-II units began to mount. Fortunately for the Japanese, the Koku Hombu had anticipated this situation and in May 1942 had instructed Mitsubishi to install their new 1,500 hp Ha-112-II engine in an improved version of the aircraft, the Ki-46-III, to increase maximum speed to 650 km/h (404 mph) and endurance by one hour. To meet the requirement for increased flight duration, despite the higher fuel consumption of the new engines, it was necessary to redesign the fuel system and add a fuselage fuel tank in front of the pilot with a resultant increase in total capacity from 1,675 litres (365 Imp gal) to 1,895 litres (417 Imp gal). Provision was also made for a ventral drop tank containing an additional 460 litres (101·2 Imp gal). The engine nacelles were also slightly enlarged to accommodate the Ha-112-II, a development of the earlier Ha-102 fitted with a direct fuel injection system. The landing gear was strengthened to cope with the increased weight and no provision was made for the single flexible machine-gun which, though installed on earlier models at the factory, had often been dispensed with in the field. However, the most significant change in external appearance was the redesign of the forward fuselage to provide a new canopy over the pilot's seat without the step between the nose and the top of the fuselage which had characterized the earlier versions of the aircraft.

Completed in December 1942, two Ki-46-III prototypes underwent accelerated flight trials leading to a production order under the designation Army Type 100 Command Reconnaissance Plane Model 3. Both the Ki-46-II, which remained in production until late in 1944, and the Ki-46-III were built at the Nagoya plant. However, when in December 1944 this plant was severely damaged by an earthquake and suffered further from the pounding inflicted by B-29s of the US 20th Air Force, production was transferred to a new plant at Toyama where only about one hundred machines were built. Late production Ki-46-IIIs coming off the Nagoya and Toyama lines were fitted with individual exhaust stacks providing some thrust augmentation and had slightly better speed and range.

Priority in delivery of the Ki-46-IIIs was given to units operating in areas where Allied forces had achieved air superiority, but often they operated alongside the older Ki-46-IIs which they never completely supplanted. Once maintenance problems with the fuel injection system of their Ha-112-IIs had been solved, the Ki-46-IIIs, benefiting from markedly improved performance between 8,000 m and 10,000 m (26,250 ft to 32,810 ft), proved to be a thorn in the Allies' side and only the faster climbing fighters under radar control could successfully intercept the fast Nipponese machines which kept constant watch over such well defended bases as the

Mitsubishi Ki-46-II KAI three-seat operational trainer.

B-29 airfields in the Marianas. However, as the war drew to its end, DINAH was no longer free from interception and losses rose alarmingly.

As the production of the Army Type 100 Command Reconnaissance Plane Model 3 gained tempo, a small number of the earlier Model 2s were modified as three-seat radio-navigation trainers. Distinguished by a stepped-up cockpit behind the pilot's seat, these aircraft were designated Army Type 100 Operations Trainer (Ki-46-II KAI) and served with the Shimoshizu Rikugun Hikogakuko (Shimoshizu Army Flying School).

A high-altitude interceptor fighter version of the Ki-46-III was developed by the Rikugun Kokugijutsu Kenkyujo (Army Aerotechnical Research Institute) as a stopgap pending production of specialized aircraft. Initially studies for this aircraft began in June 1943 and its development was

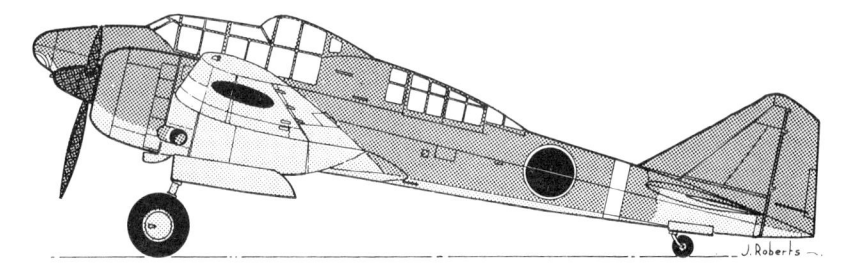

This drawing of the Mitsubishi Ki-46-II KAI operational trainer shows some detail not visible in the photograph on page 173.

pursued actively from May 1944 onwards. A modification programme was initiated at the Tachikawa Dai-Ichi Rikugun Kokusho (First Army Air Arsenal at Tachikawa) where the photographic equipment of the standard Ki-46-III was removed. Modifications also included the redesign of the nose to provide space for two 20 mm Ho-5 cannon and the replacement of the top centre fuselage fuel tank by an obliquely mounted forward-firing 37 mm Ho-203 cannon. The first Army Type 100 Air Defence Fighter (Ki-46-III KAI) was completed in October 1944 and, a month later, aircraft of this type were issued to various units operating in defence of Japan. Operational results were disappointing as the Ki-46-III KAIs did not have the climbing speed required for an interceptor, but further developments of this variant resulted in the Army Type 100 Assault Plane (Ki-46-IIIb), of which only a few were built, and the Ki-46-IIIc which remained on the drawing boards.

Retaining the Ki-46-III airframe but powered by two Ha-112-II Ru engines fitted with exhaust-driven turbosuperchargers, four Ki-46-IV prototypes were built in 1943–44. With a military rating of 1,100 hp at 10,200 m (33,465 ft), the Ha-112-II Ru gave the aircraft superior performance at altitude. Compared with the Ki-46-III, the Ki-46-IV differed by the installation, in the lower rear portion of the engine nacelles, of the turbo-

A Mitsubishi Ki-46-III KAI of the 16th Dokuritsu Hikotai. (*Aireview.*)

superchargers, the intake air being methanol-cooled as space restriction prevented the use of an intercooler, and by an increase in internal fuel capacity to 1,977 litres (435 Imp gal). Tests began in February 1944, but difficulties with the turbosupercharging system delayed the production of the Army Type 100 Command Reconnaissance Plane Model 4A (Ki-46-IVa) and its fighter version, the Ki-46-IVb with nose-mounted cannon, both aircraft being finally deleted from the production priority list.

While the Ki-46-IIs and Ki-46-IIIs operated until the end of the war, two Ki-46-IVs demonstrated in February 1945 that the DINAH was still one of the best reconnaissance aircraft of the time by covering, with the help of strong tailwinds, 2,301 km (1,430 miles) at an average speed of 700 km/h (435 mph).

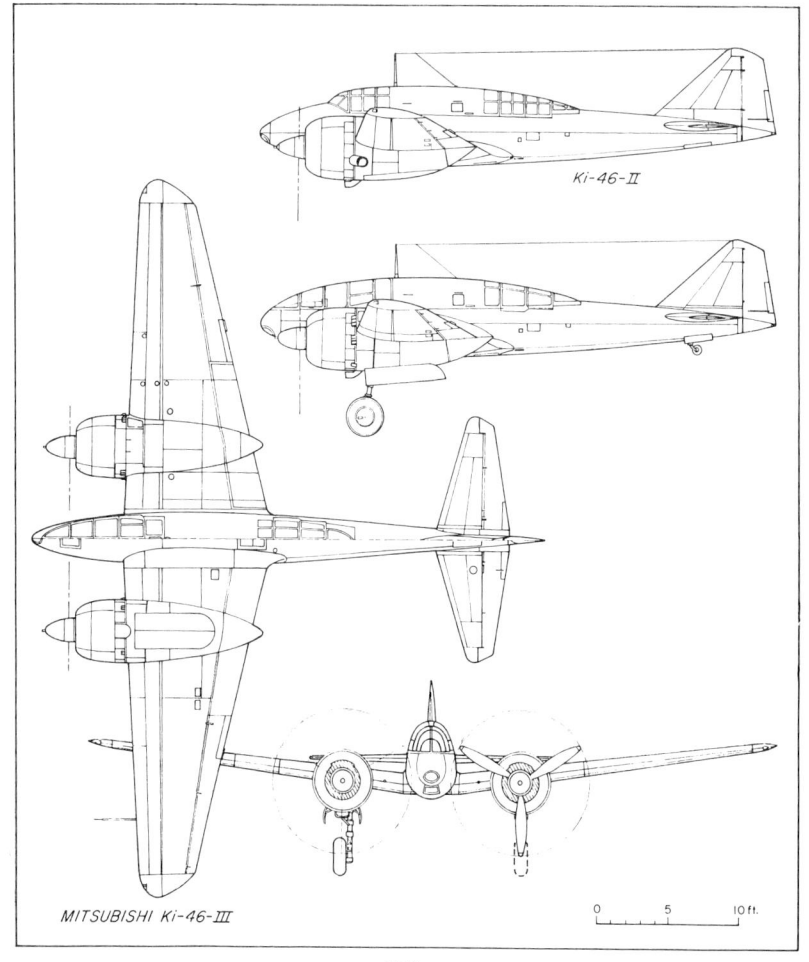

MITSUBISHI Ki-46-III

A Mitsubishi Ki-46-IV powered by two turbosupercharged Ha-112-II Ru engines. (*Aireview*.)

UNITS ALLOCATED

2nd, 8th, 10th, 15th, 38th, 81st, 82nd and 88th Sentais; 17th, 18th, 19th, 50th, 51st, 55th, 63rd, 70th, 74th, 76th, 81st and 85th Dokuritsu Dai Shijugo Chutais; 38th Dokuritsu Hikotai; Shimoshizu Rikugun Hikogakuko (Shimoshizu Army Flying School); and Tokorozawa Rikugun Koku Seibigakuko (Tokorozawa Army Air Maintenance School). (Army Type 100 Command Reconnaissance Plane.)

28th and 106th Sentais; 4th, 16th, 81st, 82nd and 83rd Dokuritsu Dai Shijugo Chutais; and 16th Dokuritsu Hikotai. (Army Type 100 Air Defence Fighter.)

TECHNICAL DATA

Description: Twin-engined two-seat reconnaissance aircraft (Ki-46-I to Ki-46-IV), operational trainer (Ki-46-II KAI), interceptor fighter (Ki-46-III KAI) and ground attack fighter (Ki-46-IIIb, -IIIc and -IVb). All-metal construction with fabric-covered control surfaces.

Accommodation: Crew of two (all versions except Ki-46-II KAI) or three (Ki-46-II KAI) in enclosed cockpits.

Powerplant: Two 900 hp Army Type 99 Model 1 fourteen-cylinder air-cooled radials (Mitsubishi Ha-26-I), rated at 780 hp for take-off and 900 hp at 3,600 m (11,810 ft), driving constant-speed three-blade metal propellers (Ki-46-I).

Two 1,050 hp Army Type 1 fourteen-cylinder air-cooled radials (Mitsubishi Ha-102), rated at 1,080 hp for take-off and 1,055 hp at 2,800 m (9,185 ft), driving constant-speed three-blade metal propellers (Ki-46-II and Ki-46-II KAI).

Two Army Type 4 fourteen-cylinder air-cooled radials (Mitsubishi Ha-112-II), rated at 1,500 hp for take-off and 1,250 hp at 5,800 m (19,030 ft), driving constant-speed three-blade metal propellers (Ki-46-IIIa, -IIIb, -IIIc and Ki-46-III KAI).

Two Mitsubishi Ha-112-II Ru fourteen-cylinder air-cooled radials, rated at 1,500 hp for take-off, 1,250 hp at 7,400 m (24,280 ft) and 1,100 hp at 10,200 m (33,465 ft), driving constant-speed three-blade metal propellers (Ki-46-IVa and -IVb).

Armament: One 7·7 mm Type 89 rear-firing flexible machine-gun (Ki-46-I and -II).

One 37 mm Ho-203 cannon obliquely-mounted in the fuselage and two 20 mm Ho-5 cannon in the nose (Ki-46-III KAI).

Two 20 mm Ho-5 cannon in the nose (Ki-46-IIIb, -IIIc and Ki-46-IVb).

Production: A total of 1,742 Ki-46s were built by Mitsubishi Jukogyo K.K. in their Nagoya and Toyama plants as follows:

    34 Ki-46 prototypes and Ki-46-I production aircraft (1939–40)
    1,093 Ki-46-II production aircraft (1940–44)
        2 Ki-46-III prototypes (1942)
    609 Ki-46-III production aircraft, including fighter conversions (1942–45)
        4 Ki-46-IV prototypes (1943–44)

	Ki-46-I	Ki-46-II	Ki-46-III	Ki-46-III KAI	Ki-46-IVa
Dimensions:					
Span	14·7 m	14·7 m	14·7 m	14·7 m	14·7 m
	(48 ft 2¾ in)	(48 ft 2¾ in)	(48 ft 2¾ in)	(48 ft 2¾ in)	(48 ft 2¾ in)
Length	11 m	11 m	11 m	11·485 m	11 m
	(36 ft 1 1/16 in)	(36 ft 1 1/16 in)	(36 ft 1 1/16 in)	(37 ft 8 3/16 in)	(36 ft 1 1/16 in)
Height	3·88 m	3·88 m	3·88 m	3·88 m	3·88 m
	(12 ft 8¾ in)	(12 ft 8¾ in)	(12 ft 8¾ in)	(12 ft 8¾ in)	(12 ft 8¾ in)
Wing area	32 sq m	32 sq m	32 sq m	32 sq m	32 sq m
	(344·444 sq ft)	(344·444 sq ft)	(344·444 sq ft)	(344·444 sq ft)	(344·444 sq ft)
Weights:					
Empty	3,379 kg	3,263 kg	3,831 kg	3,831 kg	4,010 kg
	(7,449 lb)	(7,194 lb)	(8,446 lb)	(8,446 lb)	(8,840 lb)
Loaded	4,822 kg	5,050 kg	5,722 kg	6,228 kg	5,900 kg
	(10,631 lb)	(11,133 lb)	(12,619 lb)	(13,730 lb)	(13,007 lb)
Maximum	—	5,800 kg	6,500 kg	—	6,500 kg
	—	(12,787 lb)	(14,330 lb)	—	(14,330 lb)
Wing loading	150·7 kg/sq m	157·8 kg/sq m	178·8 kg/sq m	194·6 kg/sq m	184·4 kg/sq m
	(30·9 lb/sq ft)	(32·3 lb/sq ft)	(36·6 lb/sq ft)	(39·9 lb/sq ft)	(37·8 lb/sq ft)
Power loading	3·1 kg/hp	2·3 kg/hp	2 kg/hp	2·1 kg/hp	2 kg/hp
	(6·8 lb/hp)	(5·1 lb/hp)	(4·4 lb/hp)	(4·6 lb/hp)	(4·4 lb/hp)
Performance:					
Maximum speed	540 km/h at 4,070 m	604 km/h at 5,800 m	630 km/h at 6,000 m	630 km/h at 6,000 m	630 km/h at 10,000 m
	(335·5 mph at 13,350 ft)	(375 mph at 19,030 ft)	(391 mph at 19,685 ft)	(391 mph at 19,685 ft)	(391 mph at 32,810 ft)
Cruising speed	—	400 km/h at 4,000 m	—	—	450 km/h at 4,000 m
	—	(249 mph at 13,125 ft)	—	—	(280 mph at 13,125 ft)
Climb to	5,000 m (16,405 ft)	8,000 m (26,250 ft)	8,000 m (26,250 ft)	8,000 m (26,250 ft)	10,000 m (32,810 ft)
in	7 min 45 sec	17 min 58 sec	20 min 15 sec	19 min	16 min 30 sec
Service ceiling	10,830 m (35,530 ft)	10,720 m (35,170 ft)	10,500 m (34,450 ft)	10,500 ft (34,450 ft)	11,000 m (36,090 ft)
Range	2,100 km	2,474 km	4,000 km	2,000 km plus 1 hr combat	4,000 km
	(1,305 miles)	(1,537 miles)	(2,485 miles)	(1,243 miles plus 1 hr combat)	(2,485 miles)

This Mitsubishi Ki-51 was one of the eleven Service trials aircraft. (*Mitsubishi Jukogyo K.K.*)

Mitsubishi Ki-51

At the suggestion of Captain Yuzo Fujita, one of the Japanese Army's leading flying officers, the Koku Hombu issued to Mitsubishi in December 1937 a specification calling for a ground attack aircraft to be developed from their successful Ki-30 light bomber. As compared to its forerunner, the new aircraft, designated Ki-51, was to be smaller, and emphasis was placed on manoeuvrability, protection and ability to operate from short fields close to the front lines. In February 1938 the specification was revised to incorporate the following requirements: (1) maximum speed, 420 km/h at 2,000 m (261 mph at 6,560 ft); (2) loaded weight, 2,700 kg (5,952 lb); (3) powerplant, one Mitsubishi Ha-26-II radial; (4) normal bomb-load consisting of twelve 15 kg (33 lb) bombs or four 50 kg (110 lb) bombs; and (5) armament consisting of two forward-firing machine-guns and one flexible rear-firing machine-gun.

Created by the same design team which had produced the Ki-30, the Ki-51 bore a close external resemblance to its larger forerunner but had a shorter cockpit, allowing better collaboration between the two crew members, a limited set of flight instruments and controls being installed in the rear cockpit. The lighter bomb-load enabled the bomb-bay to be dispensed with and the wing was lowered to reduce undercarriage length. The Ha-26-II radial was closely cowled and drove a three-blade propeller fitted with a large spinner. One 7·7 mm Type 89 machine-gun was mounted in each outboard wing section and a similar gun was provided for rear defence.

The first and second prototypes were completed in June and August 1939 respectively and followed by eleven Service trials aircraft built between September and December 1939. During the construction of the Service trials aircraft, a few modifications were introduced and included the replacement of the side-hinging canopy sections with rear-sliding units, the fitting of fixed leading-edge slots to improve handling characteristics at low speed and the installation of 6 mm steel armour plate under the engine cowling and cockpit. One of the Service trials aircraft was also modified in accordance with an Army request of December 1938 by replacing the flight instruments and controls in the rear cockpit with cameras. This aeroplane was intended as a prototype for the projected Army Type 99 Tactical Reconnaissance Plane (Ki-51a) but, following tests conducted at

A Mitsubishi Ki-51 Army Type 99 Assault Plane of the Kumagaya Flying School.

Kashizu, it was decided not to build this specialized version but rather to incorporate in the design of production Ki-51s provision for tactical reconnaissance equipment. Consequently no differences were mentioned in the official aircraft specification, and the aircraft could be quickly modified in the field for either tactical reconnaissance sorties or ground support missions, all 1,459 production Ki-51s built by Mitsubishi between 1940 and 1944 being designated Army Type 99 Assault Planes. During its production the Ki-51 was only modified twice to (1) install two 68 litre (15 Imp gal) wing leading edge fuel tanks and (2) replace the wing-mounted 7·7 mm Type 89 machine-guns with two 12·7 mm Type 1 machine-guns.

After initial operations in China the Ki-51s, known as SONIA to the Allies, were deployed throughout the Pacific where they served with distinction. Despite its unspectacular maximum speed which made it rather an easy prey for Allied fighters, the Ki-51 was liked by its crews as it was well protected, manoeuvrable, easy to fly and maintain, and because it could operate from small airfields at the front lines. The aircraft was so successful that, as late as 1944, a new assembly line was set up by the Tachikawa Dai-Ichi Rikugun Kokusho (First Army Air Arsenal at Tachikawa). During the closing months of the war the aircraft was finally assigned to kamikaze missions for which it carried a 250 kg (551 lb) bomb under the fuselage. After the Japanese surrender, several Ki-51s found abandoned on Java and Sumatra were briefly used against Dutch forces by the fledgling Indonesian Air Force.

In 1941, engineers from Mansyu Hikoki Seizo K.K. (Manchurian Aeroplane Manufacturing Co Ltd) were sent to the Tachikawa Dai-Ichi Rikugun Kokusho to develop an advanced version of the aircraft as the Ki-71 Army Experimental Tactical Reconnaissance Plane. Powered by one 1,500 hp Mitsubishi Ha-112-II radial, armed with two wing-mounted 20 mm Ho-5 cannon and featuring a retractable undercarriage, three Ki-71 prototypes were built at the Army Arsenal. Despite a more powerful engine and the use of a retractable undercarriage, the Ki-71 had a maximum speed of only 470 km/h (292 mph) and the design was not accepted for production. However, the development of the aircraft had been discovered by the Allies who assigned it the code name EDNA.

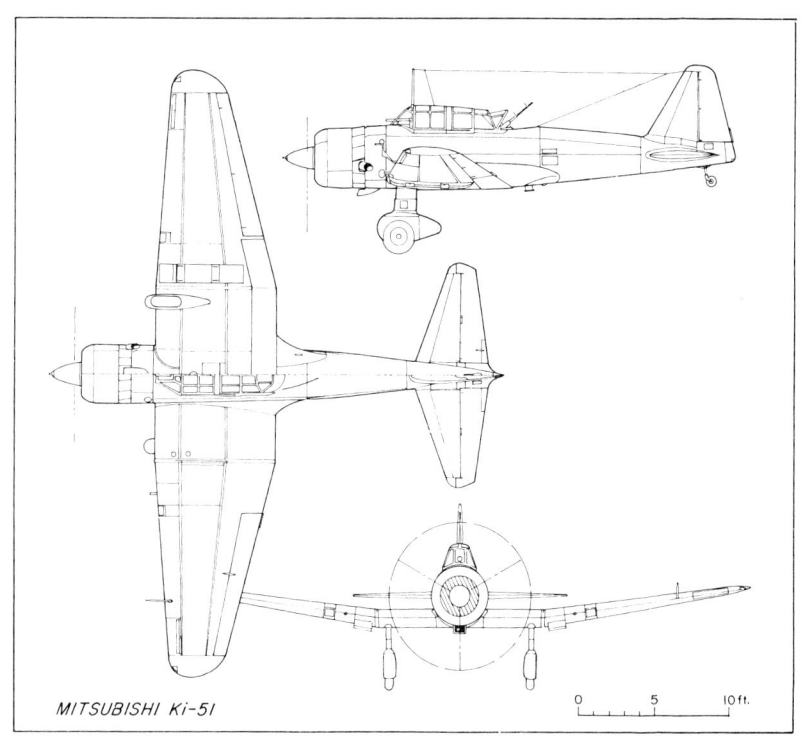

MITSUBISHI Ki-51

A Mitsubishi Ki-51 abandoned on Okinawa. (*US Navy Department.*)

UNITS ALLOCATED

6th, 27th, 32nd, 44th, 65th, 66th, 67th and 83rd Sentais. 41st, 45th, 47th, 48th, 49th, 52nd, 53rd, 71st, 73rd, 83rd, 89th, 90th and 91st Dokuritsu Hiko Chutais. 4th Kokugun Shireibu Hikodan. Koku Shikan Gakko (Army Air Academy).

TECHNICAL DATA

Description: Single-engined ground attack and tactical reconnaissance aircraft. All-metal construction with fabric-covered control surfaces.

Accommodation: Crew of two seated in tandem enclosed cockpits.

Powerplant: One 900 hp Army Type 99 Model 2 fourteen-cylinder air-cooled radial (Mitsubishi Ha-26-II), rated at 940 hp for take-off and 950 hp at 2,300 m (7,545 ft), driving a variable-pitch three-blade metal propeller.

Armament: Two wing-mounted 7·7 mm Type 89 machine-guns and one flexible rear-firing 7·7 mm Type 89 machine-gun (prototypes and early production aircraft).

Two wing-mounted 12·7 mm Type 1 machine-guns and one flexible rear-firing 7·7 mm Type 89 machine-gun (late production Ki-51).

Bomb-load—normal, 200 kg (441 lb)
—suicide operation, 250 kg (551 lb).

Dimensions: Span 12·1 m (39 ft 8⅜ in); length 9·21 m (30 ft 2 19/32 in); height 2·73 m (8 ft 11½ in); wing area 24·02 sq m (258·548 sq ft).

Weights: Empty 1,873 kg (4,129 lb); loaded 2,798 kg (6,169 lb); maximum 2,920 kg (6,415 lb); wing loading 116·5 kg/sq m (23·9 lb/sq ft); power loading 3 kg/hp (6·6 lb/hp).

Performance: Maximum speed 424 km/h at 3,000 m (263 mph at 9,845 ft); climb to 5,000 m (16,405 ft) in 9 min 55 sec; service ceiling 8,270 m (27,130 ft); range 1,060 km (660 miles).

Production: A total of 2,385 Ki-51s were built by Mitsubishi Jukogyo K.K. at Nagoya and the Tachikawa Dai-Ichi Rikugun Kokusho at Tachikawa as follows:

Mitsubishi Jukogyo K.K.:

2 Ki-51 prototypes (June and Aug 1939)
11 Ki-51 Service trials aircraft (Sept–Dec 1939)
1,459 Ki-51 production aircraft (Jan 1940–Mar 1944)

Tachikawa Dai-Ichi Rikugun Kokusho:

913 Ki-51 production aircraft (July 1941–July 1945)

In addition Tachikawa Dai-Ichi Rikugun Kokusho built three Ki-71 prototypes.

Two Mitsubishi Ki-57 Army Type 100 Transport Model 1s. (*US Navy Department.*)

Mitsubishi Ki-57

Standard personnel transport of the Imperial Japanese Army, the Ki-57 originated in early 1939 as a commercial transport developed by Mitsubishi from their Ki-21 heavy bomber at the request of Nippon Koku K.K. (Japan Air Lines). For service on their international routes the airline sought an aircraft of Japanese design with payload, speed and range performance similar to that of the military bomber. Preliminary design studies impressed the Army which had a requirement for a paratroop and staff transport and, when in August 1939 the airline was reorganized with government financial participation as Dai Nippon Koku K.K. (Greater Japan Air Line Co Ltd), the Koku Hombu issued to Mitsubishi a design specification covering the joint needs of the commercial airline and the military service. Requirements included: (1) ability to carry 11 passengers and 300 kg (661 lb) of freight over 1,400 km (870 miles) at a cruising speed of 300 km/h (186 mph) at between 2,000 m and 4,000 m (6,560 ft and 13,125 ft); (2) maximum range with commercial load, 2,000 km (1,243 miles) and ferry range, 3,000 km (1,864 miles); (3) crew of four; and (4) loaded weight not to exceed 7,900 kg (17,417 lb).

Retaining the wings, tail and cockpit sections, undercarriage and powerplant installation of the Ki-21-I, the transport aircraft, carrying the civil designation MC-20 and the military Kitai number Ki-57, featured a new fuselage accommodating eleven passengers in two rows of single seats, and had its wings mounted low on the fuselage whereas its bomber forerunner

A Mitsubishi MC-20-II of Dai Nippon Koku K.K. (*Aireview.*)

had mid-mounted wings. Completed in July 1940 the prototype made its first flight in August, and by the end of the year, despite the loss of the fourth aircraft during a test flight off Chiba on Tokyo Bay, quantity production was authorized for both commercial and military use. A total of 101 aircraft of the first production model were built by Mitsubishi between 1940 and 1942 and designated Army Type 100 Transport Model 1 (Ki-57-I) by the Army and MC-20-I by the civil authorities. A small number of Ki-57-Is were transferred to the Japanese Navy and designated Navy Type 0 Transport Model 11 or L4M1 by that Service.

Operated by the Army and Navy as a paratroop transport, communication and logistic support aircraft and by Dai Nippon Koku K.K. as a passenger transport on scheduled services as well as on military contract operations, the aircraft, named TOPSY by the Allies, was met in all theatres of operation. Although most of the time the type performed unspectacular but necessary tasks, it earned its share of fame on 14 February, 1942, during the Japanese paratroop attack on the aerodrome and oil refineries around Palembang.

In May 1942 an improved version of the aircraft, powered by two 1,080 hp Mitsubishi Ha-102 radials housed in redesigned nacelles and incor-

Mitsubishi MC-20-II camouflaged and carrying Dai Nippon Koku K.K. markings and green surrender crosses.

porating minor equipment changes, replaced the Ki-57-I on the assembly lines. A total of 406 of these aircraft were built for use by Dai Nippon Koku K.K. as the MC-20-II and by the Japanese Army as the Ki-57-II, Army Type 100 Transport Model 2. Plans to have the aircraft manufactured by Nippon Kokusai Kogyo K.K. failed to materialize and the last Ki-57-II was delivered by Mitsubishi in January 1945. After seeing active service throughout the war a few MC-20/Ki-57 aircraft survived and were operated under strict Allied control by Dai Nippon Koku K.K. until 10 October, 1945, when all Japanese air activities were prohibited.

UNITS ALLOCATED

108th and 109th Sentais. 20th Dokuritsu Hiko Chutai. 7th Hikodan, Shireibu Hikodan. 4th and 9th Hikoshidans, Shireibu Hikodan. 2nd Shudan, Shireibu Hikodan. 2nd, 3rd, 4th and 6th Kokuguns, Shireibu Hikodan. 1st Teishin Hikosentai.

TECHNICAL DATA

Description: Twin-engined personnel transport. All-metal construction with fabric-covered control surfaces.
Accommodation: Crew of four and eleven troops.
Powerplant: Two 850 hp Army Type 97 fourteen-cylinder air-cooled radials (Nakajima Ha-5 KAI), rated at 950 hp for take-off and 1,080 hp at 4,000 m (13,125 ft), driving variable-pitch three-blade metal propellers (Ki-57-I and MC-20-I).

Two 1,050 hp Army Type 100 fourteen-cylinder air-cooled radials (Mitsubishi Ha-102), rated at 1,080 hp for take-off and 1,055 hp at 2,800 m (9,185 ft), driving constant-speed three-blade metal propellers (Ki-57-II and MC-20-II).

Armament: None.

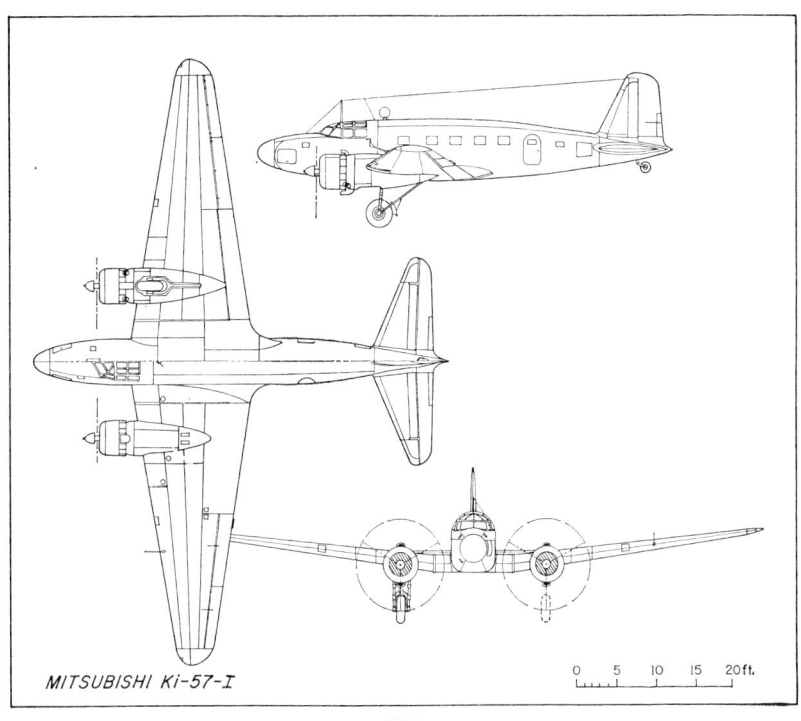

MITSUBISHI Ki-57-I

	Ki-57-I	Ki-57-II
Dimensions:		
Span	22·6 m	22·6 m
	(74 ft 1¾ in)	(74 ft 1¾ in)
Length	16·1 m	16·1 m
	(52 ft 9⅞ in)	(52 ft 9⅞ in)
Height	4·77 m	4·86 m
	(15 ft 7⅘ in)	(15 ft 11½ in)
Wing area	70·08 sq m	70·08 sq m
	(754·332 sq ft)	(754·332 sq ft)
Weights:		
Empty	5,522 kg	5,585 kg
	(12,174 lb)	(12,313 lb)
Loaded	7,860 kg	8,173 kg
	(17,328 lb)	(18,018 lb)
Maximum	8,437 kg	9,120 kg
	(18,600 lb)	(20,106 lb)
Wing loading	112·2 kg/sq m	116·6 kg/sq m
	(23 lb/sq ft)	(23·9 lb/sq ft)
Power loading	4·1 kg/hp	3·8 kg/hp
	(9·1 lb/hp)	(8·3 lb/hp)
Performance:		
Maximum speed	430 km/h at 3,400 m	470 km/h at 5,800 m
	(267 mph at 11,155 ft)	(292 mph at 19,030 ft)
Cruising speed	320 km/h at 3,000 m	—
	(199 mph at 9,840 ft)	—
Climb to	5,000 m (16,405 ft)	5,000 m (16,405 ft)
in	12 min 10 sec	15 min 45 sec
Service ceiling	7,000 m	8,000 m
	(22,965 ft)	(26,250 ft)
Range—normal	1,500 km	1,500 km
	(932 miles)	(932 miles)
—maximum	3,000 km	3,000 km
	(1,865 miles)	(1,865 miles)

Production: A total of 507 aircraft, including 101 Ki-57-Is and MC-20-Is and 406 Ki-57-IIs and MC-20-IIs, were built by Mitsubishi Jukogyo K.K. between July 1940 and January 1945.

A Mitsubishi Ki-67-1b Hiryu (Flying Dragon) of the 98th Sentai, 3rd Chutai.

Mitsubishi Ki-67 Hiryu (Flying Dragon)

Undoubtedly the best bomber to serve during the Pacific War with either the Japanese Army or the Navy, the Army Type 4 Heavy Bomber Hiryu (Flying Dragon) compared favourably with contemporary Allied twin-engined bombers. However, despite its official classification as a heavy bomber, the Ki-67 could better be compared to the American B-26 Marauder medium bomber. Had the Hiryu been available before the Allies were able to gain air superiority, the story of the war in the Pacific might indeed have been very different. Fortunately for the Allies the aircraft was thrown into combat operations in the hands of young crews fresh out of training school and operated under almost suicidal conditions against swarms of Allied fighters.

Late in 1940, while the Nakajima Ki-49 was undergoing Service trials, the Koku Hombu began drafting the specifications for its potential successor. At that time the JAAF were still preparing themselves for an eventual conflict against the Soviet Union along the Manchukuo–Siberia border and thus wanted a tactical heavy bomber. In February 1941, the Koku Hombu had finalized their specifications and instructed Mitsubishi to design and build three prototypes to meet the following requirements: (1) operating altitude, 4,000 m to 7,000 m (13,125 ft to 22,965 ft); (2) maximum speed, 550 km/h (342 mph); (3) radius of action, 700 km (435 miles) with 500 kg (1,102 lb) of bombs; (4) maximum bomb-load, eight 100 kg (220 lb) bombs, or three 250 kg (551 lb) bombs, or one 500 kg (1,102 lb) bomb; (5) normal crew of six to eight and maximum crew of nine to ten; (6) defensive armament including one 7·7 mm machine-gun in each of the nose and port and starboard positions and one 12·7 mm machine-gun in the dorsal and tail turrets; and (7) powerplants, either two

A Mitsubishi Ki-67-Ib Hiryu. The North American P-51 Mustang in the background emphasizes the relatively small dimensions of the Hiryu heavy bomber.

1,450 hp Mitsubishi Ha-101 radials, two 1,870 hp Nakajima Ha-103 radials or two 1,900 hp Mitsubishi Ha-104 radials.

To meet this specification Chief Engineer Ozawa designed a slim clean mid-wing monoplane powered by a pair of fan-cooled Mitsubishi Ha-104 radials driving four-blade constant-speed propellers. The wing and tail surfaces of the aircraft bore a strong resemblance to those of the Mitsubishi G4M1 bomber which was then entering service with the Navy but there ended its resemblance to any other Japanese aircraft. In a commendable departure from traditional Japanese design methods, Ozawa paid considerable attention to ease of production—construction by sub-assemblies being adopted from the start of the programme—and to safety of operation, all fuel and oil tanks being of the self-sealing type with armour protection. This attention to detail somewhat delayed the construction of the Ki-67 prototypes but was to be regarded as a strong asset when the aircraft had to be built, maintained and flown under the adverse conditions prevailing during the last year of the war.

The three prototypes originally ordered were completed in December 1942 and February and March 1943 respectively, but by that time Mitsubishi had already been instructed to build additional prototypes and Service

Mitsubishi Ki-67-Ib Army Type 4 Heavy Bomber Model 1B Hiryu (Flying Dragon).

Dorsal turret and side blister of a Mitsubishi Ki-67-Ib Hiryu (Flying Dragon).

trials aircraft. The first prototype made its maiden flight at Kagamigahara on 27 December, 1942, and, like the next two prototypes, carried defensive armament comprising one 7·92 mm Type 98 machine-gun in each of the nose and port and starboard beam positions and one 12·7 mm Type 1 machine-gun in dorsal and tail turrets. Despite some longitudinal stability problems and excessive control sensitivity under certain flight conditions, the flight test programme proved extremely rewarding to the Mitsubishi team. Although the maximum speed of 537 km/h at 6,090 m (334 mph at 19,980 ft) fell slightly below specification requirements, the Ki-67 easily exceeded all other requirements, and the Service trials aircraft, modified as a result of early tests to improve their flight handling characteristics, were highly manoeuvrable. Without bombs the Ki-67 could easily make loops and vertical turns, and its controls remained smooth and effective in a dive at indicated airspeeds up to 600 km/h (373 mph IAS). The additional prototypes and Service trials aircraft (Ki-67 c/ns 4 to 19) featured an increase in fuel capacity from 2,566 litres to 3,886 litres (565 Imp gal to 855 Imp gal) with resultant increase in range and had revised defensive armament comprising one 12·7 mm Type 1 machine-gun in the nose position and tail turret, one 20 mm Ho-5 cannon in the dorsal turret and one 7·92 mm Type 98 machine-gun in each of the lateral blisters—these replacing the flush-mounted gun positions of the first three aircraft.

In December 1942 suggestions were made that the Ki-67 be modified as a torpedo-bomber and accordingly on 5 January, 1943, Mitsubishi were instructed to fit torpedo racks on 100 production aircraft. To test the aircraft in its new role, the 17th and 18th Ki-67s were modified, and Major Sakamoto of the Army's Koku Shinsabu (Air Examination Department) took these two aircraft and their crews to Yokosuka Naval Air Station where torpedo launching procedures were tried out. These tests proved so successful that plans to produce only 100 torpedo-carrying Ki-67s were modified and Mitsubishi were instructed to fit torpedo racks on all Ki-67s commencing with the 161st aircraft, and the Koku Hombu agreed to release some of these aircraft for Naval service, when they were assigned the name Yasukuni, after a shrine dedicated to an Unknown Soldier.

The Army were so pleased with the aircraft that they were continually planning additional equipment and for a while its production appeared in jeopardy as there could be no agreement on a standard configuration. The demands of war finally forced the Koku Hombu to freeze the design and on 2 December, 1943, Mitsubishi were instructed to produce a single version of the aircraft—in which defensive armament was further increased by replacing the hand-held 7·92 mm machine-guns in the lateral blisters with 12·7 mm Type 1 machine-guns—as the Army Type 4 Heavy Bomber Model 1 Hiryu (Ki-67-I).

The Ki-67-I, or PEGGY as it was known to the Allies, was first flown

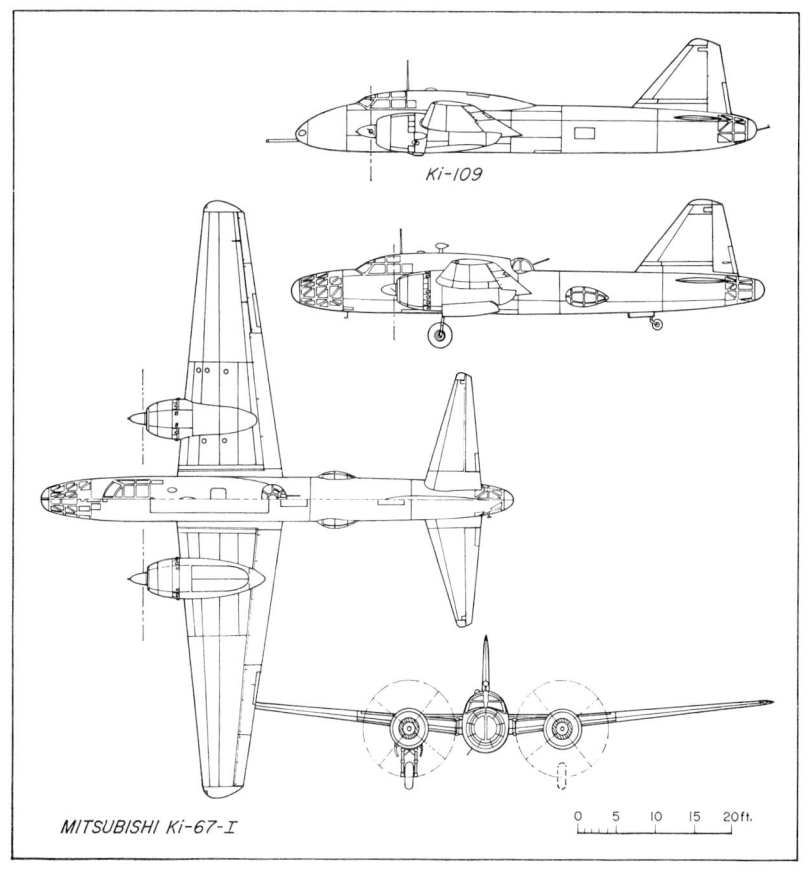

MITSUBISHI Ki-67-I

in combat by the Army's 7th and 98th Sentais and the Navy's 762nd Kokutai in torpedo attacks during the air–sea battle off Formosa in October 1944. From then on torpedo-carrying Ki-67 units of both Services operated side-by-side in many operations and were particularly active during the American landing on Okinawa. In its original role of heavy bomber the Ki-67 was operated in China, and Hamamatsu-based Hiryus, using Iwo Jima as a staging point, made repeated attacks against B-29 airfields in the Marianas.

The production of the Ki-67-I was assigned highest priority and in addition to the Mitsubishi's 5th Airframe Works at Nagoya (Oe-Machi) which had produced the first Hiryus, the following plants were included in the Ki-67 production programme: Mitsubishi's Chita and Kumamoto plants, Kawasaki Kokuki Kogyo K.K. at Gifu, Tachikawa Dai-Ichi Rikugun Kokusho at Tachikawa and Nippon Kokusai Koku Kogyo K.K. Production changes were kept to a minimum but included the replacement of the single 12·7 mm machine-gun in the tail turret by a twin-mounting, this starting with the 451st Mitsubishi-built machine, and the intended increase of the bomb-load to 1,250 kg (2,756 lb), planned for the 751st and following aircraft. However, production was seriously impaired by Allied bombings and by the earthquake of December 1944 which particularly affected engine production and only 698 Ki-67s had been built when the war ended.

Several experimental or special versions of the aircraft were designed and included:

Ha-104 Ru powered Ki-67: The 21st and 22nd Ki-67s were modified to test the turbosupercharged Ha-104 Ru radials intended for the Ki-109 heavy interceptor fighter.

Ki-67-II: Projected production version powered by two 2,400 hp Mitsubishi Ha-214 radials but not built; the 16th and 17th Ki-67s were used to flight test this type of engine.

Ki-67-I glider tug: Standard Ki-67-Is used to tow the Kokusai-built Army Experimental Transport Glider Manazuru (Crane).

Ki-67-I KAI: Modification of the Ki-67-I for suicide attack. Aircraft modified by the Tachikawa Dai-Ichi Rikugun Kokusho. All turrets removed and faired over and crew reduced to three. Long rod projecting from the nose to explode on impact either two standard 800 kg (1,764 lb) bombs or a special charge of explosives weighing 2,900 kg (6,393 lb).

I-Go-1A carrier: One specially modified Ki-67-I carrying the radio-controlled I-Go-1A anti-shipping missile under its fuselage.

Ki-69: Projected escort fighter version of the Ki-67. Not proceeded with.

Ki-97: Projected transport aircraft utilizing the wings, tail surfaces, powerplant and undercarriage of the Ki-67. Accommodation for 21 passengers. Not proceeded with.

Ki-109: Heavy fighter version, described on page 194.
Ki-112: Projected multi-seat fighter. Not proceeded with.

UNITS ALLOCATED

JAAF: 7th, 14th, 16th, 60th, 61st, 62nd, 74th, 98th and 110th Sentais. Hamamatsu Army Bomber Flying School.

JNAF: 762nd Kokutai.

TECHNICAL DATA

Description: Twin-engined heavy bomber. All-metal construction.

Accommodation: Normal crew of six to eight in enclosed cabin. Crew reduced to three for suicide attacks.

Powerplant: Two Army Type 4 eighteen-cylinder air-cooled radials (Mitsubishi Ha-104), rated at 1,900 hp for take-off, 1,810 hp at 2,200 m (7,220 ft) and 1,610 hp at 6,100 m (20,015 ft), driving constant-speed four-blade metal propellers (all Ki-67s except for the following experimental machines).

Two Mitsubishi Ha-214 eighteen-cylinder air-cooled radials, rated at 2,400 hp for take-off, 2,130 hp at 1,800 m (5,905 ft) and 1,930 hp at 8,300 m (27,230 ft), driving constant-speed four-blade metal propellers (16th and 17th Ki-67s).

Two Mitsubishi Ha-104 Ru eighteen-cylinder air-cooled radials, rated at 1,900 hp for take-off and 1,810 hp at 7,360 m (24,150 ft), driving constant-speed four-blade metal propellers (21st and 22nd Ki-67s).

Armament: One flexible 7·92 mm Type 98 machine-gun in each of the nose, and port and starboard beam positions, and one flexible 12·7 mm Type 1 machine-gun in the dorsal and tail turrets (1st, 2nd and 3rd prototypes).

One flexible 7·92 mm Type 98 machine-gun in each of the port and starboard beam positions, one flexible 12·7 mm Type 1 machine-gun in the nose and tail turrets, and one flexible 20 mm Ho-5 cannon in the dorsal turret (4th–19th Ki-67s).

One flexible 12·7 mm Type 1 machine-gun in each of the nose, port and starboard beam, and tail positions, and one flexible 20 mm Ho-5 cannon in the dorsal turret (20th–450th Ki-67s).

One flexible 12·7 mm Type 1 machine-gun in each of the nose and port and starboard beam positions, twin flexible 12·7 mm Type 1 machine-guns in the tail turret, and one flexible 20 mm Ho-5 cannon in the dorsal turret (451st and subsequent Ki-67s).

Bomb-load—normal, 500 kg (1,102 lb)
—maximum, 800 kg (1,764 lb)
—torpedo attack, one 800 kg (1,764 lb) or 1,070 kg (2,359 lb) torpedo
—suicide attack, 2,900 kg (6,393 lb).

Dimensions: Span 22·5 m (73 ft 9 $\frac{19}{16}$ in); length 18·7 m (61 ft 4 $\frac{7}{32}$ in); height 7·7 m (25 ft 3 $\frac{5}{32}$ in); wing area 65·85 sq m (708·801 sq ft).

Weights: Empty 8,649 kg (19,068 lb); loaded 13,765 kg (30,347 lb); wing loading 209 kg/sq m (42·8 lb/sq ft); power loading 3·6 kg/hp (8 lb/hp).

Performance: Maximum speed 537 km/h at 6,090 m (334 mph at 19,980 ft); cruising speed 400 km/h at 8,000 m (249 mph at 26,245 ft); climb to 6,000 m (19,685 ft) in 14 min 30 sec; service ceiling 9,470 m (31,070 ft); range—normal 2,800 km (1,740 miles), maximum 3,800 km (2,360 miles).

Production: A total of 698 Ki-67s were built as follows:

Mitsubishi Jukogyo K.K. at Nagoya, Kumamoto and Chita:
606 Ki-67s

Kawasaki Kokuki Kogyo K.K. at Gifu:
91 Ki-67s

Tachikawa Dai-Ichi Rikugun Kokusho at Tachikawa:
1 Ki-67

Nippon Kokusai Koku Kogyo K.K. at Okubo:
None (assembled 29 Mitsubishi-built Ki-67s)

One of the four Mitsubishi Ki-83 prototypes.

Mitsubishi Ki-83

The Mitsubishi Ki-83, one of the cleanest Japanese aircraft of World War II, was designed by a team led by Tomio Kubo to meet the requirements of a specification issued in May 1943 by the Koku Hombu calling for a long-range escort fighter. In answer to this specification Tomio Kubo, assisted by Engineers Mizuno, Kato and Sugiyama, first investigated the possibility of meeting the requirements with a single-engined design, the Ki-73, powered by a 2,600 hp Mitsubishi Ha-203-II twenty-four-cylinder horizontal-H liquid-cooled engine. When development problems with the Ha-203 engine delayed the programme, the Ki-73 was abandoned before construction had actually started. Yet, as captured documents led them to believe that the Ki-73 was about to enter service with the Japanese Army, the Allies gave it the code name STEVE.

After this inauspicious start, Tomio Kubo called on his experience with the Ki-46 and designed the Ki-83, an exceptionally clean all-metal mid-wing two-seat aircraft powered by two 2,200 hp Mitsubishi Ha-211 Ru turbosupercharged eighteen-cylinder air-cooled radials. Armament consisted of two 30 mm Ho-105 and two 20 mm Ho-5 cannon mounted in the lower nose of the aircraft, and the first prototype, completed in October 1944, made its maiden flight on 18 November, 1944. During successive test flights, often interrupted by Allied bombing raids and fighter sweeps, the aircraft demonstrated exceptional manoeuvrability for its size, and performance was truly spectacular. However, engine and tail vibration delayed the flight trial programme and three additional prototypes had modified engine mountings and strengthened horizontal tail surfaces with external mass balances.

The manoeuvrability and performance of the aircraft—a maximum speed of 686 km/h at 8,000 m (426 mph at 26,250 ft) being demonstrated—attracted the attention of the Japanese Navy and arrangements were made for that Service to receive some of the production aircraft, but the war ended before actual production had started. At the time of the Japanese surrender an advanced version of the aircraft, designated Ki-103, was under development while the Ki-95 was a projected version of the aircraft being developed to replace the Mitsubishi Ki-46 as a Command Reconnaissance Plane equipped with aerial cameras, armament to be reduced to two 20 mm Ho-5 cannon.

Plans for the production of the Ki-83 were never finalized, because in 1945 the JAAF had to give priority to the production of interceptor fighters. Had the war lasted longer, the Ki-83 would have been a formidable weapon as its performance compared favourably with that of the contemporary Grumman F7F Tigercat and de Havilland D.H.103 Hornet.

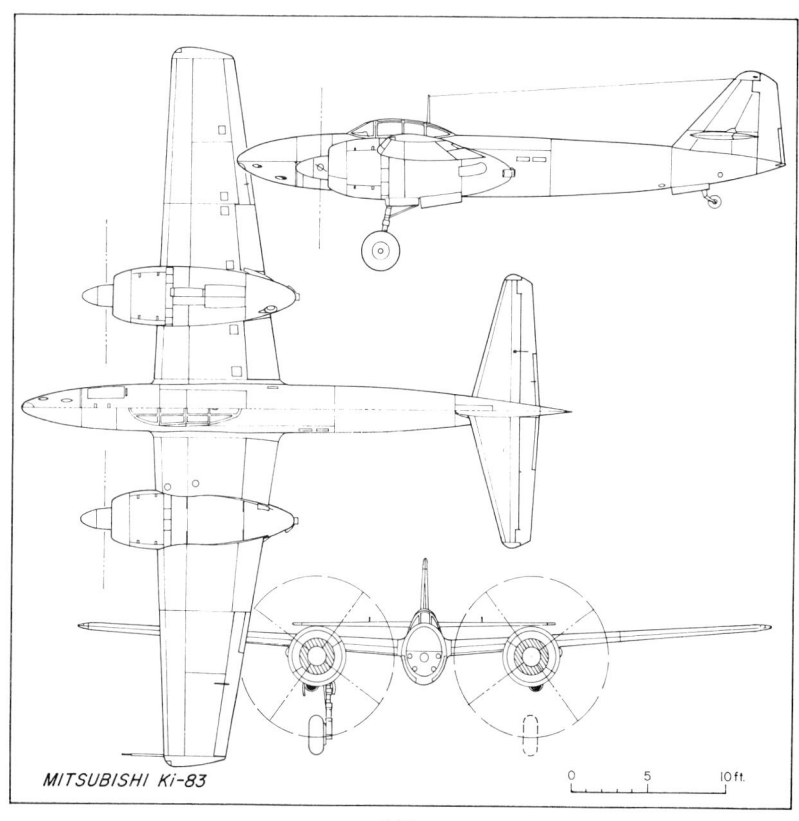

MITSUBISHI Ki-83

TECHNICAL DATA

Description: Twin-engined long-range high-altitude fighter. All-metal construction.
Accommodation: Crew of two in enclosed cockpit.
Powerplant: Two Mitsubishi Ha-211 Ru ([Ha-43] 11) eighteen-cylinder air-cooled radials, rated at 2,200 hp for take-off, 2,070 hp at 1,000 m (3,280 ft), 1,930 hp at 5,000 m (16,405 ft) and 6,400 m (21,000 ft) and 1,720 hp at 9,500 m (31,170 ft), driving constant-speed four-blade metal propellers.
Armament: Two 30 mm Ho-105 cannon and two 20 mm Ho-5 cannon in the lower forward fuselage section. Two 50 kg (110 lb) bombs carried internally.
Dimensions: Span 15·5 m (50 ft 10¼ in); length 12·5 m (41 ft 0⅛ in); height 4·6 m (15 ft 1 3/32 in); wing area 33·52 sq m (360·805 sq ft).
Weights: Empty 5,980 kg (13,184 lb); loaded 8,795 kg (19,390 lb); maximum 9,430 kg (20,790 lb); wing loading 262·4 kg/sq m (53·7 lb/sq ft); power loading 2 kg/hp (4·4 lb/hp).
Performance: Maximum speed 704·5 km/h at 9,000 m (438 mph at 29,530 ft) and 655 km/h at 5,000 m (407 mph at 16,405 ft); cruising speed 450 km/h at 4,000 m (280 mph at 13,125 ft); climb to 10,000 m (32,810 ft) in 10 min; service ceiling 12,660 m (41,535 ft); range—normal 1,953 km (1,213 miles), maximum 3,500 km (2,175 miles).
Production: Four Ki-83 prototypes built between October 1944 and May 1945 by Mitsubishi Jukogyo K.K.

Mitsubishi Ki-109

Early in the war when Japanese fighter pilots were in control of the skies, the few B-17 Flying Fortresses available in the Southwest Pacific area were the only Allied aircraft to challenge their superiority effectively. As the war developed in favour of the Allies, the longer-ranging Consolidated B-24 Liberators, better suited to the island-hopping war, replaced the B-17s. But for the Japanese the problem of attempting to destroy high flying, well protected and formidably armed bombers remained the same. The Koku Hombu were also aware of the US development of a still more formidable four-engined bomber, the Boeing B-29 Superfortress, and by 1943 they were feverishly studying every means of defence against this feared enemy aircraft.

In early 1943 the Mitsubishi Ki-67 heavy bomber then undergoing flight trials had proved that despite its size and weight it was fast and remarkably manoeuvrable. Consequently in November 1943, officers of the Rikugun Kokugijutsu Kenkyujo (Army Aerotechnical Research Institute) at Tachikawa suggested that the Ki-67 be used as a basis for a hunter–killer aircraft. The project received the designation Ki-109 and two versions were to be built: the Ki-109a, the killer, was to mount in the rear fuselage two oblique-firing 37 mm Ho-203 cannon while the Ki-109b, the hunter, was to be equipped with radar and a 40 cm searchlight. However, soon thereafter, the project was re-directed at the instigation of Major Sakamoto who suggested that a standard 75 mm Type 88 anti-aircraft cannon be mounted in the nose of a modified Ki-67. It was hoped that with this large cannon the aircraft would be able to fire on the B-29s while staying well

Mitsubishi Ki-109 with nose-mounted 75 mm Type 88 cannon.

out of range of their defensive armament. As the Koku Hombu anticipated that, initially at least, the B-29s would have to operate without fighter escort, the project was found sound and feasible and, accordingly, Mitsubishi were instructed in January 1944 to begin designing the aircraft, which retained the Ki-109 designation.

Modification of the Ki-67 to mount a 75 mm cannon in the nose was entrusted to a team led by Engineer Ozawa and the first prototype was completed in August 1944, two months after the B-29s had made their first bombing raid over Japan. Except for its nose, in the lower part of which was mounted the Type 88 cannon, the Ki-109 prototype was identical to the Ki-67 and retained the waist gun positions and dorsal and tail turrets of the bomber. Ground and inflight test firing of the heavy gun were effected by Major Makiura of the Rikugun Kokugijutsu Kenkyujo and was sufficiently successful to warrant the placing of an initial order for 44 aircraft. The first twenty-two were each to be powered by two 1,900 hp Mitsubishi Ha-104 radials but subsequent aircraft were each to receive a pair of Ha-104 Ru fitted with Ru-3 exhaust-driven turbosuperchargers to improve performance at the cruising altitude of the B-29s. These engines were actually tested on the second Ki-109 prototype, but no production aircraft were powered by Ha-104 Ru radials. Another attempt to improve climbing speed was made when a solid propellant rocket battery was installed in the rear bomb-bay of the first prototype but this scheme was abandoned.

Starting with the third Ki-109, the dorsal turret and lateral blisters were dispensed with and no bomb-bay fitted. Fifteen shells were carried for the 75 mm Type 88 cannon which was hand-loaded by the co-pilot, and the sole defensive armament consisted of a flexible 12·7 mm Type 1 machine-gun in the tail turret. The rest of the airframe and the powerplant were identical to those of the Ki-67. Despite the lack of high-altitude performance the Ki-109 was pressed into service with the 107th Sentai but, by the time enough aircraft were on hand, the B-29s had switched to low-altitude night operations.

UNITS ALLOCATED

107th Sentai.

TECHNICAL DATA

Description: Twin-engined heavy interceptor. All-metal construction.
Accommodation: Crew of four with pilot, co-pilot and radio-operator in forward cabin and gunner in rear turret.
Powerplant: Two Army Type 4 eighteen-cylinder air-cooled radials (Mitsubishi Ha-104), rated at 1,900 hp for take-off, 1,810 hp at 2,200 m (7,220 ft) and 1,610 hp at 6,100 m (20,015 ft), driving constant-speed four-blade metal propellers.
Armament: One forward-firing 75 mm Type 88 cannon and one flexible 12·7 mm Type 1 machine-gun in the tail turret.
Dimensions: Span 22·5 m (73 ft 9 18/16 in); length 17·95 m (58 ft 10 11/16 in); height 5·8 m (19 ft 1 3/32 in); wing area 65·85 sq m (708·801 sq ft).
Weights: Empty 7,424 kg (16,367 lb); loaded 10,800 kg (23,810 lb); wing loading 164 kg/sq m (33·6 lb/sq ft); power loading 2·8 kg/hp (6·3 lb/hp).
Performance: Maximum speed 550 km/h at 6,090 m (342 mph at 19,980 ft); range 2,200 km (1,367 miles).
Production: A total of 22 Ki-109s were built by Mitsubishi Jukogyo K.K. between August 1944 and March 1945.

Nakajima Ki-27

When on 7 July, 1937, hostilities broke out between Japan and China for the third time in a decade, the Japanese Army was in the midst of a re-equipment programme and had to leave the brunt of the fighting to the better equipped air elements of the Navy. At that time the JAAF was assigned the responsibility of providing air support to the advancing ground forces in Northern China and of defending the air space of the Japanese protectorate of Manchukuo. The Koku Hombu took advantage of this relatively quiet period to overhaul the Army air units and to put into service modern combat aircraft including the Army Type 97 Heavy Bomber (Mitsubishi Ki-21), the Army Type 97 and 98 Light Bombers (Mitsubishi Ki-30 and Kawasaki Ki-32), the Army Type 97 Command Reconnaissance Plane (Mitsubishi Ki-15) and the Army Type 97 Fighter (Nakajima Ki-27). The last of these was a low-wing cantilever monoplane with enclosed cockpit and fixed undercarriage which, although not as fast as the Hawker Hurricane I and Messerschmitt Bf 109B which saw service shortly before the Japanese machine, did much to turn the JAAF into an effective air force.

In 1934, the Army had issued a specification calling for a replacement type for the Army Type 92 Fighter (Kawasaki KDA-5), then standard equipment for their fighter units. In answer to this specification Kawasaki submitted their Ki-10, a refinement of their older biplane, and Nakajima entered the Ki-11, a wire-braced low-wing monoplane inspired by the Boeing P-26. Although powered by a Nakajima Ha-8 with a maximum rating of only 640 hp versus the 800 hp rating of the Kawasaki Ha-9-II of the Ki-10, the Ki-11 was considerably faster. However, the Service pilots were not yet ready for such novelties as low-wing monoplanes and enclosed cockpits, and the Ki-10, more manoeuvrable and faster climbing than the Ki-11, was selected for production as the Army Type 95 Fighter and became the JAAF's last combat biplane. Nakajima, despite their failure to obtain a production contract for the Ki-11, had acquired enough test data with this aircraft and the Ki-12, an experimental low-wing monoplane powered by a liquid-cooled Hispano-Suiza 12Ycrs with hub-mounted cannon, to be satisfied with the potential of the monoplane fighter configuration and to embark on their own on the design of a more advanced machine, the Type P.E. The P.E. design was still in its early phase when, in June 1935, the Koku Hombu instructed Mitsubishi, Kawasaki and Nakajima each to build two prototypes of advanced fighter aircraft. Nakajima's wisdom in pursuing the development of the monoplane fighter was vindicated when Kawasaki submitted their Ki-28 low-wing cantilever monoplane powered by an 800 hp Kawasaki Ha-9-IIa liquid-cooled engine, while Mitsubishi submitted the Ki-33, a version of their A5M monoplane then being manufactured for the JNAF as the Navy Type 96 Carrier Fighter. In the meantime, Nakajima had decided as a private venture to carry on with the design of their Type P.E. and to enter in the forthcoming competition a development of this machine which received the military designation Ki-27.

The single Type P.E. produced was completed in July 1936 and was followed in October 1936 by the first prototype Ki-27. Both machines, designed by T. Koyama, were low-wing cantilever monoplanes each powered by a 650 hp Nakajima Ha-1a and fitted with fixed spatted undercarriages; they differed in minor details affecting the design of the cowling, canopy, vertical tail surfaces and wheel spats. The Type P.E. was retained by Nakajima and provided useful information which was incorporated in the prototype Ki-27 during its construction. Before its retirement, the

The Nakajima Type P.E. was aerodynamically identical to the Ki-27 which first flew three months later.

A Nakajima Ki-27b in service with the Manchurian Air Force.

Type P.E. was also used to flight test the 'butterfly' combat flaps which Nakajima used with considerable success to improve the manoeuvrability of their wartime fighters. In designing the Type P.E. and the Ki-27, T. Koyama had selected an extremely light structure and made use of a new aerofoil section developed by Nakajima which gave the aircraft its remarkable manoeuvrability.

The first prototype Ki-27, flying from Ojima Airfield on 15 October, 1936, had a wing area of 16·4 sq m (176·527 sq ft) and was joined in December 1936 by a second machine on which the wing area was increased to 17·6 sq m (189·444 sq ft). Following manufacturer's trials, the two aircraft were handed over to the Rikugun Kokugijutsu Kenkyujo (Army Aerotechnical Research Institute) at Tachikawa where they were pitted against the Mitsubishi Ki-33 and Kawasaki Ki-28. During competitive trials, the second Ki-27 reached a maximum speed of 468 km/h at 4,000 m (291 mph at 13,125 ft) versus the Ki-28's speed of 485 km/h (301 mph) at the same altitude and the Ki-33's 474 km/h at 3,000 m (295 mph at 9,845 ft). An altitude of 5,000 m (16,405 ft) was reached in 5 min 10 sec by the Ki-28, in 5 min 38 sec by the Ki-27 and in 5 min 56 sec by the Ki-33. Despite its slightly inferior performance the Ki-27 was found the best of the three because of its superlative manoeuvrability, and ten pre-production aircraft, built between June and December 1937, were ordered. During the competitive trials, the incidence of the wings of the second Ki-27 had been increased by 1·5 degrees to improve handling characteristics and, despite its larger wing area, the aircraft was only 7 km/h (4·35 mph) slower than the less manoeuvrable first prototype. To improve manoeuvrability further it was decided to increase the wing span of the pre-production aircraft from 10·4 m (34 ft $1\frac{7}{16}$ in) to 11·31 m (37 ft $1\frac{1}{4}$ in) and the wing area from 17·6 sq m (189·444 sq ft) to 18·56 sq m (199·777 sq ft). Although retaining the long streamlined forward section housing the telescopic gunsight, the pre-production aircraft's canopy was modified by replacing the metal headrest by a fixed clear vision section and by fitting rearward sliding panels over the cockpit. Tests were completed late in 1937 and the aircraft was placed in production as the Army Type 97 Fighter Model A (Ki-27a).

Like the pre-production aircraft, the production Ki-27a was fitted with the larger wings, but the canopy was once again modified by adopting a more conventional windshield and using a metal-covered rear section, while the more powerful Nakajima Ha-1b rated at 780 hp at 2,900 m (9,515 ft) was fitted. The aircraft carried a pair of synchronized 7·7 mm Type 89 machine-guns mounted in the upper fuselage forward decking. In March 1938 the aircraft saw operation over Northern China where they quickly wrested control of the sky away from the hard-pressed Chinese forces. Shortly thereafter, the Imperial Japanese Army reorganized their air units by replacing the mixed units made up of fighter, bomber and reconnaissance aircraft with specialized sentais made up of only one type of aircraft, and the 59th Fighter Sentai, activated at Kagamigahara, Gifu Prefecture, on 1 July, 1938, was the first unit to be equipped exclusively with Army Type 97 Fighters. As fast as deliveries allowed, Ki-27s were delivered to the 64th, 13th, 4th, 5th and 11th Sentais in that order before September 1938. As production gained tempo the Ki-27a gave place to the Ki-27b characterized by the clear vision panels of the canopy's rear section, modified oil cooler, and provision under the wing centre-section for four 25 kg (55 lb) bombs. These bombs could be replaced by two 130 litre (28·6 Imp gal) slipper drop tanks lying flat under the wings on both sides of the fuselage. For gunnery training a cine-gun could be attached on the port wing near the root. Production of the Ki-27b was also entrusted to Mansyu Hikoki Seizo K.K. (Manchurian Aeroplane Manufacturing Co Ltd) at Harbin, Manchukuo.

Nakajima Ki-27b Army fighters of the 59th Sentai, 2nd Chutai, during the Nomonhan incident. (*US Navy Department*.)

A Nakajima Ki-27b Army Type 97 Fighter Model B. (*US Navy Department.*)

When on 4 May, 1939, fighting began on the Manchukuo/Outer Mongolia border in the Nomonhan area between the Japanese and Russian forces, the Japanese Army committed, along with other air units, five Ki-27 equipped Fighter Sentais—the 1st, 11th, 24th, 59th and 64th—mustering some 80 machines. At the peak of the fighting, Japanese forces had increased to 200 fighters, mostly Ki-27s but including also some Ki-10s. When hostilities ceased, the Japanese claimed to have shot down no fewer than 1,340 Russian aeroplanes and destroyed a further 30 Soviet machines on the ground, and they reported that the Russians had committed up to 3,000 aircraft during the five-month Nomonhan Incident. The Russian counter-claim of committing only 450 aircraft suggests that the Japanese overstated their claims to hide what was actually a defeat, as they admitted losing 120 aircraft against Russian reports that 215 Nipponese planes had been destroyed. The Nomonhan Incident was settled

A Nakajima Ki-27b after capture by Chinese Forces. The Chinese blue and white national markings can be seen beneath the wing.

A formation of Nakajima Ki-27b fighters of the 84th Dokuritsu Dai Shijugo Chutai. The engine cowlings and fuselage stripes were red. (*Aireview*.)

NAKAJIMA Ki-27b

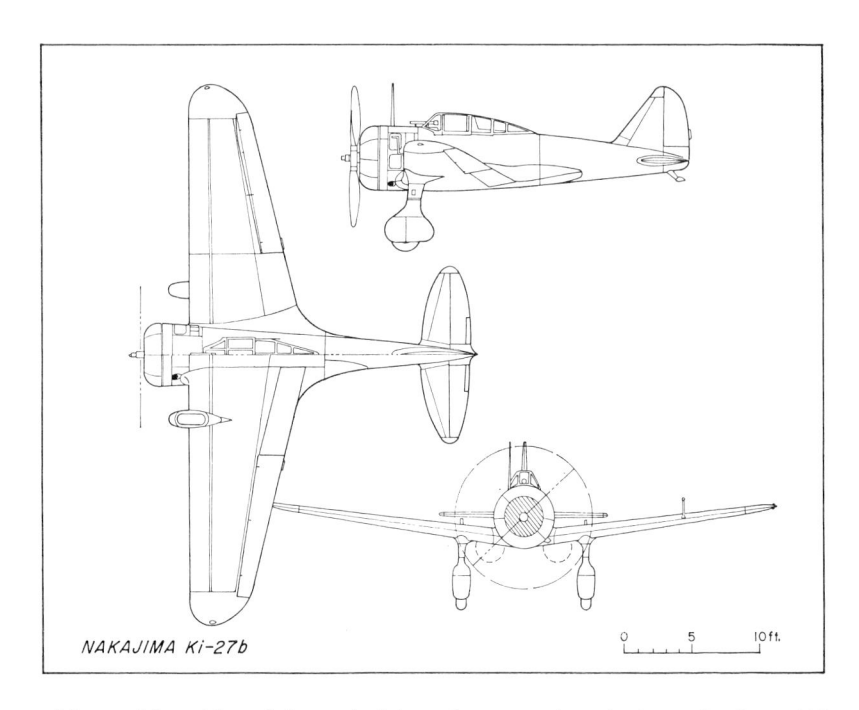

without either side gaining a decisive advantage, but the loss of at least 120 aircraft and their experienced crews was disastrous for the Japanese; however, the fighting had given them an opportunity to test their aircraft against a determined adversary and the Ki-27 had proved itself to be superior to the Russian Polikarpov I-15 fighter biplanes but hard pressed against the faster Polikarpov I-16 fighter monoplanes.

In December 1941, when the Japanese began operations against the Allies, the 1st, 11th, 50th, 54th and 77th Sentais flying Army Type 97 Fighters were deployed in support of the invasion of the Philippines, Burma, Malaya and the Netherlands East Indies, while other Ki-27 equipped Sentais were operating on the Chinese mainland, in Manchukuo and in Japan. Although obsolescent the aircraft obtained some remarkable successes against the overwhelmed Allied forces. The Ki-27 was assigned the Allied code names ABDUL (China–Burma–India theatre) and NATE (Southwest Pacific Area theatre), the latter being exclusively used from 1943 onwards. As the JAAF expanded, the Ki-27 was delivered to many new units in Japan, but most of these re-equipped with modern machines before deployment overseas while the remainder of the Ki-27s provided air defence for the Japanese homeland until 1943. However, throughout the war Ki-27s served as front-line fighters with the Manchurian Air Force. As the aircraft were replaced by Ki-43, Ki-44 and Ki-61 fighters, the Ki-27s were increasingly used as advanced trainers. To suit the Ki-27 to its new duty, the wheel spats were removed, a tailwheel replaced the skid previously used and, so modified, the aircraft was redesignated Army Type 97 Fighter Trainer. In the last months of the war some Ki-27 trainers were used in suicide attacks carrying a 500 kg (1,102 lb) bomb-load.

In 1940, as the Ki-43 was experiencing considerable difficulties, Nakajima designed a lightweight version of the Ki-27 and two machines of this type, the Ki-27 KAI, were built in July and August 1940. Maximum speed was increased to 475 km/h (295 mph) and wing loading reduced to 80 kg/sq m (16·4 lb/sq ft) but further development was not warranted as the Ki-43 had finally overcome its teething troubles.

UNITS ALLOCATED

1st, 4th, 5th, 9th, 11th, 13th, 18th, 21st, 24th, 33rd, 50th, 54th, 59th, 63rd, 64th, 70th, 77th, 78th, 85th, 87th, 144th and 246th Sentais; 9th, 10th, 28th, 47th and 84th Dokuritsu Dai Shijugo Chutais; 17th, 27th and 32nd Kyo-iku Hikotais; 5th Lensei Hikotai; Akeno Army Fighter Training School.

TECHNICAL DATA

Description: Single-seat light fighter. All-metal construction with fabric-covered control surfaces.
Accommodation: Pilot in enclosed cockpit.
Powerplant: One 650 hp Army Type 97 nine-cylinder air-cooled radial (Nakajima Ha-1a), rated at 710 hp for take-off and 650 hp at 2,000 m (6,560 ft), driving a variable-pitch two-blade propeller (Type P.E., Ki-27 prototypes and pre-production aircraft).

One 650 hp Army Type 97 nine-cylinder air-cooled radial (Nakajima Ha-1b), rated at 710 hp for take-off and 780 hp at 2,900 m (9,515 ft), driving a variable-pitch two-blade propeller (Ki-27a, Ki-27b, Ki-27 KAI and Ki-27 Trainer).

Armament: Two synchronized 7·7 mm Type 89 machine-guns (all Ki-27 versions).
　External stores: four 25 kg (55 lb) bombs, or two 130 litre (28·6 Imp gal) drop tanks (Ki-27b, Ki-27 KAI and Ki-27 Trainer).
Dimensions: Span 11·31 m (37 ft 1¼ in); length 7·53 m (24 ft 8 $\frac{7}{16}$ in); height 3·25 m (10 ft 7 $\frac{19}{32}$ in); wing area 18·56 sq m (199·777 sq ft).
Weights: Empty 1,110 kg (2,447 lb); loaded 1,790 kg (3,946 lb); wing loading 96·5 kg/sq m (19·75 lb/sq ft); power loading 2·35 kg/hp (5·2 lb/hp).
Performance: Maximum speed 470 km/h at 3,500 m (292 mph at 11,480 ft); cruising speed 350 km/h at 3,500 m (217 mph at 11,480 ft); climb to 5,000 m (16,405 ft) in 5 min 22 sec; range—normal 627 km (390 miles), maximum 1,710 km (1,060 miles).
Production: A total of 3,399 Ki-27s were built as follows:
　Nakajima Hikoki K.K. at Ota:
　　1 P.E. (July 1936)
　　2 Ki-27 prototypes (Oct–Dec 1936)
　　10 Ki-27 pre-production aircraft (June–Dec 1937)
　　2,005 Ki-27a and Ki-27b production aircraft, including Ki-27 Trainer conversions (Dec 1937–Dec 1942)
　　2 Ki-27 KAI prototypes (July–Aug 1940)
　Mansyu Hikoki Seizo K.K. at Harbin:
　　1,379 Ki-27a and Ki-27b production aircraft.

An early production Nakajima AT-2 transport of Japan Air Transport. This was the forerunner of the Japanese Army Ki-34. (*US National Archives.*)

Nakajima Ki-34

Having acquired the manufacturing rights for the Douglas DC-2, in 1935 Nakajima undertook the design of a smaller twin-engined aircraft for use on short-range light traffic routes. Engineer Akegawa was assigned the responsibility of designing the aircraft then known as the Nakajima Aerial Transport No. 1, or AT-1, and took his inspiration from the Douglas DC-2, Northrop 5A and Clark GA-43. During its design the aircraft was extensively modified and when completed in 1936 was designated Nakajima AT-2, the letter A then standing for Akegawa, the chief engineer's name. Powered by two 580 hp Nakajima Kotobuki 2-1 radials driving fixed-pitch two-blade propellers, the prototype was first flown on 12 September, 1936, from Ojima Airfield. During its tests the aircraft was flown by pilots from the manufacturer, Japan Air Transport Co, Manchurian Airlines Co, the Japanese Civil Aeronautics Authority and the two military Services. The AT-2 demonstrated excellent performance and was quite stable, but minor problems arose with engine cooling, equipment and undercarriage retraction mechanism. These deficiencies were corrected on the production machines and, powered by two 710 hp Nakajima Kotobuki 41 engines, thirty-two aircraft were built between 1937 and 1940 for Dai Nippon Koku K.K. (Greater Japan Air Lines Co Ltd) and Manchurian Airlines Co with which they served until the end of the war.

In 1937, the aircraft was also adopted by the JAAF as a communication and paratroop transport aircraft and the Army machines were designated Army Type 97 Transport or Ki-34. Powered by two 710 hp Nakajima Ha-1b engines enclosed in smooth NACA-type cowlings similar to those fitted to late production civil AT-2s, nineteen Ki-34s were built by Nakajima between 1937 and 1940. However, more Ki-34s were manufactured by Tachikawa Hikoki K.K. which delivered 299 machines of this type. Some Ki-34s were handed over to the Japanese Navy and were designated

NAKAJIMA Ki-34

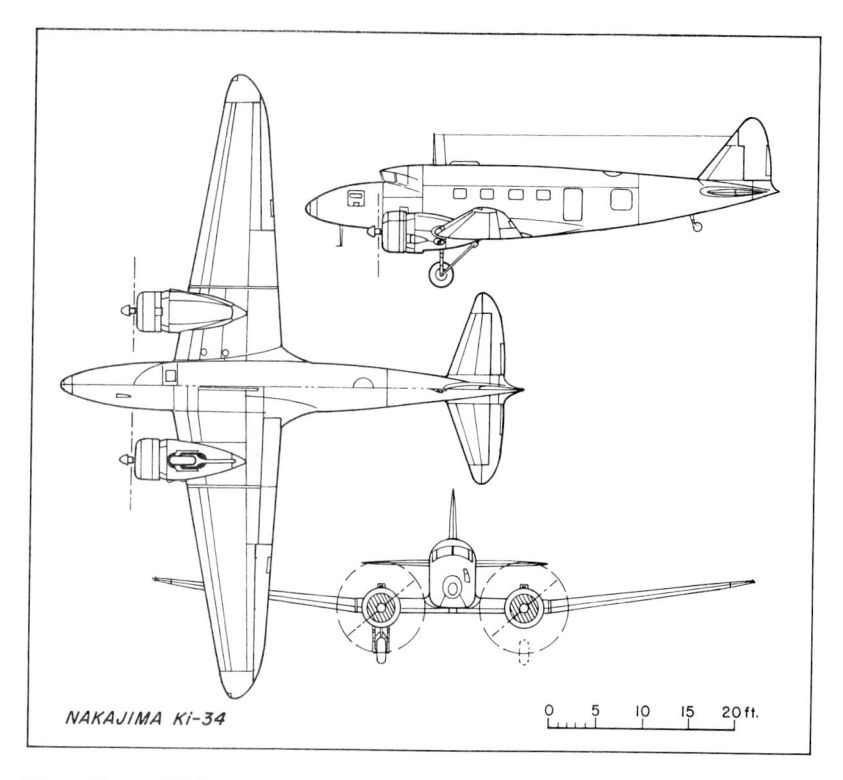

Navy Type AT-2 Transport (Nakajima L1N1) by that Service. The code name THORA applied to the military and civil machines alike.

TECHNICAL DATA

Description: Twin-engined transport aircraft. All-metal construction with fabric-covered control surfaces.
Accommodation: Crew of three and eight passengers in enclosed cabin.
Powerplant: Two 580 hp Nakajima Kotobuki 2-1 nine-cylinder air-cooled radials, driving fixed-pitch two-blade wooden propellers (AT-2 prototype).

Two Nakajima Kotobuki 41 or Nakajima Ha-1b nine-cylinder air-cooled radials, rated at 710 hp for take-off and 780 hp at 2,800 m (9,185 ft), driving variable-pitch two-blade propellers (production AT-2, L1N1 and Ki-34).

Dimensions: Span 19·916 m (65 ft 0⅛ in); length 15·3 m (50 ft 2⅜ in); height 4·15 m (13 ft 7⅜ in); wing area 49·2 sq m (529·582 sq ft).
Weights: Empty 3,500 kg (7,716 lb); loaded 5,250 kg (11,574 lb); wing loading 106·7 kg/sq m (21·9 lb/sq ft); power loading 3·7 kg/hp (8·15 lb/hp).
Performance: Maximum speed 360 km/h at 3,360 m (224 mph at 11,025 ft); cruising speed 310 km/h (193 mph); climb to 3,000 m (9,840 ft) in 6 min 38 sec; service ceiling 7,000 m (22,965 ft); range 1,200 km (745 miles).
Production: A total of 351 AT-2, Ki-34 and L1N1 were built as follows:

Nakajima Hikoki K.K. at Ota:
    1 AT-2 prototype (Oct 1936)
    32 AT-2 production aircraft (1937–40)
    19 Ki-34 and L1N1 production aircraft (1937–40)

Tachikawa Hikoki K.K. at Tachikawa:
    299 Ki-34 and L1N1 production aircraft (1939–42)

A Nakajima Ki-43-IIb Hayabusa. (*Copyright 'Maru'*.)

Nakajima Ki-43 Hayabusa (Peregrine Falcon)

In early December 1941, the Western Powers, remaining blind to the ominous war signs and confident in their technical superiority, possessed only outdated fighters to defend their possessions in the Pacific. Relying on wholly inaccurate and incomplete intelligence reports and believing that no fighters with retractable undercarriages had yet attained operational status with the Imperial Japanese Army, the future Allies had despatched to Southeast Asia and the Pacific only those aircraft which had become obsolete in the air war over Europe.

With the entry of Japan into the war the Japanese Army revealed themselves as a far more dangerous enemy than expected. One of their trumps was a new single-seat aircraft fitted with a retractable undercarriage, the Army Type 1 Fighter Model 1 Hayabusa (Peregrine Falcon), which made its combat début over Burma and the Malay peninsula during the early weeks of the war.

Design work on the Hayabusa began in December 1937 when the Army, giving up their long-standing policy of awarding competitive contracts to Japanese manufacturers, instructed Nakajima Hikoki K.K. to design a single-seat fighter to supersede the Army Type 97 Fighter (Nakajima Ki-27). The specification, quite exacting by Japanese standards, called for a fighter with (1) a maximum speed of 500 km/h (311 mph); (2) a climb rate of 5 min to 5,000 m (16,405 ft); (3) a range of 800 km (500 miles); (4) an armament of two 7·7 mm machine-guns; and (5) manoeuvrability at least equal to that of the Ki-27.

To meet these stringent requirements Nakajima assembled a team of designers led by Hideo Itokawa. Within one year the first prototype (c/n 4301) was completed at Nakajima's Ota plant and, following its secret roll-out on 12 December, 1938, flew for the first time early the following month from Ojima Airfield. Two further prototypes (c/ns 4302 and 4303) were completed in February and March 1939 and joined the first aircraft in the company's flight test programme. With the exception of minor problems, the test programme went smoothly and soon after the machines were handed over to the JAAF for Service trials.

The three prototypes were each powered by a 925 hp Nakajima Ha-25 double-row fourteen-cylinder radial with single-speed supercharger and carried an armament of two 7·7 mm Type 89 machine-guns. These aircraft were distinguishable by the lack of engine cowling gills, the metal panels in the rear cockpit hood, the cockpit-mounted radio antenna mast, a fully retractable main undercarriage and a telescopic gunsight protruding through the windshield.

Although the Ki-43 met the performance requirements of the JAAF, Nakajima were criticized by Service pilots for failing to meet the manoeuvrability requirement. To most Army pilots the retractable undercarriage was a purely technical luxury, adding weight, and they believed that future air combats would be fought as classic dog-fights. For a while the future of the Ki-43 was in doubt. However, the JAAF decided to conduct further testing with ten Service trials aircraft built by Nakajima between November 1939 and September 1940. C/ns 4304 to 4310 inclusive were basically similar to the three prototypes except for minor equipment changes and the fitting of a new all-round-vision canopy. An experimental Nakajima Ha-105 engine with two-speed supercharger was also installed on the second Service trials machine (c/n 4305) while c/n 4310 mounted a pair of 12·7 mm Ho-103 machine-guns.

The twelfth prototype Nakajima Ki-43 after suffering an undercarriage failure on landing.

A Nakajima Ki-43-Ia Hayabusa (Peregrine Falcon) of the Akeno Fighter Training School. (*Aireview*.)

The next Service trials aircraft (c/n 4311) was fitted with 'butterfly' combat flaps which could be extended in action to increase control sensitivity, to provide greater lift and to make possible a much tighter turning circle. This modification proved so effective that Service pilots commented favourably on the aircraft's handling characteristics. C/n 4313 had an alclad-treated duralumin outer skin, cowling gills, and a radio mast on the starboard side of the fuselage—these modifications being previously tested on the ninth Service trials machine (c/n 4312)—and was powered by a Ha-105 radial and armed with two 12·7 mm Ho-103 machine-guns. It also incorporated a new fuselage of smaller diameter and re-designed tail surfaces and wings similar to those of the production aircraft.

A Nakajima Ki-43-Ib carrying United States markings. The oil cooler is mounted within the engine cowling.

Following intensive tests of these aircraft, the Koku Hombu agreed that the use of butterfly combat flaps sufficiently improved the Ki-43's manoeuvrability to warrant a production order for a version using a similar airframe to that of the last Service trials machine (c/n 4313) but powered by a 950 hp Army Type 99 radial, the production version of the Nakajima Ha-25. The initial production variant, designated Army Type 1 Fighter Model 1A and named Hayabusa, was fitted with a fixed-pitch two-blade wooden propeller which was soon replaced with a two-pitch two-blade metal unit (Hamilton type). Two synchronized 7·7 mm Type 89 machine-guns were mounted in the upper cowling and two attachment points for fuel tanks were located under the wing centre-section behind and inboard of the main undercarriage units. Aircraft of this type were initially delivered to the 59th and 64th Sentais which, following training in Japan, moved to China with forty aircraft shortly before the war started.

This variant was followed on the assembly lines by the Ki-43-Ib, or Army Type 1 Fighter Model 1B, and by the Army Type 1 Fighter Model 1C (Ki-43-Ic). These aircraft differed from the Ki-43-Ia solely in their armament comprising respectively one 12·7 mm Type 1 (Ho-103) machine-gun and one 7·7 mm Type 89 machine-gun, and two 12·7 mm Type 1 machine-guns.

A Nakajima Ki-43-Ic Army Type 1 Fighter Model 1C. (*US Navy Department.*)

Early war operations established the Hayabusa as one of the most feared Japanese aircraft despite its lack of pilot and fuel tank protection and its light armament. When code names were first allocated to Japanese aircraft the Ki-43 retained much of its mystery and became known as OSCAR in the Southwest Pacific theatre and as JIM in the China–Burma–India theatre. JIM was assigned to a 'Type 1 retractable gear fighter' thought to be a derivative of NATE; OSCAR was the code name finally retained when it was found that JIM was actually the same aircraft.

Shortly after the Ki-43-I's service début five airframes were modified to mount the 1,150 hp Type 1 engine (Nakajima Ha-115, a development of the earlier Ha-25) with a two-speed supercharger and driving a constant-speed three-blade metal propeller. First flown in February 1942, the five Ki-43-II prototypes were followed by three identical pre-production machines. Except for minor engine teething troubles flight trials were

A Nakajima Ki-43-IIb Army Type 1 Fighter Model 2B. (*US Navy Department.*)

entirely satisfactory and the improved model entered production as the Army Type 1 Fighter Model 2A (Ki-43-IIa) in November 1942. The Ki-43-IIa differed from the Model 1 in several respects. The supercharger air intake was moved from under the cowling to its upper lip while the carburettor intake remained under the cowling. The wing span was reduced by 0·6 m (1 ft 11⅝ in) and wing area by 0·6 sq m (6·46 sq ft) to improve speed at low and medium altitude. Other minor changes included the heightening of the windscreen and canopy, the fitting of a new reflector gunsight and the strengthening of the wing attachment points to carry 250 kg (551 lb) bombs. Pilot's protection was introduced in the form of 13 mm head and back armour plating, and a rudimentary form of self-sealing fuel tank was installed in the wings.

Early in its production life the Ki-43-IIa had its carburettor intake deepened. However, comparatively few aircraft of this variant were built and the mass production version of Hayabusa was the Army Type 1

A Nakajima Ki-43-IIb Hayabusa photographed in Arizona during the 1950s.

Fighter Model 2B (Ki-43-IIb). Identical to the -IIa apart from minor equipment changes, the -IIb was initially identified by further modifications of the carburettor intake. The oil cooler, which so far had been mounted in a ring within the cowling ahead of the engine and around the propeller shaft just behind the spinner, was replaced by a honeycomb unit incorporated in a still deeper carburettor intake. Late production Ki-43-IIbs had their wing attachment points moved outboard of the main gear primarily to prevent bombs from crashing into the propeller during dive-bombing attacks at steep angles, while still later machines had the oil cooler removed from the carburettor intake and relocated under the centre fuselage. All these modifications progressively introduced on the Ki-43-IIb were standardized on the next variant to attain production status, the Ki-43-II KAI. This aircraft was also fitted with individual exhaust stacks

A Nakajima Ki-43-II KAI Hayabusa captured on Luzon in 1945. (*US National Archives.*)

offering some thrust augmentation and replacing the exhaust collector ring of earlier versions. Minor airframe modifications were incorporated to ease production and maintenance.

Soon after the introduction of the Ki-43-IIa, the JAAF endeavoured to augment Nakajima's production of the Hayabusa by selecting two additional manufacturing facilities, the Tachikawa Dai-Ichi Rikugun Kokusho (First Army Air Arsenal) and the Tachikawa Hikoki K.K. (Tachikawa Aeroplane Co Ltd), both at Tachikawa. However, the first of these did not have enough skilled personnel to cope with mass production of fighter aircraft and was instructed to cease production after delivering forty-nine Ki-43-IIas, mostly built from components supplied by Nakajima, between October 1942 and November 1943. Tachikawa Hikoki K.K. were better prepared to mass produce modern fighters and built 2,629 Hayabusas starting in May 1943.

The last variant designed by Nakajima was the Ki-43-IIIa of which ten prototypes were built, starting in May 1944. Similar in airframe and armament to the Ki-43-II KAI, it was powered by a Nakajima Ha-115-II

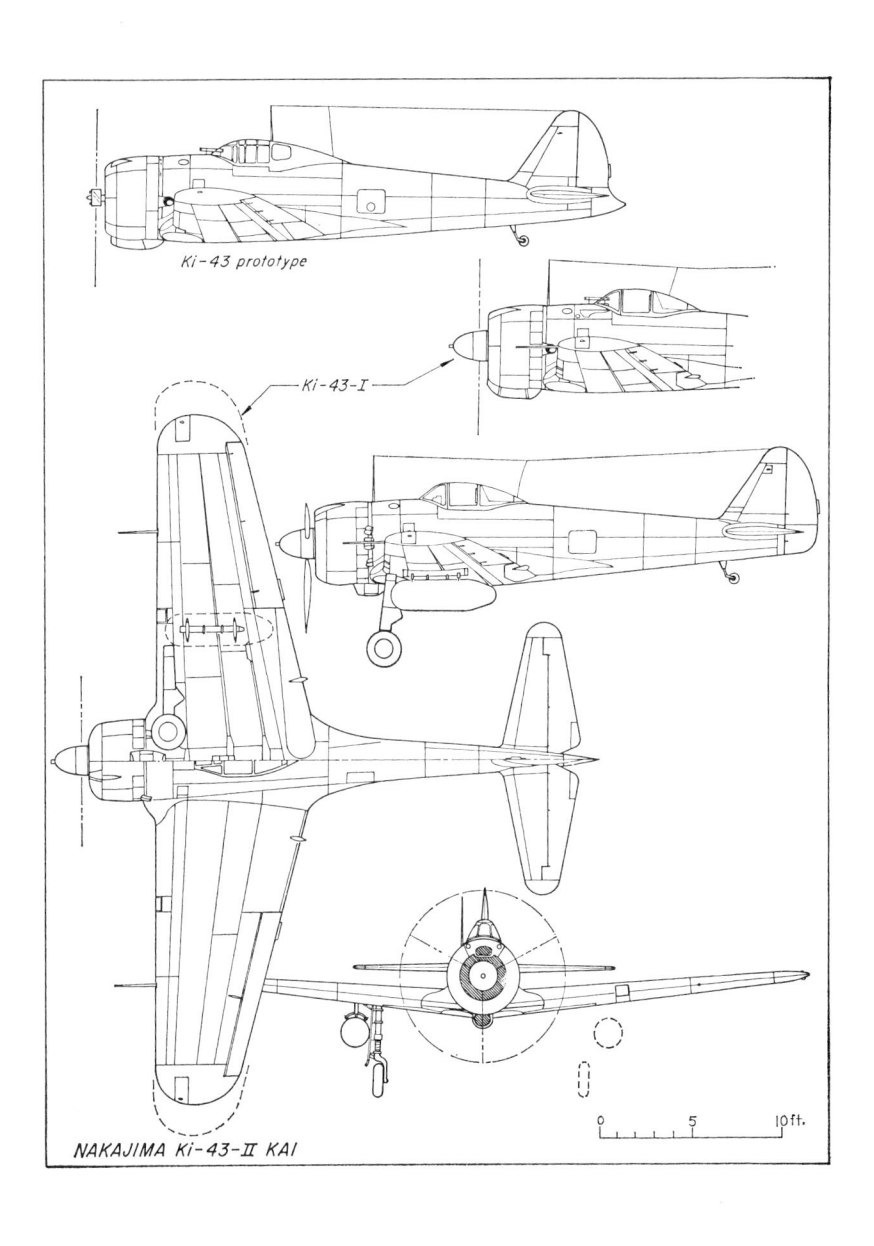

Ki-43 prototype

Ki-43-I

NAKAJIMA Ki-43-II KAI

0　　5　　10 ft.

rated at 1,230 hp at 2,800 m (9,185 ft). Production aircraft, designated Army Type 1 Fighter Model 3A, were built by Tachikawa Hikoki K.K., which company also built two prototypes of the Ki-43-IIIb, a specialized interceptor fighter, which was still undergoing tests at the end of the war. To improve climbing speed and overall performance at high altitude, a 1,250 hp Mitsubishi [Ha-33] 42 (Ha-112) was fitted while the pair of 12·7 mm Type 1 machine-guns, which constituted the standard fixed armament of Hayabusa since the Ki-43-Ic, was replaced by two 20 mm Ho-5 cannon.

Numerically, the Hayabusa was the most important aircraft of the JAAF and as such served on every front to which that Service was committed. In the closing stage of the war it had been replaced by newer types in most front-line units, and the type was extensively used on taiatari, or suicide, missions. The Ki-43-I was also operated by the Royal Thai Air Force during the war, a few being supplied to the puppet Thai government and used for limited operations against the US 14th Air Force in Southern China.

After the war, salvaged Hayabusas were flown by pilots of the Indonesian People's Security Force against the Dutch and, for a brief period only, by pilots of the French Groupes de Chasse I/7 and II/7 against Communist insurgents in Indo-China.

UNITS ALLOCATED

1st, 11th, 13th, 17th, 18th, 19th, 20th, 21st, 23rd, 24th, 25th, 26th, 30th, 31st, 33rd, 48th, 50th, 54th, 59th, 63rd, 64th, 65th, 71st, 72nd, 73rd, 77th, 101st, 102nd, 103rd, 104th, 112th, 203rd, 204th and 248th Sentais; 1st, 2nd, 4th, 5th, 13th, 14th, 17th, 19th, 24th, 26th, 47th and 71st Dokuritsu Dai Shijugo Chutais. Akeno, Hitachi and Kumagaya Army Fighter Training Schools.

TECHNICAL DATA

Description: Single-seat fighter and fighter bomber. All-metal construction with fabric-covered control surfaces.

Accommodation: Pilot in enclosed cockpit.

Powerplant: One 950 hp Army Type 99 fourteen-cylinder air-cooled radial (Nakajima Ha-25), rated at 980 hp for take-off and 970 hp at 3,400 m (11,155 ft), driving a fixed-pitch two-blade wooden propeller (Ki-43 prototypes and Service trials aircraft, and Ki-43-Ia) or two-pitch two-blade metal propeller (Ki-43-Ia, -Ib and -Ic).

One 1,100 hp Nakajima Ha-105 fourteen-cylinder air-cooled radial, driving a two-blade metal propeller (2nd and 10th Service trials Ki-43).

One Army Type 1 fourteen-cylinder air-cooled radial (Nakajima Ha-115), rated at 1,150 hp for take-off, 1,150 hp at 2,450 m (8,040 ft) and 980 hp at 5,600 m (18,375 ft), driving a constant-speed three-blade metal propeller (all versions of the Ki-43-II).

One 1,150 hp Army Type 1 fourteen-cylinder air-cooled radial (Nakajima Ha-115-II), rated at 1,190 hp for take-off, 1,230 hp at 2,800 m (9,185 ft) and 950 hp at 6,800 m (22,310 ft), driving a constant-speed three-blade metal propeller (Ki-43-IIIa).

One 1,250 hp Mitsubishi [Ha-33] 42 (Ha-112) fourteen-cylinder air-cooled radial, rated at 1,300 hp for take-off, 1,200 hp at 3,000 m (9,845 ft) and 1,100 hp at 6,200 m (20,340 ft), driving a constant-speed three-blade metal propeller (Ki-43-IIIb).

Armament: Two 7·7 mm Type 89 machine-guns (Ki-43-Ia).

One 7·7 mm Type 89 machine-gun and one 12·7 mm Type 1 (Ho-103) machine-gun (Ki-43-Ib).

Two 12·7 mm Type 1 (Ho-103) machine-guns (Ki-43-Ic, Ki-43-IIa, Ki-43-IIb, Ki-43-II KAI and Ki-43-IIIa).

Two 20 mm Ho-5 cannon (Ki-43-IIIb).

External stores: two 15 kg (33 lb bombs) (Ki-43-I)
two 30 kg (66 lb) or 250 kg (551 lb) bombs (Ki-43-II and -III)
two 200 litre (44 Imp gal) drop tanks (all versions).

	Ki-43-Ia	Ki-43-IIb	Ki-43-IIIa
Dimensions:			
Span	11·437 m	10·84 m	10·84 m
	(37 ft 6 5/16 in)	(35 ft 6¾ in)	(35 ft 6¾ in)
Length	8·832 m	8·92 m	8·92 m
	(28 ft 11¾ in)	(29 ft 3 5/16 in)	(29 ft 3 5/16 in)
Height	3·27 m	3·27 m	3·27 m
	(10 ft 8¾ in)	(10 ft 8¾ in)	(10 ft 8¾ in)
Wing area	22 sq m	21·4 sq m	21·4 sq m
	(236·805 sq ft)	(230·367 sq ft)	(230·367 sq ft)
Weights:			
Empty	1,580 kg	1,910 kg	1,920 kg
	(3,483 lb)	(4,211 lb)	(4,233 lb)
Loaded	2,048 kg	2,590 kg	2,560 kg
	(4,515 lb)	(5,710 lb)	(5,644 lb)
Maximum	2,583 kg	2,925 kg	3,060 kg
	(5,695 lb)	(6,450 lb)	(6,746 lb)
Wing loading	93·1 kg/sq m	121 kg/sq m	119·7 kg/sq m
	(19 lb/sq ft)	(28 lb/sq ft)	(24·5 lb/sq ft)
Power loading	2·1 kg/hp	2·25 kg/hp	2·1 kg/hp
	(4·6 lb/hp)	(5 lb/hp)	(4·6 lb/hp)
Performance:			
Maximum speed	495 km/h at 4,000 m	530 km/h at 4,000 m	576 km/h at 6,680 m
	(308 mph at 13,125 ft)	(329 mph at 13,125 ft)	(358 mph at 21,920 ft)
Cruising speed	320 km/h at 2,500 m	440 km/h	442 km/h
	(199 mph at 8,200 ft)	(273 mph)	(275 mph)
Climb to	5,000 m (16,405 ft)	5,000 m (16,405 ft)	5,000 m (16,405 ft)
in	5 min 30 sec	5 min 49 sec	5 min 19 sec
Service ceiling	11,750 m (38,500 ft)	11,200 m (36,750 ft)	11,400 m (37,400 ft)
Range—normal	—	1,760 km (1,095 miles)	2,120 km (1,320 miles)
—maximum	1,200 km (745 miles)	3,200 km (1,990 miles)	3,200 km (1,990 miles)

Production: A total of 5,919 Ki-43s were manufactured as follows:

Nakajima Hikoki K.K. at Ota:

    3 Ki-43 prototypes (Dec 1938–Mar 1939)
   10 Ki-43 Service trials aircraft (Nov 1939–Sept 1940)
 716 Ki-43-I production aircraft (Apr 1941–Feb 1943)
    5 Ki-43-II prototypes (Feb–May 1942)
    3 Ki-43-II Service trials aircraft (June–Aug 1942)
2,492 Ki-43-II production aircraft (Nov 1942–Oct 1944)
  10 Ki-43-IIIa prototypes (May 1944–Aug 1945)

3,239

Tachikawa Hikoki K.K. at Tachikawa:

2,629 Ki-43-II and Ki-43-IIIa production aircraft (May 1943–Aug 1945)
    2 Ki-43-IIIb prototypes (spring 1945)

Tachikawa Dai-Ichi Rikugun Kokusho at Tachikawa:

  49 Ki-43-IIa production aircraft (Oct 1942–Nov 1943).

Nakajima Ki-44 Shoki (Devil-Queller)

When China-based B-29s of the US XX Bomber Command, soon joined by Marianas-based Superfortresses of the US XXI Bomber Command, began their bombing campaign against the Japanese mainland, the Japanese Army had only one type of interceptor fighter on strength: the Army Type 2 Single-seat Fighter Model 2B Shoki (Devil-Queller) or Ki-44-IIb. Reaching an altitude of 5,000 m (16,405 ft) in 4 min 17 sec, it was the fastest climbing Japanese fighter and demonstrated its superior performance in the defence of Japan's Home Islands.

Shortly after instructing Nakajima to proceed with the design of the Ki-43, the Koku Hombu gave them their specification for an interceptor fighter. In a pronounced departure from previous Japanese standards, speed and climb rate were emphasized at the expense of manoeuvrability. The Ki-44, as the project became known, was required to climb to 4,000 m (13,125 ft) in less than 5 min, to reach a speed of 600 km/h (373 mph) at that altitude and to carry an armament of two 7·7 mm and two 12·7 mm

The first Nakajima Ki-44 (c/n 4401). The engine outlet louvres can be seen immediately behind the cooling gills.

Nakajima Ki-44-Ic Shoki (Devil-Queller) fighters of the Akeno Fighter Training School.

machine-guns. To meet these requirements T. Koyama, project engineer for Nakajima, needed an engine of higher power than that of the Nakajima Ha-25, the powerplant then emerging as the standard engine of Japanese fighter aircraft, and selected the 1,250 hp Nakajima Ha-41. Despite its fairly large diameter the Ha-41, a fourteen-cylinder double-row radial developed primarily for use on bomber aircraft, was faired smoothly to a fuselage of narrow cross section. To improve the aircraft's characteristics as a gun platform the fuselage had a large side area and the fin and rudder were mounted well to the rear of the horizontal tail surfaces, a feature found on later aircraft designed by T. Koyama. The wings had a small area of only 15 sq m (161·458 sq ft) and were fitted with 'butterfly' combat flaps.

The first prototype (c/n 4401) was completed and flown for the first time in August 1940 at Ojima Airfield, Ota, and was soon followed by two additional prototypes (c/ns 4402 and 4403). When first delivered these machines

Nakajima Ki-44-IIb Army Type 2 Single-seat Fighter Model 2B. (*Aireview*.)

were characterized by their canopy built in three sections, the front and the rear being fixed and the central one sliding to the rear, the cockpit-mounted radio antenna mast, the fixed tailwheel, the rounded rudder similar to that of the Ki-43 and the single drop-tank rack under the fuselage centreline. Early test flights were successful and the aircraft's handling characteristics were found satisfactory despite its heavy wing loading resulting in high landing speed. In the three-point attitude on the ground, frontal visibility was seriously restricted by the massive engine, but inflight visibility was judged excellent. Troubles appeared when performance trials were conducted and, at a weight of 2,550 kg (5,622 lb), a maximum speed of only 550 km/h (342 mph)—8·3 per cent below specification—was reached and the aircraft climbed to 5,000 m (16,405 ft) in 5 min 54 sec. The failure to meet the performance requirements could have meant the abandonment of the first JAAF interceptor fighter, and Nakajima, at the same time experiencing difficulties with their Ki-43 programme, had good reasons to worry. In an effort to reduce drag, the rigidity of the engine mounting was increased, the shape and frontal area of the supercharger's intake revised six times and the cowling flaps modified. Thus modified, and with

A Nakajima Ki-44-IIb Shoki (Devil-Queller) in the Philippines. Two Kawasaki Ki-45 Toryu (Dragon Killer) heavy fighters are in the background. (*US Navy*.)

armament removed, a speed of 570 km/h (354 mph)—still some 5 per cent below specification—was attained. The firewall installation was then modified to improve the engine cooling, thus making it possible to dispense with the five cooling vents mounted on both sides of the forward fuselage behind the cowling gills. With these vents sealed up, drag was substantially reduced and, still without armament, the aircraft exceeded the speed requirement when it reached a maximum of 626 km/h (389 mph). Based on these results and on weight calculations, it was estimated that production aircraft would reach a maximum speed of 580 km/h (360 mph).

Embodying the latest modifications, seven pre-production aircraft (c/ns 4404 to 4410) were built, the last being delivered in September 1941. These aircraft had a new canopy built in two sections, the aft one sliding to the rear, a radio antenna mast mounted on the forward starboard fuselage side, a redesigned rudder, and provision was made under the wing centre-section for two 130 litre (28·6 Imp gal) drop tanks. Like the prototypes,

A Nakajima Ki-44-IIb Shoki of the 246th Sentai, 2nd Chutai.

the pre-production aircraft were armed with a pair of synchronized 7·7 mm Type 89 machine-guns and one 12·7 mm Type 1 (Ho-103) machine-gun in each wing outboard of the main undercarriage well, and a telescopic gunsight protruded through the windshield. On 15 September, 1941, these seven aircraft and the second and third prototypes, brought up to similar standard, were handed over to an experimental squadron, the Kawasemi Butai, for Service trials. Assigned to the South Defence Area Army, the unit was sent to China and in May 1942 was renamed 47th Dokuritsu Dai Shijugo Chutai.

In September 1942 all tests were completed and the aircraft was accepted by the JAAF as the Army Type 2 Single-seat Fighter Model 1—single-seat being included in the designation to differentiate the aircraft from the Army Type 2 Two-seat Fighter (Kawasaki Ki-45 KAI)—and was named Shoki (Devil-Queller). When met in action over China, the Ki-44 was coded TOJO by the China–Burma–India theatre. An initial batch of Ki-44s had already been in production since January 1942, and early machines, similar

Front view of the 246th Sentai Nakajima Ki-44-IIb.

to the pre-production aircraft, were retroactively designated Model 1A (Ki-44-Ia). They were followed by the Army Type 2 Single-seat Fighter Model 1B (Ki-44-Ib) with armament increased to four 12·7 mm Type 1 (Ho-103) machine-guns. On the Ki-44-Ib, the oil cooler was removed from inside the cowling and placed under the cowling gills. Few Ki-44-Ic, or Model 1C, were built and, apart from the transfer of the lower hinged portions of the mainwheel fairings from the legs to the fuselage, were identical to the Ki-44-Ib. Only forty production Ki-44-Is were built and one of these machines was experimentally fitted with two-blade contra-rotating propellers.

Although the Ki-44-I was the fastest Japanese fighter aircraft in service it was unable to intercept the Army Type 100 Command Reconnaissance Plane (Mitsubishi Ki-46) and the JAAF was anxious to increase Shoki's

A Nakajima Ki-44-IIb Shoki with drop tanks inboard and aft of the main undercarriage units. The aircraft in the background is a Kawasaki Ki-102. (*US Navy Department.*)

speed and rate of climb. The obvious solution was to use an engine of higher power, and Nakajima selected their Ha-109 which was in production as the 1,450 hp Army Type 2 radial. Developing 1,520 hp for take-off, the Ha-109 had a diameter identical to that of the Ha-41 and, consequently, could easily be mounted on the Ki-44 airframe. Starting in August 1942, five Ki-44-II prototypes and three pre-production aircraft were built and the type replaced the Ki-44-I on Nakajima's Ota assembly lines. Few Ki-44-IIas, armed with two synchronized 7·7 mm Type 89 machine-guns and two wing-mounted 12·7 mm Type 1 (Ho-103) machine-guns, were built and the mass production variant was the Army Type 2 Single-seat Fighter Model 2B (Ki-44-IIb) with an airframe and armament identical to those of the Ki-44-Ic. These aircraft operated in Japan—where daring attacks on Tokyo, Yokohama, Kobe and Nagoya by North American B-25 bombers launched from the USS *Hornet* had demonstrated the need for an effective force of interceptor fighters—in China, Malaya and Burma, and in Sumatra where Shokis were assigned the task of defending the vital oil fields at Palembang.

Wing-mounted 40 mm Ho-301 cannon of a Nakajima Ki-44-IIc Shoki. (*US Navy Department*.)

The next variant of the Ki-44-II to enter production was the Model 2C which, armed with four 20 mm Ho-3 cannon, proved particularly effective against the B-29s attacking Japan. Some of the Ki-44-IIcs were armed with a pair of synchronized 12·7 mm Type 1 (Ho-103) machine-guns and two wing-mounted 40 mm Ho-301 cannon. The Ho-301 cannon was a very light weapon for its calibre but, having a very low muzzle velocity, was effective only at close range. The ammunition, 10 rounds per gun, was rather unusual as no cartridge case was used and the propelling charge was contained in a cavity in the rear of the projectile. Twelve exhaust ports in the base plate permitted the expanding gases to escape and drive the projectile forward. A copper band on the projectile acted as a gas seal and the propellant burned completely before leaving the barrel. As the effective range of the Ho-301 did not exceed 150 yards, some Ki-44-IIcs were fitted with a pair of 37 mm Ho-203 cannon with an effective range of 1,000 yards. However, both types of heavy cannon were only moderately successful and saw limited operation. A small number of Ki-44-IIs fitted with individual exhaust stacks providing some thrust augmentation were tested by personnel of the 2nd Air Army and one of these aircraft is known to have been used by the commanding officer of the 47th Sentai. This unit earned an enviable reputation among JAAF squadrons operating in the defence of Tokyo when in November 1944 one of its Chutais, known as the Shinten Seikutai, was formed as an air-to-air kamikaze unit specializing in ramming attacks.

The final model of the Shoki to be built, the Ki-44-III, was powered by a 2,000 hp Nakajima Ha-145 eighteen-cylinder air-cooled radial featuring thrust augmentation exhaust stacks. To improve take-off and landing characteristics despite an increase in loaded weight, the wing area was increased to 19 sq m (204·514 sq ft) and the tail surfaces were enlarged. First flown in June 1943, relatively few Ki-44-IIIs were built as the aircraft was rendered obsolete by the Ki-84-I. Two variants were built, the Army Type 2 Single-seat Fighter Model 3A armed with four 20 mm Ho-5 cannon and the Model 3B armed with two 20 mm Ho-5 cannon and two 37 mm Ho-203 cannon.

In late 1944, Shoki production terminated as the aircraft was replaced on Nakajima's assembly lines by the Ki-84 and, when the war ended, only three Sentais were still equipped with them. Early in its operational life Shoki was disliked by Service pilots because of its high landing speed and comparative lack of manoeuvrability. However, later in the war the JAAF pilots, particularly the younger ones without previous experience on the lighter Ki-27s and Ki-43s, learned to take full advantage of the Ki-44's rate of climb and diving speed. The Ki-44 was restricted against snap rolls, spins, stalls and inverted flight at high speeds, and pilot protection and

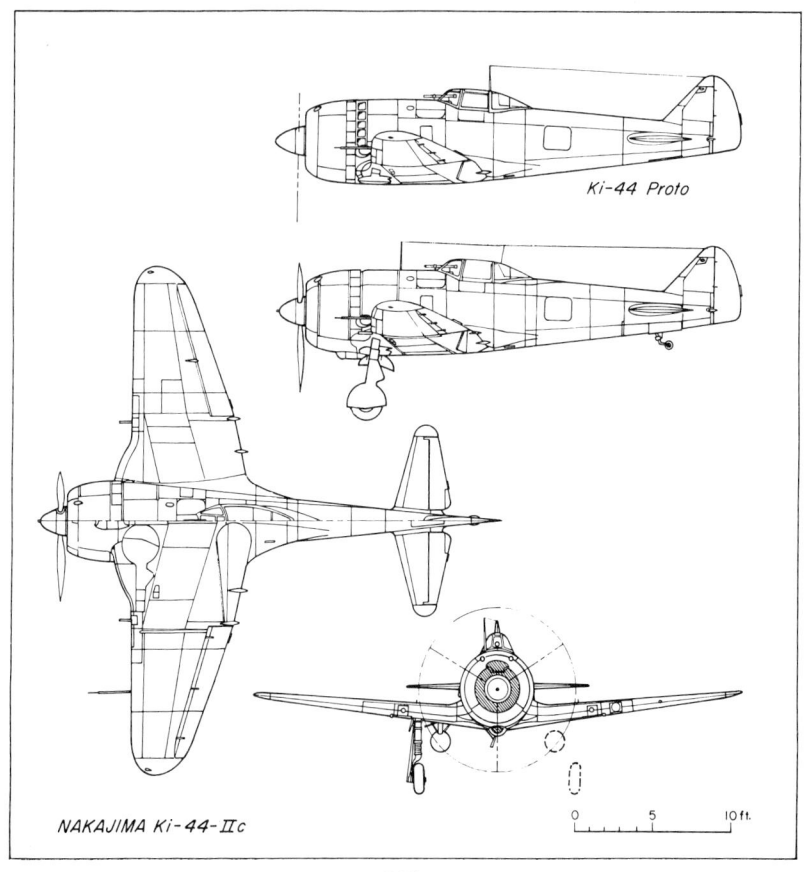

NAKAJIMA Ki-44-IIc

self-sealing fuel tanks were found ineffective against the standard Allied 0·5 in machine-guns. Despite these shortcomings the aircraft performed effectively, and the JAAF which, after competitive trials, had selected the Ki-44 over the Messerschmitt Bf 109E as the standard Army interceptor fighter, had no reason to regret their choice.

UNITS ALLOCATED

9th, 22nd, 29th, 47th, 70th, 85th, 87th and 246th Sentais; 47th Dokuritsu Dai Shijugo Chutai; Akeno and Hitachi Army Fighter Training Schools.

TECHNICAL DATA

Description: Single-seat interceptor fighter. All-metal construction with fabric-covered control surfaces.
Accommodation: Pilot in enclosed cockpit.
Powerplant: One 1,250 hp Army Type 100 fourteen-cylinder air-cooled radial (Nakajima Ha-41), rated at 1,200 hp for take-off and 1,260 hp at 3,700 m (12,140 ft), driving a constant-speed three-blade metal propeller (Ki-44 prototypes and Ki-44-I).

One 1,450 hp Army Type 2 fourteen-cylinder air-cooled radial (Nakajima Ha-109), rated at 1,520 hp for take-off, 1,440 hp at 2,150 m (7,055 ft) and 1,320 hp at 5,250 m (17,220 ft), driving a constant-speed three-blade metal propeller (Ki-44-II).

One Nakajima Ha-145 eighteen-cylinder air-cooled radial, rated at 2,000 hp for take-off, 1,880 hp at 2,000 m (6,560 ft) and 1,450 hp at 8,000 m (26,245 ft), driving a constant-speed four-blade metal propeller (Ki-44-III).

Armament: Two fuselage-mounted 7·7 mm Type 89 machine-guns and two wing-mounted 12·7 mm Type 1 (Ho-103) machine-guns (Ki-44 prototypes and pre-production aircraft, Ki-44-Ia and Ki-44-IIa).

Two fuselage-mounted 12·7 mm Type 1 (Ho-103) machine-guns and two wing-mounted 12·7 mm Type 1 (Ho-103) machine-guns (Ki-44-Ib, Ki-44-Ic and Ki-44-IIb).

Two fuselage-mounted 20 mm Ho-3 cannon and two wing-mounted 20 mm Ho-3 cannon, or two fuselage-mounted 12·7 mm Type 1 (Ho-103) machine-guns and two wing-mounted 40 mm Ho-301 cannon, or two fuselage-mounted 12·7 mm Type 1 (Ho-103) machine-guns and two wing-mounted 37 mm Ho-203 cannon (Ki-44-IIc).

Two fuselage-mounted 20 mm Ho-5 cannon and two wing-mounted 20 mm Ho-5 cannon (Ki-44-IIIa).

Two fuselage-mounted 20 mm Ho-5 cannon and two wing-mounted 37 mm Ho-203 cannon (Ki-44-IIIb).

External stores: two 130 litre (28·6 Imp gal) drop tanks.

	Ki-44-Ia	**Ki-44-IIb**
Dimensions:		
Span	9·45 m	9·45 m
	(31 ft 0 $\frac{1}{16}$ in)	(31 ft 0 $\frac{1}{16}$ in)
Length	8·75 m	8·785 m
	(28 ft 8$\frac{1}{4}$ in)	(28 ft 9$\frac{7}{8}$ in)
Height	3·25 m	3·25 m
	(10 ft 8 in)	(10 ft 8 in)
Wing area	15 sq m	15 sq m
	(161·458 sq ft)	(161·458 sq ft)
Weights:		
Empty	1,944 kg	2,106 kg
	(4,286 lb)	(4,643 lb)
Loaded	2,550 kg	2,764 kg
	(5,622 lb)	(6,094 lb)
Maximum	2,886 kg	2,993 kg
	(6,363 lb)	(6,598 lb)
Wing loading	170 kg/sq m	184 kg/sq m
	(34·8 lb/sq ft)	(37·7 lb/sq ft)
Power loading	2 kg/hp	1·8 kg/hp
	(4·4 lb/hp)	(4 lb/hp)

	Ki-44-Ia	Ki-44-IIb
Performance:		
Maximum speed	580 km/h at 3,700 m	605 km/h at 5,200 m
	(360 mph at 12,140 ft)	(376 mph at 17,060 ft)
Cruising speed	400 km/h at 4,000 m	400 km/h at 4,000 m
	(249 mph at 13,125 ft)	(249 mph at 13,125 ft)
Climb to	5,000 m (16,405 ft)	5,000 m (16,405 ft)
in	5 min 54 sec	4 min 17 sec
Service ceiling	10,820 m (35,500 ft)	11,200 m (36,745 ft)
Range—normal	926 km (575 miles)	1,296 km (805 miles)
—maximum	1,722 km (1,070 miles)	1,700 km (1,056 miles)

Production: A total of 1,225 Ki-44s were built by Nakajima Hikoki K.K. in their Ota plant as follows:
   3 Ki-44 prototypes (1940–41)
   7 Ki-44 pre-production aircraft (1941)
   40 Ki-44-I production aircraft (Jan–Oct 1942)
   5 Ki-44-II prototypes (summer 1942)
   3 Ki-44-II pre-production aircraft (autumn 1942)
   1,167 Ki-44-II and Ki-44-III production aircraft (Nov 1942–Dec 1944)

A Nakajima Ki-49-I Donryu (Storm Dragon) of the Hamamatsu Heavy Bomber Flying School.

Nakajima Ki-49 Donryu (Storm Dragon)

The Nakajima Ki-49 was designed to a JAAF specification issued in early 1938 which sought a replacement type for the Army Type 97 Heavy Bomber (Mitsubishi Ki-21), then just entering service with the 14th Sentai, and called for an aircraft capable of operating without fighter escort and relying for protection on its speed and heavy armament. The requirements of the Ki-49 specification included a maximum speed of 500 km/h (311 mph), an improvement of some 16 per cent over that of the contemporary Ki-21, a range of 3,000 km (1,864 miles), a bomb-load of 1,000 kg

223

(2,205 lb) and defensive armament comprising one flexible 20 mm cannon in a dorsal turret and several flexible 7·7 mm machine-guns including one in a tail turret. The crew had to be adequately protected from enemy gunfire and the fuel tanks self-sealing.

Nakajima assigned to the Ki-49 project their senior engineers, Nishimura, Itokawa and T. Koyama, the latter being appointed project leader, and work began in the summer of 1938. When in 1937 the Mitsubishi Ki-21

Nakajima Ki-49-I Army Type 100 Model 1 Heavy Bomber seen during early operations against Darwin. (*US National Archives.*)

had been selected over their Ki-19, Nakajima had received a production contract for the Ki-21 thus gaining an intimate knowledge of the aircraft, and they made good use of the data in designing its intended replacement. In designing the aircraft particular attention was paid to the handling requirement, and a mid-mounted wing of unusually low aspect-ratio was selected to obtain good stability and manoeuvrability at medium to low altitudes. The wing centre-section had a wider chord than the outboard panels to provide space for six self-sealing fuel tanks, three on each side of the fuselage, while reducing drag and allowing the engine nacelles to be mounted well ahead of the flaps. To improve take-off and climb performance Fowler-type flaps were adopted and extended from the fuselage to the ailerons. Two self-sealing fuel tanks and one protected oil tank were mounted in each outboard wing panel. Defensive armament consisted of one flexible 20 mm Ho-1 cannon mounted on the port side of a dorsal turret and one flexible 7·7 mm Type 89 machine-gun in each of the nose, ventral and port and starboard positions. An additional 7·7 mm Type 89 machine-gun was fitted in a tail turret, the first to be used on an Imperial Japanese Army aircraft. Bombs were carried in a fuselage bomb-bay extending almost the entire length of the wing centre-section.

The first prototype (c/n 4901) was completed and flown in August 1939. Powered by two Nakajima Ha-5 KAI radials, rated at 950 hp for take-off and 1,080 hp at 4,000 m (13,125 ft), driving Hamilton Standard two-pitch three-blade propellers, the aircraft was used primarily for handling trials and Service pilots reported favourably on its manoeuvrability. The second and third prototypes were fitted with the 1,250 hp Nakajima Ha-41, the powerplant selected for the projected production variant, and were delivered in the last quarter of 1939. Seven pre-production machines, identical to the second and third prototypes apart from the adoption of constant-speed three-blade propellers, were built in 1940 and all ten aircraft underwent a protracted flight trial programme. During this period minor changes in armament, protection and seating arrangement were tested and the aircraft was finally accepted for production as the Army Type 100 Heavy Bomber Model 1 (Ki-49-I) in March 1941.

While the prototypes and pre-production Ki-49s were being tested, alarming reports were received from China where Army Type 97 Heavy Bombers were suffering heavy losses due to the inability of available fighter aircraft to escort them all the way to and from their targets. Much in the same way as the B-40 and B-41 escort fighters were later developed in the US from the Boeing B-17 and Consolidated B-24, Engineer Matsumura designed for Nakajima the Ki-58, an escort fighter version of the Ki-49. Powered by two Nakajima Ha-109s, three prototypes were built between December 1940 and March 1941. The Ki-58 had its bomb-bay sealed and

A Nakajima Ki-49-IIb, the mass production version of the Donryu, in 110th Sentai markings.

replaced by a ventral gondola, better armour protection and armament increased to five flexible 20 mm Ho-1 cannon and three 12·7 mm Ho-103 machine-guns. The aircraft were intended to fly on the flanks of Ki-49 formations, but the idea was abandoned when the Army Type 1 Fighter Hayabusa (Nakajima Ki-43) proved to be able to escort the bombers all the way to their targets.

The Ki-80, two of which were built in October 1941, was a version of the Ki-49 intended for the use of formation leaders but was also cancelled, and the two prototypes were used as test-beds for the 2,420 hp Nakajima Ha-117.

The Ki-49-I Donryu (Storm Dragon) production aircraft were identical to the pre-production machines and deliveries started in August 1941.

A Nakajima Ki-49-IIb. Flap guides and bomb doors can be seen. (*US Navy Department*.)

When the war broke out, the 61st Sentai were exchanging their Ki-21s for Ki-49s but, because of the low initial delivery rate of Donryus, kept some of the older aircraft on strength until February 1942. As production gained tempo the Donryu made its Service début in China. Later the Ki-49, which became known as HELEN to Allied personnel, was frequently encountered over New Britain and New Guinea, and it took an active part in the JAAF operations over Australia's Northern Territory. However, early war operations confirmed the doubts expressed by Service pilots in finding that the Ki-49 was underpowered and more difficult to fly than the Ki-21. Speed, although superior to that of the older type, was insufficient to avoid interception and effective bomb-load fell below that of the Ki-21. On the positive side Donryu's crews commented favourably on the aircraft's armour and self-sealing tanks and on its defensive armament offering no blind spots except immediately above and below the aircraft.

In the spring of 1942 the decision was taken to install a pair of 1,450 hp Army Type 2 radials (Nakajima Ha-109) driving Ratier-type constant-speed three-blade propellers. The engine nacelles were only slightly modified as both types of engines had identical diameter, but the oil cooler, mounted on the front of the Ha-41 engine, was moved to the underside of the Ha-109 cowling. Other modifications dictated by combat experience, such as improved self-sealing tanks, relocated armour plating of heavier grade and a new bombsight, were incorporated in two pre-production Ki-49-IIs. The new version of the Donryu was accepted for production as the Army Type 100 Heavy Bomber Model 2A (Ki-49-IIa) with defensive armament identical to that of the Model 1 and deliveries commenced in August 1942. However, as Allied fighters were found difficult to destroy with rifle-calibre weapons, the single 7·7 mm Type 89 machine-gun in each of the nose, ventral and tail positions were replaced by 12·7 mm Type 1 (Ho-103) machine-guns in late production Ki-49-IIbs.

The Ki-49-IIs never wholly supplanted the Ki-21-IIs in the JAAF bomber units and were assigned to Sentais operating in New Guinea and China/Manchuria. When the Allies returned to the Philippines Donryus were heavily committed to the new battle front where they were severely mauled until December 1944 when most surviving aircraft were used in kikusui suicide attacks against the Allied fleet supporting the landing on Mindoro. Although the aircraft was provided with better armament and protection than any other Japanese bomber until the advent of the Mitsubishi Ki-67, the JAAF did not find its performance satisfactory. In particular, Service pilots found the speed at low and medium altitudes still insufficient, and its flight characteristics were not as pleasant as those of the older Ki-21-II. In an effort to improve Donryu's performance even more, Nakajima designed a newer version fitted with the most powerful fourteen-cylinder radial engines ever developed, the 2,420 hp Nakajima Ha-117. These engines were test flown on the Ki-80 and it was hoped that maximum rating could be increased to 2,800 hp. However, engine teething troubles were never eradicated and only six aircraft of this variant, the Ki-49-III, were built by Nakajima between March and December 1943. Standard Ki-49s were also built by Tachikawa which, after experiencing serious difficulties due to errors in the jigs supplied by Nakajima, delivered fifty machines in 1943–44, but plans to have the aircraft manufactured by Mansyu Hikoki Seizo K.K. were not realized.

Despite its shortcomings the type was adapted to perform various missions. Ki-49-Is fitted with electronic and magnetic detection gear served in an anti-submarine role. Some Ki-49-IIs operated as troop transports; others were modified in the field as night fighters in which role, operating

Close-up of Nakajima Ki-49-IIb, c/n 3567, at Nielson Field in the Philippines in March 1945. (*US Navy Department.*)

NAKAJIMA Ki-49-IIb

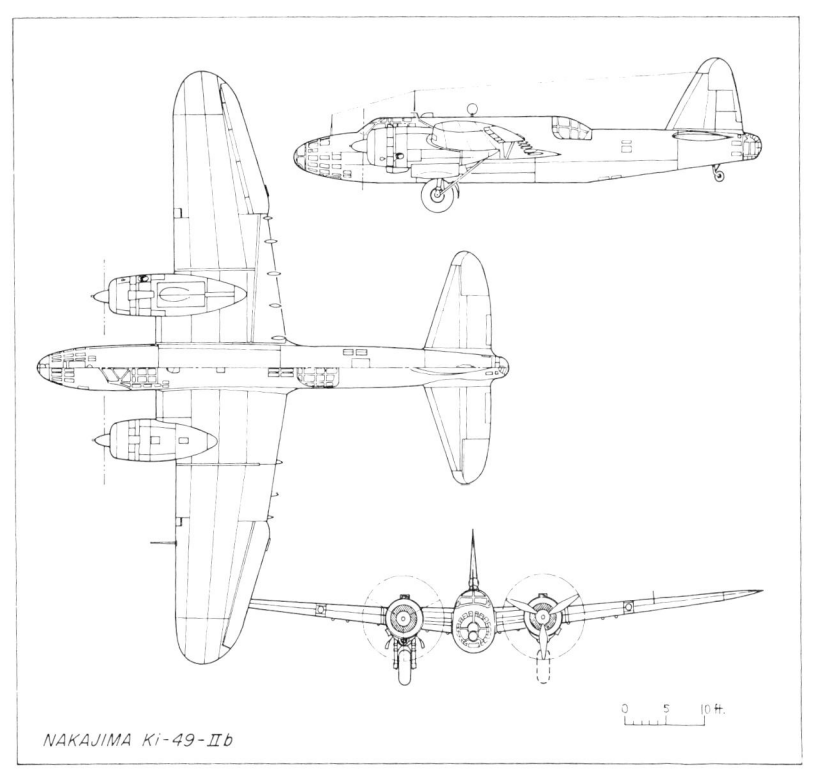

in pairs, one aircraft was fitted with a searchlight in the nose as a 'hunter' while the 'killer' mounted a 75 mm cannon in the fuselage, but they proved disappointing as they lacked the necessary performance. In the suicide bomber role the Ki-49-II had all armament removed, crew being reduced to two pilots, but carried 1,600 kg (3,527 lb) of bombs. Although Donryu's operational life was comparatively brief and colourless, it earned a special place in the history of aviation in Japan as it was the first Army bomber to be fitted with a tail turret.

UNITS ALLOCATED

61st, 62nd, 74th, 95th and 110th Sentais; 11th Hikoshidan; Hamamatsu Army Heavy Bomber Flying School.

TECHNICAL DATA

Description: Twin-engined heavy bomber. All-metal construction.
Accommodation: Crew of eight including pilot, co-pilot, bombardier, navigator, radio-operator/gunner and three gunners in enclosed cockpits.
Powerplant: Two Nakajima Ha-5 KAI fourteen-cylinder air-cooled radials, rated at 950 hp for take-off and 1,080 hp at 4,000 m (13,125 ft), driving two-pitch three-blade metal propellers (first prototype).

Two Army Type 100 fourteen-cylinder air-cooled radials (Nakajima Ha-41), rated at 1,250 hp for take-off and 1,260 hp at 3,700 m (12,140 ft), driving two-pitch three-blade metal propellers (prototypes c/ns 4902 and 4903) or constant-speed three-blade metal propellers (pre-production aircraft, c/ns 4904 to 4910, and Ki-49-I).

Two 1,450 hp Army Type 2 fourteen-cylinder air-cooled radials (Nakajima Ha-109), rated at 1,500 hp for take-off and 1,300 hp at 5,280 m (17,330 ft), driving constant-speed three-blade metal propellers (Ki-49-II and Ki-58).

Two Nakajima Ha-117 fourteen-cylinder air-cooled radials, rated at 2,420 hp for take-off and 2,250 hp at 4,900 m (16,075 ft), driving constant-speed three-blade metal propellers (Ki-49-III and Ki-80).

Armament: One flexible 20 mm Ho-1 cannon in the dorsal turret and one flexible 7·7 mm Type 89 machine-gun in each of the nose, ventral, port and starboard beam, and tail positions (prototypes, pre-production aircraft, Ki-49-I and Ki-49-IIa).

One flexible 20 mm Ho-1 cannon in the dorsal turret, one flexible 12·7 mm Type 1 (Ho-103) machine-gun in the nose, ventral and tail positions, and one flexible 7·7 mm Type 89 machine-gun in the port and starboard beam positions (Ki-49-IIb and Ki-49-III).

Five flexible 20 mm Ho-1 cannon and three flexible 12·7 mm Type 1 (Ho-103) machine-guns (Ki-58).

Bomb-load—normal, 750 kg (1,653 lb)
—maximum, 1,000 kg (2,205 lb)
—suicide attack, 1,600 kg (3,527 lb)

	Ki-49-I	Ki-49-IIa
Dimensions:		
Span	20·424 m	20·424 m
	(67 ft 0⅛ in)	(67 ft 0⅛ in)
Length	16·808 m	16·5 m
	(55 ft 1¾ in)	(54 ft 1⅜ in)
Height	4·25 m	4·25 m
	(13 ft 11 5/16 in)	(13 ft 11 5/16 in)
Wing area	69·05 sq m	69·05 sq m
	(743·245 sq ft)	(743·245 sq ft)
Weights:		
Empty	6,070 kg	6,530 kg
	(13,382 lb)	(14,396 lb)
Loaded	10,150 kg	10,680 kg
	(22,377 lb)	(23,545 lb)
Maximum	10,675 kg	11,400 kg
	(23,534 lb)	(25,133 lb)
Wing loading	·147 kg/sq m	154·7 kg/sq m
	(30·1 lb/sq ft)	(31·7 lb/sq ft)
Power loading	4·1 kg/hp	3·6 kg/hp
	(8·9 lb/hp)	(7·8 lb/hp)
Performance:		
Maximum speed	—	492 km/h at 5,000 m
	—	(306 mph at 16,405 ft)
Cruising speed	—	350 km/h at 3,000 m
	—	(217 mph at 9,845 ft)
Climb to	—	5,000 m (16,405 ft)
in	—	13 min 39 sec
Service ceiling	—	9,300 m (30,510 ft)
Range—normal	—	2,000 km (1,243 miles)
—maximum	—	2,950 km (1,833 miles)

Production: A total of 819 Ki-49s and derivatives were built as follows:

Nakajima Hikoki K.K. at Ota:

3 Ki-49 prototypes (summer 1939)
7 Ki-49 pre-production aircraft (Jan–Dec 1940)
129 Ki-49-I production aircraft (Aug 1941–Aug 1942)
2 Ki-49-II prototypes (Aug–Sept 1942)
617 Ki-49-II production aircraft (Sept 1942–Dec 1944)
6 Ki-49-III prototypes (Mar–Dec 1943)
3 Ki-58 prototypes (Dec 1940–Mar 1941)
2 Ki-80 prototypes (Oct 1941)

Tachikawa Hikoki K.K. at Tachikawa:

50 Ki-49-II production aircraft (Jan 1943–Jan 1944)

A Shotai (Section) of three Nakajima Ki-84 Hayates of the 52nd Sentai about to take-off. (*Aireview*.)

Nakajima Ki-84 Hayate (Gale)

The Nakajima Ki-84 Hayate (Gale), undoubtedly the best Japanese fighter aircraft to see large-scale operation during the last year of the war, was as feared by Allied crews as it was praised by Japanese pilots. Well protected, well armed, fast and manoeuvrable, this fighter gave a good account of itself in the desperate battles over the Philippines, the Ryukyu Islands and the Japanese Home Islands, and Japan's faith in it is emphasized by the fact that at the close of the war they were building underground factories with a planned rate of 200 Hayates per month.

The Ki-43 Hayabusas were just starting to fire their guns in anger when the Koku Hombu instructed Nakajima to design for their replacement. The specification called for an all-purpose, long-range fighter with a top speed of 640/680 km/h (398/423 mph) and capable of operating at combat rating for 1·5 hours at 400 km (250 miles) from base. A wing area of 19 to 21 sq m (204·5 to 226 sq ft) and wing loading not exceeding 170 kg/sq m (34·8 lb/sq ft) were recommended. Power was to be supplied by a Nakajima Ha-45 eighteen-cylinder double-row radial, and the specified armament comprised two 12·7 mm Type 1 (Ho-103) machine-guns and two 20 mm Ho-5 cannon. Provision for armour protection and self-sealing fuel tanks was also mandatory.

Design work on the Ki-84 was initiated by Nakajima with T. Koyama as project engineer in early 1942 and culminated in March 1943 with the completion of the first prototype (c/n 8401). The aircraft was a conventional low-wing monoplane powered by a 1,800 hp Nakajima [Ha-45] 11 and, like the Ki-62 and Ki-63 projects designed earlier by T. Koyama, had its tailplane set well ahead of the vertical surfaces. The muzzles of the engine-

The prototype Nakajima Ki-84 (c/n 8401) with its single ventral drop tank.

mounted 12·7 mm Ho-103 machine-guns protruded from the cowling, and a 20 mm Ho-5 cannon was mounted in each wing outboard of the main undercarriage. Provision was made under the fuselage centreline for a single drop tank and a big exhaust collecter pipe was mounted on each side of the engine behind the cowling gills.

The aircraft flew for the first time from Ojima Airfield in April 1943 and was joined in the company's flight test programme by a second prototype (c/n 8402) in June the same year. Tests progressed rapidly and smoothly without the usual teething troubles, and the two prototypes, together with some of the first aircraft of a Service trials batch of 83 machines, were handed over to the Tachikawa Army Air Arsenal for service tests. The JAAF pilots, who by now had learned to recognize the value of speed and protection, commented favourably on the aircraft's performance even though the maximum speed was below that specified by the Koku Hombu. During flight trials the Ki-84 reached a top speed of 624 km/h (388 mph), climbed to 5,000 m (16,405 ft) in 6 min 26 sec and reached a service ceiling of 12,400 m (40,680 ft), thus demonstrating the best performance of any Japanese aircraft suitable for immediate production.

One of the first Service trials batch of Nakajima Ki-84s. (*Richard Ward.*)

The eighty-three aircraft of the first Service trials batch, which were built between August 1943 and March 1944, differed one from the other in minor details but, progressively, fuselage changes were incorporated to ease production, and the shape and area of the fin and rudder were modified to improve control on take-off as the aircraft suffered from propeller-induced torque. Some of these machines were fitted with two wing racks for bombs of up to 250 kg (551 lb) in addition to the fuselage centreline rack used to carry a drop tank, while still other aircraft were used to test a partially-retractable ski undercarriage.

The first unit to fly the Ki-84, which did so prior to the aircraft being placed in quantity production, was an experimental Chutai which conducted intensive Service tests in Japan under operational conditions, starting in October 1943. In view of the promising results of these tests, the Ki-84 was accepted for Service operation and the Ministry of Munitions instructed Nakajima to start mass production of the aircraft as the Army Type 4 Fighter Model 1A Hayate (Gale), or Ki-84-Ia.

A second pre-production batch of 42 Ki-84s, started in April 1944, was already under construction, and production aircraft were built alongside these machines. Both types were fitted with individual exhaust stacks providing some thrust augmentation, and the fuselage centreline rack was deleted, each of the two wing racks being adapted to carry either a 200 litre (44 Imp gal) drop tank or a 250 kg (551 lb) bomb.

In March 1944, the experimental Chutai which had conducted the Ki-84's Service trials was disbanded and most of its personnel transferred to the 22nd Sentai. Equipped with production Hayates, this unit, led by Major Iwashi, moved to China where it was pitted against the US Fourteenth Air Force. During the five weeks preceding its transfer to the Philippines the 22nd Sentai did much to establish the Ki-84-Ia as a formidable foe possessing most of the virtues and few of the vices of earlier Japanese fighters and comparing favourably with the best Allied fighters. In the Philippines, where the aircraft received the code name FRANK, ten Sentais fought desperately in an effort to halt the Allied offensive. However, Japan had lost the initiative and, under the exacting conditions then prevailing, the outnumbered Hayates suffered from failures of fuel pressure and hydraulic systems and from weak landing-gear struts.

In Japan, Nakajima did their best to increase production by opening a second manufacturing line at their Utsonomiya plant and, despite the lack of skilled workers and limited supplies of aluminium and special steel alloy, delivered 373 Ki-84s in December 1944, the highest monthly production rate of any JAAF aircraft. Construction of Hayate was also assigned to Mansyu Hikoki Seizo K.K. which, starting in the spring of 1945, built 95 Ki-84s in their Harbin plant in Manchuria. The production Ki-84-I was powered by a 1,900 hp Army Type 4 radial (Nakajima Ha-45), early production machines using the [Ha-45] 11 or [Ha-45] 12 models with take-off ratings of 1,800 hp and 1,825 hp respectively, and late production aircraft receiving a [Ha-45] 21 delivering 1,990 hp for take-off, driving a constant-speed four-blade propeller. The Army Type 4 Fighter Model 1A was followed on the assembly lines by the Model 1B (Ki-84-Ib) in which the synchronized machine-guns were replaced by two 20 mm Ho-5 cannon, thus giving the aircraft a fixed armament of four 20 mm cannon. A few Model 1C (Ki-84-Ic) aircraft, specialized bomber destroyers armed with two synchronized 20 mm Ho-5 cannon and two wing-mounted 30 mm Ho-105 cannon, were also built.

Sudden loss of fuel pressure was a constant source of difficulty and the problem was never satisfactorily solved prior to the adoption of the 1,900 hp Army Type 4 radial Model 23 ([Ha-45] 23), a modification of the standard [Ha-45] 21 fitted with a low-pressure fuel injection system. But lack of engines was to slow down the Ki-84's production when Nakajima's engine plant at Musashi was destroyed by the US 20th Air Force, and the Ha-45's production, transferred to an underground plant at Asakawa and a new plant at Hamamatsu, never again reached its previous peak.

In an effort to conserve the dwindling supply of aluminium, Nakajima developed the Hayate Kai embodying wooden rear fuselage, certain fittings and modified wingtips, the wooden parts being built in a shadow factory at Tanuma. Powered by a Nakajima [Ha-45] 21, [Ha-45] 25 or [Ha-45] 23 with low-pressure fuel injection, the type was known as Ki-84-II in Nakajima's nomenclature but, depending on the armament fitted,

A Nakajima Ki-84-Ia of the 11th Sentai. The 'butterfly' combat flaps can be seen depressed below the wing trailing edge. (*US Navy Department.*)

Nakajima Ki-84-Ia Army Type 4 Fighter Model 1A Hayate in the Philippines. In the background is a Kawasaki Ki-102. (*US Navy Department*.)

retained the Ki-84-Ib or -Ic designations in the official Army nomenclature. The Ki-84-III was a high-altitude version, powered by a Ha-45 Ru engine with a turbosupercharger mounted in the fuselage belly, which was still on the drawing boards when the war ended. Plans were also made for a two-seat, dual control version but none were built. Instead some two-seat Ki-84-Is, lacking dual control equipment, were produced in the field by removing the back armour plating and radio equipment and installing a jump seat behind the pilot's seat.

Although the Hayate Kai represented a step in the right direction it was felt that further saving of aluminium would result from a complete redesign of the airframe, and Tachikawa Hikoki K.K. were entrusted by the Ministry of Munitions with the task of designing an all-wood version of the Ki-84. Three airframes, designated Ki-106, were built in 1945 for Tachikawa by Ohji Koku K.K. (Prince Aircraft Co Ltd) at Ebetsu, Ishikari Prefecture, on Hokkaido. Completed by Tachikawa and each powered by a 1,990 hp Nakajima [Ha-45] 21, the aircraft were characterized by vertical surfaces of increased area and by the smooth external finish obtained by

The Nakajima Ki-84-Ia Hayate belonging to the Air Museum, Ontario, California. (*Air Museum photo.*)

applying a thick coat of lacquer to the plywood skin. During flight trials the skin bonding had to be strengthened, but tests, which had started in July 1945, were satisfactory in all other respects. Four 20 mm Ho-5 cannon were carried by the first Ki-106 but, to save weight, armament was reduced to only two cannon on the second and third prototypes. Tachikawa were working on a weight reduction programme when the end of the war brought the Ki-106 project to a halt.

Several versions of the Ki-84 were designed during the last year of the war and included the Ki-84N, a high-altitude interceptor powered by a 2,500 hp Nakajima [Ha-44] 13 (Ha-219) and with wing area increased to 249·19 sq ft, which was in the initial design phase at the war's end and scheduled to go into production as the Ki-117. The Ki-84P was another projected high-altitude version also powered by a Nakajima [Ha-44] 13, but having its wing area further increased to 263·72 sq ft. However, the Ki-84P was abandoned in favour of the less ambitious Ki-84R using a standard Ki-84-I airframe married to a 2,000 hp Nakajima [Ha-45] 44 with a mechanically-driven two-stage three-speed supercharger. The Ki-113 was a variant of the [Ha-45] 21 powered Ki-84-Ib partially built of steel: carbon steel for the cockpit section, ribs and bulkheads, and steel sheet skinning. Designed in the autumn of 1944, a prototype Ki-113 was completed in early 1945 but not flown as it was decidedly overweight.

The Tachikawa Ki-106 which was a wooden version of the Nakajima Ki-84 Hayate. (*Aircraft Photos.*)

The last variant of Hayate to enter flight trials was the Ki-116, the fourth Mansyu-built Ki-84-I adapted to take a 1,500 hp Mitsubishi [Ha-33] 62 (Ha-112-II) driving a three-blade propeller borrowed from a Ki-46-III. The conversion was very successful, a reduction of 1,000 lb in empty weight being registered, and the aircraft was undergoing tests at the time of Japan's final defeat.

Although production Hayates were plagued by inferior workmanship, they were the most successful Japanese aircraft operating during the Okinawa campaign and in the defence of the homeland, and Nakajima and Mansyu delivered 3,382 production Ki-84s in seventeen months, no mean feat considering the chaos brought about by the B-29 raids. As demonstrated by a captured aircraft restored at the Middletown Air Depot, Pennsylvania, in the spring of 1946, the Ki-84's performance was truly spectacular: at a weight of 7,490 lb, considered representative of combat operations, the aircraft reached a speed of 427 mph at 20,000 ft using War Emergency Power. This speed exceeded that of the North American P-51D-25-NA Mustang and Republic P-47D-35-RA Thunderbolt at the same altitude by 3 mph and 22 mph respectively.

UNITS ALLOCATED

1st, 11th, 13th, 14th, 20th, 22nd, 25th, 29th, 47th, 50th, 51st, 52nd, 64th, 71st, 72nd, 73rd, 85th, 101st, 102nd, 103rd, 104th, 111th, 112th, 200th and 246th Sentais; 24th Dokuritsu Dai Shijugo Chutai.

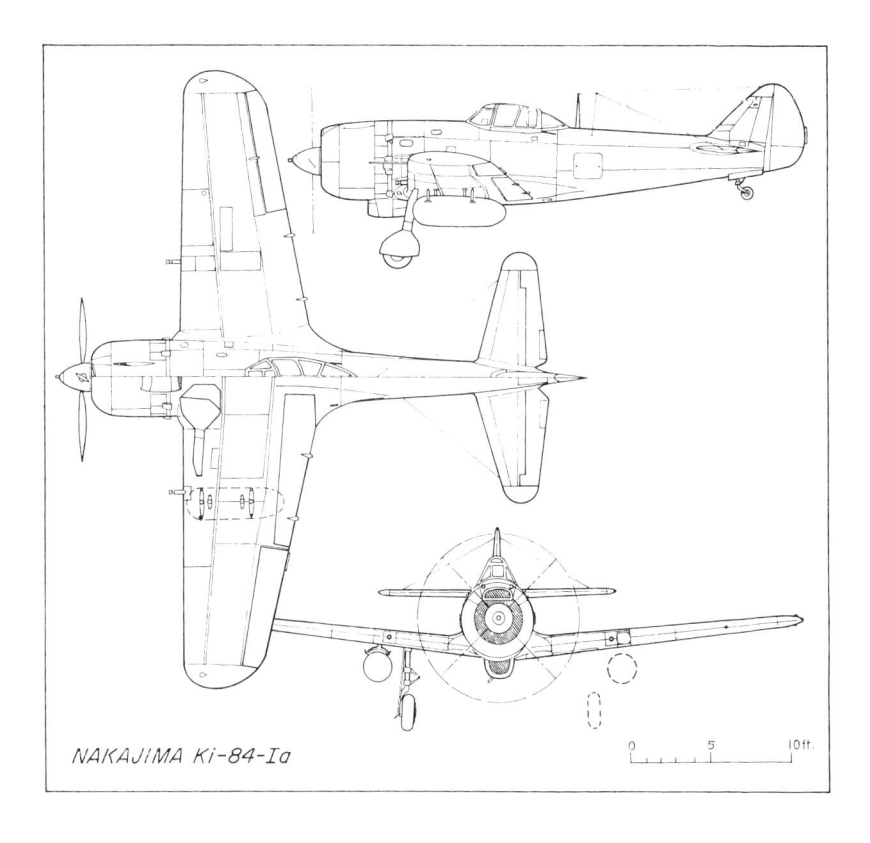

NAKAJIMA Ki-84-Ia

TECHNICAL DATA

Description: Single-seat fighter and fighter-bomber. All-metal construction with fabric-covered control surfaces (Ki-84-I). Wood rear fuselage section, wingtips and control rods (Ki-84-II). Carbon steel ribs, bulkheads and cockpit section, and steel sheet skinning (Ki-113). All-wood construction (Ki-106).
Accommodation: Pilot in enclosed cockpit.
Powerplant: One 1,900 hp Army Type 4 eighteen-cylinder air-cooled radial (Nakajima Ha-45) driving a constant-speed four-blade metal propeller. The following engine models were used:

Take-off rating	Military Power
[Ha-45] 11 1,800 hp	1,650 hp at 2,000 m (6,560 ft) (Ki-84, Ki-84-I))
[Ha-45] 12 1,825 hp	1,670 hp at 2,400 m (7,875 ft) (Ki-84-I)
[Ha-45] 21 1,990 hp	1,850 hp at 1,750 m (5,740 ft) (Ki-84-I and -II, Ki-106 and Ki-113)
[Ha-45] 23 1,900 hp	1,670 hp at 1,440 m (4,725 ft) (Ki-84-I, Ki-84-II)
[Ha-45] 25 2,000 hp	1,700 hp at 6,000 m (19,685 ft) (Ki-84-II).

One Army Type 4 fourteen-cylinder air-cooled radial (Mitsubishi [Ha-33] 62), rated at 1,500 hp for take-off, 1,350 hp at 2,000 m (6,560 ft) and 1,250 hp at 5,800 m (19,030 ft), driving a constant-speed three-blade metal propeller (Ki-116).

Armament: Two fuselage-mounted 12·7 mm Type 1 (Ho-103) machine-guns and two wing-mounted 20 mm Ho-5 cannon (Ki-84 prototypes and Service trials aircraft, Ki-84-Ia and Ki-116).

Two fuselage-mounted 20 mm Ho-5 cannon and two wing-mounted 20 mm Ho-5 cannon (Ki-84-Ib, Ki-106 and Ki-113).

Two fuselage-mounted 20 mm Ho-5 cannon and two wing-mounted 30 mm Ho-105 cannon (Ki-84-Ic). External stores: two 250 kg (551 lb) bombs, or two 200 litre (44 Imp gal) drop tanks.

	Ki-84-Ia	Ki-106	Ki-113	Ki-116
Dimensions:				
Span	11·238 m (36 ft 10 7/16 in)	11·238 m (36 ft 10 7/16 in)	11·238 m (36 ft 10 7/16 in)	11·238 m (36 ft 10 7/16 in)
Length	9·92 m (32 ft 6 9/16 in)	9·95 m (32 ft 7 3/4 in)	9·92 m (32 ft 6 9/16 in)	—
Height	3·385 m (11 ft 1 1/4 in)	3·59 m (11 ft 9 1/8 in)	3·385 m (11 ft 1 1/4 in)	3·45 m (11 ft 3 13/16 in)
Wing area	21 sq m (226·041 sq ft)	21 sq m (226·041 sq ft)	21 sq m (226·041 sq ft)	21 sq m (226·041 sq ft)
Weights:				
Empty	2,660 kg (5,864 lb)	2,948 kg (6,499 lb)	2,880 kg (6,349 lb)	2,240 kg (4,938 lb)
Loaded	3,613 kg (7,955 lb)	3,900 kg (8,598 lb)	3,950 kg (8,708 lb)	3,193 kg (7,039 lb)
Maximum	3,890 kg (8,576 lb)	—	—	—
Wing loading	172 kg/sq m (35·1 lb/sq ft)	186 kg/sq m (38 lb/sq ft)	188 kg/sq m (38·5 lb/sq ft)	152 kg/sq m (31·1 lb/sq ft)
Power loading	1·8 kg/hp (4 lb/hp)	2 kg/hp (4·4 lb/hp)	2 kg/hp (4·4 lb/hp)	1·6 kg/hp (3·5 lb/hp)
Performance:				
Maximum speed	631 km/h at 6,120 m (392 mph at 20,080 ft)	620 km/h at 6,400 m (385 mph at 21,000 ft)	620 km/h at 6,500 m (385 mph at 21,325 ft)	—
Cruising speed	445 km/h (277 mph)	—	—	—
Climb to in	5,000 m (16,405 ft) 5 min 54 sec	5,000 m (16,405 ft) 5 min	5,000 m (16,405 ft) 6 min 54 sec	—
Service ceiling	10,500 m (34,450 ft)	11,000 m (36,090 ft)	10,300 m (33,800 ft)	—
Range: normal	1,695 km (1,053 miles)	800 km plus 1·5 hr combat (497 miles plus 1·5 hr combat)	1,000 km plus 1·5 hr combat (621 miles plus 1·5 hr combat)	—
maximum	2,168 km (1,347 miles)	—	—	—

Production: A total of 3,514 Ki-84s and derivatives were built as follows:
Nakajima Hikoki K.K. at Ota and Utsonomiya:
  2 Ki-84 prototypes (March–June 1943)
  83 Ki-84 Service trials aircraft (Aug 1943–Mar 1944)
  42 Ki-84 pre-production aircraft (Apr–June 1944)
  3,288 Ki-84-I and Ki-84-II production aircraft (Apr 1944–Aug 1945)
  1 Ki-113 prototype (autumn 1944)
Mansyu Hikoki Seizo K.K. at Harbin:
  94 Ki-84-I production aircraft (1945)
  1 Ki-116 prototype (1945)
Tachikawa Hikoki K.K. at Tachikawa:
  3 Ki-106 prototypes (1945)

The sole example of the Nakajima Ki-87, photographed soon after completion.

Nakajima Ki-87

In mid-1942 the Technical Branch of the Koku Hombu approached Nakajima with a preliminary specification for a heavily armed high-altitude fighter capable of reaching a maximum speed of 800 km (497 mph) and having a maximum range of 3,000 km (1,864 miles). As these performance requirements appeared somewhat unrealistic they were soon revised and the endurance requirement was lowered to 30 min at combat rating at 500–800 km (310–497 miles) from its base plus one hour loiter time. The maximum speed was no longer specified, but the aircraft was to be armed with two 20 mm and two 30 mm cannon. An agreement between Nakajima and the JAAF was reached in November 1942, and an order was placed for three Ki-87 prototypes, expected to be completed between November 1944 and January 1945, and seven pre-production machines, to be completed between February and April 1945.

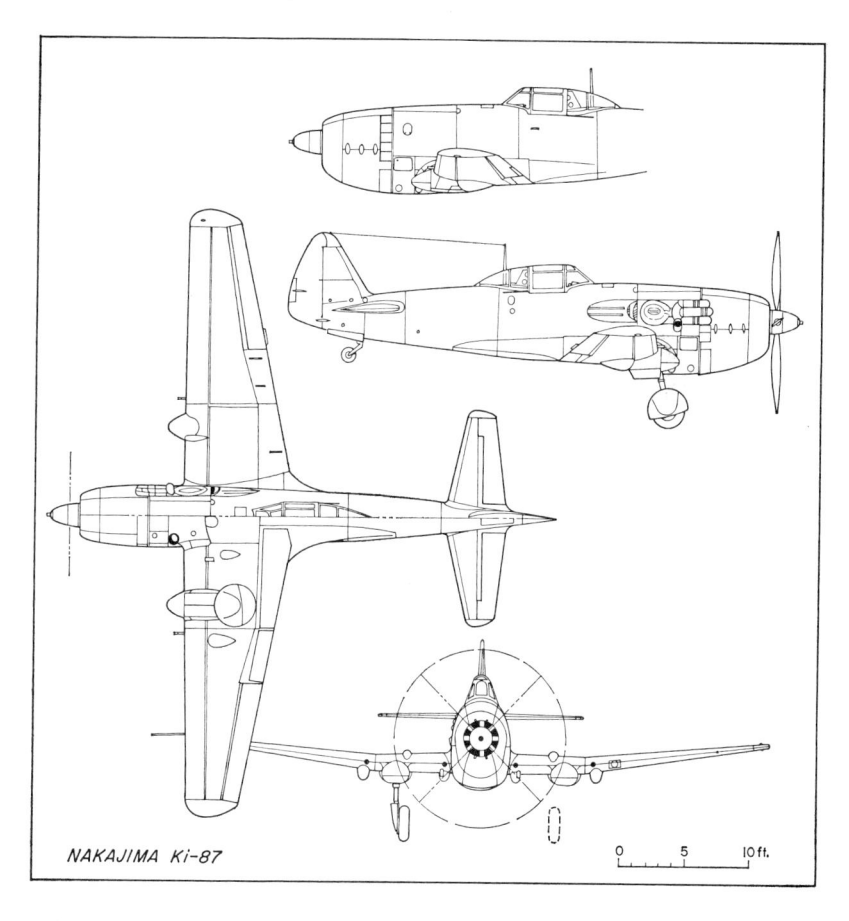

NAKAJIMA Ki-87

A 2,400 hp Nakajima [Ha-44] 11 or [Ha-44] 21 (Ha-219 Ru) with a turbosupercharger mounted on the starboard forward fuselage side was selected, and a 16-blade cooling fan, geared to run at 150 per cent of the speed of the propeller, was mounted in the cowling. One synchronized 20 mm Ho-5 cannon was mounted in each wing root, and one 30 mm Ho-105 cannon was placed in each wing outboard of the wheel well. Before completion of the first machine changes were already planned and, despite Nakajima's objections, the JAAF required that the turbosupercharger be placed in the rear fuselage on the sixth and subsequent aircraft. In addition, Nakajima intended to change the engine reduction gear ratio from 0·578 to 0·431 starting with the third aircraft and to improve cooling on the tenth aircraft by using a faster-running fan. To provide room in the wings for the heavy armament and the self-sealing fuel tanks, Nakajima had to design a novel undercarriage—by Japanese standards—inspired by the one fitted to the Curtiss P-40 in which the main undercarriage members retracted rearwards and the wheels turned through 90 degrees to lie flat.

Due to the numerous difficulties with the electrical undercarriage retraction mechanism and to teething troubles with the engine's turbosupercharger, only one prototype (c/n 8701) was completed in February 1945. Test flights began in April 1945, but only five were made during which no attempts were made to retract the troublesome undercarriage and no performance data were recorded. Although the aircraft demonstrated good flying characteristics, thought to be superior to those of the Ki-84, difficulties with the engine prevented further testing.

An improved model, the Ki-87-II, powered by a 3,000 hp Nakajima [Ha-46] 11 (Ha-217) with a turbosupercharger mounted in the fuselage belly, was still on the drawing boards when the war ended. It was anticipated that this aircraft would have had a top speed of 738 km/h (459 mph) at 11,000 m (33,530 ft) and a service ceiling of 12,850 m (42,160 ft).

TECHNICAL DATA

Description: Single-seat high-altitude interceptor fighter. All-metal construction.

Accommodation: Pilot in pressurized cockpit.

Powerplant: One Nakajima [Ha-44] 11 eighteen-cylinder air-cooled radial, rated at 2,400 hp for take-off, 2,200 hp at 1,500 m (4,920 ft), 2,050 hp at 6,000 m (19,685 ft) and 1,850 hp at 10,500 m (34,450 ft), driving a constant-speed four-blade metal propeller.

Armament: Two 20 mm Ho-5 cannon and two 30 mm Ho-105 cannon in the wings.
External store: one 250 kg (551 lb) bomb.

Dimensions: Span 13·423 m (44 ft 0½ in); length 11·82 m (38 ft 9¾ in); height 4·503 m (14 ft 9 ⅛ in); wing area 26 sq m (279·860 sq ft).

Weights: Empty 4,387 kg (9,672 lb); loaded 5,632 kg (12,416 lb); maximum 6,100 kg (13,448 lb); wing loading 216·6 kg/sq m (44·3 lb/sq ft); power loading 2·3 kg/hp (5·2 lb/hp).

Performance: (Manufacturer's estimates) Maximum speed 706 km/h at 11,000 m (439 mph at 36,090 ft); climb to 10,000 m (32,810 ft) in 14 min 12 sec; service ceiling 12,855 m (42,175 ft); endurance 2 hr.

Production: One Ki-87 prototype was completed in February 1945 by Nakajima Hikoki K.K. in their Ota plant.

The prototype Nakajima Ki-115 Tsurugi (Sabre). Lack of shock absorbers made the aircraft difficult to handle on the ground.

Nakajima Ki-115 Tsurugi (Sabre)

Anticipating that the varied collection of obsolescent combat aircraft and trainers set aside for taiatari suicide attacks in the event of an invasion of the homeland would be insufficient to rout the Allied forces, on 20 January, 1945, the Japanese Army instructed Nakajima to build a specially designed suicide attack aeroplane. The aircraft was to be easy to build, maintain and fly, and provision had to be made in its design for carrying a single bomb. Power was to be supplied by any air-cooled radial engine with a rating of 800 hp to 1,300 hp. Maximum speed was specified at 340 km/h (211 mph) with the undercarriage in position and 515 km/h (320 mph) after jettisoning.

Assisted by personnel of Mitaka Kenkyujo (Mitaka Research Institute) and Ota Seisakusho K.K. (Ota Manufacturing Co Ltd), Engineer Aori Kunihiro designed the Ki-115a Suicide Attacker Tsurugi (Sabre). Planned to be built by semi-skilled labour, the aircraft was the essence of simplicity. The all-metal wings had stressed-skin outer surfaces, the fuselage had a steel structure with tin engine cowling and steel panels on the front- and centre-sections, and the fabric-covered tail surfaces had a wooden structure. A variety of surplus engines could be used and were to be attached to the fuselage by four bolts, but all aircraft built were fitted with the Nakajima [Ha-35] 23 (Ha-25). The pilot sat in an open cockpit above the wing trailing edges and provision was made for a single bomb of up to 800 kg (1,764 lb) attached to a recessed crutch under the fuselage centre-section. The non-retractable legs of the main undercarriage were to be jettisoned after take-off for a suicide mission.

NAKAJIMA Ki-115

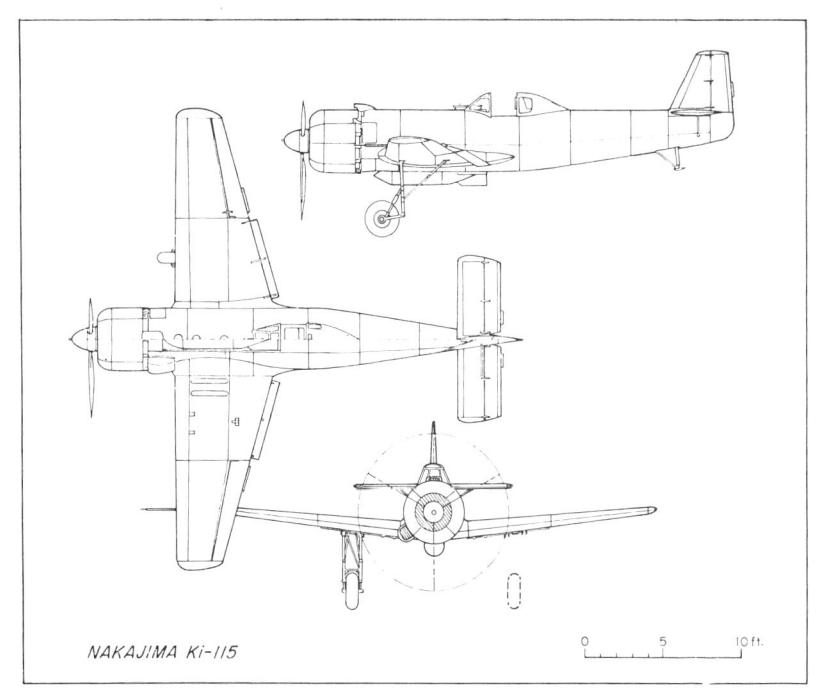

The first prototype was completed in March 1945 and flight tests began immediately. As could be expected from such a crash programme, the results were disappointing and the aircraft suffered from extremely poor handling characteristics on the ground. The crudity of the undercarriage, built of welded steel piping and lacking shock absorbers, combined with poor forward vision from the cockpit, rendered the aircraft difficult to handle, and modifications were required before handing the aircraft to pilots with limited experience. By the time basic flight tests were completed

This view shows the simplicity of the Nakajima Ki-115 Tsurugi Special Attack (Suicide) aircraft. (*USAF.*)

in June 1945, a redesigned undercarriage with shock absorbers was fitted and auxiliary flaps attached to the inboard wing trailing edges were added. Provision was made on the 104 production aircraft for two solid-fuel rockets under each wing to boost the aircraft's speed in its final dive. None of these aircraft became operational, but two were delivered to Showa Hikoki K.K. (Showa Aeroplane Co Ltd) which had been selected as the prime contractor for the proposed Toka (Wistaria) Suicide Attacker, the JNAF version of the Ki-115 which was to be powered by various reconditioned surplus engines.

The Ki-115b was a projected version with wooden wings of increased area fitted with flaps and in which the pilot's seat was moved forward. None had been completed when Japan surrendered, and the Ki-230, a development of the basic design, remained on the drawing boards.

TECHNICAL DATA

Description: Single-seat suicide attack aircraft. Mixed construction as detailed above.
Accommodation: Pilot in open cockpit.
Powerplant: One 1,150 hp Nakajima [Ha-35] 23 fourteen-cylinder air-cooled radial, rated at 1,130 hp for take-off and 980 hp at 6,000 m (19,685 ft), driving a fixed-pitch three-blade metal propeller.
Armament: One 250 kg (551 lb), 500 kg (1,102 lb), or 800 kg (1,764 lb) bomb semi-recessed under the fuselage.

	Ki-115a	Ki-115b
Dimensions:		
Span	8·6 m	9·72 m
	(28 ft 2 9/16 in)	(31 ft 10 11/16 in)
Length	8·55 m	8·55 m
	(28 ft 0⅝ in)	(28 ft 0⅝ in)
Height	3·3 m	3·3 m
	(10 ft 9 15/16 in)	(10 ft 9 15/16 in)
Wing area	12·4 sq m	14·5 sq m
	(133·472 sq ft)	(156·076 sq ft)
Weights:		
Empty	1,640 kg	1,690 kg
	(3,616 lb)	(3,726 lb)
Loaded	2,580 kg	2,630 kg
	(5,688 lb)	(5,798 lb)
Maximum	2,880 kg	—
	(6,349 lb)	—
Wing loading	208 kg/sq m	181 kg/sq m
	(42·6 lb/sq ft)	(37·1 lb/sq ft)
Power loading	2·3 kg/hp	2·3 kg/hp
	(5·1 lb/hp)	(5·1 lb/hp)
Performance:		
Maximum speed	550 km/h at 2,800 m	620 km/h at 5,800 m
	(342 mph at 9,185 ft)	(385 mph at 19,030 ft)
Cruising speed	300 km/h	—
	(186 mph)	—
Service ceiling	—	6,500 m
	—	(21,325 ft)
Range	1,200 km	1,200 km
	(745 miles)	(745 miles)

Production: A total of 105 Ki-115as were built between March and August 1945 as follows:
    1 Ki-115a prototype by Mitaka Kenkyujo at Mitaka
   22 Ki-115a production aircraft by Nakajima Hikoki K.K. at Iwate
   82 Ki-115a production aircraft by Nakajima Hikoki K.K. at Ota

Rikugun Ki-93

The Ki-93 was the last heavy fighter and ground attack aircraft built in Japan during the war and was the only design of the Rikugun Kokugijutsu Kenkyujo (Army Aerotechnical Research Institute) to be flown. Powered by two 2,400 hp Mitsubishi Ha-214 eighteen-cylinder air-cooled radials driving six-blade propellers, the Ki-93 was designed specially to carry large calibre cannon in its under-fuselage gondola. From its inception the aircraft was designed to perform as a high-altitude heavy bomber destroyer as well as a low-altitude anti-shipping aircraft. In its bomber destroyer form (Ki-93-Ia) the aircraft carried offensive armament comprising one 57 mm Ho-401 cannon and two 20 mm Ho-5 cannon, while for the anti-shipping missions (Ki-93-Ib) its offensive armament comprised one 75 mm Type 88 cannon and two 250 kg (551 lb) bombs. In both instances defensive armament consisted of a single hand-held 12·7 mm Type 1 machine-gun. The cockpit and engine nacelles were heavily armoured, and all fuel tanks were self-sealing and had an automatic fire-extinguishing system.

First prototype Rikugun Ki-93.

Production of the Ki-93 was entrusted to the Dai-Ichi Rikugun Kokusho (First Army Air Arsenal) at Tachikawa, and the first prototype, fitted with the armament intended for the Ki-93-Ia, was completed and flown in April 1945. The chaotic conditions prevailing in Japan at this late stage of the war delayed the flight trial programme and the tests were not completed prior to the Japanese surrender. A second prototype, in Ki-93-Ib ground attack configuration, was completed but not flown before the final collapse.

RIKUGUN Ki-93

TECHNICAL DATA

Description: Twin-engined heavy fighter and ground attack aircraft. All-metal construction.
Accommodation: Crew of two in enclosed cockpit.
Powerplant: Two Mitsubishi Ha-214 eighteen-cylinder air-cooled radials, rated at 2,400 hp for take-off, 1,970 hp at 1,500 m (4,920 ft) and 1,730 hp at 8,300 m (27,730 ft), driving six-blade metal propellers.
Armament: One 57 mm Ho-401 cannon and two 20 mm Ho-5 cannon in a ventral gondola and one flexible rear-firing 12·7 mm Type 1 machine-gun (Ki-93-Ia).
One forward-firing 75 mm Type 88 cannon and one flexible rear-firing 12·7 mm Type 1 machine-gun (Ki-93-Ib).
Bomb-load: two 250 kg (551 lb) bombs (Ki-93-Ib).
Dimensions: Span 19 m (62 ft 4 in); length 14·215 m (46 ft 7$\frac{23}{32}$ in); height 4·85 m (15 ft 10$\frac{13}{16}$ in); wing area 54·75 sq m (589·322 sq ft).
Weights: Empty 7,686 kg (16,945 lb); loaded 10,660 kg (23,501 lb); wing loading 194·7 kg/sq m (39·9 lb/sq ft); power loading 2·2 kg/hp (4·9 lb/hp).
Performance: Maximum speed 624 km/h at 8,300 m (388 mph at 27,230 ft); cruising speed 350 km/h (217 mph); climb to 6,000 m (19,685 ft) in 9 min 3 sec; service ceiling 12,050 m (39,530 ft); maximum range 3,000 km (1,864 miles).
Production: Two Ki-93 prototypes were built by the Dai-Ichi Rikugun Kokusho at Tachikawa in 1945.

Tachikawa Ki-9 KAI Army Type 95-1 Medium Grade Trainer Model B. (*USAF.*)

Tachikawa Ki-9

In 1933 the private-venture R-5 primary trainer powered by a 125 hp A.D.C. Cirrus IV and built by Tachikawa Hikoki K.K. was tested by the Japanese Army which found the aircraft too small for their use. However, as a result of these tests, Tachikawa were invited in March 1934 to discuss with personnel of the Tokorozawa Army Flying School the requirements for future Army trainers. A month later the Koku Hombu instructed Tachikawa to design an aircraft which, by fitting different engines, could serve as a primary trainer or as an intermediate trainer. The intermediate trainer version was to be powered by a 350 hp Hitachi Ha-13a and equipped with full blind-flying instrumentation. With this engine the aircraft was required to have a top speed of 220 km/h (137 mph) and an endurance of 3·5 hours, and was to be stressed for 12 g manoeuvres. The primary trainer version was to be powered by a 150 hp Nakajima NZ and all special equipment was eliminated to reduce weight. Despite the fact that Tachikawa were not in favour of this type of interchangeability, the Koku Hombu, noting that the problems presented by this requirement had been successfully solved by aircraft designers in Poland and Sweden, insisted on having the Ki-9 designed along these lines.

Designed by Ryokichi Endo, three Ki-9 prototypes were built in late 1934 and the first Ha-13a powered intermediate trainer made its first flight on 7 January, 1935. Controls were found to be rather heavy and manoeuvrability was disappointing as the aircraft's centre of gravity was located too far forward, while the main undercarriage's shock absorbers were excessively hard. Minor modifications were quickly made and, on 9 January, during the second flight the stall characteristics were checked, the aircraft being delivered immediately after for Service trials at Tokorozawa.

A second intermediate trainer prototype was delivered shortly after while the third aircraft was powered by the 150 hp Nakajima NZ and served as prototype for the primary trainer version. With the lighter engine the centre of gravity was located too far back and the aircraft suffered from poor handling characteristics on take-off.

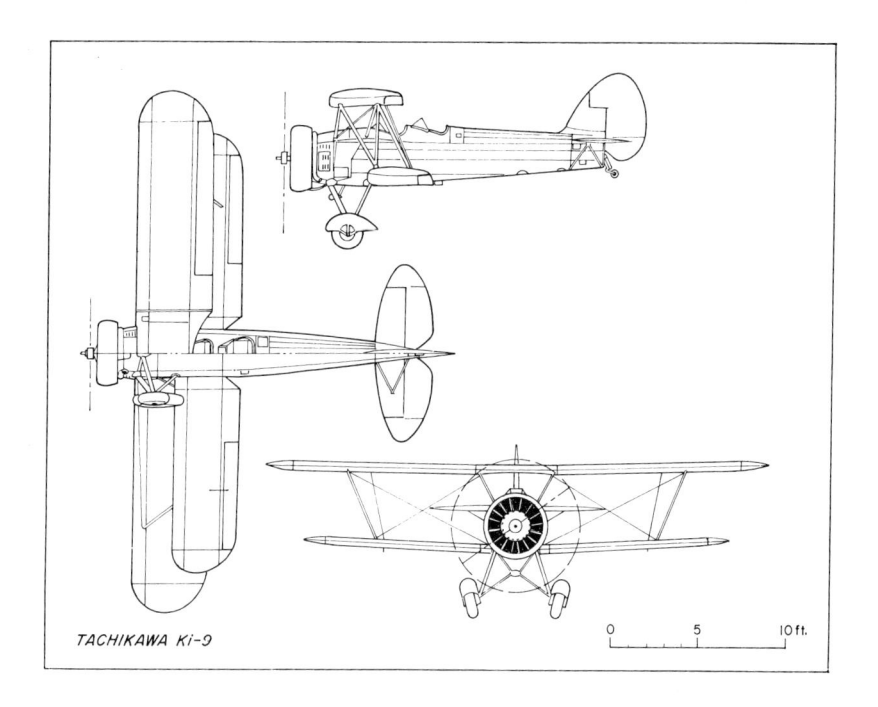

TACHIKAWA Ki-9

Following completion of Service trials at Tokorozawa, only the Ha-13a powered intermediate trainer was accepted for production as the Army Type 95-1 Medium Grade Trainer Model A. Later an improved version of the aircraft was produced as the Army Type 95-1 Medium Grade Trainer Model B (Ki-9 KAI). This version was lighter and featured a sturdier landing gear and shorter fuselage. This last modification resulted in a rearward shift of the centre of gravity which improved manoeuvrability.

The Ki-9s remained in service with the Japanese Army throughout the Sino-Japanese conflict and the Pacific War and was coded SPRUCE by the Allies. The aircraft was also operated during the war by the Cochin China, Manchurian and Thai air forces and, after the war, by the fledgling air arm of the Indonesian People's Security Forces.

UNITS ALLOCATED
Kumagaya, Mito, Tachiarai and Utsonomiya Army Flying Schools; Koku Shikan Gakko (Air Academy).

TECHNICAL DATA

Description: Single-engined basic trainer. Metal structure with fabric covering.
Accommodation: Pupil and instructor in tandem open cockpits.
Powerplant: One Army Type 95 nine-cylinder air-cooled radial (Hitachi Ha-13a), rated at 350 hp for take-off, driving a two-blade wooden propeller (first and second Ki-9 prototypes and production aircraft).
   One Nakajima NZ seven-cylinder air-cooled radial, rated at 150 hp for take-off, driving a two-blade wooden propeller (third prototype).
Dimensions: Span 10·32 m (33 ft 10 ⁵⁄₁₆ in); length 7·525 m (24 ft 8¼ in); height 3 m (9 ft 10⅛ in); wing area 24·5 sq m (263·715 sq ft).
Weights: Empty 1,015 kg (2,238 lb); loaded 1,425 kg (3,142 lb); wing loading 58·2 kg/sq m (11·9 lb/sq ft); power loading 4·1 kg/hp (9 lb/hp).
Performance: Maximum speed 240 km/h (149 mph); cruising speed 150 km/h (93 mph); climb to 1,000 m (3,280 ft) in 4 min 55 sec; endurance 3·5 hours.
Production: A total of 2,618 Ki-9s were built as follows:
   Tachikawa Hikoki K.K. at Tachikawa:
      3 Ki-9 prototypes (1934)
      2,395 Ki-9 production aircraft (1935–42)
   Tokyo Koku K.K.:
      220 Ki-9 production aircraft (1944–45)

Tachikawa Ki-17

When, early in 1935, the 150 hp Nakajima NZ powered primary trainer version of the Ki-9 failed to give satisfaction, the Japanese Army finally decided to review their earlier decision to select a common type for primary and intermediate training. Accordingly, in April 1935, Tachikawa were instructed to design a new primary trainer which received the designation Ki-17. The specification called for an aircraft with a loaded weight not exceeding 1,000 kg (2,205 lb) and a wing loading of less than 35 kg/sq m (7·2 lb/sq ft). Whereas the Ki-9 was stressed for 12 g manoeuvres the Ki-17 was to be stressed for only 6 g. Tachikawa were instructed to have two prototypes ready by August 1935 as the Army were anxious to have the aircraft as soon as possible to train the large number of pilots required for their expansion programme.

Despite Engineer Fujita's suggestion that the wing loading be increased over the 35 kg/sq m requirement of the specification the Technical Department of the Koku Hombu insisted on its being retained. The result was a remarkably light biplane with a loaded weight of only 900 kg (1,984 lb) which bore a strong family resemblance to the earlier Ki-9. The principal external difference lay in the wings which were of equal span, whereas on the Ki-9 they were of unequal span, resulting in the Ki-17 having a larger wing area despite the fact that it had a shorter span. Powered by a 150 hp Hitachi Ha-12, the first of two Ki-17 prototypes was completed in July 1935. In its original form the aircraft was fitted with ailerons on both the

Tachikawa Ki-17 Army Type 95-3 Primary Trainer. (*USAF.*)

upper and lower wings, as was the Ki-9, but during flight trials these ailerons proved over-sensitive and those on the upper wing were deleted.

Following this modification the aircraft was placed in production as the Army Type 95-3 Primary Trainer (Allied code name CEDAR) and a total of 560 aircraft of this type were built up to 1944.

UNITS ALLOCATED

Kumagaya, Mito, Tachiarai and Utsonomiya Army Flying Training Schools; Koku Shikan Gakko (Air Academy).

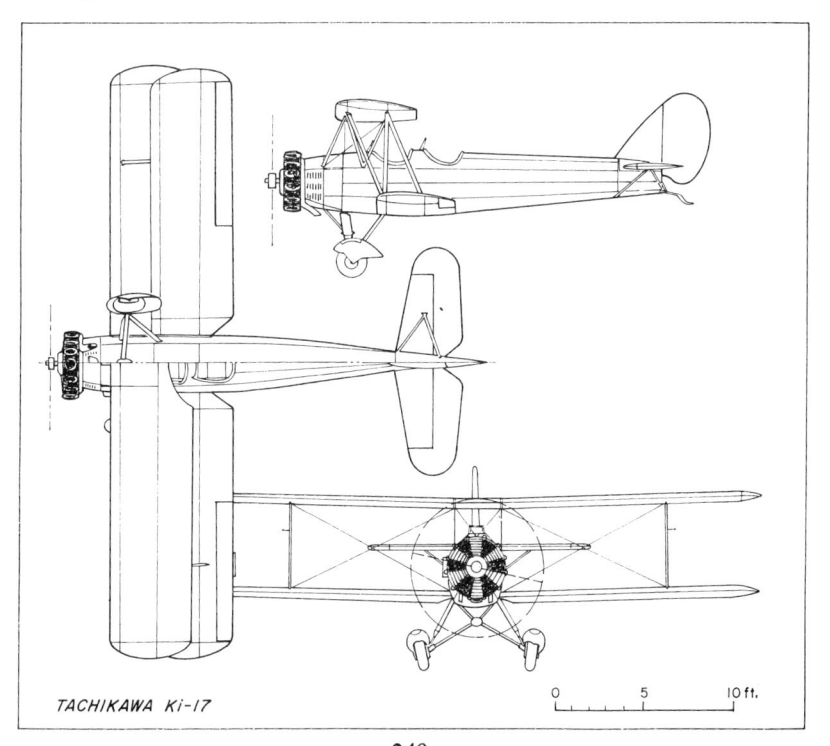

TACHIKAWA Ki-17

TECHNICAL DATA

Description: Single-engined primary trainer. Metal structure with fabric covering.
Accommodation: Pupil and instructor in tandem open cockpits.
Powerplant: One Army Type 95 seven-cylinder air-cooled radial (Hitachi Ha-12), rated at 150 hp for take-off, driving a two-blade wooden propeller.
Dimensions: Span 9·82 m (32 ft 2⅝ in); length 7·8 m (25 ft 7 3/32 in); height 2·95 m (9 ft 8 5/32 in); wing area 26·02 sq m (280·076 sq ft).
Weights: Empty 618 kg (1,362 lb); loaded 900 kg (1,984 lb); wing loading 34·6 kg/sq m (7·1 lb/sq ft); power loading 6 kg/hp (13·2 lb/hp).
Performance: Maximum speed 170 km/h (106 mph); cruising speed 130 km/h (81 mph); service ceiling 5,300 m (17,390 ft); endurance 3·45 hr.
Production: A total of 560 Ki-17s, including two prototypes, were built by Tachikawa Hikoki K.K. at Tachikawa between 1935 and 1944.

Tachikawa Ki-36 and Ki-55

In May 1937 the Koku Hombu issued a specification calling for a two-seat army co-operation machine. The aircraft was to be a fast single-engined monoplane capable of operating from small rough strips immediately behind the front lines. Good downward visibility from the cockpit and extreme manoeuvrability at low altitudes were among the prime requirements for the aircraft, which was to incorporate provision for photographic and radio equipment in addition to bomb racks for light anti-personnel bombs.

Competitive designs to this specification were submitted by Mitsubishi Jukogyo K.K. (Ki-35) and Tachikawa Hikoki K.K. (Ki-36), but only the

Tachikawa Ki-36 Army Type 98 Direct Co-operation Plane. (*USAF.*)

TACHIKAWA Ki-36

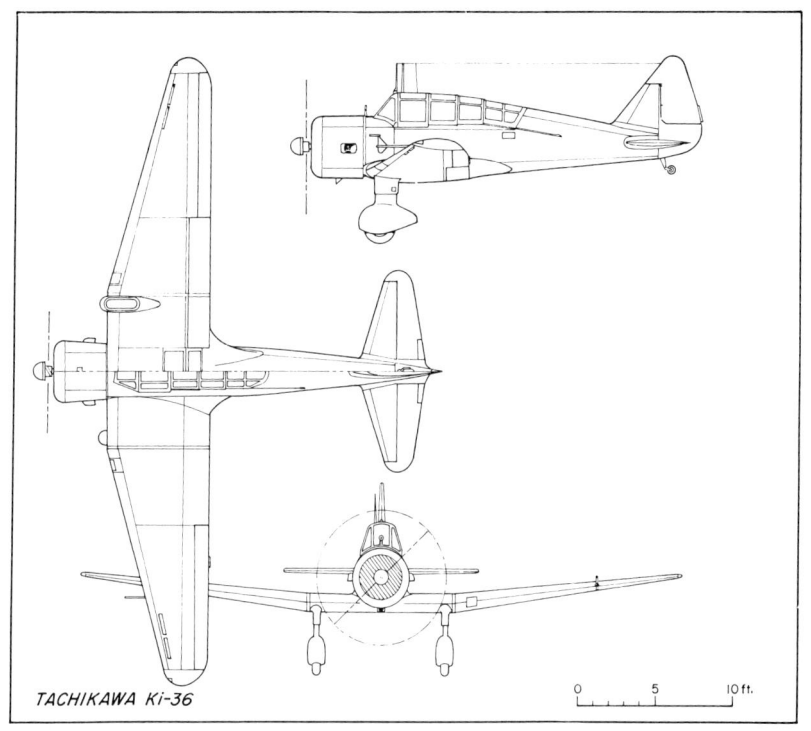

construction of Tachikawa Ki-36 prototypes was authorized by the Koku Hombu. Despite the stringent demands for good cockpit visibility, manoeuvrability and short-field performance, Ryokichi Endo, who led the Tachikawa engineering team, selected a conventional low-wing monoplane configuration with fixed spatted undercarriage. To obtain the necessary low speed handling characteristics Endo strove to design a light airframe which, combined with a large wing area, resulted in a low wing loading. Sensitivity of controls was achieved by using large-size elevators and rudder. Despite the cockpit location over the wings, the pilot had a good field of view forward and downward due to the large degree of sweepback incorporated in the wing leading edges, while large windows under the wing centre-section provided a good field of view for the observer.

Powered by a 450 hp Hitachi Ha-13 nine-cylinder air-cooled radial driving a two-blade wooden propeller, the first prototype was completed in March 1938 and made its maiden flight at Tachikawa on 20 April, 1938. During flight tests the aircraft performed satisfactorily and demonstrated brisk take-off and flight performance. Because the first Ki-36 suffered from wingtip stall, the second prototype had fixed leading edge slots near the wingtips to correct this deficiency. Both prototypes were armed with a fixed forward-firing 7·7 mm Type 89 machine-gun mounted offset to

Tachikawa Ki-55 of the Kumagaya Army Flying School. (*Aireview.*)

starboard within the engine cowling and with a similar flexible rear-firing machine-gun manned by the observer, and racks were mounted under the wings for ten 12·5 kg (27·5 lb) or 15 kg (33 lb) anti-personnel bombs. In this form the aircraft was ordered into production as the Army Type 98 Direct Co-operation Plane, beginning at Tachikawa in November 1938, and in 1940 production was also initiated by Kawasaki Kokuki Kogyo K.K. Late production aircraft built by Tachikawa and Kawasaki featured a two degree wing wash-out to improve stall characteristics.

Assigned in small detachments to ground units of the Japanese Army, the Ki-36s operated successfully during the second Sino-Japanese conflict. The ability of the aircraft to utilize small airstrips close to the battlefields made it popular with ground commanders, and the Ki-36 contributed significantly to the demoralization of the hard-pressed Chinese troops. However, when the Pacific War began, the Ki-36s suffered heavy losses when faced by Allied fighters and, from 1943 onwards, the aircraft was relegated to units operating in China where they encountered fewer Allied aircraft, while a small number of Ki-36s were supplied to Thailand.

The ease of piloting and good handling characteristics of the Ki-36 combined with good performance rendered it ideally suited for adaptation to the advanced training role. All unnecessary equipment was removed to conserve weight, as were the observation windows under the fuselage and the wheel spats. Designated Ki-55, the trainer was adopted as the Army Type 99 Advanced Trainer and was manufactured in large numbers by Tachikawa and Kawasaki. In the normal flight training syllabus, Army single-engined pilots received their wings after flying the Ki-55 solo, and the aircraft was operated by civil flying schools operating under military contracts as well as by regular Army Flying Schools. Ki-55s were also delivered to the wartime Japanese satellite air forces of Thailand, Manchukuo and Cochin China, while three aircraft of this type abandoned on Java by the Japanese were flown against the Dutch by the revolutionary Indonesian Air Force.

During the last year of the war a number of Ki-36s and Ki-55s, both types being known as IDA to the Allied forces, were expended in suicide sorties for which they carried externally a single 250 kg (551 lb) or 500 kg (1,102 lb) bomb.

An advanced version of the Ki-36 featuring a retractable undercarriage and powered by a 600 hp Hitachi Ha-38 nine-cylinder radial driving a three-blade propeller was designed by Tachikawa under the Ki-72 designation but was not built.

UNITS ALLOCATED

Ki-36: 29th and 44th Sentais; 17th, 44th, 45th, 66th and 74th Dokuritsu Dai Shijugo Chutais; Korean Command; Central Command; 7th and 8th Ground Support Units.

Ki-55: Kumagaya, Mito, Tachiarai and Utsonomiya Army Flying Schools.

TECHNICAL DATA

Description: Single-engined army co-operation aircraft (Ki-36) or two-seat advanced trainer (Ki-55). All-metal structure with metal and fabric covering.
Accommodation: Crew of two in tandem enclosed cockpits.
Powerplant: One 450 hp Army Type 98 nine-cylinder air-cooled radial (Hitachi Ha-13a), rated at 510 hp for take-off and 470 hp at 1,700 m (5,580 ft), driving a two-blade wooden propeller.
Armament: One forward-firing 7·7 mm Type 89 machine-gun in the engine cowling and one flexible rear-firing 7·7 mm Type 89 machine-gun (Ki-36).

One forward-firing 7·7 mm Type 89 machine-gun in the engine cowling (Ki-55).

External load: ten 12·5 kg (27·5 lb) or 15 kg (33 lb) bombs (Ki-36). Suicide sorties: one 250 kg (551 lb) or 500 kg (1,102 lb) bomb (Ki-36 and Ki-55).

	Ki-36	Ki-55
Dimensions:		
Span	11·8 m	11·8 m
	(38 ft 8 9/16 in)	(38 ft 8 9/16 in)
Length	8 m	8 m
	(26 ft 2 31/32 in)	(26 ft 2 31/32 in)
Height	3·64 m	3·64 m
	(11 ft 11 5/16 in)	(11 ft 11 5/16 in)
Wing area	20 sq m	20 sq m
	(215·277 sq ft)	(215·277 sq ft)
Weights:		
Empty	1,247 kg	1,292 kg
	(2,749 lb)	(2,848 lb)
Loaded	1,660 kg	1,721 kg
	(3,660 lb)	(3,794 lb)
Wing loading	83 kg/sq m	86·1 kg/sq m
	(17 lb/sq ft)	(17·6 lb/sq ft)
Power loading	3·3 kg/hp	3·4 kg/hp
	(7·2 lb/hp)	(7·4 lb/hp)
Performance:		
Maximum speed	348 km/h at 1,800 m	349 km/h at 2,200 m
	(216 mph at 5,905 ft)	(217 mph at 7,220 ft)
Cruising speed	236 km/h	235 km/h
	(147 mph)	(146 mph)
Climb to	3,000 m (9,845 ft)	3,000 m (9,845 ft)
in	6 min 39 sec	6 min 55 sec
Service ceiling	8,150 m	8,200 m
	(26,740 ft)	(26,900 ft)
Range	1,235 km	1,060 km
	(767 miles)	(659 miles)

Production: A total of 2,723 Ki-36s and Ki-55s were built as follows:

Tachikawa Hikoki K.K. at Tachikawa:
    2 Ki-36 prototypes (spring 1938)
    860 Ki-36 production aircraft (Nov 1938–Jan 1944)
    1 Ki-55 prototype (Sept 1939)
    1,077 Ki-55 production aircraft (Oct 1939–Apr 1943 and Nov–Dec 1943)

Kawasaki Kokuki Kogyo K.K. at Gifu and Akashi:
    472 Ki-36 production aircraft (June 1940–May 1942) (Gifu)
    251 Ki-55 production aircraft (Feb 1941–Mar 1943) (Gifu)
    60 Ki-55 production aircraft (Sept 1941–Nov 1942) (Akashi)

Tachikawa Ki-54

In late 1939, at the request of the Koku Hombu, Ryokichi Endo began designing for Tachikawa a twin-engined multi-purpose trainer. The aircraft was required to duplicate closely the handling characteristics and performance of the series of modern twin-engined bombers which the Army had operated since 1937. It was to be used for the simultaneous training of a complete bomber's crew including pilot, bombardier, navigator, gunner and radio-operator. To achieve the necessary performance Endo selected a low-wing design with retractable undercarriage and adopted a pair of 510 hp Hitachi Ha-13a radials with Hamilton-type variable-pitch propellers to power the aircraft.

Designated Ki-54, the first prototype was completed and flown during the summer of 1940. Following minor modifications which partially corrected a nose-heavy tendency during landings, the aircraft was placed

Tachikawa Ki-54a advanced trainer. (*Archivio Fotografico Italo de Marchi.*)

in production in 1941 as the Army Type 1 Advanced Trainer Model A (Ki-54a). Like the prototype, the aircraft of this first production series were primarily designed for pilot training. However, the Ki-54a was soon supplanted by the Ki-54b (Army Type 1 Operations Trainer Model B) which had full provision for bomber crew training and had four gunnery stations each mounting a flexible 7·7 mm Type 89 machine-gun. Operated by all military multi-engined training schools and communications schools as well as by civil training schools under Japanese Army contracts, the Ki-54b was built in greater numbers than any other variants of the Ki-54.

The Ki-54c or Army Type 1 Transport Model C was a light transport and communications version characterized by its smooth upper fuselage

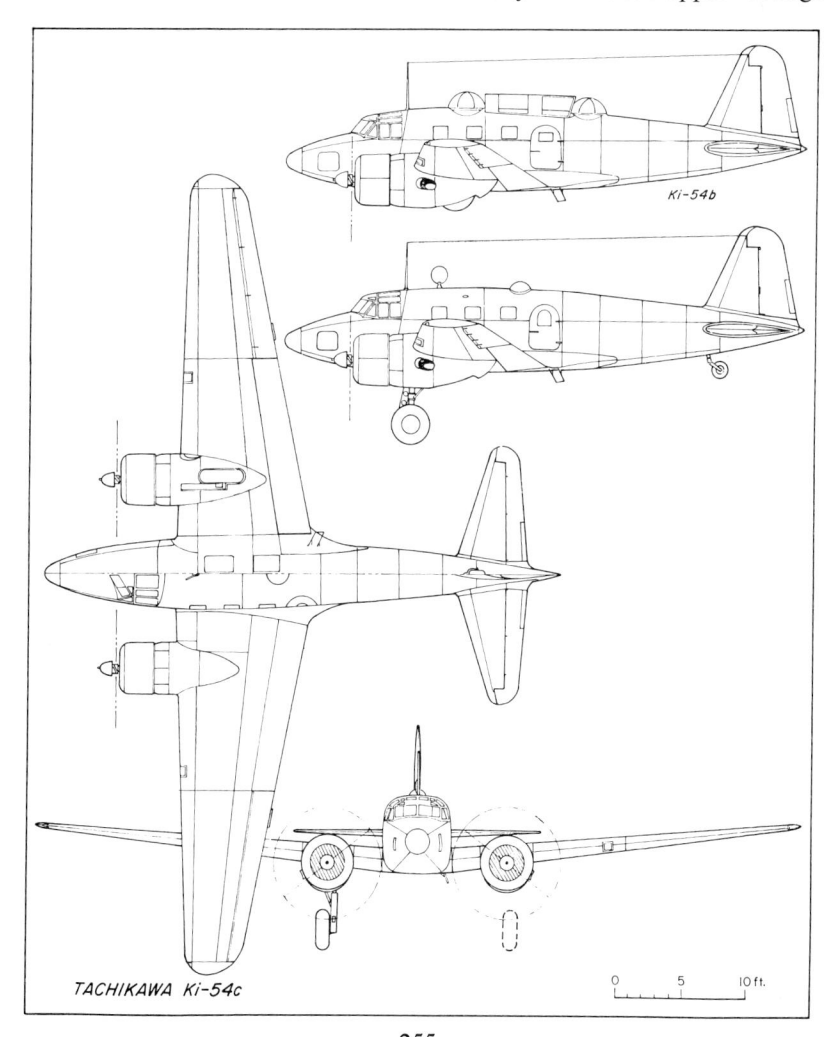

TACHIKAWA Ki-54c

A Tachikawa Ki-54c Army Type 1 Transport Model C with surrender markings, photographed at Morotai in the summer of 1945. (*Frank Smith.*)

line and was fitted with eight seats. A similar version was built in small numbers as the Y-59 for civil operators. Late in the war an all-wood version of the Ki-54c, the Ki-110, was built, but the aircraft was destroyed during an American raid. The Ki-111 was a projected fuel tanker version and the Ki-114 was an advanced version of the all-wood Ki-110, but neither could be completed prior to the Japanese surrender.

The Army Type 1 Patrol Bomber Model D (Ki-54d) was an antisubmarine patrol aircraft carrying eight 60 kg (132 lb) depth-charges, developed from the basic Ki-54 and powered by the same engines, but few were built and they saw action for only a brief period.

As a crew trainer and light transport, the Ki-54 was one of the most successful Japanese aircraft of the war and was well known to the Allies which named it HICKORY regardless of the versions. The code name JOYCE was erroneously assigned to a non-existent light bomber version.

UNITS ALLOCATED
108th Sentai; 20th and 25th Hikodans; Army Air Communication School.

TECHNICAL DATA
Description: Twin-engined crew trainer (Ki-54a and Ki-54b), light transport (Ki-54c, Ki-110, Ki-111 and Ki-114) and anti-submarine patrol aircraft (Ki-54d). All-metal construction with fabric-covered control surfaces.

Accommodation: Crew of five to nine in enclosed cabin (Ki-54a, b and d), crew of two and eight passengers (Ki-54c, Ki-110 and Ki-114) or crew of two (Ki-111).

Powerplant: Two 450 hp Army Type 98 nine-cylinder air-cooled radials (Hitachi Ha-13a), rated at 510 hp for take-off and 470 hp at 1,700 m (5,580 ft), driving two-blade propellers.

Armament: Four flexible 7·7 mm Type 89 machine-guns and practice bombs (Ki-54b). 480 kg (1,058 lb) of depth-charges (Ki-54d).

Dimensions: Span 17·9 m (58 ft 8⅚ in); length 11·94 m (39 ft 2⅛ in); height 3·58 m (11 ft 8⅞ in); wing area 40 sq m (430·555 sq ft).

Weights: Empty 2,954 kg (6,512 lb); loaded 3,897 kg (8,591 lb); wing loading 97·4 kg/sq m (20 lb/sq ft); power loading 3·8 kg/hp (8·4 lb/hp).

Performance: Maximum speed 376 km/h at 2,000 m (234 mph at 6,560 ft); cruising speed 240 km/h (149 mph); climb to 5,000 m (16,405 ft) in 20 min 18 sec; service ceiling 7,180 m (22,555 ft); range 960 km (597 miles).

Production: A total of 1,368 Ki-54s were built by Tachikawa Hikoki K.K. as follows: 7 in 1940, 101 in 1941, 236 in 1942, 386 in 1943, 500 in 1940, 138 in 1945.

Tachikawa Ki-70

Designed as a replacement for the Mitsubishi Ki-46, the Tachikawa Ki-70 (code name CLARA) never entered production as its performance fell below that of advanced versions of its predecessor. In March 1939, two years after issuing the specification to which the Ki-46 was designed and eight months before the first flight of that aircraft, the Koku Hombu instructed Tachikawa Hikoki K.K. to design a still faster and longer-range reconnaissance aircraft which received the Kitai number Ki-70. The aircraft proposed by Tachikawa was a twin-engined mid-wing cantilever monoplane with laminar flow aerofoil. The crew of three included an observer manning a flexible 7·7 mm machine-gun in the glazed nose, the pilot seated just forward of the wing leading edge and the radio-operator manning a flexible 12·7 mm machine-gun in the rear fuselage. To improve the field of fire of the rear-firing machine-gun, twin fins and rudders were adopted. With two 1,900 hp Mitsubishi Ha-104M eighteen-cylinder radials, a top speed of 647 km/h at 5,400 m (402 mph at 17,715 ft) was anticipated.

Construction of two prototypes progressed slowly, and the first Ki-70 was not completed until February 1943. When flight tests began, the results were immediately disappointing as the Ki-70's weight exceeded calculated values by a considerable amount. Consequently, wing loading was excessive and the aircraft was hard to handle during take-off and landing. Inflight handling characteristics could hardly be considered satisfactory and the maximum speed reached during the trials was 580 km/h (360 mph), which compared poorly with the top speed of 604 km/h and 630 km/h (375 mph and 391 mph) respectively reached by the Ki-46-II and Ki-46-III. In an effort to improve performance a third prototype was built with 2,200 hp turbosupercharged Mitsubishi Ha-211-I Ru radials. However, the Ha-211-I Ru was unreliable and the Ki-70 was still overweight, forcing the Koku Hombu to abandon its support of the programme.

Tachikawa Ki-70 Army Experimental Command Reconnaissance Plane. (*Aireview*.)

TACHIKAWA Ki-70

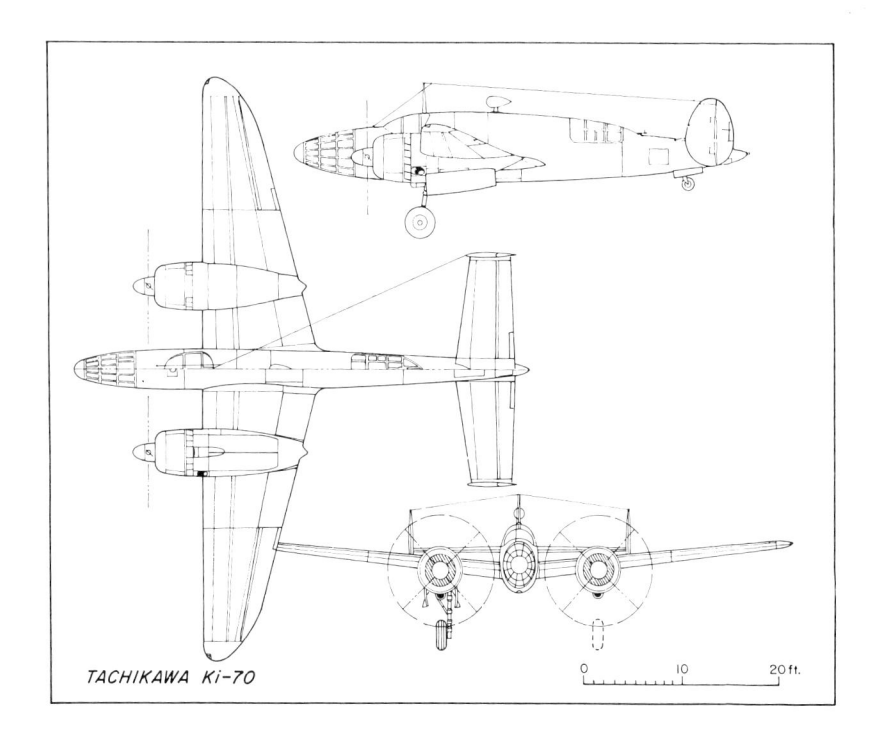

TECHNICAL DATA

Description: Twin-engined reconnaissance aircraft. All-metal construction with fabric-covered control surfaces.

Accommodation: Crew of three in enclosed cockpits.

Powerplant: Two Mitsubishi Ha-104M eighteen-cylinder air-cooled radials, rated at 1,900 hp for take-off, 1,810 hp at 2,200 m (7,220 ft) and 1,610 hp at 6,100 m (20,015 ft), driving four-blade metal propellers (first and second prototypes).

Two Mitsubishi Ha-211-I Ru eighteen-cylinder air-cooled radials, rated at 2,200 hp for take-off, 2,070 hp at 1,000 m (3,280 ft) and 1,720 hp at 9,500 m (31,170 ft), driving four-blade metal propellers (third prototype).

Armament: One flexible forward-firing 7·7 mm Type 89 machine-gun and one flexible rear-firing 12·7 mm Type 1 (Ho-103) machine-gun.

Dimensions: Span 17·8 m (58 ft 4$\frac{23}{32}$ in); length 14·5 m (47 ft 6$\frac{7}{8}$ in); height 3·46 m (11 ft 4$\frac{7}{32}$ in); wing area 43 sq m (462·846 sq ft).

Weights: (with Ha-104M) Empty 5,895 kg (12,996 lb); loaded 9,855 kg (21,727 lb); maximum 10,700 kg (23,589 lb); wing loading 229·2 kg/sq m (46·9 lb/sq ft); power loading 2·6 kg/hp (5·7 lb/hp).

Calculated Performance: (with Ha-104M) Maximum speed 647 km/h at 5,400 m (402 mph at 17,715 ft); cruising speed 490 km/h at 5,400 m (304 mph at 17,715 ft); climb to 5,000 m (16,405 ft) in 5 min; service ceiling 11,000 m (36,090 ft); range 2,480 km (1,541 miles).

Production: A total of three Ki-70s were built in 1943 by Tachikawa Hikoki K.K.

The thirteenth pre-production Tachikawa Ki-74. (*Aireview*.)

Tachikawa Ki-74

Although first conceived as early as 1939, the Tachikawa Ki-74 had not been placed in full production when the Pacific War ended. During those six years its intended role had been changed from that of long-range reconnaissance to that of long-range stratospheric bombing.

Under the guidance of Dr Kimura, the Ki-74 was originally designed in the spring of 1939 to meet the requirements of a specification issued by the Koku Hombu and calling for a long-range reconnaissance aircraft capable of operating west of Lake Baikal from Manchurian bases. The aircraft was to have a range of 5,000 km (3,107 miles) at a cruising speed of at least 450 km/h (280 mph). To meet these performance requirements, Dr Kimura proposed using a pair of 2,400 hp Mitsubishi Ha-214M radials driving six-blade propellers and fitting a pressure cabin. However, pending development of the pressure cabin system tested on the Tachikawa SS-1 and Ki-77, the project was temporarily suspended.

View of the Tachikawa Ki-74 showing bomb-bay and ventral entrance hatch. (*Aireview*.)

Late in 1941 the project was revived as a long-range high-altitude bomber-reconnaissance aircraft capable of bombing the United States mainland. To fit the aircraft for its new role, Tachikawa added bombing equipment, self-sealing fuel tanks and armour to the original design and

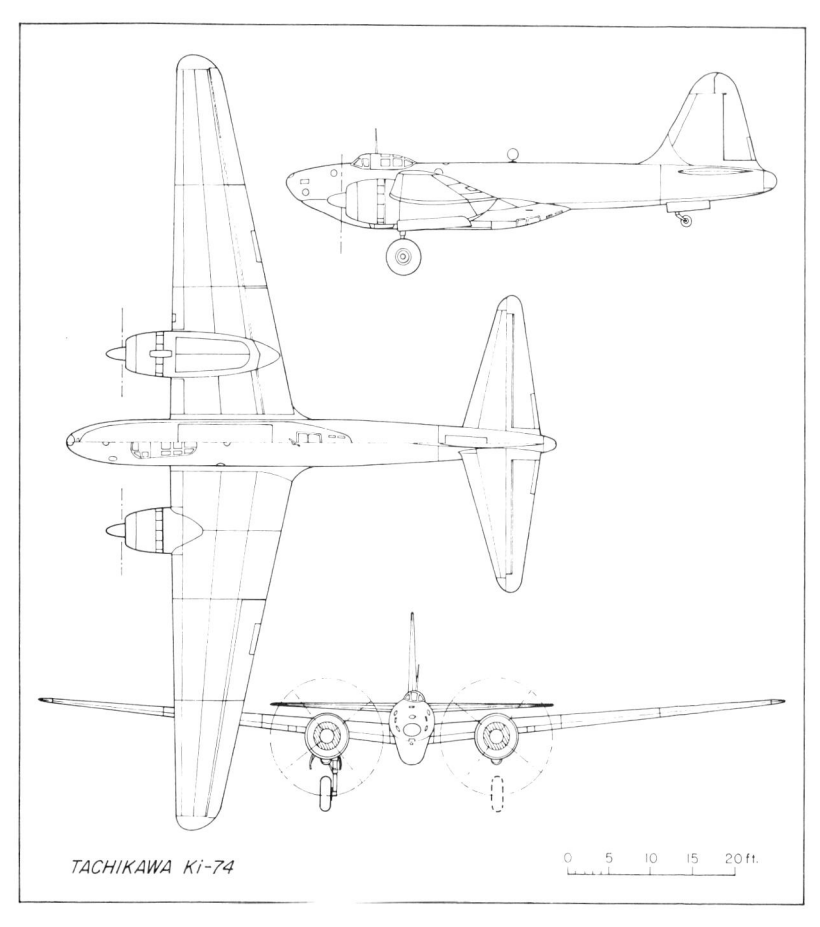

TACHIKAWA Ki-74

decided to replace the Ha-214M engines with a pair of 2,200 hp Mitsubishi Ha-211-I radials. The design of the aircraft was approved by the Koku Hombu in September 1942 and construction of three prototypes was authorized. The first prototype, completed in March 1944, was followed by two externally identical aircraft which were powered by 2,200 hp turbosupercharged Ha-211-I Ru radials. However, during the flight trial programme both versions of the Mitsubishi Ha-211 suffered from teething troubles and it was decided to replace them on the pre-production aircraft with the lower-powered but more reliable turbosupercharged Mitsubishi Ha-104 Ru.

Thirteen Ha-104 Ru powered pre-production aircraft were built and were still undergoing tests when the war ended. All five crew members were seated in a pressure cabin in the forward fuselage, and the aircraft was armed with a single remotely-controlled 12·7 mm machine-gun in the tail and carried a bomb-load of 1,000 kg (2,205 lb). Plans were made to use the Ki-74s in bombing attacks against the B-29 bases on Saipan as soon as sufficient aircraft were available, but the Japanese surrender terminated the project. Although the Ki-74 was never encountered during the war, the Allies were aware of its development, but thinking at first that it was a 'super-range, high-speed fighter' intended for long-range escort duty they accordingly assigned to it a male name: PAT; when the true role of the aircraft was discovered the code name was changed to PATSY.

The fourth pre-production aircraft (Ki-74 c/n 7) was modified in 1944 to undertake non-stop flights between Japan and Germany, but the Third Reich capitulated before the first of these flights could be made. Other developments included a pure bomber version, the Ki-74-II, with a bomb-load increased to 2,000 kg (4,410 lb), and a transport version, but both these projects were abandoned before completion.

TECHNICAL DATA

Description: Twin-engined high-altitude long-range reconnaissance-bomber. All-metal construction.
Accommodation: Crew of five in pressure cabin.
Powerplant: Two Mitsubishi Ha-211-I eighteen-cylinder air-cooled radials, rated at 2,200 hp for take-off, 2,070 hp at 1,000 m (3,280 ft) and 1,930 hp at 5,000 m (16,405 ft), driving four-blade metal propellers (first prototype).

Two Mitsubishi Ha-211-I Ru eighteen-cylinder air-cooled radials, rated at 2,200 hp for take-off, 2,070 hp at 1,000 m (3,280 ft) and 1,720 hp at 9,500 m (31,170 ft), driving four-blade metal propellers (second and third prototypes).

Two Mitsubishi Ha-104 Ru eighteen-cylinder air-cooled radials, rated at 2,000 hp for take-off, 1,900 hp at 2,000 m (6,560 ft) and 1,750 hp at 6,000 m (19,685 ft), driving four-blade metal propellers (4th–16th aircraft).
Armament: One remotely-controlled 12·7 mm Type 1 (Ho-103) machine-gun in the tail.
 Bomb-load: 1,000 kg (2,205 lb) (Ki-74-I).
Dimensions: Span 27 m (88 ft 7 in); length 17·65 m (57 ft 10⅜ in); height 5·1 m (16 ft 8⁴⁹⁄₆₄ in); wing area 80 sq m (861·11 sq ft).
Weights: Empty 10,200 kg (22,487 lb); loaded 19,400 kg (42,770 lb); wing loading 242·5 kg/sq m (49·7 lb/sq ft); power loading 4·4 kg/hp (9·7 lb/hp).
Performance: Maximum speed 570 km/h at 8,500 m (354 mph at 27,890 ft); cruising speed 400 km/h at 8,000 m (249 mph at 26,245 ft); climb to 8,000 m (26,245 ft) in 17 min; service ceiling 12,000 m (39,370 ft): range 8,000 km (4,971 miles).
Production: A total of 16 Ki-74s were built between March 1944 and August 1945 by Tachikawa Hikoki K.K. at Tachikawa.

The Tachikawa Ki-77 which, in July 1944, set an unofficial closed-circuit distance record by flying 10,212 miles (16,435 km) non-stop in 57 hr 12 min. (*Aireview*.)

Tachikawa Ki-77

During the thirties the strong rivalry existing between the largest newspapers in Japan had resulted in several famous record flights and, in late 1939, the *Asahi Shimbun* (Asahi Press) were studying the possibility of bettering the recent round-the-word flight by J-BACI, a modified Mitsubishi G3M2, which had been sponsored by their rivals the *Mainichi Shimbun*. The management of *Asahi Shimbun* agreed that the most promising way to recapture the interest of the Japanese populace was to sponsor a non-stop flight between Tokyo and New York. As no aircraft then available had sufficient range for this flight, *Asahi Shimbun* approached the Aeronautical Research Institute of the University of Tokyo in January 1940 with a request that they design a new aircraft with a range exceeding 15,000 km (9,321 miles) at a minimum cruising speed of 300 km/h (186 mph). The aircraft was to fly in the sub-stratosphere and, besides its primary use as a long-distance record-breaking machine, was to serve in the development of a future stratospheric transport.

With the approval of the Japanese Army work began in earnest in March 1940, the project receiving the designation A-26—the 'A' referring to the sponsoring *Asahi Shimbun* and the '26' standing for the first two digits of the current Japanese year, 2600 (A.D. 1940). Members of the

Aeronautical Research Institute of the University of Tokyo, led by Dr H. Kimura, were responsible for the basic design while Tachikawa Hikoki K.K., which appointed Ryokichi Endo as their chief project engineer, were responsible for detailed engineering drawings and the manufacture of the aircraft. Dr Kimura decided to power the A-26 with two 1,000 hp Nakajima Ha-105 fourteen-cylinder double-row radials enclosed in close-fitting cowlings inspired by those of the Curtiss-Wright CW-20, but eventually the aircraft was powered by two 1,170 hp Nakajima Ha-115, a development of the earlier Ha-105 with a lower reduction ratio. Initially it was hoped that the 'sealed oxygen cabin', unpressurized but sealed to prevent loss of oxygen, would necessitate only minimum use of oxygen masks by the crew, but in the event the crew members were to suffer the discomfort of wearing their masks continuously. A wing of laminar flow section, designed by Professor Fukazu of the University of Tokyo, with six-degrees dihedral and an aspect ratio of 11 was adopted as it offered the best compromise between the conflicting requirements imposed by long-range operation and ease of production. In the wing were located the fuel tanks with a total

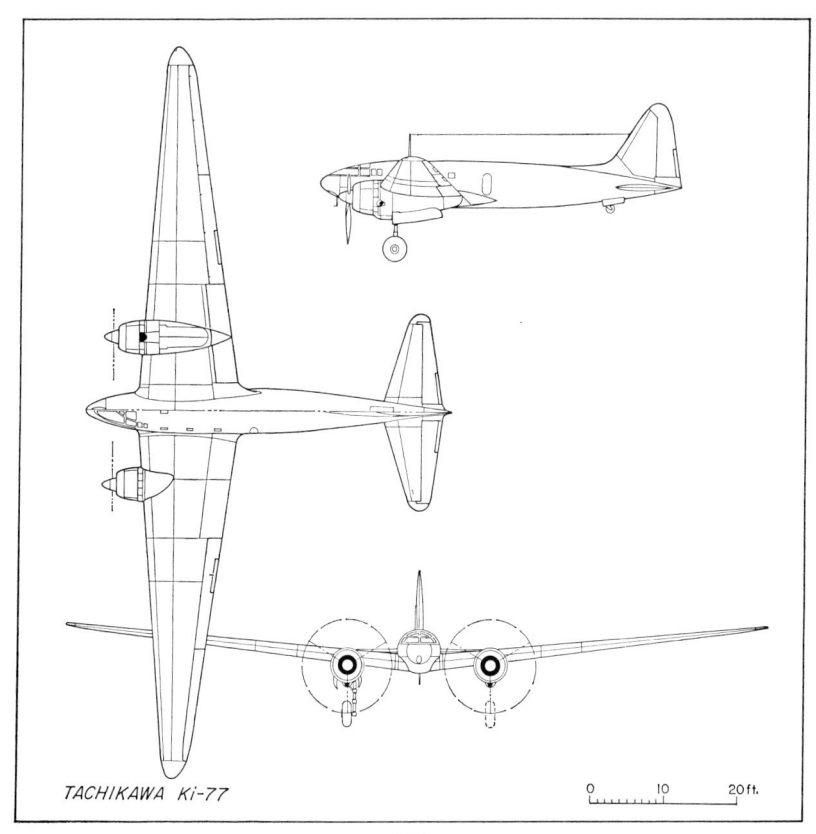

TACHIKAWA Ki-77

capacity of 11,155 litres (2,542 Imp gal). Having resolved the basic configuration of the aircraft, detailed engineering drawing began in the autumn of 1940, the first flight being tentatively scheduled for November 1941. Minor design problems forced a first postponement until February 1942, but the beginning of hostilities in the Pacific compromised the future of the aircraft as Tachikawa were instructed to concentrate on military programmes.

In the summer of 1942 the project was revived again as a long-range communication aeroplane by the Japanese Army which wished to maintain a line of communication with the other Axis powers. Now bearing the military designation Ki-77, the aircraft was completed in September 1942 and, after delays caused by engine cooling difficulties, made its first flight from Tachikawa Airfield on 18 November, 1942, with pilots Kamada and Nagatomo at the controls. Flying characteristics were found fully satisfactory during flight trials, but the engine cowlings had to be modified several times due to overheating on the ground. Finally the problem was solved and the Ki-77 gave a first demonstration of its capability on 20–21 April, 1943, when it flew non-stop from Fussa, Tokyo Prefecture, to Singapore covering 5,330 km (3,312 miles) in 19 hr 13 min. A second prototype began flight trials the following month to be readied for the Seiko (Success) flight between Japan and Germany. This flight was actually attempted on 7 July, 1943, but the aircraft was lost over the Indian Ocean, possibly due to an encounter with British fighters, on its way from Singapore to Berlin.

Despite their preoccupation with the ever gloomier war situation, the Japanese decided to attack, unofficially, the world closed-circuit distance record. An 865 km (537·5 miles) circuit between Sinking, Peichengtu and Harbin, Manchuria, was selected and, starting on 2 July, 1944, at Sinking airfield, the first prototype Ki-77—the aircraft originally intended to fly non-stop from Tokyo to New York—flew nineteen circuits (16,435 km or 10,212 miles) in 57 hr 12 min, thus gaining for Japan an unrecognized world record.

Surviving the war, the aircraft was last flown between Yamanashi Airfield and Yokosuka in US markings to be shipped to the United States where it was eventually scrapped.

TECHNICAL DATA

Description: Twin-engined long-range experimental aircraft. All-metal construction.
Accommodation: Crew of five in sealed oxygen cabin.
Powerplant: Two Nakajima Ha-115 fourteen-cylinder air-cooled radials, rated at 1,170 hp for take-off and 1,000 hp at 4,300 m (14,110 ft), driving constant-speed three-blade metal propellers.
Dimensions: Span 29·438 m (96 ft 6¾ in); length 15·3 m (50 ft 2⅜ in); height 3·85 m (12 ft 7⅝ in); wing area 79·56 sq m (856·373 sq ft).
Weights: Empty 7,237 kg (15,955 lb); loaded 16,725 kg (36,872 lb); wing loading 210·2 kg/sq m (43·1 lb/sq ft); power loading 7·15 kg/hp (15·75 lb/hp).
Performance: Maximum speed 440 km/h at 4,600 m (273 mph at 15,090 ft); cruising speed 300 km/h (186 mph); climb to 6,000 m (19,685 ft) in 24 min; service ceiling 8,700 m (28,545 ft); range 18,000 km (11,185 miles).
Production: Two aircraft built by Tachikawa Hikoki K.K. in 1942 and 1943.

Tachikawa Ki-94

Preliminary discussions regarding a heavily armed high-altitude fighter were held between the Koku Hombu and Tachikawa Hikoki K.K. in mid-1942. At that time the Japanese Army wanted to obtain a fighter fitted with a pressure cabin and capable of reaching a top speed of 800 km/h (497 mph) and having a maximum range of 3,000 km (1,864 miles). As these performance requirements were rather stringent, the Koku Hombu decided to instruct Tachikawa to proceed with the design of the aircraft while they placed a contract with Nakajima for another high-altitude fighter with less stringent range requirement. The aircraft proposed by Tachikawa, which received the Kitai designation Ki-94, was of highly unconventional design. The aircraft was a large twin-boom monoplane powered by two 2,200 hp Mitsubishi Ha-211 Ru eighteen-cylinder air-cooled radials which were mounted fore and aft of the pilot's cockpit and drove four-blade tractor and pusher propellers. Proposed armament included two 37 mm Ho-203 cannon and two 30 mm Ho-105 cannon, and a maximum speed of 780 km/h (485 mph) at 10,000 m (32,810 ft) was anticipated. A full-size wooden mock-up was completed late in 1943, but development of the aircraft was discontinued as the Technical Department of the Koku Hombu judged the project too complex and its calculated performance unduly optimistic.

Soon after, Tachikawa submitted a new proposal designed to meet the same requirements as the competitive Nakajima Ki-87. The new aircraft was a single-engined single-seat high-altitude fighter of conventional design with laminar-flow wing and featuring a pressure cabin mounted in

Full-scale mock-up of the twin-boom Tachikawa Ki-94.
(*Courtesy Richard M. Bueschel.*)

TACHIKAWA Ki-94-II

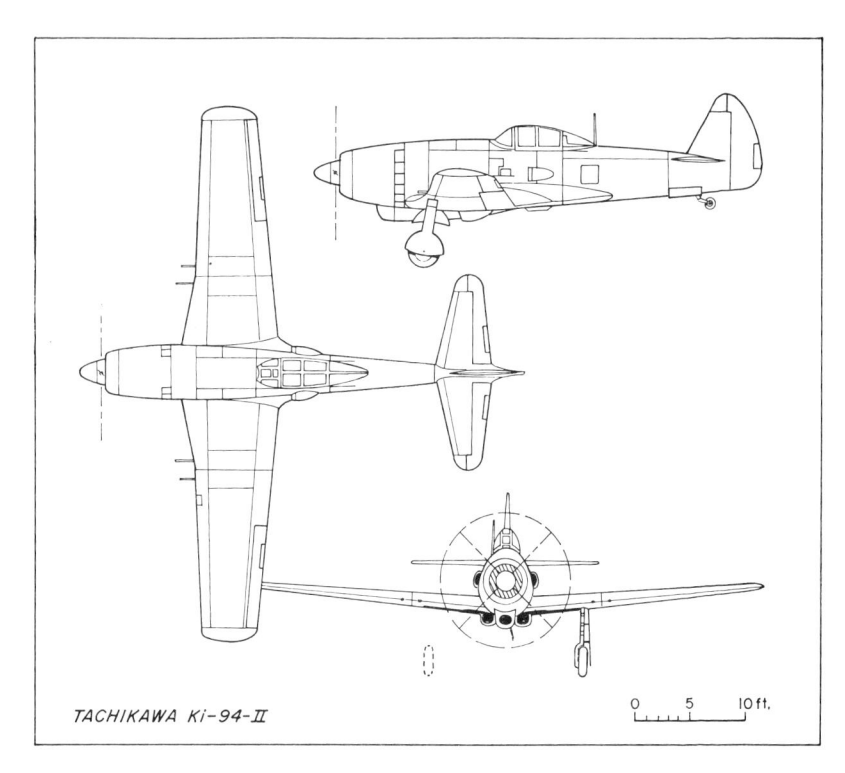

the fuselage behind the wing trailing edges. The aircraft was to be powered by a fan-cooled turbosupercharged 2,400 hp Nakajima [Ha-44] 12 eighteen-cylinder radial driving a six-blade propeller, and the wing-mounted armament was to include two 30 mm Ho-105 cannon and two 20 mm Ho-5

First prototype Tachikawa Ki-94, temporarily fitted with four-blade propeller. (*Aireview*.)

cannon. The proposal was accepted by the Koku Hombu which ordered one static test airframe, three prototypes and eighteen pre-production aircraft under the designation Ki-94-II, the earlier twin-engined project being redesignated Ki-94-I. The first Ki-94-II was scheduled for completion on 20 July, 1945, but eventually was completed two weeks behind schedule. The six-blade propeller planned for the Ki-94-II was not ready in time, and it was decided to begin testing of the first prototype on 18 August, 1945, by temporarily fitting a four-blade airscrew. A second prototype, intended to be fitted with the six-blade propeller, was under construction, but the end of the war prevented it from being completed, while the first aircraft was still being readied for its intended maiden flight three days later.

TECHNICAL DATA

Description: Single-engined high-altitude fighter. All-metal construction.
Accommodation: Pilot in pressurized cockpit.
Powerplant: One 2,400 hp Nakajima [Ha-44] 12 eighteen-cylinder air-cooled radial, rated at 2,450 hp for take-off, 2,350 hp at 1,100 m (3,610 ft), 2,200 hp at 4,400 m (14,435 ft) and 2,040 hp at 11,000 m (36,090 ft), driving a constant-speed four-blade (first prototype) or six-blade (planned production aircraft) metal propeller.
Armament: Two wing-mounted 30 mm Ho-105 cannon and two wing-mounted 20 mm Ho-5 cannon. External load: one 500 kg (1,102 lb) bomb.
Dimensions: Span 14 m (45 ft 11 $\tfrac{3}{16}$ in); length 12 m (39 ft 4 $\tfrac{7}{16}$ in); height 4·65 m (15 ft 3 $\tfrac{1}{16}$ in); wing area 28 sq m (301·388 sq ft).
Weights: Empty 4,690 kg (10,340 lb); loaded 6,450 kg (14,220 lb); wing loading 230·4 kg/sq m (47·2 lb/sq ft); power loading 2·6 kg/hp (5·8 lb/hp).
Performance: Maximum speed 712 km/h at 12,000 m (442 mph at 39,370 ft); cruising speed 440 km/h at 9,000 m (273 mph at 29,530 ft); climb to 10,000 m (32,810 ft) in 17 min 38 sec; service ceiling 14,680 m (48,170 ft); range 2,100 km (1,305 miles).
Production: One prototype completed by Tachikawa Hikoki K.K. in August 1945.

IMPERIAL JAPANESE NAVY AIRCRAFT
Aichi D1A

When in 1933 it became apparent that the performance of the prototypes of two Nakajima-designed carrier dive-bombers produced to the 6-Shi and 7-Shi specifications would not be satisfactory, the Imperial Japanese Navy instructed Aichi, Nakajima and Dai-Ichi Kaigun Koku Gijitsusho to submit designs meeting the requirements of a new 8-Shi specification calling for two-seat carrier-borne dive-bombers. In the specification emphasis was placed on structural strength and manoeuvrability but overall performance had to substantially exceed that of the ill-fated Nakajima Experimental 6-Shi and 7-Shi Carrier Dive Bombers.

An Aichi D1A2 Navy Type 96 Carrier Bomber of this type sank the United States gunboat *Panay* in 1937.

Through their technical arrangements with Ernst Heinkel Flugzeugwerke A.G., Aichi were able to import from Germany a single example of the He 66, a single-seat dive-bomber biplane powered by a 715 hp Siemens SAM-22B nine-cylinder air-cooled radial. Shortly after the He 66's arrival in Japan a team led by Tokuhishiro Goake modified it to meet the requirements of the 8-Shi specification. Modifications included redesign and strengthening of the undercarriage to withstand the pounding of carrier landings, the replacement of the Siemens engine by a 560 hp Nakajima Kotobuki 2 Kai 1 nine-cylinder air-cooled radial and the addition of a second seat behind the pilot's seat. Known as the Aichi Special Bomber, the modified aircraft was intensively tested in competition with the Nakajima entry while Tokuhishiro Goake was modifying the basic design to ensure that production aircraft would meet all the requirements. During

Aichi D1A2 with Nakajima Hikari engine. (*USAF.*)

the competitive trials the aircraft proved more stable and manoeuvrable than either the Nakajima or the Yokosuka design, and late in 1934 Aichi were awarded a production contract for their proposed design.

The production aircraft, bearing the constructor's model number AB-9, were officially designated the Navy Type 94 Carrier Bomber or Aichi D1A1. Compared with the prototype the production D1A1 featured a Townend ring around the engine cylinders, five-degree sweepback on both wings and the rudder was modified while the tailskid was replaced by a fixed tailwheel. Defensive armament comprised two forward-firing 7·7 mm Type 92 machine-guns and a flexible rear-firing 7·7 mm Type 92, and bomb-load included two 30 kg (66 lb) bombs under the wings and one 250 kg (551 lb) bomb on a swing-down yoke under the fuselage. The first 118 aircraft were powered by the 580 hp Nakajima Kotobuki 2 Kai 1, but the last 44 received the Kotobuki 3 of slightly higher rating. The D1A1, along with the D1A2, was among the first aircraft operating during the initial phase of the second Sino-Japanese conflict, but by the time the Pacific War started they had almost completely disappeared from the aircraft inventory of the Japanese Navy, the last surviving D1A1 aircraft being operated only in a training capacity.

In 1935, Tokuhishiro Goake designed the D1A2, an improved version of the aircraft. Power was increased through the use of a 730 hp Nakajima Hikari 1 nine-cylinder air-cooled radial enclosed in a NACA cowling, and performance was also increased by fitting of spats and improved windshields. The first prototype D1A2 was completed in the autumn of 1936 and production began soon after under the designation Navy Type 96 Carrier Bomber. The D1A2 was actively used throughout the second Sino-Japanese conflict and achieved notoriety in 1937 when aircraft of this type sank the American gunboat *Panay*. At the time of the Japanese attack on Pearl Harbor, 68 D1A2s served in second-line units and the aircraft received the Allied code name SUSIE. Attrition and availability of more modern equipment led to the retirement of this aircraft soon after.

AICHI D1A2

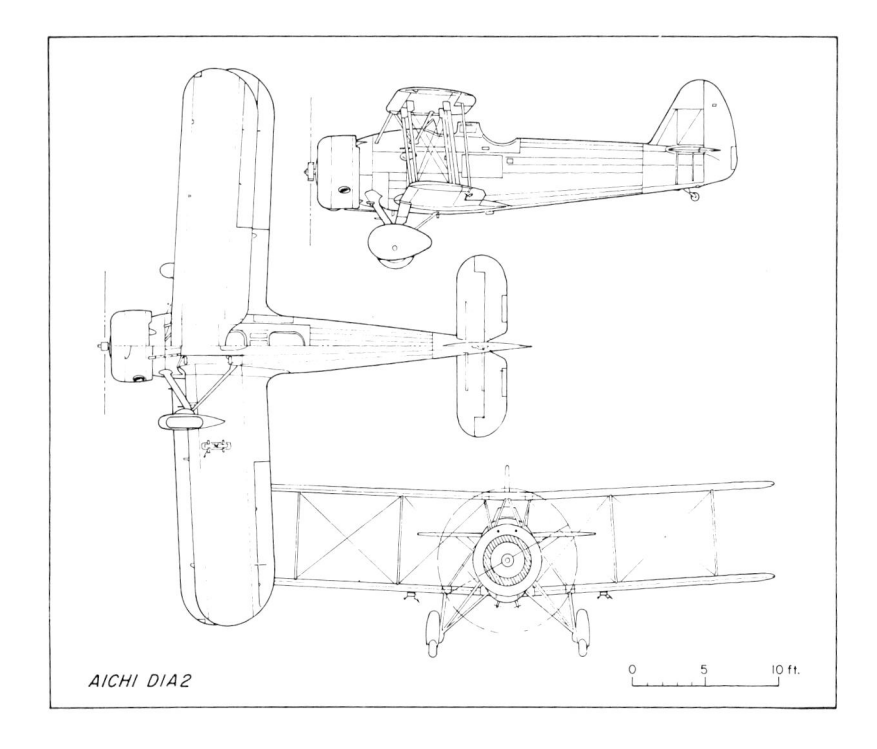

UNITS ALLOCATED
Carriers: *Akagi, Kaga* and *Ryujo*; 12th, 13th, 14th and 15th Kokutais.

TECHNICAL DATA
Description: Single-engined carrier-borne biplane dive-bomber. Metal structure with metal and fabric covering.
Accommodation: Pilot and radio-operator/gunner in tandem open cockpits.
Powerplant: One Nakajima Kotobuki 2 Kai 1 nine-cylinder air-cooled radial, rated at 580 hp for take-off and 460 hp at 1,500 m (4,920 ft), driving a two-blade propeller (modified He 66 and first 118 D1A1s).

One Nakajima Kotobuki 3 nine-cylinder air-cooled radial, rated at 640 hp for take-off and 715 hp at 2,800 m (9,185 ft), driving a two-blade propeller (last 44 D1A1s).

One Nakajima Hikari 1 nine-cylinder air-cooled radial, rated at 730 hp for take-off and 670 hp at 3,500 m (11,485 ft), driving a two-blade propeller (D1A2).
Armament: Two fixed forward-firing 7·7 mm Type 92 machine-guns in the engine cowling and one flexible rear-firing 7·7 mm Type 92 machine-gun.

Bomb-load: one 250 kg (551 lb) bomb under the fuselage and two 30 kg (66 lb) bombs under the wings.

	D1A1	D1A2
Dimensions:		
Span	11·37 m	11·4 m
	(37 ft 3⅝ in)	(37 ft 4¹³⁄₁₆ in)
Length	9·4 m	9·3 m
	(30 ft 10¹⁄₁₆ in)	(30 ft 6⅛ in)
Height	3·45 m	3·41 m
	(11 ft 2¹³⁄₁₆ in)	(11 ft 2¼ in)
Wing area	34·05 sq m	34·7 sq m
	(366·51 sq ft)	(373·506 sq ft)

	D1A1	D1A2
Weights:		
Empty	1,400 kg	1,516 kg
	(3,086 lb)	(3,342 lb)
Loaded	2,400 kg	2,500 kg
	(5,291 lb)	(5,512 lb)
Maximum	—	2,610 kg
	—	(5,754 lb)
Wing loading	70·5 kg/sq m	72 kg/sq m
	(14·4 lb/sq ft)	(14·8 lb/sq ft)
Power loading	4·3 kg/hp	3·8 kg/hp
	(9·1 lb/hp)	(8·4 lb/hp)
Performance:		
Maximum speed	151·5 kt at 2,050 m	167 kt at 3,200 m
	(174 mph at 6,725 ft)	(192 mph at 10,500 ft)
Cruising speed	—	120 kt at 1,000 m
	—	(138 mph at 3,280 ft)
Climb to	3,000 m (9,845 ft)	3,000 m (9,845 ft)
in	9 min 30 sec	7 min 51 sec
Service ceiling	7,000 m	6,980 m
	(22,965 ft)	(22,900 ft)
Range	570 naut miles	500 naut miles
	(656 st miles)	(576 st miles)

Production: In addition to the Heinkel-built prototype modified by Aichi, 590 production aircraft were built by Aichi Tokei Denki K.K. at Nagoya as follows:
162 D1A1 (1934–37)
428 D1A2 (1936–40)

Aichi D3A

When on 7 December, 1941, the Japanese Navy launched their surprise attack against military installations on Oahu Island, the Aichi D3A1, soon to be named VAL by the Allies, became the first Japanese aircraft to drop bombs on American targets. Despite its apparent obsolescence—the D3A being the last type of Japanese carrier-borne aircraft to use a fixed spatted undercarriage—the aircraft achieved considerable success during the first ten months of the war and sank more Allied fighting ships than any other single type of Axis aircraft.

During the summer of 1936, the Japanese Navy issued an 11-Shi specification calling for a carrier-based dive-bomber of monoplane design to supplant the obsolescent Navy Type 96 Carrier Bomber (Aichi D1A2). In answer to this specification, design proposals were submitted by Aichi Tokei Denki K.K., Nakajima Hikoki K.K. and Mitsubishi Jukogyo K.K., and the first two companies each received a contract from the Navy for the manufacture of two prototypes. Designed by a team led by Tokuhishiro Goake, the Aichi entrant (constructor's project designation AM-17) was

The second prototype Aichi 11-Shi Navy Experimental Carrier Bomber.

a monoplane with low-mounted elliptical wings inspired by those of the Heinkel He 70. Despite the inherent drag of a fixed undercarriage, this type of landing gear was retained as performance gains stemming from the use of a fully retractable unit were found insufficient to justify the extra weight and maintenance problems.

The first prototype, powered by a 710 hp Nakajima Hikari 1 nine-cylinder air-cooled radial, was completed in December 1937 and flight trials began a month later. Initial results were disappointing as the aircraft was underpowered and suffered from directional instability in wide turns. The dive brakes—similar to those used on the Junkers-Ju 87—vibrated alarmingly when turned through 90 degrees to present a flat area to the airflow during dives and, as diving speed requirement was increased from 200 kt to 240 kt, it became imperative to increase their area and strengthen their mounting. On the positive side, the aircraft possessed a strong airframe and overall handling characteristics were satisfactory with the exception of a tendency to snap roll during tight turns.

To correct the numerous deficiencies experienced with the first prototype, the second aircraft was extensively modified prior to entering its flight trial programme. Power was increased by replacing the Hikari 1 with an 840 hp Mitsubishi Kinsei 3 fourteen-cylinder air-cooled radial enclosed

Aichi D3A1 dive-bombers.

An Aichi D3A1 Navy Type 99 Carrier Bomber Model 11 of the 33rd Kokutai. (*Aireview.*)

in a redesigned cowling, the area of the vertical tail surfaces was enlarged and strengthened dive brakes were fitted. However, the main modification affected the wings which had the span increased from 14·1 m (46 ft 3⅛ in) to 14·5 m (47 ft 6⅞ in), thus increasing wing area by 2 sq m (21·528 sq ft) to 35 sq m (376·735 sq ft), while the outer-sections of the leading edges were cambered down to prevent the snap rolling in tight turns. Thus modified, the D3A1 won the competitive trials over the Nakajima D3N1 and, in December 1939, Aichi were awarded a production contract for the aircraft under the designation Navy Type 99 Carrier Bomber Model 11.

The production D3A1s were further improved and featured slightly smaller wings. Powered by the 1,000 hp Mitsubishi Kinsei 43 or 1,070 hp Kinsei 44, these aircraft incorporated numerous internal changes increasing loaded weight to 3,650 kg (8,047 lb). The directional instability problem was finally eradicated with the fitting of a large dorsal fin, the aircraft became highly manoeuvrable, a characteristic which enabled it occasionally to be used as a fighter despite the fact that armament comprised only two forward-firing 7·7 mm Type 97 machine-guns and one flexible rear-firing 7·7 mm Type 92 machine-gun. Normal offensive load was a single 250 kg

Aichi D3A2 Navy Type 99 Carrier Bomber Model 22s at Misawa, Aomori, in October 1945. (*USAF.*)

(551 lb) bomb carried under the fuselage and swung down and forward on arms before release, but two additional 60 kg (132 lb) bombs could be carried on wing racks located under each wing outboard of the dive brakes.

Carrier qualification trials were conducted aboard the *Kaga* and the *Akagi* in 1940 and the D3A1s saw limited combat operations from land bases in China and Indo-China during the fourteen months preceding the beginning of the Pacific War. Starting with the Hawaiian operation, in which 126 D3A1s took part, the Navy Type 99 Carrier Bomber Model 11 took part in all major Japanese carrier operations in the first ten months of the war. They achieved fame during the campaign in the Indian Ocean

An Aichi D3A2 abandoned on Guam. (*US Navy Department.*)

when the D3A1s placed respectively 87 per cent and 82 per cent of their bombs on target during attacks on the cruisers HMS *Cornwall* and HMS *Dorsetshire* and the carrier HMS *Hermes*. However, the heavy losses in élite crews, aircraft and aircraft carriers suffered in the Coral Sea battle, at Midway, around Guadalcanal and off Santa Cruz, and the American offensive in the Solomons, compelled the Japanese Navy to assign an increasing number of Navy Type 99 Carrier Bombers to land-based Kokutais.

In June 1942, an improved version of the D3A powered by a 1,300 hp Kinsei 54 made its début when Aichi began testing the sole prototype of the D3A2 Model 12. As the earlier D3A1 had insufficient range for operations in the Solomons, the production version of the D3A2 featured increased fuel tankage with a total capacity of 1,079 litres (237·4 Imp gal). Externally the aircraft was almost identical to the D3A1 with the exception of the fitting of a propeller spinner and the use of a longer, more pointed rear canopy section. Designated Navy Type 99 Carrier Bomber Model 22, this version began to replace the Model 11 in front-line units in the autumn of 1942, and its production was also undertaken by Showa Hikoki Kogyo K.K. When the much faster Yokosuka Suisei became available the D3A2s were relegated to land-based units and to those operating from the smaller carriers which had a deck inadequate for the Suisei's higher landing speed. When in 1944 the American forces returned to the Philippines the D3A2s took an active part in the bitter fighting but were hopelessly out-performed and losses were heavy. By then many D3A1s and D3A2s were operated by training units in Japan and several were modified as Navy Type 99 Bomber Trainer Model 12s (D3A2-K). However, during the last year of the war the D3A2s were pressed back into combat for kamikaze sorties during which their loss rate reached frightening proportions without compensating results.

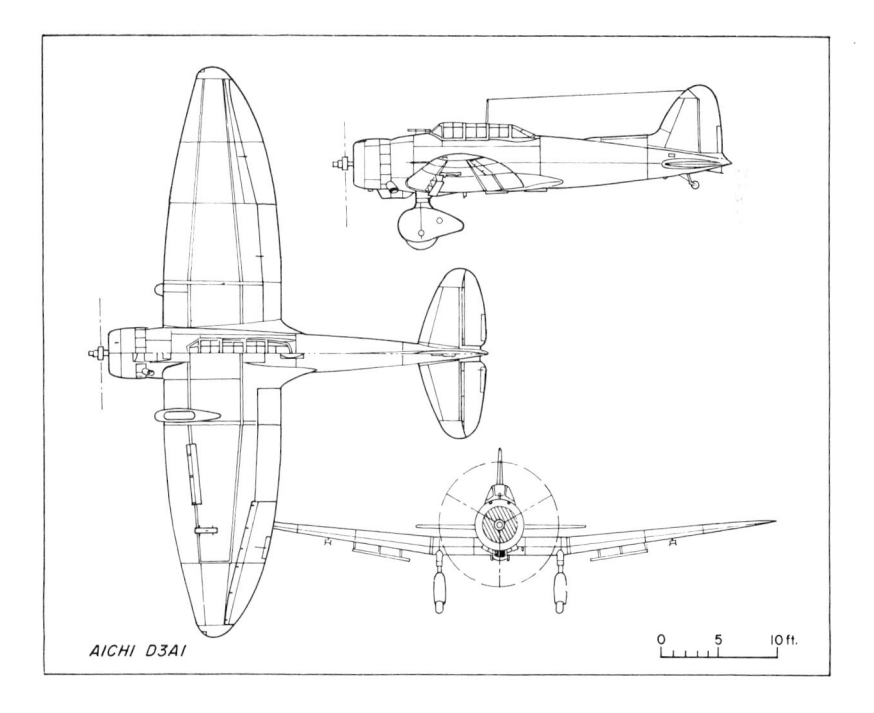

AICHI D3A1

UNITS ALLOCATED

Carriers: *Kaga, Akagi, Ryujo, Soryu, Hiryu, Shokaku, Zuikaku, Shoho, Zuiho, Chitose, Chiyoda*, etc; 12th, 14th, 31st, 33rd, 35th, 40th, 541st and 582nd Kokutais.

TECHNICAL DATA

Description: Single-engined carrier-borne and land-based dive-bomber (D3A1 and D3A2) or bomber trainer (D3A2-K). All-metal construction with fabric-covered control surfaces.

Accommodation: Crew of two in tandem enclosed cockpits.

Powerplant: One Nakajima Hikari 1 nine-cylinder air-cooled radial, rated at 710 hp for take-off and 800 hp at 3,500 m (11,485 ft), driving a three-blade metal propeller (first prototype).

One Mitsubishi Kinsei 3 fourteen-cylinder air-cooled radial, rated at 840 hp for take-off and 730 hp at 1,600 m (5,250 ft), driving a three-blade metal propeller (second prototype).

One Mitsubishi Kinsei 43 fourteen-cylinder air-cooled radial, rated at 1,000 hp for take-off and 990 hp at 2,800 m (9,185 ft), driving a three-blade metal propeller (early production D3A1 Model 11).

One Mitsubishi Kinsei 44 fourteen-cylinder air-cooled radial, rated at 1,070 hp for take-off and 1,080 hp at 2,000 m (6,560 ft), driving a three-blade metal propeller (late production D3A1 Model 11).

One Mitsubishi Kinsei 54 fourteen-cylinder air-cooled radial, rated at 1,300 hp for take-off, 1,200 hp at 3,000 m (9,845 ft) and 1,100 hp at 6,200 m (20,340 ft), driving a three-blade metal propeller (D3A2 Model 12, D3A2 Model 22 and D3A2-K Model 12).

Armament: Two forward-firing 7·7 mm Type 97 machine-guns in the engine cowling and one flexible rear-firing 7·7 mm Type 92 machine-gun.

Bomb-load: one 250 kg (551 lb) bomb under the fuselage, and two 60 kg (132 lb) bombs under the wings.

	D3A1	D3A2
Dimensions:		
Span	14·365 m	14·365 m
	(47 ft 1 3/16 in)	(47 ft 1 3/16 in)
Length	10·195 m	10·195 m
	(33 ft 5 3/8 in)	(33 ft 5 3/8 in)
Height	3·847 m	3·847 m
	(12 ft 7 15/32 in)	(12 ft 7 15/32 in)
Wing area	34·9 sq m	34·9 sq m
	(375·659 sq ft)	(375·659 sq ft)
Weights:		
Empty	2,408 kg	2,570 kg
	(5,309 lb)	(5,666 lb)
Loaded	3,650 kg	3,800 kg
	(8,047 lb)	(8,378 lb)
Wing loading	104·6 kg/sq m	108·9 kg/sq m
	(21·4 lb/sq ft)	(22·3 lb/sq ft)
Power loading	3·65 kg/hp	2·92 kg/hp
	(8 lb/hp)	(6·4 lb/hp)
Performance:		
Maximum speed	209 kt at 3,000 m	232 kt at 6,200 m
	(240 mph at 9,845 ft)	(267 mph at 20,340 ft)
Cruising speed	160 kt at 3,000 m	160 kt at 3,000 m
	(184 mph at 9,845 ft)	(184 mph at 9,845 ft)
Climb to	3,000 m (9,845 ft)	3,000 m (9,845 ft)
in	6 min 27 sec	5 min 48 sec
Service ceiling	9,300 m	10,500 m
	(30,050 ft)	(34,450 ft)
Range	795 naut miles	730 naut miles
	(915 st miles)	(840 st miles)

Production: A total of 1,495 D3As were built as follows:

Aichi Kokuki K.K. at Funakata, Nagoya:

    2 11-Shi prototypes (1937–38)

    6 D3A1 Service trials aircraft (1939)

    470 D3A1 Model 11 production aircraft (Dec 1939–Aug 1942)

    1 D3A2 Model 12 prototype (June 1942)

    815 D3A2 Model 22 production aircraft (Aug 1942–June 1944)

1,294

Showa Hikoki Kogyo K.K. in Tokyo:

    201 D3A2 Model 22 production aircraft (Dec 1942–Aug 1945)

Aichi E13A

Faced with the need to provide escorts for maritime convoys often operating far out of range of land-based aircraft, the Japanese Navy relied extensively on the use of reconnaissance floatplanes, and during the second World War Japan operated more aircraft of this type than any other nation. Consequently, the Aichi E13A1—numerically the most important Japanese floatplane—occupies a significant place among the combat aircraft operated during the Pacific War.

In 1937, the Japanese Navy began to evince considerable interest in obtaining a replacement for the ageing Kawanishi E7K2 three-seat twin-float seaplane. In June of that year the Naval Staff issued to Aichi, Nakajima and Kawanishi a 12-Shi specification calling for a two-seat reconnaissance floatplane. Each of these manufacturers respectively began in September 1937 designing the E12A1, E12N1 and E12K1 but, while all these activities were taking place, another 12-Shi specification—this time calling for three-seat reconnaissance floatplanes with higher speed and longer range—was issued to the same companies. The three additional designs, which complemented rather than supplanted the earlier designs, received the designations E13A1, E13N1 and E13K1.

Of the three competing companies Aichi was the only one which decided to proceed with the development of two designs to meet the requirements of both specifications while Nakajima decided to concentrate on the two-seater and Kawanishi to build prototypes of a three-seater. The design of the E13A1, drawn up by a design team led by Kishiro Matsuo, bore a strong resemblance to the E12A1, being merely a larger and more powerful version of the two-seat aircraft. Powered by a 1,060 hp Mitsubishi Kinsei 43 fourteen-cylinder air-cooled radial, the first prototype E13A1 was completed in late 1938 almost simultaneously with the two E12A1 prototypes which were powered by 870 hp Mitsubishi Zuisei fourteen-cylinder air-cooled radials. During manufacturer's trials the E13A1 proved itself to be the best of the two designs since despite its larger size and heavier weight it had better performance and was more stable and manoeuvrable than the E12A1. Since the Japanese Navy had by then indicated that they favoured a three-seat aircraft, the development of the E12A1 and E12N1 was suspended and the E13A1 was intensively tested by Service pilots in competition with the two prototypes of the Kawanishi E13K1.

In December 1940 the E13A1 won the competition and was accepted for production as the Navy Type 0 Reconnaissance Seaplane Model 1 (later Model 11). Production was initially entrusted to Aichi Tokei Denki K.K.

which built, including the prototypes, a total of 133 E13A1s until 1942 when they were instructed to concentrate on producing the D3A and D4Y carrier bombers. At that time the prime responsibility for the production of the Navy Type 0 Reconnaissance Seaplane was entrusted to K.K. Watanabe Tekkosho (later reorganized as Kyushu Hikoki K.K.) while limited production of the aircraft was undertaken by the Dai-Juichi Kaigun Kokusho (11th Naval Air Arsenal) at Hiro.

The E13A1 made its combat début in late 1941 when, operating from cruisers and seaplane tenders, the aircraft was used for attacks on the Canton–Hankow railway and for anti-shipping patrols. Shortly thereafter E13A1s launched from cruisers of the 8th Cruiser Division (*Tone*, *Chikuma* and *Kinugasa*) flew reconnaissance missions during the Hawaiian operation. From then on Navy Type 0 Reconnaissance Seaplanes operating from ships as well as from shore bases were found wherever the Japanese Navy were active. Despite its lack of fuel tankage and crew protection and its limited defensive armament, this aircraft was eminently successful and its maximum endurance of almost fifteen hours suited it admirably to long patrol reconnaissance missions. On occasions the E13A1, known to the

A prototype Aichi 12-Shi Navy Experimental Three-seat Reconnaissance Seaplane. (*USAF.*)

An Aichi E13A1 Navy Type 0 Reconnaissance Seaplane Model 11. (*S. Tanaka.*)

Allies as JAKE, was used for bombing missions whenever Allied air opposition was limited. Other missions performed by the Navy Type 0 Reconnaissance Seaplane included air–sea rescue, staff transport, shipping attack and, late in the war, kamikaze sorties.

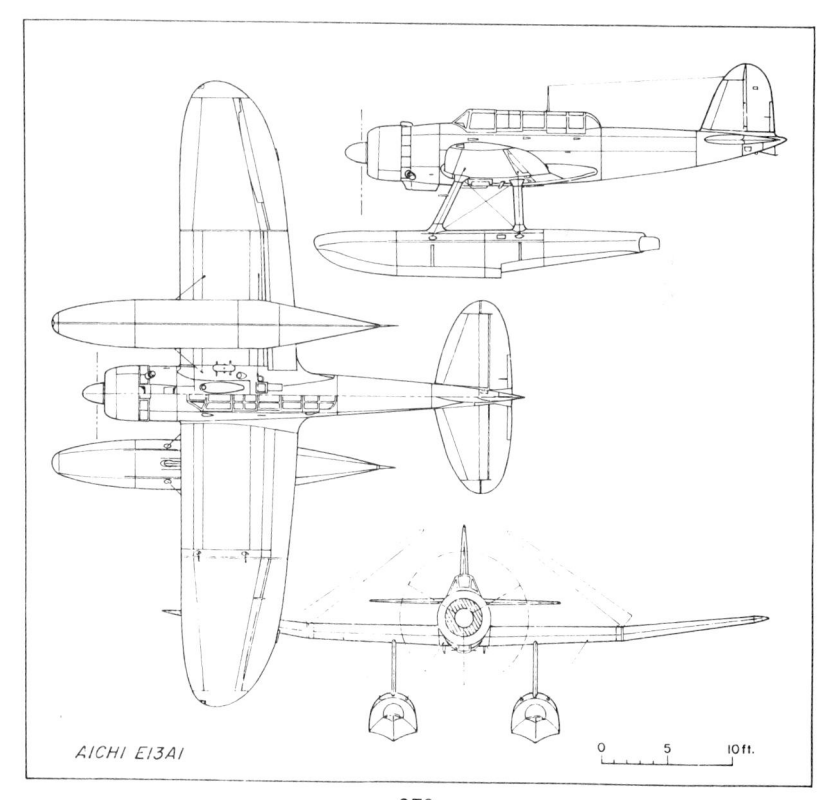

For almost four years no model changes were made and when in November 1944 two new versions appeared they could only be distinguished by the fitting of two additional pairs of inward sloping float bracing struts and a propeller spinner. Retaining the Kinsei 43 radial of the initial model, the E13A1a Model 11A was fitted with improved radio equipment while the E13A1b Model 11B was equipped with air-to-surface radar with antennae on the wing leading edges and the rear fuselage sides. For night operations aircraft of each of these versions could be fitted with exhaust flame dampers while for operations against P.T. boats a flexible 20 mm cannon firing from the fuselage belly could be mounted. Some E13A1s were also fitted with a magnetic airborne submarine detection device known as Jikitanchiki but results were poor unless the aircraft flew at a mere 30 to 40 ft above the surface.

Crew boarding an Aichi E13A1. (*S. Tanaka.*)

UNITS ALLOCATED

Aircraft tenders: *Chitose, Chiyoda, Kimikawa Maru*; Battleship: *Haruna*; Cruisers: *Kinugasa, Atago, Takao, Chokai, Maya, Kumano, Chikuma, Tone, Suzuya*, etc; 5th, 7th, 19th, 21st, 36th, 40th, 901st, 932nd, 955th, Chichijima and Sasebo Kokutais.

TECHNICAL DATA

Description: Single-engined twin-float reconnaissance seaplane. All-metal construction with fabric-covered control surfaces.
Accommodation: Crew of three in tandem enclosed cockpits.
Powerplant: One Mitsubishi Kinsei 43 fourteen-cylinder air-cooled radial, rated at 1,060 hp for take-off and 1,080 hp at 2,000 m (6,560 ft), driving a three-blade metal propeller.
Armament: One flexible rear-firing 7·7 mm Type 92 machine-gun.
    One flexible rear-firing 7·7 mm Type 92 machine-gun and one flexible downward-firing 20 mm Type 99 Model 1 cannon (field modification on late production aircraft).
    External load: one 250 kg (551 lb) bomb, or four 60 kg (132 lb) bombs or depth-charges.
Dimensions: (E13A1a) Span 14·5 m (47 ft 6⅞ in); length 11·3 m (37 ft 0⅞ in); height 7·4 m (24 ft 3½ in); wing area 36 sq m (387·499 sq ft).
Weights: (E13A1a) Empty 2,642 kg (5,825 lb); loaded 3,640 kg (8,025 lb); maximum 4,000 kg (12,192 lb); wing loading 101·1 kg/sq m (20·7 lb/sq ft); power loading 3·4 kg/hp (7·6 lb/hp).
Performance: (E13A1a) Maximum speed 203 kt at 2,180 m (234 mph at 7,155 ft); cruising speed 120 kt at 2,000 m (138 mph at 6,560 ft); climb to 3,000 m (9,845 ft) in 6 min 5 sec; service ceiling 8,730 m (28,640 ft); range 1,128 naut miles (1,298 st miles).
Production: A total of 1,418 E13A1s were built as follows:
    Aichi Tokei Denki K.K., Funakata:
        133 aircraft (1938–42)
    Dai-Juichi Kaigun Kokusho, Hiro:
        48 aircraft (1940–42)
    Kyushu Hikoki K.K., Zasshonokuma:
        1,237 aircraft (1942–45)

Aichi H9A

Despite its colourless operational history the Aichi H9A was noteworthy among the aircraft of the fighting powers because it was the only type of flying-boat specially designed as a pilot and crew trainer to be placed in quantity production. Development of this aircraft began in January 1940 when the Japanese Navy instructed Aichi to design a twin-engined training flying-boat to provide advanced training for the future crews of the high-performance Kawanishi H8K1 maritime reconnaissance flying-boat.

Designed between May and December 1940 by a team led by Morishige Mori, the H9A1 was a parasol monoplane powered by a pair of 710 hp Nakajima Kotobuki 41 Kai 2 nine-cylinder air-cooled radials and fitted with a semi-retractable tricycle beaching gear. The normal crew comprised pilot, co-pilot, observer, flight engineer and radio-operator, but seating was also provided for three pupils. For armament training and to suit the aircraft for its secondary mission of anti-submarine patrol, provision was made for one flexible 7·7 mm machine-gun in each of the bow and dorsal open positions and two 250 kg (551 lb) depth-charges.

The first of three prototypes was completed and flown in September 1940 but flying and alighting characteristics were unsatisfactory. To correct

One of the few known photographs of an Aichi H9A1 flying-boat. (*Copyright Toshio Fukui.*)

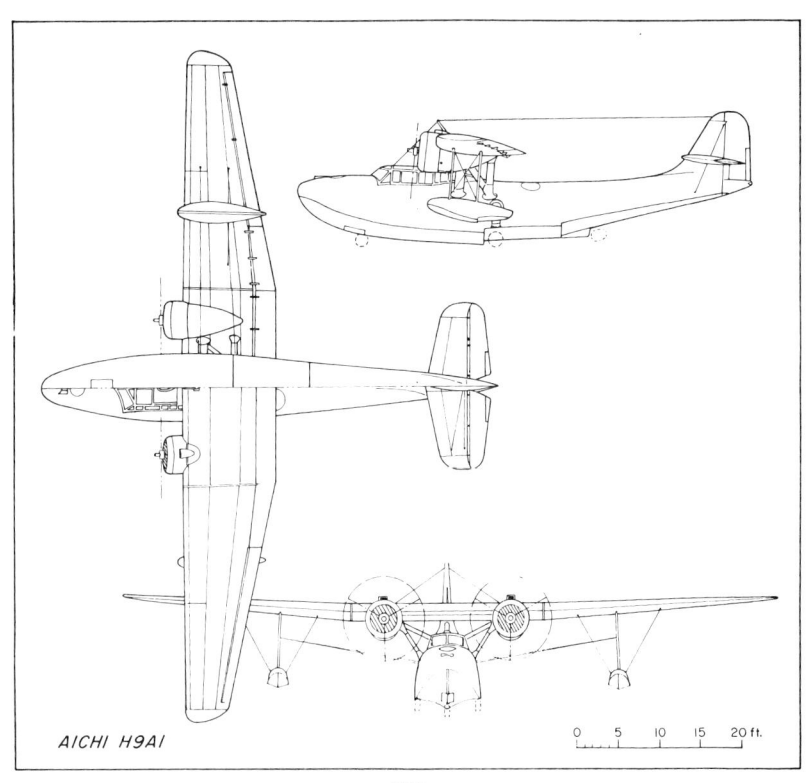

AICHI H9A1

this deficiency the engines were mounted lower on the wings, the flaps were modified, and span and wing area were respectively increased from 21 m (69 ft 10$\frac{25}{32}$ in) to 24 m (78 ft 8$\frac{7}{8}$ in) and from 58·62 sq m (630·978 sq ft) to 63·3 sq m (681·353 sq ft).

So modified, the aircraft displayed markedly improved handling characteristics and was placed in limited production at Aichi's Eitoku plant where twenty-four aircraft designated Navy Type 2 Training Flying-Boat Model 11 were built in 1942 and 1943. Four additional aircraft were built in 1944 by Nippon Hikoki K.K. Service use was limited to training missions and some coastal patrols around Japan and the aircraft remained unknown to the Allies until 1945.

TECHNICAL DATA

Description: Twin-engined training and anti-submarine patrol flying-boat. All-metal structure with light alloy, ply and fabric covering.

Accommodation: Normal crew of five plus three pupils.

Powerplant: Two Nakajima Kotobuki 41 Kai 2 nine-cylinder air-cooled radials, rated at 710 hp for take-off and 780 hp at 2,900 m (9,515 ft), driving two-blade wooden propellers (13-Shi prototypes).

Two Nakajima Kotobuki 42 or 43 nine-cylinder air-cooled radials, rated at 710 hp for take-off and 610 hp at 3,000 m (9,845 ft), driving three-blade propellers (production aircraft).

Armament: One hand-held 7·7 mm Type 92 machine-gun in an open bow position and in an open dorsal position.

External load: up to 250 kg (551 lb) of bombs or depth-charges.

Dimensions: Span 24 m (78 ft 8$\frac{7}{8}$ in); length 16·95 m (55 ft 7$\frac{3}{16}$ in); height 5·25 m (17 ft 2$\frac{11}{16}$ in); wing area 63·3 sq m (681·353 sq ft).

Weights: Empty 4,900 kg (10,803 lb); loaded 7,000 kg (15,432 lb); maximum 7,500 kg (16,535 lb); wing loading 110·6 kg/sq m (22·6 lb/sq ft); power loading 4·9 kg/hp (10·9 lb/hp).

Performance: Maximum speed 171 kt at 3,000 m (197 mph at 9,845 ft); cruising speed 120 kt at 1,000 m (138 mph at 3,280 ft); climb to 3,000 m (9,845 ft) in 11 min 14 sec; service ceiling 6,780 m (22,245 ft); range 1,160 naut miles (1,335 st miles).

Production: A total of 31 H9A1s were built as follows:

Aichi Kokuki K.K., Eitoku:

   3 prototypes (1940)
   24 production aircraft (1942–43)

Nippon Hikoki K.K., Tomioka:

   4 production aircraft (1944)

Aichi 16-Shi Navy Experimental Reconnaissance Seaplane with cut-away rear cockpit sides. The Japanese wartime censor is responsible for the white patches in the background.

Aichi E16A Zuiun (Auspicious Cloud)

As few airfields were available on the islands dispersed over the vast area of the Pacific Ocean it was logical for the Japanese Navy to rely heavily on the use of float seaplanes, and more types of reconnaissance float seaplanes were designed for that Service than any other class of aircraft. In 1939 the Aichi E13A1, intended to replace the ageing Kawanishi E7K2 aboard the Navy's seaplane tenders and cruisers, had not yet been accepted for production when Naval Headquarters began drafting a 14-Shi specification calling for a successor to the E13A. Disagreements regarding the requirements to be met by the new reconnaissance float seaplane prevented the manufacturers from submitting specific designs. However, in October 1940, Engineers Kishiro Matsuo and Yasushiro Ozawa began designing the Aichi AM-22 and in January 1941 the Navy drafted a new 16-Shi specification around the design of the AM-22. Requirements were once again modified in July 1941 but after that date the Aichi design was finalized.

The first Aichi AM-22, officially designated Navy Experimental 16-Shi Reconnaissance Seaplane (E16A1), was completed in May 1942. Except

An Aichi E16A1 Zuiun (Auspicious Cloud). The dive-brakes form part of the structure of the forward float struts.

for wooden wingtips and tailplane and fabric-covered control surfaces, the aircraft was of all-metal construction and was powered by a 1,300 hp Mitsubishi MK8A Kinsei 51 radial and armed with two wing-mounted 7·7 mm machine-guns and one flexible rear-firing 7·7 mm machine-gun. The twin single-step metal floats were attached to the wings by vertical N-struts and to the fuselage by inclined I-struts. The wings folded upward for stowage aboard cruisers or seaplane tenders. Designed to operate as a dive-bomber, the E16A1 was fitted with hydraulically-operated dive brakes mounted on the front leg of the N-struts. Two additional prototypes with wing span increased from 12·7 m (41 ft 8 in) to 12·81 m (42 ft $0\frac{11}{32}$ in)

An Aichi E16A1 of the 634th Kokutai, after capture. (*Eckert*.)

were built and were used to test various dive-brake designs as the original set caused excessive buffeting when extended. Like the production aircraft these prototypes were armed with two wing-mounted 20 mm cannon and one flexible 13 mm machine-gun and could carry one 250 kg (551 lb) bomb under the fuselage.

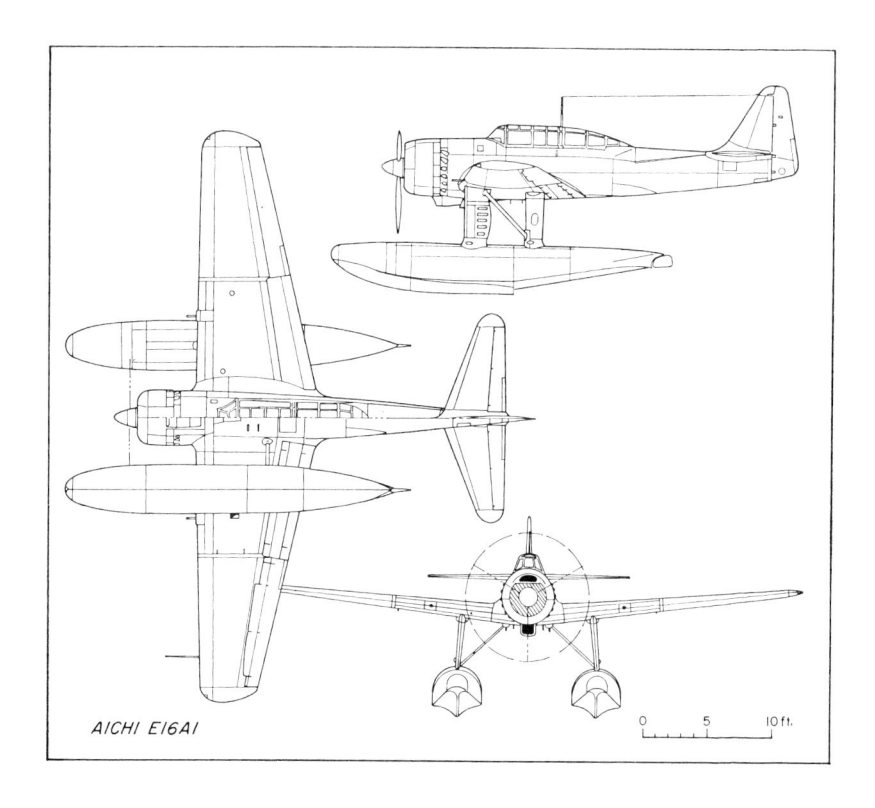

AICHI E16A1

With perforated dive brakes, redesigned rear canopy section, strengthened floats and improved flap actuation mechanism the E16A1 was accepted for production in August 1943 as the Navy Reconnaissance Seaplane Zuiun (Auspicious Cloud) Model 11. Early production aircraft were powered by the Mitsubishi MK8A Kinsei 51 radial, but this engine was replaced by the MK8D Kinsei 54 on late production aircraft, most of these being built by Nippon Hikoki K.K. The E16A2, powered by a 1,560 hp Mitsubishi MK8P Kinsei 62, was still undergoing tests at the time of the Japanese surrender.

Entering service at a time when Japan had lost air superiority, the E16A1s (code name PAUL) suffered heavy losses during the Philippines campaign of 1944 and most surviving Zuiuns were expended in suicide attacks in the Okinawa area.

UNITS ALLOCATED

301st, 634th and Yokosuka Kokutais.

TECHNICAL DATA

Description: Single-engined twin-float reconnaissance seaplane. All-metal structure with stressed-skin covering, wooden wingtips and tailplane, and fabric-covered control surfaces.

Accommodation: Crew of two in tandem enclosed cockpits.

Powerplant: One Mitsubishi MK8A Kinsei 51 fourteen-cylinder air-cooled radial, rated at 1,300 hp for take-off, 1,200 hp at 3,000 m (9,845 ft) and 1,100 hp at 6,200 m (20,340 ft), driving a three-blade constant-speed metal propeller (prototypes and early production aircraft).

One Mitsubishi MK8D Kinsei 54 fourteen-cylinder air-cooled radial, rated at 1,300 hp for take-off, 1,200 hp at 3,000 m (9,845 ft) and 1,100 hp at 6,200 m (20,340 ft), driving a three-blade constant-speed metal propeller (late production aircraft).

One Mitsubishi MK8P Kinsei 62 fourteen-cylinder air-cooled radial, rated at 1,560 hp for take-off, 1,340 hp at 2,100 m (6,890 ft) and 1,190 hp at 5,800 m (19,030 ft), driving a three-blade constant-speed metal propeller (E16A2 prototype).

Armament: Two wing-mounted 7·7 mm Type 97 machine-guns and one flexible rear-firing 7·7 mm Type 92 machine-gun (first prototype).

Two wing-mounted 20 mm Type 99 Model 2 cannon and one flexible rear-firing 13 mm Type 2 machine-gun (all aircraft except first prototype).

    External load: 180 kg (397 lb) of bombs (first prototype), or 250 kg (551 lb) of bombs (all other E16A1s).

Dimensions: Span 12·81 m (42 ft 0$\frac{11}{32}$ in); length 10·833 m (35 ft 6½ in); height 4·791 m (15 ft 8⅝ in); wing area 28 sq m (301·388 sq ft).

Weights: Empty 2,945 kg (6,493 lb); loaded 3,900 kg (8,598 lb); maximum 4,553 kg (10,038 lb); wing loading 139·3 kg/sq m (28·5 lb/sq ft); power loading 3 kg/hp (6·6 lb/hp).

Performance; Maximum speed 237 kt at 5,500 m (273 mph at 18,045 ft); cruising speed 180 kt at 5,000 m (207 mph at 16,405 ft); climb to 3,000 m (9,845 ft) in 4 min 40 sec; service ceiling 10,000 m (32,810 ft); range—normal 635 naut miles (731 st miles), maximum 1,307 naut miles (1,504 st miles).

Production: A total of 256 E16As were built as follows:

    Aichi Kokuki K.K. at Eitoku:

        3 E16A1 prototypes (1942)
      193 E16A1 production aircraft (Jan 1944–May 1945)
        1 E16A2 prototype (1944)

    Nippon Hikoki K.K. at Tomioka:

       59 E16A1 production aircraft (Aug 1944–Aug 1945)

The seventh Aichi B7A1 Navy Experimental 16-Shi Carrier Attack Bomber.

Aichi B7A Ryusei (Shooting Star)

Exceptionally large for a Japanese carrier-borne aircraft, the Ryusei (Shooting Star) was designed by Chief Engineer Norio Ozaki, assisted by Morishige Mori and Yasushiro Ozawa, to a 16-Shi specification prepared by the Japanese Navy. The Navy's specification called for a carrier-borne attack bomber to supplement and eventually replace both the Nakajima B6N torpedo-bomber and the Yokosuka D4Y dive-bomber. The requirements for this aircraft included: (1) offensive load, two 250 kg (551 lb) bombs or six 60 kg (132 lb) bombs carried internally or one 800 kg (1,764 lb) torpedo carried externally; (2) defensive armament, two forward-firing 20 mm cannon and one flexible 13 mm machine-gun; (3) maximum speed, 300 kt (354 mph); (4) normal range, 1,000 naut miles (1,151 st miles) and maximum range, 1,800 naut miles (2,072 st miles); and (5) manoeuvrability equal to that of the Mitsubishi A6M Carrier Fighter. As the aircraft was intended to operate from a new class of aircraft carriers the traditional restriction on aircraft length to 11 m (36 ft $1\frac{1}{16}$ in)—stemming from the size of deck elevators on the older aircraft carriers—was waived.

To meet the payload, range and speed requirements a powerful engine had to be selected and Aichi were instructed to use a Nakajima Homare eighteen-cylinder radial, a powerplant which was then favoured by the Navy to become their standard aircraft engine in the 1,800 hp to 2,200 hp class. The need to select a mid-wing configuration to provide space in the fuselage for a ventral bomb-bay combined with the necessity to provide adequate clearance for the 3·5 m (11 ft $5\frac{25}{32}$ in) diameter four-blade pro-

Aichi B7A1 Ryusei (Shooting Star). This view shows the extremely wide-track undercarriage.

peller made it necessary to select an inverted gull wing to reduce the length of the undercarriage legs. The wings were also fitted with drooping ailerons, which could be deflected 10 degrees to serve as auxiliary flaps, and dive brakes were mounted on the undersurface ahead of the flaps between the fuselage and ailerons. For carrier stowage the wings folded hydraulically upwards outboard of the flaps.

Designated AM-23 by its manufacturers and Navy Experimental 16-Shi Carrier Attack Bomber (B7A1) by the Japanese Navy, the first prototype was completed in May 1942. As the aircraft was the first to be powered by the still experimental 1,800 hp Homare 11 engine, the flight trial programme was constantly interrupted by engine teething troubles, but when the Homare 11 performed smoothly the B7A1 demonstrated sparkling performance (maximum speed: 310 kt—367 mph) and excellent handling characteristics. A total of nine Homare 11 powered B7A1 prototypes were built and were progressively modified to eradicate minor airframe and equipment problems. In April 1944 an improved engine version, the 1,825 hp Homare 12, became available and powered by this engine the aircraft

An Aichi B7A2 Navy Carrier Attack Bomber Ryusei (Shooting Star) of the 752nd Kokutai.

AICHI B7A2

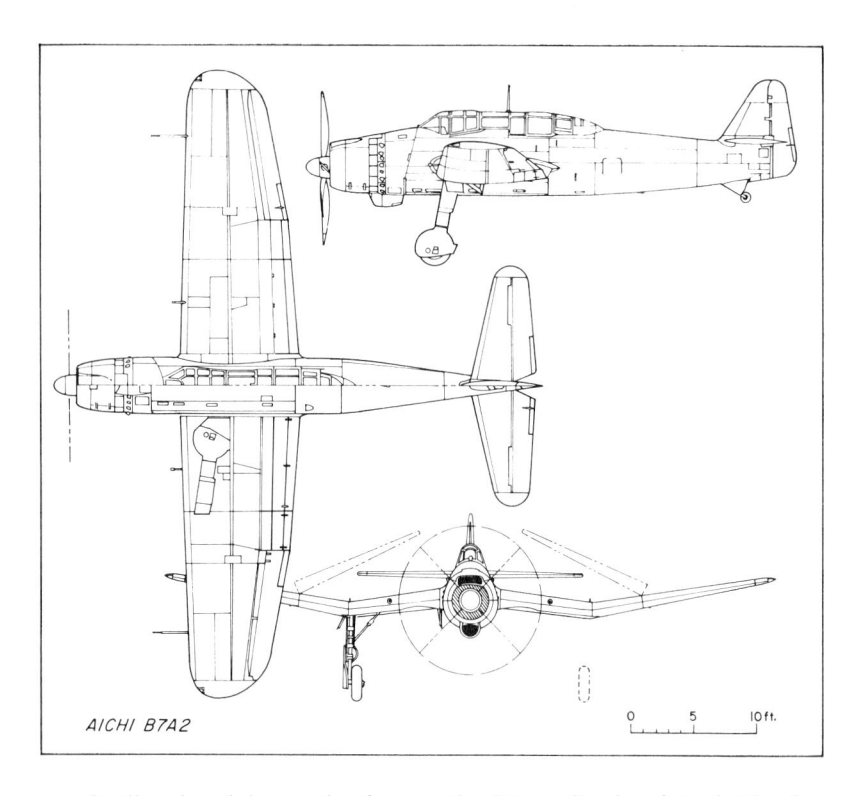

was finally placed in production as the Navy Carrier Attack Bomber Ryusei.

Assembly lines for the Homare 12 powered B7A2 were set up by Aichi Kokuki K.K. at Funakata and the 21st Naval Air Arsenal (Dai-Nijuichi Kaigun Kokusho) at Omura, but production was slow in gaining tempo despite the fact that the B7A was easier to build than the much smaller Yokosuka D4Y which Aichi had been building for many years. Initial production aircraft retained the flexible rear-firing 7·92 mm Type 1 machine-gun but late production B7A2s mounted a 13 mm Type 2 machine-gun in its place. Production of the B7A2 by Aichi was finally brought to a standstill when the Funakata plant was destroyed by the earthquake which, in May 1945, rocked the Tokai district. However, this no longer affected the outcome of the war because the Japanese Navy had lost their carrier fleet and the small number of B7A2s (code name GRACE) built saw limited service from land bases with the Yokosuka and 752nd Kokutais.

One B7A2 was experimentally fitted with a 2,000 hp Nakajima Homare 23 intended for future production aircraft but because of the earthquake the projected B7A3 Ryusei Kai powered by a 2,200 hp Mitsubishi MK9A was not realized. Towards the end of the war a successor to the Ryusei was under development. This aircraft, the Mokusei (Jupiter), was to have been much smaller and faster but its design did not progress further than the initial layout phase.

UNITS ALLOCATED
752nd and Yokosuka Kokutais.

TECHNICAL DATA
Description: Single-engined carrier-borne torpedo and dive-bomber. All-metal construction with fabric-covered control surfaces.
Accommodation: Crew of two in tandem enclosed cockpits.
Powerplant: One Nakajima NK9B Homare 11 eighteen-cylinder air-cooled radial, rated at 1,800 hp for take-off, 1,440 hp at 1,800 m (5,905 ft) and 1,560 hp at 6,400 m (21,000 ft), driving a constant-speed four-blade metal propeller (B7A1 prototypes).

One Nakajima NK9C Homare 12 eighteen-cylinder air-cooled radial, rated at 1,825 hp for take-off, 1,670 hp at 2,400 m (7,875 ft) and 1,560 hp at 6,550 m (21,490 ft), driving a constant-speed four-blade metal propeller (production B7A2).

One Nakajima NK9H-S Homare 23 eighteen-cylinder air-cooled radial, rated at 2,000 hp for take-off and 1,570 hp at 6,850 m (22,475 ft), driving a constant-speed four-blade metal propeller (one experimental B7A2).

One Mitsubishi MK9A ([Ha-43] 11) eighteen-cylinder air-cooled radial, rated at 2,200 hp for take-off, 2,070 hp at 1,000 m (3,280 ft) and 1,930 hp at 5,000 m (16,405 ft), driving a constant-speed four-blade metal propeller (B7A3).

Armament: Two wing-mounted 20 mm Type 99 Model 2 cannon and one flexible rear-firing 7·92 mm Type 1 machine-gun (B7A1 and early production B7A2).

Two wing-mounted 20 mm Type 99 Model 2 cannon and one flexible rear-firing 13 mm Type 2 machine-gun (late production B7A2).

Bomb-load: one 800 kg (1,764 lb) torpedo or up to 800 kg (1,764 lb) of bombs.

Dimensions: (B7A2) Span 14·4 m (47 ft 2 $\frac{18}{18}$ in); length 11·49 m (37 ft 8 $\frac{1}{2}$ in); height 4·075 m (13 ft 4 $\frac{7}{16}$ in); wing area 35·4 sq m (381·041 sq ft).
Weights: (B7A2) Empty 3,810 kg (8,400 lb); loaded 5,625 kg (12,401 lb); maximum 6,500 kg (14,330 lb); wing loading 158·9 kg/sq m (32·5 lb/sq ft); power loading 3·1 kg/hp (6·8 lb/hp).
Performance: (B7A2) Maximum speed 306 kt at 6,550 m (352 mph at 21,490 ft); climb to 4,000 m (13,125 ft) in 6 min 55 sec; service ceiling 11,250 m (36,910 ft); range—normal 1,000 naut miles (1,151 st miles), maximum 1,640 naut miles (1,888 st miles).
Production: A total of 114 B7As were built as follows:

Aichi Kokuki K.K. at Funakata:

9 B7A1 prototypes (May 1942–Feb 1944)
80 B7A2 production aircraft (May 1944–July 1945)

Dai-Nijuichi Kaigun Kokusho at Omura (Sasebo):

25 B7A2 production aircraft (Apr 1944–Aug 1945)

Aichi M6A Seiran (Mountain Haze)

Bearing the distinction of being the only submarine-borne aircraft to have been built anywhere in the world with offensive missions as its primary role, the Aichi M6A1 Seiran (Mountain Haze) is assured a place in history even though the second World War ended before the aircraft could fly its first sortie.

In their Fourth Reinforcement Programme the Japanese Navy included a request for eighteen submarines of the I-400 Class. These very large submarines, each displacing 4,500 tons, were to have a cruising radius of

41,575 naut miles at 14 kt and were to be equipped with a large watertight hangar capable of accommodating two attack aircraft and with a catapult on the forward deck. However, the pressing need for more conventional submarines forced a revision of the plan and only five of this class were actually ordered with an enlarged hangar accommodating three aircraft.

In 1942 Aichi were instructed to design a Navy Experimental 17-Shi Special Attack Bomber for use aboard the submarines of the I-400 Class. The original 17-Shi specification called for a fast catapult-launched aircraft without undercarriage but this was later revised to provide for twin detachable floats. The design of the aircraft bearing the Aichi model number AM-24 was assigned to a team led by Norio Ozaki, Yasushiro Ozawa and Morishige Mori and, despite the added complexity stemming from the need to provide easy stowage in the small watertight hangar, the project progressed smoothly. Two versions of the aircraft were designed, the M6A1 Seiran with detachable floats and intended for attack missions and the trainer version, the M6A1-K Seiran Kai, with retractable undercarriage. The popular name of the M6A1-K was later changed to Nanzan (Southern Mountain).

Completed in November 1943, the first prototype M6A1 Seiran was powered by a 1,400 hp Aichi AE1P Atsuta 30 twelve-cylinder inverted-vee liquid-cooled engine. The aircraft was characterized by the complicated wing and tail folding system. The wings swivelled on their rear spar to lie flat along the fuselage, the tip of the vertical tail surfaces folded to starboard and the horizontal tail surfaces folded downward. Despite the apparent complexity of the folding mechanism and the lack of space aboard the submarine, the M6A1 could be readied for flight in less than 7 min by four trained personnel. To facilitate night assembly fluorescent paint was applied to all important parts.

The Aichi M6A1 Seiran (Mountain Haze) entered service with the 631st Kokutai during the winter of 1944–45.

An Aichi M6A1 Navy Special Attack Bomber Seiran (Mountain Haze). The large cantilever floats were designed to be jettisoned in combat.

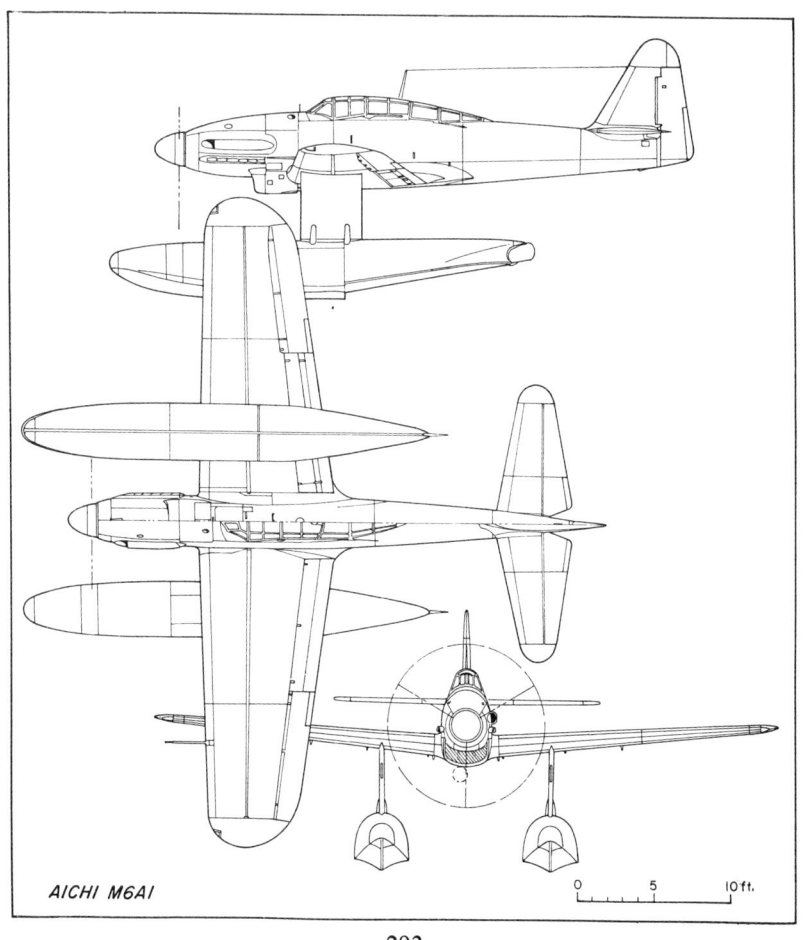

AICHI M6A1

Aichi M6A1-K Nanzan (Southern Mountain), land-based trainer version of the M6A1 Seiran floatplane.

Five additional prototypes powered by the Atsuta 31 engine were followed by two M6A1-K Nanzan with Atsuta 32 engine and by eighteen Atsuta 32 powered M6A1 production aircraft. The Nanzan was fitted with an inwardly-retracting undercarriage, and the folding tip of the rudder was dispensed with as the absence of floats improved directional stability. Plans were on hand for an attack on the lock gates of the Panama Canal by the First Submarine Flotilla made up of I-400 and I-401 submarines, each carrying three M6A1s, and of the I-13 and I-14 submarines, each carrying two Seirans. However, the target was changed to the US Navy's anchorage at Ulithi Atoll and the First Submarine Flotilla put to sea in late July 1945. The war ended before the attack could take place.

TECHNICAL DATA

Description: Single-engined submarine-borne attack bomber with twin detachable floats (M6A1). Single-engined land-based combat trainer with retractable undercarriage (M6A1-K). All-metal construction with fabric-covered control surfaces.

Accommodation: Crew of two in tandem enclosed cockpits.

Powerplant: One Aichi AE1P Atsuta 30 or Atsuta 31 twelve-cylinder inverted-vee liquid-cooled engine, rated at 1,400 hp for take-off, 1,250 hp at 1,700 m (5,580 ft) and 1,290 hp at 5,000 m (16,405 ft), driving a constant-speed three-blade metal propeller (M6A1 prototypes).

One Aichi Atsuta 32 twelve-cylinder inverted-vee liquid-cooled engine, rated at 1,400 hp for take-off, 1,340 hp at 1,700 m (5,580 ft) and 1,290 hp at 5,000 m (16,405 ft), driving a constant-speed three-blade metal propeller (M6A1 production aircraft and M6A1-K prototypes).

Armament: One flexible rear-firing 13 mm Type 2 machine-gun.
 Bomb-load: two 250 kg (551 lb) bombs, or one 800 kg (1,764 lb) or 850 kg (1,874 lb) bomb.

Dimensions: (M6A1) Span 12·262 m (40 ft 2¾ in); length 11·64 m (38 ft 2¼ in); height 4·58 m (15 ft 0 6/16 in); wing area 27 sq m (290·624 sq ft).

Weights: (M6A1) Empty 3,301 kg (7,277 lb); loaded 4,040 kg (8,907 lb); maximum 4,445 kg (9,800 lb); wing loading 149·6 kg/sq m (30·6 lb/sq ft); power loading 2·1 kg/hp (4·6 lb/hp).

Performance: (M6A1) Maximum speed 256 kt at 5,200 m (295 mph at 17,060 ft); cruising speed 160 kt at 3,000 m (184 mph at 9,845 ft); climb to 3,000 m (9,845 ft) in 5 min 48 sec; service ceiling 9,900 m (32,480 ft); range 642 naut miles (739 st miles).

Production: A total of 28 M6A1s were built between October 1943 and July 1945 by Aichi Kokuki K.K. at Eitoku as follows:

  6 M6A1 prototypes (Oct 1943–Oct 1944)
  20 M6A1 production aircraft (Oct 1944–July 1945)
  2 M6A1-K prototypes (1945)

Aichi S1A Denko (Bolt of Light)

The development of night fighters was long neglected by the Japanese and when the Marianas-based B-29s began to mount low-level night attacks Japan's defence against this type of operation was left to an assorted collection of aircraft. The only operational radar-equipped night fighters available at the end of the war were a small number of the Navy's Nakajima J1N1-S Gekko, and their intended replacement, the Aichi S1A1, had yet to be flown.

Late in 1943, the Japanese Navy issued for the first time a specification for a night fighter which was to possess a maximum speed of 370 kt at 9,000 m (426 mph at 29,530 ft), an endurance of five hours and a rate of climb of 6,000 m (19,685 ft) in 8 min. The aircraft's armament was to include two 30 mm cannon, and airborne radar equipment was mandatory. In answer to this specification Aichi designed the Navy Experimental 18-Shi Night Fighter Denko (Bolt of Light) incorporating many advanced features such as drooping ailerons acting as auxiliary landing flaps, and air-brakes were installed under the wing and fuselage centre-section to be used in the final stage of interception to avoid overtaking the enemy bomber. Radar was installed in the nose, and armament consisted of two 30 mm Type 5 and two 20 mm Type 99 Model 2 cannon mounted in the lower forward fuselage section and two 20 mm Type 99 Model 2 cannon installed in a remotely-controlled dorsal turret. The crew of two was housed in separate cockpits, the pilot over the wing leading edge and the radar-operator/gunner above the trailing edge.

The main difficulties faced by the Aichi design team stemmed from the need to meet the performance requirements since the Navy insisted on using two Nakajima Homare engines which had insufficient power at altitude. Maximum speed with two fan-cooled 2,000 hp Nakajima NK9K-S

Full-scale mock-up of the Aichi S1A1 Denko (Bolt of Light) twin-engined night fighter.

Homare 22 engines was initially calculated at 340 kt (391 mph) but later revised to only 318 kt (366 mph) as the weight of the aircraft kept increasing. With two turbosupercharged Nakajima NK9K-L Homare 24s it was hoped that production aircraft would have a top speed of 367 kt (422 mph).

However, no aircraft were completed before the Japanese surrender as the first prototype, 70 per cent complete, was destroyed during an Allied raid on the Aichi plant and the second prototype suffered the same fate when 90 per cent complete.

TECHNICAL DATA

Description: Twin-engined night fighter. All-metal construction with fabric-covered control surfaces.

Accommodation: Pilot and radar-operator/gunner in separate enclosed cockpits.

Powerplant: Two Nakajima NK9K-S Homare 22 eighteen-cylinder air-cooled radials, rated at 2,000 hp for take-off, 1,885 hp at 1,750 m (5,740 ft) and 1,620 hp at 6,400 m (21,000 ft), driving constant-speed four-blade metal propellers.

Armament: Two forward-firing 30 mm Type 5 cannon and two forward-firing 20 mm Type 99 Model 2 cannon in the forward fuselage, and two 20 mm Type 99 Model 2 cannon in a dorsal turret.
  Bomb-load: 250 kg (551 lb).

Dimensions: Span 17·5 m (57 ft 4$\frac{33}{64}$ in); length 15·1 m (49 ft 6$\frac{1}{2}$ in); height 4·61 m (15 ft 1$\frac{1}{2}$ in); wing area 47 sq m (505·902 sq ft).

Weights: Empty 7,320 kg (16,138 lb); loaded 10,180 kg (22,443 lb); maximum 11,510 kg (25,375 lb); wing loading 126·6 kg/sq m (44·4 lb/sq ft); power loading 2·5 kg/hp (5·6 lb/hp).

Performance: Maximum speed 318 kt at 8,000 m (366 mph at 26,245 ft); cruising speed 240 kt at 4,000 m (276 mph at 13,125 ft); climb to 9,000 m (29,530 ft) in 14 min 45 sec; service ceiling 12,000 m (39,370 ft); range—normal 916 naut miles (1,054 st miles), maximum 1,373 naut miles (1,580 st miles).

Production: No aircraft completed by the end of the war.

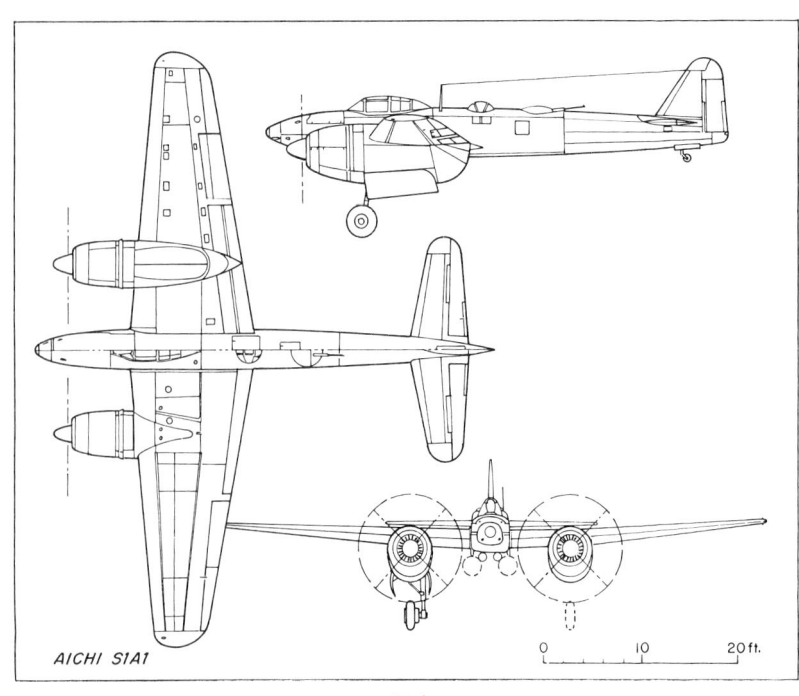

AICHI S1A1

Kawanishi E7K1 floatplanes of the Kure Kokutai. (*Eckert.*)

Kawanishi E7K

Development of a three-seat long-range reconnaissance twin-float seaplane intended to replace the Navy Type 90-3 Reconnaissance Seaplane (Kawanishi E5K1) was begun in March 1932 by Kawanishi and Aichi in answer to a 7-Shi specification issued during the previous month by the Japanese Navy. The Kawanishi design, designated Model J by the manufacturers and E7K1 by the Navy, was the work of a team led by Eiji Sekiguchi and the first prototype was completed in less than a year. Flown for the first time on 6 February, 1933, the E7K1 was a twin-float biplane powered by a 500 hp Hiro Type 91 twelve-cylinder W liquid-cooled engine driving a two-blade wooden propeller. Defensive armament included a fixed forward-firing 7·7 mm Type 92 machine-gun, one flexible rear-firing 7·7 mm Type 92 machine-gun and a similar flexible weapon firing downward to the rear. Racks for four 30 kg (66 lb) or two 60 kg (132 lb) bombs were installed under the wing centre-section. The crew—consisting of a pilot, an observer and a radio-operator/gunner—was seated in three separate open cockpits.

In May 1933 the first prototype completed its manufacturer's flight test programme and was handed over to the Navy for competitive Service trials against the Aichi AB-6. Performance and handling characteristics of the E7K1 were found markedly superior to those of the AB-6 but no order was placed for several months. Finally, in May 1934, following delivery of a second E7K1 prototype in late 1933, the Navy ordered the aircraft into production as the Navy Type 94 Reconnaissance Seaplane Model 1. Initial production aircraft received the 500 hp Hiro Type 91 engine as fitted to the prototypes but late production E7K1s received an uprated version of this engine, the 600 hp Type 91, with a maximum take-off rating of 750 hp and driving a four-blade wooden propeller. In service the E7K1 was lauded by its crews for its ease of handling and its reliability and was operated from warships, seaplane tenders and shore bases for maritime reconnaissance and coastal patrol. It was also used for a number of test projects as well as mother aircraft for the MXY3 Experimental Target Glider or its powered radio-controlled version, the Navy Type 1 Target Plane (MXY4). For this task the aircraft was fitted with a metal frame above the upper wing centre-section. A total of 183 Navy Type 94 Reconnaissance Seaplane Model 1 aircraft were built by Kawanishi and production was also undertaken by Nippon Hikoki K.K. beginning in April 1937.

Three years after production of the E7K1 had begun the Japanese Navy began to evince considerable interest in the E7K2, a proposed version of the aircraft powered by an 870 hp Mitsubishi Zuisei 11 fourteen-cylinder air-cooled radial driving a two-blade propeller. The first E7K2 flew in August 1938 and production began in November 1938 under the designation Navy Type 94 Reconnaissance Seaplane Model 2 (later Model 12).

When the Pacific War began the E7K1s had been relegated to training duties but the E7K2s (code name ALF), despite their obsolescence, remained in first-line service until early 1943. The aircraft was initially used for convoy escort, anti-submarine patrol and reconnaissance. Later in the war, the E7K2s were retained in the liaison and training roles and as mother aircraft for the MXY4 radio-controlled target plane.

A Kawanishi E7K2 Navy Type 94 Reconnaissance Seaplane Model 2. In the background is a Nakajima E8N1 Type 95 Reconnaissance Seaplane.

The radial-engined Kawanishi E7K2 aboard ship. (*US Navy Department*.)

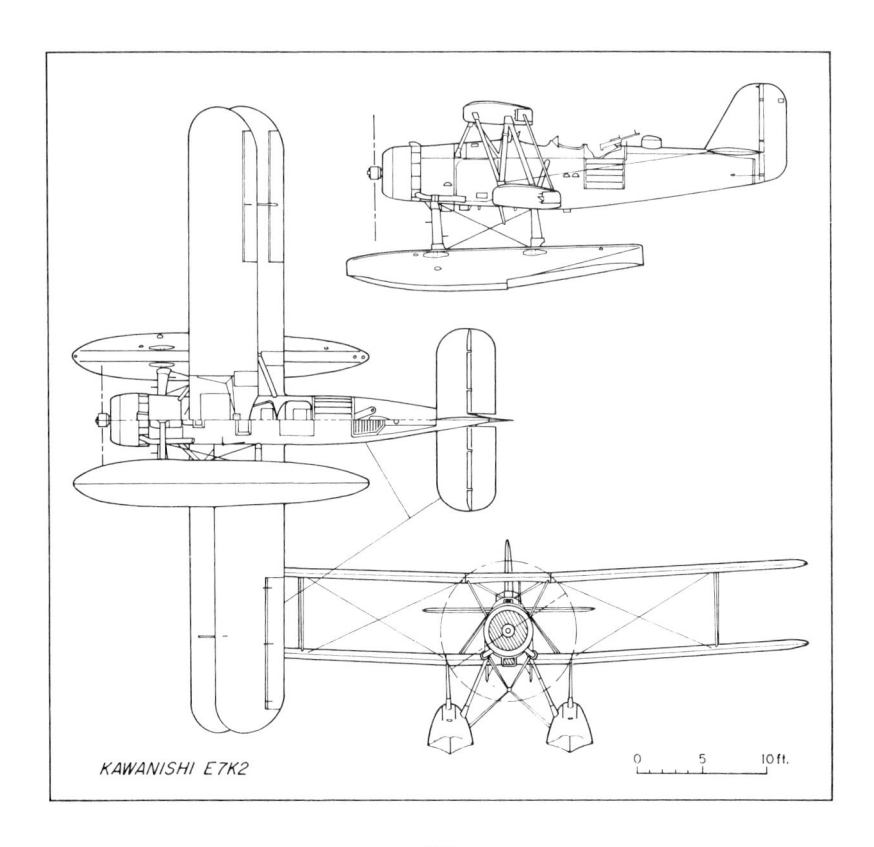

KAWANISHI E7K2

UNITS ALLOCATED

Seaplane tenders: *Chitose, Chiyoda*; Cruisers: *Mikuma, Furutaka, Kako, Kitakami, Kuma, Kiso, Kinu, Nagara, Yura, Isuzu, Natori, Kashii, Kashima, Abukuma*, etc; 19th, Chinkai and Kure Kokutais.

TECHNICAL DATA

Description: Single-engined twin-float reconnaissance seaplane. All-metal structure with fabric covering.

Accommodation: Crew of three in tandem open cockpits.

Powerplant: One 500 hp Hiro Type 91 twelve-cylinder W liquid-cooled engine, rated at 620 hp for take-off and 520 hp at 1,000 m (3,280 ft), driving a two-blade wooden propeller (prototypes and early production E7K1s).

One 600 hp Hiro Type 91 twelve-cylinder W liquid-cooled engine, rated at 750 hp for take-off and 600 hp at 1,500 m (4,920 ft), driving a four-blade wooden propeller (late production E7K1s).

One 870 hp Mitsubishi Zuisei 11 fourteen-cylinder air-cooled radial, rated at 870 hp for take-off and 850 hp at 2,300 m (7,545 ft), driving a two-blade metal propeller (E7K2s).

Armament: One forward-firing 7·7 mm Type 92 machine-gun, one flexible rear-firing 7·7 mm Type 92 machine-gun and one flexible downward-firing 7·7 mm Type 92 machine-gun.

Bomb-load: four 30 kg (66 lb) or two 60 kg (132 lb) bombs.

	E7K1 (late production)	E7K2
Dimensions:		
Span	14 m	14 m
	(45 ft 11 $\frac{3}{16}$ in)	(45 ft 11 $\frac{3}{16}$ in
Length	10·41 m	10·5 m
	(34 ft 1 $\frac{27}{32}$ in)	(34 ft 5 $\frac{3}{8}$ in)
Height	4·81 m	4·85 m
	(15 ft 9 $\frac{3}{8}$ in)	(15 ft 10 $\frac{15}{16}$ in)
Wing area	43·6 sq m	43·6 sq m
	(469·305 sq ft)	(469·305 sq ft)
Weights:		
Empty	1,970 kg	2,100 kg
	(4,343 lb)	(4,630 lb)
Loaded	3,000 kg	3,300 kg
	(6,614 lb)	(7,275 lb)
Wing loading	68·8 kg/sq m	75·7 kg/sq m
	(14·1 lb/sq ft)	(15·5 lb/sq ft)
Power loading	4 kg/hp	3·8 kg/hp
	(8·8 lb/hp)	(8·4 lb/hp)
Performance:		
Maximum speed	129 kt at 500 m	149 kt at 2,000 m
	(148 mph at 1,805 ft)	(171 mph at 6,560 ft)
Cruising speed	—	100 kt at 1,000 m
	—	(115 mph at 3,280 ft)
Climb to	3,000 m (9,845 ft)	3,000 m (9,845 ft)
in	10 min 45 sec	9 min 6 sec
Service ceiling	—	7,060 m
	—	(23,165 ft)
Endurance	12 hr	11·32 hr

Production: A total of 530 E7Ks were built as follows:

Kawanishi Kokuki K.K. at Naruo:

    2 E7K1 prototypes (1933)
    183 E7K1 production aircraft (1934–38)
    1 E7K2 prototype (1938)
    287 E7K2 production aircraft (1938–41)

Nippon Hikoki K.K. at Tomioka:

    57 E7K1 and E7K2 production aircraft (1937–39)

Kawanishi Navy Experimental 9-Shi Large-size Flying-Boat, the prototype of the H6K series. (*Aireview*.)

Kawanishi H6K

Operated throughout the Pacific War as a long-range maritime reconnaissance aircraft, bomber and transport, the Kawanishi H6K was one of the best combat aircraft available to the Japanese Navy when the war broke out. The aircraft originated in early 1933 when a Navy Experimental 8-Shi Large Flying-Boat specification was issued to Kawanishi. In answer to this specification Kawanishi submitted design proposals for two separate aircraft: the Type Q with four engines and the Type R with three engines. Both types were of monoplane design, and extensive studies, including model testing in wind tunnel and water tank, were made between March and September 1933. However, the Navy were not satisfied with the calculated performance of either type and, in early 1934, a Navy Experimental 9-Shi Large Flying-Boat specification was issued.

The new specification, incorporating the knowledge acquired with the design of the Type Q and the Type R, reflected the Navy's increased performance requirements and called for a four-engined flying-boat of monoplane design with overall performance—including a range of 2,500 naut miles at a cruising speed of 120 kt—superior to that of the American Sikorsky S-42. Benefiting from the information obtained by Kawanishi's personnel during a visit to Short Brothers, a team led by Yoshio Hashiguchi and Shizuo Kikahura designed a flying-boat bearing the company designation of Type S and characterized by its parasol wing mounted above the hull on inverted-V struts and braced by parallel struts attached low on the hull and running to half-span. Powered by four 840 hp Nakajima Hikari 2 nine-cylinder air-cooled radials, the first prototype made its maiden flight on 14 July, 1936, with test pilot Katsuji Kondo at the controls.

Immediately after the first test flight, the forward step was moved back 50 cm (1 ft $7\frac{11}{16}$ in) to improve water handling characteristics. Manufacturer's trials proceeded swiftly, the aircraft being handed over to the Japanese Navy on 25 July, 1936. Service trials indicated that the H6K1 was satisfactory in every respect except that it was somewhat underpowered. Water handling was particularly satisfactory, the hull having good stability and spray characteristics. Defensive armament comprised three flexible 7·7 mm Type 92 machine-guns mounted in an open bow position, in a power-operated dorsal turret—the first such installation on a Japanese aircraft—and in a non-powered tail turret, while offensive armament included either two 800 kg (1,764 lb) torpedoes or up to 1,000 kg (2,205 lb) of bombs attached to the parallel wing-supporting struts. Two additional prototypes were delivered in 1937, with a fourth being completed early in 1938. Initially these three aircraft were each powered by four Hikari 2 radials and differed from the first aircraft in featuring ailerons of increased span, enlarged fins and redesigned dorsal turret installation.

Following completion of Service trials the first, third and fourth prototypes were re-engined with 1,000 hp Mitsubishi Kinsei 43 fourteen-cylinder air-cooled radials and these aircraft entered service with the Japanese Navy in January 1938 under the designation Navy Type 97 Flying-Boat Model 1 (H6K1). At the same time the type was placed in full production, the initial production machines being designated H6K2 Model 2 (the full designation of this version was changed to Navy Type 97 Flying-Boat Model 11 in April 1940). With the exception of minor internal equipment changes the H6K2s were identical to the re-engined H6K1s and ten of this version were built. Two of these aircraft, the seventh and eighth H6K2s, were modified as prototypes for a transport version and the H6K2 production batch was followed by two aircraft built from the start as staff transports under the designation of H6K3. A requirement for a military VIP transport as well as for a civil version existed, but the need for the basic long-range maritime reconnaissance flying-boat was even more pressing and, consequently, priority was given to the production of the H6K4.

The Navy Type 97 Flying-Boat Model 2-2 or H6K4 was the major production version of the aircraft and this had the fuel capacity increased from 7,765 litres (1,708 Imp gal) to 13,409 litres (2,950 Imp gal). The power-operated dorsal turret was replaced by two beam blisters which each contained a hand-held 7·7 mm Type 92 machine-gun, and two similar weapons were provided in an open bow position and an open dorsal position while a hand-held 20 mm Type 99 Model 1 cannon was installed in the tail turret. The Kinsei 43 powered H6K4 Model 2-2 was followed in August 1941 by the H6K4 Model 2-3 powered by four Kinsei 46s and a total of 127 aircraft of both versions—later jointly redesignated Navy Type 97 Flying-Boat Model 22—were built between 1939 and 1942. At the beginning of the war sixty-six H6K4s were operated by first-line units of

Kawanishi H6K4 Navy Type 97 Flying-Boat Model 22. (*Aireview.*)

the Japanese Navy. Besides performing the normal long-range maritime reconnaissance sorties for which they had been conceived, these aircraft flew bombing missions against land targets in the Netherlands East Indies and at Rabaul. However, the Navy Type 97 Flying-Boat, dubbed MAVIS by the Allies, was lacking armour protection and self-sealing fuel tanks and soon had to be withdrawn from bombing operations as Allied fighter defence became more effective. In the maritime reconnaissance role, when usually little or no fighter opposition was encountered, the aircraft was more successful and its remarkable endurance proved extremely valuable in patrolling the vast expanses of the Pacific.

As a safeguard against potential problems with the Kawanishi H8K1, in 1941 the 119th H6K was fitted with four 1,300 hp Mitsubishi Kinsei 53 radials, and the open gun position in the bow was replaced by a turret housing a 7·7 mm Type 92 machine-gun located immediately aft of the flight deck. This aircraft served as prototype for the Navy Type 97 Flying-Boat Model 23 (H6K5) which supplanted the H6K4 Model 22 on Kawanishi's assembly lines and was powered by either four Kinsei 51 or 53

Kawanishi H6K5 Navy Type 97 Flying-Boat Model 23. (*US Navy Department.*)

radials. In 1942, the thirty-sixth H6K5 was completed, bringing total production of the maritime reconnaissance version of the aircraft to 175 machines, including the four prototypes but excluding the two H6K2s modified as transports and the two H6K3s. As the production of the later H8K gained tempo, the surviving H6K4s and H6K5s were withdrawn from first-line duties and, fitted with troop benches, were relegated to military transport duties.

As previously related, two H6K2s had been modified in 1939 as prototypes for a transport version intended for military staff transport and for

A Kawanishi H6K5 Navy Type 97 Flying-Boat under attack by Allied aircraft.

operation over the long over-water routes of Dai Nippon Koku K.K. (Greater Japan Air Lines). In 1940, once the production of the H6K4 maritime reconnaissance model was well established, Kawanishi began to produce a small number of transport flying-boats designated Navy Type 97 Transport Flying-Boat (H6K2-L) which, despite their designation, were based on the H6K4 with increased fuel tankage. Modifications included the removal of all armament, and the interior fuselage arrangement was revised to provide for the following installations: mail and cargo compartment in the hull forward of the cockpit, galleys behind the cockpit, a midship cabin with seats for eight or sleeping accommodation for four followed by an aft cabin with ten seats and, aft of this again, toilets and cargo compartment. Sixteen Kinsei 43 powered H6K2-Ls were followed by twenty H6K4-Ls powered by four Kinsei 46 radials, and featuring additional cabin windows but retaining, although without armament, the glazed tail turret. Two additional H6K4-L transports were obtained by converting two H6K4 patrol flying-boats. Twenty Navy Type 97 Transport Flying-Boats, code named TILLIE by the Allies, were used by the Japanese

J-BFOZ *Ayanami* (*Waves whose beauty suggests figures woven in silk*), one of sixteen Kawanishi H6K2-L flying-boats operated by Dai Nippon Koku K.K.

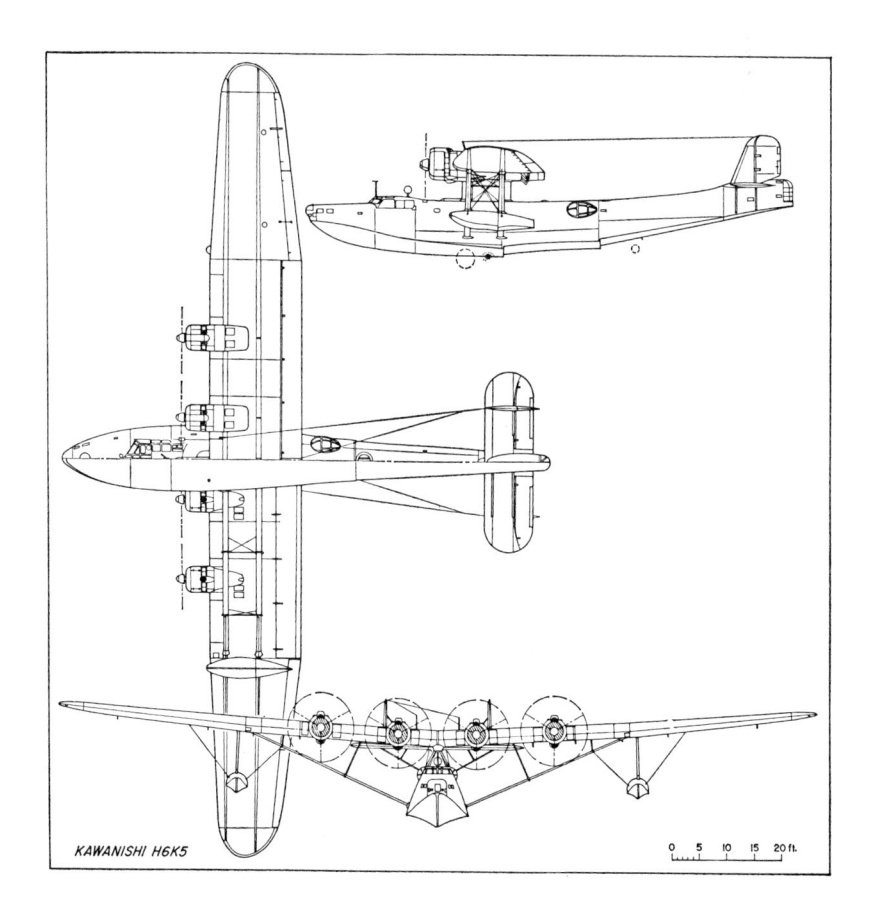

KAWANISHI H6K5

305

Navy for staff transport, and the other eighteen aircraft were delivered to the Kaiyo (Ocean) Division of Dai Nippon Koku K.K. which assigned the type to their Yokohama–Saipan–Palau–Timor, Saigon–Bangkok and Saipan–Truk–Ponape–Jaluit routes. Several of these aircraft were destroyed by the Allies but the surviving H6K2-Ls and H6K4-Ls were retained in service by both the Navy and Dai Nippon Koku K.K. until the end of the war.

UNITS ALLOCATED

8th, 14th, 801st, Toko and Yokohama Kokutais.

TECHNICAL DATA

Description: Four-engined long-range maritime reconnaissance flying-boat (H6K1, H6K2, H6K4 and H6K5) and transport flying-boat (H6K2-L, H6K3 and H6K4-L). All-metal construction with fabric-covered control surfaces.

Accommodation: Normal crew of nine (H6K1, H6K2, H6K4 and H6K5).

Crew of eight and 10–18 passengers (H6K2-L, H6K3 and H6K4-L).

Powerplant: Four Nakajima Hikari 2 nine-cylinder air-cooled radials, rated at 840 hp for take-off and 700 hp at 1,200 m (3,940 ft), driving three-blade metal propellers (H6K1 prototypes).

Four Mitsubishi Kinsei 43 fourteen-cylinder air-cooled radials, rated at 1,000 hp for take-off and 990 hp at 2,800 m (9,185 ft), driving three-blade metal propellers (H6K1 Model 1, H6K2, H6K2-L, H6K3 and H6K4 Model 2-2).

Four Mitsubishi Kinsei 46 fourteen-cylinder air-cooled radials, rated at 930 hp for take-off and 1,070 hp at 4,200 m (13,780 ft), driving three-blade metal propellers (H6K4 Model 2-3 and H6K4-L).

Four Mitsubishi Kinsei 51 or Kinsei 53 fourteen-cylinder radials, rated at 1,300 hp for take-off, 1,200 hp at 3,000 m (9,845 ft) and 1,100 hp at 6,200 m (20,340 ft), driving three-blade metal propellers (H6K5).

Armament: One flexible 7·7 mm Type 92 machine-gun in an open bow position, one flexible 7·7 mm Type 92 machine-gun in a power-operated dorsal turret and one hand-held 7·7 mm Type 92 machine-gun in a tail turret (H6K1 and H6K2).

One flexible 7·7 mm Type 92 machine-gun in an open bow position (H6K4) or forward turret (H6K5), one 7·7 mm Type 92 machine-gun in an open dorsal position, one 7·7 mm Type 92 machine-gun in each beam blister and one flexible 20 mm Type 99 Model 1 cannon in a tail turret (H6K4 and H6K5).

Bomb-load: two 800 kg (1,764 lb) torpedoes, or up to 1,000 kg (2,205 lb) of bombs (H6K1, H6K2, H6K4 and H6K5).

	H6K2	H6K2-L	H6K4	H6K5
Dimensions:				
Span	40 m (131 ft 2 25/32 in)	40 m (131 ft 2 25/32 in)	40 m (131 ft 2 25/32 in)	40 m (131 ft 2 25/32 in)
Length	25·625 m (84 ft 0 27/32 in)	24·9 m (81 ft 8 5/16 in)	25·625 m (84 ft 0 27/32 in)	25·625 m (84 ft 0 27/32 in)
Height	6·27 m (20 ft 6 27/32 in)	6·27 m (20 ft 6 27/32 in)	6·27 m (20 ft 6 27/32 in)	6·27 m (20 ft 6 27/32 in)
Wing area	170 sq m (1,829·858 sq ft)	170 sq m (1,829·858 sq ft)	170 sq m (1,829·858 sq ft)	170 sq m (1,829·858 sq ft)
Weights:				
Empty	10,340 kg (22,796 lb)	12,025 kg (26,511 lb)	11,707 kg (25,810 lb)	12,380 kg (27,117 lb)
Loaded	16,000 kg (35,274 lb)	17,100 kg (37,699 lb)	17,000 kg (37,479 lb)	17,500 kg (38,581 lb)
Maximum	— —	23,000 kg (50,706 lb)	21,500 kg (47,399 lb)	23,000 kg (50,706 lb)
Wing loading	94·1 kg/sq m (19·3 lb/sq ft)	100·6 kg/sq m (20·6 lb/sq ft)	100 kg/sq m (20·5 lb/sq ft)	102·9 kg/sq m (21·1 lb/sq ft)
Power loading	4 kg/hp (8·8 lb/hp)	4·3 kg/hp (9·5 lb/hp)	4·3 kg/hp (9·5 lb/hp)	3·4 kg/hp (7·4 lb/hp)

Performance:

	H6K2	H6K2-L	H6K4	H6K5
Maximum speed	179 kt at 2,100 m (206 mph at 6,890 ft)	180 kt at 2,610 m (207 mph at 8,565 ft)	183·5 kt at 4,000 m (211 mph at 13,125 ft)	208 kt at 6,000 m (239 mph at 19,685 ft)
Cruising speed	— —	130 kt at 1,000 m (150 mph at 3,280 ft)	120 kt at 4,000 m (138 mph at 13,125 ft)	140 kt at 4,000 m (161 mph at 13,125 ft)
Climb to in	5,000 m (16,405 ft) 13 min 58 sec	— — —	5,000 m (16,405 ft) 13 min 31 sec	5,000 m (16,405 ft) 13 min 23 sec
Service ceiling	7,600 m (24,935 ft)	— —	9,610 m (31,530 ft)	9,560 m (31,365 ft)
Normal range	2,230 naut miles (2,567 st miles)	2,337 naut miles (2,690 st miles)	2,590 naut miles (2,981 st miles)	2,667 naut miles (3,070 st miles)
Maximum range	— —	— —	3,283 naut miles (3,779 st miles)	3,656 naut miles (4,208 st miles)

Production: A total of 215 H6Ks were built by Kawanishi Kokuki K.K. in their Naruo plant as follows:

    4 H6K1 prototypes (1936–38)
  (3) H6K1 Model 1 modified from prototypes (1938)
  10 H6K2 Model 11 (1938–39)
  (2) H6K2 modified as experimental transports (1939)
    2 H6K3 (1939)
 127 H6K4 Model 22 (1939–42)
  36 H6K5 Model 23 (1942)
  16 H6K2-L (1940–42)
  20 H6K4-L (1942–43)
  (2) H6K4-L modified from H6K4 airframes (1942)

Kawanishi H8K

During the summer of 1938 Kawanishi Kokuki K.K. obtained a development contract from the Navy for a large four-engined maritime reconnaissance flying-boat intended to supplant the Navy Type 97 Flying-Boat. The Navy Experimental 13-Shi Large Flying-Boat specification called for an aircraft with overall performance superior to that of the British Short Sunderland and American Sikorsky XPBS-1 and possessing a top speed of 240 kt (276 mph), a cruising speed of 180 kt (207 mph) and a maximum patrol range of 4,500 naut miles (5,180 st miles).

    Design work began in August 1938 and model testing in wind tunnel and water tank led to the selection of an extremely clean, high-wing cantilever monoplane design. To meet the stringent range requirement the Kawanishi engineering team decided to use eight comparatively small unprotected wing fuel tanks and to install six large tanks in the hull. The hull tanks were fitted with a carbon dioxide fire extinguisher system and were partially self-sealing. Furthermore these tanks were arranged in such a way that if punctured the fuel would drain into bilges whence it could be pumped back into undamaged tanks. Total fuel capacity was 17,040 litres (3,749 Imp gal) and fuel weight represented some 29 per cent of the aircraft's maximum

Kawanishi Navy Experimental 13-Shi Flying-Boat, prototype of the H8K series. (*Courtesy Heinz J. Nowarra.*)

take-off weight. Armour protection was also extensively provided, and provision for a defensive armament comprising one flexible 20 mm Type 99 Model 1 cannon in each of the nose, dorsal and tail turrets and in port and starboard beam blisters and one flexible 7·7 mm Type 92 machine-gun in each of two side hatches and one ventral position was incorporated.

Powered by four 1,530 hp Mitsubishi MK4A Kasei 11 fourteen-cylinder air-cooled radials driving four-blade propellers, the prototype H8K1 was completed on 31 December, 1940, and made its maiden flight in January 1941. The aircraft's behaviour during high-speed taxi-ing and take-off proved highly disappointing as, soon after the nose was lifted, it was extremely unstable and water was thrown into the propellers and over the wings. To remedy this the H8K1 prototype was returned to the factory where the hull depth was increased by 50 cm (1 ft $7\frac{11}{16}$ in), the planing bottom was modified and longitudinal steps were added on the forward portion of the hull between the keel and the main chine. As soon as these modifications had been incorporated the H8K1 was returned to its flight test crew. Water handling characteristics, although still inferior to those of the H6K series, were markedly improved and flying characteristics and flight performance were substantially better than those of the earlier

A captured Kawanishi H8K2 which had been operated by the 801st Kokutai. (*Eckert.*)

flying-boat. Late in 1941, on the basis of the results of the Service trials programme, the Navy authorized the production of the aircraft as the Navy Type 2 Flying-Boat Model 11 (H8K1).

Already two pre-production aircraft, with hulls similar to that of the modified prototype, had been flown and the second of these featured the modified vertical tail surfaces adopted for all production H8K1s. Powered by four 1,530 hp Mitsubishi MK4A Kasei 11 or MK4B Kasei 12 radials, the H6K1 Model 11 had defensive armament reduced to two 20 mm Type 99 Model 1 cannon (dorsal and tail turrets) and four flexible 7·7 mm Type 92 machine-guns. Offensive load, carried under the wings, consisted of either two 800 kg (1,764 lb) torpedoes, eight 250 kg (551 lb) bombs or

This view of the Kawanishi H8K2 shows its hull shape to advantage. The apparent growths along the top of the rear hull are trees on the far shore. (*US Navy Department*.)

sixteen 60 kg (132 lb) bombs or depth-charges. The first combat sortie of the H8K1 took place on the night of 4–5 March, 1942, when two aircraft of the Yokohama Kokutai (Yokohama Naval Air Corps), operating from Wotje Atoll in the Marshall Islands and refuelled by a submarine at French Frigate Shoals, made a bombing attack on Oahu Island. Due to heavy cloud cover in the Honolulu area the results were disappointing but a similar mission, timed to coincide with the Japanese attack against Midway, was even less successful for it had to be cancelled when the refuelling submarine found French Frigate Shoals occupied by US Forces. However, in its intended maritime reconnaissance role the H8K1 proved extremely successful as its heavy defensive armament, effective armour and fuel tank protection, and its high speed enabled the aircraft to defend itself adequately.

Remarkable as it was, the performance of the H8K1 Model 11 was surpassed by that of the H8K2 Model 12 powered by four 1,850 hp Mitsubishi MK4Q Kasei 22s fitted with water injection. The installation of four Kasei 22s in modified nacelles was first tested on the H8K1 prototype and improved performance to such an extent that Kawanishi switched to the Kasei 22 powered H8K2 Model 12 after producing only sixteen Kasei

A Kawanishi H8K2 under test in the United States. (*US Navy Department.*)

11/12 powered H8K1s. Once again the vertical tail surfaces were modified but otherwise the aircraft was externally identical to the H8K1. The increased power enabled Kawanishi to increase maximum take-off weight from 31,000 kg (68,343 lb) to 32,500 kg (71,650 lb) and maximum fuel capacity to 18,880 litres (4,154 Imp gal). At the same time defensive armament was revised and the H8K2 carried armament similar to that of the first prototype but for the addition of a flexible 7·7 Type machine-gun firing through openings on either side of the pilot's cockpit. Being the most heavily defended and fastest flying-boat to serve with any of the combatants, the H8K2, dubbed EMILY, was respected by Allied fighter pilots who considered it to be the most difficult Nipponese aircraft to shoot down. Making its début in 1943, the Navy Type 2 Flying-Boat Model 12 supplanted the Navy Type 97 Flying-Boat as the standard Japanese long-range maritime reconnaissance aircraft. Most late production aircraft were fitted with ASV radar and the type served with first-line units until the final Japanese surrender.

After serving as an engine test bed for the Kasei 22 powered H8K2, the original H8K1 experimental aircraft was again modified as the prototype for a transport version of the H8K series. The deep hull made possible the installation of two decks, the lower deck extending from the nose to the rear hull step and the upper extending from the wing centre-section to the

A Kawanishi H8K2 Navy Type 2 Flying-Boat Model 12. (*US Navy Department.*)

rear of the hull. Accommodation was provided for either twenty-nine passengers or sixty-four troops, and armament was reduced to one flexible 13 mm Type 2 machine-gun in the nose turret and one 20 mm Type 99 Model 1 cannon in the tail turret. The installation of the lower deck cabin necessitated the removal of most of the hull tanks, and total fuel capacity was reduced to 13,414 litres (2,951 Imp gal). Following successful completion of its flight trials the aircraft was delivered to the Headquarters of Naval Activity at Yokosuka where it served as a staff transport, and production of the similar H8K2-L Model 32 was authorized as the Navy Type 2 Transport Flying-Boat Seiku (Clear Sky). A total of thirty-six H8K2-Ls were built between 1943 and 1945 and exclusively operated by Naval transport units.

When design of the H8K had begun, it was originally intended to use retractable stabilizing floats but these were abandoned in favour of fixed floats to save weight. However, in 1943 the idea was revived in an attempt to increase further the top speed of the H8K. Two Kasei 22 powered prototypes fitted with retractable stabilizing floats were completed in 1944

A Kawanishi H8K2 photographed immediately before being shot down by a US aircraft.

and these aircraft, designated H8K3 Model 22, underwent extensive flight testing. The H8K3 carried the same total defensive armament as the H8K2, but the side blisters were replaced by sliding hatches—this modification being also adopted as standard on late production H8K2s—and the non-retractable dorsal turret was replaced by a fully retractable unit. In 1945, these two aircraft were re-engined with four 1,825 hp Mitsubishi MK4T-B Kasei 25b radials and were redesignated H8K4 Model 23. Neither the H8K4 Model 23 nor its contemplated transport version, the H8K4-L Model 33, were placed in production since by then the Navy had a far more pressing need for interceptor fighters, and Kawanishi were instructed to concentrate on the production of the N1K2-J Shiden Kai.

KAWANISHI H8K3

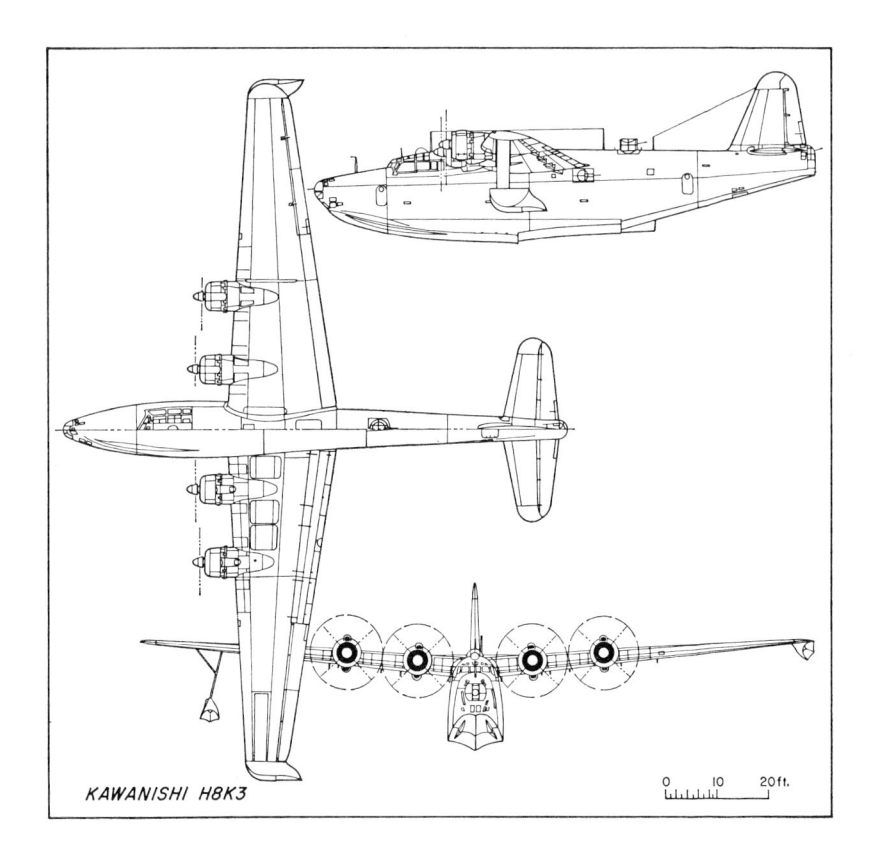

Even though far fewer H8Ks were built than contemporary British Short Sunderlands or American Consolidated PBY Catalinas, the Japanese flying-boat emerged from the conflict as the most outstanding water-based combat aircraft of the second World War.

UNITS ALLOCATED

14th, 801st, 851st, 1001st, 1021st, Takuma, Toko, Yokohama and Yokosuka Chinjufu Kokutais.

TECHNICAL DATA

Description: Four-engined long-range maritime reconnaissance flying-boat (H8K1 to H8K4) or transport flying-boat (H8K2-L). All-metal construction.

Accommodation: Crew of ten (H8K1 to H8K4).

Crew of nine and 29 passengers or 64 troops (H8K2-L).

Powerplant: Four Mitsubishi MK4A Kasei 11 fourteen-cylinder air-cooled radials, rated at 1,530 hp for take-off, 1,410 hp at 2,000 m (6,560 ft) and 1,340 hp at 4,000 m (13,125 ft), driving four-blade metal propellers (13-Shi prototype and early production H8K1s).

Four Mitsubishi MK4B Kasei 12 fourteen-cylinder air-cooled radials, rated at 1,530 hp for take-off, 1,480 hp at 2,000 m (6,560 ft) and 1,380 hp at 4,000 m (13,125 ft), driving four-blade metal propellers (late production H8K1s).

Four Mitsubishi MK4Q Kasei 22 fourteen-cylinder air-cooled radials, rated at 1,850 hp for take-off, 1,680 hp at 2,100 m (6,890 ft) and 1,540 hp at 5,500 m (18,045 ft), driving four-blade metal propellers (H8K2, H8K2-L and H8K3).

Four Mitsubishi MK4T-B Kasei 25b fourteen-cylinder air-cooled radials, rated at 1,825 hp for take-off, driving four-blade metal propellers (H8K4).

Armament: 20 mm Type 99 Model 1 cannon in bow, dorsal and tail turrets and two beam blisters, and 7·7 mm Type 92 machine-guns in ventral, port and starboard hatches (13-Shi prototype).

20 mm Type 99 Model 1 cannon in dorsal and tail turrets, and 7·7 mm Type 92 machine-guns in two beam blisters, ventral and cockpit hatches and bow turret (production H8K1s).

20 mm Type 99 Model 1 cannon in bow, dorsal and tail turrets and two beam hatches, and 7·7 mm Type 92 machine-guns in ventral, port and starboard fuselage sides and cockpit hatches (H8K2, H8K3 and H8K4).

External load: two 800 kg (1,764 lb) torpedoes, or eight 250 kg (551 lb) bombs, or sixteen 60 kg (132 lb) bombs or depth-charges (H8K1 to H8K4).

	H8K1	H8K2	H8K3	H8K2-L
Dimensions:				
Span	38 m	38 m	38 m	38 m
	(124 ft 8 $\frac{1}{16}$ in)	(124 ft 8 $\frac{1}{16}$ in)	(124 ft 8 $\frac{1}{16}$ in)	(124 ft 8 $\frac{1}{16}$ in)
Length	28·13 m	28·13 m	28·13 m	28·13 m
	(92 ft 3 $\frac{19}{16}$ in)	(92 ft 3 $\frac{19}{16}$ in)	(92 ft 3 $\frac{19}{16}$ in)	(92 ft 3 $\frac{19}{16}$ in)
Height	9·15 m	9·15 m	9·15 m	9·15 m
	(30 ft 0¼ in)	(30 ft 0¼ in)	(30 ft 0¼ in)	(30 ft 0¼ in)
Wing area	160 sq m	160 sq m	160 sq m	160 sq m
	(1,722·219 sq ft)	(1,722·219 sq ft)	(1,722·219 sq ft)	(1,722·219 sq ft)
Weights:				
Empty	15,502 kg	18,380 kg	18,570 kg	16,900 kg
	(34,176 lb)	(40,521 lb)	(40,940 lb)	(37,258 lb)
Loaded	24,500 kg	24,500 kg	24,500 kg	26,683 kg
	(54,013 lb)	(54,013 lb)	(54,013 lb)	(58,826 lb)
Maximum	31,000 kg	32,500 kg	32,500 kg	30,000 kg
	(68,343 lb)	(71,650 lb)	(71,650 lb)	(66,139 lb)
Wing loading	153·1 kg/sq m	153·1 kg/sq m	153·1 kg/sq m	166·8 kg/sq m
	(31·4 lb/sq ft)	(31·4 lb/sq ft)	(31·4 lb/sq ft)	(34·2 lb/sq ft)
Power loading	4 kg/hp	3·3 kg/hp	3·3 kg/hp	3·6 kg/hp
	(8·8 lb/hp)	(7·3 lb/hp)	(7·3 lb/hp)	(7·9 lb/hp)
Performance:				
Maximum speed	234 kt at 5,000 m	252 kt at 5,000 m	—	227 kt at 4,000 m
	(269 mph at 16,405 ft)	(290 mph at 16,405 ft)	—	(261 mph at 13,125 ft)
Cruising speed	160 kt at 4,000 m	160 kt at 4,000 m	—	160 kt at 4,000 m
	(184 mph at 13,125 ft)	(184 mph at 13,125 ft)	—	(184 mph at 13,125 ft)
Climb to	5,000 m	5,000 m	—	4,000 m
	(16,405 ft)	(16,405 ft)	—	(13,125 ft)
in	14 min 33 sec	10 min 12 sec	—	10 min 37 sec
Service ceiling	7,630 m	8,850 m	—	—
	(25,035 ft)	(29,035 ft)	—	—
Maximum range	3,888 naut miles	3,862 naut miles	—	2,397 naut miles
	(4,475 st miles)	(4,445 st miles)	—	(2,759 st miles)

Production: A total of 167 H8Ks were built by Kawanishi Kokuki K.K. in their Naruo and Konan plants as follows:
    1 H8K1 prototype (Dec 1940)
    2 H8K1 pre-production aircraft (1941)
   14 H8K1 production aircraft (1941–42)
 112 H8K2 production aircraft (1943–45)
    2 H8K3 prototypes (1944)
  (2) H8K4 prototypes modified from H8K3 airframes (1945)
  36 H8K2-L production aircraft (1943–45)

The Kawanishi E15K1 Navy High-speed Reconnaissance Seaplane Shiun (Violet Cloud) Model 11.

Kawanishi E15K Shiun (Violet Cloud)

When conceived the Kawanishi E15K1 was one of the most advanced reconnaissance seaplanes of its time and its design represented a significant advance in the state of the art. However, lack of reliability of the complex float system, disappointing performance and lack of armour and fuel tank protection contributed to the dismal failure of an interesting effort to produce a fast floatplane capable of holding its own against enemy fighters.

In 1939 the Japanese Navy granted to the Kawanishi Kokuki K.K. a development contract for a two-seat high-speed reconnaissance float seaplane. The 14-Shi specification covering this aircraft was remarkably free of the usual list of stringent requirements, Kawanishi being merely instructed to design a floatplane capable of out-performing enemy land-based fighters. This in itself was an extremely difficult requirement to meet and led to the adoption of an unusual float system. The cantilever pylon-mounted central float was attached to the fuselage by two pins and, in an emergency, the forward pin could be removed thus releasing the entire float and increasing maximum speed by some 50 knots (58 mph). The stabilizing floats were fitted with metal planing bottoms and rubberized-fabric tops which were inflated when the floats were extended. Under normal take-off and alighting conditions these floats were extended but, if the central float had been jettisoned, the stabilizing floats were to be kept retracted to act as flotation buoys. The powerplant installation was equally ingenious as the aircraft was powered by a 1,500 hp Mitsubishi MK4D

Kasei 14 air-cooled radial driving a pair of two-blade contra-rotating propellers, the first of their kind to be installed on a Japanese-built aircraft. The concern of the manufacturers to meet the performance requirements was also shown by the selection of a laminar-flow aerofoil conceived by Professor Ichiro Tani of the Tokyo Imperial University.

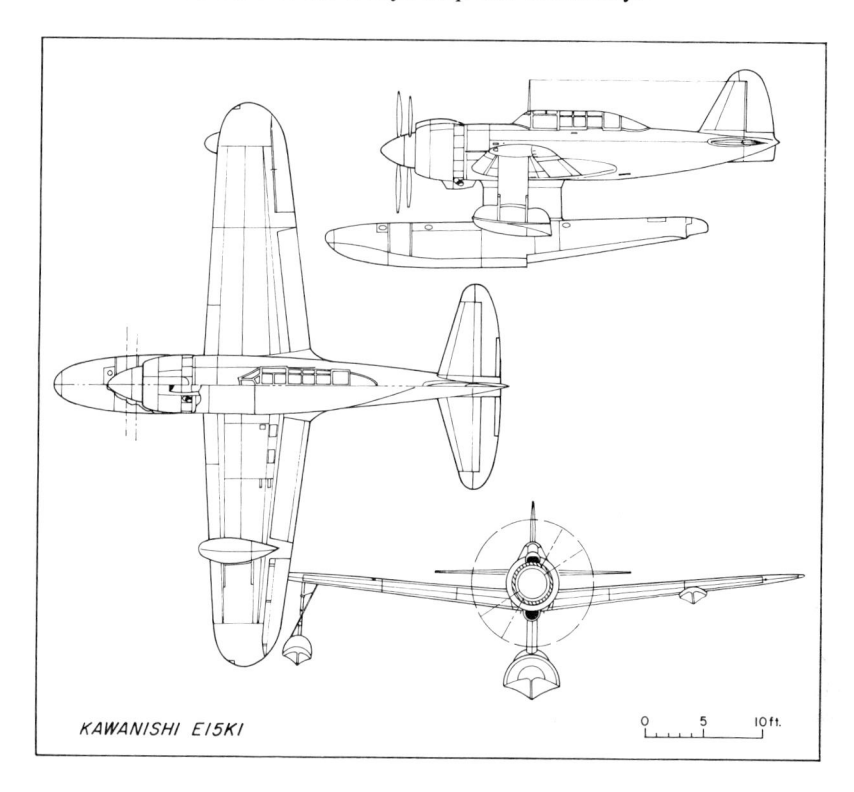

KAWANISHI E15K1

The design of the aircraft, which bore the designation K-10 under the newly established Service Aeroplane Development Programme system, began in July 1939 but engineering difficulties delayed the completion of the aircraft until late in 1941. On 5 December, 1941, the first prototype, now bearing the E15K1 designation, made its maiden flight. Flying characteristics were found satisfactory but problems were encountered with the pitch control system for the contra-rotating propellers and with the stabilizing float retraction mechanism. In October 1942 the aircraft was handed over to the Navy but was extensively damaged on alighting when a flap failure prevented the lowering of the stabilizing floats. The aircraft was repaired and a ventral fin added to improve directional stability.

Despite repeated failures of the float retraction mechanism necessitating the elimination of the inflation system, the E15K1 was placed in limited production as the Navy High-speed Reconnaissance Seaplane Shiun

(Violet Cloud) Model 11. Finally the original stabilizing floats, which were still unreliable, had to be replaced by fixed units attached to the wings by slim cantilever struts, and the added drag was partially compensated by an increase in power by the use of a 1,850 hp Mitsubishi MK4S Kasei 24 fitted with individual exhaust stacks.

Six E15K1s, to be named NORM by the Allies, were sent to Palau for combat evaluation but were quickly shot down by Allied fighters as the ventral float jettisoning system, never previously tested, failed to operate. With the float attached, the aircraft was too slow and its single 7·7 mm machine-gun and lack of armour and fuel tank protection made it an easy prey. Consequently, production was terminated in February 1944 and only fifteen Shiuns, including prototypes, were built.

UNIT ALLOCATED
Cruiser *Oyodo*.

TECHNICAL DATA

Description: Single-engined high-speed reconnaissance float seaplane. All-metal construction.

Accommodation: Crew of two in tandem enclosed cockpits.

Powerplant: One Mitsubishi MK4D Kasei 14 fourteen-cylinder air-cooled radial, rated at 1,500 hp for take-off, 1,620 hp at 2,100 m (6,890 ft) and 1,480 hp at 5,500 m (18,045 ft), driving two-blade contra-rotating propellers (prototypes and early production aircraft).

One Mitsubishi MK4S Kasei 24 fourteen-cylinder air-cooled radial, rated at 1,850 hp for take-off, 1,680 hp at 2,100 m (6,890 ft) and 1,540 hp at 5,500 m (18,045 ft), driving two-blade contra-rotating propellers (late production aircraft).

Armament: One flexible rear-firing 7·7 mm Type 92 machine-gun.
Bomb-load: two 60 kg (132 lb) bombs.

Dimensions: Span 14 m (45 ft 11 $\frac{1}{16}$ in); length 11·587 m (38 ft 0 $\frac{3}{16}$ in); height 4·95 m (16 ft 2 $\frac{7}{8}$ in); wing area 30 sq m (322·916 sq ft).

Weights: Empty 3,165 kg (6,978 lb); loaded 4,100 kg (9,039 lb); maximum 4,900 kg (10,803 lb); wing loading 136·7 kg/sq m (28 lb/sq ft); power loading 2·2 kg/hp (4·9 lb/hp).

Performance: Maximum speed, with float attached, 253 kt at 5,700 m (291 mph at 18,700 ft); cruising speed 160 kt at 2,500 m (184 mph at 8,205 ft); climb to 6,000 m (19,685 ft) in 10 min; service ceiling 9,830 m (32,250 ft); range 1,820 naut miles (2,095 st miles).

Production: A total of 15 E15K1s were built by Kawanishi Kokuki K.K. in their Naruo plant as follows:
6 prototypes and Service trials aircraft (1941–42)
9 production aircraft (1943–44)

Kawanishi N1K Kyofu (Mighty Wind)

Appearing too late to serve in its intended role, the Kawanishi N1K1 Kyofu (Mighty Wind) floatplane fighter participated only briefly in combat operations but its sound design led to its adaptation into one of the most successful land-based fighter aircraft of the war.

A Kawanishi N1K1 Kyofu (Mighty Wind) floatplane fighter. The type was used in the defence of Japan during the last year of the war. (*Richard M. Bueschel.*)

Development of a series of floatplane fighters intended to provide air support to Japanese amphibious landing forces in areas where no airfield existed was initiated in 1940 and, while Nakajima Hikoki K.K. undertook the development of an interim aircraft—the A6M2-N—Kawanishi Kokuki K.K. were instructed to initiate the design of an aircraft specially conceived for that purpose. The 15-Shi specification covering this aircraft was issued by the Japanese Navy in September 1940 and planning began immediately in the Kawanishi engineering office. Basing their efforts on the advanced technology developed for the E15K1 Shiun, a team of engineers including Toshihara Baba, Shizuo Kikuhara, Hiroyuki Inoue and Elizaburo Adachi, designed a compact floatplane with mid-mounted wings of laminar-flow section. Like the Shiun, the projected floatplane fighter, then known by the SADP designation of K-20, was to be powered by a 1,460 hp Mitsubishi

MK4D Kasei 14 driving two contra-rotating two-blade propellers to offset the anticipated propeller torque on take-off. The central float was to be attached to the fuselage by a V-strut forward and an I-strut at the rear, but the proposed use of retractable stabilizing floats with metal planing bottoms and inflatable rubberized-fabric tops could be traced to the Shiun's design philosophy. Difficulties encountered with this type of float during the early part of the E15K1 flight trial programme led to their replacement by fixed cantilever floats prior to the aircraft's first flight.

Following its completion at Kawanishi's Naruo plant the first N1K1 made its successful maiden flight on 6 May, 1942. However, teething

A Kawanishi N1K1 Kyofu with three-blade propeller driven by an extension shaft.

troubles with the contra-rotating propeller gear box—similar to those experienced in the E15K1 programme—led to the decision to replace the Kasei 14 by a MK4C Kasei 13 driving a conventional three-blade propeller via an extension shaft. The Kasei 13 powered second prototype was delivered soon after but the gain in powerplant reliability was partially offset by a powerful torque on take-off requiring extreme skill on the part of the pilot. Despite this shortcoming, Service trials aircraft were delivered to the Navy starting in August 1942. Once in the air the N1K1 was an extremely pleasant aircraft to handle and the use of combat flaps gave it remarkable manoeuvrability. Like the A6M2 Reisen which by then had achieved air superiority over the Pacific, the N1K1 was armed with two wing-mounted 20 mm cannon and two fuselage-mounted 7·7 mm machine-guns and its performance was almost as spectacular as that of the famous Reisen.

Satisfied with the results of the flight trial programme the Navy ordered the aircraft into quantity production as the Navy Fighter Seaplane Kyofu Model 11, and deliveries of production aircraft began in the spring of 1943 following the completion of eight prototypes and Service trials aircraft. But production was slow in gaining tempo and by December 1943, when the delivery rate had reached fifteen aircraft per month, the decision was taken to cease manufacture of the Kyofu and the last N1K1 was delivered in March 1944. This decision did not indicate any misgiving on the aircraft's capability but merely reflected the fact that war had taken an unfavourable turn for Japan which now no longer needed a fighter designed to support offensive operations.

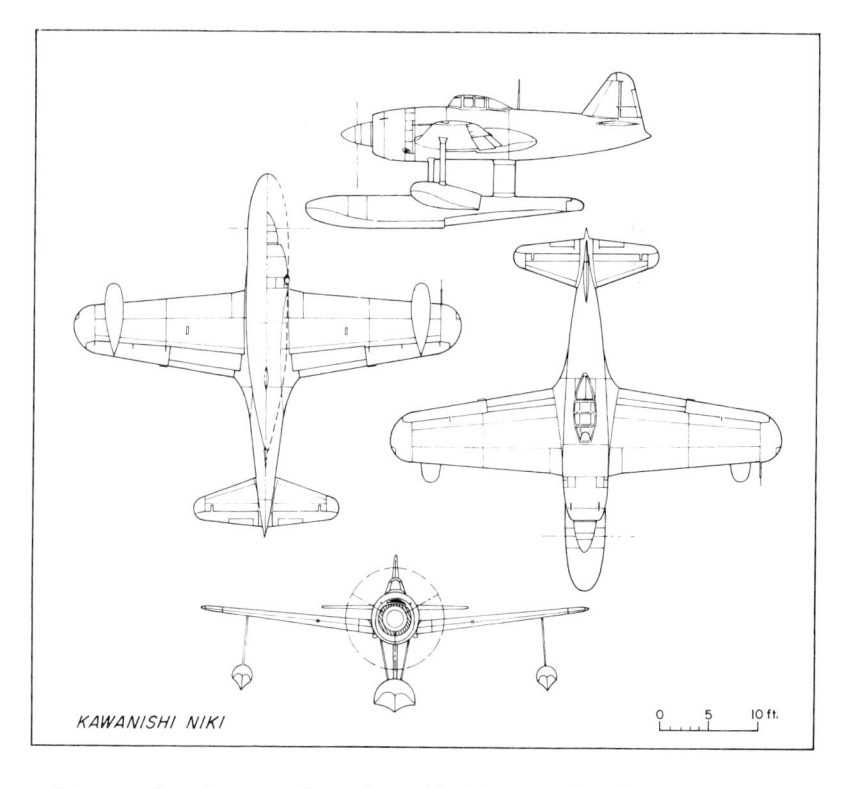

KAWANISHI N1K1

The war situation was also reflected in the operational use of the aircraft in a defensive role and N1K1s (code name REX) were assigned as interceptors at Balikpapan, Borneo. Late in the war, the Kyofu was assigned to similar duties with the Otsu Kokutai operating from Lake Biwa as an air defence unit.

The curtailment of the Kyofu production in favour of the Shiden, its land-based development, prevented the realization of an advanced floatplane version, the N1K2, which was to have been powered by a 1,900 hp Mitsubishi MK4R Kasei 23.

UNIT ALLOCATED

Otsu Kokutai.

TECHNICAL DATA

Description: Single-engined float seaplane fighter. All-metal construction.
Accommodation: Pilot in enclosed cockpit.
Powerplant: One Mitsubishi MK4D Kasei 14 fourteen-cylinder air-cooled radial, rated at 1,460 hp for take-off, 1,400 hp at 2,700 m (8,860 ft) and 1,260 hp at 6,100 m (20,045 ft), driving two contra-rotating two-blade metal propellers (first prototype).

One Mitsubishi MK4C Kasei 13 fourteen-cylinder air-cooled radial, rated at 1,460 hp for take-off, 1,420 hp at 2,000 m (6,560 ft) and 1,300 hp at 6,000 m (19,685 ft), driving a three-blade metal propeller (second and subsequent prototypes and early production aircraft).

One Mitsubishi MK4E Kasei 15 fourteen-cylinder air-cooled radial, rated at 1,530 hp for take-off, 1,400 hp at 2,600 m (8,530 ft) and 1,280 hp at 6,000 m (19,685 ft), driving a three-blade metal propeller (late production aircraft).
Armament: Two fuselage-mounted 7·7 mm Type 97 machine-guns and two wing-mounted 20 mm Type 99 Model 1 cannon.
External stores: two 30 kg (66 lb) bombs.
Dimensions: Span 12 m (39 ft 4$\frac{7}{16}$ in); length 10·589 m (34 ft 8$\frac{7}{8}$ in); height 4·75 m (15 ft 7 in); wing area 23·5 sq m (252·951 sq ft).
Weights: Empty 2,752 kg (6,067 lb); loaded 3,500 kg (7,716 lb); maximum 3,712 kg (8,184 lb); wing loading 148·9 kg/sq m (30·5 lb/sq ft); power loading 2·3 kg/hp (5 lb/hp).
Performance: Maximum speed 264 kt at 5,700 m (304 mph at 18,700 ft); cruising speed 200 kt at 2,000 m (230 mph at 6,560 ft); climb to 5,000 m (16,405 ft) in 5 min 32 sec; service ceiling 10,560 m (34,645 ft); range—normal 570 naut miles (656 st miles), maximum 900 naut miles (1,036 st miles).
Production: A total of 97 N1K1s were built by Kawanishi Kokuki K.K. in their Naruo plant as follows:
8 prototypes and Service trials aircraft (May 1942–July 1943)
89 production aircraft (July 1943–Mar 1944)

Kawanishi N1K1-J Shiden (Violet Lightning) and N1K2-J Shiden Kai

In December 1941, while detailed design work on the N1K1 floatplane was still in progress, the Kawanishi engineering team put to their management a proposal to develop a land-based version of their floatplane fighter. The estimated performance of the land-based fighter was sufficiently attractive to justify the development of the aircraft and Kawanishi decided to go ahead as a private venture. Initially, with the exception of the replacement of the ventral float and outrigger floats by a fully retractable land undercarriage, few modifications were planned. However, it was soon decided to exchange the fourteen-cylinder Kasei engine powering the N1K1 Kyofu for the new eighteen-cylinder Nakajima Homare radial which was expected to deliver 2,000 hp and thus would boost the performance of the aircraft. To take full advantage of the power available a four-blade propeller with a diameter of 3·3 m (10 ft 9$\frac{29}{32}$ in) was selected. The large diameter of the propeller, combined with the location of the wings at mid-fuselage, necessitated the adoption of lengthy main undercarriage legs

A Kawanishi N1K1-J Shiden (Violet Lightning) of the 341st Kokutai, in the Philippines. (*US Navy Department*.)

which contracted as they retracted into the wing wells. Modifications were also made to the combat flap system, and, whereas flap extension was manually controlled on the Kyofu, the flaps were operated automatically on the land-based fighter. Despite the problems encountered with the design of the landing gear the construction of the prototype progressed rapidly at the Naruo plant of Kawanishi and the prototype was completed in December 1942.

On 27 December, 1942, a mere seven months and three weeks after the first flight of the N1K1, the prototype of the land-based fighter made its maiden flight at Itami Airport. Designated Model X-1 Experimental Land-based Fighter by its manufacturers, the aircraft was powered by a 1,820 hp Nakajima Homare 11 radial and was armed with two fuselage-mounted 7·7 mm Type 97 machine-guns and two 20 mm Type 99 Model 2 cannon suspended under the wings in gondolas. From the start the flight trials programme was marred by engine and undercarriage teething troubles and the early Homare engine failed to develop its rated power. The company

A Kawanishi Model X-1 Experimental Land-based Fighter. (*NA&SM*.)

test pilot also complained of poor visibility during taxi-ing, resulting from the exceptionally long undercarriage, and of excessive propeller torque during take-off. However, in flight the aircraft possessed pleasant handling characteristics and was almost as manoeuvrable as the Mitsubishi Reisen. By July 1943 four prototypes had been built and one of these was handed over to the Navy. Naval personnel, prejudiced by the fact that the aircraft had been developed as a private venture, were initially quite critical of the aircraft and Service engineers insisted that the design of the aircraft left much to be desired. Performance was also disappointing and the aircraft achieved a top speed of only 310 kt (357 mph) whereas its calculated maximum speed had been estimated at 350 kt (403 mph). This speed, however, exceeded that of the A6M5, and the Kawanishi fighter was more manoeuvrable and had a longer range than the slightly faster Mitsubishi J2M2. Consequently, the Navy, which by then had a pressing need for a fighter aircraft capable of meeting the US Navy's Hellcats and Corsairs on equal terms, decided to instruct Kawanishi to suspend the development of their J3K1 and J6K1 land-based fighters, which were designed respectively to Navy Experimental 17-Shi and 18-Shi Interceptor Fighter specifications, and, with the help of Service engineers and technicians, to concentrate on improving their land-based version of the N1K1. Concurrently with this decision the aircraft became officially known as the N1K1-J Shiden (Violet Lightning) Interceptor Fighter.

Additional prototypes and Service trials aircraft, built during 1943 at Kawanishi's Naruo Works, were fitted with the 1,990 hp Nakajima NK9H Homare 21 engine enclosed in a modified cowling featuring an additional lower lip scoop, individual exhaust stacks and an external oil cooler mounted on the port side of the cowling behind and below the cooling gills. These aircraft were also armed with two additional 20 mm Type 99 Model

A Kawanishi N1K1-J Shiden with underwing cannon gondola.

Shiden Model 11A with 400-litre drop tank and four 20 mm wing cannon.

2 cannon mounted in the wings just outboard of the external cannon gondolas. By the end of 1943, seventy N1K1-J aircraft had been built at the Naruo Works, a first aircraft of the type had been delivered by the Himeji Works and quantity production had been authorized as the Navy Interceptor Fighter Shiden Model 11.

Pilot training and familiarization was conducted in Japan but operations were plagued by undercarriage malfunctions and engine teething troubles. However, as American landings in the Philippines were anticipated, the 201st Kokutai took their Shidens to Cebu where several were destroyed on the ground during pre-landing fighter sweeps by US Navy aircraft. Further aircraft losses resulted from persistent engine troubles and undercarriage weakness, and aircraft availability was also reduced by insufficient maintenance crews and by logistic problems. In combat, however, the Shiden was a superlative aircraft and experienced pilots had little difficulty in engaging American aircraft, and, under the code name GEORGE, it was considered by Allied personnel to be one of the best Japanese aircraft.

Development of the Shiden was pursued actively in Japan and four major versions, all powered by the Homare 21 engine, were built. The N1K1-J Shiden Model 11, the original variant armed with two fuselage-mounted 7·7 mm Type 97 machine-guns, two wing-mounted 20 mm Type 99 Model 2 cannon and two 20 mm Type 99 Model 2 cannon in underwing gondolas, was built in larger numbers than any other models. The N1K1-Ja Model 11A carried its four 20 mm cannon inside the wings and had no fuselage-mounted machine-guns. The N1K1-Jb Model 11B was armed with four improved 20 mm cannon inside the wings, was fitted with two underwing racks for bombs of up to 250 kg (551 lb) and featured square-tipped horizontal tail surfaces. Finally a specialized fighter-bomber version with four underwing bomb-racks but otherwise identical to the N1K1-Jb was built as the N1K1-Jc Shiden Model 11C. Experimental versions included a rocket-boosted N1K1-J Kai interceptor which was fitted with a solid-propellant rocket beneath the rear fuselage. As the war drew to its end, a

KAWANISHI N1K1-J

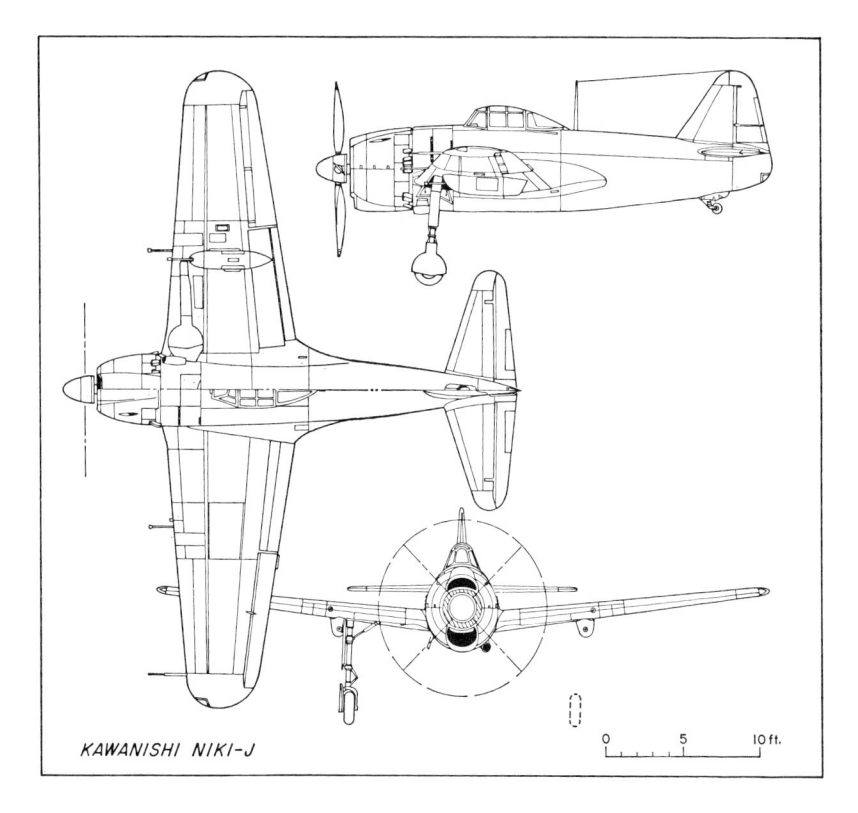

number of early Shidens were modified to serve in the defence of the homeland as dive-bombers against the anticipated Allied invasion fleet. For this mission the aircraft were fitted with a ventral pannier housing a 250 kg (551 lb) bomb and six air-to-ground unguided rocket-powered bombs, but this version never attained operational status.

In 1943, while the N1K1-J was being evaluated by the Japanese Navy, preliminary design work on an advanced version of the aircraft had already begun at Kawanishi and the N1K1-J was placed in production only as a stop-gap measure pending availability of the new version designated N1K2-J. The prime reason for designing the N1K2-J was to eliminate the need for the long and complex undercarriage of the earlier version, and consideration was also given to simplifying construction and maintenance. To achieve this goal, the wings were moved to the lower fuselage, conventional main gear legs of reduced length were adopted and the fuselage and tail surfaces were entirely redesigned. The result was a virtually new aircraft retaining only the wings and armament of the N1K1-Jb. In prototype form the aircraft featured a cleaner cowling for the Homare 21 engine but, to achieve production standardization, this was replaced on production aircraft by a cowling similar to that fitted to the N1K1-J.

Built at the Naruo Works of Kawanishi, the prototype of the N1K2-J was flown for the first time on 31 December, 1943, and successfully completed its manufacturer's trials within fifteen weeks before being handed over to the Navy in April 1944. Despite persistent difficulties with the unreliable Homare 21 engine, the N1K2-J had all the qualities of a successful fighter aircraft and the Navy demonstrated their confidence by authorizing quantity production before completion of Service trials. By June 1944 seven additional prototypes had been built, and production aircraft, designated Navy Interceptor Fighter Shiden Kai (Violet Lightning Modified) Model 21, began rolling off the assembly lines at Naruo while a second variant, the N1K2-Ja Model 21A fighter-bomber fitted with wing racks for four 250 kg (551 lb) bombs, was being readied. Following favourable reports from Service test pilots the N1K2-J was adopted by the Navy as their standard land-based fighter and fighter-bomber and the aircraft was also placed in production at Kawanishi's Himeji Works, at the Dai-Nana Kokuki Seisakusho (7th Airframe Works) of Mitsubishi, at the Shinonoi plant of Showa, at the Eitoku plant of Aichi and in the Naval Air Arsenals at Hiro, Koza and Omura. Unfortunately for the Japanese, production fell considerably behind schedule as bombing by B-29 Superfortresses led to shortage of engines and equipment and, with the exception of Kawanishi's Naruo and Himeji plants, the companies involved in the Shiden Kai production programme delivered only a token number of aircraft. Production of a two-seat version, the N1K2-K Shiden Kai Rensen (Violet Lightning Modified Fighter Trainer), was also planned, but only a limited number of aircraft were produced by fitting a second seat behind the pilot's seat of some existing N1K2-J airframes.

In operation the N1K2-J revealed itself as a truly outstanding fighter capable of meeting on equal terms the best Allied fighter aircraft. Its qualities were demonstrated spectacularly by such pilots as Warrant Officer Kinsuke Muto of the 343rd Kokutai who, in February 1945, engaged single-handed twelve US Navy Hellcats, destroying four American aircraft and forcing the others to break off combat. Against the high-flying B-29s the Shiden Kai was less successful as its climbing speed was insufficient and the power of its Homare 21 fell rapidly at high altitudes.

One of the major faults of the Shiden Kai Model 21 lay in its centre of gravity being too far back and to overcome this shortcoming Kawanishi produced the N1K3-J Shiden Kai 1 Model 31 on which the Homare 21 engine was moved forward six inches, this modification providing space for two fuselage-mounted 13·2 mm Type 3 machine-guns. Two N1K3-J prototypes were built at Himeji but neither this model nor its carrier-borne variant, the N1K3-A Shiden Kai 2 Model 41, were put into production. The N1K4-J Shiden Kai 3 Model 32 and the carrier-borne N1K4-A Shiden Kai 4 Model 42 were powered by the improved 2,000 hp NK9H-S Homare 23 radial fitted with low-pressure fuel-injection system, and two prototypes of the N1K4-J and one prototype of the N1K4-A were built in the spring of 1945 at Naruo.

The N1K2-J prototype in overall orange (E18) scheme with black anti-glare panel.

A Kawanishi N1K2-J Shiden Kai of the Yutani Special Unit. (*NA&SM*.)

The Kawanishi N1K2-J Shiden Kais were the best Japanese Navy operational fighters but for Japan they were too few and too late. (*US Air Force Museum*.)

Up to this time the development of the Shiden and Shiden Kai had resulted in production of an outstanding series of all-purpose fighter aircraft but, at this stage of the war, the Japanese Navy needed an aircraft with good high-altitude performance. To meet this pressing requirement Kawanishi designed two specialized versions. The N1K5-J Shiden Kai 5 Model 25, armed with two fuselage-mounted 13·2 mm Type 3 machine-

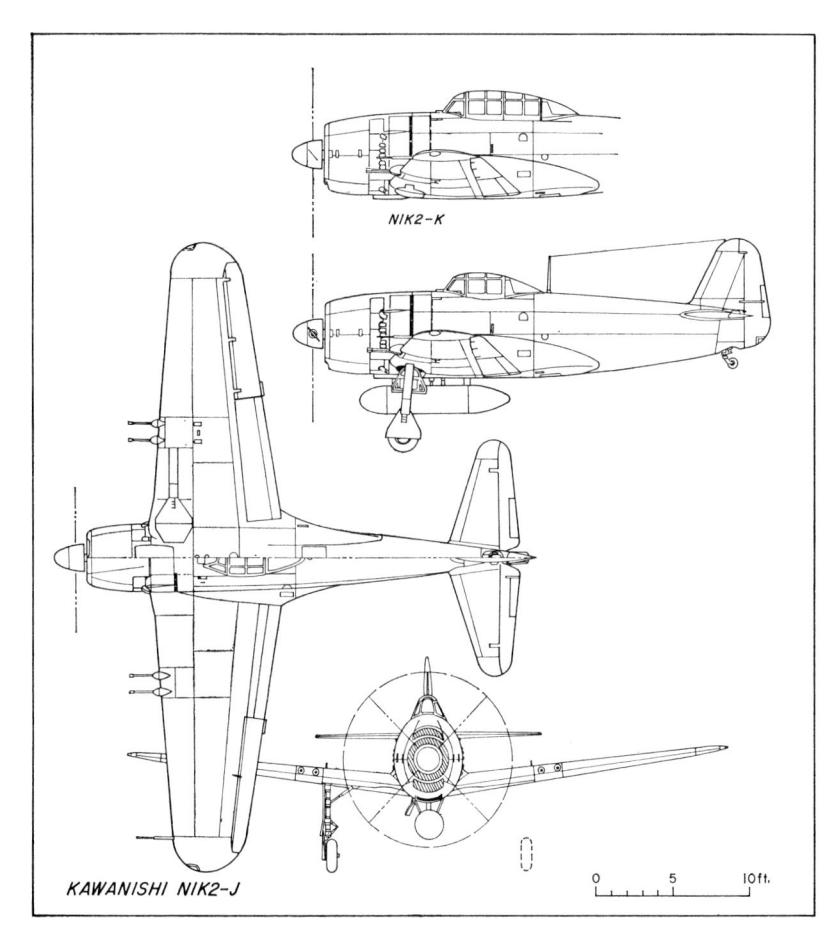

KAWANISHI N1K2-J

N1K2-K

guns and four wing-mounted 20 mm Type 99 cannon, was to be powered by a 2,200 hp Mitsubishi MK9A eighteen-cylinder air-cooled radial while another high-altitude interceptor version was planned around the Homare 44 with mechanically-driven three-speed supercharger. A prototype of the N1K5-J was destroyed prior to completion during a Superfortress attack and the final Japanese collapse brought an end to these promising projects.

A Kawanishi N1K2-J Navy Interceptor Fighter Shiden Kai Model 21.

UNITS ALLOCATED
201st, 341st, 343rd and Genzan Kokutais.

TECHNICAL DATA
Description: Single-seat land-based interceptor fighter (N1K1-J, N1K2-J, N1K3-J, N1K4-J and N1K5-J), single-seat carrier-based fighter (N1K3-A and N1K4-A) or two-seat advanced fighter trainer (N1K2-K). All-metal construction.

Accommodation: Pilot in enclosed cockpit (all fighter versions), or pilot and instructor in enclosed tandem cockpits (N1K2-K).

Powerplant: One Nakajima NK9B Homare 11 eighteen-cylinder air-cooled radial, rated at 1,820 hp for take-off, 1,600 hp at 2,000 m (6,560 ft) and 1,440 hp at 5,700 m (18,700 ft), driving a four-blade metal propeller (N1K1-J prototypes).

One Nakajima NK9H Homare 21 eighteen-cylinder air-cooled radial, rated at 1,990 hp for take-off, 1,825 hp at 1,750 m (5,740 ft) and 1,625 hp at 6,100 m (20,015 ft), driving a four-blade metal propeller (production N1K1-J, N1K2-J, N1K2-K, N1K3-J and N1K3-A).

One Nakajima NK9H-S Homare 23 eighteen-cylinder air-cooled radial, rated at 2,000 hp for take-off and 1,570 hp at 6,850 m (22,475 ft), driving a four-blade metal propeller (N1K4-J and N1K4-A).

One Mitsubishi [Ha-43] 11 (MK9A) eighteen-cylinder air-cooled radial, rated at 2,200 hp for take-off, 2,070 hp at 1,000 m (3,280 ft) and 1,800 hp at 6,000 m (19,685 ft), driving a four-blade metal propeller (N1K5-J).

One Nakajima Homare 44 eighteen-cylinder air-cooled radial, rated at 2,000 hp for take-off, 1,880 hp at 2,000 m (6,560 ft) and 1,800 hp at 8,000 m (26,245 ft), driving a four-blade metal propeller (projected version).

Armament: Two fuselage-mounted 7·7 mm Type 97 machine-guns and two 20 mm Type 99 Model 2 cannon in wing gondolas (N1K1-J prototypes).

Two fuselage-mounted 7·7 mm Type 97 machine-guns, two wing-mounted 20 mm Type 99 Model 2 cannon and two 20 mm Type 99 Model 2 cannon in wing gondolas (N1K1-J).

Four wing-mounted 20 mm Type 99 Model 2 cannon (N1K1-Ja, N1K1-Jb, N1K1-Jc, N1K2-J, N1K2-Ja and N1K2-K).

Two fuselage-mounted 13·2 mm Type 3 machine-guns and four wing-mounted 20 mm Type 99 Model 2 cannon (N1K3-J, N1K3-A, N1K4-J, N1K4-A and N1K5-J).

External stores: one 400 litre (88 Imp gal) drop tank, or two 60 kg (132 lb) bombs (N1K1-J and N1K1-Ja), or two 250 kg (551 lb) bombs (N1K1-Jb, N1K2-J, N1K3-J, N1K3-A, N1K4-J, N1K4-A and N1K5-J), or four 250 kg (551 lb) bombs (N1K1-Jc and N1K2-Ja). One 250 kg (551 lb) bomb and six air-to-ground rockets in ventral pannier (experimental installation on some N1K1-J).

	N1K1-J	N1K2-J
Dimensions:		
Span	12 m	12 m
	(39 ft 4 7/16 in)	(39 ft 4 7/16 in)
Length	8·885 m	9·345 m
	(29 ft 1 23/32 in)	(30 ft 7 29/32 in)
Height	4·06 m	3·96 m
	(13 ft 3 27/32 in)	(12 ft 11 29/32 in)
Wing area	23·5 sq m	23·5 sq m
	(252·951 sq ft)	(252·951 sq ft)
Weights:		
Empty	2,897 kg	2,657 kg
	(6,387 lb)	(5,858 lb)
Loaded	3,900 kg	4,000 kg
	(8,598 lb)	(8,818 lb)
Maximum	4,321 kg	4,860 kg
	(9,526 lb)	(10,714 lb)
Wing loading	166 kg/sq m	170·2 kg/sq m
	(34 lb/sq ft)	(34·9 lb/sq ft)
Power loading	2 kg/hp	2 kg/hp
	(4·4 lb/hp)	(4·4 lb/hp)
Performance:		
Maximum speed	315 kt at 5,900 m	321 kt at 5,600 m
	(363 mph at 19,355 ft)	(369 mph at 18,375 ft)
Cruising speed	200 kt at 2,000 m	200 kt at 3,000 m
	(230 mph at 6,560 ft)	(230 mph at 9,845 ft)
Climb to	6,000 m (19,685 ft)	6,000 m (19,685 ft)
in	7 min 50 sec	7 min 22 sec
Service ceiling	12,500 m	10,760 m
	(41,010 ft)	(35,300 ft)
Range—normal	773 naut miles	926 naut miles
	(890 st miles)	(1,066 st miles)
—maximum	1,374 naut miles	1,293 naut miles
	(1,581 st miles)	(1,488 st miles)

Production: A total of 1,435 Shidens and Shiden Kais were built as follows:

Kawanishi Kokuki K.K. at Naruo:
   9 N1K1-J prototypes (1942–43)
  530 N1K1-J production aircraft (1943–44)
   8 N1K2-J prototypes (1943–44)
  351 N1K2-J and N1K2-K production aircraft (1944–45)
   2 N1K4-J prototypes (1945)
   1 N1K4-A prototype (1945)
  ―
 901

Kawanishi Kokuki K.K. at Himeji:
  468 N1K1-J production aircraft (1943–45)
   42 N1K2-J production aircraft (1945)
    2 N1K3-J prototypes (1945)
  ―
 512

Mitsubishi Jukogyo K.K. at Tsurashima:
  9 N1K2-J production aircraft (1945)
Aichi Kokuki K.K. at Eitoku:
  1 N1K2-J production aircraft (1945)
Showa Hikoki K.K. at Shinonoi:
  1 N1K2-J production aircraft (1945)

Dai-Juichi Kaigun Kokusho at Hiro:
  1 N1K2-J production aircraft (1945)
Omura Kaigun Kokusho at Omura:
  10 N1K2-J production aircraft (1945)
Koza Kaigun Kokusho at Koza:
  — N1K2-J production not realized

A Kyushu K11W1 Shiragiku (White Chrysanthemum), with surrender markings, at Shanghai in late 1945. The aircraft in the background are Curtiss C-46s. (*Edgar Deigan.*)

Kyushu K11W Shiragiku (White Chrysanthemum)

In late 1940 work on a single-engined crew trainer began at K.K. Watanabe Tekkosho to meet the requirements set by the Japanese Navy in their 15-Shi specification calling for an aircraft intended to replace the Navy Type 90 Operations Trainer (Mitsubishi K3M). Even though the aircraft was to be used to train a complete bomber crew, Watanabe retained a single-engine configuration and, with its wing mounted at mid-fuselage, deep belly and retractable main undercarriage, the aircraft bore a strong resemblance to the North American O-47 observation monoplane. The pilot and radio-operator/gunner were seated above the wing under a transparent canopy while the instructor, navigator and bombardier were housed in a cabin under the wing.

Powered by a 515 hp Hitachi GK2B Amakaze 21 nine-cylinder air-cooled radial, the prototype K11W1 made its first flight in November 1942, and the flight trials programme was completed rapidly, as no major problems were encountered. Shortly after the reorganization of K.K. Watanabe Tekkosho into Kyushu Hikoki K.K., the company received a production contract for the K11W1 which entered service in the summer of 1943 as the Navy Operations Trainer Shiragiku (White Chrysanthemum) Model 11. For armament training the Shiragiku carried a single flexible rear-firing 7·7 mm machine-gun and two 30 kg (66 lb) bombs, but late in the war the aircraft was modified to carry a single 250 kg (551 lb) bomb for kamikaze sorties.

KYUSHU K11W1

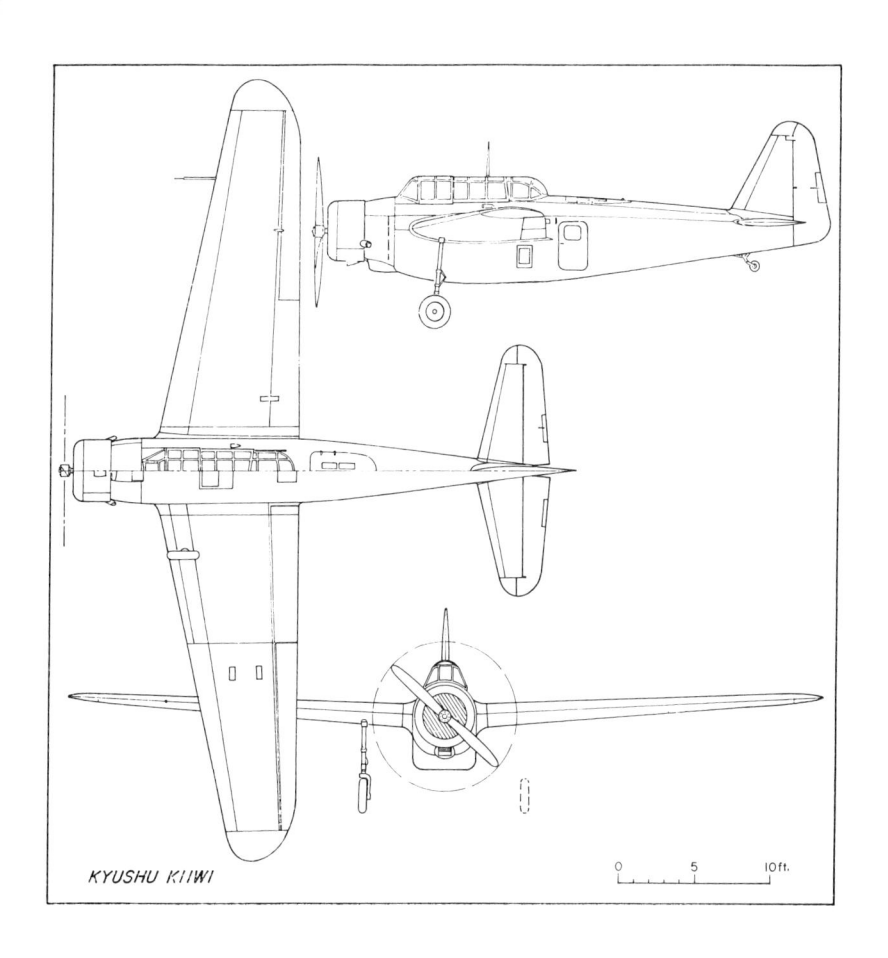

A Kyushu K11W1 Shiragiku with lower engine cowling removed.

Development of the Shiragiku led to the K11W2, an all-wood version, which was built in small numbers and saw limited service as a utility transport and anti-submarine aircraft. Experience with this version led to the design of a specialized anti-submarine patrol aircraft, the Q3W1 Nankai (South Sea). The Nankai was a two-seater retaining much of the structure of the K11W2 and fitted with redesigned square-tipped tail surfaces, but its development was suspended when in January 1945 the maiden flight of the single prototype ended in a wheels-up landing.

TECHNICAL DATA

Description: Single-engined crew trainer. All-metal construction with fabric-covered control surfaces (K11W1) or all-wood construction (K11W2).
Accommodation: Crew of five in enclosed cabin.
Powerplant: One Hitachi GK2B Amakaze 21 nine-cylinder air-cooled radial, rated at 515 hp for take-off and 480 hp at 1,500 m (4,920 ft), driving a two-blade metal propeller.
Armament: One rear-firing flexible 7·7 mm Type 92 machine-gun.
    External stores: two 30 kg (66 lb) bombs (training missions), or one 250 kg (551 lb) bomb (kamikaze missions).
Dimensions: Span 14·98 m (49 ft 1¾ in); length 10·24 m (33 ft 7$\frac{9}{32}$ in); height 3·93 m (12 ft 10$\frac{22}{32}$ in); wing area 30·5 sq m (328·298 sq ft).
Weights: Empty 1,677 kg (3,697 lb); loaded 2,640 kg (5,820 lb); maximum 2,800 kg (6,173 lb); wing loading 86·6 kg/sq m (17·7 lb/sq ft); power loading 5·1 kg/hp (11·3 lb/hp).
Performance: Maximum speed 124 kt at 1,700 m (143 mph at 5,580 ft); cruising speed 95 kt at 1,000 m (109 mph at 3,280 ft); climb to 3,000 m (9,845 ft) in 19 min 35 sec; service ceiling 5,620 m (18,440 ft); range 950 naut miles (1,093 st miles).
Production: A total of 798 K11Ws were built by K.K. Watanabe Tekkosho, later renamed Kyushu Hikoki K.K. between November 1942 and August 1945.

Kyushu Q1W Tokai (Eastern Sea)

Development of Japan's first specialized anti-submarine patrol aircraft was initiated by K.K. Watanabe Tekkosho in 1942 when the Navy issued their 17-Shi specification calling for a three-seat aircraft with long endurance and comparatively low speed. The aircraft was to be able to launch its attacks in a fairly steep dive and to operate safely over the ocean. Furthermore the Navy demanded that it be quickly completed.

Ten Kyushu Q1W1 Tokai (Eastern Sea) land-based patrol bombers at Mizutani, Hokkaido. One propeller had been removed from each aircraft to prevent their use following the Japanese surrender. (*USAF.*)

Two views of a Kyushu Q1W1 Tokai (Eastern Sea). Weapon attachment points can be seen beneath the fuselage in the three-quarter front view. (*Courtesy William Green.*)

To meet these requirements Eng Nojiri opted for a twin-engined configuration and, to provide good forward visibility and ease of communication between the members of the crew, adopted a cockpit arrangement similar to that of the Junkers-Ju 88. At the same time Nojiri decided to simplify production by designing wings of constant taper on the leading and trailing edges. Powered by two 610 hp Hitachi GK2C Amakaze 31 nine-cylinder air-cooled radials driving three-blade variable-pitch propellers, the aircraft was to be fitted with a new type of small search radar. However, delays in the production of this equipment necessitated the use of the larger Type 3 radar which was supplemented by a magnetic anomaly detection gear. The aircraft's standard armament included a single flexible rear-firing 7·7 mm machine-gun and two 250 kg (551 lb) depth-charges, but provision was made in the nose for the installation of one or two 20 mm Type 99 cannon.

Completed in September 1943, the Q1W1 prototype was found to possess pleasant handling characteristics and easily met all the Navy's requirements. Quantity production of the aircraft—designated Navy Patrol Plane Tokai (Eastern Sea) Model 11 by the JNAF and coded LORNA by the Allies—was authorized in the spring of 1944 but comparatively few Q1W1s were built before the end of the war. Tokais were operated from bases in Japan,

Enlarged picture of the left-hand Kyushu Q1W1 seen in the line-up photograph on page 332. (*USAF*.)

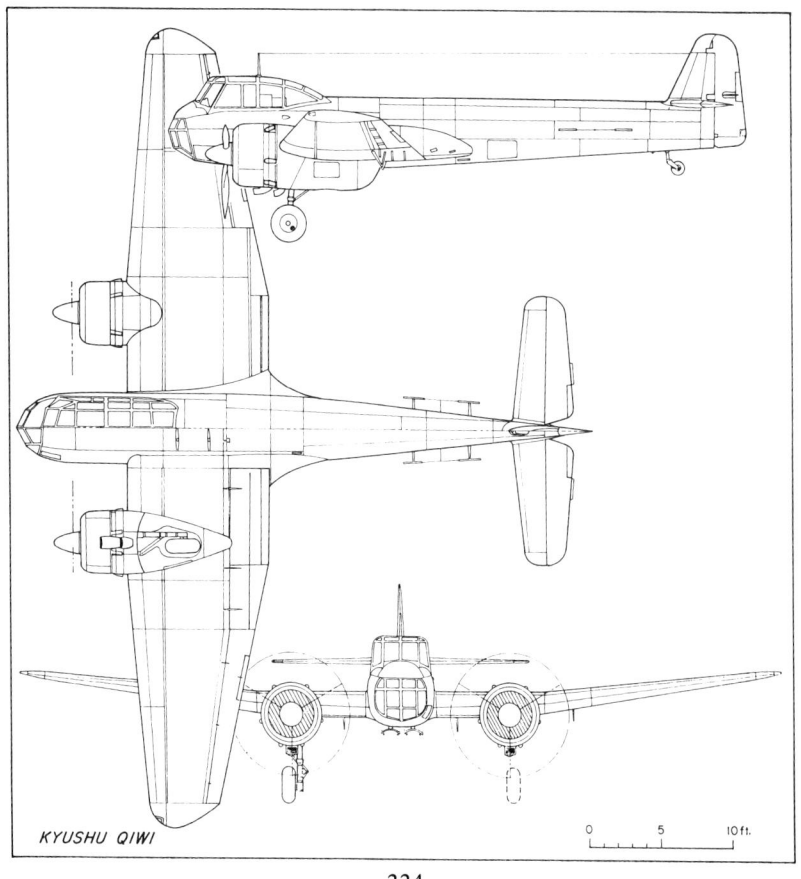

KYUSHU Q1W1

Formosa and China to protect Japanese convoys bringing badly needed raw materials and oil from the Netherlands East Indies and Malaya, but their effectiveness was badly impaired by their slow speed and wholly insufficient defensive armament which rendered them easy prey for Allied aircraft.

The Q1W2 Tokai Model 21 was a version with wooden rear fuselage built in small numbers, while the Q1W1-K Tokai Ren (Eastern Sea Trainer), of which only one prototype was completed, was an all-wood four-seat version intended for the training of operators of electronic equipment.

TECHNICAL DATA

Description: Twin-engined anti-submarine patrol aircraft (Q1W1 and Q1W2) and crew trainer (Q1W1-K). All-metal construction (Q1W1), mixed metal and wood construction (Q1W2) or all-wood construction (Q1W1-K).
Accommodation: Crew of three (Q1W1 and Q1W2) or four (Q1W1-K) in enclosed cockpits.
Powerplant: Two 610 hp Hitachi GK2C Amakaze 31 nine-cylinder air-cooled radials, rated at 610 hp for take-off and 480 hp at 1,500 m (4,920 ft), driving three-blade variable-pitch metal propellers.
Armament: One flexible rear-firing 7·7 mm Type 92 machine-gun and (optional) one or two forward-firing 20 mm Type 99 cannon.
  External stores: two 250 kg (551 lb) bombs or depth-charges.
Dimensions: Span 16 m (52 ft 5¾ in); length 12·085 m (39 ft 7⅞ in); height 4·118 m (13 ft 6⅛ in); wing area 38·21 sq m (411·287 sq ft).
Weights: Empty 3,102 kg (6,839 lb); loaded 4,800 kg (10,582 lb); maximum 5,318 kg (11,724 lb); wing loading 125·6 kg/sq m (25·7 lb/sq ft); power loading 3·9 kg/hp (8·5 lb/hp).
Performance: Maximum speed 174 kt at 1,340 m (200 mph at 4,395 ft); cruising speed 130 kt at 1,000 m (150 mph at 3,280 ft); climb to 2,000 m (6,560 ft) in 8 min 44 sec; service ceiling 4,490 m (14,730 ft); range 725 naut miles (834 st miles).
Production: A total of 153 Q1Ws were built by Kyushu Hikoki K.K. between September 1943 and August 1945.

Kyushu J7W Shinden (Magnificent Lightning)

The Kyushu J7W1 Shinden (Magnificent Lightning) was the only aircraft of canard configuration to be ordered in quantity production anywhere in the world during the second World War, and was one of the most unusual types built in Japan. The concept of the aircraft's unique configuration was due to Captain Masaoki Tsuruno of the Technical Staff of the Japanese Navy, who from the outset contemplated the possibility of replacing the rear-mounted radial engine, which drove a six-blade propeller, with a turbojet.

Following some initial work on Captain Tsuruno's concept, the Staff of the Dai-Ichi Kaigun Koku Gijitsusho (First Naval Air Technical Arsenal) designed the MXY6 glider to test the proposed aircraft's handling qualities at low speed. Three prototypes of the MXY6 were built for the Navy by Chigasaki Seizo K.K., and these all-wood gliders with moderately swept wings supporting tall tail surfaces inboard of the ailerons began flight

The Kyushu J7W1 Shinden (Magnificent Lightning) prototype before installation of the nose-mounted armament.

trials in the autumn of 1943. Later one of these aircraft was experimentally fitted with a 22 hp Semi 11 ([Ha-90] 11) four-cylinder air-cooled engine.

The feasibility of the canard configuration being proven by the unpowered and powered versions of the MXY6, the Navy decided to instruct Kyushu Hikoki K.K. to design an Otsu (B) Type Interceptor Fighter along these lines, to meet the requirement of an 18-Shi specification. In spite of their lack of previous experience with high performance aircraft, Kyushu were selected because both their design team and production facilities were relatively unburdened, but the Navy decided to assign a team from the Dai-Ichi Kaigun Koku Gijitsusho, led by Captain Tsuruno, to strengthen Kyushu's design capabilities.

Work on the J7W1 began in earnest in June 1944, and the first prototype

The Kyushu J7W1 Shinden at Wright Field, Ohio. This view shows to advantage the unorthodox layout. (*US Air Materiel Command.*)

was completed within a mere ten months. The nose, to which were attached the horizontal control surfaces with elevators, contained four forward-firing 30 mm Type 5 cannon and housed the nosewheel. The pilot sat in the centre of the fuselage forward of the aft-mounted swept wings. The main undercarriage legs and wheels retracted laterally into the wings, and small auxiliary wheels retracted into the base of the two vertical fins and rudders attached to the wings. The 2,130 hp Mitsubishi MK9D ([Ha-43] 12) eighteen-cylinder radial and its supercharger were installed in the fuse-

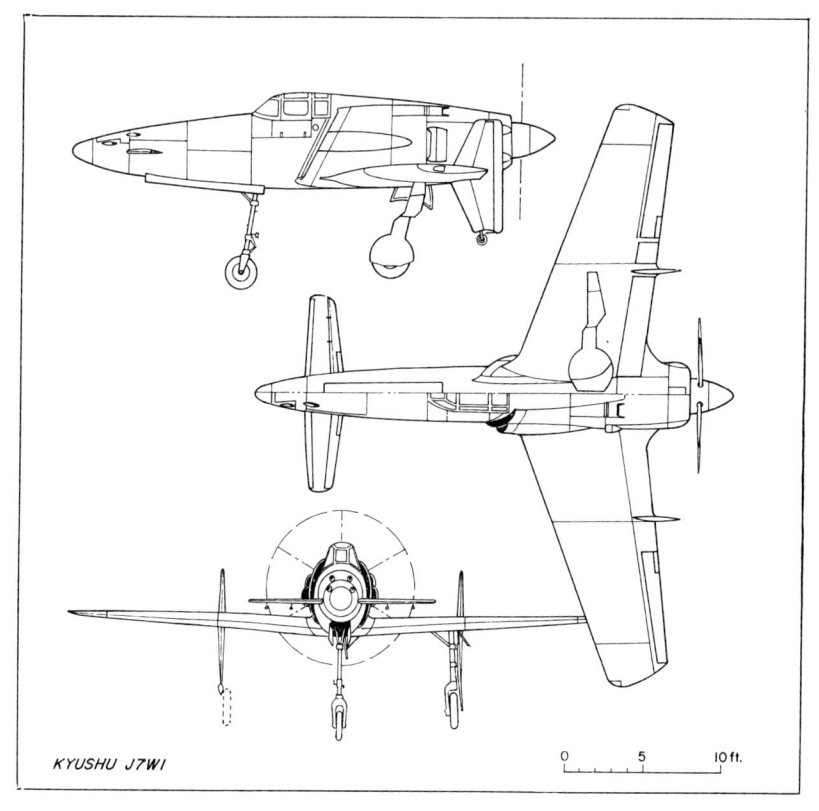

KYUSHU J7W1

lage behind the pilot's cockpit and drove a six-blade pusher propeller via an extension shaft. Engine cooling air was supplied by long, narrow, obliquely mounted intakes on each side of the fuselage.

The Navy, desperately needing a heavily armed high-performance interceptor fighter, decided prior to the aircraft's maiden flight to order it into production at Kyushu's Zasshonokuma factory and at Nakajima's Handa plant. Considering the difficult conditions under which the Japanese aircraft industry was working at this stage of the war, the anticipated monthly output of 30 Shindens at Zasshonokuma and 120 at Handa appears unduly optimistic; and the Japanese surrender settled this plan.

The Yokosuka MXY6 research glider. (*USAF.*)

Difficulties with engine cooling on the ground and the unavailability of some items of equipment delayed the first flight of the J7W1 until 3 August, 1945, when Captain Tsuruno took the aircraft for a short flight at Fukuoka Airport. Two other short flights, bringing total flight time to some 45 min, were made prior to the end of the war and revealed the need to correct a strong torque pull to starboard on take-off and marked vibrations in the propeller and its extended drive shaft.

At war's end a second prototype had been completed but not flown, this aircraft being eventually dismantled and shipped to the United States. Plans were also made for a J7W2 version in which the radial engine was to be replaced with a 900 kg (1,984 lb) thrust Ne-130 turbojet.

TECHNICAL DATA

Description: Single-engined interceptor fighter of canard configuration. All-metal construction.
Accommodation: Pilot in enclosed cockpit.
Powerplant: One Mitsubishi [Ha-43] 12 (MK9D) eighteen-cylinder air-cooled radial, rated at 2,130 hp for take-off, 2,020 hp at 1,180 m (3,870 ft) and 1,160 hp at 8,700 m (28,545 ft), driving a six-blade metal pusher propeller (J7W1).
One 900 kg (1,984 lb) thrust Ne-130 axial-flow turbojet (J7W2).
Armament: Four forward-firing nose-mounted 30 mm Type 5 cannon.
External stores: two 60 kg (132 lb) or four 30 kg (66 lb) bombs.
Dimensions: (J7W1) Span 11·114 m (36 ft 5 9/16 in); length 9·66 m (31 ft 8 5/16 in); height 3·92 m (12 ft 10 11/32 in); wing area 20·5 sq m (220·659 sq ft).
Weights: (J7W1) Empty 3,645 kg (7,639 lb); loaded 4,928 kg (10,854 lb); maximum 5,228 kg (11,526 lb); wing loading 240·4 kg/sq m (49·1 lb/sq ft); power loading 2·3 kg/hp (5·1 lb/hp).
Performance: (J7W1) Maximum speed 405 kt at 8,700 m (466 mph at 28,545 ft); cruising speed 228 kt at 4,000 m (263 mph at 13,125 ft); climb to 8,000 m (26,245 ft) in 10 min 40 sec; service ceiling 12,000 m (39,370 ft); normal range 460 naut miles (529 st miles).
Production: Two J7W1 prototypes were completed in the spring of 1945 at the Zasshonokuma plant of Kyushu Hikoki K.K. Quantity production in this plant and in the Handa plant of Nakajima Hikoki K.K. had been undertaken, but no production aircraft had been completed by the end of the war.

Mitsubishi K3M

The development of a single-engined crew trainer was begun as a private venture by Mitsubishi in 1928 when that company commissioned the British engineer Herbert Smith, formerly with Sopwith Aviation Co Ltd, to design an aircraft which, in addition to the pilot, would provide accommodation for an instructor and three or four pupils. In December 1928 Smith submitted a design for an all-wood biplane which became known by the manufacturer's designation M-13, but no prototype was built as Mitsubishi failed to interest the Japanese Navy in it.

The project was revived in 1929 when the Navy placed an order for two prototypes of a completely new design, the Ka-2, which had been designed for Mitsubishi by Eng Hattori. The new aircraft was of high-wing parasol configuration and had a metal fuselage with fabric covering. Also known as the 4MS1 by its manufacturers and as the K3M1 by the Navy, the first prototype was completed in May 1930 and made its maiden flight shortly after with pilot Nakawa at the controls. Powered by a 340 hp Mitsubishi-built Hispano-Suiza eight-cylinder vee liquid-cooled engine, the aircraft suffered from poor stability in flight. The second prototype was identical, but the third and fourth aircraft had dihedral to improve stability. However, the aircraft was still unsatisfactory as its engine suffered from excessive vibration and poor cooling and, before accepting the aircraft, the Navy requested that the liquid-cooled engine be replaced by a 340 hp Hitachi Amakaze 11 radial. With this powerplant the aircraft, now designated K3M2, entered production at Mitsubishi as the Navy Type 90 Crew Trainer Model 1. Later this version was also built by Aichi Tokei Denki K.K.

In 1933 the Japanese Army evinced considerable interest in the K3M2, and a modified version for that Service was designed by Masakishi Mizumo. Bearing the Kitai designation Ki-7, the first prototype for the

A Watanabe-built K3M3. The overturn crash pylon and underwing fuel tank can be seen.

Three derelict Mitsubishi K3M3s, with enlarged tail surfaces. (*Eckert*.)

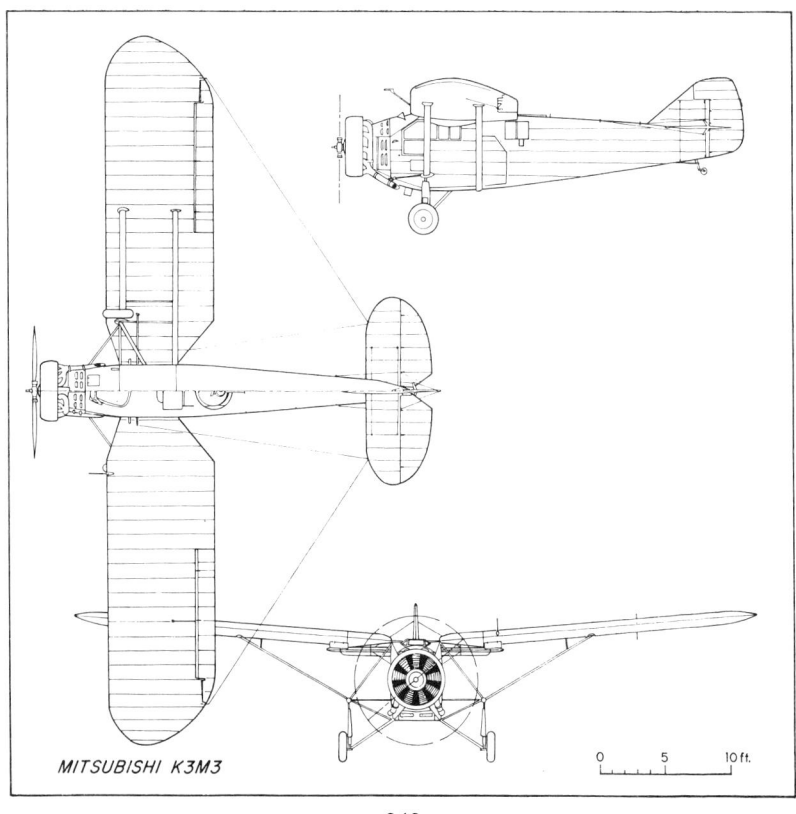

MITSUBISHI K3M3

A Mitsubishi A6M3 Navy Type 0 Carrier Fighter Model 32 during operations in the Solomons. Unit markings on the tail have been deleted by the censor.

Damaged and abandoned Mitsubishi A6M3 Model 32.

A captured Mitsubishi A6M3 with drop tank in position. (*USAF.*)

Captured Mitsubishi A6M3 Model 32 with United States markings.

cylinder radial equipped with a two-speed supercharger instead of a single-speed unit as used on the earlier Sakae 12. The installation of the new engine necessitated moving the firewall 8 inches aft, resulting in a reduction in fuselage fuel tank capacity from 98 litres (21·6 Imp gal) to 60 litres (13·2 Imp gal) and changing the shape of the engine cowling to incorporate the supercharger air intake in its upper lip. Although the aircraft performed satisfactorily, the flight trials of the A6M3 were rather disappointing as performance fell substantially below calculated data, and production was delayed until sufficient Sakae 21 engines were available. Starting with the fourth aircraft, the ammunition supply for the wing-mounted 20 mm cannon was increased from 60 rpg to 100 rpg, and soon thereafter, at the suggestion of operational units, the folding wingtips were removed, reducing the span to 11 m (36 ft $1\frac{1}{16}$ in) and wing area to 21·53 sq m (231·746 sq ft). This modification, which resulted in a slight increase in level speed at the cost of negligible reduction in overall performance and manoeuvrability, was introduced to ease production and maintenance. In this form the A6M3 was designated Navy Type 0 Carrier Fighter Model 32. Three hundred and forty-three were built by Mitsubishi, while an unspecified number of identical aircraft were built at Koizumi by Nakajima.

Following limited service in Japan the A6M3 Model 32s were deployed to the New Guinea/Solomons area in the late spring of 1942 where the Japanese were getting ready to mount an amphibious assault on northern Australia. The inconclusive Coral Sea battle and the defeat off Midway were soon followed by the American landing on Guadalcanal.

The lack of airfields close to the combat area forced the A6M3s to operate from bases located some 560 naut miles from Guadalcanal.

MITSUBISHI A6M2

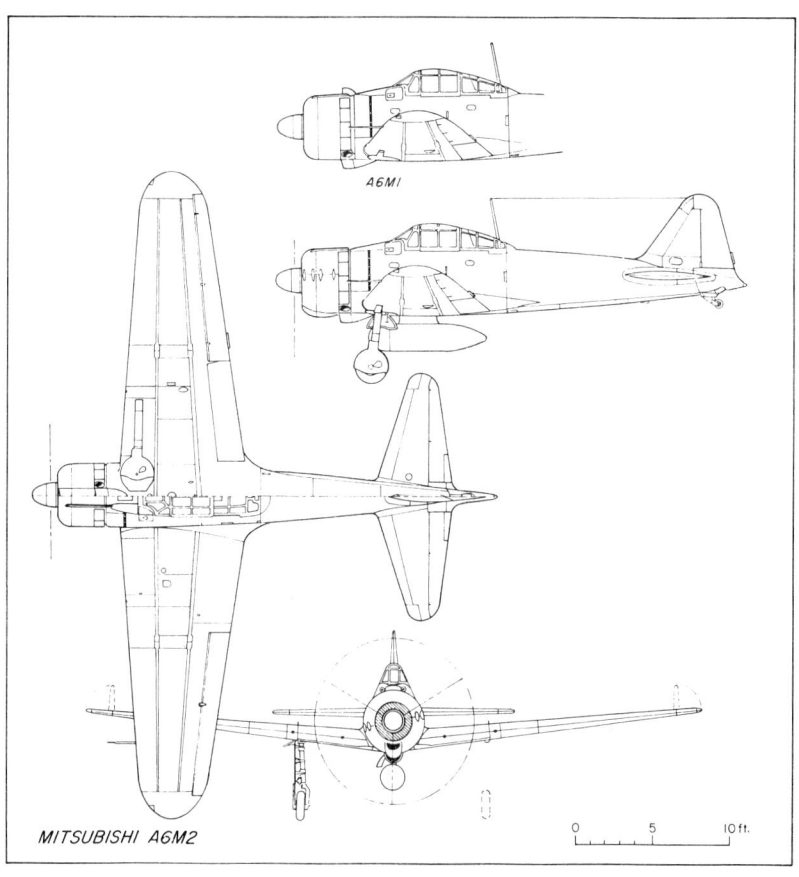

equipped land-based Kokutais led the Japanese Forces in the conquest of the Philippines and the Netherlands East Indies. Concentrating their numerically inferior fighter units, the Japanese Navy was able to inflict severe losses on all of its opponents. Then, in spite of an impressive victory-to-loss ratio, the Reisen units began to lose ground when losses of aircraft and experienced pilots could not be made good by accelerated aircraft production and pilot training just as the Allied war machine was gaining tempo. On 7 and 8 May, 1942, the Japanese Navy and the US Navy carriers met in the Coral Sea, after which in spite of heavier Allied losses the Japanese had to call off their intended invasion of Australia. Four weeks later, on 3 and 4 June, four Japanese carriers and their aircraft were lost in the Battle of Midway. The Japanese advance had been stopped, and from then on the Reisens were to operate in a defensive role in which their lack of armour and fuel tank protection was to prove extremely costly.

Six months before the war began Mitsubishi started testing a new version of the Reisen—the A6M3, powered by a 1,130 hp Sakae 21 fourteen-

unexplained loss of the second A6M1, the initial trials were completed in July 1940, and on 21 July the Navy decided to assign fifteen A6M2s to the 12th Rengo Kokutai (12th Combined Naval Air Corps) for combat trials in China, while on the last day of the month the aircraft was accepted for production as the Navy Type 0 Carrier Fighter Model 11. In China the pre-production A6M2s of the 12th Rengo Kokutai drew their first blood on 13 September, 1940, and later, reinforced with a number of production aircraft, the A6M2s destroyed 99 Chinese aircraft for the loss of two of their own to ground fire. In September 1941 they were redeployed in preparation for the impending war with the Allies.

Prior to the beginning of the Pacific War several modifications were introduced on the assembly lines, the first being a reinforcement of the rear wing spar introduced on the 22nd A6M2. Beginning with the 65th aircraft, manually folding wingtips were incorporated to fit the standard 11 m (36 ft $1\frac{1}{16}$ in) deck elevators of the Navy's carriers. So modified, the aircraft was redesignated the Navy Type 0 Carrier Fighter Model 21, and was also

Mitsubishi A6M3 Navy Type 0 Carrier Fighter Model 22s of the 251st Kokutai. (*Copyright 'Maru'*.)

built by Nakajima at their Koizumi plant. Finally a modified aileron tab balance was incorporated on the 192nd and subsequent A6M2 aircraft.

When the war in the Pacific broke out, the Japanese Navy had a total of 521 carrier fighters on strength of which 328 were A6M2s equipping most of its first-line units. On the first day of the war these Reisens spearheaded a two-prong attack on the American forces at Pearl Harbor and in the Philippines. In two hours they virtually eliminated any possibility of effective US airborne counter attacks. Under their cover the Japanese bombers had wiped out the battleship forces of the US Pacific Fleet. Moving quickly through the entire Pacific and Indian Oceans, the Rengo Kantai (Combined Fleet) and its Zero Fighters swept the area in a series of successes marked by victories over Wake, Darwin and Ceylon while the Reisen-

A captured Mitsubishi A6M2 Navy Type 0 Carrier Fighter Model 21 undergoing flight test in the San Diego area early in 1943. (*USAF*.)

with provision for two 60 kg (132 lb) bombs; (5) provison for full radio equipment including direction finding equipment; (6) take-off run, less than 70 m (230 ft) with 27 kt headwind; and (7) manoeuvrability at least equal to that of the Navy Type 96 Carrier Fighter (Mitsubishi A5M).

Nakajima elected to pull out of the competition, but Jiro Horikoshi and his Mitsubishi team pressed forward with the design of their A6M1, an all-metal low-wing monoplane powered by a 780 hp Mitsubishi Zuisei 13. The first prototype was completed in March 1939, and on 1 April, 1939, the aircraft made its first flight at Kagamigahara with test pilot Katsuzo Shima at the controls. During the flight test programme the two-blade variable-pitch propeller was replaced by a three-blade constant-speed unit, and, apart from maximum speed, all requirements were either met or exceeded. Accordingly Mitsubishi was instructed to install Nakajima NK1C Sakae 12 engines in the third prototype and subsequent aircraft. The first Sakae 12 powered A6M2 began flight trials on 28 December, 1939, and the aircraft proved to be far more successful than the Navy's most optimistic expectations.

Production of an initial Service trials batch of A6M2s had been authorized by the Navy, and military trials progressed rapidly. In spite of the

Captured Mitsubishi A6M2 with flaps lowered and undercarriage extended.

A Mitsubishi A6M2 Reisen (Zero Fighter) of the 12th Rengo Kokutai shortly after the type's entry into service. (*Aireview*.)

Naval Staff's intention was to begin development of an aircraft to replace the Navy Type 96 Carrier Fighter (Mitsubishi A5M) which had recently become operational, and the new requirements far exceeded those of its predecessor. A team led by Chief Engineer Jiro Horikoshi was assigned by Mitsubishi to work swiftly on this project even though it meant pulling out of the design competition for the Navy Experimental 11-Shi Carrier Bomber.

In October 1937 the Navy, in the light of combat reports from China, issued a revised specification including the following requirements: (1) maximum speed, 270 kt at 4,000 m (311 mph at 13,125 ft); (2) climbing speed, 3,000 m (9,840 ft) in 9 min 30 sec; (3) endurance, 1·5 to 2 hr at normal rated power or 6 to 8 hr at economical cruising speed with drop tanks; (4) armament, two 20 mm cannon and two 7·7 mm machine-guns

A Mitsubishi A6M2 of the 341st Kokutai.

TECHNICAL DATA

Description: Single-engined observation float seaplane (F1M1 and F1M2) or seaplane trainer (F1M2-K). All-metal construction with fabric-covered control surfaces.

Accommodation: Pilot and radio operator/gunner in tandem open cockpits.

Powerplant: One Nakajima Hikari 1 nine-cylinder air-cooled radial rated at 820 hp for take-off and 660 hp at 3,500 m (11,485 ft), driving a two-blade propeller (F1M1).

One Mitsubishi Zuisei 13 fourteen-cylinder air-cooled radial rated at 875 hp for take-off and 800 hp at 4,000 m (13,125 ft), driving a three-blade propeller (F1M2 and F1M2-K).

Armament: Two fixed forward-firing 7·7 mm Type 97 machine-guns and one flexible rear-firing 7·7 mm Type 92 machine-gun.

External stores: two 60 kg (132 lb) bombs (standard) or one 250 kg (551 lb) (experimental installation).

Dimensions: (F1M2) Span 11 m (36 ft 1 $\frac{1}{16}$ in); length 9·5 m (31 ft 2 in); height 4 m (13 ft 1 $\frac{10}{32}$ in); wing area 29·54 sq m (317·965 sq ft).

Weights: (F1M2) Empty 1,928 kg (4,251 lb); loaded 2,550 kg (5,622 lb); wing loading 86·3 kg/sq m (17·7 lb/sq ft); power loading 2·9 kg/hp (6·4 lb/hp).

Performance: (F1M2) Maximum speed 200 kt at 3,440 m (230 mph at 11,285 ft); climb to 5,000 m (16,405 ft) in 9 min 36 sec; service ceiling 9,440 m (30,970 ft); range 400 naut miles (460 st miles).

Production: A total of 1,118 F1Ms were built as follows:

Mitsubishi Jukogyo K.K., Nagoya:

4 F1M1 prototypes
524 F1M2 production aircraft

Dai-Nijuichi Kaigun Kokusho, Sasebo:

590 F1M2 production aircraft

Mitsubishi A6M Reisen (Zero Fighter)

From the attack on Pearl Harbor to the last desperate attempts to ward off the swarms of Allied carrier-based aircraft and Marianas-based B-29s, the Mitsubishi A6M Reisen (Zero Fighter) took part in almost every major action in which the Japanese Navy was committed. Its extreme manoeuvrability and exceptional range became almost legendary and to this day Zero Fighter remains for the Japanese and their former enemies alike the symbol of Japanese air power. Its world-wide fame was won in a series of victories against all types of land- and carrier-based Allied aircraft during the first six months of the Pacific War and, because the Japanese Navy failed to introduce another operational fighter matching the speed, armament and protection of the modern Allied fighters which began arriving in the Pacific theatre in late 1942, the Mitsubishi A6M was forced to bear the brunt of the actions until the end of the war. Despite its avowed obsolescence after 1943, the aircraft was kept in production until the Japanese surrender, and more Reisens were built than any other type of Japanese aircraft.

On 19 May, 1937, preliminary specifications for a Navy Experimental 12-Shi Carrier Fighter were submitted to Mitsubishi and Nakajima. The

characteristics on the water and in the air were markedly improved, and the F1M2 entered production as the Navy Type 0 Observation Seaplane Model 11. Production of the F1M2 was initially the sole responsibility of Mitsubishi Jukogyo K.K. which built 524. Later production was also undertaken by the Dai-Nijuichi Kaigun Kokusho (21st Naval Air Arsenal) at Sasebo. Highly manoeuvrable, the Navy Type 0 Observation Seaplane saw considerable service throughout the war from seaplane tenders, cruisers and shore bases. Its operations were not limited to reconnaissance, coastal patrol and convoy escort duties. Despite its armament comprising only two forward-firing 7·7 mm machine-guns, one flexible 7·7 mm machine-gun and two 60 kg (132 lb) bombs, it was successfully operated as a fighter and dive-bomber in support of amphibious operations. The results obtained in this last role led to the experimental installation of a 250 kg (551 lb) bomb, but the scheme was not adopted for production. A more successful modification programme led to the conversion of a limited number of F1M2s for the advanced training role, the aircraft being then designated F1M2-K.

UNITS ALLOCATED

Aircraft tenders: *Kimikawa Maru, Kiyokawa Maru, Kunikawa Maru, Sagara Maru, Sanuki Maru* and *Sanyo Maru*; Battleships: *Fuso, Hiei, Kirishima, Kongo, Musashi, Mutsu, Nagato* and *Yamato*; Cruisers: *Aoba, Ashigara, Atago, Haguro, Kinu, Maya, Myoko, Nachi* and *Takao*; 21st, 32nd, 453rd, 902nd, 938th, 954th, Amakusa, Fukuyama, Otsu and Tateyama Kokutais.

A Mitsubishi F1M2 with its floats buried in sand. This example was shot down during the battle of the Coral Sea and is seen on an island in the Louisiade Archipelago, southeast of New Guinea.

Mitsubishi F1M2 Navy Type 0 Observation Seaplane Model 11.

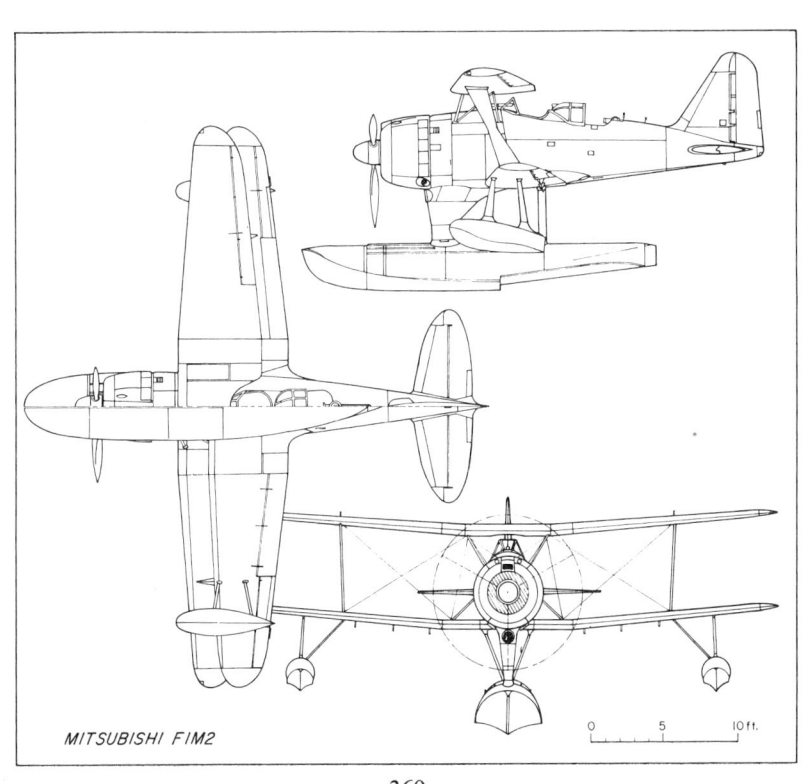

MITSUBISHI F1M2

The first Mitsubishi Zuisei powered Mitsubishi F1M2. (*US Navy Department.*)

number of interplane struts, its performance was substantially superior to that of the competitive Aichi design. However, the F1M1 suffered from a strong tendency to porpoise on the water, and in flight directional stability was poor.

After producing four F1M1 prototypes Mitsubishi redesigned the aircraft to eradicate the problems encountered during the flight test programme. The improved F1M2 was powered by an 875 hp Mitsubishi Zuisei 13 fourteen-cylinder radial fitted with a cleaner and longer cowling, improving forward visibility. It featured redesigned wings with straight leading edges instead of the elliptical design used on the F1M1. To improve stability dihedral was increased from 2 to 3 degrees, and vertical fin and rudder areas were respectively increased by 85 and 30 per cent. In this form the handling

A beached and badly damaged Mitsubishi F1M2.

A Mitsubishi F1M2 Navy Type 0 Observation Seaplane in a typical South Seas setting. (*Aireview*.)

Mitsubishi F1M

The Mitsubishi F1M2 was unique among Japanese naval aircraft as it was the only type in the observation seaplane class to be accepted for quantity production by the Japanese Navy. Despite its obsolete configuration the F1M2, which was known as PETE to the Allies, was intended to fulfil the requirements for a short-range observation float seaplane, but its exceptional manoeuvrability led to its use as an interceptor fighter, dive-bomber, convoy escort and coastal patrol aircraft, in which roles it earned for itself a commendable war record.

A 10-Shi specification outlining the Navy requirement for a catapult-launched short-range observation seaplane intended to replace the Navy Type 95 Reconnaissance Seaplane (Nakajima E8N1) was issued in late 1934 to Aichi, Kawanishi and Mitsubishi. Of similar external configuration to the Hikari 1 powered Aichi AB-13, the only other contender built in prototype form, the Mitsubishi Ka-17 was designed by a team led by Joji Hattori. The first Mitsubishi prototype, designated F1M1 by the Japanese Navy, was completed and flown in June 1936. Also powered by an 820 hp Nakajima Hikari 1 nine-cylinder radial, it was an extremely clean biplane with a central float and two outboard stabilizing floats, and due to Hattori's efforts to obtain a clean aerodynamic aircraft by reducing the

One flexible 20 mm Type 99 Model 1 cannon in a dorsal turret, and one flexible 7·7 mm Type 92 machine-gun in each of the lateral blisters and a retractable dorsal turret. A fourth flexible 7·7 mm Type 92 machine-gun could be fired from cockpit windows (G3M2 Model 22 and G3M3).

One flexible 7·7 mm Type 92 machine-gun in a dorsal turret (L3Y1 and L3Y2).

Bomb-load: one 800 kg (1,764 lb) torpedo or 800 kg (1,764 lb) of bombs carried externally under the fuselage.

	Ka-15 1st prototype	G3M1 Model 11	G3M2 Model 22	G3M3 Model 23
Dimensions:				
Span	25 m (82 ft 0¼ in)	25 m (82 ft 0¼ in)	25 m (82 ft 0¼ in)	25 m (82 ft 0¼ in)
Length	16·45 m (53 ft 11⅝ in)	16·45 m (53 ft 11⅝ in)	16·45 m (53 ft 11⅝ in)	16·45 m (53 ft 11⅝ in)
Height	3·685 m (12 ft 1 1/16 in)	3·685 m (12 ft 1 1/16 in)	3·685 m (12 ft 1 1/16 in)	3·685 m (12 ft 1 1/16 in)
Wing area	75 sq m (807·3 sq ft)	75 sq m (807·3 sq ft)	75 sq m (807·3 sq ft)	75 sq m (807·3 sq ft)
Weights:				
Empty	4,400 kg (9,700 lb)	4,770 kg (10,516 lb)	4,965 kg (10,936 lb)	5,243 kg (11,551 lb)
Loaded	7,250 kg (15,984 lb)	7,642 kg (16,848 lb)	8,000 kg (17,637 lb)	8,000 kg (17,637 lb)
Wing loading	96·7 kg/sq m (19·8 lb/sq ft)	101·9 kg/sq m (20·9 lb/sq ft)	106·7 kg/sq m (21·8 lb/sq ft)	106·7 kg/sq m (21·8 lb/sq ft)
Power loading	4·8 kg/hp (10·7 lb/hp)	3·6 kg/hp (7·9 lb/hp)	3·7 kg/hp (8·1 lb/hp)	3·1 kg/hp (6·8 lb/hp)
Performance:				
Maximum speed	170·3 kt at 1,500 m (196 mph at 4,920 ft)	188 kt at 2,000 m (216 mph at 6,560 ft)	201·5 kt at 4,180 m (232 mph at 13,715 ft)	224·5 kt at 5,900 m (258 mph at 19,360 ft)
Cruising speed	—	—	150 kt at 4,000 m (173 mph at 13,125 ft)	160 kt at 4,000 m (184 mph at 13,125 ft)
Climb to	3,000 m (9,845 ft)	3,000 m (9,845 ft)	3,000 m (9,845 ft)	3,000 m (9,845 ft)
in	9 min 40 sec	9 min 47 sec	8 min 19 sec	5 min 29 sec
Service ceiling	— —	7,480 m (24,540 ft)	9,130 m (29,950 ft)	10,280 m (33,730 ft)
Maximum range	— —	— —	2,365 naut miles (2,722 st miles)	3,363 naut miles (3,871 st miles)

Production: A total of 1,048 G3Ms were built by Mitsubishi Jukogyo K.K. at Nagoya and Nakajima Hikoki K.K. at Koizumi as follows:

Mitsubishi:

21 Ka-15 prototypes (1935–36)
34 G3M1 production aircraft (1936–37)
343 G3M2 Model 21 production aircraft (1937–39)
238 G3M2 Model 22 production aircraft (1939–41)

636

Nakajima:

412 G3M2 Model 22 and G3M3 production aircraft (1941–43)

A formation of Mihoro Kokutai Mitsubishi G3M2 Navy Type 96 Attack Bomber Model 22s during early operations in Malaya.

engined aircraft. But by 1943 few Navy Type 96 Attack Bombers were still operating in their intended role, most surviving aircraft serving until the end of the war in second-line units as glider tugs, bomber trainers and as maritime reconnaissance aircraft often fitted with search radar.

During the war the Dai-Ichi Kaigun Kokusho (First Naval Air Arsenal) at Kasumigaura converted a number of aircraft to Navy Type 96 Transports, known to the Allies as TINA, with a row of cabin windows, and a door on the port side, and two versions were built. The L3Y1 Model 11, powered by the Kinsei 3, was modified from the G3M1 while the L3Y2 Model 12 was converted from the Kinsei 45 powered G3M2. Defensive armament consisted of a single 7·7 mm machine-gun.

UNITS ALLOCATED

762nd, 1001st, Chitose, Genzan, Kanoya, Kisarazu, Matsushima, Mihoro, Misawa, Ominato and Takao Kokutais.

TECHNICAL DATA

Description: Twin-engined bomber (G3M series) and transport (L3Y series). All-metal construction with fabric-covered control surfaces.

Accommodation: Normal crew of five (Ka-15, G3M1 and G3M2 Model 12) or seven (G3M2 Model 22 and G3M3).

Powerplant: Two Hiro Type 91 twelve-cylinder liquid-cooled engines, rated at 750 hp for take-off and 600 hp at sea level, driving four-blade fixed-pitch propellers (1st, 2nd, 5th and 6th Ka-15 prototypes).

Two Mitsubishi Kinsei 2 fourteen-cylinder air-cooled radials, rated at 830 hp for take-off and 680 hp at 1,500 m (4,920 ft), driving four-blade fixed-pitch wooden propellers (3rd, 7th to 10th, and 12th through 21st Ka-15 prototypes).

Two Mitsubishi Kinsei 3 fourteen-cylinder air-cooled radials, rated at 910 hp for take-off and 790 hp at 2,000 m (6,560 ft), driving either four-blade fixed-pitch wooden propellers or three-blade variable-pitch metal propellers (4th and 11th Ka-15 prototypes, G3M1 and L3Y1).

Two Mitsubishi Kinsei 41 or 42 fourteen-cylinder air-cooled radials, rated at 1,075 hp for take-off and 990 hp at 2,800 m (9,185 ft), driving three-blade variable-pitch metal propellers (G3M2).

Two Mitsubishi Kinsei 45 fourteen-cylinder air-cooled radials, rated at 1,075 hp for take-off and 1,000 hp at 4,180 m (13,715 ft), driving three-blade variable-pitch metal propellers (G3M2, and L3Y2).

Two Mitsubishi Kinsei 51 fourteen-cylinder air-cooled radials, rated at 1,300 hp for take-off and 1,200 hp at 3,000 m (9,845 ft), driving three-blade variable-pitch metal propellers (G3M3).

Armament: One flexible 7·7 mm Type 92 machine-gun in each of the two retractable dorsal turrets and one retractable ventral turret (Ka-15, G3M1 and G3M2 Model 21).

finder units, first used on the Model 21, were adopted as standard equipment for the Model 22 aircraft, thus enhancing the ability of the G3M2 to operate on long over-water flights.

In December 1941, the Japanese Navy had 204 Mitsubishi G3M2 Models 21, 22 and 23 operating in first-line units, and a further fifty-four of this type were operated by second-line units. When hostilities began, Navy Type 96 Attack Bombers took part in the operation against the US Forces on Wake Island, the Philippines and the Marianas, while on 10 December, 1941, sixty G3M2s of the Genzan and Mihoro Kokutais, operating with twenty-six G4M1s of the Kanoya Kokutai, succeeded in sinking the two British battleships, HMS *Prince of Wales* and HMS *Repulse* off Malaya. As Japanese forces moved swiftly through the Southwest Pacific islands, so did the Navy Type 96 Bombers. However, the aircraft had already been replaced by the G4M1 on the Mitsubishi assembly line, and Nakajima was left as the sole supplier. In 1941 this company had introduced a new version, the G3M3 Model 23, powered by two 1,300 hp Kinsei 51 engines. Externally identical to the G3M2 Model 22, the G3M3 was the fastest variant of the aircraft, and with fuel capacity increased to 5,182 litres (1,140 Imp gal) possessed a truly spectacular range for a twin-

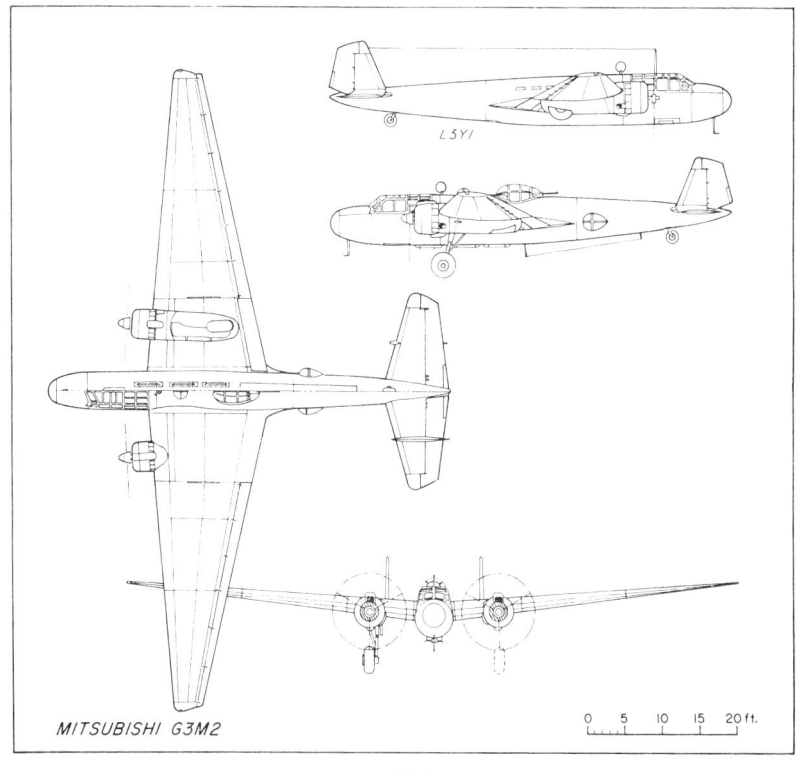

MITSUBISHI G3M2

Mitsubishi G3M2 bombers of the Mihoro Kokutai. The nearest aircraft is a Model 22 version and the other a Model 21. (*S. Tanaka*.)

In the late thirties few high-performance transport aircraft were available in Japan, and consequently several modifications of the G3M series were developed to fill military and civil needs. The designation G3M1-L applied to some G3M1s converted for use as military transports and these aircraft were re-engined with two 1,075 hp Kinsei 45 engines. Beginning in 1938, some two dozen G3M2s were converted as Mitsubishi Twin-Engined Transports for civil operators. Most of these aircraft were used by Nippon Koku K.K. (Japan Air Lines) and its successor Dai Nippon Koku K.K. (Greater Japan Air Lines), but this variant is best remembered for a number of goodwill flights. J-BEOA flew from Tokyo to Teheran, J-BEOC from Tokyo to Rome and J-BACI, *Nippon* (G3M2 No. 328), made a round-the-world flight sponsored by the *Mainichi Shimbun* (Mainichi Press), beginning on 26 August, 1939, and ending on 20 October, a distance of 32,850 miles being covered in 194 flying hours. During the war the Mitsubishi Twin-Engined Transports, supplemented by a number of L3Y1 and L3Y2 transports, were operated by Dai Nippon Koku K.K. on their military contract routes throughout the war zone.

While these transport versions of the aircraft were showing the Japanese flag abroad, newer bomber variants were being delivered to the Navy. In answer to the pressing requests of operational units for a version with increased offensive armament, Mitsubishi designed the G3M2 Model 22. The retractable ventral and rear dorsal turrets were eliminated, and a large 'turtle back' turret, housing a manually operated flexible 20 mm Type 99 Model 1 cannon, was mounted above the fuselage. Reduced-size wing fillets allowed for the fitting of a blister-type position, on each side of the rear fuselage, for a flexible 7·7 mm machine-gun. The front retractable dorsal turret was retained and late production Navy Type 96 Attack Bomber Model 22s received a fourth 7·7 mm machine-gun which could be fired from either side of the cockpit. Various equipment changes were incorporated and licence-built Sperry automatic pilot and radio direction

original requirements, this variant saw only limited service, as an improved version of the Kinsei engine allowed a further increase in performance.

Powered by two Kinsei 41 or 42 engines, the G3M2 Model 21 differed from the early production aircraft in minor internal details, including an increase in fuel capacity from 3,805 litres (837 Imp gal) to 3,874 litres (852 Imp gal). Defensive armament still comprised only three 7·7 mm machine-guns, but two different types of dorsal turrets were fitted. On 14 August, 1937, a week after the second Sino-Japanese conflict had begun, the Kanoya Kokutai based at Taipei (Formosa) sent its G3M2 Model 21 bombers against targets in the Hangchow and Kwangteh areas on the Chinese mainland. Despite poor weather these aircraft flew 1,250 miles

Close-up of a Mitsubishi G3M2 Navy Type 96 Attack Bomber Model 21.
(*S. Tanaka.*)

over water and made the first trans-oceanic bombing raid in aviation history, this feat being matched the next day by G3M2s of the Kisarazu Kokutai operating from their Omura base on Kyushu. Soon thereafter, the G3M2s were moved to bases on the mainland from which they mounted attacks deep into Chinese territory. However, operating beyond the range of Japanese fighter aircraft, the Navy Type 96 Attack Bombers suffered heavy losses as their defensive armament was wholly inadequate. Despite these losses the G3M2 force operating in China was slowly increased and in this theatre of operations a peak inventory of 130 machines, serving in four Kokutais, was reached in the summer of 1940, three years after the first operational sortie. Mitsubishi built 343 Navy Type 96 Attack Bomber Model 21s (Nos. 56 through 398 inclusive) and Nakajima began manufacturing this G3M variant under a Navy production contract. Late production aircraft were powered by a pair of Kinsei 45 engines which maintained their normal rating up to 4,180 m (13,715 ft) instead of only 2,800 m (9,185 ft) for the Kinsei 41 or 42 used in early production G3M2s.

353

a single torpedo carried under the fuselage and no provisions were made in the design for an internal bomb-bay. Powered by two 750 hp Hiro Type 91 liquid-cooled engines, the first Ka-15 was completed in June 1935.

In July 1935, at Kagamigahara, Mitsubishi test pilot Kajima assisted by Lieut Sada of the Japanese Navy took the Ka-15 on its maiden flight. The elated JNAF officers and the designers knew at once that Japan possessed a medium bomber equal to most foreign aircraft. Within a year twenty additional prototypes had been delivered, and the test programme progressed smoothly despite the loss of the second aircraft. The twenty-one Ka-15s were completed in six configurations:

Ka-15, Nos. 1, 2, 5 and 6. Unglazed nose with bomb-aiming window under the pilot's cockpit. Two 750 hp Hiro Type 91 liquid-cooled engines, driving fixed-pitch four-blade MW 116 wooden propellers. One aircraft tested with ski undercarriage.

Ka-15 No. 3. Identical airframe. Two 830 hp Mitsubishi Kinsei 2 fourteen-cylinder air-cooled radials, driving fixed-pitch four-blade MW 126 wooden propellers.

Ka-15 No. 4. Identical airframe. Two 910 hp Mitsubishi Kinsei 3 fourteen-cylinder air-cooled radials, driving variable-pitch three-blade Hamilton Standard CS 16 metal propellers.

Ka-15, Nos. 7, 9, 10 and 12 through 21. Glazed nose accommodating the bomb aimer/navigator and incorporating an optically-flat aiming window and an astrodome. Powerplant identical to that of the third Ka-15 (Kinsei 2 with MW 126 propellers).

Ka-15 No. 8. Identical to the 7th Ka-15 except for increased dihedral.

Ka-15 No. 11. Identical to the seventh Ka-15 with the exception of the powerplant which consisted of two Kinsei 3s, driving Hamilton Standard CS 16 variable-pitch propellers.

In June 1936 the aircraft was put into production as the Navy Type 96 Attack Bomber Model 11 (G3M1) while most of the prototypes were delivered to the Tateyama Kokutai for accelerated Service trials. At that time the 'solid nose' version received the unofficial designations G3M1a (Hiro Type 91 powered aircraft) and G3M1b (Kinsei powered aircraft), while the version with the glazed nose became known as the G3M1c. Thirty-four production G3M1 (Nos. 22 through 55 inclusive) were built and each powered by two Kinsei 3 radials, as these engines had demonstrated during flight tests an increased maximum speed from 196 mph to 216 mph. However, due to a shortage of variable-pitch propellers, some of these aircraft had to be temporarily fitted with MW 126 fixed-pitch four-blade propellers with resultant loss of performance. The production aircraft could be distinguished from the prototypes by the redesigned canopy covering the enlarged cockpits and, in addition, internal equipment changes were incorporated. Even though the G3M1 exceeded most of the Navy's

was strictly intended to serve as an aerodynamic prototype possessing the necessary performance required from a future attack bomber, but the designers were freed from meeting specific military requirements. Bearing the manufacturer's designation Ka-9, the aircraft was designed by Sueo Honjo assisted by Tomio Kubo and Nobuhiko Kusabake, and was powered by two 500 hp Hiro Type 91 twelve-cylinder liquid-cooled engines. It made its first flight in April 1934, with Yoshitaka Kajima at the controls. Possessing an exceptionally clean airframe characterized by a typical Junkers 'double wing' and twin fins and rudders, the Ka-9 demonstrated exceptional manoeuvrability and handling characteristics and achieved a

A Mitsubishi G3M1 with presentation marking Hokoku 205 on the rear fuselage. On the left is a Mitsubishi Navy Type 96 Carrier Fighter Model 2-2 with cockpit canopy closed. (*US Navy Department*.)

maximum range of 3,265 naut miles (3,760 st miles). The results of the flight test programme were received with enthusiasm by the Navy which soon thereafter issued to Mitsubishi a new 9-Shi specification which this time called for a fully developed attack bomber carrying an 800 kg (1,764 lb) offensive load and a defensive armament of three 7·7 mm machine-guns. Although this specification had been issued to Mitsubishi on a non-competitive basis, Nakajima attempted unsuccessfully to enter its privately developed LB-2 against the Mitsubishi Ka-15. However, the success of the earlier Ka-9 had already won the battle for the Ka-15, and the Navy gave Mitsubishi its full assistance as they were anxious to take delivery of the aircraft.

In designing the Ka-15 to meet the requirements of the 9-Shi specification, Kiro Honjo married the wing of the Ka-9 to a wider fuselage providing space for three retractable turrets—two dorsal and one ventral—each housing one 7·7 mm Type 92 machine-gun. To improve aerodynamic flow over the wing the corrugated metal panels used on the wing trailing edge of the Ka-9 were replaced with smooth-skinned panels. Other modifications included the enlargement of the tail surfaces to cope with the increased longitudinal movement at the centre of gravity and to improve stability during the bomb-run, and the retractable undercarriage was simplified and strengthened. The aircraft being primarily intended to operate in support of naval units, the main offensive weapon consisted of

One of the fifteen Mitsubishi Ka-15 prototypes with glazed nose.
(*Mitsubishi Jukogyo K.K.*)

Mitsubishi G3M

The horror that Admiral Sir Tom Phillips and the officers and men of HMS *Repulse* and HMS *Prince of Wales* must have felt when the first salvo of bombs fell on their ships when operating beyond the known range of the 'obsolete' Japanese air force was due to the foresight of Admiral Isoroku Yamamoto who had initiated the development of the Navy Type 96 Attack Bomber (NELL), one of the two types of bombers participating in this operation.

In 1933, while serving as chief of the Technical Division of the Naval Bureau of Aeronautics, Admiral Yamamoto convinced the Naval Staff of the urgent need to develop a land-based long-range aircraft supplementing carrier-based aircraft in support of naval units operating in the vastness of the Pacific where established air bases were widely spread. Towards fulfilling this requirement Mitsubishi was issued, on a non-competitive basis, an 8-Shi specification calling for a land-based twin-engined long-range reconnaissance aircraft. From the inception of the programme the aircraft

Mitsubishi G3M1 Navy Type 96 Attack Bomber Model 11 in natural metal finish with red fins and rudders.

350

A5M4-K

MITSUBISHI A5M4

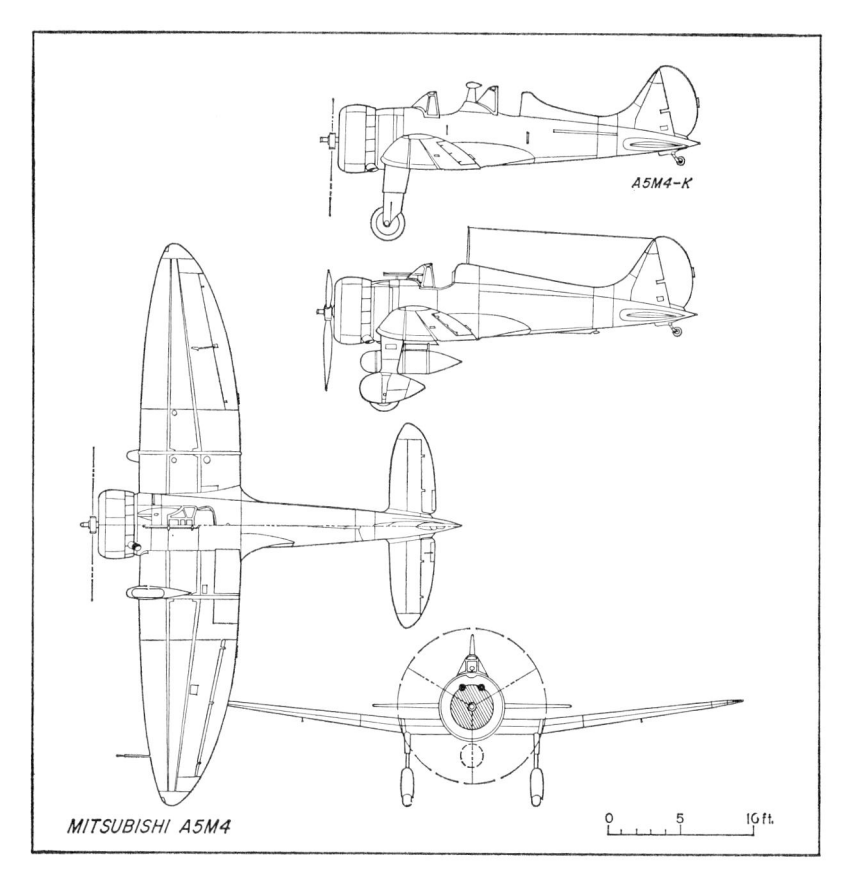

Production: A total of 1,094 A5Ms and derivatives were built as follows:

Mitsubishi Jukogyo K.K., Nagoya:

    6 Ka-14 prototypes (1935–36)
    782 A5M1 to A5M4 (1936–40)
    1 Ki-18 prototype (1935)
    2 Ki-33 prototypes (1936)
    ―
    791

K.K. Watanabe Tekkosho:

    39 A5M4 (1939–42)

Dai-Nijuichi Kaigun Kokusho, Omura:

    161 A5M4 (1939–41)
    103 A5M4-K (1942–44)
    ―
    264

	Ka-14 (1st prototype)	A5M1	A5M4	Ki-18	Ki-33
Dimensions:					
Span	11 m (36 ft 1 1/16 in)	11 m (36 ft 1 1/16 in)	11 m (36 ft 1 1/16 in)	11 m (36 ft 1 1/16 in)	11 m (36 ft 1 1/16 in)
Length	7·67 m (25 ft 1 31/32 in)	7·71 m (25 ft 3 1/2 in)	7·565 m (24 ft 9 27/32 in)	7·655 m (25 ft 1 3/8 in)	7·545 m (24 ft 9 1/16 in)
Height	3·265 m (10 ft 8 1/2 in)	3·2 m (10 ft 6 in)	3·27 m (10 ft 8 3/4 in)	3·15 m (10 ft 4 in)	3·19 m (10 ft 5 1/2 in)
Wing area	17·8 sq m (191·597 sq ft)	17·8 sq m (191·597 sq ft)	17·8 sq m (191·597 sq ft)	17·8 sq m (191·597 sq ft)	17·8 sq m (191·597 sq ft)
Weights:					
Empty	— —	1,075 kg (2,370 lb)	1,216 kg (2,681 lb)	1,110 kg (2,447 lb)	1,132 kg (2,496 lb)
Loaded	1,373 kg (3,087 lb)	1,500 kg (3,307 lb)	1,671 kg (3,684 lb)	1,422 kg (3,135 lb)	1,462 kg (3,223 lb)
Wing loading	77·2 kg/sq m (16·1 lb/sq ft)	84·3 kg/sq m (17·3 lb/sq ft)	93·8 kg/sq m (19·2 lb/sq ft)	79·9 kg/sq m (16·4 lb/sq ft)	82·1 kg/sq m (16·8 lb/sq ft)
Power loading	2·5 kg/hp (5·6 lb/hp)	2·6 kg/hp (5·7 lb/hp)	2·4 kg/hp (5·2 lb/hp)	2·6 kg/hp (5·7 lb/hp)	2·1 kg/hp (4·5 lb/hp)
Performance:					
Maximum speed	243·5 kt at 3,200 m (280 mph at 10,500 ft)	219 kt at 2,100 m (252 mph at 6,890 ft)	235 kt at 3,000 m (270 mph at 9,845 ft)	445 km/h at 3,050 m (276·5 mph at 10,000 ft)	475 km/h at 3,000 m (295 mph at 9,845 ft)
Climb to	5,000 m (16,405 ft)	5,000 m (16,405 ft)	3,000 m (9,845 ft)	5,000 m (16,405 ft)	5,000 m (16,405 ft)
in	5 min 54 sec	8 min 30 sec	3 min 35 sec	6 min 26 sec	5 min 56 sec
Service ceiling	— —	— —	9,800 m (32,150 ft)	— —	— —
Range	— —	— —	648 naut miles (746 st miles)	— —	— —

UNITS ALLOCATED

Carriers: *Akagi, Hosho, Kaga, Ryujo* and *Zuiho*; 12th, 13th, 14th, 15th, Oita, Ominato, Omura, Sasebo and Yokosuka Kokutais.

TECHNICAL DATA

Description: Single-seat carrier-borne fighter (A5M1 to A5M4), or single-seat land-based fighter (Ki-18 and Ki-33), or two-seat fighter-trainer (A5M4-K). All-metal construction with fabric-covered control surfaces.

Accommodation: Pilot in open cockpit (all versions except for A5M2b Model 22, Ki-33 and A5M4-K). Pilot in enclosed cockpit (A5M2b Model 22 and Ki-33). Student pilot and instructor in tandem open cockpits (A5M4-K).

Powerplant: One Nakajima Kotobuki 5 nine-cylinder air-cooled radial, rated at 550 hp for take-off and 600 hp at 3,100 m (10,170 ft), driving a two-blade propeller (Ka-14 No. 1 and Ki-18).

One Nakajima Kotobuki 3 nine-cylinder air-cooled radial, rated at 640 hp for take-off and 715 hp at 2,800 m (9,185 ft), driving a two-blade propeller (Ka-14 No. 2) or three-blade propeller (A5M2b).

One Nakajima Hikari 1 nine-cylinder air-cooled radial, rated at 700 hp for take-off and 800 hp at 3,500 m (11,485 ft), driving a two-blade propeller (Ka-14 Nos. 3 to 5).

One Nakajima Kotobuki 2 KAI 1 nine-cylinder air-cooled radial, rated at 580 hp for take-off and 630 hp at 1,500 m (4,920 ft), driving a two-blade propeller (A5M1).

One Nakajima Kotobuki 2 KAI 3A nine-cylinder air-cooled radial, rated at 610 hp for take-off and 690 hp at 3,250 m (10,665 ft), driving a three-blade propeller (A5M2a).

One Hispano-Suiza 12Xcrs twelve-cylinder vee liquid-cooled engine, rated at 610 hp for take-off and 690 hp at 3,900 m (12,795 ft), driving a three-blade propeller (A5M3a).

One Nakajima Kotobuki 41 or 41 KAI nine-cylinder air-cooled radial, rated at 710 hp for take-off and 785 hp at 3,000 m (9,845 ft), driving a three-blade propeller (A5M4 and A5M4-K).

One 720 hp Mitsubishi Kinsei A-8 or A-9 fourteen-cylinder air-cooled radial, driving a three-blade propeller (experimental installation on one Ka-14 prototype).

One Nakajima Ha-1a nine-cylinder air-cooled radial, rated at 710 hp for take-off and 745 hp at 3,700 m (12,140 ft), driving a two-blade propeller (Ki-33).

Armament: Two 7·7 mm Type 89 machine-guns in the upper fuselage decking (all versions except as noted).

Two 20 mm Oerlikon FF cannon (A5M1a).

One engine-mounted 20 mm Hispano cannon (A5M3a).
External stores: two 30 kg (66 lb) bombs (A5M2b and A5M4), or one 160 litre (35·2 Imp gal) drop tank (A5M4).

A Mitsubishi A5M4 with drop tank. The arrester hook can be clearly seen under the rear fuselage. (*US Navy Department.*)

Mitsubishi A5M4 of the 13th Rengo Kokutai during operations in China. (*Aeroplane Photo Supply.*)

designated Model 34, but both versions of the A5M4 were being phased out from first-line units during 1941.

When the Pacific War began, the Allies still thought that the Mitsubishi A5M4 equipped the bulk of the Japanese Navy fighter units and they assigned the code name CLAUDE to the aircraft while reserving the name SANDY for what they thought was a version of the aircraft with inverted gull wings. Of course no SANDY was ever met in combat, as the only version of the aircraft with inverted gull wings was the original prototype of 1935 which had long been destroyed in structural tests. Actually the only units still equipped with A5M4s, which the Japanese had intended to use in their initial attacks, were the carriers *Ryujo*, *Zuiho* and *Hosho*. It was planned that the A5M4s based aboard these carriers would provide fighter cover for the Formosa-based bombers attacking the Philippines, but the phenomenal range of the A5M's successor, the Mitsubishi A6M2, enabled the Navy to relieve the three carriers and their A5M4s of their intended mission. With the exception of the attack against Davao, no A5M4 participated in front-line actions against the Allies, and most aircraft of this type were retained in Japan by second-line and training units.

Development of a two-seat trainer version of the Navy Type 96 Carrier Fighter Model 24 to a 15-Shi specification began in 1940 at the Dai-Nijuichi Kaigun Kokusho. Powered by a Kotobuki 41, the A5M4-K was characterized by the removal of the wheel spats and the fitting of two tandem open cockpits with large headrests. A turn-over pylon mounted between the two cockpits and small horizontal fins on both sides of the rear fuselage were added to improve safety and spin recovery. After serving in their intended role of advanced fighter trainer, beginning in late 1942, the A5M4-Ks ended their life among the few remaining A5M4 single-seat fighters in kamikaze attacks against Allied ships cruising off the coast of Japan.

refuelled and, partly due to the superior training and *esprit de corps* of their pilots, the A5M2s maintained their superiority over the much faster Polikarpov I-16s used by the Chinese. At the same time the Japanese fighter proved that despite its lightweight structure it was able to absorb considerable battle damage, as demonstrated by Petty Officer Kashimura who brought his A5M2 back to its base after losing one third of its port wing in a ramming attack by a Chinese fighter.

Powered by a 610 hp Hispano-Suiza twelve-cylinder vee liquid-cooled engine imported from France, two A5M3a prototypes were built to test the novel engine and its 20 mm cannon firing through the propeller hub. Even though the A5M3a was slightly faster than any other variants of the Navy Type 96 Carrier Fighter, no production order was placed, because the Navy did not want to have to rely on foreign suppliers, and the next production model was the A5M4.

Developed to meet the requirements for increased range stemming from the Chinese decision to move their aircraft beyond the effective range of the A5M2s, the A5M4 was externally identical to the late production A5M2b with open cockpit. Powered by a Kotobuki 41 and fitted with a 160 litre (35·2 Imp gal) ventral drop tank, this version of the Navy Type 96 Carrier Fighter was first designated Model 4, being changed to Model 24 when the new designation system identifying airframe and engine modifications was introduced. Delivered to combat units in China in 1938, the A5M4s increased markedly the area of Japanese air superiority and once again forced the Chinese to move their decimated air units further away from the battle area. The A5M4 was built in larger numbers than any other variants of the Navy Type 96 Carrier Fighter and remained in production at Mitsubishi's Nagoya plant until 1940, while two hundred aircraft of this type were also built by K.K. Watanabe Tekkosho and the Dai-Nijuichi Kaigun Kokusho (21st Naval Air Arsenal) at Omura. Late production aircraft with Kotobuki 41 KAI engines and minor airframe changes were

A Mitsubishi A5M2b Navy Type 96 Carrier Fighter Model 2-2 of the Hyakurihara Kokutai. This version had an enclosed cockpit.

Mitsubishi A5M2a Navy Type 96 Carrier Fighter Model 2-1.

types based on the Ki-18 but featuring an enclosed cockpit and powered by a Nakajima Ha-1a. During competitive trials the lighter Nakajima entry, the Ki-27, was found more manoeuvrable than the Ki-33 and won a production contract.

Fortunately for Mitsubishi, the naval pilots were less adamant in their quest for extreme manoeuvrability, and the A5M1 proved a complete success following its delivery to Service units in early 1937. However, by the time the second Sino-Japanese conflict flared up in July 1937, the A5M1 had been replaced on the assembly lines by the Navy Type 96 Carrier Fighter Model 2-1 (A5M2a) powered by a Nakajima Kotobuki 2 KAI 3A. In the early stage of the conflict, when the only fighters available in quantity to the Japanese were the obsolete carrier-based Nakajima A2N1s and A4N1s, losses reached a dangerous level, but with the arrival at Shanghai of the A5M2-equipped 12th and 13th Kokutais, the Japanese gained complete air superiority. In Japan the aircraft was used for various experiments such as the testing of the ventral drop tank designed for the Mitsubishi A6M2, which was fitted on the 205th Navy Type 96 Carrier Fighter, and the testing of Oerlikon FF 20 mm cannon, which were mounted on a modified A5M1 designated A5M1a.

With the accelerated tempo of air operations in China, the development of the Navy Type 96 Carrier Fighter was actively pursued, and the A5M2b Model 2-2 was placed in production. Having an enclosed cockpit, the A5M2b was powered by a 640 hp Kotobuki 3 driving a three-blade propeller. To improve forward visibility a NACA cowling with cooling flaps was adopted, and at the same time minor equipment changes dictated by early combat experience were incorporated. Despite its advantages the enclosed cockpit was disliked by Japanese pilots and was soon discarded on late production A5M2bs. On the war front the three variants of the A5M2 continued to achieve considerable success and forced the Chinese to pull back their air units beyond the range of the Navy Type 96 Carrier Fighter. This move was countered by the establishment of intermediate landing fields between Shanghai and Nanking where the A5M2s could be

Bearing the manufacturer's designation Ka-14 and powered by a 550 hp Nakajima Kotobuki 5 radial, the first prototype was fitted with inverted gull wings with 16° 24′ anhedral from the roots to the undercarriage attachment points and 9° 30′ dihedral outboard to the wingtips. Flight trials began at Kagamigahara on 4 February, 1935, and it was soon evident that the aircraft exceeded the most sanguine expectations of its designers, as it reached a top speed of 243 kt (280 mph). However, the aircraft tended to suffer from pitching oscillations in flight and from a tendency to balloon when landing, and it was found necessary to modify the second prototype considerably. Powered by a 640 hp direct-drive Nakajima Kotobuki 3, the second Ka-14 featured new wings with straight centre-section and 2° 40′ dihedral outboard of the undercarriage while split trailing-edge flaps were installed on the centre-section. Four additional prototypes, differing in minor details, were built and tested by the Navy with a variety of engines, including the Nakajima Hikari 1 and the Mitsubishi A-8 and A-9 radials. Following satisfactory completion of Service trials the aircraft, now powered by the 580 hp Nakajima Kotobuki 2 KAI 1, was placed in production as the Navy Type 96 Carrier Fighter Model 1 (A5M1).

The remarkable performance demonstrated by the second Ka-14 attracted the attention of the Japanese Army which ordered a similar machine under the Ki-18 designation. Powered by a Nakajima Kotobuki 5, the Ki-18 was identical to the naval aircraft except that all its carrier equipment was removed. Tested at Tachikawa by Army pilots, the Ki-18 was 45 km/h (28 mph) faster than the Kawasaki Ki-10-I fighter biplane then entering service with Army units, but was found inferior in dog-fighting. Consequently, the Koku Hombu decided to request the development of competitive prototypes capable of equalling or surpassing the Ki-18's performance while having a manoeuvrability equal to that of the Ki-10. In answer to this request Mitsubishi produced two Ki-33 proto-

The sole example of the Mitsubishi Ki-18, developed for the Japanese Army from the Navy's A5M series.

The inverted gull winged Mitsubishi Ka-14 which was the prototype for the A5M series of carrier-borne fighters. (*Mitsubishi Jukogyo K.K.*)

Mitsubishi A5M

The delivery of A5M1 single-seat fighters to operational units of the Navy marked Japanese aviation's entry into an age of self-sufficiency. When, in April 1932, the Naval Staff began an ambitious re-equipment programme aimed at ending their reliance on foreign-designed aircraft, two types of carrier fighters were designed to a 7-Shi specification, Mitsubishi's entry being a low-wing monoplane while Nakajima's design was a parasol monoplane. However, both aircraft failed to meet the stringent requirements of the specification, and the Navy were compelled to order another biplane, the Nakajima A4N1, developed from that firm's earlier design, the A2N1. From its inception the Nakajima A4N1 had been conceived as a stopgap and, in February 1934, the Navy issued their 9-Shi specification for a new single-seat fighter.

The 9-Shi specification called for a fighter meeting the following requirements: (1) maximum speed 350 km/h at 3,000 m (217·5 mph at 9,845 ft); (2) climb to 5,000 m (16,405 ft) in 6 min 30 sec; (3) span and length not to exceed 11 m (36 ft $1\frac{1}{16}$ in) and 8 m (26 ft $2\frac{31}{32}$ in); and (4) armament two 7·7 mm machine-guns. Operation from the deck of aircraft carriers, a normal requirement for a naval fighter, was intentionally omitted from the original specification to ease the designers' task in meeting the rather stringent performance requirements. Under the direction of Jiro Horikoshi, Mitsubishi's team designed a low-wing inverted gull monoplane with spatted undercarriage in which great attention was paid to minimizing drag by adopting an airframe of small cross section with flush-riveted aluminium stressed-skin covering.

JAAF was completed in December 1933. Powered by a 475 hp Mitsubishi Type 92 radial, the Ki-7 differed from its naval counterpart in having a reinforced engine mounting and forward fuselage structure, but the aircraft crashed during the early part of its development programme. A second Ki-7 prototype, powered by a 450 hp Nakajima Kotobuki radial, was handed over to Tokyo Koku K.K. for modification as a light civil transport when the Japanese Army lost interest in the project. Registered J-BABQ and known as the Mitsubishi MS-1 Civil Transport Plane, the sole civilian aircraft of this type was re-engined with a 420 hp Nakajima-built Bristol Jupiter VI radial and could be fitted with either fixed landing gear or twin floats.

In 1939 the production of the naval trainer was transferred to K.K. Watanabe Tekkosho which introduced a new version, the Navy Type 90 Crew Trainer Model 2 (K3M3). Powered by a 580 hp Nakajima Kotobuki 2 KAI 2 radial, the K3M3 was fitted with the enlarged tail surfaces first introduced on the civil MS-1. Both the K3M2 and K3M3 versions were extensively used as trainers during the war, the aircraft being coded PINE by the Allies, and a small number of K3M3s were modified as utility transports under the designation K3M3-L.

TECHNICAL DATA

Description: Single-engined crew trainer (K3M1, K3M2, K3M3 and Ki-7), light civil transport (MS-1) or utility transport (K3M3-L). Mixed construction.

Accommodation: Pilot and gunner in separate open cockpits and instructor and two pupils in enclosed cabin (K3M1, K3M2, K3M3 and Ki-7), or pilot in open cockpit and four to five passengers or light cargo in enclosed cabin (MS-1 and K3M3-L).

Powerplant: One Mitsubishi-built Hispano-Suiza eight-cylinder vee liquid-cooled engine, rated at 340 hp for take-off and 300 hp at 1,000 m (3,280 ft), and driving a two-blade wooden propeller (K3M1).

One Hitachi Amakaze 11 nine-cylinder air-cooled radial, rated at 340 hp for take-off and 300 hp at sea level, and driving a two-blade wooden propeller (K3M2).

One Nakajima Kotobuki 2 KAI 2 nine-cylinder air-cooled radial, rated at 580 hp for take-off, and driving a two-blade metal propeller (K3M3).

One Mitsubishi Type 92 nine-cylinder air-cooled radial, rated at 475 hp for take-off and 420 hp at sea level, and driving a two-blade metal propeller (first Ki-7).

One Nakajima Kotobuki nine-cylinder air-cooled radial, rated at 450 hp for take-off, and driving a two-blade wooden propeller (second Ki-7).

One Nakajima-built Bristol Jupiter VI nine-cylinder air-cooled radial, rated at 420 hp for take-off, and driving a two-blade wooden propeller (MS-1).

Armament: (Applying only to the K3M1, K3M2, K3M3 and Ki-7) One flexible rear-firing 7·7 mm Type 92 machine-gun. Four 30 kg (66 lb) bombs.

Dimensions: (K3M3) Span 15·78 m (51 ft 9¼ in); length 9·54 m (31 ft 3$\frac{19}{32}$ in); height 3·82 m (12 ft 6$\frac{13}{32}$ in); wing area 34·5 sq m (371·354 sq ft).

Weights: (K3M3) Empty 1,360 kg (2,998 lb); loaded 2,200 kg (4,850 lb); wing loading 63·8 kg/sq m (13·1 lb/sq ft); power loading 3·8 kg/hp (8·4 lb/hp).

Performance: (K3M3) Maximum speed 127 kt at 1,000 m (146 mph at 3,280 ft); climb to 5,000 m (16,405 ft) in 9 min 30 sec; service ceiling 6,390 m (20,965 ft); range 432 naut miles (497 st miles).

Production: A total of 624 K3Ms and derivatives were built as follows:

Mitsubishi Jukogyo K.K.:
 4 K3M1 (1930–31)
 70 K3M2 (1932–35)
 2 Ki-7 (1933)
 (1) MS-1 (1934)

Aichi Tokei Denki K.K.:
 247 K3M2

K.K. Watanabe Tekkosho:
 301 K3M3 (1939–41)

Reisen losses mounted alarmingly, as, in addition to combat losses arising from the Japanese attempt to throw back the first Allied amphibious operation, a large number of A6M3 Model 32s were lost because they had insufficient range. The Sakae 21 was found to have a higher fuel consumption than the Sakae 12, and furthermore the tank capacity had been reduced when this engine had been installed. At the request of operational units Mitsubishi fitted a 45 litre (9·9 Imp gal) tank in each wing outboard of the cannon bay, and in order to retain a low wing loading, in spite of the increased weight, the folding wingtips were again fitted. Still retaining the short designation A6M3 this version was known as the Navy Type 0 Carrier Fighter Model 22, or Model 22A (A6M3a) when long-barrel 20 mm Type 99 Model 2 Mk 3 cannon were installed. The installation of these wing tanks restored the range of the Reisen to its original level, but the Model 22 suffered heavy losses when modern Allied fighters such as the Lockheed P-38 Lightning, Chance-Vought F4U-1 Corsair and Supermarine Spitfire were introduced in the Pacific theatre. A small number of A6M3s were tested operationally at Rabaul with wing-mounted experimental 30 mm cannon.

When Allied Intelligence began to assign code names to Japanese aircraft the Reisen became known as the ZEKE. However, faulty identification and lack of co-operation with Intelligence officers in the China–Burma–India theatre of operation resulted in the temporary assignment of duplicate code names for the Reisen, RAY and BEN, but these were soon dropped in favour of ZEKE. Similarly, the name HAP—in honour of General Arnold, the US Army Air Forces' Chief of Staff—was first assigned to 'a new Japanese fighter with square wingtips', the A6M3 Model 32. HAP was changed for HAMP to spare General Arnold's feelings, but finally became ZEKE 32 when Allied Intelligence realized that the aircraft was not a new design but merely a version of the ZEKE. Partly as a result of the confusion existing in Intelligence circles and because Reisen's official Japanese designation was known early in the war, these various code names were not often used, and to this day this aircraft is better known as the Zero.

During the inconclusive Japanese strike in the Aleutians in June 1942, an A6M2 had made a forced landing on Akutan Island and the aircraft was captured by the Allies. Transported to San Diego, California, this A6M2 was repaired and tested, proving an invaluable prize for Allied technical intelligence. During exhaustive tests in the United States all qualities and weaknesses of the aircraft were carefully studied and the information passed to operational units which were able to improve their tactics against the nimble Nipponese fighter which had ruled the Pacific sky during the first six months of the war.

In Japan at that time Mitsubishi and the Navy were attempting to improve the Reisen. At low altitude it could still hold its own against Allied aircraft, but at medium and high altitude it was hopelessly outclassed by the Lightnings and Corsairs. In an attempt to correct this situation two A6M2s were modified by Dai-Ichi Kaigun Koku Gijitsusho

Captured Mitsubishi A6M3 Model 32 with flaps lowered. (*USAF.*)

at Yokosuka and, designated A6M4s, were powered by an experimental turbosupercharged Sakae engine. Major teething troubles with the experimental engine precluded the placing of a production order, and the Navy had to settle for an interim version of the aircraft, the A6M5, pending availability of the new Mitsubishi A7M Reppu. Delays in the development of the Reppu resulted in production of the interim A6M5 being continued until the end of the war.

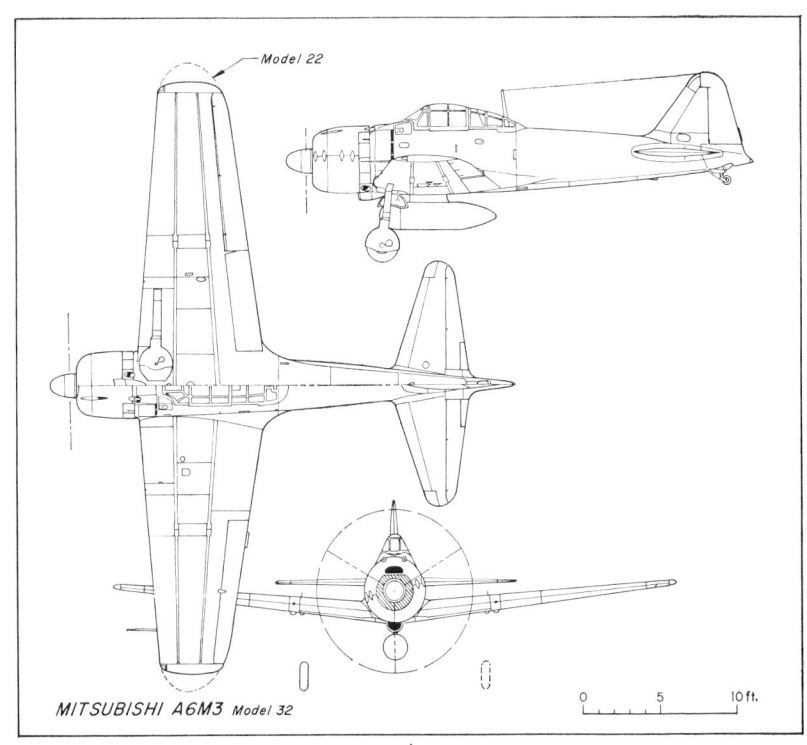

MITSUBISHI A6M3 Model 32

One of the main weaknesses of the early Reisen against the new Allied fighter aircraft was its insufficient diving speed, and often the Reisens lost sure victims as the Allied aircraft dived out of reach. To improve diving speed Mitsubishi modified the 904th A6M3 in August 1943 by fitting a new set of wings with heavier gauge skin and with redesigned non-folding rounded wingtips, reducing span to 11 m (36 ft $1\frac{1}{16}$ in) and wing area to 21·3 sq m (229·27 sq ft). The standard A6M3 armament, consisting of two 7·7 mm Type 97 machine-guns and two 20 mm Type 99 Model 2 Mk 3 cannon, was retained, as were the two 45 litre wing fuel tanks and the Sakae 21 engine, but new individual exhaust stacks providing some thrust augmentation were fitted. Although there was an increase in normal loaded weight of 416 lb, the A6M5 was faster than the A6M3 Model 32

A Mitsubishi A6M5 captured on Peleliu in the Central Pacific Area. White borders have been omitted from the Hinomarus. (*USAF.*)

and reached a maximum level speed of 351 mph at 19,685 ft—a gain of 13 mph, and could be dived at speeds up to 410 mph IAS. Put into production as the Navy Type 0 Carrier Fighter Model 52, the A6M5 was rushed to front-line units in the autumn of 1943 in time to meet the new threat presented by the appearance of the superlative Grumman F6F Hellcat. Although in performance the A6M5 could hold its own against the slightly less manoeuvrable Hellcat, the American fighter gained decisive superiority as it was more strongly built and better protected, and because its heavier armament tore easily through the light construction of the Nipponese fighter.

Appearing in prototype form in late 1943, the A6M5a began rolling off the Mitsubishi and Nakajima production lines in March 1944. This variant was fitted with a still heavier gauge wing skin which allowed a further increase in diving speed to 460 mph, armament being improved by replacing the drum-fed 20 mm Type 99 Model 2 Mk 3 cannon of 100 rpg with belt-fed 20 mm Type 99 Model 2 Mk 4 cannon of 125 rpg. The A6M5a Model 52A was soon followed by the A6M5b, jointly developed by Mitsubishi and Dai-Ichi Kaigun Kokusho to correct the two major weaknesses of the Reisen—insufficient armament and lack of armour and fuel tank protection. Armour glass was installed just behind the windshield glass, and the fuel tanks had automatic fire extinguishers. Also, one of the fuselage-mounted 7·7 mm Type 97 machine-guns was replaced with a 13·2 mm Type 3 machine-gun. Although the A6M5b Model 52B

A Mitsubishi A6M5 Navy Type 0 Carrier Fighter Model 52 on evaluation flight in the United States. The US markings have been partly painted out.

was probably the best version of the Reisen to see combat duty, its first operational sortie was a complete failure. Delivered to the fighter units serving aboard the carriers of the Third Koku Kantai in time to participate in Operation AGO, the battle of the Philippines, the A6M5bs suffered a crushing defeat at the hands of the US Navy Hellcats during the Marianas 'turkey shoot'.

When the Allies landed at Leyte most Japanese Navy fighter units were equipped with the A6M5, A6M5a and A6M5b. The Reisens were no match for the numerically and technically superior US fighters and many A6M5s with a 250 kg (551 lb) bomb fitted to the ventral drop tank rack were expended in kamikaze attacks starting on 25 October, 1944, when five Reisens of the Shikishima unit formed by volunteers of the 201st Kokutai sank the escort carrier *St Lo* and damaged the carriers

A captured Mitsubishi A6M5 Model 52.

Kalinin Bay, *Kitkun Bay* and *White Plains*. When finally the Philippines were secured by the Allies, most of the Reisens assigned to this campaign had been destroyed.

In Japan the development of the Reisen continued, as production of the Mitsubishi J2M Raiden was slow in gaining speed and the Mitsubishi A7M Reppu was not yet ready for production. The Japanese Navy was painfully aware of the obsolescence of the A6M, but the need for as many fighter aircraft as possible was too pressing to phase it out of production. The crushing defeat suffered during the battle of the Philippines resulted, on 23 July, 1944, in an urgent request from the Navy to modify the Reisen by (1) installing two additional 13·2 mm Type 3 machine-guns in the wing outboard of the cannon; (2) mounting an armour plate behind the pilot's seat; (3) fitting a 140 litre (30·8 Imp gal) self-sealing fuel tank behind the cockpit; and by (4) installing wing racks for unguided air-to-air missiles. Eitaro Sano, who had replaced Jiro Horikoshi as chief engineer for the Reisen programme, requested that the Mitsubishi Kinsei engine be substituted for the Sakae to cope with the anticipated weight increase, but the Navy refused to give its approval and instructed Mitsubishi to retain the

Mitsubishi A6M5a with green and white surrender markings. (*Peter Selinger*.)

Sakae 21 engine until the Sakae 31 with water-methanol injection became available. The first A6M5c, modified from an A6M5 airframe, was completed in September 1944. Following flight trials during which it was found necessary to increase the thickness of the wing covering in the area of the gun bays, the aircraft was put into production as the Navy Type 0 Carrier Fighter Model 52C. Mitsubishi built only 93 of these prior to delivering, in November 1944, the prototype of the A6M6c with water-methanol boosted Sakae 31 engine. Production of the A6M6c Model 53C was assigned to Nakajima, and self-sealing wing tanks were substituted for the previously unprotected tanks.

Although with the Sakae 31 a maximum speed of 346 mph was possible, performance often fell below this level as the engine suffered from teething troubles and as workmanship on airframe and engine deteriorated.

Operational units had developed a modification of the Reisen's drop tank fitting to carry a 250 kg (551 lb) bomb, permitting the aircraft to be used as fighter-bomber. When most of the large aircraft carriers were lost, the Navy instructed Mitsubishi to design a more reliable bomb rack and to produce a version of the Reisen suitable for use as a dive-bomber to operate from the smaller carriers. The A6M7 was designed to meet this requirement and differed from the A6M6c by the installation of the special bomb rack, a reinforced tailplane and the provision of two 350 litre (77 Imp gal) wing drop tanks attached outboard of the 13·2 mm machine-guns. Production of this aircraft as the Model 63 began in May 1945.

Apart from their use in growing numbers as a suicide attack aircraft, the Reisens still equipped most first-line fighter units when the war finally reached the Japanese homeland, and the lack of sufficient night fighters led to their use in yet another role. Some of the units operating at night, including the 302nd Kokutai, modified their A6M5s to mount an oblique-firing 20 mm cannon in the rear fuselage, the aircraft so modified being unofficially designated A6M5d-S.

The disappointing performance of the A6M5c and A6M6c finally convinced the Navy that they should yield to Mitsubishi's request to

A Mitsubishi A6M6c with the heavier armament carried by this late version of Reisen. (*Copyright 'Maru.'*)

MITSUBISHI A6M8

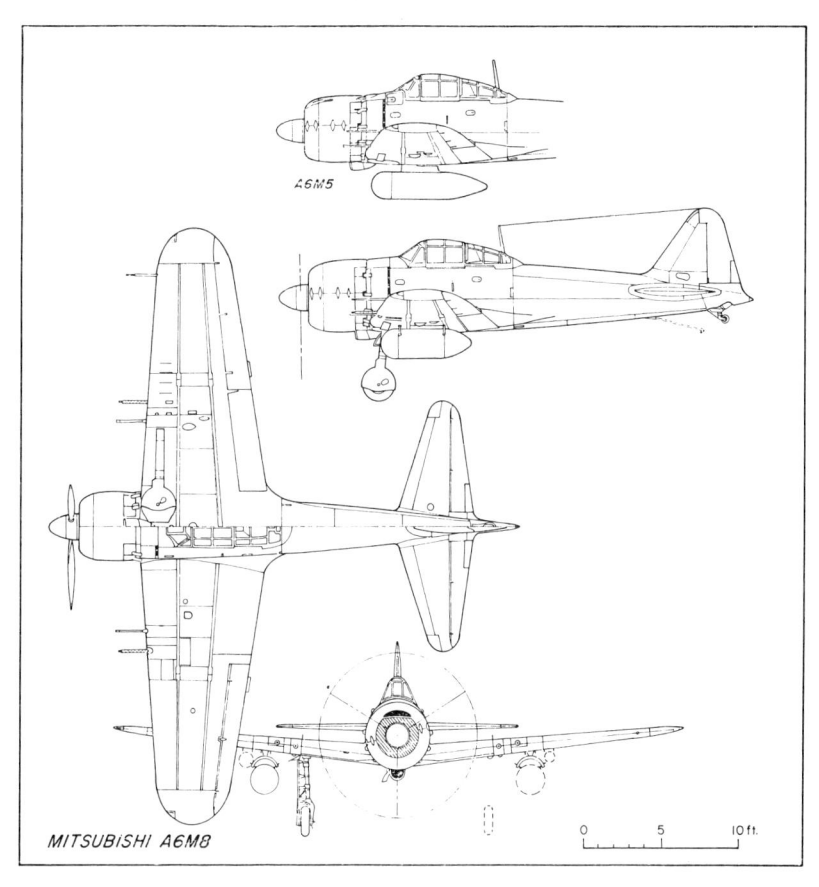

replace the Sakae engine with the more powerful Mitsubishi Kinsei and, as the Nakajima Musashi engine plant had ceased production of the Sakae to concentrate on production of the Homare, the manufacture of two Kinsei powered A6M8 prototypes was finally approved in November 1944. Using an airframe similar to that of the A6M7, the first A6M8 was completed in April 1945. The forward fuselage was redesigned to accommodate the 1,560 hp Mitsubishi MK8P Kinsei 62 which had a larger diameter than the Sakae engine, necessitating the removal of the fuselage-mounted guns. At the same time, the fuel tank fire-extinguishing system was also improved. After completion of the Service trials at Aomori, during which the oil-cooling system had to be revised, the A6M8 received top priority for production in dispersal plants as the Navy Type 0 Carrier Fighter Model 64. The Navy had hoped that the A6M8 would be able to meet the US Navy Hellcats on better terms, but none of the 6,300 production aircraft which had been ordered could be completed before the end of the war, due to the chaotic conditions then prevailing in the Japanese aircraft industry.

UNITS ALLOCATED

All wartime Japanese aircraft carriers; 2nd, 3rd, 6th, 12th, 202nd, 204th, 205th, 221st, 251st, 252nd, 261st, 281st, 302nd, 331st, 341st, 343rd, 381st, 601st, 652nd, 653rd, 721st, Genzan, Konoike, Oita, Tainan, Tsukuba, Yatabe and Southern Islands Kokutais.

TECHNICAL DATA

Description: Single-seat carrier-borne fighter, all-metal construction with fabric-covered control surfaces.
Accommodation: Pilot in enclosed cockpit.
Powerplant: One Mitsubishi Zuisei 13 fourteen-cylinder air-cooled radial, rated at 780 hp for take-off and 875 hp at 3,600 m (11,810 ft), driving a two- or three-blade metal propeller (A6M1).

One Nakajima NK1C Sakae 12 fourteen-cylinder air-cooled radial, rated at 940 hp for take-off and 950 hp at 4,200 m (13,780 ft), driving a three-blade metal propeller (A6M2).

One Nakajima NK1F Sakae 21 fourteen-cylinder radial rated at 1,130 hp for take-off, 1,100 hp at 2,850 m (9,350 ft) and 980 hp at 6,000 m (19,685 ft), driving a three-blade metal propeller (A6M3, A6M5, A6M5a, A6M5b and A6M5c).

One Nakajima Sakae 31 fourteen-cylinder air-cooled radial, rated at 1,130 hp for take-off, 1,100 hp at 2,850 m (9,350 ft) and 980 hp at 6,000 m (19,685 ft), driving a three-blade metal propeller (A6M6c and A6M7).

One Mitsubishi MK8P Kinsei 62 fourteen-cylinder radial, rated at 1,560 hp for take-off, 1,340 hp at 2,100 m (6,890 ft) and 1,180 hp at 5,800 m (19,030 ft), driving a three-blade metal propeller (A6M8).

Armament: Two 7·7 mm Type 97 machine-guns in the upper fuselage decking and two wing-mounted 20 mm Type 99 cannon. (A6M1, A6M2, A6M3, A6M5 and A6M5a).

One 7·7 mm Type 97 machine-gun and one 13·2 mm Type 3 machine-gun in the upper fuselage decking, and two wing-mounted 20 mm Type 99 cannon (A6M5b).

One 13·2 mm Type 3 machine-gun in the upper fuselage decking, two wing-mounted 13·2 mm Type 3 machine-guns and two wing-mounted 20 mm Type 99 cannon (A6M5c, A6M6c and A6M7).

Two wing-mounted 13·2 mm Type 3 machine-guns and two wing-mounted 20 mm Type 99 cannon (A6M8).

Two 7·7 mm Type 97 machine-guns in the upper fuselage decking and two wing-mounted 30 mm cannon (experimental installation on A6M3).

Two 7·7 mm Type 97 machine-guns in the upper fuselage decking, two wing-mounted 20 mm Type 99 cannon and one fuselage-mounted oblique-firing 20 mm Type 99 cannon (night fighter version of A6M5).

External Stores:
—Normal — two 60 kg (132 lb) bombs
—Suicide missions — one 250 kg (551 lb) bomb
—Maximum — one 500 kg (1,102 lb) bomb (A6M7 and A6M8)
—Air-to-air rockets — eight 10 kg (22 lb) or two 60 kg (132 lb) rockets (A6M6c and A6M8)
—Drop tanks — one 330 litre (72·6 Imp gal) (all versions except A6M7 and A6M8)
two 350 litre (77 Imp gal) (A6M7 and A6M8)

	A6M2 Model 21	A6M3 Model 32	A6M5 Model 52	A6M8 Model 64
Dimensions:				
Span	12 m (39 ft 4 7/16 in)	11 m (36 ft 1 1/8 in)	11 m (36 ft 1 1/8 in)	11 m (36 ft 1 1/8 in)
Length	9·06 m (29 ft 8 11/16 in)	9·06 m (29 ft 8 11/16 in)	9·121 m (29 ft 11 3/32 in)	9·237 m (30 ft 3 21/32 in)
Height	3·05 m (10 ft 0 1/8 in)	3·509 m (11 ft 6 5/32 in)	3·509 m (11 ft 6 5/32 in)	3·638 m (11 ft 11 7/32 in)
Wing area	22·44 sq m (241·541 sq ft)	21·53 sq m (231·746 sq ft)	21·3 sq m (229·27 sq ft)	21·3 sq m (229·27 sq ft)
Weights:				
Empty	1,680 kg (3,704 lb)	1,807 kg (3,984 lb)	1,876 kg (4,136 lb)	2,150 kg (4,740 lb)
Loaded	2,410 kg (5,313 lb)	2,544 kg (5,609 lb)	2,733 kg (6,025 lb)	3,150 kg (6,945 lb)

	A6M2 Model 21	A6M3 Model 32	A6M5 Model 52	A6M8 Model 64
Weights contd.:				
Maximum	2,796 kg (6,164 lb)	— —	— —	— —
Wing loading	107·4 kg/sq m (22 lb/sq ft)	118·1 kg/sq m (24·2 lb/sq ft)	128·3 kg/sq m (26·3 lb/sq ft)	147·9 kg/sq m (30·3 lb/sq ft)
Power loading	2·5 kg/hp (5·5 lb/hp)	2·3 kg/hp (5 lb/hp)	2·4 kg/hp (5·3 lb/hp)	2 kg/hp (4·4 lb/hp)
Performance:				
Maximum speed	288 kt at 4,550 m (331·5 mph at 14,930 ft)	294 kt at 6,000 m (338 mph at 19,685 ft)	305 kt at 6,000 m (351 mph at 19,685 ft)	309 kt at 6,000 m (356 mph at 19,685 ft)
Cruising speed	180 kt (207 mph)	200 kt (230 mph)	200 kt (230 mph)	— —
Climb to	6,000 m (19,685 ft)	6,000 m (19,685 ft)	6,000 m (19 685 ft)	6,000 m (19,685 ft)
in	7 min 27 sec	7 min 19 sec	7 min 1 sec	6 min 50 sec
Service ceiling	10,000 m (32,810 ft)	11,050 m (36,250 ft)	11,740 m (38,520 ft)	11,200 m (37,075 ft)
Normal range	1,010 naut miles (1,160 st miles)	— —	— —	— —
Maximum range	1,675 naut miles (1,930 st miles)	1,284 naut miles (1,477 st miles)	1,037 naut miles (1,194 st miles)	— —

Production: Conflicting production figures for the single-seat carrier- and land-based variants of the A6M have been reported by Mitsubishi, Nakajima and various Japanese Government agencies. The production figures based on the Japanese fiscal year appear to be the most accurate and are quoted below:

	Mitsubishi Jukogyo K.K.	Nakajima Hikoki K.K.	Total
Mar 1939–Mar 1942	722	115	837
Apr 1942–Mar 1943	729	960	1,689
Apr 1943–Mar 1944	1,164	2,268	3,432
Apr 1944–Mar 1945	1,145	2,342	3,487
Apr 1945–Aug 1945	119	885	1,004
	3,879	6,570	10,449

Production figures for the A6M2-N, A6M2-K and A6M5-K are reported separately in the appropriate sections of this book.

Mitsubishi G4M1 Navy Type 1 Attack Bomber Model 11. (*USAF.*)

Mitsubishi G4M

Built in larger numbers than any other Japanese bomber and flown in action from Australia to the Aleutians, and in use from the first day of the war until it transported the Japanese surrender delegation, the Navy Type 1 Attack Bomber—dubbed BETTY by the Allies—remains to this day the most famous Japanese bomber. Contemporary with the Reisen it shared fame and success with that aircraft during the first year of the war, when its stupendous range offset the small number in service and enabled the Japanese Navy to strike at Allied forces in their furthest retreats. However, when in the second half of 1942 the American forces took the offensive in the Solomons, the G4M was called upon to fight a defensive war in which range was no longer the most important factor.

The G4M's lack of armour and its unprotected fuel tanks made it a comparatively easy prey for the Allied fighters even though it carried heavy defensive armament, and soon the aircraft became known to friend and foe alike as the 'Flying Lighter'. In spite of this major shortcoming, not an oversight but the result of a requirement for maximum range which brought a new dimension to air–sea warfare, the Navy Type 1 Attack Bomber earned a place among the outstanding aircraft of World War II.

Development of the G4M series began in September 1937 when the Navy issued a 12-Shi specification to Mitsubishi, calling for a land-based attack bomber with a top speed of 215 kt at 3,000 m (247 mph at 9,845 ft) and a range of 2,600 naut miles (2,993 st miles) without bomb-load and a range of 2,000 naut miles (2,302 st miles) with an 800 kg torpedo (1,764 lb).

The aircraft, intended as a replacement for the Navy Type 96 Attack

Bomber which had made its début against China two months earlier, was to be powered by a pair of 1,000 hp radial engines and was to carry a crew of seven to nine. The task facing the design team, led by Kiro Honjo, was particularly difficult as both speed and range requirements exceeded those of the G3M1 which at that time had the best performance of any land-based naval bomber in the world. It soon appeared that these performance requirements could not be met with a total of only 2,000 hp as suggested by the Navy, and Kiro Honjo opted to power the aircraft with a pair of Mitsubishi Kasei, a new fourteen-cylinder air-cooled radial which was expected to develop a minimum of 1,500 hp for take-off. The two-spar wings were fitted with unprotected integral tanks with a total capacity of 4,900 litres (1,078 Imp gal), and were mid-set on a fat cigar-shaped semi-monocoque fuselage. The size and section of the fuselage were selected to facilitate crew movements in flight and to provide space for a bomb-bay under the wing centre-section, and its shape was dictated by the desire to facilitate mass production. The defensive armament, one of the major weaknesses of the G3M, was considerably increased over that of the Navy Type 96 Attack Bomber and included one 7·7 mm Type 92 machine-gun in a nose cone rotating mechanically through 360 degrees about the aircraft's axis, one flexible 7·7 mm Type 92 machine-gun in the dorsal blister, one flexible 7·7 mm Type 92 machine-gun in each of the port and starboard fuselage blisters behind the wing trailing edge and one hand-held flexible 20 mm Type 99 Model 1 cannon in a tail turret.

Inspections of a full-scale mock-up were held in August and September 1938, but construction of the prototype progressed slowly as the Mitsubishi engineering team had to share its time between two major projects, the Navy Experimental 12-Shi Carrier Fighter (A6M1) and the Navy Experimental 12-Shi Attack Bomber (G4M1). Powered by two 1,530 hp Mitsubishi Kasei 11 fourteen-cylinder air-cooled radials, the first G4M1 prototype was finally completed in September 1939 and was transferred to Kagamigahara Airfield to begin its flight test programme. On 23 October, 1939, the aircraft made its maiden flight with Mitsubishi test pilot Katsuzo

One of the two Mitsubishi G4M1s which carried the Japanese surrender delegation to Ie-Shima. The aircraft was painted white and carried green crosses. The aircraft in the background is a Boeing B-17H with droppable lifeboat. (*USAF.*)

Shima at the controls. The flight test results were highly encouraging, and only minor modifications had to be made prior to its delivery to the Yokosuka Experimental Air Corps for Service trials in January 1940. The second prototype, completed in February 1940 and delivered to the Navy during the following month, featured a vertical fin of increased area and was fitted with aileron tab balances. During performance testing this aircraft easily exceeded the official requirements and obtained the notable top speed of 240 kt (276 mph) and possessed a maximum range of 3,000 naut miles (3,453 st miles).

In spite of its remarkable performance the aircraft was not immediately placed in production for its intended role, due to the change in policy brought about by war experience in China. At that time, not having taken delivery of the Navy Type 0 Carrier Fighter Model 12 (Mitsubishi A6M2), the Navy did not have a fighter aircraft with sufficient range to escort its Navy Type 96 Attack Bombers on their raids deep into China. Bomber losses were heavy and, since late in 1938, the Yokosuka Experimental Air Corps was actively recommending that the G4M be fitted with heavy defensive armament to serve as 'wingtip' escort fighters for the bomb-carrying G3M2s. As a result, in 1939 production of the G4M1 was temporarily shelved in favour of the G6M1, a heavy escort fighter version of the aircraft. The bomb-bay was faired over and a ventral gondola housing two 20 mm Type 99 Model 1 cannon, one forward firing and one rearward, was mounted under the fuselage while a single 20 mm Type 99 Model 1 cannon, which could be fired from either side, replaced the two light machine-guns in the fuselage blister positions. The tail cannon and nose-mounted flexible machine-gun were retained while the dorsal machine-gun was eliminated; this brought total armament of the G6M1 to four 20 mm cannon and one 7·7 mm machine-gun. A large number of reserve ammunition drums were carried in the fuselage, increasing weight considerably and necessitating the reduction in fuel capacity to 3,640 litres (800 Imp gal) to maintain the take-off weight at 9,500 kg (20,944 lb). Thirty G6M1s, designated Navy Type 1 Wingtip Convoy Fighter, were built in 1940. However, the combat weight of the aircraft was too high, and the G6M1s were slower than the G3M2s once their warload had been dropped. Following limited training operations the type was modified as a crew trainer and redesignated Navy Type 1 Large Land Trainer (G6M1-K). Eventually it was again modified as Navy Type 1 Transport (G6M-L2) and used as a paratroop transport during the Pacific War.

Production of the original G4M1 bomber version was finally authorized in 1940 under the designation Navy Type 1 Attack Bomber Model 11, and the first production aircraft, preceded by thirteen Service trials aircraft, was completed in April 1941. Within six weeks the First Kokutai had completed its working-up period, and this unit took its G4M1s into operation with an attack on Chungking. During the summer of 1941, by which time the Chinese Air Force was putting up only token resistance, this unit operated with conspicuous success against targets deep in China.

Mitsubishi G4M2a with bulged bomb-bay doors.

On the eve of the Pacific War the Japanese Navy transferred twenty-seven G4M1s of the Kanoya Kokutai to bases in Indo-China to strengthen its air striking force poised to attack the battleships of Admiral Sir Tom Phillips, while retaining on Formosan bases ninety-three other Navy Type 1 Attack Bombers for operations against the American forces in the Philippines. Within a week of the initial Japanese attack these aircraft had effectively contributed to the sinking of HMS *Prince of Wales* and HMS *Repulse* and to eliminating American air power in the Philippines. Encountering only token fighter opposition, the G4M1s were able to provide support to Japanese ground forces and to deny naval reinforcement to the hard-pressed Allied forces in Southeast Asia Area. Soon the Navy Type 1 Attack Bomber began operations in the Netherlands East Indies, New Guinea and the Solomons, and on 19 February, 1942, they joined carrier-based aircraft in the first Japanese attack on Darwin. Up to that time the G4M1, nicknamed Hamaki (Cigar) by its crews because of the shape of the fuselage, had been remarkably successful, and was rapidly supplanting the older G3M2 in first-line units; but when the G4M1s began to attack targets around Port Moresby, losses rose sharply against increased fighter opposition as they carried neither armour nor fuel tank protection.

In an attempt partially to remedy these shortcomings Mitsubishi

A damaged Mitsubishi G4M2a of the 763rd Kokutai abandoned in the Philippines. (*US Navy Department.*)

Captured Mitsubishi G4M2a undergoing flight evaluation.

developed the Navy Type 1 Attack Bomber Model 12. This model, which retained the short designation of G4M1, was powered by a pair of Kasei 15 engines with increased power ratings at altitude to enable the aircraft to fly above the effective ceiling of light anti-aircraft guns. The lateral fuselage gun blisters were changed for glazed flush panels, and the shape of the tail cone, housing a flexible 20 mm cannon, was altered. The underside of the wing tanks was protected by rubber sheeting, and layers of rubber sheet and sponge protected the fuselage tanks. All tanks were fitted with carbon dioxide fire-extinguisher systems. As a result of the modifications the aircraft gross weight increased and performance deteriorated, maximum speed being reduced by some 5 kt (6 mph) and maximum range decreasing from 3,256 naut miles (3,749 st miles) to 3,086 naut miles (3,553 st miles). The ability of the aircraft to sustain battle damage was somewhat improved, but losses during the Solomons campaign remained heavy and included the two G4M1s carrying Admiral Isoroku Yamamoto and his staff which were shot down over Bougainville on 18 April, 1943.

In November 1942, the prototype of a new version, the G4M2, was completed. Featuring a new wing with laminar flow and powered by two 1,800 hp Mitsubishi MK4P Kasei 21s with water-methanol injection, this version had several modifications intended to improve performance, handling characteristics and armament. These included (1) increased tailplane area to improve stability; (2) rounded wing and tail tips; (3) greatly increased nose glazing area; (4) new bomb-aimer's window to improve night bombing accuracy; (5) the addition of a flexible 7·7 mm machine-gun firing through small ports on either side of the nose; (6) replacement of the dorsal gun blister by an hydraulically operated dorsal turret housing a 20 mm cannon; and (7) provision for an auxiliary fuselage tank increasing total fuel capacity by 350 Imp gal to 1,428 Imp gal (6,490 litres). The rest of the airframe was initially identical to that of the G4M1 Model 12, but the third G4M2 prototype was tested with bomb-bay doors, no such doors being used on the G4M1 when bombs or torpedoes were carried. This feature was incorporated as standard equipment on the 65th and subsequent G4M2s. In July 1943, following completion of its flight trials programme, the G4M2 was put into production at the Nagoya plant as the Navy Type 1 Attack Bomber Model 22. Production of the

G4M1 continued in the same plant until January 1944, but by that time sufficient Kasei 21s were available, and the G4M2 replaced the G4M1, a second G4M2 production line being set up at the Okayama plant. Two other versions of the G4M2 were built, the Model 22A in which the laterally positioned 7·7 mm machine-guns were replaced by 20 mm Type 99 Model 1 cannon, and the Model 22B in which all four 20 mm cannon were Type 99 Model 2.

In late 1943, as the high expectations of newer types of attack bombers, such as the Nakajima G5N1 Shinzan and Mitsubishi G7M1 Taizan, failed to materialize, the development of the basic G4M series was accelerated, and, after producing some 350 G4M2 Model 22, 22A and 22B, Mitsubishi began delivering the G4M2a. This aircraft was powered by two 1,850 hp Mitsubishi MK4T Kasei 25s with improved fuel consumption and fitted with bulged bomb-bay doors. Four versions were built: the Navy Type 1 Attack Bomber Model 24, of which only fourteen were built, carried the same defensive armament as the G4M2 Model 22; the G4M2a Model 24A and 24B carried respectively the same armament as the G4M2 Model 22A and 22B; while the G4M2a Model 24C was identical to the Model 24B except that the 7·7 mm machine-gun in the nose was supplemented by a 13 mm Type 2 machine-gun. The main production types were the G4M2a Model 24B and Model 24C, and late production aircraft were fitted with air-surface radar.

Experimental versions built in 1943 and 1944 included the single G4M2b Model 25, the second G4M2a prototype modified to flight test the Mitsubishi MK4V Kasei 27, two G4M2c Model 26s used to test the turbosupercharged MK4T-B Ru Kasei 25b Ru, while the third G4M2 prototype was tested with a pair of MK4T-B Kasei 25b engines. Yet another version of the G4M2 series was to acquire fame as the carrier for the MXY7 Navy Suicide Attacker—Ohka. A substantial number of G4M2a Model 24B and 24C aircraft had their bomb-bay doors removed and were fitted with special shackles to carry the Ohka piloted missile. This modification was redesignated G4M2e Model 24J. This aircraft was very heavy and had poor handling characteristics when carrying the Ohka and proved an easy target for Allied fighter aircraft.

From the summer of 1943 onwards the G4M2s and G4M2as began to

Captured Mitsubishi G4M2a Navy Type 1 Attack Bomber Model 24. (*USAF.*)

supplement the G4M1s in front-line units, and by October 1944, when American forces landed on Leyte, the G4M1s had been relegated to training, transport and maritime reconnaissance duties. During the Philippines campaign of 1944 and the air–sea battles off Formosa, the Mariana and Ryuku archipelagos, the Navy Type 1 Attack Bombers Model 22 and 24 suffered heavy losses during almost suicidal attacks against Allied naval task forces. Further south the G4M2s based on Timor kept up constant pressure against Australian forces at Darwin, but there also the losses were disproportionate to results achieved. While the G4M2s and G4M2as remained in service until the Japanese surrender, the Ohka-carrying G4M2es saw only limited action as on 21 March, 1945, sixteen of the aircraft taking part in the first Ohka sortie were shot down before being able to fly their piloted missiles to the launching point.

Mitsubishi G4M3s of the Yokosuka Kokutai. This version had dihedral tailplanes and modified tail turrets.

The propensity of the G4M1 and G4M2 to catch fire easily when hit led to excessive combat losses. To remedy this major shortcoming Mitsubishi undertook in November 1942 to redesign the aircraft, emphasis being placed on fuel tank and crew protection. The wing construction was changed to a single-spar structure housing self-sealing rubber tanks with a capacity of only 4,490 litres (988 Imp gal) against a capacity of 6,490 litres (1,428 Imp gal) for the G4M2, with armour plating throughout the crew areas. The tail turret was modified to a design similar to that used on contemporary American aircraft, and the consequent reduction in fuselage length resulted in the forward shift of the centre of gravity, this in turn necessitating the adoption of dihedral on the horizontal tail surfaces to restore the aircraft's stability. Designated the G4M3 Model 34, the first of three prototypes was completed in January 1944, and limited production began in October 1944. The G4M3a Model 34A was a proposed version with revised armament and was eventually intended for transport and anti-submarine duties. The final development of the aircraft took place in January 1945 when the third and fifteenth G4M3s were each re-engined with two 1,825 hp MK4T-B Ru Kasei 25b Ru with exhaust driven turbo-superchargers as prototypes for the G4M3 Model 36. These aircraft were still undergoing flight trials when the war ended.

MITSUBISHI G4M3

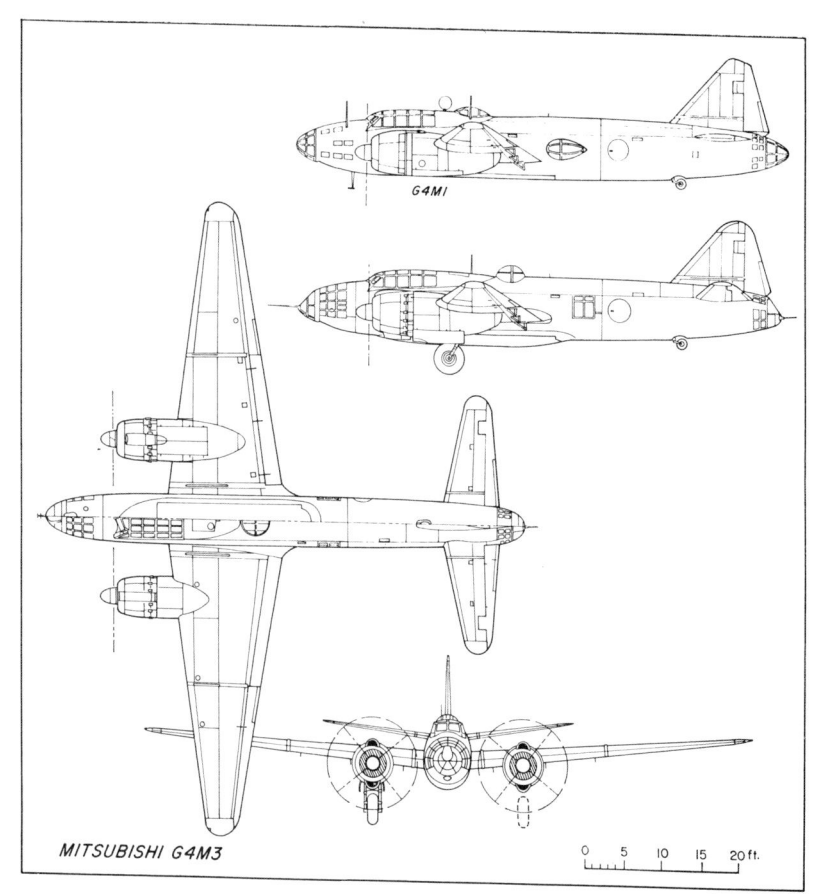

On 19 August, 1945, four days after the cessation of hostilities, two all-white G4M1s bearing green crosses flew to Ie-Shima with the Japanese surrender delegation led by Lieut-General Torashiro Kawabe. Japan and the G4M were finally ready for peace.

UNITS ALLOCATED

1st, 4th, 702nd, 705th, 706th, 721st, 722nd, 751st, 752nd, 753rd, 755th, 761st, 762nd, 763rd, 765th, 951st, 1021st, Chitose, Genzan, Kanoya, Kisarazu, Misawa, Takao and Yokosuka Kokutais.

TECHNICAL DATA

Description: Twin-engined land-based bomber (G4M), heavy escort fighter (G6M1), bomber crew trainer (G6M1-K) or transport (G6M1-L2). All-metal construction with fabric-covered control surfaces.

Accommodation: (G4M) Normal crew of seven. (G6M1) Crew of ten.

Powerplant: Two 1,530 hp Mitsubishi MK4A Kasei 11 fourteen-cylinder air-cooled radials rated at 1,530 hp for take-off, 1,410 hp at 2,000 m (6,560 ft) and 1,340 hp at 4,000 m (13,125 ft), driving three-blade metal propellers (12-Shi prototypes, G4M1 Model 11 and G6M1).

Two Mitsubishi MK4E Kasei 15 fourteen-cylinder air-cooled radials rated at 1,530 hp for take-off, 1,400 hp at 2,600 m (8,530 ft) and 1,280 hp at 6,000 m (19,685 ft), driving three-blade metal propellers (G4M1 Model 12).

Two Mitsubishi MK4P Kasei 21 fourteen-cylinder air-cooled radials rated at 1,800 hp for take-off, 1,575 hp at 1,800 m (5,905 ft) and 1,410 hp at 4,800 m (15,750 ft), driving four-blade metal propellers (G4M2 Model 22, 22A and 22B).

Two Mitsubishi MK4T Kasei 25 fourteen-cylinder air-cooled radials rated at 1,825 hp for take-off, 1,680 hp at 2,100 m (6,890 ft) and 1,540 hp at 5,500 m (18,045 ft), driving four-blade metal propellers (G4M2a Model 24, 24A and 24B, G4M2e Model 24J, G4M3 Model 34 and G4M3a Model 34A).

Two Mitsubishi MK4T-B Kasei 25b fourteen-cylinder air-cooled radials rated at 1,825 hp for take-off, driving four-blade metal propellers (G4M2d Model 27).

Two Mitsubishi MK4T-B Ru Kasei 25b Ru fourteen-cylinder air-cooled radials rated at 1,825 hp for take-off and 1,500 hp at 7,200 m (23,620 ft), driving four-blade metal propellers (G4M2c Model 26 and G4M3 Model 36).

Two Mitsubishi MK4V Kasei 27 fourteen-cylinder air-cooled radials rated at 1,795 hp for take-off, 1,670 hp at 2,600 m (8,530 ft) and 1,480 hp at 6,580 m (21,590 ft), driving four-blade metal propellers (G4M2b Model 25).

	G4M1 Model 11	G4M2 Model 22	G4M3 Model 34	G6M1
Dimensions:				
Span	25 m (82 ft 0¼ in)	25 m (82 ft 0¼ in)	25 m (82 ft 0¼ in)	25 m (82 ft 0¼ in)
Length	20 m (65 ft 7 43/48 in)	20 m (65 ft 7 43/48 in)	19·5 m (63 ft 11 23/32 in)	20 m (65 ft 7 43/48 in)
Height	6 m (19 ft 8 7/32 in)	6 m (19 ft 8 7/32 in)	6 m (19 ft 8 7/32 in)	6 m (19 ft 8 7/32 in)
Wing area	78·125 sq m (840·927 sq ft)	78·125 sq m (840·927 sq ft)	78·125 sq m (840·927 sq ft)	78·125 sq m (840·927 sq ft)
Weights:				
Empty	6,800 kg (14,991 lb)	8,160 kg (17,990 lb)	8,350 kg (18,409 lb)	7,000 kg (15,432 lb)
Loaded	9,500 kg (20,944 lb)	12,500 kg (27,558 lb)	12,500 kg (27,558 lb)	9,500 kg (20,944 lb)
Wing loading	121·6 kg/sq m (24·9 lb/sq ft)	160 kg/sq m (32·8 lb/sq ft)	160 kg/sq m (32·8 lb/sq ft)	121·6 kg/sq m (24·9 lb/sq ft)
Power loading	3·1 kg/hp (6·8 lb/hp)	3·5 kg/hp (7·7 lb/hp)	3·4 kg/hp (7·6 lb/hp)	3·1 kg/hp (6·8 lb/hp)
Performance:				
Maximum speed	231 kt at 4,200 m (266 mph at 13,780 ft)	236 kt at 4,600 m (272 mph at 15,090 ft)	254 kt at 5,150 m (292 mph at 16,895 ft)	—
Cruising speed	170 kt at 3,000 m (196 mph at 9,845 ft)	170 kt at 4,000 m (196 mph at 13,125 ft)	170 kt at 4,000 m (196 mph at 13,125 ft)	—
Climb to	7,000 m (22,965 ft)	8,000 m (26,245 ft)	7,000 m (22,965 ft)	—
in	18 min	30 min 24 sec	20 min 10 sec	—
Service ceiling	—	8,950 m (29,365 ft)	9,220 m (30,250 ft)	—
Maximum range	3,256 naut miles (3,749 st miles)	3,270 naut miles (3,765 st miles)	2,340 naut miles (2,694 st miles)	—

Production: A total of 2,446 G4Ms and G6M1s were built by Mitsubishi Jukogyo K.K. as follows:

  2 12-Shi prototypes (Nagoya plant Sept 1939 and Feb 1940)
  30 G6M1 (Nagoya plant 1940)
  1,200 G4M1 (Nagoya plant Jan 1941–Jan 1944)
  1,154 G4M2 (Nagoya plant 640 aircraft and Okayama plant 514 aircraft Nov 1942–Aug 1945)
  60 G4M3 (Nagoya and Okayama plants Dec 1943–Aug 1945)

G4M Armament:

	Nose	Dorsal blister	Dorsal turret	Beam blisters/ beam hatches	Tail turret	Ventral Gondola Forward-firing	Rear-firing
12-Shi prototypes G4M1 Model 11 G4M1 Model 12	7·7 mm × 1 Type 92	7·7 mm × 1 Type 92	—	7·7 mm × 2 Type 92	20 mm × 1 Type 99 Model 1	—	—
G4M2 Model 22 G4M2a Model 24 G4M2b Model 25 G4M2d Model 27 G4M3 Model 34	7·7 mm × 2 Type 92	—	20 mm × 1 Type 99 Model 1	7·7 mm × 2 Type 92	20 mm × 1 Type 99 Model 1	—	—
G4M2 Model 22A G4M2a Model 24A G4M3a Model 34A	7·7 mm × 2 Type 92	—	20 mm × 1 Type 99 Model 1	20 mm × 2 Type 99 Model 1	20 mm × 1 Type 99 Model 1	—	—
G4M2 Model 22B G4M2a Model 24B G4M2e Model 24J G4M2c Model 26 G4M3 Model 36	7·7 mm × 2 Type 92	—	20 mm × 1 Type 99 Model 2	20 mm × 2 Type 99 Model 2	20 mm × 1 Type 99 Model 2	—	—
G4M2a Model 24C	13 mm × 1 Type 2 7·7 mm × 1 Type 92	—	20 mm × 1 Type 99 Model 2	20 mm × 2 Type 99 Model 2	20 mm × 1 Type 99 Model 2	—	—
G6M1	7·7 mm × 1 Type 92	—	—	20 mm × 1 Type 99 Model 1	20 mm × 1 Type 99 Model 1	20 mm × 1 Type 99 Model 1	20 mm × 1 Type 99 Model 1

Bomb-load —one 800 kg (1,764 lb) torpedo or similar load of bombs (G4M1)
—one 800 kg (1,764 lb) torpedo or up to 1,000 kg (2,205 lb) of bombs (G4M2 and G4M3)
—one Navy Special Attacker Ohka Model 11 (G4M2e)
—none (G6M1)

A pair of Mitsubishi J2M3 Raiden (Thunderbolt) Model 21s captured by British Forces and seen over Malaya. (*Imperial War Museum*.)

Mitsubishi J2M Raiden (Thunderbolt)

The Japanese Navy's decision to stress speed and rate of climb rather than manoeuvrability and range as the most important requirements for a new land-based interceptor fighter was a bold departure from their established procedure and indicated remarkable insight on the part of the Naval Staff. Development of this new specialized weapon in the Japanese armoury began in October 1938, when Jiro Horikoshi held preliminary discussions with the technical staff of the JNAF, but its realization was to be plagued by numerous delays.

For almost a year the project was kept in limbo as Jiro Horikoshi and his team were kept fully occupied with the development of the Mitsubishi A6M1, and consequently the official 14-Shi specification was not drawn up until September 1939. The specification called for a single-seat, single-engined interceptor fighter with a maximum speed of 600 km/h at 6,000 m (373 mph at 19,685 ft). The aircraft was required to climb to 6,000 m in less than 5½ min; to have a landing speed of not more than 130 km/h (81 mph); to take-off in overload, no-wind conditions, in 300 m (984 ft); and to have an endurance of 45 minutes at full rated power. Armament was to be identical to that of the A6M2, but for the first time the Navy requested that armour plating be incorporated behind the pilot's seat. No mention of manoeuvrability requirements were made in the specification, and the choice of engine was left to Jiro Horikoshi.

After evaluating the respective advantages of the 1,200 hp Aichi Atsuta twelve-cylinder liquid-cooled engine and the 1,430 hp Mitsubishi Kasei fourteen-cylinder radial engine, Jiro Horikoshi decided to select the more powerful engine in spite of its larger frontal area and higher fuel consumption. To minimize drag the large Kasei 13 radial was fitted with an extension shaft and an air-driven fan allowing the use of a fully tapered cowling of comparatively narrow cross section. A low aspect ratio wing of laminar section was selected and combat flaps were fitted to improve manoeuvrability. Further attention to drag reduction resulted in the adoption of an extremely shallow curved windscreen canopy. Design of the aircraft progressed rapidly, but development problems with the engine cooling system and the laminar flow aerofoil section, combined with the priority given to the development of the A6M series, delayed the completion of the first prototype J2M1, which also bore the Service Aeroplane Development Programme number M-20, until February 1942.

The first flight took place at Kasumigaura on 20 March, 1942, with Mitsubishi test pilot Katsuzo Shima at the controls. Technical difficulties soon began to interrupt the flight test programme. The main undercarriage members, which initially could not be retracted at speeds in excess of 100 mph, were twice modified, but as the aircraft possessed good stability and controllability the Navy decided to go ahead with its Service trials at Suzuka Naval Air Base. As was to be expected from the manufacturer's test pilots' reports the J2M1 was severely criticized by the Naval pilots who were adamant in their complaints of distorted vision on landing, caused by the sloping windscreen. The propeller pitch change mechanism proved unreliable, speed and rate of climb fell well below specification and visibility from the cockpit was found insufficient. As a result the Navy instructed Mitsubishi to modify the fourth aircraft and try to improve the overall characteristics.

The first modification consisted of replacing the shallow extended curved windscreen with a more conventional unit with optically flat bullet-proof panels. The troublesome Kasei 13 and its complicated extension shaft was replaced by a MK4R-A Kasei 23a modified to incorporate the fan cooling system and fitted with individual exhaust stacks and water-methanol

A captured Mitsubishi J2M3 Navy Interceptor Fighter Raiden Model 21 in April 1945. (*US Navy Department.*)

A Mitsubishi J2M3 in front of the partly completed underground final assembly building at Atsugi. (*USAF.*)

injection. With the new engine, the length of the nose could be reduced, further improving the pilot's view during landing, and Mitsubishi were confident that the J2M2 would meet the Navy requirements.

These hopes appeared to be vindicated when the J2M2 was accepted for production as the Navy Interceptor Fighter Raiden (Thunderbolt) Model 11 in October 1942. Unfortunately, protracted troubles with the Kasei 23a, the first Japanese-developed engine with water-methanol injection, constantly delayed the programme. Excessive emission of smoke at maximum rated power was eliminated by adjusting the fuel and water-methanol injection systems, but engine vibration proved a more difficult problem to solve. At certain engine and propeller speeds critical and uncontrollable vibration frequency occurred. This was finally eradicated by improved engine mounting shock dampers and propeller modifications. The combined effect of these teething troubles, and the production priorities given to the A6M, resulted in an extremely slow delivery rate, and at the end of the fiscal year 1942–43 (March 1943), six months after the aircraft had been accepted for production, only fourteen aircraft, including the three

A Mitsubishi J2M3 Raiden Model 21 abandoned on Dewey Boulevard in the suburbs of Manila. On the left is a Mitsubishi A6M. (*US Navy Department.*)

J2M1 prototypes, had been delivered. Production was finally picking up when two incidents within three months caused new delays.

The first of these, in which the second J2M2 and its pilot were lost, occurred shortly after take-off on 16 June, 1943, and Mitsubishi engineers were at a loss to explain its cause. A month later, the tenth J2M2 suffered the same trouble, but the pilot was successful in regaining control of the aircraft by promptly lowering the undercarriage. Examination of this aircraft revealed that the tailwheel struts had pressed against the torque tube lever after retraction, jamming the controls in the dive position. Once the cause had been found, the controls were properly modified to prevent occurrence of similar accidents, and the Raiden Model 11 was ready for initial deliveries to the 381st Kokutai at Toyohashi, southeast of Nagoya in Aichi Prefecture.

A dramatic view of a captured Mitsubishi J2M3 Raiden. (*USAF.*)

Unfortunately, delivery to an operational unit did not end teething troubles, and with several new models under development the production rate remained low for wartime, 141 aircraft being produced in the fiscal year 1943–44. Concurrent with the formation of the 381st Kokutai, the first J2M3 was produced. Still powered by the Kasei 23a, the J2M3 was characterized by a stronger wing housing four 20 mm Type 99 cannon—two Model 2 cannon with projecting muzzles and two slower firing Model 1s completely within the wing, the fuselage-mounted machine-guns being

J2M4

MITSUBISHI J2M3

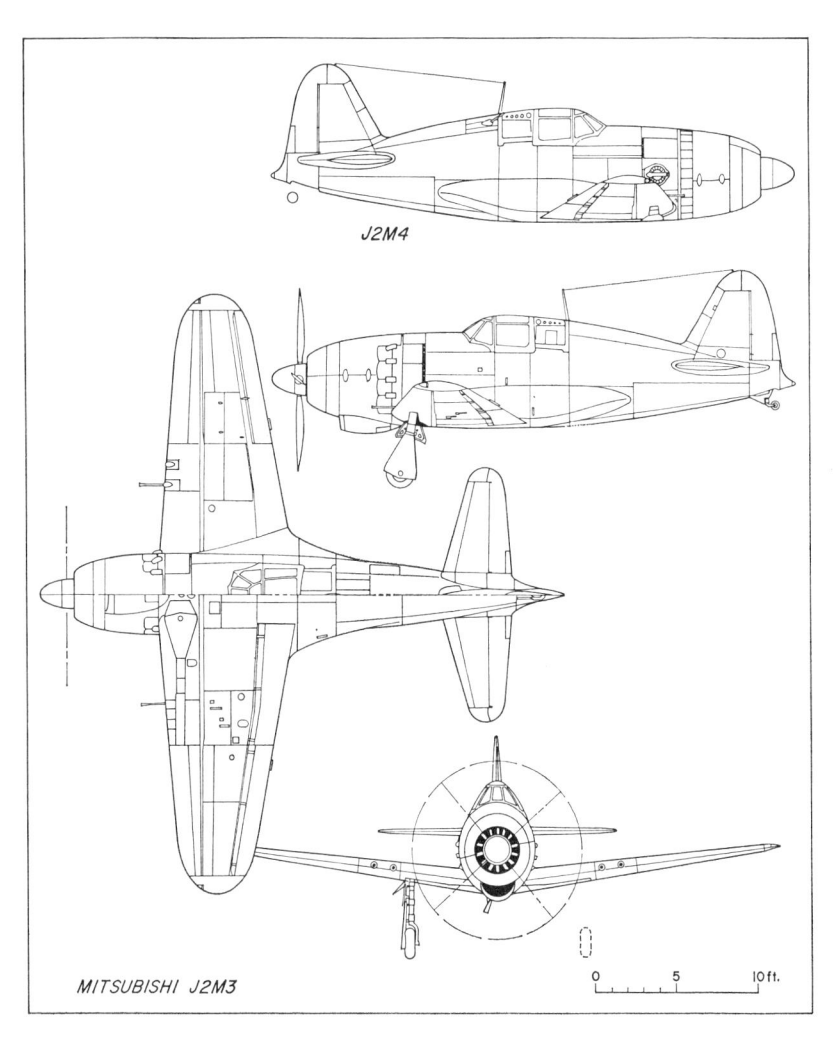

Three almost completed Mitsubishi J2M3s found by United States Forces at Atsugi in September 1945. (*USAF.*)

Mitsubishi MK4R-A Kasei 23a installation in a Mitsubishi J2M3 Raiden (Thunderbolt). (*USAF.*)

dispensed with. Manufactured initially alongside the J2M2, the J2M3 Model 21 soon supplanted it and became the major production model of the Raiden series. Service pilots still complained about the poor lateral and rear visibility, and performance, which with the J2M2 had almost reached the specification requirements, once again fell below par when the heavier but better armed Raiden Model 21 was built. Accordingly in June 1944, the Navy decided to adopt the faster Kawanishi Shinden as its main interceptor fighter and to continue Raiden production at reduced pace until the Mitsubishi Reppu could be placed in production. However this decision did not prevent the realization of two additional variants of the Raiden with better high-altitude performance.

The most ambitious of these two variants was the J2M4 Model 34 powered by a turbosupercharged MK4R-C Kasei 23c. Mounted in the fuselage behind the cockpit and fitted with a large air intake on the port side of the cowling, the turbosupercharger allowed the rated power of 1,420 hp to be maintained up to 9,200 m (30,185 ft) instead of only 4,800 m (15,750 ft) as on the standard Kasei 23a. Room was still found in the fuselage to mount two oblique-firing 20 mm cannon. Capable of reaching a speed of 362 mph at 30,185 ft, the J2M4 would have been a valuable addition to the units attempting to ward off the B-29s which flew over Japan at altitudes exceeding the practical combat ceiling of most Japanese fighter aircraft, but teething troubles with the complex turbosupercharger forced the cancellation of the project after the completion of only two

J2M4s. The second high-altitude version of the Raiden, the J2M5 Model 33, proved more successful. Retaining the airframe of the J2M4 with its wider and roomier cockpit offering improved visibility, the J2M5 was powered by a MK4U-A Kasei 26a with a mechanically-driven, three-stage supercharger, and was the fastest version of the Raiden, reaching a speed of 382 mph at 22,310 ft.

By the time the J2M5, which had begun its test programme in May 1944, had completed its Service trials, the war situation had again materially deteriorated for Japan, which was now being bombed by the USAAF Boeing B-29s. As a result the Raiden was again in great demand, and the J2M5 version was placed in production at the Koza Kaigun Kokusho (Koza Naval Air Arsenal) while Mitsubishi built 260 Raiden Model 21s and some thirty-four Raiden Model 33s, bringing total production by the parent company to 476 aircraft.

Several other versions were built or designed by Mitsubishi, but all differed only in minor details from the major production models. The J2M3a Model 21A, of which twenty-one were built, was identical to the J2M3 except that the two wing-mounted 20 mm Type 99 Model 1 cannon were replaced by two 20 mm Type 99 Model 2 cannon carried in under-wing pods. By fitting the J2M3 airframe with the wider cockpit and with the domed canopy of the J2M5, one J2M6 Model 31 was built. A similar modification of the J2M3a, never realized, would have produced the J2M6a Model 31A. The projected J2M7 Model 23 was to be a variant of the J2M3 airframe mounting the Kasei 26a, while the J2M5a Model 33A and the

Turbosupercharger installation in experimental Mitsubishi J2M4.
(*US Navy Department.*)

J2M7a Model 23A were to be externally similar machines with Kasei 26a engines, domed cockpit canopies and four 20 mm Type 99 Model 2 cannon. The J2M5a was to be built as a new aircraft, while the J2M7a was a planned modification of the J2M3 airframe, but neither of these was built prior to the end of the war. A final version designed to overcome the pilots' persistent complaints of poor visibility was to feature a cut-down rear fuselage and a canopy similar to that of the Zero Fighter—but the project remained on the drawing board.

Although a small number of Raidens had been deployed to the Philippines, where they earned the code name JACK, they were mainly used in the defence of Japan. In this role its good performance, powerful armament and adequate protection as the attributes of a successful fighter were at last recognized by their pilots who preferred it to all other Japanese operational fighters as a bomber destroyer. During the hectic months preceding the end of the war, field units frequently modified the aircraft, and oblique-firing 20 mm cannon, such as those tested on the J2M4, were often mounted on experimental Raidens. Persistently plagued by technical troubles and indecision over the future of its production, the Raidens, fortunately for the Allies, were too few and too late.

UNITS ALLOCATED

302nd, 332nd, 352nd, 381st, Genzan and Tainan Kokutais.

TECHNICAL DATA

Description: Single-seat interceptor fighter. All-metal construction with fabric-covered control surfaces.
Accommodation: Pilot in enclosed cockpit.
Powerplant: One Mitsubishi MK4C Kasei 13 fourteen-cylinder air-cooled radial, rated at 1,430 hp for take-off, 1,400 hp at 2,700 m (8,860 ft) and 1,260 hp at 6,100 m (20,015 ft), driving a three-blade constant-speed metal propeller (J2M1).

One Mitsubishi MK4R-A Kasei 23a fourteen-cylinder air-cooled radial, rated at 1,800 hp for take-off, 1,575 hp at 1,800 m (5,905 ft) and 1,410 hp at 4,800 m (15,750 ft), driving a four-blade constant-speed metal propeller (J2M2, J2M3, J2M3a, J2M6 and J2M6a).

One Mitsubishi MK4R-C Kasei 23c fourteen-cylinder air-cooled radial, rated at 1,820 hp for take-off, and 1,420 hp at 9,200 m (30,185 ft), driving a four-blade constant-speed metal propeller (J2M4).

One Mitsubishi MK4U-4 Kasei 26a fourteen-cylinder air-cooled radial, rated at 1,820 hp for take-off, 1,510 hp at 2,800 m (9,185 ft), 1,400 hp at 6,800 m (22,310 ft) and 1,310 hp at 7,200 m (23,295 ft), driving a four-blade constant-speed metal propeller (J2M5, J2M5a, J2M7 and J2M7a).

Armament: Two 7·7 mm Type 97 machine-guns in the upper fuselage decking and two wing-mounted 20 mm Type 99 Model 2 cannon (J2M1 and J2M2).

Two wing-mounted 20 mm Type 99 Model 2 cannon and two wing-mounted 20 mm Type 99 Model 1 cannon (J2M3, J2M5, J2M6 and J2M7).

Four wing-mounted 20 mm Type 99 Model 2 cannon (J2M3a, J2M5a, J2M6a and J2M7a).

Two fuselage-mounted oblique-firing 20 mm Type 99 Model 1 cannon, two wing-mounted 20 mm Type 99 Model 2 cannon and two wing-mounted 20 mm Type 99 Model 1 cannon (J2M4 and field modification of some J2M3s).

External stores: two 60 kg (132 lb) bombs, or two 200 litre (44 Imp gal) drop tanks.

Production: A total of 476 aircraft were built by Mitsubishi Jukogyo K.K. In addition a number of J2M5s were built by the Koza Kaigun Kokusho (Koza Naval Air Arsenal). Production at Mitsubishi's Nagoya and Suzuka plants was as follows:

3 J2M1 prototypes	2 J2M4 prototypes
155 J2M2 production aircraft	34 J2M5 production aircraft
260 J2M3 production aircraft	1 J2M6 production aircraft
21 J2M3a production aircraft	

	J2M1	J2M2	J2M3	J2M4	J2M5
Dimensions:					
Span	10·8 m (35 ft 5·⁵⁄₁₆ in)	10·8 m (35 ft 5·⁵⁄₁₆ in)	10·8 m (35 ft 5·⁵⁄₁₆ in)	10·8 m (35 ft 5·⁵⁄₁₆ in)	10·8 m (35 ft 5·⁵⁄₁₆ in)
Length	9·9 m (32 ft 5·¾ in)	9·695 m (31 ft 9·¹⁄₁₆ in)	9·945 m (32 ft 7·³¹⁄₃₂ in)	10·145 m (33 ft 3·¹⁹⁄₃₂ in)	9·945 m (32 ft 7·³¹⁄₃₂ in)
Height	3·82 m (12 ft 6·³³⁄₆₄ in)	3·875 m (12 ft 8·⁵⁄₆₄ in)	3·945 m (12 ft 11·⁵⁄₁₆ in)	3·945 m (12 ft 11·⁵⁄₁₆ in)	3·945 m (12 ft 11·⁵⁄₁₆ in)
Wing area	20·05 sq m (215·816 sq ft)	20·05 sq m (215·816 sq ft)	20·05 sq m (215·816 sq ft)	20·05 sq m (215·816 sq ft)	20·05 sq m (215·816 sq ft)
Weights:					
Empty	2,191 kg (4,830 lb)	2,348 kg (5,176 lb)	2,460 kg (5,423 lb)	2,823 kg (6,202 lb)	2,510 kg (5,534 lb)
Loaded	2,861 kg (6,307 lb)	3,210 kg (7,077 lb)	3,435 kg (7,573 lb)	3,947 kg (8,702 lb)	3,482 kg (7,676 lb)
Wing loading	142·7 kg/sq m (29·2 lb/sq ft)	160·1 kg/sq m (32·8 lb/sq ft)	171·3 kg/sq m (35·1 lb/sq ft)	196·9 kg/sq m (40·3 lb/sq ft)	173·7 kg/sq m (35·6 lb/sq ft)
Power loading	2 kg/hp (4·4 lb/hp)	1·8 kg/hp (3·9 lb/hp)	1·9 kg/hp (4·2 lb/hp)	2·2 kg/hp (4·8 lb/hp)	1·9 kg/hp (4·2 lb/hp)
Performance:					
Maximum speed	312 kt at 6,000 m (359 mph at 19,685 ft)	322 kt at 5,450 m (371 mph at 17,880 ft)	317 kt at 5,300 m (365 mph at 17,390 ft)	315 kt at 9,200 m (362 mph at 30,185 ft)	332 kt at 6,800 m (382 mph at 22,310 ft)
Cruising speed	—	—	190 kt (219 mph)	200 kt (230 mph)	200 kt (230 mph)
Climb to	—	6,000 m (19,685 ft)	6,000 m (19,685 ft)	10,000 m (32,810 ft)	6,000 m (19,685 ft)
in	—	5 min 38 sec	6 min 14 sec	19 min 30 sec	6 min 20 sec
Service ceiling	11,000 m (36,090 ft)	—	11,700 m (38,385 ft)	11,550 m (37,895 ft)	11,250 m (36,910 ft)
Normal range	—	—	1,025 naut miles (1,180 st miles)	500 naut miles (575 st miles)	680 naut miles (783 st miles)

Mitsubishi A6M2-K two-seat advanced trainer version of Reisen (Zero Fighter).

Mitsubishi A6M2-K and A6M5-K

Although during the second World War many of the fighting powers developed two-seat trainer versions of some of their first-line single-seat aircraft (e.g. Focke-Wulf Fw 190A-8/U1, Republic TP-47G, Fiat G.50B), none of these nations, except for the Soviet Union and Japan, made much use of these aircraft. In Japan the Navy became the champion of the two-seat fighter trainer, and already in the early thirties the Nakajima A3N1, a two-seat version of the Navy Type 90 Carrier Fighter, had been built for that purpose. During the war two-seat trainer versions of the Mitsubishi A5M4, Kawanishi N1K2-J and Mitsubishi A6M2 and A6M5 were built to fill the gap in the training programme between the Navy Type 93 Intermediate Trainer and the operational single-seat fighter aircraft.

Designed by the engineering staff of the Dai-Nijuichi Kaigun Kokusho at Omura, near Sasebo, to a 17-Shi specification, the first A6M2-K was completed in November 1943. Much of the A6M2 airframe was retained and modifications included the fitting of a new two-seat cockpit with dual controls and the mounting of small horizontal fins on the rear fuselage sides to improve spin recovery characteristics. To save weight the two wing-mounted 20 mm cannon and the main wheel covers were removed. Powered by the standard Nakajima Sakae 12, the A6M2-K completed its flight test programme successfully and was placed in production at the Dai-Nijuichi Kaigun Kokusho starting in late 1943, and at the Hitachi Kokuki K.K. starting in May 1944.

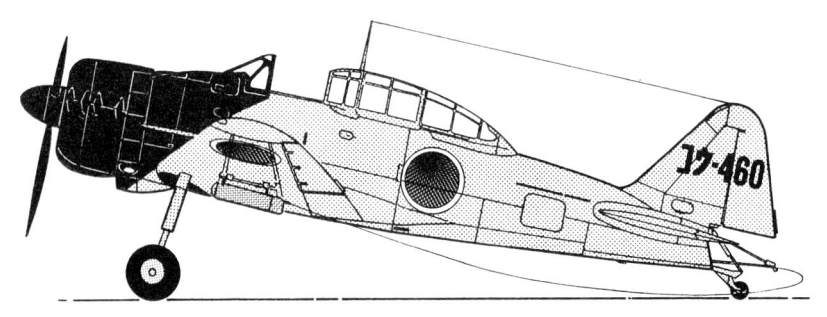

Mitsubishi A6M2-K, of the Konoike Kokutai, modified for target towing.

Development of a similar two-seat trainer based on the A6M5 airframe began at the Dai-Nijuichi Kaigun Kokusho in August 1944, and the first of seven experimental A6M5-K, built by Hitachi Kokuki K.K., was completed in March 1945. Except for the fitting of a Sakae 21 with individual exhaust stacks and the use of the shorter A6M5 wing with a span of 11 m (36 ft $1\frac{1}{16}$ in) and an area of 21·3 sq m (229·27 sq ft), the A6M5-K was identical to the A6M2-K.

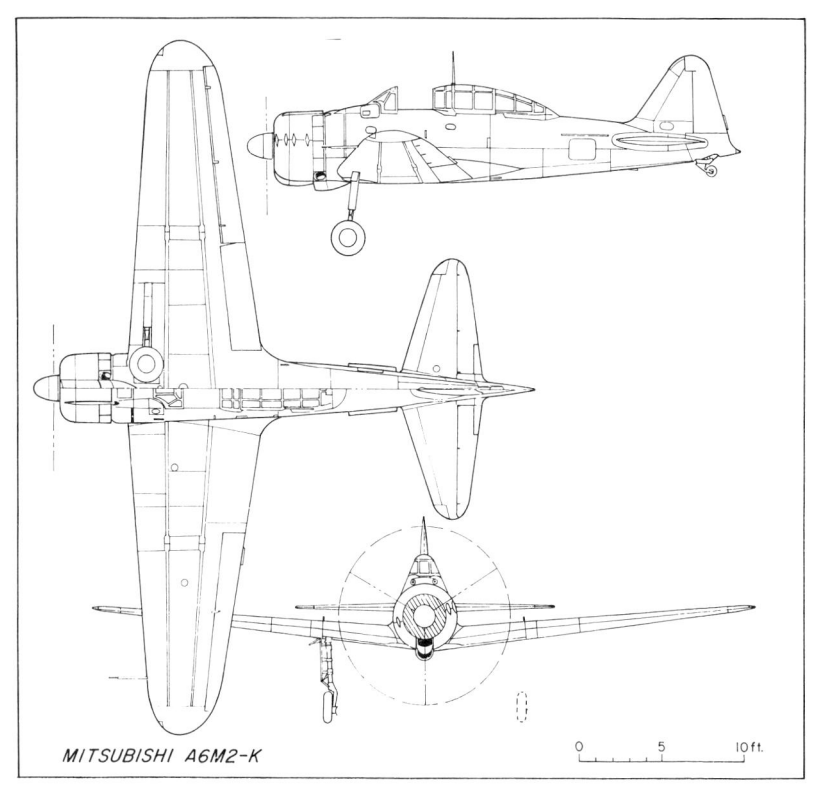

MITSUBISHI A6M2-K

UNITS ALLOCATED

Konoike and Yatabe Kokutais.

TECHNICAL DATA

Description: Two-seat fighter trainer, all-metal construction with fabric-covered control surfaces.

Accommodation: Student pilot and instructor seated in tandem in partially enclosed cockpit.

Powerplant: One Nakajima NK1C Sakae 12 fourteen-cylinder air-cooled radial, rated at 940 hp for take-off and 950 hp at 4,200 m (13,780 ft), driving a three-blade constant-speed metal propeller (A6M2-K).

One Nakajima NK1F Sakae 21 fourteen-cylinder air-cooled radial rated at 1,130 hp for take-off, 1,100 hp at 2,850 m (9,350 ft) and 980 hp at 6,000 m (19,685 ft), driving a three-blade constant-speed metal propeller (A6M5-K).

Armament: Two fuselage-mounted 7·7 mm Type 97 machine-guns.

External stores—normal, two 60 kg (132 lb) bombs

—suicide, one 250 kg (551 lb) bomb

Dimensions: (A6M2-K) Span 12 m (39 ft 4$\frac{7}{16}$ in); length 9·15 m (30 ft 0¼ in); height 3·535 m (11 ft 7$\frac{3}{16}$ in); wing area 22·44 sq m (241·541 sq ft).

Weights: (A6M2-K) Empty 1,819 kg (4,010 lb); loaded 2,334 kg (5,146 lb); maximum 2,627 kg (5,792 lb); wing loading 104 kg/sq m (21·3 lb/sq ft); power loading 2·5 kg/hp (5·5 lb/hp).

Performance: (A6M2-K) Maximum speed 476 km/h at 4,000 m (296 mph at 13,125 ft); cruising speed 345 km/h (214 mph); climb to 6,000 m (19,685 ft) in 7 min 56 sec; service ceiling 10,180 m (33,400 ft); normal range 745 naut miles (860 st miles).

Production: A total of 515 A6M2-K and A6M5-K were built as follows:

Dai-Nijuichi Kaigun Kokusho at Omura (Sasebo):

236 A6M2-K (Nov 1943–Aug 1945)

Hitachi Kokuki K.K.:

272 A6M2-K (May 1944–Aug 1945)
7 A6M5-K (Mar–Aug 1945)

Mitsubishi A7M Reppu (Hurricane)

Even though as early as 1940 the Japanese Navy had foreseen the need to develop a new type of carrier-borne fighter to replace the Mitsubishi A6M Reisen, and they had issued to this effect a 16-Shi specification, the overburdened Mitsubishi company could only deliver a single production aircraft meeting this requirement prior to the end of the war. From its inception, the programme ran into difficulties through shortage of design staff, and preoccupation with modifications to production types forced the Naval Staff to withdraw the 16-Shi specification. The project was revived in April 1942 when Mitsubishi were instructed to begin the design of the M-50 Reppu (Hurricane) shipboard fighter to a 17-Shi specification. As three years would be required before the aircraft could be delivered to operational units, Jiro Horikoshi insisted that the Mitsubishi MK9A or MK9B eighteen-cylinder air-cooled engine, then under development with the company's designation A-20, be selected to ensure that the aircraft would have the necessary performance to engage successfully all types of aircraft expected to be encountered in 1945. Following preliminary discussions between Mitsubishi and the Navy, the 17-Shi specification was officially issued on 6 July, 1942. Requirements included: (1) maximum speed 345 kt at 6,000 m (397 mph at 19,685 ft); (2) climb to 6,000 m (19,685

Mitsubishi Navy Experimental 17-Shi Carrier Fighter Reppu (Hurricane). (*US Navy Department.*)

ft) in less than 6 min; (3) endurance of 2½ hr at 250 kt (288 mph) plus 30 min at maximum power rating; (4) dive speed of 450 kt (518 mph); (5) manoeuvrability at least equal to that of the A6M3 Model 32; and (6) armament of two 20 mm cannon and two 13·2 mm machine-guns. Disregarding Jiro Horikoshi's statement that the required performance could only be attained by use of the Mitsubishi MK9A or MK9B engine, the Navy first elected to postpone its engine selection for the M-50 Reppu until April 1943, but in September 1942 the Navy instructed Mitsubishi to install in it the lower powered NK9K Homare.

Powered by the Homare 22 and fitted with self-sealing petrol tanks, bullet-proof windshield and armour plate behind the pilot's seat, the first prototype Reppu, now bearing the short designation A7M1, was not completed until April 1944, as the Mitsubishi engineering team was required to give priority to the development of newer variants of the A6M and the J2M. The A7M1 was a large aircraft having a wing span of 14 m (45 ft 11$\frac{3}{16}$ in) and a wing area of 30·86 sq m (332·173 sq ft), almost half as much again as that of the A6M5 Model 52, and hydraulically operated folding outer wing panels had to be fitted to allow the use of the aircraft aboard carriers.

On 6 May, 1944, the first A7M1 made its maiden flight with Eisaku Shibayama at the controls. With the exception of minor landing gear troubles the flight was successful, and three weeks later the aircraft was handed over to the Navy for Service trials. The Service pilots commented favourably on the aircraft's stability and handling characteristics and reported that with the use of the specially designed combat flaps the A7M1 was as manoeuvrable as the Reisen. Unfortunately, Jiro Horikoshi's warnings that with the Homare 22 the aircraft would be underpowered were well founded. At 6,000 m (19,685 ft) the engine developed only 1,300 hp against a calculated rating of 1,700 hp and at this altitude maximum speed was only 300–310 knots (345–357 mph). Similarly the climb to 19,685 ft took 10 to 11 min whereas the specification had called for not more than 6 min. As a result of this poor performance, on 30 July, 1944, the Navy decided to suspend further trials and Mitsubishi were instructed to stop work on the third to sixth prototypes which were then on the production lines. Soon after this Jiro Horikoshi succeeded in obtaining the Navy's authorization to install the Mitsubishi MK9A engine on the sixth airframe, which became the first prototype of the A7M2 series.

The MK9A had a larger diameter than the Homare 22, and its installation necessitated complete redesign of the forward fuselage, work being completed in October 1944, and the A7M2 made its first flight on the 13th of that month. It soon became apparent that the Navy had at last found a potential successor to the A6M Reisen. Plans were immediately made to start mass production of the aircraft, as the Navy Carrier Fighter Reppu Model 22, at Mitsubishi's Oe Airframe Works at Nagoya and Nankai Works in Osaka. Production aircraft, armed with either four 20 mm Type 99 Model 2 cannon or two 20 mm Type 99 Model 2 cannon and two 13·2 mm Type 3 machine-guns, were expected to reach a maximum speed of 339 knots at 6,600 m (390 mph at 21,655 ft) and hopes ran high in the Navy that the supremacy of the US Navy F4U-1 Corsairs and F6F-5 Hellcats would soon be challenged, but misfortunes continued to plague the Japanese programme. In December 1944 a violent earthquake in the Nagoya area was soon followed by massive bombing raids by B-29s in which the Daiko engine plant, responsible for the manufacture of the MK9A, was severely damaged. Later, the second A7M2 prototype was lost in a landing accident while the first, third and fifth were destroyed on the ground by US aircraft. As the war ended, only the fourth, sixth and seventh prototypes were still in flying condition, and only one production aircraft (Allied code name SAM) had been completed.

Development of an Otsu (B) Type Land-based Interceptor Fighter, based on the Reppu, was initiated in February 1944. Emphasis was placed on increased rate of climb and maximum speed at high altitude, while armament was to include four wing-mounted 30 mm Type 5 cannon, with two similar weapons mounted at an oblique angle in the aft fuselage. To meet these requirements the fuselage had to be modified extensively and the wing thickness increased to mount the heavier weapons and larger main

Mitsubishi A7M2 Reppu with Mitsubishi MK9A engine. (*US Navy Department.*)

Front view of Mitsubishi A7M2 Reppu without propeller. (*US Navy Department*.)

wheels. Designated A7M3-J Model 34, the aircraft was to be powered by a turbosupercharged version of the MK9A. A maximum speed of 350 kt (403 mph) was expected to be reached at 10,000 m (32,810 ft), this altitude being attained in 15 min. Engineering drawings for the A7M3-J were completed in November 1944, and a mock-up was inspected by the Navy in February 1945. A prototype was planned for completion in October 1945, but work on the aircraft was stopped when Japan surrendered.

As the Japanese industry had acquired only limited experience in the field of turbosupercharged engines, a further variant of the Reppu, the A7M3 Model 23, was designed around the Mitsubishi MK9C with a

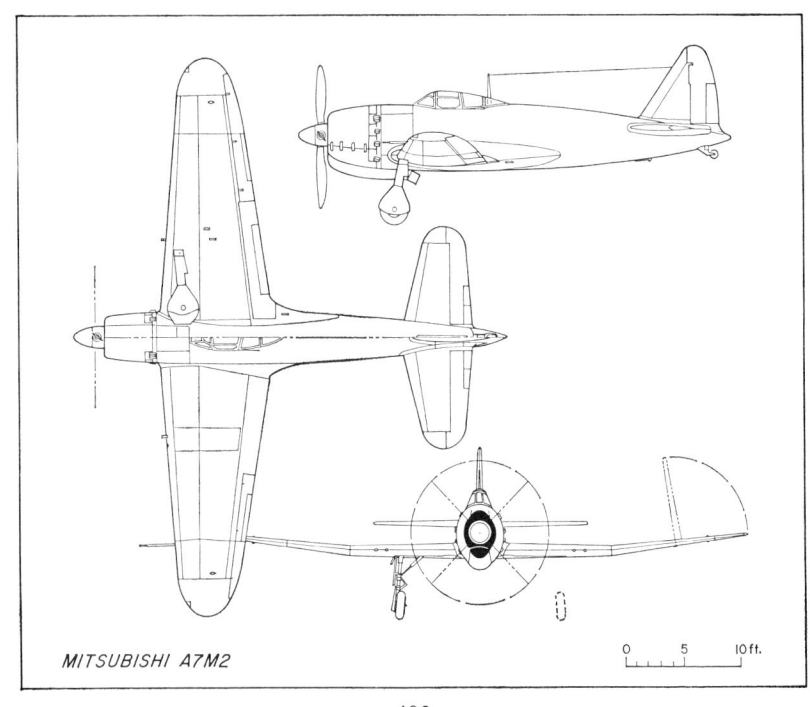

MITSUBISHI A7M2

mechanically-driven three-speed supercharger. While the A7M3-J required a major redesign of the Reppu airframe, the A7M3 was designed around the standard A7M2 airframe. Modifications were to include the elimination of the folding wing mechanism and the installation of an additional fuel tank in the aft fuselage. Pilot protection was also to be improved by fitting bullet-proof glass behind the seat. With an armament of six wing-mounted 20 mm Type 99 Model 2 cannon, the A7M3 Model 23 was intended to reach a maximum speed of 347 kt at 8,700 m (399 mph at 28,545 ft), but the first prototype, scheduled for completion in December 1945, was still under construction when war ended.

Another derivative of the Reppu, named Rifuku (Land Wind), was being jointly developed by Mitsubishi and Nakajima to meet the requirements of a 20-Shi specification calling for a Ko(A) Type Carrier Fighter, issued on 7 April, 1945. The Rifuku was to make use of the A7M3-J airframe and was to be powered by either a Nakajima [Ha-41] 21 or a Nakajima [Ha-44] 13. This aircraft was still in its initial design stage when Japan surrendered.

TECHNICAL DATA

Description: Single-seat carrier-borne or land-based fighter (A7M1, A7M2 and A7M3), or land-based interceptor fighter (A7M3-J). All-metal construction with fabric-covered control surfaces.

Accommodation: Pilot in enclosed cockpit.

Powerplant: One Nakajima NK9K Homare 22 eighteen-cylinder air-cooled radial, rated at 2,000 hp for take-off, and 1,570 hp at 6,850 m (22,475 ft), driving a four-blade constant-speed metal propeller (A7M1).

One Mitsubishi MK9A eighteen-cylinder air-cooled radial rated at 2,200 hp for take-off, 2,070 hp at 1,000 m (3,280 ft) and 1,800 hp at 6,000 m (19,685 ft), driving a four-blade constant-speed metal propeller (A7M2).

One Mitsubishi MK9C eighteen-cylinder air-cooled radial rated at 2,250 hp for take-off, 2,000 hp at 1,800 m (5,905 ft), 1,800 hp at 5,000 m (16,405 ft) and 1,660 hp at 8,700 m (28,545 ft), driving a four-blade constant-speed metal propeller (A7M3).

One Mitsubishi [Ha-43] 11 Ru eighteen-cylinder air-cooled radial rated at 2,200 hp for take-off, 2,130 hp at 6,800 m (22,310 ft) and 1,920 hp at 10,300 m (33,795 ft), driving a four-blade constant-speed metal propeller (A7M3-J).

Armament: Two wing-mounted 13·2 mm Type 3 machine-guns and two wing-mounted 20 mm Type 99 Model 2 cannon (A7M1 and A7M2).

Four wing-mounted 20 mm Type 99 Model 2 cannon (A7M2).

Six wing-mounted 20 mm Type 99 Model 2 cannon (A7M3).

Two fuselage-mounted oblique-firing 30 mm Type 5 cannon and four wing-mounted 30 mm Type 5 cannon (A7M3-J).

External load: two 250 kg bombs (551 lb) or two 350 litre (77 Imp gal) drop tanks.

	A7M1	A7M2	A7M3	A7M3-J
Dimensions:				
Span	14 m	14 m	14 m	14 m
	(45 ft 11 $\frac{3}{16}$ in)	(45 ft 11 $\frac{3}{16}$ in)	(45 ft 11 $\frac{3}{16}$ in)	(45 ft 11 $\frac{3}{16}$ in)
Length	10·995 m	11 m	11m	11·964 m
	(36 ft 0$\frac{7}{8}$ in)	(36 ft 1 $\frac{1}{16}$ in)	(36 ft 1 $\frac{1}{16}$ in)	(39 ft 0 $\frac{1}{16}$ in)
Height	4·28 m	4·28 m	4·28 m	4·28 m
	(14 ft 0$\frac{1}{2}$ in)	(14 ft 0$\frac{1}{2}$ in)	(14 ft 0$\frac{1}{2}$ in)	(14 ft 0$\frac{1}{2}$ in)
Wing area	30·86 sq m	30·86 sq m	30·86 sq m	31·3 sq m
	(332·173 sq ft)	(332·173 sq ft)	(332·173 sq ft)	(336·909 sq ft)

	A7M1	A7M2	A7M3	A7M3-J
Weights:				
Empty	3,110 kg	3,226 kg	3,392 kg	3,955 kg
	(6,856 lb)	(7,112 lb)	(7,478 lb)	(8,719 lb)
Loaded	4,410 kg	4,720 kg	5,040 kg	5,732 kg
	(9,722 lb)	(10,406 lb)	(11,111 lb)	(12,637 lb)
Wing loading	142·9 kg/sq m	152·9 kg/sq m	163·3 kg/sq m	183·1 kg/sq m
	(29·3 lb/sq ft)	(31·3 lb/sq ft)	(33·4 lb/sq ft)	(37·5 lb/sq ft)
Power loading	2·2 kg/hp	2·1 kg/hp	2·2 kg/hp	2·6 kg/hp
	(4·9 lb/hp)	(4·7 lb/hp)	(4·9 lb/hp)	(5·7 lb/hp)
Performance:				
Maximum speed	310 kt at 6,190 m	339 kt at 6,600 m	347 kt at 8,700 m	350 kt at 10,000 m
	(357 mph at	(390 mph at	(399 mph at	(403 mph at
	20,310 ft)	21,655 ft)	28,545 ft)	32,810 ft)
Cruising speed	—	225 kt at 4,000 m	—	—
	—	(259 mph at	—	—
		13,125 ft)		
Climb to	6,000 m	6,000 m	10,000 m	10,000 m
	(19,685 ft)	(19,685 ft)	(32,810 ft)	(32,810 ft)
in	9 min 54 sec	6 min 7 sec	13 min 6 sec	15 min
Service ceiling	—	10,900 m	11,300 m	11,500 m
	—	(35,760 ft)	(37,075 ft)	(37,730 ft)
Endurance	—	2·5 hr at cruising	—	—
	—	speed + 30 min	—	—
		combat		

Production: A total of 10 A7Ms were built by Mitsubishi Jukogyo K.K. at Nagoya as follows:

    2 A7M1 prototypes
    7 A7M2 prototypes and Service trials aircraft
    1 A7M2 production aircraft

Mitsubishi J8M Shusui (Sword Stroke)

The arrival of the B-29 Superfortress over Japan suddenly created an urgent need for a fast-climbing interceptor fighter, a weapon long neglected by the Japanese armed forces. Fortunately for them, their Military Attachés in Germany had been aware of the development of the Messerschmitt Me 163B, a spectacular rocket-powered fighter and, in late 1943, had obtained for Japan the manufacturing rights for the German machine and its Walter HWK 109-509 engine. Unfortunately, one of the two submarines taking to Japan technical data on the Me 163B and its engine was sunk en route and only incomplete data were taken back by Cdr Eiichi Iwaya. In spite of this setback the Japanese Navy issued a 19-Shi specification, in July 1944, covering the development of a rocket-powered interceptor fighter inspired by the German aircraft. The task of designing and producing the aircraft was assigned to Mitsubishi. From its inception the project became a joint Navy–Army venture as the Army intended to adopt the aircraft,

A Mitsubishi J8M1 Shusui (Sword Stroke) rocket fighter, captured by United States Forces.

while modifications of the Walter HWK 109-509 motor to Japanese production techniques was carried out as a joint Navy–Army–Mitsubishi project.

Design of the aircraft, designated J8M1 by the Navy and Ki-200 by the Army, proceeded rapidly under the direction of Mijiro Takahashi of Mitsubishi, and a mock-up was completed in September 1944. Three weeks later the final mock-up was inspected and approved by both Services, clearing the way for construction of prototypes.

Shortly after instructing Mitsubishi to undertake the design of the J8M1, the Navy had initiated at their Dai-Ichi Kaigun Koku Gijitsusho (First Naval Air Technical Arsenal), in Yokosuka, the development of a full-scale glider version which was intended to provide data on the handling characteristics of the tailless J8M1 and to be used for the training of J8M1 pilots. The first prototype of the tailless glider, designated MXY8 Akigusa (Autumn Grass), was completed in December 1944, and the aircraft was transported to Hyakurigahara Airfield in Ibaragi Prefecture where its flight trials programme began on 8 December.

For its first flight the Akigusa was towed to altitude by a Kyushu K10W1 of the 312th Kokutai, and was piloted by Lieut-Cdr Toyohiko Inuzuka, the J8M1 project pilot. Notwithstanding its unusual configuration, the MXY8 handled satisfactorily and two additional prototypes were built at Yokosuka, one being delivered to the Rikugun Kokugijutsu Kenkyujo (Army Aerotechnical Research Institute), at Tachikawa, for evaluation by the Army. Production of a heavier version of the MXY8, intended as a training glider for J8M1 pilots and fitted with water ballast tanks to approximate the weight of the operational aircraft, was undertaken for the Navy by Maeda Koku Kenkyujo (Maeda Aircraft Institute) and for the Army by Yokoi Koku K.K. (Yokoi Aircraft Co) as the Ku-13 Training

MITSUBISHI J8M1

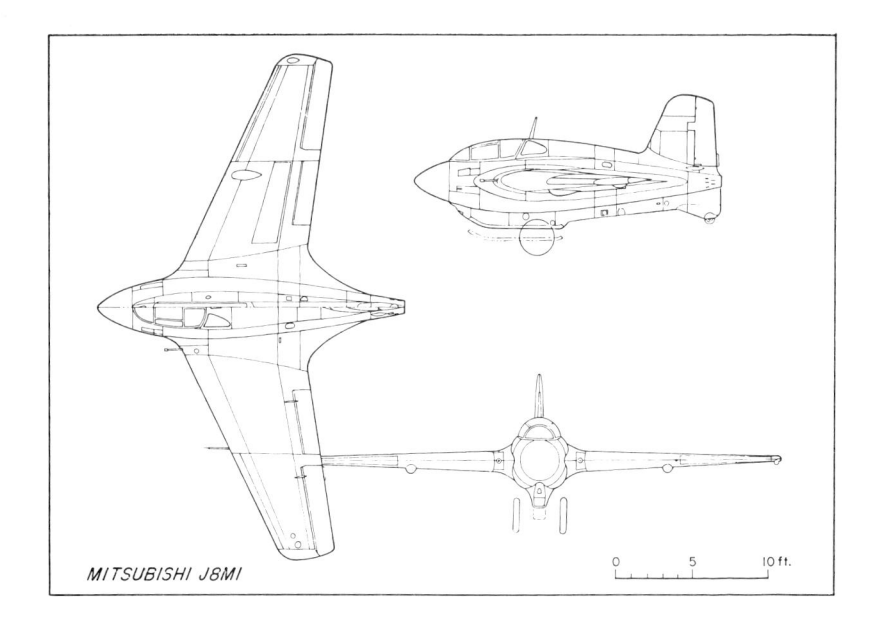

Glider. The Navy also planned to build the MXY9 Shuka (Autumn Fire), a modified version powered by a 200 kg (441 lb) thrust Tsu-11 ducted fan engine, but none were completed before the Japanese surrender.

To assess more extensively the handling characteristics of the fully-loaded Shusui, Mitsubishi completed the first two J8M1s with ballast replacing the rocket motor and its fuel. Towed by a Nakajima B6N1 the first aircraft was flown at Hyakurigahara beginning on 8 January, 1945, and confirmed the soundness of the design whilst powered prototypes were being readied under the designations J8M1 Navy Experimental Rocket-Powered Interceptor Fighter Shusui and Ki-200 Army Experimental Rocket-Powered Interceptor Fighter Shusui. The first prototype for the Navy was completed at Nagoya in June 1945 and was transferred to Yokoku for final checks. On 7 July, 1945, the J8M1 was ready to start flight trials, but on its maiden flight the engine failed during the steep climb after take-off and the aircraft crashed, killing its pilot, Lieut-Cdr Toyohiko Inuzuka. The fuel system of the sixth and seventh prototypes was being modified when the war ended, and no other J8M1 or Ki-200 was tested. At the end of the war Shusui production was already under way, and the Navy had instructed Mitsubishi, Nissan and Fuji to produce two versions of the aircraft, the J8M1 armed with two 30 mm Type 5 cannon, and the J8M2 Shusui-Kai in which one of the wing-mounted cannon was replaced by additional fuel tanks. An enlarged version of the Ki-200 with increased fuel tankage, the Ki-202 developed by the Rikugun Kokugijutsu Kenkyujo, had been selected by the Army as their priority interceptor project.

Yokosuka MXY8 Akigusa (Autumn Grass). (*Edward T. Maloney.*)

TECHNICAL DATA

Description: Single-seat short-range rocket-powered interceptor fighter (J8M, Ki-200 and Ki-202) or tailless glider (MXY8 and Ku-13). Mixed construction.

Accommodation: Pilot in enclosed cockpit.

Powerplant: One 1,500 kg (3,307 lb) thrust Toko Ro.2 (KR10) bi-fuel liquid rocket (J8M, Ki-200 and Ki-202).

Armament: Two wing-mounted 30 mm Type 5 cannon (J8M1).

One wing-mounted 30 mm Type 5 cannon (J8M2).

Two wing-mounted 30 mm Ho-105 cannon (Ki-200 and Ki-202).

Dimensions: (J8M1) Span 9·5 m (31 ft 2 in); length 6·05 m (19 ft 10 $\frac{3}{16}$ in); height 2·7 m (8 ft 10 $\frac{3}{16}$ in); wing area 17·73 sq m (190·843 sq ft).

Weights: (J8M1) Empty 1,505 kg (3,318 lb); loaded 3,885 kg (8,565 lb); wing loading 219·1 kg/sq m (44·9 lb/sq ft).

Performance: (J8M1) Maximum speed 900 km/h at 10,000 m (559 mph at 32,810 ft); climb to 10,000 m (32,810 ft) in 3 min 30 sec; service ceiling 12,000 m (39,370 ft); powered endurance 5 min 30 sec.

Production: Seven Shusui aircraft were built in 1945 by Mitsubishi Jukogyo K.K., three MXY8 light gliders were built by the Dai-Ichi Kaigun Koku Gijitsusho and some fifty to sixty Akigusa and Ku-13 Shusui heavy gliders were built by Maeda Koku Kenkyujo and Yokoi Koku K.K.

A formation of Nakajima E8N2 floatplanes and a Kawanishi E7K2.

Nakajima E8N

When in 1933 the Japanese Navy issued a specification calling for a two-seat aircraft intended to replace the Navy Type 90-2-2 Reconnaissance Seaplane (Nakajima E4N2) as a standard light reconnaissance floatplane aboard their aircraft tenders, battleships and cruisers, two of the competitive manufacturers, Aichi and Kawanishi, decided to enter low-wing monoplane designs. The third competitor, however, Nakajima Hikoki K.K., decided to submit a modernized version of their earlier E4N2 biplane.

Bearing the manufacturer's designation Type MS, the Nakajima floatplane differed from its predecessor in featuring wings of reduced chord and area and was characterized by increased sweep of its upper wing and by taller vertical tail surfaces without dorsal fin. Designated E8N1 by the Navy, the aircraft was, like the E4N2, powered by a 580 hp Nakajima Kotobuki 2 KAI 1 nine-cylinder radial driving a two-blade propeller, and was designed by a team led by Eng Kishiro Matsuo. Completed and flown in March 1934, the first prototype was followed by six additional experimental machines which were extensively tested against the single prototype of the Kawanishi E8K1 monoplane and the two prototypes of the Aichi E8A1 monoplane.

NAKAJIMA E8N2

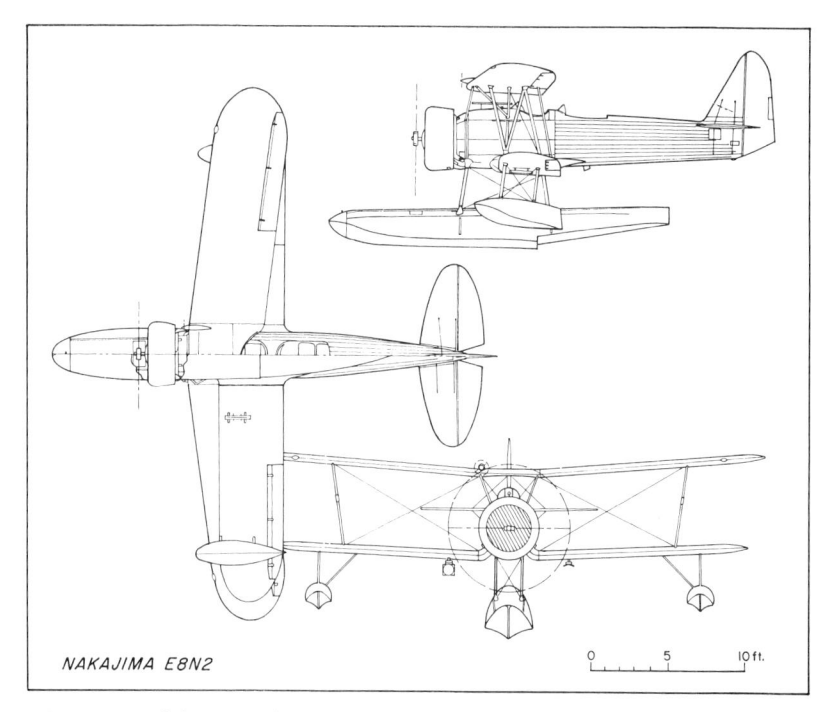

Because of its superior manoeuvrability and better handling characteristics, the Nakajima E8N1 won the competition and in October 1935 was accepted for operation as the Navy Type 95 Reconnaissance Seaplane Model 1. Later the E8N2 with Kotobuki 2 KAI 2 engine and improved equipment was produced, and the type remained in production with both Nakajima and Kawanishi until 1940.

Operating as a catapult-launched reconnaissance aircraft, the E8N1 saw considerable service aboard aircraft tenders, battleships and cruisers,

Nakajima E8N2 from the battleship *Kirishima*.

409

and during the second Sino-Japanese war distinguished itself on several occasions by destroying opposing Chinese fighters. During that same war the aircraft was occasionally operated as a dive-bomber but more often was employed as a reconnaissance and artillery spotting aircraft. At the onset of the Pacific War the Navy Type 95 Reconnaissance Seaplane was in process of being replaced in first-line units with Navy Type 0 Reconnaissance Seaplanes (Aichi E13A1) and Navy Type 0 Observation Seaplanes (Mitsubishi F1M2). However, during the first year of the war the E8N2 was still operated from Navy vessels and the type was coded DAVE by the Allies. Later in the war the aircraft was retained for second-line duties such as communications, liaison and training.

UNITS ALLOCATED

Aircraft tenders: Chiyoda, Kamoi, Kiyokawa Maru, Sagara Maru and Sanuki Maru.

Battleships: Fuso, Haruna, Hyuga, Ise, Kirishima, Kongo, Mutsu, Nagato and Yamashiro.

Cruisers: Aoba, Ashigara, Atago, Chokai, Haguro, Kako, Kashima, Katori, Kumano, Maya, Mikuma, Mogami, Myoko, Nachi, Suzuya, Takao and Tone.

TECHNICAL DATA

Description: Single-engined two-seat reconnaissance floatplane. All-metal structure with fabric covering.

Accommodation: Crew of two in open cockpits.

Powerplant: One Nakajima Kotobuki 2 KAI 1 nine-cylinder air-cooled radial, rated at 580 hp for take-off and 460 hp at 3,000 m (9,845 ft), driving a two-blade propeller (E8N1).

One Nakajima Kotobuki 2 KAI 2 nine-cylinder air-cooled radial, rated at 630 hp for take-off and 460 hp at 3,000 m (9,845 ft), driving a two-blade propeller (E8N2).

Armament: One fixed forward-firing 7·7 mm machine-gun and one flexible rear-firing 7·7 mm machine-gun. External stores: two 30 kg (66 lb) bombs.

Dimensions: Span 10·98 m (36 ft 0 $\frac{8}{32}$ in); length 8·81 m (28 ft 10 $\frac{27}{32}$ in); height 3·84 m (12 ft 7 $\frac{8}{16}$ in); wing area 26·5 sq m (285·243 sq ft).

Weights: Empty 1,320 kg (2,910 lb); loaded 1,900 kg (4,189 lb); wing loading 71·7 kg/sq m (14·7 lb/sq ft); power loading 3 kg/hp (6·6 lb/hp).

Performance: Maximum speed 162 kt at 3,000 m (186 mph at 9,845 ft); cruising speed 100 kt (115 mph); climb to 3,000 m (9,845 ft) in 6 min 31 sec; service ceiling 7,270 m (23,850 ft); range 485 naut miles (558 st miles).

Production: A total of 755 E8Ns were built by Nakajima Hikoki K.K. at Koizumi and Kawanishi Kokuki K.K. at Konan, as follows:

Nakajima:
  7 prototypes (1934)
  700 production aircraft (1934–40)

Kawanishi:
  48 production aircraft (1938–40)

Nakajima B5N1 Navy Type 97 Carrier Attack Bomber Model 1 of the Yokosuka Kokutai.

Nakajima B5N

When the Pacific War began the Japanese Navy possessed in the Nakajima B5N2 the most modern type of carrier-borne torpedo bomber to be operated by any of the world's navies, and on 7 December, 1941, manned by the élite of the Service, 144 aircraft of this type crippled the battleship force of the US Pacific Fleet anchored at Pearl Harbor. During the following twelve months carrier-based B5N2s were to deliver fatal blows to three US Navy carriers, the *Lexington*, the *Yorktown* and *Hornet*, during three separate encounters, while land- and carrier-based B5N2s supported Japanese amphibious attacks on the entire war front. But by 1944 the accelerated technical developments brought by the war had rendered the aircraft obsolete, and it ended its war service in second-line units.

Development of a new series of carrier attack bombers, as the torpedo

Nakajima B5N1-K trainer.

bombers were known in Japan, had been initiated in 1932 with the issuance by the Navy of a 7-Shi specification. Aichi, Mitsubishi and Nakajima each delivered a prototype in answer to the specification, but none were found satisfactory, and the Navy had to issue a 9-Shi specification to obtain a replacement for the obsolescent Navy Type 92 Attack Bomber B3Y1. The requirements contained in the 9-Shi specification were met by the design submitted by the Dai-Ichi Kaigun Koku Gijitsusho at Yokosuka, and this aircraft was placed in production as the Navy Type 96 Carrier Attack Bomber (B4Y1).

The B4Y1 was, however, regarded as a stopgap pending availability of

Nakajima B5N2 Navy Type 97 Carrier Attack Bomber Model 12.

a more modern aircraft possessing performance more compatible with that of the Navy Type 96 Carrier Fighter. To obtain this aircraft the Navy issued in 1935 a 10-Shi specification calling for a single-engined carrier attack bomber of monoplane design. Requirements included: (1) span, less than 16 m (52 ft $5\frac{29}{32}$ in) with provision for wing folding mechanism to reduce span to not more than 7·5 m (24 ft $7\frac{9}{32}$ in); (2) armament, one 800 kg (1,764 lb) torpedo or equivalent bomb-load and one 7·7 mm machine-gun; (3) maximum speed, 180 kt at 2,000 m (207 mph at 6,560 ft); (4) endurance at 135 kt (155 mph), 4 hr normal and 7 hr maximum; (5) crew of three; and (6) powerplant, either one Nakajima Hikari or Mitsubishi Kinsei radial engine.

Under the leadership of Katsuji Nakamura, the Nakajima design team adopted for their Type K a clean low-wing configuration fitted with a hydraulically-operated retractable undercarriage. The large wing could be folded upwards, and the hinge points were arranged so that the wingtips overlapped each other when folded above the cockpit. When compared with the massive wing, the fuselage appeared small as overall length was kept to 10·3 m (33 ft $9\frac{1}{2}$ in) to enable the aircraft to be accommodated on the standard deck elevators of the Navy carriers. Other innovations incorporated in the Type K included Fowler flaps and variable-pitch propeller. Bearing the official designation B5N1, the prototype powered by a Nakajima Hikari 2 nine-cylinder air-cooled radial was completed in December 1936 and made its first flight in January 1937. Difficulties with

Captured Nakajima B5N2 at Anacostia Naval Air Station. This example has ASV radar antennae on the fuselage sides. (*US Navy Department*.)

the hydraulic system marred the initial flight testing operations, but soon the troubles were eradicated and the aircraft reached a maximum speed of 230 mph, thus far exceeding the requirements of the 10-Shi specification. However, the many technical innovations incorporated in the aircraft were a source of worries for the Navy who feared that the aircraft would be excessively difficult to maintain. Accordingly, starting with the second prototype, the hydraulic wing-folding mechanism was replaced by a manual-folding system and the Fowler flaps were changed for more conventional units. Further changes to the second B5N1 included replacement of the Hikari 2 by a Hikari 3 driving a constant-speed propeller and the installation of integral wing tanks with increased capacity. In this form the aircraft won the competitive trials over the Mitsubishi B5M1 and went into production at Koizumi in November 1937 as the Navy Type 97 Carrier Attack Bomber Model 1.

After an initial crew training period in Japan, the aircraft, later redesignated Navy Type 97 Carrier Attack Bomber Model 11, went into service aboard the Japanese carriers. Meanwhile land-based units took the aircraft into combat operations on the Chinese mainland where, armed with bombs, it served as a tactical bomber in support of ground operations. Operating under the cover of escorting Navy Type 96 Carrier Fighters, the B5N1 was quite successful in spite of its lack of protection for crew and fuel tank and its modest defensive armament, comprising a single flexible 7·7 mm Type 92 machine-gun manned by the radio operator. In level bombing sorties, such as those flown over China, the observer was responsible for aiming the bombs. Seated between the pilot and the radio operator, he could see the target by opening a pair of small folding doors in the floor of the fuselage. During the Sino-Japanese war no major modification was found necessary, and the only changes incorporated in the B5N1 affected its internal equipment, such as radio, for which an antenna mast was provided on late production aircraft to replace the trailing aerial fitted to earlier machines. Later the need to improve the aircraft's performance, to enable it to survive when faced with more modern fighters than those operated by the Chinese, led to the design in 1939 of a new variant.

First flown in December 1939, the B5N2, which entered production soon after as the Navy Type 97 Carrier Attack Bomber Model 12, was externally identical to the B5N1 but was powered by a 1,000 hp Nakajima Sakae 11 radial engine. As the fourteen-cylinder double-row Sakae 11 had a smaller diameter than the nine-cylinder single-row Hikari 3, Nakajima engineers decided to use a smaller cowling providing better pilot view and reducing drag, and a small spinner was fitted over the propeller hub to reduce drag further and increase engine cooling. In spite of a 36 per cent increase in power as compared to the B5N1, the B5N2 was not appreciably faster, but the Navy decided to accept the change as the Sakae engine was more reliable than the Hikari, a quality of major importance in the case of a single-engined aircraft required to operate long distances over water.

At the time of the Japanese attack on Pearl Harbor, the B5N2s had completely replaced the earlier B5N1s and B4Y1s in first-line units of the Navy. Participating in all carrier operations until replaced in 1944 by the Navy Carrier Attack Bomber Tenzan, the B5N2 received the Allied code name KATE. The Navy Type 97 Carrier Attack Bombers were also operated from land bases, taking an active part in the Solomons campaign, and were last used actively in their intended role during the 1944 campaign in the Philippines. When staggering losses and insufficient performance forced their relegation to second-line units, the B5N2s found a new lease of life because their long endurance made them particularly adaptable to maritime reconnaissance and anti-submarine roles. Operating in areas where Allied fighters were not normally found, the B5N2s gave Japanese surface convoys desperately needed air cover against Allied submarines. Visual reconnaissance as initially used in this role gave place to electronic warfare methods when some B5N2s were fitted with Air-to-Surface Vessel Radar, with aerials fitted along the rear fuselage sides and along the wing leading edges, while others received Jikitanchiki magnetic airborne submarine detection devices. Other war weary B5N2s supplemented the B5N1-K—an advanced trainer developed by Nakajima from the B5N1 when that variant

Nakajima B5N2 Navy Type 97 Carrier Attack Bomber Model 12. (*Eckert.*)

NAKAJIMA B5N2

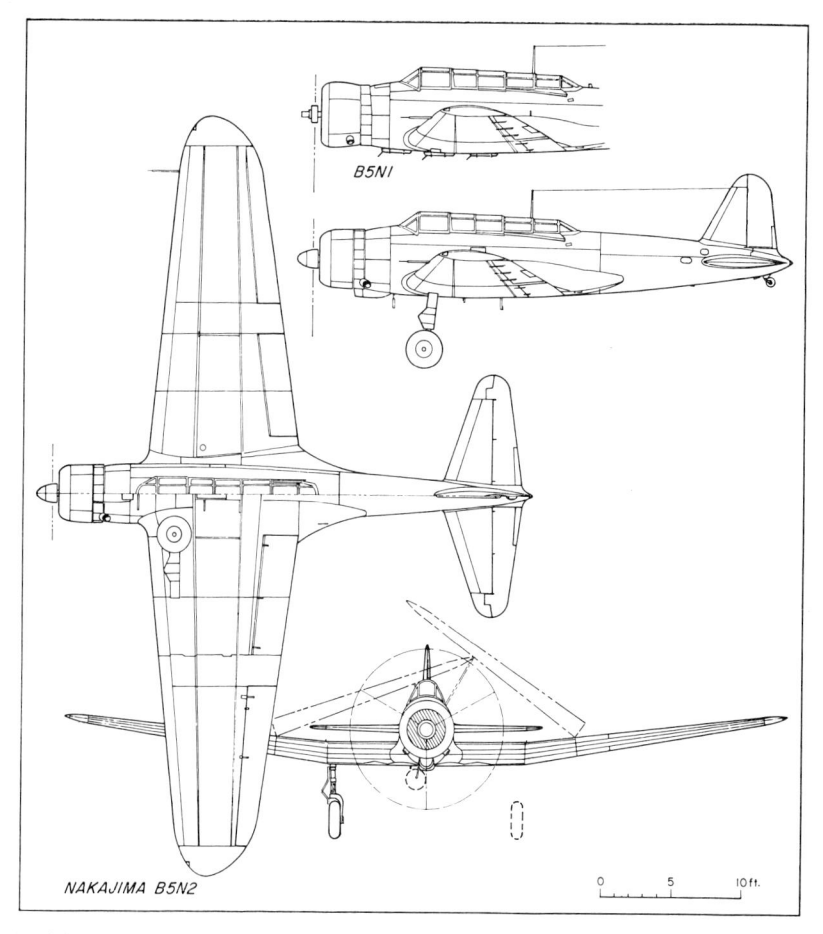

had been replaced in first-line units by the B5N2—in training and target-towing units and for towing the Chikara Special Training Gliders.

UNITS ALLOCATED

All Japanese wartime aircraft carriers; 601st, 653rd, 931st, Himeji, Omura and Usa Kokutais.

TECHNICAL DATA

Description: Single-engined three-seat carrier-borne torpedo-bomber. All-metal construction with fabric-covered control surfaces.

Accommodation: Crew of three comprising pilot, observer/navigator/bomb-aimer and radio operator/gunner, in enclosed cockpit.

Powerplant: One Nakajima Hikari 2 nine-cylinder air-cooled radial rated at 700 hp for take-off, and 800 hp at 3,500 m (11,485 ft), driving a three-blade variable-pitch propeller (first prototype).

One Nakajima Hikari 3 nine-cylinder air-cooled radial rated at 770 hp for take-off, and 840 hp at 3,000 m (9,845 ft), driving a three-blade constant-speed metal propeller (B5N1).

One Nakajima NK1B Sakae 11 fourteen-cylinder air-cooled radial rated at 1,000 hp for take-off, and 970 hp at 3,000 m (9,845 ft), driving a three-blade constant-speed metal propeller (B5N2).

Armament: One flexible rear-firing 7·7 mm Type 92 machine-gun.

Bomb-load: 800 kg (1,764 lb) of bombs or one 800 kg (1,764 lb) torpedo.

	B5N1	B5N2
Dimensions:		
Span	15·518 m	15·518 m
	(50 ft 10 18/18 in)	(50 ft 10 18/18 in)
Length	10·3 m	10·3 m
	(33 ft 9½ in)	(33 ft 9½ in)
Height	3·7 m	3·7 m
	(12 ft 1 21/32 in)	(12 ft 1 21/32 in)
Wing area	37·7 sq m	37·7 sq m
	(405·798 sq ft)	(405·798 sq ft)
Weights:		
Empty	2,106 kg	2,279 kg
	(4,643 lb)	(5,024 lb)
Loaded	3,700 kg	3,800 kg
	(8,157 lb)	(8,378 lb)
Maximum	4,015 kg	4,100 kg
	(8,852 lb)	(9,039 lb)
Wing loading	98·1 kg/sq m	100·8 kg/sq m
	(20·1 lb/sq ft)	(20·6 lb/sq ft)
Power loading	4·8 kg/hp	3·8 kg/hp
	(11·5 lb/hp)	(8·4 lb/hp)
Performance:		
Maximum speed	199 kt at 2,000 m	204 kt at 3,600 m
	(229 mph at 6,560 ft)	(235 mph at 11,810 ft)
Cruising speed	138 kt at 2,000 m	140 kt at 3,000 m
	(159 mph at 6,560 ft)	(161 mph at 9,845 ft)
Climb to	3,000 m	3,000 m
	(9,845 ft)	(9,845 ft)
in	7 min 50 sec	7 min 40 sec
Service ceiling	7,400 m	8,260 m
	(24,280 ft)	(27,100 ft)
Range—normal	590 naut miles	528 naut miles
	(679 st miles)	(608 st miles)
—maximum	1,220 naut miles	1,075 naut miles
	(1,404 st miles)	(1,237 st miles)

Production: A total of 1,149 B5Ns were built by Nakajima Hikoki K.K. at Koizumi, Aichi Tokei Denki K.K. at Nagoya, and the Dai-Juichi Kaigun Kokusho at Hiro, as follows:

Nakajima:

669 B5N1, B5N1-K and B5N2 (1936–41)

Aichi:

200 B5N2 (1942–43)

Dai-Juichi Kaigun Kokusho:

280 B5N2 (1942–43)

First prototype Nakajima J1N1-C Gekko (Moonlight) reconnaissance aircraft. (*US Navy Department.*)

Nakajima J1N Gekko (Moonlight)

After nine months of bitter fighting in China the Japanese Navy began to receive requests from its senior air officers in the theatre of operations, urging the Naval Staff to initiate the development of a long-range fighter aircraft. These officers pointed out that the Chinese consistently kept their fighters on bases out of range of the Navy Type 96 Carrier Fighters and that this tactic resulted in heavy losses of Navy Type 96 Attack Bombers operating without escort deep in Chinese territory. To meet this requirement the Japanese Naval Bureau of Aeronautics staff began in the spring of 1938 to draft a 13-Shi specification inspired by the Potez 63 which was about to enter service with units of the French Armée de l'Air. After reviewing the preliminary draft with senior fighter pilots of the 12th Kokutai (Naval Air Corps), in 1938 the Japanese Navy officially issued to Mitsubishi and Nakajima a 13-Shi specification calling for a three-seat twin-engined long-range fighter. Emphasis was placed on good combat manoeuvrability so that the aircraft could successfully engage single-engined enemy fighters. Other requirements included: (1) maximum speed, 280 kt (322 mph); (2) normal range, 1,300 naut miles (1,496 st miles) and maximum range 2,000 naut miles (2,302 st miles); and (3) armament to include forward-firing 20 mm cannon and 7·7 mm machine-guns, and flexible rear-firing 7·7 mm machine-guns.

To meet the exacting 13-Shi specifications, Katsuji Nakamura designed a clean low-wing monoplane featuring several technical innovations. Two 1,130 hp Nakajima Sakae radial engines were chosen but, to offset the effect of propeller torque, handed engines were used and these were the Sakae 21 and 22 driving propellers rotating in opposite directions. Armament consisted of a 20 mm Type 99 Model 1 cannon and two 7·7 mm Type 97 machine-guns mounted in the nose and firing forward, while two tandem-mounted remotely-controlled barbettes each housing two 7·7 mm machine-guns were mounted on the fuselage behind the pilot's cockpit. These barbettes were hydraulically operated as were the cowling flaps and retractable landing gear. The first prototype of the Navy Experimental 13-Shi Three-seat Escort Fighter, bearing the short designation J1N1, made its first flight in May 1941, but serious teething troubles plagued the flight trials. To improve manoeuvrability the second prototype was fitted with trailing-edge flaps which could be deflected 20 degrees during combat manoeuvring and 40 degrees on landing, and also with leading-edge slots. Both aircraft were delivered to the Navy for Service trials in August 1941, but these were an abysmal failure because the aircraft was considerably overweight and there was excessive trouble with the opposite rotating propellers and complex hydraulic systems. The remote-controlled barbettes were found to be difficult to aim and too heavy. The J1N1 suffered severe aileron vibration during rolls, and the pilots found manoeuvrability to be inadequate although quite remarkable for a twin-engined aircraft. Pitted against the single-engined Mitsubishi A6M2 in comparative trials,

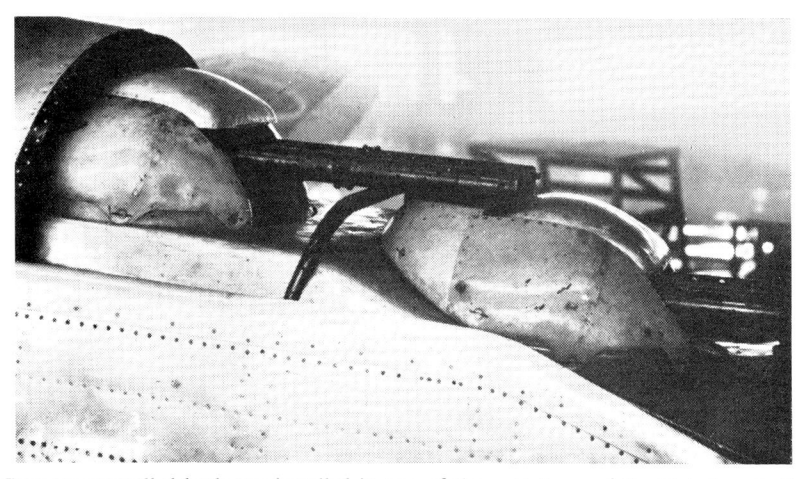

Remote-controlled barbettes installed in one of the prototypes of the Nakajima-built Navy Experimental 13-Shi Three-seat Escort Fighters. (*USAF.*)

the J1N1 was found inferior on all counts except range, and as a result the Navy decided in October 1941 to reject it as a long-range escort fighter. As the aircraft was almost as fast as the A6M2, Nakajima was authorized to modify the nearly completed examples already on the assembly lines to serve as prototypes for a fast land-based long-range reconnaissance aircraft.

In redesigning the aircraft for its new role, careful attention was given to reducing weight and improving reliability. Weight savings resulted from a reduction in internal fuel capacity from 2,270 litres (499 Imp gal) to 1,700 litres (374 Imp gal) and by removing all armament including the troublesome dorsal barbettes. Reliability and ease of maintenance were

A Nakajima J1N1-R Gekko (Moonlight) with experimental turret installation housing a 20 mm cannon. (*US Navy Department*.)

improved by replacing the handed Sakae 21 and 22 engines driving opposite rotating propellers with a pair of unhanded Sakae 21s. To provide sufficient range in spite of reduction in internal fuel capacity, provisions were made under the wing centre-section for two 330 litre (72·6 Imp gal) drop tanks. The fuselage was redesigned to accommodate a forward cockpit for the pilot and for the radio operator/gunner who operated a flexibly-mounted rear-firing 13 mm Type 2 machine-gun. A navigator/observer was seated in a separate cockpit located behind the trailing edge. In this form the aircraft, now designated J1N1-C, successfully passed its Service trials in July 1942 and was put into production as the Navy Type 2 Reconnaissance Plane. Production was kept at a low rate as the need for specialized reconnaissance aircraft was less pressing than for other combat types, and between April 1942 and March 1943 Nakajima delivered only fifty-four J1N1-Cs including prototypes. Delivered to operational units in the autumn of 1942, the J1N1-C was first encountered by the Allies during

A Nakajima J1N1-C KAI Gekko Model 11 of the Yokosuka Kokutai.

NAKAJIMA J1N1-C KAI

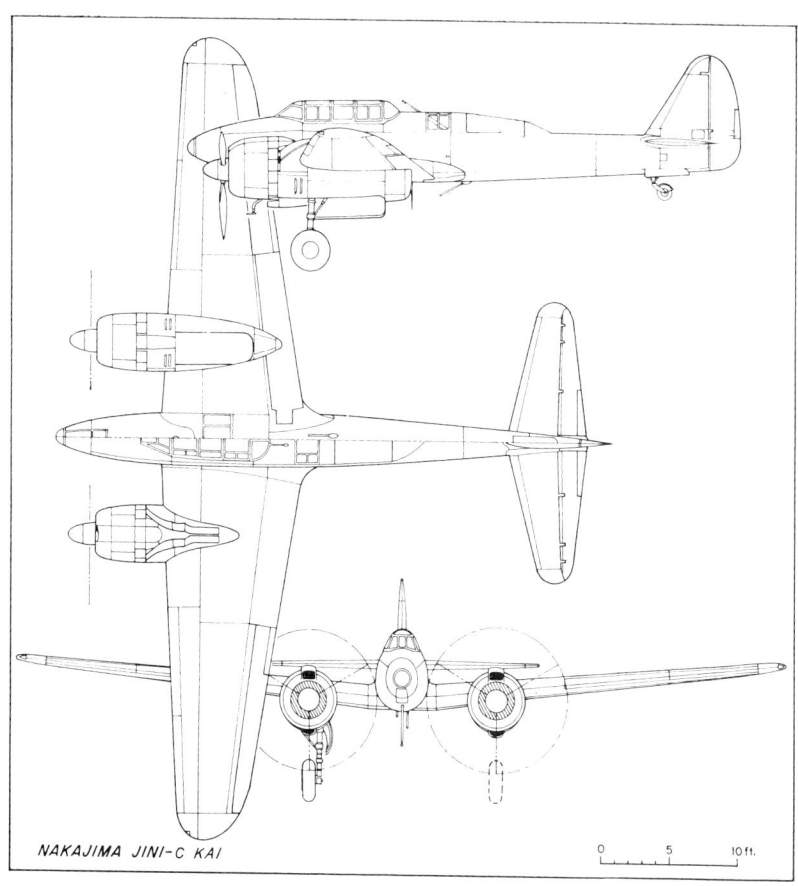

the Solomons campaign when it was initially identified as a fighter and received the code name IRVING, whereas a reconnaissance aircraft would have been given a feminine name. Later, the aircraft was redesignated J1N1-R by the Navy, and a small number of them were armed with a 20 mm Type 99 Model 1 cannon mounted in a spherical turret installed behind the pilot's seat. In the spring of 1943, Commander Yasuna Kozono, commanding officer of the 251st Kokutai then based at Vunakanau Airfield at Rabaul, suggested that obliquely-mounted cannon be installed in the observer's cockpit of the J1N1-C for night-fighting operations. The maintenance crews at Rabaul removed all equipment from the observer's cockpit and mounted two fixed 20 mm cannon firing forward and upward at an angle of 30 degrees, and two similar weapons firing forward and downward, the modified aircraft being designated J1N1-C KAI. Soon afterwards, two B-24 Liberators were intercepted and destroyed, proving that Commander Kozono's idea was practical. This success attracted the attention of the Naval Staff who had begun to recognize the need for a specialized night fighter and accordingly Nakajima was instructed to begin manufacture of a version built from scratch as a night fighter.

Production of the J1N1-S Gekko (Moonlight) Model 11 began in August 1943 at Koizumi, and the importance given to it by the Navy is shown by the fact that 183 aircraft of the J1N series, mostly night fighters, were produced between April 1943 and March 1944 as against only 54 aircraft in the previous twelve months. A further 240 Gekkos were built until December 1944 when the type was phased out of production. Carrying the same armament as the J1N1-C KAI, the J1N1-S featured a redesigned upper fuselage eliminating the step between the rear of the observer's cockpit and the base of the vertical fin. Individual exhaust stacks replaced the collector ring fitted to earlier machines. Combat experience indicated that the downward-firing cannon were not as effective as the upward-firing weapons, and consequently they were not installed on late production aircraft, designated J1N1-Sa Gekko Model 11A. Most of the J1N1-Sa and some of the J1N1-S night fighters were fitted with AI radar with external antenna attached to the nose of the aircraft, while a few aircraft carried a small searchlight in the nose. When no searchlight or radar equipment was fitted, the J1N1-Sa was armed with a nose-mounted forward-firing 20 mm Type 99 Model 2 cannon. In operation the Gekko proved effective against the comparatively slow B-24, but seldom more than one firing pass could be made at the much faster B-29s. Production of the J1N1 series terminated in December 1944, and before the war ended most Gekko and surviving J1N1-R reconnaissance aircraft were expended in kamikaze attacks in which they carried two 250 kg (551 lb) bombs.

UNITS ALLOCATED

133rd, 141st, 153rd, 251st, 302nd and 322nd Kokutais.

A Nakajima J1N1-Sa of the 302nd Kokutai. This aircraft had three upward-firing 20 mm cannon and was fitted with nose-mounted centimetric radar.

TECHNICAL DATA

Description: Twin-engine long-range escort fighter (J1N1), reconnaissance aircraft (J1N1-C and J1N1-R) or night fighter (J1N1-S and J1N1-Sa). All-metal construction with fabric-covered control surfaces.

Accommodation: Crew of three (J1N1, J1N1-C and J1N1-R), or two (J1N1-C KAI, J1N1-S and J1N1-Sa) in enclosed cockpit.

Powerplant: Two Nakajima NK1F Sakae (one Sakae 21 and one Sakae 22) fourteen-cylinder air-cooled radials, rated at 1,130 hp for take-off, 1,100 hp at 2,850 m (9,350 ft) and 980 hp at 6,000 m (19,685 ft), driving opposite rotating three-blade constant-speed metal propellers (J1N1).

Two 1,130 hp Nakajima NK1F Sakae 21 fourteen-cylinder air-cooled radials with the same rating at altitude as listed above but with propellers rotating in the same direction.

Armament: One forward-firing 20 mm Type 99 Model 1 cannon, two forward-firing 7·7 mm Type 97 machine-guns and four 7·7 mm Type 97 machine-guns in two remotely controlled dorsal barbettes (J1N1).

One rear-firing hand-held 13 mm Type 2 machine-gun (J1N1-C and J1N1-R).

One 20 mm Type 99 Model 1 cannon in a dorsal turret (some J1N1-R).

Two fuselage-mounted upward-firing 20 mm Type 99 cannon and two 20 mm Type 99 downward-firing cannon (J1N1-C KAI and J1N1-S).

Two fuselage-mounted upward-firing 20 mm Type 99 cannon and, optional, one forward-firing 20 mm Type 99 cannon (J1N1-Sa).

	J1N1 (13-Shi)	J1N1-C	J1N1-S
Dimensions:			
Span	16·98 m	16·98 m	16·98 m
	(55 ft 8½ in)	(55 ft 8½ in)	(55 ft 8½ in)
Length	12·18 m	12·18 m	12·77 m
	(39 ft 11 47/64 in)	(39 ft 11 47/64 in)	(41 ft 10¾ in)
Height	4·562 m	4·562 m	4·562 m
	(14 ft 11 19/32 in)	(14 ft 11 19/32 in)	(14 ft 11 19/32 in)
Wing area	40 sq m	40 sq m	40 sq m
	(430·555 sq ft)	(430·555 sq ft)	(430·555 sq ft)
Weights:			
Empty	5,020 kg	4,852 kg	4,840 kg
	(11,067 lb)	(10,697 lb)	(10,670 lb)
Loaded	7,250 kg	6,890 kg	7,010 kg
	(15,984 lb)	(15,190 lb)	(15,454 lb)
Maximum	8,030 kg	7,527 kg	8,184 kg
	(17,703 lb)	(16,594 lb)	(18,043 lb)
Wing loading*	181·3 kg/sq m	172·3 kg/sq m	175·3 kg/sq m
	(37·1 lb/sq ft)	(35·3 lb/sq ft)	(35·9 lb/sq ft)
Power loading	3·6 kg/hp	3·3 kg/hp	3·7 kg/hp
	(7·8 lb/hp)	(7·3 lb/hp)	(8·0 lb/hp)
Performance:			
Maximum speed	274 kt at 5,000 m	286 kt at 6,000 m	274 kt at 5,840 m
	(315 mph at 16,405 ft)	(329 mph at 19,685 ft)	(315 mph at 19,160 ft)
Cruising speed	180 kt at 4,000 m	150 kt at 4,000 m	180 kt at 4,000 m
	(207 mph at 13,125 ft)	(173 mph at 13,125 ft)	(207 mph at 13,125 ft)
Climb to	—	4,000 m	5,000 m
	—	(13,125 ft)	(16,405 ft)
in	—	5 min 37 sec	9 min 35 sec
Service ceiling	—	10,300 m	9,320 m
	—	(33,795 ft)	(30,610 ft)
Range—normal	—	1,457 naut miles	1,374 naut miles
	—	(1,677 st miles)	(1,581 st miles)
—maximum	—	—	2,040 naut miles
	—	—	(2,348 st miles)

* At normal loaded weight.

Production: A total of 479 J1Ns were built by Nakajima Hikoki K.K. at Koizumi as follows:
 2 J1N1 prototypes (spring 1941)
 7 J1N1-C prototypes (1941–42)
 470 J1N1-C, J1N1-R, J1N1-C KAI, J1N1-S and J1N1-Sa production aircraft (July 1942–Dec 1944)

Nakajima G5N Shinzan (Mountain Recess)

In 1938, though the range capability of the Mitsubishi G4M1, then still in the design stage and yet untried, was quite phenomenal by contemporary standards, the Japanese Naval Staff began to show considerable interest in acquiring an attack bomber with a range of 3,000 to 3,500 naut miles (3,450 to 4,030 st miles). It was obvious that such a range would necessitate use of a four-engine configuration, and as the Japanese industry lacked sufficient experience in the design and manufacture of such a large aircraft, the Navy made arrangements for Japan Air Lines Co (Nippon Koku K.K.) to acquire the sole prototype of the four-engined Douglas DC-4E transport. At the same time the Navy told Nakajima to be ready to develop a long-range heavy bomber from the DC-4E.

Shortly after its arrival in Japan in 1939, the DC-4E was secretly handed over to Nakajima who dismantled it for study, and before the end of the year Nakajima had built the first prototype of the Experimental 13-Shi Attack Bomber Shinzan (Mountain Recess) G5N1. The new aircraft retained the wing, powerplant installation and undercarriage of the American transport, but featured a new fuselage with glazed nose and ventral bomb-bay, new tail surfaces with twin fins and rudders, and was powered by four 1,870 hp Nakajima NK7A Mamoru 11 fourteen-cylinder radials. When the G5N1 flew on 10 April 1941 it became the first four-engined land-based aircraft designed for the Navy and the first retractable tricycle undercarriage aircraft built in Japan.

Unfortunately Nakajima engineers had based their design on an unsuccessful aircraft already rejected by American airlines, and their in-

The Navy Experimental Type D Transport was the Douglas DC-4E tested by the Japanese Navy.

NAKAJIMA G5N1

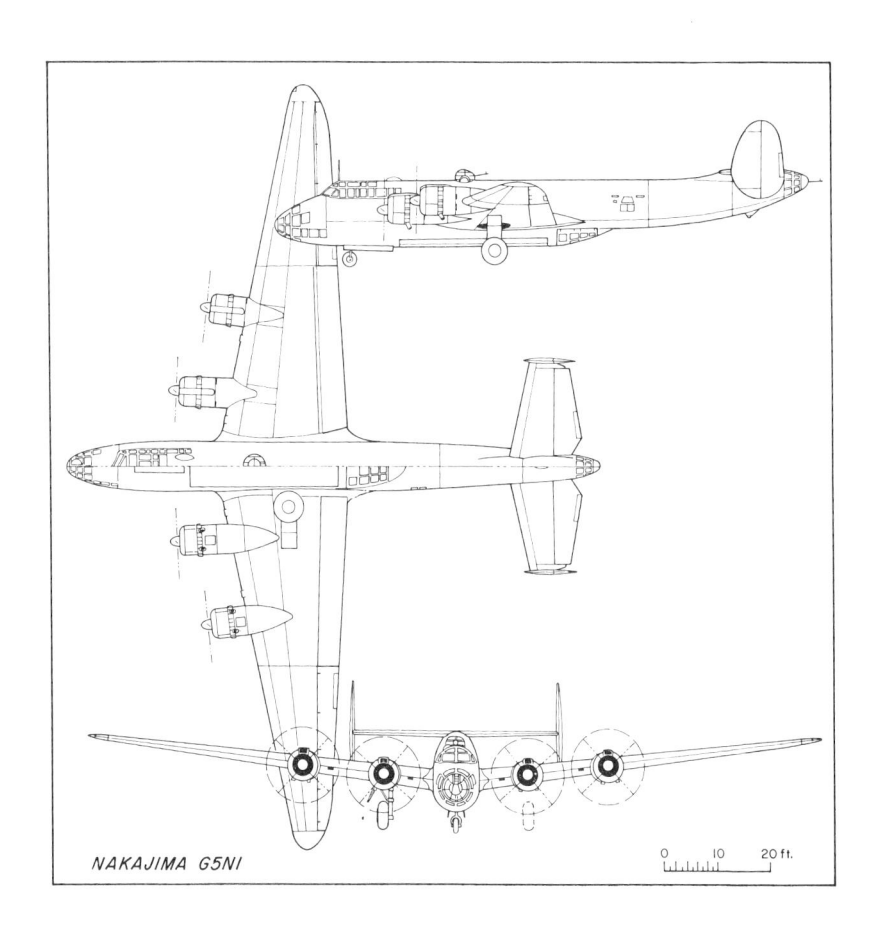

A Nakajima G5N1 Shinzan (Mountain Recess) with, in the foreground, a Mitsubishi Reisen (Zero Fighter). (*Courtesy William Green.*)

A Nakajima G5N2 Shinzan (Mountain Recess) at Atsugi in September 1945. (*USAF.*)

experience with aircraft of this size led them to excessive weight increases. The combined effects of the complex Douglas design, overweight, and unreliable engines, resulted in very poor performance, and only three additional G5N1 prototypes were built. In an attempt to save the design, two further prototypes, designated G5N2, were built and fitted with four 1,530 hp Mitsubishi Kasei 12 engines but, as the basic airframe problems remained and the aircraft was underpowered, the project was finally cancelled. Projected versions for the Japanese Army, the Nakajima Ki-68, powered by either four Mitsubishi Ha-101 or four Nakajima Ha-103 engines, and the Kawanishi designed Ki-85, powered by four Mitsubishi Ha-111Ms, were not proceeded with.

Finally two G5N1s, re-engined with the Kasei 12, and the two G5N2s ended their lives as freight transports and were then designated Shinzan-Kai Model 12 Transport—G5N2-L (Allied code name LIZ).

TECHNICAL DATA

Description: Four-engined heavy bomber. All-metal construction with fabric-covered control surfaces.
Accommodation: Crew of seven to ten.
Powerplant: Four Nakajima NK7A Mamoru 11 fourteen-cylinder air-cooled radials rated at 1,870 hp for take-off, 1,750 hp at 1,400 m (4,595 ft) and 1,600 hp at 4,900 m (16,075 ft), driving four-blade constant-speed propellers (G5N1).

Four Mitsubishi Kasei 12 fourteen-cylinder air-cooled radials rated at 1,530 hp for take-off, 1,480 hp at 2,200 m (7,220 ft) and 1,380 hp at 4,100 m (13,450 ft), driving four-blade constant-speed propellers (G5N2).

Armament: 20 mm Type 99 Model 1 cannon in the dorsal and tail turrets and one 7·7 mm Type 97 machine-gun in each of the nose, ventral, port and starboard beam positions.
    Bomb-load—normal, 2,000 kg (4,409 lb)
    —maximum, 4,000 kg (8,818 lb)
Dimensions: Span 42·14 m (138 ft 3 $\frac{1}{16}$ in); length 31·02 m (101 ft 9¼ in); wing area 201·8 sq m (2,172·149 sq ft).
Weights: Empty 20,100 kg (44,313 lb); loaded 28,150 kg (62,060 lb); maximum 32,000 kg (70,768 lb); wing loading 139·5 kg/sq m (28·6 lb/sq ft); power loading 3·8 kg/hp (8·3 lb/hp).
Performance: Maximum speed 227 kt at 4,100 m (261 mph at 13,450 ft); cruising speed 200 kt at 4,000 m (230 mph at 13,125 ft); climb to 2,000 m (6,560 ft) in 5 min 17 sec; service ceiling 7,450 m (24,440 ft); range 2,300 naut miles (2,647 st miles).
Production: Four G5N1s and two G5N2s were built in 1941–42 by Nakajima Hikoki K.K. in their Koizumi plant.

Nakajima A6M2-N

Bearing the distinction of being one of the only two types of single-seat float seaplane fighters of modern design—the other being its successor the Kawanishi N1K1 Kyofu—to participate in combat operations during the second World War, the Nakajima A6M2-N has earned a special place in history in spite of the fact that changes in the military situation forced its use in a purely defensive role rather than in the more offensive role for which it was conceived.

In the autumn of 1940 the Japanese Navy had issued a 15-Shi specification calling for a single-seat fighter seaplane to provide air cover during the early phases of amphibious landing operations or over military bases in the smaller islands where the construction of airfields was not practicable. Kawanishi began design of the N1K1 to meet this requirement, but it was soon obvious that it would not be ready in time to take part in the impending conflict with the United States. Accordingly the Navy instructed Nakajima to develop a float fighter version of the Mitsubishi A6M2 which they were building. Using the airframe of the A6M2 Model 11, without folding wingtips, as a basis for their project, engineers Niitake and Tajima began working on the new aircraft, then known as the AS-1, in February 1941. The landing gear was removed, all wheel-wells being faired over, and in its place was mounted a large central float attached by means of a forward sloping pylon and aft V-strut, two stabilizing cantilever floats being fitted outboard under the wings. The standard armament and powerplant of the A6M2 were retained, but the vertical tail surfaces had to be enlarged and a small ventral fin was added. Because the main pylon for the ventral float was attached beneath the fuselage, no drop tank could be fitted, but this was offset by the installation of an auxiliary tank in the float itself. The prototype A6M2-N float seaplane made its maiden flight on the first day of the war, and production began soon afterwards under the designation Navy Type 2 Floatplane Fighter Model 11.

Notwithstanding the weight and drag of the float installation, the A6M2-N, code name RUFE, was quite fast and manoeuvrable, and aircraft of this type were first deployed with the Yokohama Kokutai to Tulagi in the Solomons where they were soon destroyed in the pre-landing bombing raids by the B-17s of the US 11th Group. Other A6M2-Ns successfully took part in the Aleutian campaign, but in its defensive role the aircraft did not stand much of a chance against Allied land-based fighters. In the closing months of the war the A6M2-Ns of the Otsu Kokutai, normally used to train pilots for the Kawanishi N1K1 Kyofu, served occasionally as interceptors in the defence of Central Honshu from their base on Lake Biwa.

The Nakajima A6M2-N Navy Type 2 Floatplane Fighter Model 11. This was a development of the Mitsubishi A6M Reisen (Zero Fighter) series of landplane fighters. (*US Navy Department.*)

NAKAJIMA A6M2-N

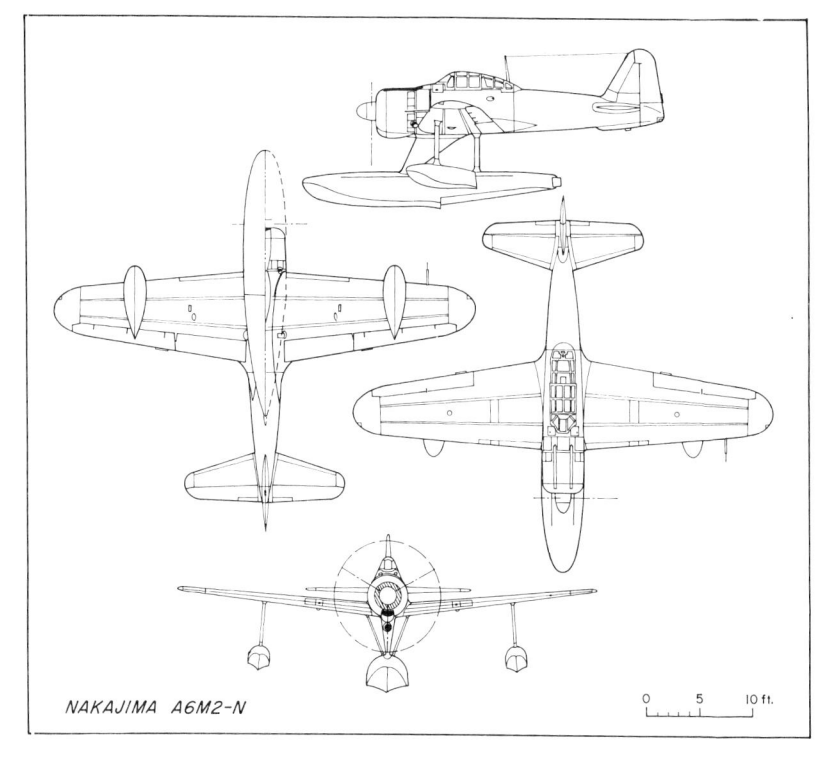

UNITS ALLOCATED
Yokosuka, Yokohama and Otsu Kokutais; 5th, 36th and 452nd Kokutais.

TECHNICAL DATA
Description: Single-engined float seaplane fighter. All-metal construction with fabric-covered control surfaces.
Accommodation: Pilot in enclosed cockpit.
Powerplant: One Nakajima NK1C Sakae 12 fourteen-cylinder air-cooled radial, rated at 940 hp for take-off, and 950 hp at 4,200 m (13,780 ft), driving a three-blade metal propeller.
Armament: Two 7·7 mm Type 97 machine-guns in the upper fuselage decking and two wing-mounted 20 mm Type 99 cannon.
  External load: two 60 kg (132 lb) bombs.
Dimensions: Span 12 m (39 ft 4 $\tfrac{7}{16}$ in); length 10·1 m (33 ft 1 $\tfrac{5}{8}$ in); height 4·3 m (14 ft 1 $\tfrac{5}{16}$ in); wing area 22·44 sq m (241·541 sq ft).
Weights: Empty 1,912 kg (4,235 lb); loaded 2,460 kg (5,423 lb); maximum 2,880 kg (6,349 lb); wing loading 109·7 kg/sq m (22·5 lb/sq ft); power loading 2·6 kg/hp (5·7 lb/hp).
Performance: Maximum speed 235 kt at 5,000 m (270·5 mph at 16,405 ft); cruising speed 160 kt (184 mph); climb to 5,000 m (16,405 ft) in 6 min 43 sec; ceiling 10,000 m (32,810 ft); range—normal 620 naut miles (714 st miles), maximum 963 naut miles (1,107 st miles).
Production: A total of 327 A6M2-Ns were built at Koizumi by Nakajima Hikoki K.K. between December 1941 and September 1943.

Nakajima B6N Tenzan (Heavenly Mountain)

Intended as a replacement for the Navy Type 97 Carrier Attack Bomber, the Nakajima B6N was designed by Kenichi Matsumura to a 14-Shi specification issued in 1939 by the Imperial Naval Staff. The specification called for a three-seat carrier-borne torpedo-bomber with a top speed of 250 kt (288 mph), a cruising speed of 200 kt (230 mph) and a range of 1,000 naut miles (1,151 st miles) with an 800 kg (1,764 lb) bomb-load, or 1,800 naut miles (2,072 st miles) without bomb-load.

The B6N introduced no major aerodynamic improvements over the B5N, the increase in performance being achieved by the use of an engine offering some 80 per cent more power than the Sakae 11 in the B5N2. In spite of a considerable increase in all-up weight, Matsumura was constrained by carrier stowage restrictions to use a wing with approximately the same span and area as that of the older aircraft. The major external difference lay in the design of the vertical tail surfaces which on the B5N were swept forward to keep the aircraft's length within the limit of 11 m (36 ft $1\frac{1}{16}$ in) imposed by the size of the deck elevators. The Navy insisted on powering the aircraft with a Mitsubishi Kasei engine, but Matsumura elected to use the new 1,870 hp Nakajima Mamoru 11 fourteen-cylinder air-cooled radial as it had lower fuel consumption and a better growth potential. With this powerplant installed the first two prototypes were readied for flight trials in the spring of 1941.

Nakajima B6N1 Tenzan (Heavenly Mountain) powered by a Nakajima Mamoru 11. (*Aireview.*)

Nakajima B6N2 Navy Carrier Attack Bomber Tenzan Model 12.
(*Copyright 'Maru.'*)

The war against the Allies had not yet started and the Japanese Navy was confident that the B6N1 would be ready to replace the B5N2 in the near future. Unfortunately, early flight test reports indicated that the design suffered from serious engineering defects. The most urgent modification affected the vertical tail surfaces which had to be moved 2 deg 10 min to the left to correct directional stability problems stemming from the powerful torque of the four-blade propeller. After this modification the aircraft displayed markedly improved flying characteristics, but teething troubles, particularly with the Mamoru engine, slowed its development. By the end of 1942 the Navy Experimental 14-Shi Carrier Attack Bomber was considered ready for carrier acceptance trials, but when the aircraft was tested aboard the *Ryuho* and the *Zuikaku* the mounting of its arrester hook proved weak, and the aircraft was involved in several landing

A Nakajima B6N2 Navy Carrier Attack Bomber Tenzan Model 12 at Atsugi. Radar antennae can be seen along the fuselage side. (*USAF.*)

430

mishaps. In early 1943, with the hook mounting strengthened, the B6N1, although requiring the use of RATOG * units for take-off at maximum gross weight, completed its carrier acceptance trials successfully.

After more than two years of testing, the type was finally accepted for production as the Navy Carrier Attack Bomber Tenzan (Heavenly Mountain) Model 11. The production aircraft introduced several modifications dictated by the result of the flight trials. The principal modifications included (1) replacement of the single exhaust stack, which produced excessive glare at night, by a series of smaller exhaust units; (2) torpedo rack under the starboard fuselage side angled down 2 deg, and provision for torpedo stabilizing tail plates to eliminate a tendency for the torpedo to bounce during low altitude release; (3) strengthening of the main landing gear attachment and of the tailplane; (4) addition of a flexible 7·7 mm

A captured Nakajima B6N2, undergoing tests, in United States markings. (*US Navy Department*.)

machine-gun firing through a ventral tunnel. Attempts were also made to replace the unprotected semi-integral fuel tanks with protected bag-type tanks, but this modification resulted in a 30 per cent reduction in tank capacity and consequently the Navy decided to retain the original semi-integral tanks. In service the Tenzan performed satisfactorily, but its high landing speed and wing loading restricted its use to the larger carriers. During the battle off the Marianas, the first major engagement in which they participated, the Tenzans failed to achieve any significant results as the overwhelming superiority of the US Navy Hellcats deprived them of their escorting Reisens.

The Tenzan production programme suffered a new blow when the Ministry of Munitions instructed Nakajima to cease manufacture of the Mamoru engine to enable concentration on the more widely used Sakae and Homare engines. Consequently Nakajima was forced to re-engine the Tenzan with the 1,850 hp Mitsubishi MK4T Kasei 25 originally specified by the Navy. The modifications required to install the new powerplant

* Rocket Assisted Take-Off Gear.

NAKAJIMA B6N2

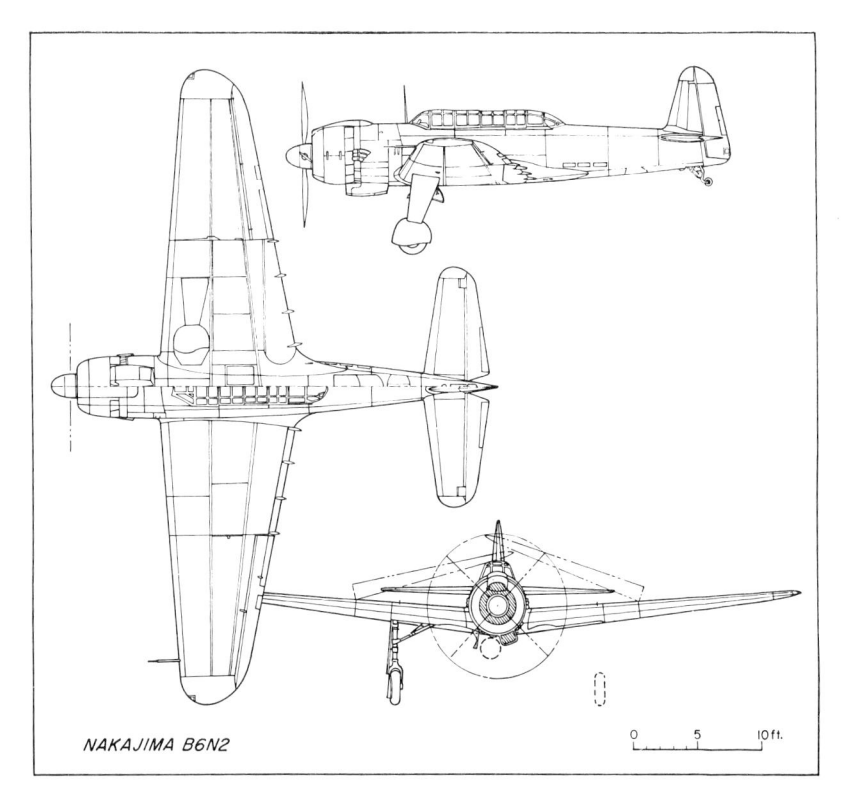

were comparatively small, and the programme suffered only minor delays. After completing 135 Mamoru-powered B6N1s—including two prototype aircraft—Nakajima began delivering the Navy Carrier Attack Bomber Tenzan Model 12 (B6N2) powered by the Kasei 25. These aircraft had also undergone a number of minor internal changes and were fitted with a non-retractable tailwheel, the tailwheel of the B6N1 being fully retractable. Late production aircraft designated B6N2a Model 12A were armed with a flexible 13 mm Type 2 machine-gun in place of the dorsal 7·7 mm Type 97 fitted to earlier machines. Like the earlier version, the B6N2 was known as JILL to the Allies, and aircraft of this type were active throughout the last two years of the war, being particularly aggressive during conventional and kamikaze attacks around Okinawa.

Two B6N2s—the 751st and 752nd production Tenzans—were modified to serve as prototypes for the B6N3 Model 13, a version powered by a 1,850 hp Mitsubishi MK4T-C Kasei 25c and featuring a strengthened undercarriage with larger wheels intended for operation from land bases with semi-prepared runways, as by then the Navy was practically without any aircraft carriers. The production of the B6N3 had not yet started when the war ended.

UNITS ALLOCATED

Carriers: *Hiyo, Junyo, Shinyo, Shokaku, Taiyo, Unryu, Unyo* and *Zuikaku*. 551st, 601st, 653rd, 705th, 752nd, 903rd and Southern Islands Kokutais.

TECHNICAL DATA

Description: Single-engined three-seat carrier-borne torpedo-bomber. All-metal construction with fabric-covered control surfaces.

Accommodation: Crew of three comprising pilot, observer/navigator/bomb-aimer and radio-operator/gunner in enclosed cockpit.

Powerplant: One Nakajima NK7A Mamoru 11 fourteen-cylinder air-cooled radial, rated at 1,800 hp for take-off, 1,750 hp at 1,400 m (4,595 ft) and 1,600 hp at 4,900 m (16,075 ft), driving a four-blade constant-speed metal propeller (14-Shi prototypes and B6N1 Model 11).

One Mitsubishi MK4T Kasei 25 fourteen-cylinder air-cooled radial, rated at 1,850 hp for take-off, 1,680 hp at 2,100 m (6,880 ft) and 1,540 hp at 5,500 m (18,040 ft), driving a four-blade constant-speed metal propeller (B6N2).

One 1,850 hp Mitsubishi MK4T-C Kasei 25c fourteen-cylinder air-cooled radial, driving a four-blade constant-speed metal propeller (B6N3).

Armament: One flexible rear-firing 7·7 mm Type 97 machine-gun (14-Shi prototypes).

One flexible rear-firing 7·7 mm Type 97 machine-gun and one flexible 7·7 mm Type 97 machine-gun firing through a ventral tunnel (B6N1 and B6N2 Model 12).

One flexible rear-firing 13 mm Type 2 machine-gun and one flexible 7·7 mm Type 97 machine-gun firing through a ventral tunnel (B6N2a Model 12A and B6N3).

Bomb-load: 800 kg (1,764 lb) of bombs, or one torpedo.

	B6N1	**B6N2**
Dimensions:		
Span	14·894 m	14·894 m
	(48 ft 10⅜ in)	(48 ft 10⅜ in)
Length	10·365 m	10·865 m
	(34 ft 0 1/16 in)	(35 ft 7¾ in)
Height	3·7 m	3·8 m
	(12 ft 1 21/32 in)	(12 ft 5 19/32 in)
Wing area	37·2 m	37·2 sq m
	(400·416 sq ft)	(400·416 sq ft)
Weights:		
Empty	3,223 kg	3,010 kg
	(7,105 lb)	(6,636 lb)
Loaded	5,200 kg	5,200 kg
	(11,464 lb)	(11,464 lb)
Maximum	5,650 kg	5,650 kg
	(12,456 lb)	(12,456 lb)
Wing loading	139·8 kg/sq m	139·8 kg/sq m
	(28·6 lb/sq ft)	(28·6 lb/sq ft)
Power loading	2·9 kg/hp	2·8 kg/hp
	(6·4 lb/hp)	(6·2 lb/hp)
Performance:		
Maximum speed	251 kt at 4,800 m	260 kt at 4,900 m
	(289 mph at 15,750 ft)	(299 mph at 16,075 ft)
Cruising speed	180 kt at 4,000 m	180 kt at 4,000 m
	(207 mph at 13,125 ft)	(207 mph at 13,125 ft)
Climb to	5,000 m	5,000 m
	(16,405 ft)	(16,405 ft)
in	11 min 1 sec	10 min 24 sec
Service ceiling	8,650 m	9,040 m
	(28,380 ft)	(29,660 ft)
Range—normal	790 naut miles	943 naut miles
	(909 st miles)	(1,085 st miles)
—maximum	1,861 naut miles	1,644 naut miles
	(2,142 st miles)	(1,892 st miles)

Production: A total of 1,268 B6Ns were built by Nakajima Hikoki K.K. as follows:
  2 14-Shi prototypes (1941–42)
  133 B6N1 production aircraft (Feb 1943–July 1943)
  1,133 B6N2 production aircraft (June 1943–Aug 1945)
  (2) B6N3 prototypes (modified from B6N2 airframes)

Of the 1,266 production B6N1s and B6N2s built, 296 were built in the Koizumi plant and 970 in the Handa plant.

Nakajima C6N Saiun (Painted Cloud)

Early combat experiences during the Pacific War indicated that the Japanese Navy's standard practice of assigning reconnaissance sorties to Attack (Torpedo) Bombers operating from aircraft carriers was not entirely satisfactory and that a fast long-range carrier-borne reconnaissance aircraft was needed. In the spring of 1942, the Naval Staff issued a 17-Shi specification to Nakajima, calling for a three-seat carrier-borne reconnaissance aircraft. Performance requirements included: (1) maximum speed of 350 kt (403 mph) at 6,000 m (19,685 ft); (2) climb to 6,000 m (19,685 ft) in less than 8 min; (3) normal range 1,500 naut miles (1,727 st miles) at 210 kt (242 mph); (4) maximum range 2,500 naut miles (3,078 st miles); and (4) landing speed not more than 70 kt (81 mph).

To meet these particularly stringent requirements Eng Yasuo Fukuda and Yoshizo Yamamoto had to pay considerable attention to reducing drag to a minimum, and initially they recommended that the aircraft be powered by two 1,000 hp radials buried in the fuselage and driving separate propellers at the leading edge of each wing by means of an extension

Nakajima C6N1 Saiun (Painted Cloud) with four-blade propeller. (*USAF.*)

Production prototype Nakajima C6N1 with three-blade propeller.

gear system. However, the impending availability of the Nakajima Homare—an eighteen-cylinder double-row air-cooled radial of comparatively small diameter—made it possible to adopt a more conventional powerplant installation offering less potential maintenance headaches. The fuselage diameter was kept to a minimum, so that the mounting of the oil cooler had to be external and offset to port, while, to keep the aircraft length within the size requirement for the carrier deck elevators, the vertical tail surfaces were canted forward. In spite of its comparatively small area, the laminar flow wing provided sufficient volume for four protected and two unprotected integral tanks with a total capacity of 1,360 litres (299·2 Imp gal). To achieve the required landing speed of 70 kt with the high wing loading, a combination of Fowler and split flaps were fitted to the wing trailing edge, and leading-edge slats were incorporated. The crew of three was seated in tandem under a long glazed canopy; camera portholes and observation windows were located in the bottom and in the sides of the fuselage. The defensive armament consisted of a single flexible rear-firing 7·92 mm Type 1 machine-gun manned by the radio operator.

Powered by a 1,820 hp Nakajima NK9B Homare 11 driving a four-blade constant-speed propeller, the first C6N1 was completed one month behind

The aerodynamically clean Nakajima C6N1 was the fastest wartime carrier-based reconnaissance aircraft.

Captured Nakajima C6N1 Saiun.

schedule in March 1943, and the aircraft made its first flight on 15 May, 1943. The C6N1 demonstrated pleasing handling characteristics during its flight trials, but its Homare engine suffered from more than its fair share of teething problems. In particular, power at altitude fell considerably below the manufacturer's calculations and consequently the C6N1 failed to meet the speed requirements contained in the 17-Shi specification, and the maximum speed reached during flight tests was 345 kt (397 mph). A total of nineteen prototypes and pre-production aircraft were built between March 1943 and April 1944, and some of these machines had the more powerful NK9H Homare 21 driving a three-blade constant-speed propeller. The Homare 21 powered C6N1 also featured a shorter oil radiator starting at the cooling gills rather than at the cowling lip.

Even though the C6N1 failed to meet the speed requirements of the 17-Shi specification, it offered a substantial increase in speed and range over the D4Y2-C then used for reconnaissance by Naval carrier-based units. In the spring of 1944 the Homare 21 powered C6N1 was placed in production as the Navy Carrier Reconnaissance Plane Saiun (Painted Cloud) Model 11. The first major operation in which the C6N1 took part was the battle of the Marianas. From then on, taking advantage of their range of over 3,000 miles, when a torpedo-shaped ventral drop-tank with a capacity of 730 litres (160·6 Imp gal) was fitted, the Saiuns effectively shadowed the US Fleet, for their speed, almost equal to that of the Grumman F6F-5 Hellcat, rendered them almost immune from interception. Dubbed MYRT by Allied intelligence officers, the C6N1 won the respect of its opponents.

While the Saiun was blooded in combat, its development continued actively at Nakajima's Koizumi plant. The C6N1-B Saiun Model 21 was a projected carrier-borne attack bomber retaining the Homare 21 engine of the reconnaissance version but featuring provision for a torpedo mounted externally, offset to starboard, under the fuselage. Forward-firing armament was to be installed, but the loss of most Japanese carriers eliminated the need for such an aircraft. Conversely, the sudden need for night fighters to defend the Japanese homeland against B-29 attacks led to the modification of the Saiun to meet this role. Designated the C6N1-S, the night fighter model had a reduced crew of two, and a pair of 20 mm Type 99 cannon mounted obliquely in the fuselage. The weight of these weapons and their ammunition was offset by the saving in weight by the omission of one crew member and his equipment, such as the flexible machine-gun, seating, etc, and consequently the original performance was retained. As the effectiveness of the Saiun was impaired by the lack of airborne radar equipment, only a few Saiuns were converted to C6N1-S configuration but they were the fastest night fighters available for defence of the Japanese homeland.

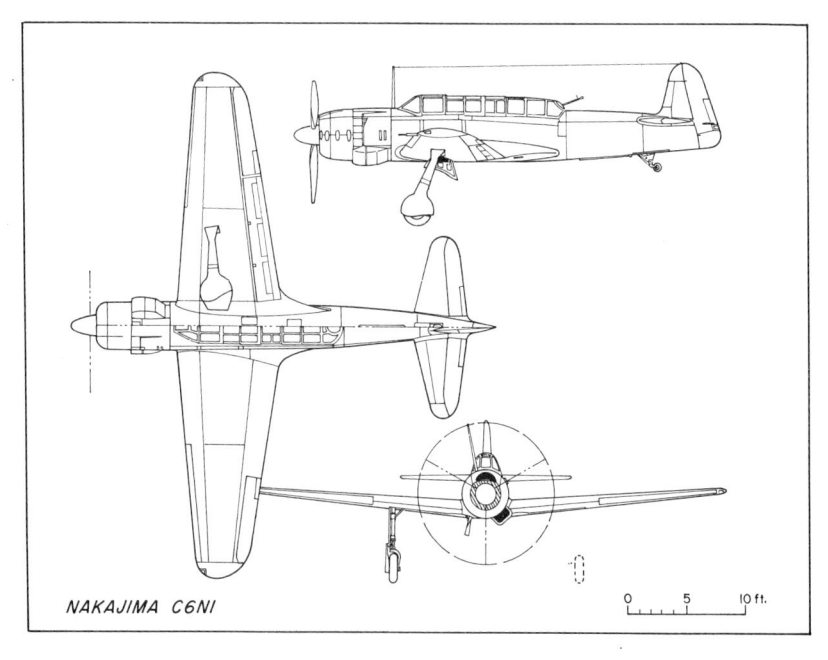

NAKAJIMA C6N1

With a view to improving the altitude performance of the reconnaissance and night fighter versions of the Saiun, Nakajima experimentally fitted a turbosupercharged NK9K-L Homare 24 in a prototype designated C6N2. Flight testing of this aircraft, which suffered from the same teething troubles as other Japanese aircraft powered by a turbosupercharged engine, was still underway when the war ended. Plans were on hand to manufacture, as the C6N3 Saiun KAI 1, a night fighter version of the aircraft powered by the turbosupercharged Homare 24 engine, but these were not realized. Three other advanced versions of the aircraft, the Mitsubishi MK9A powered C6N4 Saiun KAI 2, the C6N5 Saiun KAI 3 and the all-wood C6N6 Saiun KAI 4, were still on the drawing board when the war ended.

A turbosupercharged Nakajima NK9K-L Homare (Honour) 24 installed in a Nakajima C6N2 Saiun (Painted Cloud). (*US Navy Department.*)

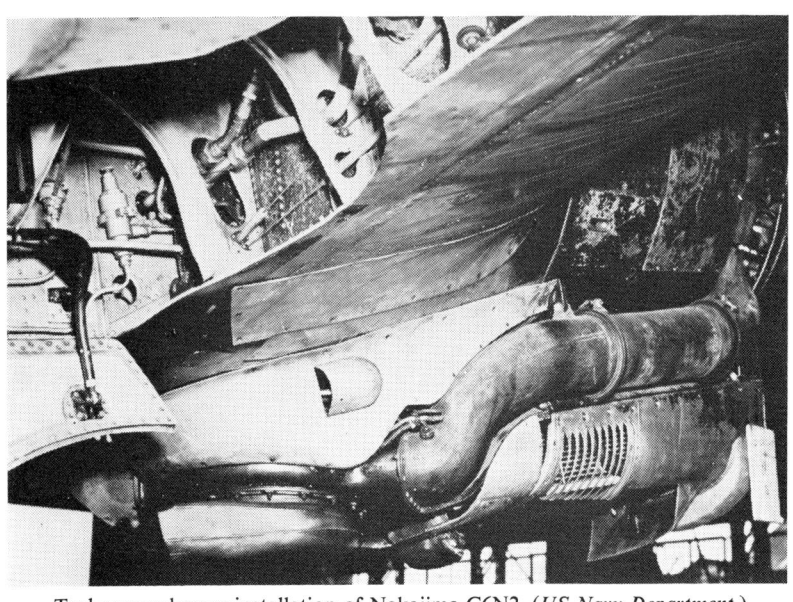

Turbosupercharger installation of Nakajima C6N2. (*US Navy Department.*)

When at 05.40 hr on 15 August, 1945, a C6N1 was shot down by Lieut-Cdr Reidy, it became the last confirmed aerial victory of the second World War. Five minutes later the war was over, and the Saiuns, like all other Japanese aircraft, were grounded.

UNITS ALLOCATED
132nd, 343rd, 601st, 653rd and 762nd Kokutais.

TECHNICAL DATA
Description: Single-engined three-seat carrier-borne reconnaissance aircraft, or land-based two-seat night fighter (C6N1-S and C6N3). All-metal construction with fabric-covered control surfaces.

Accommodation: (Reconnaissance aircraft) Crew of three, comprising pilot, navigator/observer and radio operator/gunner in enclosed cockpit. (Night fighter version) Crew of two, comprising pilot and radio operator/navigator in enclosed cockpit.

Powerplant: One Nakajima NK9B Homare 11 eighteen-cylinder air-cooled radial, rated at 1,820 hp for take-off, 1,600 hp at 2,000 m (6,560 ft) and 1,500 hp at 6,500 m (21,325 ft), driving a four-blade constant-speed metal propeller (17-Shi prototype).

One Nakajima NK9H Homare 21 eighteen-cylinder air-cooled radial, rated at 1,990 hp for take-off, 1,870 hp at 2,000 m (6,560 ft) and 1,700 hp at 6,500 m (21,325 ft), driving a three-blade constant-speed metal propeller (C6N1 and C6N1-S).

One Nakajima NK9K-L Homare 24 eighteen-cylinder air-cooled radial, rated at 1,980 hp for take-off, and 1,780 hp at 9,000 m (29,530 ft), driving a four-blade constant-speed metal propeller (C6N2 and C6N3).

Armament: One flexible rear-firing 7·92 mm Type 2 machine-gun (all versions except C6N1-S and C6N3).

Two fuselage-mounted oblique-firing 20 mm Type 99 cannon (C6N1-S and C6N3).

External stores: one 730 litre (160·6 Imp gal) ventral drop tank.

Dimensions: (C6N1) Span 12·5 m (41 ft 0⅛ in); length 11 m (36 ft 1 1/16 in); height 3·96 m (12 ft 11 39/32 in); wing area 25·5 sq m (274·479 sq ft).

Weights: (C6N1) Empty 2,968 kg (6,543 lb); loaded 4,500 kg (9,921 lb); maximum 5,260 kg (11,596 lb); wing loading 176·5 kg/sq m (36·1 lb/sq ft); power loading 2·3 kg/hp (5 lb/hp).

Performance: (C6N1) Maximum speed 329˙kt at 6,100 m (379 mph at 20,015 ft); cruising speed 210 kt (242 mph); climb to 6,000 m (19,685 ft) in 8 min 9 sec; service ceiling 10,470 m (35,236 ft); range—normal 1,663 naut miles (1,914 st miles), maximum 2,866 naut miles (3,300 st miles).

Production: A total of 463 C6Ns were built by Nakajima Hikoki K.K. at Koizumi and Handa between March 1943 and August 1945.

The Nakajima G8N1 Renzan (Mountain Range) was too late to enter service as the Japanese Navy's first operational four-engined bomber.

Nakajima G8N Renzan (Mountain Range)

By the end of 1942 the Japanese Navy had proved the value of long-ranging land-based attack bombers operating in support of the fleet and effecting deep-penetration offensive missions against enemy bases. At that time the Imperial Staff was studying the calculated performance of the Mitsubishi G7M1 (Navy Experimental 16-Shi Attack Bomber) and of the Kawanishi K-100 (Navy Experimental 17-Shi Attack Bomber) which had been designed to specifications calling for a bomber with a maximum speed of 320 kt (368 mph) and a range of 4,000 naut miles (4,605 st miles) to replace the then operational Mitsubishi G4M. Both the Mitsubishi G7M1 and the Kawanishi K-100 were twin-engined aircraft, and the Navy concluded that this time they would have to abandon their insistence on this configuration if they wanted the specifications to be met. Consequently, in February 1943, they instructed Nakajima to design a four-engined attack bomber as the Navy Experimental 18-Shi Attack Bomber Renzan (Mountain Range) G8N1.

The G8N1 specification issued on 14 September, 1943, called for: (1) a maximum speed of 320 kt (368 mph); (2) climb to 8,000 m (26,245 ft) in 20 min; (3) a range of 2,000 naut miles (2,300 st miles) with full bomb-load and a maximum range of 4,000 naut miles (4,605 st miles); (4) a bomb-load of 4,000 kg (8,816 lb); and (5) good protective and defensive armament in all directions. To meet these requirements Nakajima selected a mid-mounted wing of comparatively small area and high aspect ratio, with laminar flow section. Four 2,000 hp Nakajima NK9K-L Homare 24 with Hitachi 92 turbosuperchargers were adopted and cooled by fans rotating

The Nakajima G8N1 second prototype. (*USAF.*)

in the opposite direction to the propellers. Defensive armament was provided by power-operated nose, dorsal, ventral and tail turrets and two free-swivelling beam machine-guns. Structural design was simplified by using large thick plate covering to ease mass production, and it was hoped that a total of forty-eight G8N1s, including sixteen prototypes and Service trials aircraft, could be produced by September 1945.

The first prototype was completed in October 1944 and was first flown on the 23rd of that month. Three additional aircraft were completed respectively in December 1944, and March and June 1945. Apart from slight problems with the turbosuperchargers, flight tests were satisfactory, but were constantly disrupted by enemy air attacks, and the third G8N1 prototype was destroyed on the ground by US Navy aircraft. The critical shortage of light alloys and the Japanese Navy's more defensive role forced the cancellation of the proposed production programme.

Prior to cancellation of the programme, the design had been modified to allow the use of the G8N1 as a parent aircraft for the Ohka 43 Special Attack Bomber, and a production version powered by four 2,200 hp Mitsubishi MK9A radials had been proposed as the Renzan-Kai Model 22, G8N2. At the time of the Japanese surrender the only version of the aircraft still under consideration for possible construction was the all-steel

Nakajima G8N1 Renzan (Mountain Range) seen in the United States after the war.

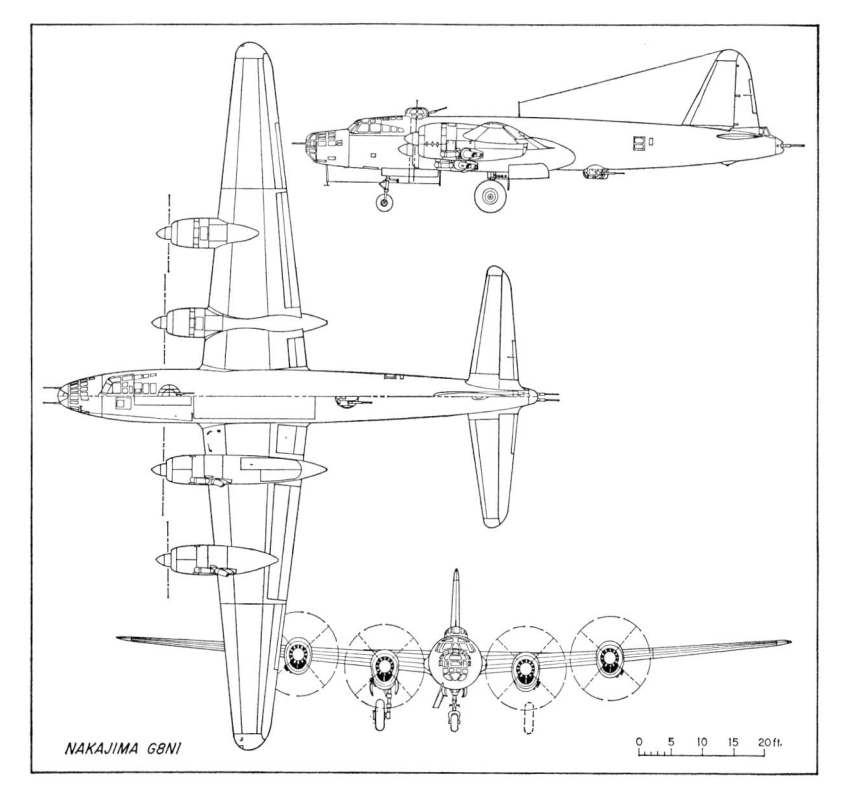

G8N3 Renzan-Kai Model 23. One of the surviving G8N1s, or RITA as it was known to the Allies, was briefly tested in the United States after the war.

TECHNICAL DATA

Description: Four-engined heavy bomber. All-metal construction with fabric-covered control surfaces.
Accommodation: Normal crew of ten.
Powerplant: Four Nakajima NK9K-L Homare 24 eighteen-cylinder air-cooled radials, rated at 2,000 hp for take-off and 1,850 hp at 8,000 m (26,245 ft), driving four-blade constant-speed metal propellers.
Armament: Twin 20 mm Type 99 cannon in power-operated dorsal, ventral and tail turrets, two 13 mm Type 2 machine-guns in a power-operated nose turret and one flexible 13 mm Type 2 machine-gun in each of the port and starboard beam positions.
    Bomb-load—normal, four 250 kg (551 lb) bombs
          —maximum, two 2,000 kg (4,409 lb) bombs
Dimensions: Span 32·54 m (106 ft 9$\frac{3}{32}$ in); length 22·935 m (75 ft 2$\frac{13}{16}$ in); height 7·2 m (23 ft 7$\frac{13}{32}$ in); wing area 112 sq m (1,205·553 sq ft).
Weights: Empty 17,400 kg (38,360 lb); loaded 26,800 kg (59,084 lb); maximum 32,150 kg (70,879 lb); wing loading 239·3 kg/sq m (49 lb/sq ft); power loading 3·4 kg/hp (7·5 lb/hp).
Performance: Maximum speed 320 kt at 8,000 m (368 mph at 26,245 ft); cruising speed 200 kt at 4,000 m (230 mph at 13,125 ft); climb to 8,000 m (26,245 ft) in 17 min 34 sec; service ceiling 10,200 m (33,465 ft); range—normal 2,130 naut miles (2,452 st miles), maximum 4,030 naut miles (4,639 st miles).
Production: Four G8N1s were built between October 1944 and June 1945 by Nakajima Hikoki K.K. in their Koizumi plant.

The turbojet Nakajima Kikka (Orange Blossom). (*Courtesy William Green.*)

Nakajima Kikka (Orange Blossom)

Design work on the Kikka (Orange Blossom)—the only Japanese jet-powered aircraft capable of taking-off on its own power, albeit only twice during the second World War—began in September 1944. The enthusiastic reports on the progress of the Messerschmitt Me 262 twin-jet fighter received from the Japanese Air Attaché in Germany had prompted the Naval Staff to instruct Nakajima to design a single-seat twin-jet attack fighter based on the German Me 262. Requirements included: (1) maximum speed 375 kt (432 mph); (2) range 110 naut miles (127 st miles) with a bomb-load of 500 kg (1,102 lb) or 150 naut miles (173 st miles) with a bomb-load of 250 kg (551 lb); (3) landing speed 80 kt (92 mph); and (4) take-off run 350 m (1,150 ft) when using two 450 kg (992 lb) thrust RATOG bottles. In addition, provisions were to be made for folding wings, to enable the aircraft to be hidden in caves and tunnels and also for ease of production by semi-skilled labour.

The aircraft, designed by Kazuo Ohno and Kenichi Matsumura, externally resembled the Me 262 but was smaller. The two turbojets were mounted in separate nacelles under the wings to allow, with a minimum of changes, the installation of engines of various types. This feature was to prove particularly useful when engine development fell behind airframe design. Initially the aircraft was to be powered by two 200 kg (441 lb) thrust Tsu-11 Campini-type engines, but these were soon replaced by two 340 kg (750 lb) thrust Ne-12 turbojets. By that time the project had been designated Navy Special Attacker Kikka, but its future was still uncertain as the Ne-12 failed to deliver sufficient thrust. Fortunately, photographs of the German BMW 003 axial-flow turbojet had been obtained by Eng

Second prototype Nakajima Kikka (Orange Blossom) shortly before completion. (*Informations Aéronautiques.*)

Eichi Iwaya of the Japanese Navy, and from these the Japanese were able to design a similar turbojet, designated Ne-20, offering a thrust of 475 kg (1,047 lb). It appeared that with two Ne-20 turbojets the Kikka would meet its design performance and the project rapidly picked up speed.

Completed in August 1945, the first Kikka made its maiden flight on 7 August at Kisarazu Naval Air Base with Lieut-Cdr Susumu Takaoka at the controls. Four days later the pilot aborted a take-off during the second flight, the accident being caused by mounting the two RATOG bottles at an incorrect angle. A second prototype was almost ready for flight trials and eighteen additional prototypes and pre-production aircraft were in various stages of assembly when on 15 August, 1945, the development of the aircraft was terminated.

The port Ne-20 axial-flow turbojet in the second prototype Nakajima Kikka (Orange Blossom). (*Edgar Deigan.*)

NAKAJIMA Kikka

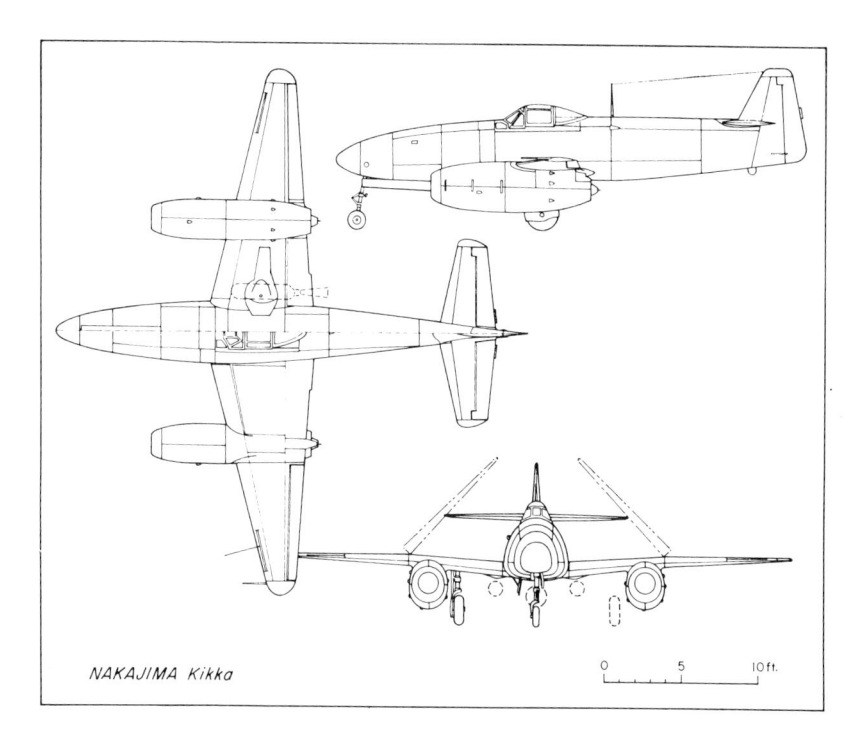

Several advanced versions of the Kikka remained on the drawing board, and included an unarmed two-seat advanced trainer, for which version the third Kikka was to serve as prototype. An unarmed two-seat reconnaissance aircraft and a single-seat fighter were also under development. The fighter version was to be armed with two 30 mm Type 5 cannon and powered with either two 900 kg (1,984 lb) thrust Ne-130 or two 885 kg (1,951 lb) thrust Ne-330 axial-flow turbojets.

TECHNICAL DATA

Description: Twin-jet single-seat attack bomber. All-metal construction with fabric-covered control surfaces.
Accommodation: Pilot in enclosed cockpit.
Powerplant: Two 475 kg (1,047 lb) static thrust Ne-20 axial-flow turbojets.
Armament: One 500 kg (1,102 lb) or 800 kg (1,764 lb) bomb.
Dimensions: Span 10 m (32 ft 9 11/16 in); length 8·125 m (26 ft 7 7/8 in); height 2·95 m (9 ft 8 5/32 in); wing area 13·2 sq m (142·083 sq ft).
Weights: Empty 2,300 kg (5,071 lb); loaded 3,500 kg (7,716 lb); maximum 4,080 kg (8,995 lb); wing loading 265 kg/sq m (54·3 lb/sq ft); power loading 3·7 kg/kg s.t. (3·7 lb/lb s.t.).
Performance: Maximum speed 336 kt (387 mph) at sea level and 376 kt at 10,000 m (433 mph at 32,810 ft); climb to 10,000 m (32,810 ft) in 26 min; service ceiling 12,000 m (39,370 ft); range 509 naut miles (586 st miles).
Production: Two aircraft were built between June and August 1945 by Nakajima Hikoki K.K.

Yokosuka K5Y

Built in larger numbers than any other Japanese training aircraft, the Yokosuka designed Navy Type 93 Intermediate Trainer was put into production in 1933 and, in spite of the advent of more modern monoplane advanced trainers, this biplane remained in production until the end of the war. Development of this prolific trainer began in 1932 when the Navy instructed Kawanishi to develop, with the help of engineers from the Dai-Ichi Kaigun Koku Gijitsusho (First Naval Air Technical Arsenal), an improved version of the Navy Type 91 Intermediate Trainer, of which two prototypes had been built in that Arsenal during 1931.

Bearing the designation K5Y1, the new aircraft primarily differed from its predecessor in a redesigned upper wing with increased dihedral and sweep, mounted closer above the fuselage, and redesigned tail surfaces. The K5Y1 was a sesquiplane with fixed undercarriage, powered by a 340 hp Hitachi Amakaze 11 radial with Townend ring. The prototype was completed and flown in December 1933. Following an abbreviated flight trials programme the aircraft was accepted by the Navy, and quantity production began at Kawanishi in January 1934 as the Navy Type 93 Intermediate Trainer. The land-based version of the aircraft bore the designation K5Y1, while the K5Y2 designation applied to a version fitted with twin floats. Only sixty K5Y1s and K5Y2s were built by Kawanishi between 1933 and 1936, but successive orders were placed with seven other manufacturers, and the aircraft, coded WILLOW by the Allies, saw extensive service throughout the war.

Three other versions of the aircraft, the K5Y3, K5Y4 and K5Y5, with more powerful models of the Amakaze radial enclosed in a smoother cowling, were planned, but only the float-equipped K5Y3 was built, two prototypes being manufactured by Nippon Hikoki K.K. The land-based K5Y4 and K5Y5 remained on the drawing board.

Yokosuka K5Y1 Navy Type 93 Intermediate Trainer of the Kasumigaura Kokutai. (*Aireview*.)

Yokosuka K5Y2 floatplane version of the K5Y1 Navy Type 93 Intermediate Trainer. The K5Y2 illustrated was used by the Kasumigaura Kokutai. (*Aireview*.)

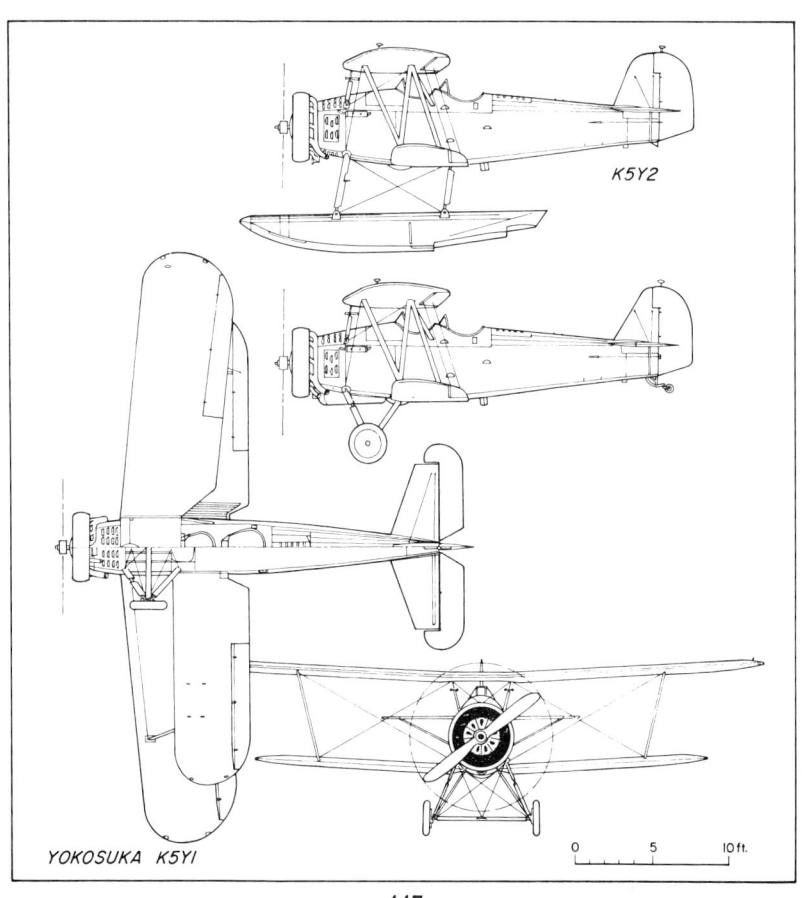

K5Y2

YOKOSUKA K5Y1

447

UNITS ALLOCATED

Kashima, Kasumigaura, Shanghai, Suzuka and Tsuchiura Kokutais.

TECHNICAL DATA

Description: Two-seat land-based intermediate trainer (K5Y1, K5Y4 and K5Y5) or twin-float seaplane intermediate trainer (K5Y2 and K5Y3). Mixed construction.

Accommodation: Pilot and instructor in tandem open cockpits.

Powerplant: One Hitachi Amakaze 11 nine-cylinder air-cooled radial rated at 340 hp for take-off and 300 hp at sea level, driving a two-blade wooden propeller (K5Y1 and K5Y2).

One 515 hp Hitachi Amakaze 21 nine-cylinder air-cooled radial rated at 515 hp for take-off and 480 hp at 1,500 m (4,920 ft), driving a two-blade wooden propeller (K5Y3).

One 480 hp Hitachi Amakaze 21A nine-cylinder air-cooled radial rated at 480 hp for take-off and 450 hp at 1,500 m (4,920 ft), driving a two-blade wooden propeller (K5Y4).

One 515 hp Hitachi Amakaze 15 nine-cylinder air-cooled radial rated at 515 hp for take-off and 450 hp at sea level, driving a two-blade wooden propeller (K5Y5).

Armament: One forward-firing 7·7 mm Type 89 machine-gun and one flexible rear-firing 7·7 mm Type 92 machine-gun.

External stores: two 30 kg (66 lb) bombs or ten 10 kg (22 lb) bombs.

	K5Y1	K5Y2
Dimensions:		
Span	11 m	11 m
	(36 ft 1 1/16 in)	(36 ft 1 1/16 in)
Length	8·05 m	8·78 m
	(26 ft 4 13/16 in)	(28 ft 9 21/32 in)
Height	3·2 m	3·68 m
	(10 ft 5 31/32 in)	(12 ft 0 7/8 in)
Wing area	27·7 sq m	27·7 sq m
	(298·159 sq ft)	(298·159 sq ft)
Weights:		
Empty	1,000 kg	1,150 kg
	(2,205 lb)	(2,535 lb)
Loaded	1,500 kg	1,650 kg
	(3,307 lb)	(3,638 lb)
Wing loading	54·2 kg/sq m	59·6 kg/sq m
	(11·1 lb/sq ft)	(12·2 lb/sq ft)
Power loading	4·4 kg/hp	4·9 kg/hp
	(9·7 lb/hp)	(10·7 lb/hp)
Performance:		
Maximum speed	115 kt at sea level	107 kt at sea level
	(132 mph at sea level)	(123 mph at sea level)
Cruising speed	75 kt at 1,000 m	75 kt at 1,000 m
	(86 mph at 3,280 ft)	(86 mph at 3,280 ft)
Climb to	3,000 m (9,845 ft)	3,000 m (9,845 ft)
in	13 min 32 sec	19 min 35 sec
Service ceiling	5,700 m	4,330 m
	(18,700 ft)	(14,205 ft)
Range	550 naut miles	379 naut miles
	(633 st miles)	(436 st miles)

Production: A total of 5,770 K5Ys were built between 1933 and 1945 as follows:

Dai-Ichi Kaigun Kokusho, Kasumigaura:	75 K5Y1 (1944)
Fuji Hikoki K.K.:	869 K5Y1 and K5Y2 (1942–45)
Hitachi Kokuki K.K.:	1,393 K5Y1 and K5Y2 (1940–44)
Kawanishi Kokuki K.K.:	60 K5Y1 and K5Y2 (1933–36)
Mitsubishi Jukogyo K.K.:	60 K5Y1
Nakajima Hikoki K.K.:	24 K5Y1 (1935–36)
K.K. Watanabe Tekkosho:	{ 393 K5Y1 (1936–39)
	{ 163 K5Y2 (1937–39)
Nippon Hikoki K.K.	{ 2,025 K5Y1 (1940–45)
	{ 708 K5Y2 and K5Y3 (1940–45)

Yokosuka B4Y1 Navy Type 96 Carrier Attack Bomber bearing the presentation marking Hokoku 130. (*US Navy Department.*)

Yokosuka B4Y

When the war against Japan began, the Yokosuka B4Y1 biplane was believed to be the major type of carrier-borne torpedo-bomber operated by the Japanese Navy, and erroneous early reports credited the sinking of HMS *Prince of Wales* and HMS *Repulse* to this aircraft. The truth, however, was quite different, as by 1941 the B4Y1, which had been developed to serve as an interim carrier-based attack bomber pending availability of the Nakajima B5N1 and the Mitsubishi B5M1 monoplanes, had been relegated to training duties, and it is rather doubtful that the type was ever encountered in combat by Allied forces.

In 1934 the Navy had an urgent need for a new type of carrier-borne attack bomber since the Navy Type 92 Carrier Attack Bomber (B3Y1) had been found to be quite unreliable. To meet this requirement the Naval Staff issued a 9-Shi specification and design proposals were submitted by Mitsubishi, Nakajima and the Dai-Ichi Kaigun Koku Gijitsusho (First Naval Air Technical Arsenal). The Arsenal's project was the work of Sanae Kawasaki, who endeavoured to design an aircraft capable of receiving various types of powerplants and making use of existing components. To realize his goal Sanae Kawasaki matched a new fuselage and tail section to the wings of the Kawanishi E7K1 which had been found highly efficient. The first B4Y1 prototype of this hybrid, powered by a 600 hp Hiro Type 91 liquid-cooled engine, was completed and flown in late 1935. During 1936 four additional prototypes were built, the second and third prototypes being powered by the 640 hp Nakajima Kotobuki 3 radial, and the fourth and fifth prototypes receiving the 840 hp Nakajima Hikari 2 radial, and these were tested against the Mitsubishi Ka-12 and the two

Yokosuka B4Y1 Navy Type 96 Carrier Attack Bombers. These have an additional interplane strut at the centre section/outer plane joints. The nearest aircraft bears the presentation number 135.

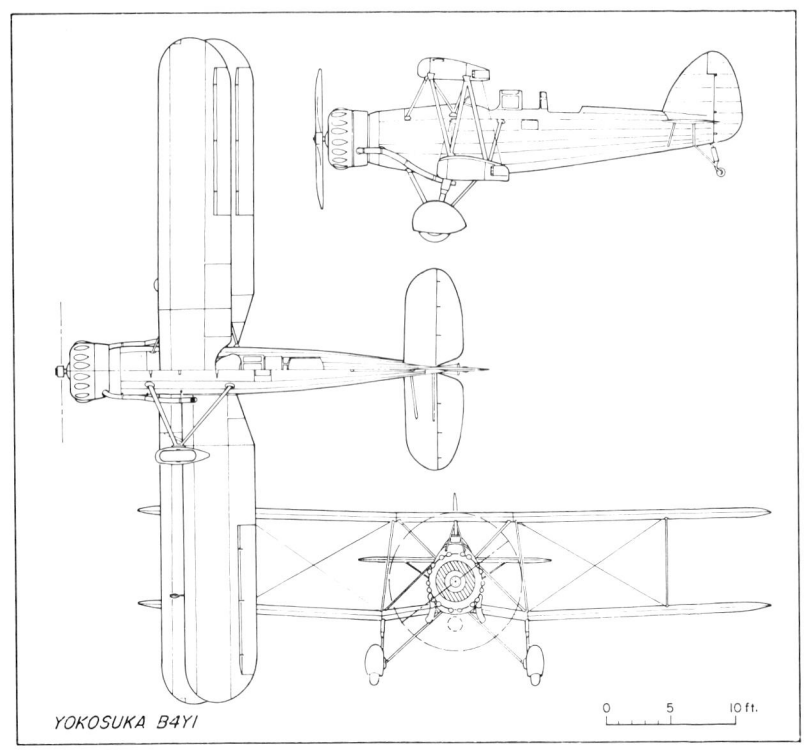

YOKOSUKA B4Y1

Nakajima B4N1s. At the conclusion of these tests, the Hikari 2 powered B4Y1 was found to be superior to the B4N1 and the Ka-12, and in November 1936 production orders for the B4Y1 were placed with Mitsubishi, Nakajima and the Dai-Juichi Kaigun Kokusho (Eleventh Naval Air Arsenal). Designated Navy Type 96 Carrier Attack Bomber, and later coded JEAN by the Allies, the production aircraft had a canopy covering the rear cockpit and were operated aboard Japanese carriers until 1940, seeing combat action during the second Sino-Japanese war. During the Pacific War, the few B4Y1s still airworthy were operated in a training capacity.

UNITS ALLOCATED
Aircraft carriers: *Akagi, Hosho, Kaga, Ryujo* and *Soryu*; 13th and 15th Kokutais.

TECHNICAL DATA
Description: Single-engined carrier-borne torpedo-bomber. All-metal structure with light alloy and fabric covering.
Accommodation: Pilot in open cockpit and navigator and radio operator/gunner in enclosed rear cockpit.
Powerplant: One 600 hp Hiro Type 91 twelve-cylinder liquid-cooled engine rated at 750 hp for take-off and 600 hp at 1,500 m (4,920 ft), driving a two-blade propeller (first prototype).
One 640 hp Nakajima Kotobuki 3 nine-cylinder air-cooled radial rated at 640 hp for take-off and 715 hp at 2,800 m (9,185 ft), driving a two-blade propeller (second and third prototypes).
One Nakajima Hikari 2 nine-cylinder air-cooled radial rated at 840 hp for take-off and 700 hp at 1,200 m (3,940 ft), driving a two-blade propeller (fourth and fifth prototypes and production aircraft).
Armament: One flexible rear-firing 7·7 mm Type 92 machine-gun.
External stores: one 800 kg (1,764 lb) torpedo, or 500 kg (1,102 lb) of bombs.
Dimensions: Span 15 m (49 ft 2 ⅛ in); length 10·15 m (33 ft 3 ⅻ in); height 4·36 m (14 ft 3 ⅔ in); wing area 50 sq m (538·194 sq ft).
Weights: Empty 2,000 kg (4,409 lb); loaded 3,600 kg (7,937 lb); wing loading 72 kg/sq m (14·7 lb/sq ft); power loading 4·3 kg/hp (9·4 lb/hp).
Performance: Maximum speed 150 kt (173 mph); climb to 3,000 m (9,845 ft) in 14 min; service ceiling 6,000 m (19,685 ft); range 850 naut miles (978 st miles).
Production: A total of 205 B4Y1s were built as follows:

Dai-Ichi Kaigun Koku Gijitsusho, Yokosuka:	5 prototypes (1935–36)
Nakajima Hikoki K.K.:	37 production aircraft (1937–38)
Mitsubishi Jukogyo K.K., Nagoya:	135 production aircraft (1937–38)
Dai-Juichi Kaigun Kokusho, Hiro:	28 production aircraft (1938)

Yokosuka E14Y

Designed by Mitsuo Yamada of the Dai-Ichi Kaigun Koku Gijitsusho (First Naval Air Technical Arsenal) to meet the requirements of a 12-Shi specification calling for a small submarine-borne reconnaissance seaplane, the E14Y1 became the only enemy aircraft to drop bombs on the American mainland when an aircraft of this type, flown by Warrant Officer Fujita operating from the submarine I-25, dropped four 76 kg (167·5 lb) phosphorus bombs in two attacks along the wooded Oregon coast.

Powered by a 340 hp Hitachi Tempu 12 nine-cylinder air-cooled radial engine, the prototype E14Y1 was completed in 1939 at Yokosuka, and comparative trials with the Watanabe E14W1, designed to meet the same 12-Shi specification, took place soon after. Destined to be carried in a watertight hangar, the E14Y1 could easily be dismantled for storage aboard the submarine. For this purpose the twin floats and supporting struts could

Prototype of the Yokosuka E14Y1, the only type of enemy aircraft to have dropped bombs on the American mainland. (*Eckert.*)

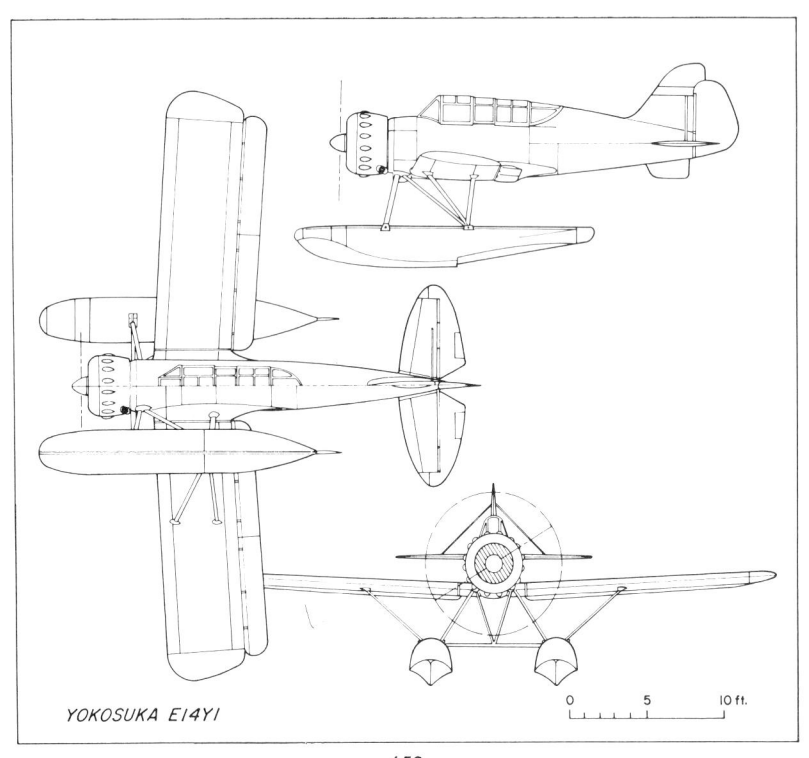

YOKOSUKA E14Y1

be detached from the fuselage while the wings could be detached from the fuselage at the spar fittings. In its original form the aircraft was fitted with low aspect ratio vertical tail surfaces, but flight trials revealed the need to substitute higher surfaces, which in turn necessitated the adoption of a detachable top fin section so as to fit into the submarine's hangar. At the end of comparative trials, the Yokosuka design was found to be superior to the E14W1, but the production contract was assigned to Watanabe. The aircraft was designated Navy Type 0 Submarine-borne Reconnaissance Seaplane Model 1-1 (later redesignated Navy Type 0 Small Reconnaissance Seaplane Model 11).

Known to the Allies as GLEN, the E14Y1 made its operational début on 17 December, 1941, when the submarine I-7 launched its aircraft for a dawn reconnaissance over Pearl Harbor to assess the damage done by the carriers' bombers. Until 1943, when the increased use of radar by the Allies made such missions impractical, the E14Y1s were used for similar reconnaissance sorties over Allied bases in Australia, New Zealand, Africa, Madagascar and the Aleutians. The aircraft was also used by commerce-raiding submarines, but its use was limited by the inability to operate in any but the smoothest sea conditions.

UNITS ALLOCATED
Submarines I-7 to I-11, and I-15 to I-35.

TECHNICAL DATA

Description: Two-seat submarine-borne twin-float reconnaissance monoplane. Welded steel-tube fuselage with fabric, wood and light alloy covering. Fabric-covered wings with light metal spars and wooden ribs.

Accommodation: Pilot and observer seated in tandem enclosed cockpits.

Powerplant: One Hitachi Tempu 12 nine-cylinder air-cooled radial engine, rated at 340 hp for take-off and 300 hp at sea level, driving a two-blade wooden propeller.

Armament: One flexible rear-firing 7·7 mm Type 92 machine-gun and 60 kg (132 lb) of bombs.*

Dimensions: Span 11 m (36 ft 1$\frac{1}{16}$ in); length 8·54 m (28 ft 0$\frac{3}{32}$ in); height 3·8 m (12 ft 5$\frac{19}{32}$ in); wing area 19 sq m (204·514 sq ft).

Weights: Empty 1,119 kg (2,469 lb); loaded 1,450 kg (3,197 lb); maximum 1,600 kg (3,527 lb); wing loading 76·3 kg/sq m (15·7 lb/sq ft); power loading 4·3 kg/hp (9·4 lb/hp).

Performance: Maximum speed 133 kt (153 mph) at sea level; cruising speed 90 kt at 1,000 m (104 mph at 3,280 ft); climb to 3,000 m (9,845 ft) in 10 min 11 sec; service ceiling 5,420 m (17,780 ft); range 476 naut miles (548 st miles).

Production: One prototype E14Y1 built by Dai-Ichi Kaigun Koku Gijitsusho at Yokosuka, and 125 production aircraft built by K.K. Watanabe Tekkosho between 1941 and 1943.

*The increased bomb-load on the Oregon flights was made possible by single-crew operation.

Yokosuka D4Y1 Suisei photographed during its Service trials.

Yokosuka D4Y Suisei (Comet)

The Suisei (Comet) was one of the most aesthetically pleasing single-engined bombers to serve with any of the fighting powers during the second World War, and it brought the design of this category of aircraft to an aerodynamic level comparable to that of the de Havilland Mosquito in the twin-engined category. Whereas the Mosquito was of wooden construction, the Yokosuka Suisei was of all-metal construction, but apart from their aerodynamic achievements both types had many points in common. Both were originally designed as bombers but were first operated in the reconnaissance role and each saw service in the night fighter role. In spite of its superb performance, however, the Suisei had a considerably shorter operational history than the Mosquito as the Japanese surrender ended its career. Today the Suisei, or JUDY as it was known to the Allies, has faded from the memory of aviation enthusiasts.

In the spring of 1938 the Japanese Navy acquired from Germany the Heinkel He 118V4 and its production rights, and the aircraft—designated DXHe1 according to the Japanese Navy short designation system—underwent flight trials at Yokosuka. Reaching a maximum speed of 260 mph on the power of its Daimler-Benz DB 601A, the DXHe1 impressed the Naval Staff and plans were on hand to produce a modified version for service aboard aircraft carriers, but the aircraft disintegrated during a test flight. Shortlived as they had been, the DXHe1 tests strongly influenced the Navy, and late in 1938 the design staff of the Dai-Ichi Kaigun Koku Gijitsusho at Yokosuka was instructed to design an aircraft, inspired by, but smaller than, the He 118V4, to meet the requirements of a Navy Experimental 13-Shi Carrier Bomber specification. These requirements included: (1) maximum speed 280 kt (322 mph); (2) cruising speed 230 kt (265 mph); (3) range 800 naut miles (921 st miles) with a 250 kg (551 lb) bomb, and 1,200 naut miles (1,381 st miles) without bomb-load; and (4) ability to operate from small carriers.

To meet these requirements, a team led by Chief Eng Masao Yamana designed a clean mid-wing monoplane of comparatively small size for a two-seat dive-bomber. Even though its wing had a span and area comparable to that of the single-seat Mitsubishi A6M2 fighter, the prototype D4Y1 designed to the 13-Shi specification had a fuel capacity almost equal to that of the much larger Aichi D3A2 it was intended to replace. The wing span was sufficiently short to preclude the need for a wing-folding system. Three electrically-operated dive-brakes were fitted beneath the wings ahead of each landing flap, and the mainwheels and undercarriage legs retracted in front of the main spar. Although the design of the D4Y1 had been inspired by the Heinkel He 118, the Japanese engineers succeeded in producing an airframe which was not only lighter and smaller, but which was also much improved aerodynamically, as indicated by the fact that the D4Y1 featured an internal bomb-bay with provision for a single bomb of up to 500 kg (1,102 lb) whereas the German aircraft carried its bomb-load externally. Plans had been made to power the aircraft with a licence-built version of the Daimler-Benz DB 601A, the Aichi Atsuta twelve-cylinder liquid-cooled engine, but the unavailability of the Japanese-built engine when the first prototype was being built forced a change to the 960 hp Daimler-Benz DB 600G, of which a few examples had been imported from Germany.

Powered by a DB 600G, the first D4Y1 was completed in November 1940 and made its maiden flight at Yokosuka the following month. Performance and flight characteristics of the aircraft exceeded the Navy's most optimistic hopes, and the trials were accelerated in 1941, when four additional prototypes, differing from the first aircraft in only minor details, were delivered. These five prototypes built at Yokosuka were all powered by the 960 hp Daimler-Benz DB 600G and carried a defensive armament including two forward-firing 7·7 mm Type 97 machine-guns mounted in the upper fuselage decking and one flexible rear-firing 7·92 mm Type 1 machine-gun manned by the radio operator. For short missions a maximum warload of 1,234 lb could be carried and included one 500 kg (1,102 lb) bomb in the fuselage bomb-bay and two 30 kg (66 lb) bombs under the wings. But when simulated dive-bombing tests were made, the aircraft ran into trouble as wing flutter developed and cracks appeared in the wing spars. Consequently, plans to mass produce the aircraft in the Nagoya plant of the Aichi Tokei Denki K.K. had to be hurriedly changed, as it was obvious that the D4Y1 was not ready to be operated in its intended role.

Initially, the pre-production D4Y1s, which began rolling off Aichi's

Yokosuka D4Y1 Navy Carrier Bomber Suisei (Comet) Model 11.

assembly lines in the spring of 1942, differed from the Yokosuka-built prototypes only in being powered by the 1,200 hp Aichi AE1A Atsuta 12. With its maximum speed substantially higher than that of the Nakajima B5N2 operated as reconnaissance aircraft, and with good range performance, the Atsuta 12 powered D4Y1 appeared to be ideally suited for that role. Accordingly the Navy instructed Aichi to modify the aircraft as the D4Y1-C carrier-borne reconnaissance aircraft by mounting a K-8 camera in the aft fuselage, while Aichi engineers combined their efforts with those of the staff of Dai-Ichi Kaigun Koku Gijitsusho in attempting to improve the rigidity of the wing.

Two pre-production D4Y1-Cs modified as carrier reconnaissance aircraft were embarked aboard the *Soryu* when this aircraft carrier sailed to take part in the Japanese attack on Midway. But these aircraft had little chance to demonstrate their worth, as they were lost when the *Soryu* was sunk in the early phase of the carrier action. In July 1942 the D4Y1-C was ordered into production as the Navy Type 2 Carrier Reconnaissance Plane Model 11. Production was slow in gaining tempo as the requirement for specialized carrier-borne reconnaissance aircraft was limited, and by the end of March 1943 Aichi had only completed twenty-five D4Y1s and D4Y1-Cs including pre-production aircraft. Small detachments of D4Y1-Cs were beginning to be assigned to aircraft carriers in the autumn of 1942, and the type remained in first-line service until the end of the war. Fitted with two 330 litre (72·6 Imp gal) drop tanks, the D4Y1-C had extensive range, and the aircraft was liked by its crews, who complained only of lack of pilot and fuel tank protection while ground crews experienced some difficulty with the liquid-cooled engine.

Development of the D4Y1 continued and, fitted with reinforced wing spars and improved dive-brakes, it was finally accepted as a dive-bomber in March 1943, entering production as the Suisei (Comet) Carrier Bomber

Model 11. As there was a demand for a fast aircraft capable of supplementing and eventually supplanting the obsolescent Aichi D3A2, production was rapidly speeded up and most of the 589 D4Y1s and D4Y1-Cs built by Aichi between April 1943 and March 1944 were of the dive-bomber variant. When in June 1944 the 1st, 2nd and 3rd Koku Sentais (Carrier Divisions) were sent to ward off the impending Allied amphibious attacks on the Marianas, the nine Japanese carriers embarked a total of 141 Suiseis and thirty-three D4Y1-Cs .When attempting to attack the US Fleet, the aircraft were intercepted long before reaching their targets and a considerable number of Suiseis were shot down during the Marianas 'turkey shoot' and they failed to sink a single American carrier. Some of the Suiseis participating in this battle were of the Model 21 variant (D4Y1 KAI) which had been converted by installing catapult equipment to enable them to operate aboard the small carriers.

In spite of the ominous lesson of the battle for the Marianas, the next production version of the aircraft still had no provision for either crew or fuel tank protection, and modifications were limited to the installation of the 1,400 hp Aichi AE1P Atsuta 32 engine. Designated Suisei Carrier Bomber Model 12 (D4Y2), this variant entered production in October 1944, and the Model 12A (D4Y2a) differed only in having a flexible rear-firing 13 mm Type 2 machine-gun in lieu of the standard 7·92 mm machine-gun. When fitted with catapult equipment, these versions became Model 22 (D4Y2 KAI) and Model 22A (D4Y2a KAI) respectively, while similar reconnaissance variants were built as the Navy Type 2 Carrier Reconnaissance Plane Model 12 and 12A (D4Y2-C and D4Y2-Ca). Entering service during the battle for the Philippines, the different D4Y2 variants were decimated by the numerically superior Allied fighter aircraft and a large number of Suiseis were expended in kamikaze attacks.

The Aichi-built Yokosuka D4Y2 Suisei (Comet) was the fastest carrier-borne dive-bomber in service during the second World War. (*Copyright 'Maru.'*)

Yokosuka D4Y3 Suisei Model 33 of the 601st Kokutai.

Maintenance difficulties with the Atsuta engine had plagued the operational career of the D4Y series since the early days, and many of the Navy officers were strongly advocating replacement of the unreliable liquid-cooled engine with an air-cooled radial. Even though the installation of a radial engine of large diameter on the Suisei airframe of narrow cross section presented considerable difficulties, the Aichi engineering team proposed to fit the 1,560 hp Mitsubishi MK8P Kinsei 62 fourteen-cylinder radial on a standard D4Y2 airframe. A close-fitting cowling, incorporating a supercharger air intake in its upper lip, was designed. By smoothly tapering the sides of the cowling the powerplant installation produced only a minimal drag increase, and in May 1944 tests with an experimental aircraft designated D4Y3 indicated that the performance of the modified aircraft was virtually identical to that of the D4Y2, while the only negative effects of the modification were reduction of pilot visibility during carrier landings and reduction of manoeuvrability on take-off. As the Kinsei engine was more reliable than the Atsuta, the Navy authorized Aichi to produce the aircraft as the Suisei Carrier Bomber Model 33 (D4Y3) and Model 33A (D4Y3a), this last variant being armed with a flexible 13 mm Type 2 machine-gun. Late production D4Y3s were fitted with three solid propellant RATOG units strapped under the fuselage to improve take-off

Yokosuka D4Y3 Suisei Model 33, c/n 3957, belonging to a land-based unit. (*US Navy Department.*)

when operating with maximum warloads from small carriers, but no reconnaissance version of the aircraft was produced, as by then the superior Nakajima C6N1 was available.

Designed in late 1944, the D4Y4 was a specialized suicide bomber. As no radio operator/gunner was required for kamikaze attacks, the D4Y4 was designed as a single-seat version of the Kinsei powered D4Y3 carrying a single 800 kg (1,764 lb) bomb semi-recessed beneath the fuselage. Fitted with three RATOG auxiliary rockets which could be used either to shorten take-off from small airstrips or boost the speed during the final dive, 296 of these aircraft were built in 1945 as the Suisei Special Attack Bomber Model 43.

The Dai-Juichi Kaigun Kokusho (11th Naval Air Arsenal) at Hiro was also responsible for the production of Suisei bombers, and between April 1944 and the end of the war, this Arsenal delivered 215 D4Y1s, D4Y2s and D4Y3s. It also undertook modification of a limited number of D4Y2s

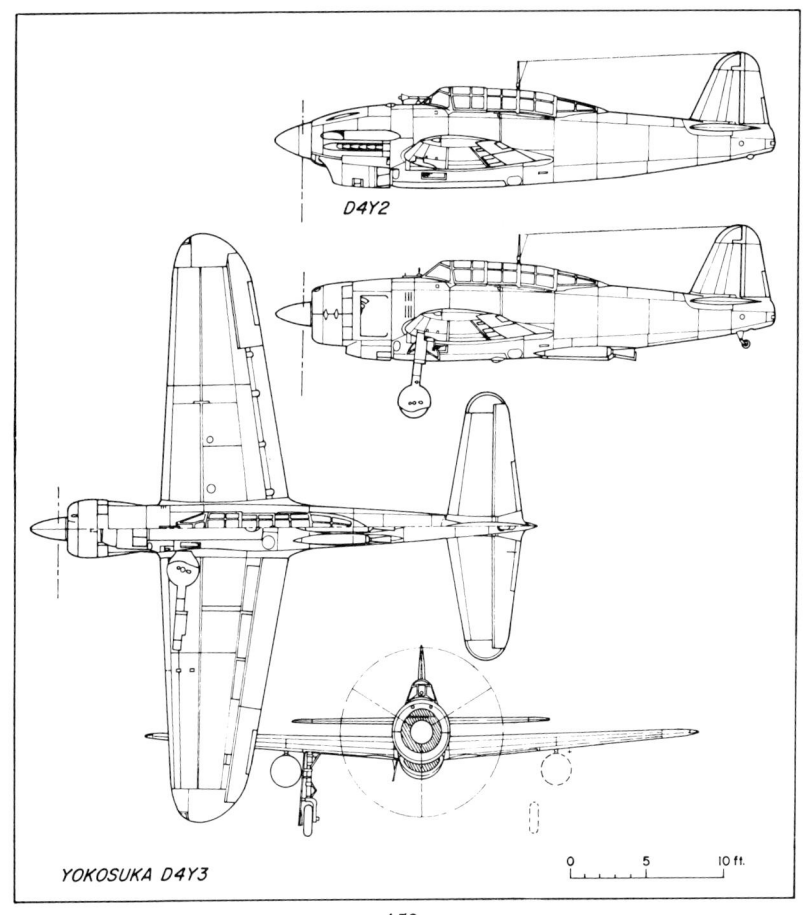

D4Y2

YOKOSUKA D4Y3

intended to operate in the night fighter role. For this duty the bomb racks, flexible rear-firing guns and carrier equipment were removed, and the internal bomb-bay was faired over. A single 20 mm Type 99 Model 2 cannon was mounted obliquely in the fuselage to fire upward and forward at a 30 deg angle. Some of these aircraft were also fitted with wing racks for air-to-air rockets. Designated Suisei-E Night Fighter (D4Y2-S), these aircraft were used with limited success from bases in Central Japan against low-flying B-29s operating at night. Lacking AI radar and having a slow climbing speed, the D4Y2-S was rather ineffective as a night fighter.

A final bomber version providing crew and fuel tank protection was under development when Japan capitulated. Intended to be powered by a 1,825 hp Nakajima NK9C Homare 12 eighteen-cylinder air-cooled radial, the D4Y5 was to have entered production in late 1945 as the Suisei Carrier Bomber Model 54.

The last sortie of the Suisei was made on 15 August, 1945, when Admiral Ugaki led eleven aircraft in a final but inconclusive kamikaze attack off Okinawa.

UNITS ALLOCATED

Carriers: *Chitose, Chiyoda, Hiyo, Junyo, Shinyo, Shokaku, Soryu, Taiyo, Unryu, Unyo* and *Zuikaku*.

121st, 131st, 503rd, 601st, 634th, 653rd, 721st, Southwest Islands and Yokosuka Kokutais.

TECHNICAL DATA

Description: Single-engined carrier-based dive-bomber and reconnaissance aircraft, and land-based night fighter (D4Y2-S). All-metal construction with fabric-covered control surfaces.

Accommodation: Crew of two in tandem enclosed cockpit (all versions except D4Y4) or pilot in enclosed cockpit (D4Y4).

Powerplant: One 960 hp Daimler-Benz DB 600G twelve-cylinder inverted vee liquid-cooled engine, driving a three-blade constant-speed metal propeller (13-Shi prototype).

One Aichi AE1A Atsuta 12 twelve-cylinder inverted vee liquid-cooled engine, rated at 1,200 hp for take-off, 1,010 hp at 1,500 m (4,920 ft) and 965 hp at 4,450 m (14,600 ft), driving a three-blade constant-speed metal propeller (D4Y1, D4Y1 KAI, and D4Y1-C).

One Aichi AE1P Atsuta 32 twelve-cylinder liquid-cooled vee engine, rated at 1,400 hp for take-off, 1,340 hp at 1,700 m (5,580 ft) and 1,280 hp at 5,000 m (16,405 ft), driving a three-blade constant-speed metal propeller (D4Y2, D4Y2a, D4Y2 KAI, D4Y2-S, D4Y2-C and D4Y2-Ca).

One Mitsubishi MK8P Kinsei 62 fourteen-cylinder air-cooled radial engine rated at 1,560 hp for take-off, 1,340 hp at 2,100 m (6,890 ft) and 1,190 hp at 5,800 m (19,030 ft), driving a three-blade constant-speed metal propeller (D4Y3, D4Y3a and D4Y4).

One Nakajima NK9C Homare 12 eighteen-cylinder air-cooled radial engine rated at 1,825 hp for take-off, 1,670 hp at 2,400 m (7,875 ft) and 1,560 hp at 6,550 m (21,490 ft), driving a four-blade constant-speed metal propeller (D4Y5).

Armament: Two fuselage-mounted 7·7 mm Type 97 machine-guns and one rear-firing flexible 7·92 mm Type 1 machine-gun (13-Shi prototype, D4Y1, D4Y1 KAI, D4Y1-C, D4Y2, D4Y2 KAI, D4Y2-C and D4Y3).

Two fuselage-mounted 7·7 mm Type 97 machine-guns, and one rear-firing flexible 13 mm Type 2 machine-gun (D4Y2a, D4Y2a KAI, D4Y2-Ca, D4Y3a and D4Y5).

Two fuselage-mounted 7·7 mm Type 97 machine-guns (D4Y4 and D4Y5).

Two fuselage-mounted 7·7 mm Type 97 machine-guns and one fuselage-mounted oblique-firing 20 mm Type 99 Model 2 cannon (D4Y2-S).

Bomb-load	
—normal, 310 kg (683 lb)	(D4Y1, D4Y1 KAI, D4Y2, D4Y2a,
—maximum, 560 kg (1,234 lb)	D4Y2 KAI, D4Y2a KAI, D4Y3 and D4Y3a)
—suicide, 800 kg (1,764 lb)	(D4Y4 and D4Y5)

External tanks: two 330 litre (72·6 Imp gal) drop tanks.

	D4Y1 Model 11	D4Y2 Model 12	D4Y3 Model 33	D4Y4 Model 43
Dimensions:				
Span	11·5 m (37 ft 8¾ in)	11·5 m (37 ft 8¾ in)	11·5 m (37 ft 8¾ in)	11·5 m (37 ft 8¾ in)
Length	10·22 m (33 ft 6⅜ in)	10·22 m (33 ft 6⅜ in)	10·22 m (33 ft 6⅜ in)	10·22 m (33 ft 6⅜ in)
Height	3·675 m (12 ft 0 11/16 in)	3·74 m (12 ft 3¼ in)	3·74 m (12 ft 3¼ in)	3·74 m (12 ft 3¼ in)
Wing area	23·6 sq m (254·027 sq ft)	23·6 sq m (254·027 sq ft)	23·6 sq m (254·027 sq ft)	23·6 sq m (254·027 sq ft)
Weights:				
Empty	2,440 kg (5,379 lb)	2,635 kg (5,809 lb)	2,501 kg (5,514 lb)	2,635 kg (5,809 lb)
Loaded	3,650 kg (8,047 lb)	3,835 kg (8,455 lb)	3,754 kg (8,276 lb)	4,542 kg (10,013 lb)
Maximum	4,250 kg (9,370 lb)	4,623 kg (10,192 lb)	4,657 kg (10,267 lb)	4,746 kg (10,463 lb)
Wing loading	154·7 kg/sq m (31·7 lb/sq ft)	162·5 kg/sq m (33·3 lb/sq ft)	159·1 kg/sq m (32·6 lb/sq ft)	192·5 kg/sq m (39·4 lb/sq ft)
Power loading	3 kg/hp (6·7 lb/hp)	2·7 kg/hp (6 lb/hp)	2·4 kg/hp (5·3 lb/hp)	2·9 kg/hp (6·4 lb/hp)
Performance:				
Maximum speed	298 kt at 4,750 m (343 mph at 15,585 ft)	313 kt at 5,250 m (360 mph at 17,225 ft)	310 kt at 6,050 m (357 mph at 19,850 ft)	304 kt at 5,900 m (350 mph at 19,355 ft)
Cruising speed	230 kt at 3,000 m (265 mph at 9,845 ft)	230 kt at 2,000 m (265 mph at 6,560 ft)	180 kt at 3,000 m (207 mph at 9,845 ft)	200 kt at 3,000 m (230 mph at 9,845 ft)
Climb to	3,000 m (9,845 ft)	3,000 m (9,845 ft)	3,000 m (9,845 ft)	5,000 m (16,405 ft)
in	5 min 14 sec	4 min 36 sec	4 min 35 sec	9 min 22 sec
Service ceiling	9,900 m (32,480 ft)	10,700 m (35,105 ft)	10,500 m (34,450 ft)	8,450 m (27,725 ft)
Normal range	850 naut miles (978 st miles)	790 naut miles (909 st miles)	820 naut miles (944 st miles)	890 naut miles (1,024 st miles)
Maximum range	2,100 naut miles (2,417 st miles)	1,945 naut miles (2,239 st miles)	1,560 naut miles (1,796 st miles)	1,400 naut miles (1,611 st miles)

Production: A total of 2,038 D4Ys were built as follows:

Dai-Ichi Kaigun Koku Gijitsusho at Yokosuka:

5 13-Shi prototypes (1940–41)

Aichi Kokuki K.K., at the Eitoku Plant, Nagoya:

660 D4Y1 production aircraft (spring 1942–Apr 1944)
326 D4Y2 production aircraft (Apr 1944–Aug 1944)
536 D4Y3 production aircraft (May 1944–Feb 1945)
296 D4Y4 production aircraft (Feb 1945–Aug 1945)

Dai-Juichi Kaigun Kokusho at Hiro:

215 D4Y1, D4Y2 and D4Y3 production aircraft (Apr 1944–July 1945)

Yokosuka P1Y Ginga (Milky Way)

For most of the air forces of the major fighting powers the fast twin-engined medium bomber was an all-important weapon. Japan, however, did not possess an equivalent aircraft until 1944 when the Japanese Army introduced their Ki-67 Hiryu, and the Navy took delivery of their P1Y1 Ginga (Milky Way). The prototype of this aircraft had made its first flight in the summer of 1943, and confidence in its performance was so high that Nakajima, the prime producer, went directly from prototype manufacture to quantity production. Including the prototypes, forty-five P1Y1s were delivered in 1943, and monthly output increased steadily, a total of 453 P1Y1s being built by the time the aircraft was finally accepted by the Navy in October 1944. Unfortunately for Japan the serviceability and reliability of the Ginga were not very satisfactory, and for a while the Navy found themselves with a large number of aircraft not yet accepted for Service use.

The development of the P1Y series was initiated by the Dai-Ichi Kaigun Koku Gijitsusho in 1940 to meet the requirements of a 15-Shi specification calling for a fast bomber capable of undertaking low-altitude attacks as well as torpedo and dive-bombing attacks. The intention was to produce an aircraft comparable to the Junkers-Ju 88, North American B-25 Mitchell and Martin B-26 Marauder. To that effect, an engineering team led by Tadanao Mitsuzi and Masao Yamana designed an extremely clean twin-engined aircraft with a narrow circular fuselage with mid-mounted wings. The powerplant selected was the Nakajima Homare eighteen-

The third prototype Yokosuka P1Y1 Ginga (Milky Way). The prototypes had single exhaust pipes and retractable tailwheels.

The third prototype Yokosuka P1Y1 after experimental installation of a Tsu-11 jet unit beneath the fuselage. (*Aireview*.)

cylinder air-cooled radial then still in the design stage. With a pair of these engines the P1Y was expected to reach a top speed of over 300 kt (345 mph) and in spite of its small size, provision was made in the wings for eight protected and six unprotected fuel tanks with a total capacity of 5,535 litres (1,218 Imp gal) to which could be added two 220 litre (48 Imp gal) drop tanks. Two oil tanks were mounted in each engine nacelle, but armour protection was restricted to a 20 mm plate behind the pilot's head. Compared with contemporary Allied aircraft, the defensive armament, limited to a single flexibly mounted gun in the nose and rear cockpit positions, was utterly inadequate and the aircraft was to rely on its speed to avoid interception. Normal offensive load was to consist of either a single 800 kg (1,764 lb) torpedo carried semi-internally under the fuselage or two 500 kg (1,102 lb) bombs carried in a ventral bomb-bay.

While detailed design work on the aircraft, then known as the Y-20, was progressing at the Dai-Ichi Kaigun Koku Gijitsusho, the Navy decided to assign its manufacture to Nakajima's Koizumi plant, where production of the Navy Type 96 Attack Bomber Model 23 (NELL) was scheduled to terminate in early 1943. In February 1943 the last five G3M3s were rolled out at Koizumi and the assembly lines quickly dismantled to make room for the P1Y production line.

Powered by a pair of 1,820 hp Nakajima Homare 11s, the first prototype was completed in August 1943 and made its maiden flight shortly after. Its high speed and ease of handling were soon commented upon favourably by the manufacturer's pilots and Service pilots, but their enthusiasm was not shared by the ground crews who were experiencing considerable difficulties with its troublesome hydraulic system and unreliable powerplants. Even under the most favourable conditions obtained during the flight trials programme, when the manufacturer's experienced mechanics were available at all times, maintenance problems caused numerous diffi-

Yokosuka P1Y1 Navy Bomber Ginga Model 11 of the Yokosuka Kokutai.
(*Copyright 'Maru.'*)

culties and, although production was rapidly growing, for over a year the Navy delayed acceptance of the P1Y1 for Service use. During that period numerous changes were introduced on the assembly lines, the first of these consisting of replacing the curved windshield with a new unit incorporating a flat bullet-proof panel, the installation of a revised cowling with individual exhaust stacks instead of a single exhaust pipe, and in using flat-headed rivets in place of the original flush rivets on the fuselage. Production aircraft also differed from the prototypes in being powered by 1,825 hp Homare 12 radials and in the fitting of a fixed tailwheel instead of the retractable one. Numerous changes were also incorporated in the defensive armament, and initial production aircraft mounted a flexible 20 mm cannon in the nose in place of the prototypes' 7·7 mm machine-gun, and, when production allowed, the slow-firing 20 mm Type 99 Model 1 cannon in the nose and dorsal positions were replaced by 13 mm Type 2 machine-guns on single or twin mountings (P1Y1a, P1Y1b and P1Y1c). Late production aircraft were also fitted with air-to-sea search radar, and it was also planned to use the P1Y1 as a parent aircraft for the Ohka Model 22 suicide aircraft.

Experimental installation of power-operated dorsal turret behind the cockpit of a Yokosuka P1Y1 of the Yokosuka Kokutai.

Finally the Navy accepted the aircraft for Service use, and the P1Y1 became known as the Navy Bomber Ginga (Milky Way) Model 11. Unrelenting maintenance problems, notably resulting from the unreliable Homare 12 engine, which seldom delivered its rated power, still kept the aircraft from combat until the early part of spring 1945. However, when the Ginga was finally committed to combat operations, it justified the Navy's most optimistic hopes, and although it was only in combat for less than six months, FRANCES, as the Allies named this new foe, was a most respected aircraft.

Late production Yokosuka P1Y1s with ASV radar antennae in the nose and on the sides of the rear fuselage. (*US Navy Department.*)

During its flight trial programme the P1Y1 with its maximum speed of 340 mph had attracted the attention of the naval pilots who were attempting to create a night fighting force against expected Allied night bombing operations over the Japanese mainland. To meet this requirement the Navy instructed Kawanishi to produce in their Konan plant a night fighter version of the P1Y1. As it was feared that Homare engine production would be insufficient to meet all demands, Kawanishi decided to install a pair of 1,850 hp Mitsubishi Kasei 25a fourteen-cylinder radials on the night fighter. Designated P1Y2-S, the Kawanishi-built aircraft retained the ventral bomb-bay, as they were intended to be operated as night intruders as well as night fighters. The nose gun of the bomber was eliminated on the P1Y2-S, but a pair of 20 mm Type 99 Model 2 cannon were mounted obliquely in the fuselage to fire up and forwards, and the flexibly mounted 20 mm Type 99 cannon in the rear cockpit was retained. First flown in June 1944, the P1Y2-S went into production as the Navy Night Fighter Kyokko (Aurora), but its performance at altitude proved somewhat disappointing. As a result on most of the ninety-six P1Y2-S built the angled guns were removed, and these aircraft were operated as bombers under the designation Navy Bomber Ginga Model 16 (P1Y2). A modification of the Nakajima-built P1Y1, the Navy Night Fighter Byakko (White

YOKOSUKA P1Y1

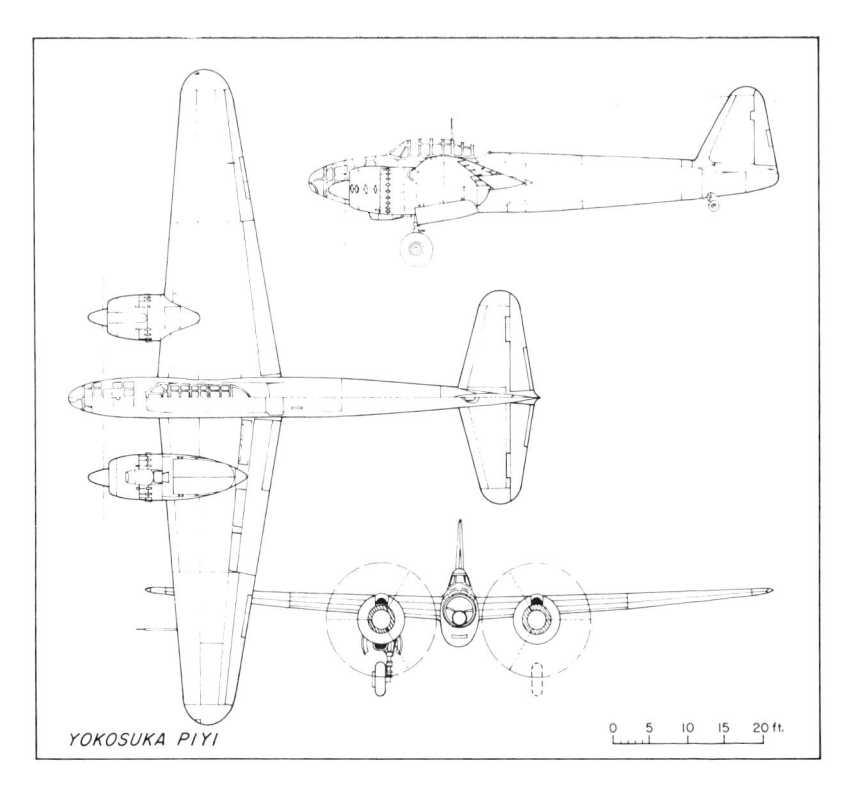

Light) (P1Y1-S), fitted with two pairs of obliquely-mounted 20 mm cannon —one forward and the other aft of the cockpit—proved equally unsuccessful.

Numerous modifications of the P1Y series were made during the last year of the war, and these included the fitting of wooden tail surfaces and rear fuselage sections on a limited number of aircraft, and the experimental testing of a power-operated dorsal turret, mounting two 20 mm cannon.

Captured Yokosuka P1Y1. (*Eckert*.)

The third prototype was used to test-fly the Tsu-11 Campini-type jet engine intended for the Ohka Model 22 series. One aircraft was also tested with ten forward-firing 20 mm cannon, and an even more formidable fire power consisting of sixteen 20 mm cannon was projected. Plans were also on hand for a version to be partially built of steel, but this did not materialize.

Several versions of the Ginga retaining the basic airframe structure were planned: the P1Y4 Model 12 was to be powered by a pair of 2,000 hp Homare 23 radials; the P1Y5 Model 14 was to have two 2,200 hp Mitsubishi MK9A radials; and Kawanishi were planning to build the Kasei 25c powered P1Y6 Model 17. The most ambitious version of the Ginga was the P1Y3 Model 33, which was specially designed to carry the rocket-powered Ohka Model 21 or jet-powered Ohka Model 22 suicide aircraft. To accommodate this weapon in its bomb-bay, the P1Y3 was to have had an enlarged fuselage, and wing span was to be increased from 20 m (65 ft $7\frac{13}{32}$ in) to 22 m (72 ft $2\frac{1}{8}$ in). However, by the end of the war the P1Y3, as well as the P1Y4, P1Y5 and P1Y6, was still on the drawing board.

UNITS ALLOCATED
522nd, 752nd, 761st, 762nd and Yokosuka Kokutais.

TECHNICAL DATA

Description: Twin-engined medium bomber (P1Y1/P1Y6), or night fighter (P1Y1-S and P1Y2-S). All-metal construction.

Accommodation: Crew of three in enclosed cockpits.

Powerplant: Two Nakajima NK9B Homare 11 eighteen-cylinder air-cooled radials rated at 1,820 hp for take-off, 1,650 hp at 2,000 m (6,560 ft) and 1,440 hp at 5,700 m (18,700 ft), driving three-blade propellers (prototypes and P1Y1).

Two Nakajima NK9C Homare 12 eighteen-cylinder air-cooled radials rated at 1,825 hp for take-off, 1,670 hp at 2,400 m (7,875 ft) and 1,500 hp at 6,600 m (21,655 ft), driving three-blade propellers (P1Y1a, P1Y1b, P1Y1c and P1Y1-S).

Two Mitsubishi MK4T-A Kasei 25a fourteen-cylinder air-cooled radials rated at 1,850 hp for take-off, 1,680 hp at 2,600 m (8,530 ft) and 1,540 hp at 5,500 m (18,045 ft), driving three-blade propellers (P1Y2 and P1Y2-S).

Two Nakajima NK9H Homare 21 eighteen-cylinder air-cooled radials rated at 1,990 hp for take-off, 1,850 hp at 1,750 m (5,740 ft) and 1,625 hp at 6,100 m (20,015 ft), driving three-blade propellers (P1Y3).

Two Nakajima NK9H-S Homare 23 eighteen-cylinder air-cooled radials rated at 2,000 hp for take-off and 1,570 hp at 6,850 m (22,475 ft), driving three-blade propellers (P1Y4).

Two Mitsubishi MK4T-C Kasei 25c fourteen-cylinder air-cooled radials rated at 1,825 hp, driving three-blade propellers (P1Y6).

Two Mitsubishi [Ha-43] 11 (MK9A) eighteen-cylinder air-cooled radials rated at 2,200 hp for take-off, 2,070 hp at 1,000 m (3,280 ft) and 1,800 hp at 6,000 m (19,685 ft), driving four-blade propellers (P1Y5).

Armament: One flexible 7·7 mm Type 92 machine-gun in the nose and one flexible rear-firing 20 mm Type 99 cannon (15-Shi prototypes).

One flexible 20 mm Type 99 cannon in the nose and one flexible rear-firing 20 mm Type 99 cannon (P1Y1 and P1Y2).

One flexible 20 mm Type 99 cannon in the nose and one flexible rear-firing 13 mm Type 2 machine-gun (P1Y1a and P1Y2a).

One flexible 20 mm Type 99 cannon in the nose and twin 13 mm Type 2 machine-guns in a dorsal turret (P1Y1b and P1Y2b).

One flexible 13 mm Type 2 machine-gun in the nose and twin 13 mm Type 2 machine-guns in a dorsal turret (P1Y1c, P1Y2c and P1Y3).

One flexible rear-firing 13 mm Type 2 machine-gun and four oblique-firing 20 mm Type 99 cannon, two forward and two behind the cockpit (P1Y1-S).

One flexible rear-firing 20 mm Type 99 cannon and two oblique-firing 20 mm Type 99 cannon (P1Y2-S).

One flexible rear-firing 13 mm Type 2 machine-gun and ten forward-firing 20 mm Type 99 cannon (experimental installation on P1Y1).

Bomb-load: one 800 kg (1,764 lb) torpedo or up to 1,000 kg (2,205 lb) of bombs (P1Y1 and P1Y2). 1,600 kg (3,525 lb) of bombs (P1Y3).

	P1Y1	P1Y3	P1Y2-S
Dimensions:			
Span	20 m	22 m	20 m
	(65 ft 7 13/32 in)	(72 ft 2 1/8 in)	(65 ft 7 13/32 in)
Length	15 m	19 m	15 m
	(49 ft 2 9/16 in)	(62 ft 4 3/32 in)	(49 ft 2 9/16 in)
Height	4·3 m	4·3 m	4·3 m
	(14 ft 1 9/32 in)	(14 ft 1 9/32 in)	(14 ft 1 9/32 in)
Wing area	55 sq m	58·4 sq m	55 sq m
	(592·013 sq ft)	(628·610 sq ft)	(592·013 sq ft)
Weights:			
Empty	7,265 kg	9,600 kg	7,800 kg
	(16,017 lb)	(21,164 lb)	(17,196 lb)
Loaded	10,500 kg	13,500 kg	10,500 kg
	(23,149 lb)	(29,762 lb)	(23,149 lb)
Maximum	13,500 kg	17,100 kg	13,500 kg
	(29,762 lb)	(37,699 lb)	(29,762 lb)
Wing loading	190·9 kg/sq m	231·2 kg/sq m	190·9 kg/sq m
	(39·1 lb/sq ft)	(47·3 lb/sq ft)	(39·1 lb/sq ft)
Power loading	2·9 kg/hp	3·4 kg/hp	2·8 kg/hp
	(8·2 lb/hp)	(7·5 lb/hp)	(8 lb/hp)
Performance:			
Maximum speed	295 kt at 5,900 m	295 kt at 6,100 m	282 kt at 5,400 m
	(340 mph at 19,355 ft)	(340 mph at 20,015 ft)	(325 mph at 17,715 ft)
Cruising speed	200 kt at 4,000 m	—	200 kt at 4,000 m
	(230 mph at 13,125 ft)	—	(230 mph at 13,125 ft)
Climb to	3,000 m	—	5,000 m
	(9 845 ft)	—	(16,405 ft)
in	4 min 15 sec	—	9 min 23 sec
Service ceiling	9,400 m	—	9,560 m
	(30,840 ft)	—	(31,365 ft)
Range—normal	1,036 naut miles	—	—
	(1,192 st miles)	—	—
—maximum	2,900 naut miles	3,500 naut miles	2,150 naut miles
	(3,338 st miles)	(4,029 st miles)	(2,475 st miles)

Production: A total of 1,098 P1Ys were built as follows:

Nakajima Hikoki K.K., Koizumi:

6 prototypes (1943)
996 P1Y1 and P1Y1-S (1943–45)

Kawanishi Kokuki K.K., Konan:

96 P1Y2 and P1Y2-S (1944–45)

Yokosuka D3Y Myojo (Venus)

By 1943 one of the most serious problems facing the Japanese aircraft industry was the expected shortage of light alloys which, coupled with the insufficient number of skilled workers available, made it virtually impossible to produce the large number of aircraft ordered by the two Services. In an attempt to alleviate this problem, the Navy instructed its various suppliers to study the possibility of using non-strategic materials such as wood in the manufacture of trainer and transport aircraft.

First production Matsushita-built Yokosuka D3Y1 Myojo (Venus). (*USAF.*)

Design of a wooden version of the Navy Type 99 Bomber Trainer Model 12 (D3A2-K) was begun in late 1943 at the Dai-Ichi Kaigun Koku Gijitsusho under the Service Aeroplane Development Programme's designation Y-50. Though the intention had been to produce an aircraft closely based on the Aichi D3A, the desire to have the aircraft manufactured by semi-skilled workers with no previous aircraft manufacturing experience led to considerable modifications. The original elliptical wing and rounded tail surfaces of the D3A2, judged too complex for wooden construction, were replaced with straight tapered surfaces, while the fuselage length was increased to improve stability. Powered by a 1,300 hp Mitsubishi Kinsei 54 fourteen-cylinder air-cooled radial, two prototypes, designated Navy Experimental Bomber Trainer Myojo (Venus) or Yokosuka D3Y1-K,

YOKOSUKA D3Y1-K

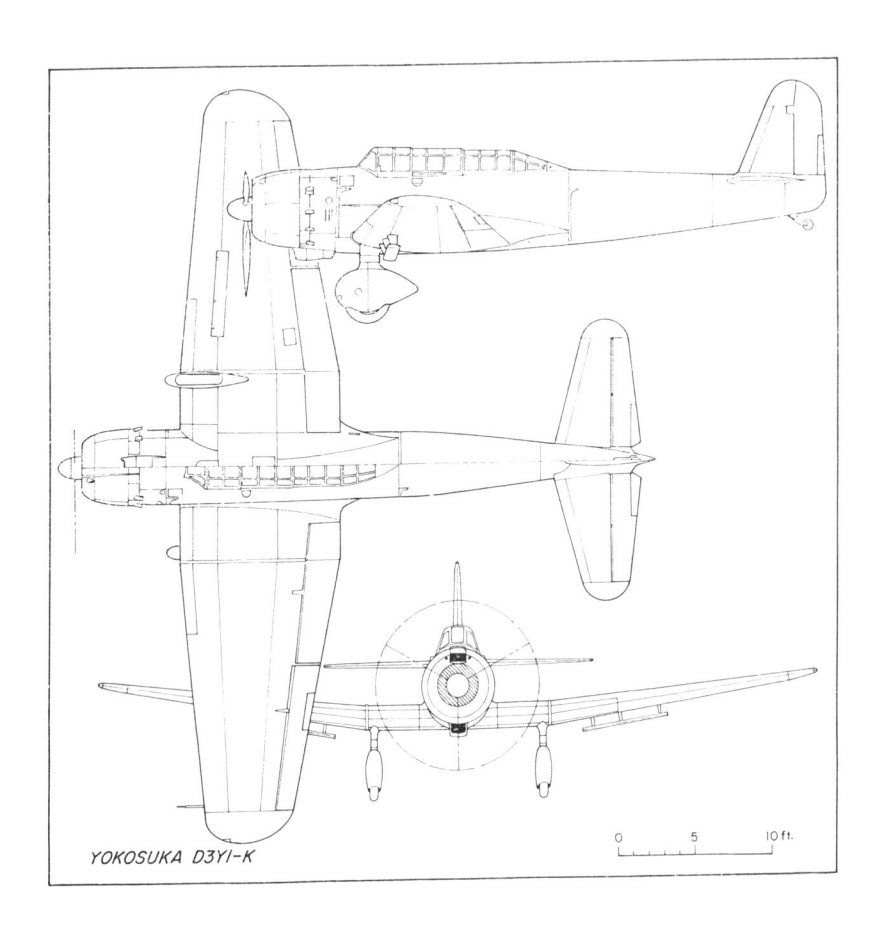

were completed in July and August 1944. However, empty weight of the aircraft substantially exceeded estimates, and the aircraft was further redesigned to reduce weight. Manufacture of the lighter production version was entrusted to Matsushita Koku Kogyo K.K. (Matsushita Air Industries Co) but only three production Navy Type 99 Bomber Trainer Myojo Model 22s could be completed before the final collapse.

Development of a single-seat D3Y2-K Special Attacker Myojo Kai (Venus Modified) was initiated early in 1945. Powered by a 1,560 hp Mitsubishi Kinsei 62 and fitted with a jettisonable undercarriage, this version was to have been armed with two 20 mm Type 99 cannon and was to carry a single bomb of up to 800 kg (1,764 lb). The prototype had not been completed when the war ended, and the planned monthly production of thirty D5Y1s, as the aircraft had been redesignated, was never undertaken.

TECHNICAL DATA

Description: Single-engine bomber trainer (D3Y1-K) or suicide attack bomber (D3Y2-K).
Accommodation: Crew of two in enclosed cockpit (D3Y1-K) or pilot in enclosed cockpit (D3Y2-K).
Powerplant: One Mitsubishi Kinsei 54 fourteen-cylinder air-cooled radial rated at 1,300 hp for take-off, 1,200 hp at 3,000 m (9,845 ft) and 1,100 hp at 6,200 m (20,340 ft), driving a three-blade metal propeller (D3Y1-K).
One Mitsubishi Kinsei 62 fourteen-cylinder air-cooled radial rated at 1,560 hp for take-off, 1,340 hp at 2,100 m (6,890 ft) and 1,190 hp at 5,800 m (19,030 ft), driving a three-blade metal propeller (D3Y2-K).
Armament: Two 20 mm Type 99 Model 1 cannon in the engine cowling (D3Y2-K).
Bomb-load: 800 kg (1,764 lb) (D3Y2-K).

	D3Y1-K	D3Y2-K
Dimensions:		
Span	14 m	14 m
	(45 ft 11 3/16 in)	(45 ft 11 3/16 in)
Length	11·215 m	11·515 m
	(36 ft 9 17/32 in)	(37 ft 9 11/32 in)
Height	4·185 m	4·2 m
	(13 ft 8 3/4 in)	(13 ft 9 11/32 in)
Wing area	32·8 sq m	30·5 sq m
	(353·055 sq ft)	(328·298 sq ft)
Weights:		
Empty	3,200 kg	3,050 kg
	(7,055 lb)	(6,724 lb)
Loaded	4,200 kg	4,630 kg
	(9,259 lb)	(10,207 lb)
Wing loading	128 kg/sq m	151·8 kg/sq m
	(26·2 lb/sq ft)	(31·1 lb/sq ft)
Power loading	3·23 kg/hp	2·97 kg/hp
	(7·1 lb/hp)	(6·5 lb/hp)
Performance:		
Maximum speed	243 kt at 6,200 m	254 kt at 5,000 m
	(280 mph at 20,340 ft)	(292 mph at 16,405 ft)
Cruising speed	160 kt at 3,000 m	160 kt at 3,000 m
	(184 mph at 9,845 ft)	(184 mph at 9,845 ft)
Climb to	6,000 m	6,000 m
	(19,685 ft)	(19,685 ft)
in	13 min 23 sec	11 min 45 sec
Service ceiling	—	9,250 m
	—	(30,350 ft)
Normal range	—	795 naut miles
	—	(915 st miles)

Production: Two D3Y1-K prototypes were built at the Dai-Ichi Kaigun Koku Gijitsusho at Yokosuka in July and August 1944, and three D3Y1-K production aircraft were built by Matsushita Koko Kogyo K.K. in the summer of 1945.

Although of poor quality this photograph is of particular interest, being one of the few known pictures of the Yokosuka R2Y Keiun (Beautiful Cloud) with shaft-driven six-blade airscrew. (*Courtesy William Green.*)

Yokosuka R2Y Keiun (Beautiful Cloud)

Early operations during the war indicated to the Japanese the need to possess long-range high-speed land-based reconnaissance aircraft whose superior speed would prevent their interception. In 1942 the Navy initiated the development of a new class of aircraft to fulfil this role. To that effect a 17-Shi specification was issued calling for an aircraft with a top speed of 360 kt at 6,000 m (414 mph at 19,685 ft), and the Dai-Ichi Kaigun Koku Gijitsusho was entrusted with the design. Bearing the SADP number Y-30 and the short designation R1Y1 and named Seiun (Blue Cloud), the projected aircraft was initially planned around the use of a new 2,500 hp twenty-four cylinder, liquid-cooled engine then under development by Mitsubishi, but anticipated late engine delivery led to a redesign around the use of two Mitsubishi MK10A radials. In this form the R1Y1 bore a strong resemblance to the P1Y1 Ginga bomber, but, as calculated performance fell short of meeting requirements, the project had to be abandoned.

To take the place of the stillborn R1Y1, the Navy decided to issue a new 18-Shi specification based on preliminary work on the Y-40 project designed by the Dai-Ichi Kaigun Koku Gijitsusho. Begun early in 1943, the Y-40 was inspired by evaluation of the Heinkel He 119V4 which had been acquired for the Navy in 1940 by Cdr Hideo Tsukada. Like the German machine, the Y-40 was to be powered by two coupled engines buried in the fuselage behind the cockpit and driving a single tractor propeller via an extension shaft.

Under the leadership of Cdr Shiro Otsuki, the design of the aircraft— now designated R2Y1 and named Keiun (Beautiful Cloud)—progressed smoothly until the early autumn of 1944 when the Japanese defeat off the

Flaps, undercarriage doors, nosewheel and opened cockpit canopy can be seen in this view of the Yokosuka R2Y. (*Aireview*.)

Marianas led to the Navy placing new emphasis on the design of fighter and bomber aircraft, while the rapid Allied advances eliminated the need for long-range reconnaissance aircraft. At this point it appeared as if the Keiun would share the fate of the Seiun; but the need for fast attack aircraft and the adaptability of the Keiun's airframe lent a new lease of life to the project.

In late 1944 the design staff of Dai-Ichi Kaigun Koku Gijitsusho suggested that the R2Y be redesigned as a jet attack bomber. For this purpose it was intended to replace the fuselage-mounted Aichi [Ha-70] 10 (twin-coupled Atsuta 30 engines) with a large-capacity fuel tank, and to attach a 1,320 kg (2,910 lb) static thrust Ne-330 turbojet under each wing outboard

This view of the Yokosuka R2Y shows the air intake above the rear fuselage, the long nosewheel door and the six-blade airscrew. (*Aireview*.)

YOKOSUKA R2Y1

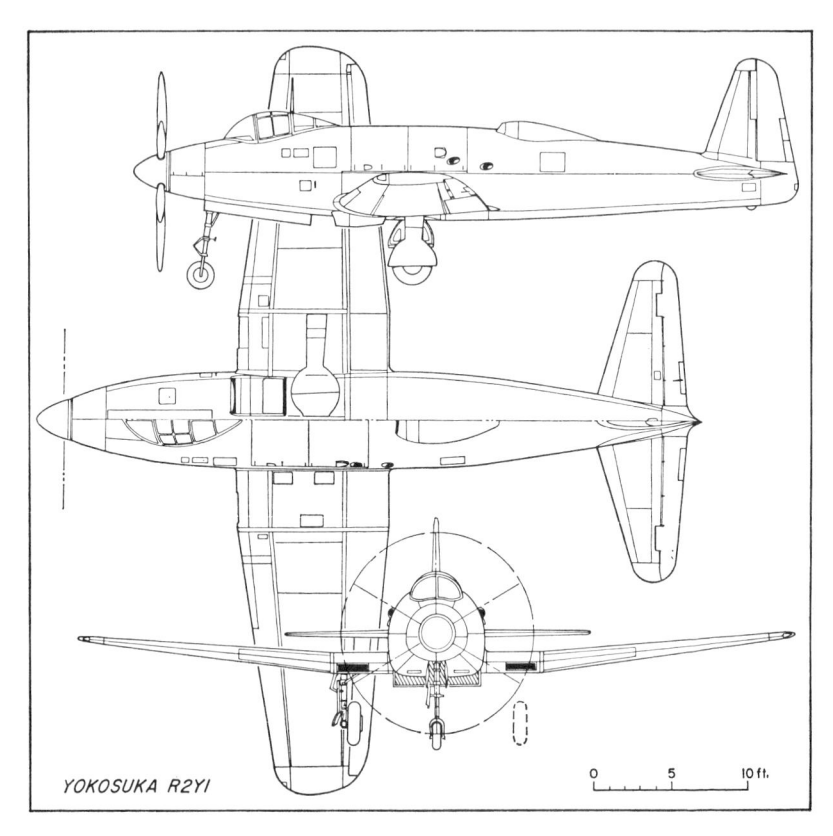

of the main undercarriage units. Armament was to consist of a single 800 kg (1,764 lb) bomb slung beneath the fuselage and a battery of cannon installed in the nose. Maximum anticipated speed at sea level was 430 kt (495 mph) compared with 388 kt at 10,000 m (447 mph at 32,810 ft) for the piston-engined version. This proposal was enthusiastically received by the Navy who, while detailed engineering design of the jet-powered R2Y2 was actively pursued, gave their authorization to complete the piston-engined R2Y1 as an aerodynamic prototype for the jet attack aircraft.

Completed in April 1945, the R2Y1 prototype was transferred to Kisarazu where taxi-ing tests were marred by nosewheel shimmy and difficulties with an overheating engine. Finally on 8 May the aircraft made its first flight with Lieut-Cdr Kitajima at the controls. Unfortunately this flight had to be cut short because there was an abnormal rise in oil temperature, while a few days later an engine fire on the ground necessitated a complete engine change. Before this could be done, the R2Y1 was destroyed by American bombs.

At the end of the war a second R2Y1 prototype was under construction, and design of the R2Y2 had almost been completed.

The second Yokosuka R2Y1 Keiun (Beautiful Cloud) under construction. (*US Navy Department.*)

TECHNICAL DATA

Description: Two-seat long-range reconnaissance aircraft (R2Y1), two-seat attack aircraft (R2Y2). All-metal construction.

Accommodation: Pilot and radio operator/navigator in enclosed cockpit.

Powerplant: One Aichi [Ha-70] 10 (twin-coupled Aichi Atsuta 30s) twenty-four cylinder liquid-cooled engine, rated at 3,400 hp for take-off and 3,100 hp at 3,000 m (9,845 ft), driving a six-blade metal propeller (R2Y1).

Two 1,320 kg (2,910 lb) thrust Ne-330 axial-flow turbojets (R2Y2).

Armament: None (R2Y1).

One 800 kg (1,764 lb) bomb and battery of forward-firing cannon (R2Y2).

Dimensions: (R2Y1) Span 14 m (45 ft 11 $\frac{3}{16}$ in); length 13·05 m (42 ft 9$\frac{23}{32}$ in); height 4·24 m (13 ft 10$\frac{15}{16}$ in); wing area 34 sq m (365·972 sq ft).

Weights: (R2Y1) Empty 6,015 kg (13,261 lb); loaded 8,100 kg (17,857 lb); maximum 9,400 kg (20,723 lb); wing loading 238·2 kg/sq m (48·8 lb/sq ft); power loading 2·4 kg/hp (5·2 lb/hp).

Performance: (R2Y1) Maximum speed 388 kt at 10,000 m (447 mph at 32,810 ft); cruising speed 250 kt at 4,000 m (288 mph at 13,125 ft); climb to 10,000 m (32,810 ft) in 10 min; service ceiling 11,700 m (38,385 ft); maximum range 1,950 naut miles (2,244 st miles).

Production: One R2Y1 was completed at the Dai-Ichi Kaigun Koku Gijitsusho in April 1945.

Yokosuka MXY7 Navy Suicide Attacker Ohka (Cherry Blossom) Model 11. (*Informations Aéronautiques.*)

Yokosuka MXY7 Ohka (Cherry Blossom)

In the summer of 1944 the resolute Japanese Naval officers, who were faced with the overwhelming material strength of the Allied Forces progressing inexorably towards Japan, had little hope of forestalling defeat by conventional tactics, and many of them began to advocate the use of drastic new combat methods. One of these officers was Ensign Mitsuo Ohta, a transport pilot serving with the 405th Kokutai, who conceived the idea of a rocket-propelled suicide aircraft. With the help of personnel from the Aeronautical Research Institute of the University of Tokyo, Ensign Ohta proceeded to draft preliminary plans for his proposed aircraft, and in August 1944 submitted his drawings to the Dai-Ichi Kaigun Koku Gijitsusho at Yokosuka. Ensign Ohta's proposal was favourably received by the Navy, who decided to proceed with the project and assigned the preparation of detailed drawings to a team of engineers led by Masao Yamana, Tadanao Mitsugi and Rokuro Hattori.

Bearing the designation MXY7, the aircraft was primarily designed as an anti-invasion or coastal defence weapon to be launched from a parent aircraft. Following an initial glide after release from the mother plane, the MXY7 was to accelerate towards its target on the power of three solid-propellant rockets mounted in the tail, being fired either singly or in unison. The tiny aircraft was built of wood and non-critical metal alloys and great care was taken in its planning to enable it to be mass produced by unskilled labour. As the aircraft was to be flown on its one-way mission by pilots with only limited flying experience, instruments were kept to a minimum and good manoeuvrability was demanded to achieve reasonable accuracy.

The design and construction of unpowered prototypes was completed in a matter of weeks, and by the end of September 1944 ten MXY7s had been completed. Named Navy Suicide Attacker Ohka (Cherry Blossom) Model 11, the initial version was to carry a 1,200 kg (2,646 lb) warhead in the nose and be transported in the bomb-bay of a specially modified Navy Type 1 Attack Bomber Model 24J (G4M2e). A battery of three Type 4 Mark 1 Model 20 rockets, providing a combined thrust of 800 kg (1,764 lb) for 8–10 sec, was fitted. Initial flight trials without power began at Sagami in October 1944, and the first powered flight was made at Kashima during the following month. These trials proved successful and performance measured during an unmanned flight at Kashima in January 1945 indicated that at 3,500 m (11,485 ft) the Ohka Model 11 could reach a top speed of 250 kt (288 mph) without power and 350 kt (403 mph) with full thrust.

Yokosuka Ohka Model 11 found on Yontan aerodrome, Okinawa. (*US Navy Department.*)

Without waiting for the results of the trials, the Navy placed the aircraft in full production, and a total of 755 Ohka Model 11s were built between September 1944 and March 1945. Of these 155 were built by the Dai-Ichi Kaigun Koku Gijitsusho at Yokosuka, and 600 by the Dai-Ichi Kaigun Kokusho at Kasumigaura, with Nippon Hikoki K.K. at Yokohama and Fuji Hikoki K.K. at Kanegawa acting as subcontractors for wings and tail units. On 21 March, 1945, the Ohka Model 11 was taken into battle by the 721st Kokutai, but the sixteen G4M2e parent aircraft were intercepted and forced to release their weapons short of the target. The first success was achieved on 1 April when Ohkas damaged the battleship *West Virginia* and three transport vessels, while the first Allied ship sunk by Ohka aircraft was the destroyer *Mannert L. Abele*, lost off Okinawa on 12 April.

The slow and cumbersome parent aircraft proved to be extremely vulnerable when approaching to within a few miles of well-defended targets, and production of the Ohka Model 11 ceased in March 1945.

Forty-five examples of the Ohka K-1, an unpowered version with water ballast replacing the warhead and the powerplant, were built by the Dai-Ichi Kaigun Koku Gijitsusho to provide pilots with limited handling experience of their weapon. The water ballast was released during the terminal phase to reduce the landing speed to 120 kt (138 mph), the aircraft landing on retractable skids.

The Ohka Model 22 was planned as an improved version of this weapon intended to be carried by the faster Navy Bomber Ginga (P1Y1). Because of the limited clearance provided by the parent aircraft, the wing span of

Yokosuka Ohka K-1 training glider version of the Ohka piloted bomb. This example is seen in the US Air Force Museum, Wright-Patterson Air Force Base, Ohio, with a German FZG 76 (V 1) on the left. (*Air Force Museum photo*.)

the Ohka Model 22 was smaller than that of the Model 11 and the warhead limited to 600 kg (1,323 lb). To increase the Ohka's range so that the parent aircraft could release it at greater distance from the intended target, the Model 22 was powered by a Tsu-11, a Campini-type jet engine with a 100 hp Hitachi four-cylinder inline engine as a gas generator. Fifty Ohka Model 22s were delivered by the Dai-Ichi Kaigun Koku Gijitsusho with follow-on production assigned to Aichi Kokuki K.K. and with Murakami Hikoki K.K., Miguro Hikoki K.K. and Fuji Hikoki K.K. acting as subcontractors. Aichi's inability to start production led to the decision to concentrate production of the Okha Model 22 in underground factories managed by the Dai-Ichi Kaigun Kokusho, but the war ended before these factories were completed. One test flight was made in July 1945, but auxiliary rockets installed under the wings went off accidentally just after release causing a stall from which the pilot could not recover.

Turbojet-powered Navy Suicide Attacker Ohka (Cherry Blossom) Model 22 (Yokosuka MXY7). Another example can be seen in the background as well as two Mitsubishi J8M Shusui (Swinging Sword) rocket fighters. (*US Navy Department.*)

The Ohka Model 33 was an enlarged version of the Model 22 which, powered by a Ne-20 turbojet and carrying an 800 kg (1,764 lb) warhead, was intended to be carried by the Navy Attack Bomber Renzan (G8N1). The low priority given to the G8N1 programme led to the cancellation of the Ohka 33 before completion. Also unbuilt was the still larger Ohka 43A intended to be catapulted from surfaced submarines. Powered by a Ne-20 turbojet, the Model 43A was to have had folding wings for storage in deck hangars. The Ohka Model 43B, basically similar to the Model 43A, was

View of the Yokosuka Ohka Model 22 showing jet tailpipe and the starboard air intake as well as mass-balanced elevator. (*US Navy Department.*)

479

Full-scale mock-up of the Yokosuka Ohka Model 43 and its Ne-20 turbojet. (*US Navy Department*.)

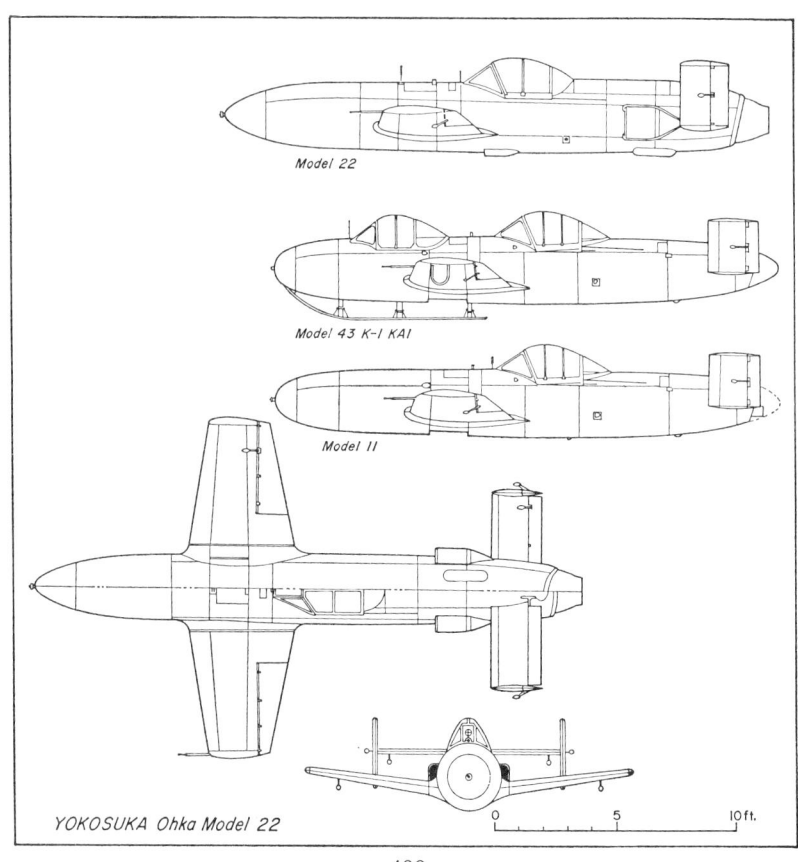

YOKOSUKA Ohka Model 22

designed for the defence of Japan's own shores and was to be launched from catapults installed in caves. Once in the air the pilot of the Ohka 43B would have released the wingtips to gain speed, but the first aircraft had not been completed at the end of the war. However, a two-seat training version, designated Ohka Model 43 K-1 KAI Wakazakura (Young Cherry), was built in limited numbers and had the warhead replaced by a second cockpit and the addition of flaps and retractable skids for landing. A single Type 4 Mark 1 Model 20 rocket was mounted in the tail to obtain limited power-handling experience.

Other developments of the Ohka series included a single Ohka Model 11 experimentally fitted with wings made by Nakajima out of thin steel; the Ohka Model 21 combining the powerplant of the Model 11 with the airframe of the Model 22; and the Model 53 which, powered by a Ne-20 turbojet, was to be towed aloft by another aircraft and released over the target.

The Hitachi four-cylinder inverted inline engine which formed part of the Tsu-11 powerplant installation of the Yokosuka Ohka Model 22. (*US Navy Department*.)

TECHNICAL DATA

Description: Single-seat suicide aircraft (Model 11, 21, 22, 23, 43A, 43B and 53). Single-seat training glider (Ohka K-1), or two-seat powered-glider (Ohka Model 43 K-1 KAI). Mixed construction.
Accommodation: Pilot in enclosed cockpit.
Powerplant: Three Type 4 Mark 1 Model 20 solid-propellant rockets with a total thrust of 800 kg (1,764 lb) (Ohka Model 11 and 21).
One 200 kg (551 lb) thrust Tsu-11 turbojet (Ohka Model 22).
One 475 kg (1,047 lb) thrust Ne-20 axial-flow turbojet (Ohka Model 33, 43A, 43B and 53).
One 260 kg (573 lb) thrust Type 4 Mark 1 Model 20 solid-propellant rocket (Ohka Model 43 K-1 KAI).
Armament: Warhead in the nose:
    Ohka 11: 1,200 kg (2,646 lb)
    Ohka 22:   600 kg (1,323 lb)
    Ohka 33: 800/900 kg (1,764/1,984 lb)
    Ohka 43:   800 kg (1,764 lb)

The spartan cockpit of an Ohka Model 11, with rudimentary instrumentation and flight controls. (*USAF.*)

	Model 11	Model 22	Model 43B
Dimensions:			
Span	5·12 m	4·12 m	9 m
	(16 ft 9 9/16 in)	(13 ft 6 7/32 in)	(29 ft 6 11/32 in)
Length	6·066 m	6·88 m	8·16 m
	(19 ft 10 13/16 in)	(22 ft 6 7/8 in)	(26 ft 9¼ in)
Height	1·16 m	1·15 m	1·15 m
	(3 ft 9 21/32 in)	(3 ft 9 9/32 in)	(3 ft 9 9/32 in)
Wing area	6 sq m	4 sq m	13 m
	(64·583 sq ft)	(43·055 sq ft)	(139·930 sq ft)
Weights:			
Empty	440 kg	545 kg	1,150 kg
	(970 lb)	(1,202 lb)	(2,535 lb)
Loaded	2,140 kg	1,450 kg	2,270 kg
	(4,718 lb)	(3,197 lb)	(5,004 lb)
Wing loading	356·7 kg/sq m	362·5 kg/sq m	174·6 kg/sq m
	(73·1 lb/sq ft)	(74·3 lb/sq ft)	(35·8 lb/sq ft)
Performance:			
Maximum speed	350 kt at 3,500 m	240 kt at 4,000 m	300 kt at 4,000 m
	(403 mph at 11,485 ft)	(276 mph at 13,125 ft)	(345 mph at 13,125 ft)
Terminal dive velocity	500 kt	—	—
	(576 mph)		
Range	20 naut miles	70 naut miles	150 naut miles
	(23 st miles)	(81 st miles)	(173 st miles)

Production: A total of 852 Ohkas were built by the following major contractors with the co-operation of a series of sub-contractors:

Dai-Ichi Kaigun Koku Gijitsusho, Yokosuka:
  155 Ohka Model 11
  50 Ohka Model 22
  45 Ohka Model K-1
  2 Ohka Model 43 K-1 KAI

Dai-Ichi Kaigun Kokusho, Kasumigaura:
  600 Ohka Model 11

APPENDIX A

Lesser Types; Imperial Japanese Army

Included in this appendix are details and illustrations of a number of minor aircraft which do not warrant lengthier treatment in the main part of this work, and of experimental aircraft of unusual design which could not be completed before the Japanese surrender. Also included here are the two major types of transport gliders developed during the Pacific War for the Japanese Army.

Mock-up of the Kawasaki Ki-88.

Kawasaki Ki-88

With its 1,500 hp Kawasaki Ha-140 liquid-cooled engine mounted behind the cockpit and driving a tractor propeller via an extension shaft, the Kawasaki Ki-88 was inspired by the Bell P-39 Airacobra of the US Army Air Forces. Proposed armament comprised a 37 mm cannon in the propeller shaft and two 20 mm cannon in the lower section of the nose. Design of the Ki-88 was undertaken in August 1942 but, following the inspection of a full-scale mock-up, development was discontinued within a year as its calculated maximum speed of 600 km/h at 6,000 m (373 mph at 19,685 ft) was only slightly higher than that of the Ki-61 already in production. Span 12·4 m (40 ft 8 $\tfrac{3}{16}$ in); length 10·2 m (33 ft 5 $\tfrac{9}{16}$ in). Loaded weight 3,900 kg (8,598 lb).

Kawasaki Ki-91

Design of a four-engine bomber with a pressurized cabin and having a radius of action of 4,500 km (2,796 st miles) with a bomb-load of 4,000 kg (8,818 lb) was undertaken by Kawasaki in May 1943. Planned production was suspended in February 1945 when tooling was destroyed during a B-29 raid before completion of the prototype. Power-operated turrets housing two 20 mm cannon were to be installed, one in the nose, one above the fuselage and two mounted beneath the fuselage. A four-cannon turret was planned for the tail position. Four 2,500 hp Mitsubishi Ha-214 Ru engines. Span 48 m (157 ft 5¾ in); length 33 m (108 ft $3\frac{7}{32}$ in). Loaded weight 58,000 kg (127,868 lb). Maximum speed 580 km/h at 10,000 m (360 mph at 32,810 ft); maximum range 10,000 km (6,214 st miles). Illustration is of a model.

Kokusai Ku-8

The design of this, the only Japanese transport glider to be met in combat, began in December 1941 when the airframe of a Ki-59 twin-engined light transport was modified as the Ku-8-I glider by removing the engines and conventional undercarriage and by fitting landing skids beneath the fuselage. Following flight trials the glider was considerably modified and fitted with a swinging nose section with ramp loading, and was placed in production as the Army Type 4 Large-size Transport Glider. Known as GANDER to the Allies, the Ku-8-II could accommodate up to 20 soldiers or a mountain cannon with crew and was normally towed by a Mitsubishi Ki-21-II. Span 23·2 m (76 ft 1⅜ in); length 13·31 m (43 ft 8 in). Loaded weight 3,500 kg (7,716 lb). Maximum towing speed 224 km/h (139 mph).

Kokusai Ku-7 Manazuru (Crane)

Largest glider built in Japan, the Ku-7 remained experimental, as by the time of its first flight in August 1944 the war was going against Japan. Design of this twin boom glider with central nacelle, accommodating either 32 fully armed troops or one 8-ton tank, was undertaken in late 1942. Fitted with four non-retractable mainwheels and one nosewheel, the Ku-7 was towed by either the Nakajima Ki-49-II or the Mitsubishi Ki-67-I and was fitted with a swinging loading door in the rear of the central nacelle. Span 35 m (114 ft 9 $\frac{10}{16}$ in); length 19·92 m (65 ft 4¼ in). Loaded weight 12,000 kg (26,455 lb).

Kokusai Ki-105 Ohtori (Phoenix)

Initially designated Ku-7-II, the Ki-105 was a powered version of the Kokusai Ku-7 fitted with two 940 hp Mitsubishi Ha-26-II fourteen-cylinder radials. Commencing in April 1945, nine prototypes were tested and plans were on hand to produce 300 aircraft of this type to be used as fuel tankers to carry supplies to Japan. In a typical flight between the Sumatra oilfields and the Japanese mainland, 80 per cent of the fuel load would have been consumed, but the critical fuel shortage in Japan rendered even this solution attractive. Span 35 m (114 ft 9 $\frac{10}{16}$ in); length 19·92 m (65 ft 4¼ in). Normal payload 3,300 kg (7,275 lb); maximum weight 12,500 kg (27,558 lb). Cruising speed 220 km/h (137 mph); maximum range 2,500 km (1,553 st miles).

Mansyu Ki-79b two-seat advanced trainer.

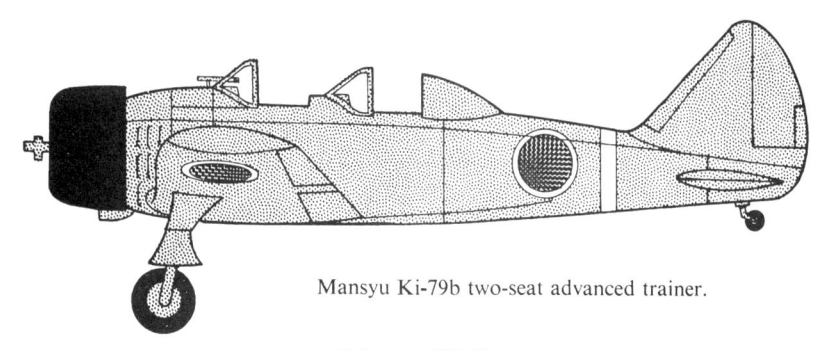

Mansyu Ki-79

While manufacturing the Nakajima Ki-27 fighter under licence, in 1942 Mansyu undertook redesign of this aircraft as an advanced trainer. Designated Army Type 2 Advanced Trainer, the aircraft was built in four versions: the Ki-79a single-seat trainer powered by a 510 hp Hitachi Ha-13a; the similarly powered Ki-79b tandem two-seat trainer; the single-seat Ki-79c, powered by a Hitachi [Ha-23] 22; and the two-seat Ki-79d with a [Ha-23] 24. All powerplants were versions of a basic type. All Ki-79 variants had open cockpits, but whereas the Ki-79a and b had all-metal airframes, the Ki-79c and d were built of wood and steel. Armament: one forward-firing 7·7 mm machine-gun. Span 11·5 m (37 ft 8¾ in); length 7·85 m (25 ft 9$\frac{1}{16}$ in). Empty weight 1,300 kg (2,866 lb). Maximum speed 340 km/h (211 mph); normal range 920 km (572 st miles).

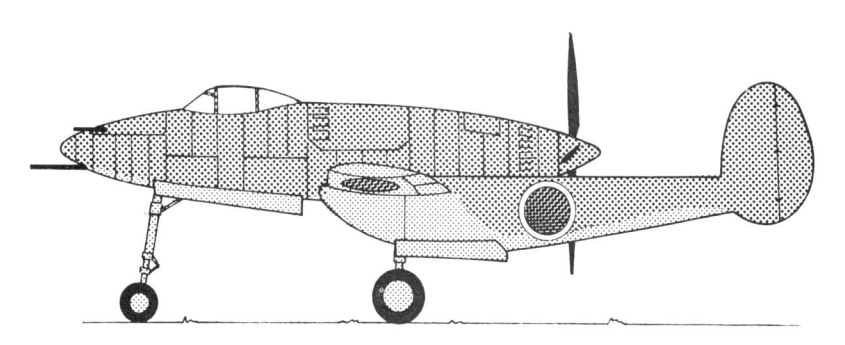

Mansyu Ki-98

Mansyu Ki-98

In 1943 Mansyu undertook design of the Ki-98 single-seat ground attack aircraft. Of twin-boom configuration, it was to be powered by a 2,200 hp turbosupercharged Mitsubishi Ha-211 Ru radial engine mounted in the central nacelle behind the pilot's seat and driving a four-blade propeller. Nose-mounted armament consisted of one 37 mm and two 20 mm cannon. A prototype was still under construction when Japan surrendered. Span 11·26 m (36 ft 11$\frac{5}{16}$ in); length 11·4 m (37 ft 4$\frac{13}{16}$ in). Loaded weight 4,500 kg (9,921 lb). Maximum speed 730 km/h at 10,000 m (454 mph at 32,810 ft).

Nakajima Ki-19

Designed to a 1935 specification calling for a twin-engined heavy bomber, four Ki-19 prototypes were built by Nakajima to compete with the Mitsubishi Ki-21. After competitive trials, the Ki-21 having been adopted by the Army, the four Ki-19s were used by Nakajima for various tests. In April 1939, the fourth prototype was sold to *Domei Tsushin-sha* (Domei Press) as the N-19 communications aircraft and registered J-BACN. Two 850 hp Nakajima Ha-5 (1st and 2nd aircraft), or Mitsubishi Ha-6. Span 22 m (72 ft 2$\frac{1}{8}$ in); length 15 m (49 ft 2$\frac{9}{16}$ in). Loaded weight 7,150 kg (15,763 lb). Maximum speed 350 km/h (217 mph); range 4,000 km (2,485 st miles).

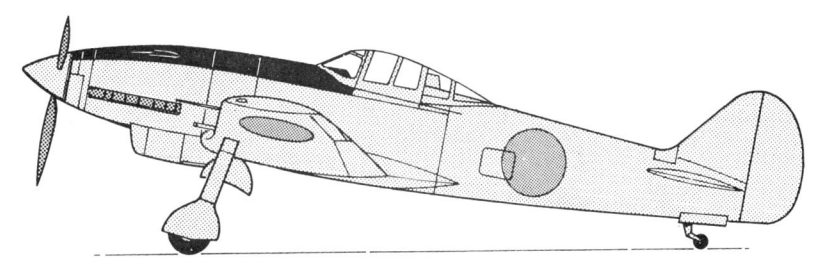

Nakajima Ki-62

The Ki-62 was a light fighter designed in 1941 by T. Koyama to compete with the Kawasaki Ki-61. Although this design appeared to be promising, its development was discontinued to enable Nakajima to concentrate on production of their Ki-43 and Ki-44. Later, the Ki-62's data and design features were incorporated in the Ki-84 design. One 1,175 hp Kawasaki Ha-40 liquid-cooled engine. Span 12 m (39 ft 4$\frac{7}{16}$ in); length 8·75 m (28 ft 8$\frac{1}{2}$ in). The Ki-63 was a projected version powered by a 1,050 hp Mitsubishi Ha-102 radial.

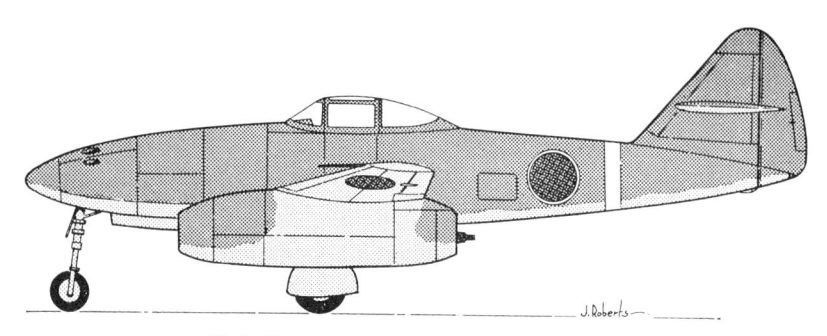

Nakajima Ki-201 Karyu (Fire Dragon)

The Karyu (Fire Dragon) twin-jet attack fighter was designed by Nakajima late in 1944 and bore a striking resemblance to the smaller Messerschmitt Me 262 fighter. The Ki-201, under construction at the end of the war, was scheduled to fly in December 1945, but quantity production of the aircraft was in doubt, as the Army had selected the Rikugun Ki-202 for priority development. Two 885 kg (1,951 lb) thrust Ne-230 turbojets or two 908 kg (2,002 lb) thrust Ne-130 turbojets. Armament: two 20 mm and two 30 mm cannon. Span 13·7 m (44 ft 11¾ in); length 11·5 m (37 ft 8¾ in). Maximum speed 852 km/h at 10,000 m (529 mph at 32,810 ft); climb to 10,000 m (32,810 ft) in 13 min 15 sec.

Tokyo Koku Ki-107

Intended as a successor to the Kokusai Ki-86, the Ki-107 was an experimental all-wood two-seat primary trainer. Powered by a 110 hp Hitachi Ha-47 inline engine, the sole prototype of the Ki-107 made its first flight in February 1944. Later in the year the aircraft was destroyed during a heavy landing, and its development was suspended. Span 10·02 m (32 ft 10½ in); length 8·05 m (26 ft 4¹⁵⁄₁₆ in). Loaded weight 829 kg (1,828 lb). Maximum speed 197 km/h (122 mph); range 475 km (295 st miles).

APPENDIX B

Lesser Types; Imperial Japanese Navy

This appendix covers interesting types developed for the Navy but of too limited significance to be covered in the main part of this book.

Aichi E11A1

In 1936 the Navy instructed Aichi and Kawanishi to draw up a night reconnaissance seaplane in answer to an 11-Shi specification calling for a successor to the Aichi E10A1 operating from cruisers and battleships. Designed by a team led by Morishige Mori, the prototype E11A1 made its first flight in June 1937 and won the competition against the Kawanishi E11K1. In April 1938, the E11A1 was put into production as the Navy Type 98 Night Reconnaissance Seaplane, and, including prototypes, a total of seventeen flying-boat biplanes of this type were built between 1937 and 1940. Armament: one flexible 7·7 mm machine-gun. Powerplant: one 620 hp Hiro Type 91 Model 22 liquid-cooled engine. Span 14·49 m (47 ft 6 $\frac{15}{32}$ in); length 10·71 m (35 ft 1 $\frac{21}{32}$ in). Loaded weight 3,300 kg (7,275 lb). Maximum speed 117 kt at 2,400 m (135 mph at 7,875 ft); range 1,050 naut miles (1,209 st miles).

Kawanishi J6K1 Jinpu (Squall)

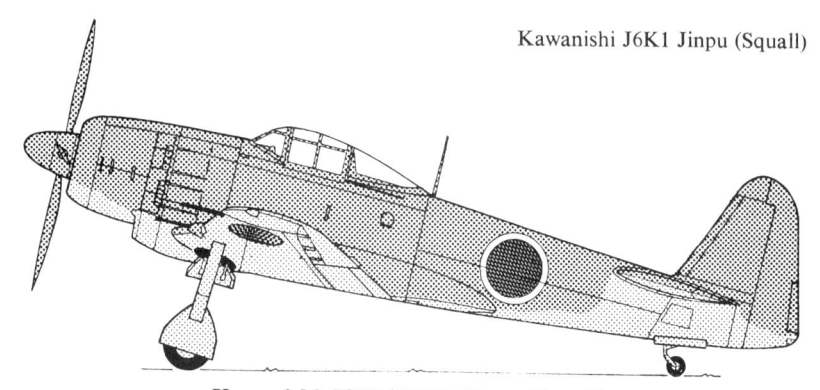

Kawanishi J3K1/J6K1 Jinpu (Squall)

In 1942 Kawanishi undertook the design of a single-seat interceptor fighter meeting the requirements of a 17-Shi specification. This aircraft, designated J3K1, was to have been powered by a Mitsubishi MK9A radial engine, but its development was suspended during the early design stage. Within a year work began anew on a Homare 42 powered derivative which received the short designation J6K1 and the popular name Jinpu (Squall). In spite of its promise the J6K1 was not proceeded with as the N1K2-J proved highly successful in meeting the Navy's requirement for a land-based interceptor fighter. Armament: two 30 mm cannon and two 13·2 mm machine-guns. Span 12·5 m (41 ft $0\frac{1}{8}$ in); length 10·118 m (33 ft $22\frac{11}{32}$ in). Loaded weight 4,370 kg (9,634 lb). Maximum speed 370 kt at 10,000 m (426 mph at 32,810 ft).

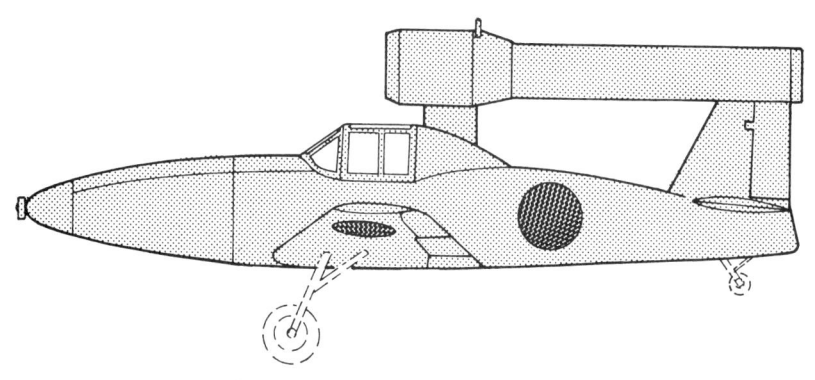

Kawanishi Baika (Plum Blossom)

Designed in co-operation with Prof Ichiro Tani of the Aeronautical Institute of Tokyo Imperial University, the Baika (Plum Blossom) was inspired by the German V 1 flying bomb. Intended as a special attacker (piloted suicide aircraft), the Baika was to be fitted with an undercarriage jettisonable after take-off. The single Maru Ka-10 pulse-jet, giving a maximum thrust of 360 kg (794 lb) at 740 km/h (460 mph), was to be mounted either above the fuselage—as in the V 1—or beneath it. A 250 kg (551 lb) explosive warhead was to be placed in the nose of the aircraft. When the war ended the Baika was still on the drawing board. Span 6·6 m (21 ft $7\frac{27}{32}$ in); length 7 m (22 ft $11\frac{19}{32}$ in). Loaded weight 1,430 kg (3,152 lb).

Mitsubishi B5M1

Of more conventional construction than the Nakajima B5N1, its competitor, the B5M1 was initially favoured by the Navy and was put into production as the Navy Type 97 Carrier Attack Bomber Model 2; but production was terminated after the delivery of 125 machines because in service the Nakajima aircraft proved highly successful. During the Pacific War, the B5M1s were operated from land bases in Southeast Asia for a brief period before being relegated to ancillary duties. One 1,000 hp Mitsubishi Kinsei 43. One flexible 7·7 mm machine-gun and 800 kg (1,764 lb) of bombs or a torpedo. Span 15·3 m (50 ft 2⅜ in); length 10·234 m (33 ft 10$\frac{16}{32}$ in). Loaded weight 4,000 kg (8,818 lb). Maximum speed 205 kt at 2,200 m (237 mph at 7,220 ft); normal range 1,188 naut miles (1,367 st miles).

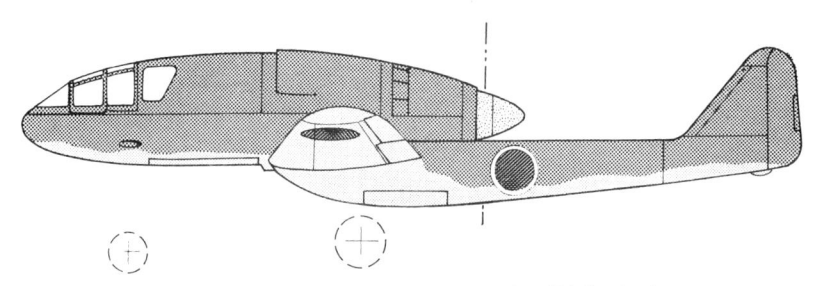

Mitsubishi J4M1 Senden (Flashing Lightning)

Although not proceeding further than the design stage, the J4M1 Senden (Flashing Lightning) was an interesting project intended to provide the Navy with a high-performance interceptor fighter. Of twin-boom design with a Mitsubishi MK9D driving a four-blade pusher propeller, the J4M1 was projected to reach a top speed of 380 kt at 8,000 m (437 mph at 26,245 ft). Armament: one 30 mm and two 20 mm cannon. Designed to a 17-Shi specification, the aircraft was abandoned in favour of the Kyushu J7W1 Shinden which had the Navy's full backing.

Nakajima J5N1 Tenrai (Heavenly Thunder)

During the spring of 1943 Nakajima undertook the design of a single-seat twin-engine aircraft to meet the requirements of an 18-Shi specification calling for an interceptor fighter capable of reaching a top speed of 360 kt at 6,000 m (414 mph at 19,685 ft). Bearing a strong resemblance to their earlier J1N1, but fitted with an all-round-vision cockpit canopy above the leading edge of the wings, the J5N1 Tenrai (Heavenly Thunder) was powered by a pair of 1,990 hp Nakajima Homare 21 radial engines and armed with two 30 mm and two 20 mm cannon. Flight trials begun in July 1944 were disappointing, and the J5N1 reached a maximum speed of only 322 kt (371 mph). Six prototypes were built, the last two being experimentally modified as two-seaters, but the type was not placed in production. Span 14·4 m (47 ft 2 $\frac{18}{}$ in); length 11·46 m (37 ft 7 $\frac{3}{16}$ in). Loaded weight 7,300 kg (16,094 lb).

A bad quality, but rare, photograph of the experimental Nakajima J5N1 Tenrai (Heavenly Thunder). Although removed when this photograph was taken Tenrai had four-blade airscrews with large-diameter spinners. (*Courtesy William Green.*)

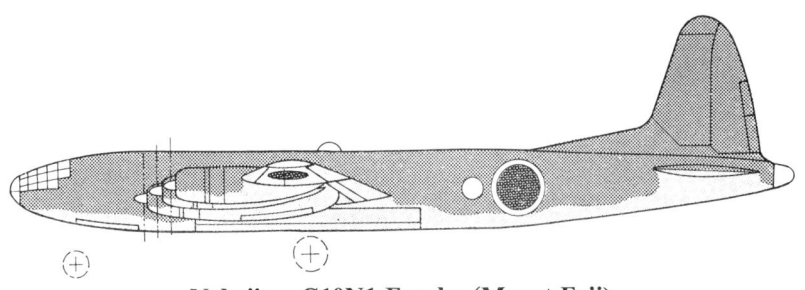

Nakajima G10N1 Fugaku (Mount Fuji)

In April 1943, as a private venture, Nakajima initiated studies for an aircraft (Project Z) capable of carrying out bombing operations against the US mainland from bases in Japan. Later during that year these studies served as the basis for a joint Navy–Army project, which initially was intended to be powered by six 5,000 hp Nakajima Ha-505 thirty-six cylinder radials. However, because of expected late availability of these powerplants, the design was scaled down to use six 2,500 hp Nakajima NK11A radials. In this form the G10N1 Fugaku (Mount Fuji) was designed to cruise at altitudes in excess of 10,000 m (32,810 ft) and to reach a top speed of 680 km/h (423 mph). Defensive armament: four 20 mm cannon; bomb-load 20,000 kg (44,092 lb) for short-range sorties, or 5,000 kg (11,023 lb) for sorties against targets in the US. Span 63 m (206 ft $8\frac{5}{16}$ in); length 40 m (131 ft $2\frac{13}{16}$ in). Loaded weight 160,000 kg (352,740 lb.). Under development at war's end.

Yokosuka K2Y2 developed from the Avro 504K.

Yokosuka K2Y1/K2Y2

Eventually replaced by the Kyushu K9W1, the antiquated Yokosuka K2Y2 was still the standard naval primary trainer when the war began. The original K2Y1—which was essentially an improved version of the Avro 504K—was first produced in 1928 and was placed in production as the Navy Type 3 Primary Trainer Model 1. However, the major production version was the K2Y2 which was introduced in 1930 and was powered by a 160 hp Hitachi Kamikaze 2 seven-cylinder air-cooled radial. Including prototypes, a total of 360 K2Y1s and K2Y2s were built between 1929 and 1930 by six manufacturers. Span 10·9 m (35 ft $9\frac{1}{8}$ in); length 8·6 m (28 ft $2\frac{19}{32}$ in). Loaded weight 890 kg (1,962 lb). Maximum speed 87 kt (100 mph) at sea level; range 226 naut miles (260 st miles).

Yokosuka K4Y1

Main type of primary floatplane trainer operated during the Pacific War by the Navy, the K4Y1 was designed in 1930 at the Dai-Ichi Kaigun Koku Gijitsusho. Following successful completion of flight trials, conducted with two Yokosuka-built prototypes, the K4Y1 was accepted for production as the Navy Type 90 Training Seaplane, and Watanabe, which had been entrusted with production, delivered 156 between 1932 and 1939. A further 53 K4Y1s were built in 1939–40 by Nippon Hikoki K.K. One 160 hp Hitachi Kamikaze 2 seven-cylinder air-cooled radial. Span 10·9 m (35 ft 9$\frac{1}{8}$ in); length 9·05 m (29 ft 8$\frac{5}{16}$ in). Loaded weight 990 kg (2,183 lb). Maximum speed 88 kt (101 mph) at sea level; range 170 naut miles (206 st miles).

Yokosuka H5Y1

Intended to complement the Kawanishi H6K series of four-engined flying-boats, the H5Y1 was designed by Dai-Ichi Kaigun Koku Gijitsusho in answer to a 9-Shi specification calling for a medium-size patrol flying-boat. As this aircraft proved to be underpowered, production, entrusted to the Dai-Juichi Kaigun Kokusho, was suspended after the delivery of twenty H5Y1s produced between 1936 and 1941. Two 1,200 hp Mitsubishi Shinten 21 fourteen-cylinder air-cooled radials. Armament: three flexible 7·7 mm machine-guns and two 250 kg (551 lb) bombs. Span 31·57 m (103 ft 6$\frac{29}{32}$ in); length 20·5 m (67 ft 3$\frac{3}{32}$ in). Loaded weight 11,500 kg (25,353 lb). Maximum speed 165 kt at 700 m (190 mph at 2,295 ft); maximum range 2,554 naut miles (2,940 st miles).

APPENDIX C

Foreign-designed Aircraft

Seven years and two days after the historic flight of the Wright brothers at Kitty Hawk, two Japanese Army officers brought Japan into the air age by flying their French Henri Farman biplane and German Grade aircraft over the Yoyogi Parade Ground in Tokyo on 19 December, 1910. Another seven years passed before the first indigenous Japanese aircraft flew, but this event had little impact on the selection of flying equipment by the Japanese Air Forces, which, during the first two decades of their existence, primarily acquired aircraft either built abroad or designed by foreign engineers and built in Japan.

This policy changed during the early 1930s when the Japanese decided to end their reliance on foreign sources of supply by encouraging their own aircraft designers and building up their aircraft industry. Consequently, with only a few notable exceptions, they limited their purchase of foreign aircraft to the acquisition of single aircraft of a few types for use in comparative trials with indigenous types and for obtaining valuable technical information, particularly with regard to equipment such as retractable undercarriages and radio direction-finding equipment. These foreign-designed aircraft are listed in the index at the end of this volume.

The Fiat B.R.20 operated in China by the Japanese Army as the Army Type I Heavy Bomber. (*Aireview*.)

In addition, the Japanese Army acquired 85 Italian Fiat B.R.20 heavy bombers (Army Type I Heavy Bomber) while the Navy purchased twelve Heinkel He 112B-0 fighters (Navy Type He Air Defence Fighters or A7He1) and twenty Seversky 2PA-B3 fighters (Navy Type S Two-seat Fighter or A8V1). These three types of aircraft were operated briefly during the second Sino-Japanese war but had been phased out of operations by the time the Pacific War began.

Photographs on opposite page. Top: This Seversky 2PA-B3 was operated by the Japanese Navy as the Type S Two-seat Fighter. Centre: Fairchild A942 tested as Navy Experimental Type F Amphibious Transport. Bottom: The Douglas DF was tested as the Navy Experimental Type D Flying-Boat. (*Top and centre photos. Aireview.*)

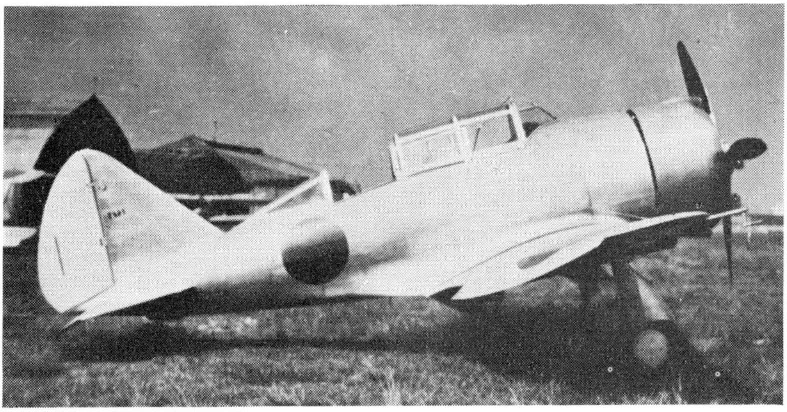

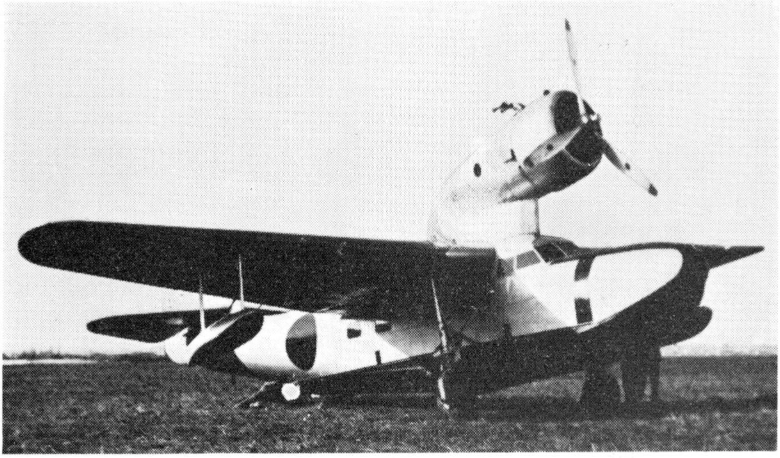

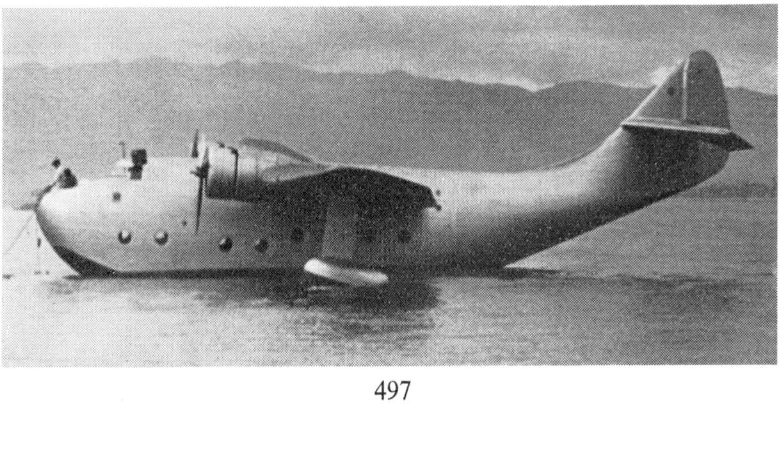

A Messerschmitt Bf 109E-3 tested by the Japanese Army. Allied code name was MIKE. (*Aireview*.)

Contrary to the popular opinion that during the war the Japanese produced several types of foreign-designed aircraft without licence (this belief was so strong that Allied aircrew erroneously reported sighting such aircraft—particularly those of German design—in Japanese markings and that many received code names, including BESS, FRED, JANICE, MIKE and MILLIE), only five types of foreign-designed aircraft were extensively used by the Japanese during the Pacific War. These aircraft, actually built under proper licence, are described hereunder.

Douglas DC-2

On 27 March, 1934, Nakajima Hikoki K.K. acquired for the sum of $80,000 the licence rights to build the Douglas DC-2 twin-engined transport, and to sell such aircraft in the Empire of Japan and Manchukuo. While the DC-2 design was being adapted to Japanese production methods under the direction of Kyoshi Akegawa, Setsuo Nichimura and Katsuji Nakamura, one Douglas-built DC-2 (NC 14284, c/n 1323) was

The Nakajima-built Douglas DC-2 which was operated by the Japanese Army.

Nakajima-built Douglas DC-2. The DC-2 and the Fokker F.VIIb-3m in the background both carry the markings of Japan Air Transport.

imported by Nihon Koku K.K. (Japan Air Transport Co Ltd), this aircraft being delivered in December 1934.

Production of the DC-2 in Japan was started in 1935, and the first of these, assembled from imported components and powered by two Wright Cyclone SGR-1820-F2 air-cooled radials, made its first flight in February 1936. Five additional aircraft, initially powered by SGR-1820-F2s but eventually re-engined with SGR-1820-F52 engines, were built by Nakajima in 1936–37 and delivered to Nihon Koku K.K. (later reorganized as Dai Nippon Koku K.K.—Greater Japan Air Lines) for operation on their routes linking Japan with Formosa.

During the Pacific War the Japanese-built DC-2s were erroneously reported in widespread use by the Navy, and they received the code name TESS. Actually only the first aircraft assembled by Nakajima from Douglas-built components was impressed, and this in fact was used by the Army.

TECHNICAL DATA
Description: Twin-engined personnel transport. All-metal construction with fabric-covered control surfaces.
Accommodation: Crew of four and 14 passengers.
Powerplant: Two 730 hp Wright Cyclone SGR-1820-F52 nine-cylinder air-cooled radials driving three-blade metal propellers.
Dimensions: Span 25·778 m (84 ft 7 in); length 18·887 m (62 ft); height 4·423 m (14 ft 6⅛ in); wing area 87·3 sq m (939·686 sq ft).
Weights: Empty 5,585 kg (12,313 lb); loaded 8,160 kg (17,990 lb); wing loading 93·5 kg/sq m (19·1 lb/sq ft); power loading 5·6 kg/hp (12·3 lb/hp).
Performance: Maximum speed 320 km/h at 760 m (199 mph at 2,315 ft); cruising speed 270 km/h (168 mph); climb to 1,000 m (3,280 ft) in 2 min 36 sec; service ceiling 5,400 m (17,715 ft); range 1,620 km (1,007 st miles).
Production: Six DC-2s were built by Nakajima Hikoki K.K. between 1936 and 1937.

Douglas L2D

Japanese interest in the Douglas DC-3 twin-engined transport materialized as early as 1937 when two trading companies, Mitsui Bussan Kaisha K.K. (Mitsui Trading Co Ltd) and Far Eastern Trading Co Ltd, began placing orders for a number of them. Consequently, thirteen Cyclone-powered DC-3s (Douglas c/ns 1979, 2025, 2026, 2049–2052 and 2096–2101 inclusive) and seven Twin Wasp powered DC-3s (Douglas c/ns 2009, 2037–2041 and 2048) were delivered between November 1937 and February 1939. Operated by Dai Nippon Koku K.K. (Greater Japan Air Lines), these aircraft, less attritions through operational and combat losses, remained in service until the end of the Pacific War when the surviving aircraft were scrapped.

An L2D2, Nakajima-built Douglas DC-3. (*US Navy Department.*)

On 24 February, 1938, Mitsui and Company Ltd, the US based subsidiary of Mitsui Bussan Kaisha K.K., acquired for $90,000 the licence rights to build and sell the DC-3. For this sum Mitsui obtained all necessary technical data but later purchased separately the parts for two unassembled DC-3s (Douglas c/ns 2055 and 2056). Unknown to the Douglas Aircraft Company, the licence and pattern aircraft had been acquired by Mitsui on instruction of the Japanese Navy. After arrival in Japan, the parts for c/ns 2055 and 2056 were delivered to Showa Hikoki Kogyo K.K. which were instructed to assemble the two aircraft and prepare for further production. At the same time Nakajima Hikoki K.K. were asked to participate in production.

The two prototypes, designated Douglas L2D1, or Navy Type D Transport, were delivered by Showa in October 1939 and April 1940. The delay resulted from late completion of Showa's facilities. Meanwhile, the engineering staff of Nakajima and Showa co-operated in modifying the type for Japanese production techniques and for adoption of the 1,000 hp Mitsubishi Kinsei 43 radials in place of the imported 1,000 hp Pratt & Whitney SB3G engines fitted to the two L2D1s. In this form seventy-one L2D2s (Navy Type 0 Transport Model 11) were delivered by Nakajima between 1940 and 1942, and the first Showa-built L2D2 was delivered in March 1941. After November 1942, when the last Nakajima-built L2D2 was delivered, the production of the Navy Type 0 Transport—which by then had been selected by the Navy as their standard transport aircraft—was the sole responsibility of Showa.

Showa-built L2D3 version of the Douglas DC-3 seen after capture. The additional flight deck windows can be clearly seen. (*US Navy Department.*)

DOUGLAS L2D3

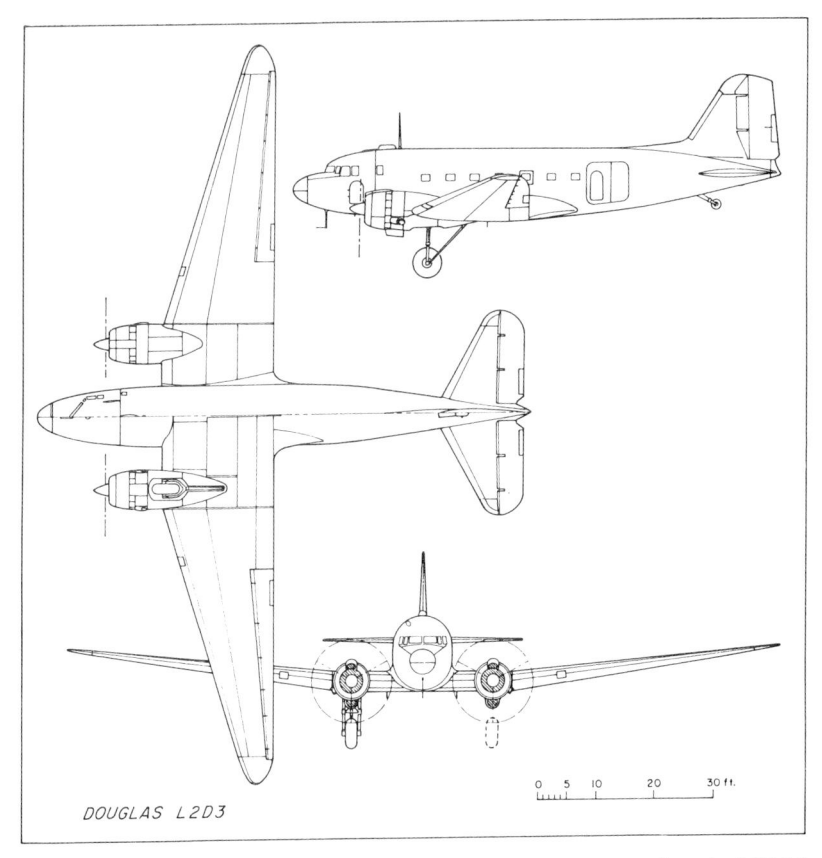

As production by Showa was gaining tempo, a cargo transport version, the L2D2-1 fitted with reinforced cargo floor and large cargo-loading doors on the port side of the rear fuselage, was produced. Still later, the Navy Type 0 Transport Model 22—characterized externally by the installation of an additional glazed window area behind the flight deck—became the main production version and appeared in four variants:

    L2D3:   Personnel transport powered by two 1,300 hp Kinsei 51 radials.
    L2D3a: Personnel transport powered by two 1,300 hp Kinsei 53 radials.
    L2D3-1: Kinsei 51 powered cargo transport.
    L2D3-1a: Kinsei 53 powered cargo transport.

The L2D4 and L2D4-1 were respectively personnel and cargo transports fitted with a dorsal turret housing a flexible 13 mm Type 2 machine-gun. Two hand-held 7·7 mm Type 92 machine-guns could be fired from fuselage hatches. Designated Navy Type 0 Transport Model 32, this version remained experimental.

Finally, the L2D5 or Navy Type 0 Transport Model 33 was a version of the L2D4 which was under construction when the war ended. Wherever possible light alloys were to be replaced by wood or steel, and the L2D5 was to have been powered by 1,560 hp Kinsei 62 radials. Named TABBY by the Allies, the Japanese-built DC-3s were met throughout the Pacific theatre of operations and often led to tragic recognition errors.

501

UNITS ALLOCATED

Southern Philippines Kokutai. Squadrons (Butais) attached to the 3rd, 4th, 6th, 11th, 12th, 13th and 14th Air Fleets (Koku Kantais), to the Combined Fleet (Rengo Kantai) and to the China Area and Southwest Area Fleets.

TECHNICAL DATA

Description: Twin-engined personnel and cargo transport. All-metal construction with fabric-covered control surfaces (L2D1 to L2D4-1) or light alloy, steel and wood construction (L2D5).

Accommodation: Crew of three to five, and either 21 passengers (L2D1 to L2D5) or 4,500 kg (9,920 lb) of freight (L2D2-1 to L2D4-1).

Powerplant: Two Pratt & Whitney SB3G fourteen-cylinder air-cooled radials, rated at 1,000 hp for take-off, driving three-blade metal propellers (L2D1).

Two Mitsubishi Kinsei 43 fourteen-cylinder air-cooled radials, rated at 1,000 hp for take-off, and 1,080 hp at 2,000 m (6,560 ft), driving three-blade metal propellers (L2D2 and L2D2-1).

Two Mitsubishi Kinsei 51 fourteen-cylinder air-cooled radials rated at 1,300 hp for take-off, and 1,200 hp at 3,000 m (9,845 ft), driving three-blade metal propellers (L2D3, L2D3-1, L2D4 and L2D4-1).

Two Mitsubishi Kinsei 53 fourteen-cylinder air-cooled radials, rated at 1,300 hp for take-off, and 1,200 hp at 3,000 m (9,845 ft), driving three-blade metal propellers (L2D3a and L2D3-1a).

Two Mitsubishi Kinsei 62 fourteen-cylinder air-cooled radials, rated at 1,560 hp for take-off, and 1,340 hp at 2,100 m (6,890 ft), driving three-blade metal propellers (L2D5).

Armament: One flexible 13 mm Type 2 machine-gun and two 7·7 mm Type 92 machine-guns (L2D4, L2D4-1 and L2D5).

	L2D2	L2D3-1a
Dimensions:		
Span	28·956 m	28·956 m
	(95 ft)	(95 ft)
Length	19·72 m	19·507 m
	(64 ft 8⅜ in)	(64 ft)
Height	7·46 m	7·46 m
	(24 ft 5¹¹⁄₁₆ in)	(24 ft 5¹¹⁄₁₆ in)
Wing area	91·6 sq m	91·6 sq m
	(985·97 sq ft)	(985·97 sq ft)
Weights:		
Empty	7,125 kg	7,218 kg
	(15,708 lb)	(15,913 lb)
Loaded	10,900 kg	12,500 kg
	(24,030 lb)	(27,558 lb)
Wing loading	119 kg/sq m	136·5 kg/sq m
	(24·4 lb/sq ft)	(28 lb/sq ft)
Power loading	5·45 kg/hp	4·8 kg/hp
	(12 lb/hp)	(10·6 lb/hp)
Performance:		
Maximum speed	191 kt at 2,400 m	212 kt at 2,800 m
	(220 mph at 7,875 ft)	(244 mph at 9,185 ft)
Cruising speed	140 kt at 2,000 m	130 kt at 3,000 m
	(161 mph at 6,560 ft)	(150 mph at 9,845 ft)
Climb to	5,000 m	5,000 m
	(16,405 ft)	(16,405 ft)
in	20 min 36 sec	16 min 2 sec
Service ceiling	10,900 m	—
	(35,760 ft)	—
Normal range	1,740 naut miles	1,620 naut miles
	(2,003 st miles)	(1,865 st miles)

Showa-built L2D4-1 cargo transport version of the Douglas DC-3 with dorsal turret and freight loading doors.

Production: Including the two L2D1s assembled from Douglas-built parts, a total of 487 L2Ds were built by Showa Hikoki Koygo K.K. and Nakajima Hikoki K.K. as follows:

	Showa	Nakajima
1939	1	—
1940	1	10
1941	22	49
1942	87	12
1943	61	—
1944	157	—
1945	87	—
Totals	416	71

Kyushu K9W Momiji (Maple) and Kokusai Ki-86

In 1938 the German company Bücker Flugzeugbau G.m.b.H. demonstrated their Bü 131B Jungmann two-seat primary trainer and Bü 133C Jungmeister single-seat aerobatic trainer in Japan. The spectacular performance put up by these two aircraft impressed the Japanese Navy, which decided to purchase the Hirth HM 504 powered Jungmann and handed it over to their 11th Rengo Kokutai where the aircraft was put through intensive flight trials. The aircraft was found easy to handle on the ground and in the air, and Service personnel commented favourably upon its simplicity of construction and maintenance. As a result, in 1939 the Navy decided to purchase from Bücker an additional twenty machines which were designated Navy Experimental Type Bu Primary Trainer (KXBu1) and were tested under actual training conditions. Again the aircraft was found extremely satisfactory, the only adverse comments being those expressed by experienced flying instructors who found the Bü 131 almost too easy to handle.

In 1939, the Navy requested K.K. Watanabe Tekkosho to design to a 14-Shi specification a primary trainer inspired by the Bü 131 but not a copy of it. Watanabe submitted two separate designs, both powered by an experimental 110 hp Hitachi 13-Shi Type 1 engine, one being a biplane and the other a monoplane. Prototypes of each of these designs as well as of a competitive Hitachi design were built in 1941, but when tested against the Bü 131 all were found markedly inferior to the German machine. Consequently, Yoshiro Uhara was sent to Germany to negotiate the acquisition of the

One of the Japanese Army's Kokusai Ki-86a Army Type 4 Primary Trainers.
(*Aireview.*)

manufacturing rights for the Jungmann. In August 1942, following the successful completion of negotiations, the Bü 131 was put into production by Watanabe (later renamed Kyushu) as the Navy Type 2 Primary Trainer Model 11 (K9W1). Named Momiji (Maple) and coded CYPRESS by the Allies, the K9W1 was powered by a 110 hp Hitachi GK4A Hatsukaze 11 air-cooled four-cylinder inverted inline engine and became the Navy's standard primary trainer.

The outstanding qualities of the K9W1 attracted the interest of the Army, which in 1943 instructed Nippon Kokusai Koku to manufacture a version of the aircraft bearing the designation Ki-86. Powered by a 110 hp Army Type 4 four-cylinder inverted inline air-cooled engine (Hitachi [Ha-47] 11), the Army version of the Hatsukaze 11, the prototype first flew in late 1943. Ki-86a production models, designated Army Type 4

A captured Kokusai Ki-86a (Bücker Jungmann) with British markings.

504

KYUSHU K9W1

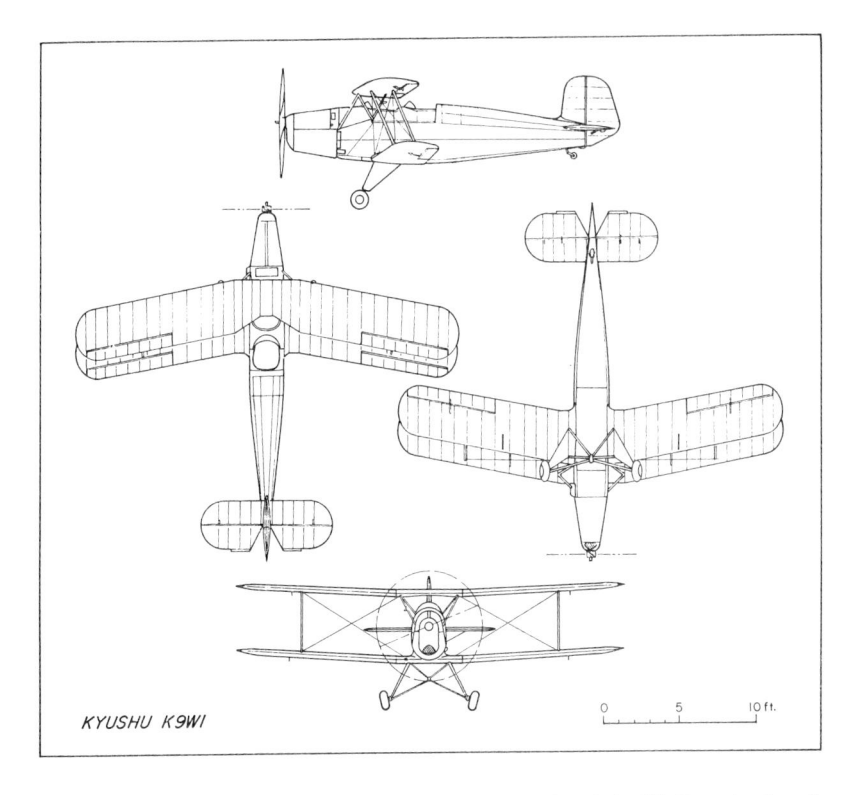

Primary Trainer, were delivered starting in 1944 and replaced the Ki-17 as the Army's standard primary trainer. One experimental Ki-86b, an all-wood version, weighing some 150 kg (331 lb) more than the standard version, was completed in February 1945.

TECHNICAL DATA

Description: Two-seat primary trainer biplane. Metal structure with mixed covering (K9W1 and Ki-86a) or all-wood construction (Ki-86b).
Accommodation: Pilot and instructor in tandem open cockpits.
Powerplant: One Hitachi GK4A Hatsukaze 11 (K9W1) or Hitachi [Ha-47] 11 (Ki-86) air-cooled four-cylinder inline engine rated at 110 hp for take-off and driving a two-blade wooden propeller.
Dimensions: (Ki-86a) Span 7·34 m (24 ft 0¾ in); length 6·616 m (21 ft 8½ in); height 2·636 m (8 ft 7²³⁄₃₂ in); wing area 14·2 sq m (152·847 sq ft).
Weights: (Ki-86a) Empty 409 kg (902 lb); loaded 639 kg (1,409 lb); wing loading 45 kg/sq m (9·2 lb/sq ft); power loading 5·8 kg/hp (12·8 lb/hp).
Performance: (Ki-86a) Maximum speed 180 km/h (112 mph); cruising speed 120 km/h at 1,000 m (75 mph at 3,280 ft); climb to 2,000 m (6,560 ft) in 13 min; service ceiling 3,880 m (12,730 ft); range 600 km (373 st miles).
Production: A total of 339 K9W1s and 1,037 Ki-86s were built:
   Kyushu Hikoki K.K.:
      278 K9W1s (1942–44)
   Hitachi Kokuki K.K.:
      61 K9W1s (1943)
   Nippon Kokusai Koku Kogyo K.K.:
      1,037 Ki-86s (1943–45)

Kyushu K10W1

In 1937 Mitsubishi Jukogyo K.K. acquired from North American Aviation Inc two aircraft of the NA-16 series of advanced trainers. Delivered in September 1937, the NA-16-4R was powered by a 450 hp Pratt & Whitney R-985-9CG driving a three-blade propeller, while the NA-16-4RW, delivered three months later, was powered by a Wright R-975-E3 driving a two-blade propeller. After their arrival in Japan both aircraft were handed over to the Navy who tested them as the KXA1 and KXA2, Navy Experimental Type A Intermediate Trainers.

Upon successful completion of evaluation, the Navy elected to acquire the manufacturing rights for the type, and a licence was obtained through an intermediary trading company. Production of an extensively modified version of the NA-16-4R was then entrusted to K.K. Watanabe Tekkosho. Designed in answer to a 14-Shi specification and designated K10W1, the Japanese-built version was completed in 1941 and had revised vertical tail surfaces and was powered by a 600 hp Nakajima Kotobuki 2 Kai air-cooled radial engine. Shortly after, the aircraft was ordered into production as the Navy Type 2 Intermediate Trainer.

After completing their twenty-sixth K10W1 in November 1942, under instruction of the Naval Staff, Watanabe handed all necessary tooling and blueprints to Nippon Hikoki K.K., who delivered an additional 150 between February 1943 and March 1944.

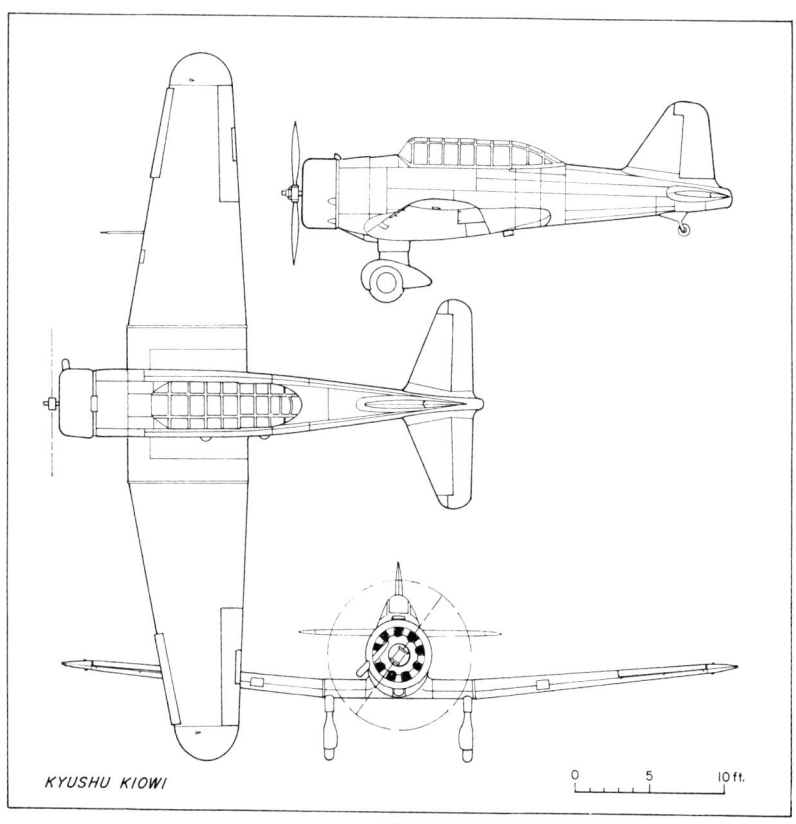

KYUSHU K10W1

North American KXA1 (NA-16-4R). (*North American Rockwell Corp.*)

Known to the Allies as OAK, the K10W1 supplanted the K5Y1 as the standard intermediate trainer in the Navy's pilot training syllabus.

TECHNICAL DATA

Description: Single-engined intermediate pilot trainer. All-metal structure with light alloy and fabric covering.

Accommodation: Pilot and instructor in tandem enclosed cockpits.

Powerplant: One Nakajima Kotobuki 2 Kai air-cooled radial, rated at 600 hp for take-off and 460 hp at 2,080 m (6,825 ft), driving a two-blade wooden propeller.

Armament: One forward-firing 7·7 mm Type 97 machine-gun.

Dimensions: Span 12·36 m (40 ft 6⅜ in); length 8·839 m (29 ft); height 2·835 m (9 ft 3⅜ in); wing area 22·3 sq m (240·034 sq ft).

Weights: Empty 1,476 kg (3,254 lb); loaded 2,033 kg (4,448 lb); maximum 2,093 kg (4,615 lb); wing loading 91·2 kg/sq m (18·5 lb/sq ft); power loading 3·4 kg/hp (7·5 lb/hp).

Performance: Maximum speed 152 kt at 2,080 m (175 mph at 6,825 ft); cruising speed 120 kt at 1,000 m (138 mph at 3,280 ft); climb to 5,000 m (16,405 ft) in 17 min 13 sec; service ceiling 7,300 m (23,950 ft); range 575 naut miles (652 st miles).

Production: A total of 176 K10W1s were built as follows:

K.K. Watanabe Tekkosho:

    26 K10W1 (1941–42)

Nippon Hikoki K.K.:

    150 K10W1 (1943–44)

Lockheed Type LO

In 1938 the Lockheed Aircraft Corporation exported to Japan a total of thirty of their Model 14-38 twin-engined passenger transports. Twenty aircraft (c/ns 1426–1428, 1433–1438, 1445, 1446, 1452 and 1455–1462) were delivered between March and July 1938 to Tachikawa Hikoki K.K. for eventual re-sale to Nihon Koku K.K. (Japan Air Transport Co Ltd) while a further ten aircraft (c/ns 1447–1449, 1453, 1454 and 1477–1481) were delivered direct to Nihon Koku K.K. between June and September 1938. Operated by that airline and its successor, Dai Nippon Koku, on its routes linking Japan to China, the aircraft was powered by a pair of 900 hp Wright R-1820-G3B fourteen-cylinder radials. Being used throughout the war, these civilian aircraft received the allied code name of TOBY.

Tachikawa, also having successfully negotiated a manufacturing licence with Lockheed, decided to submit to the Army a proposal covering Japanese production of a modified version. As the Army urgently required air transport to support their operations

A civil Type LO Transport, built by Tachikawa. (*Koku Fan*.)

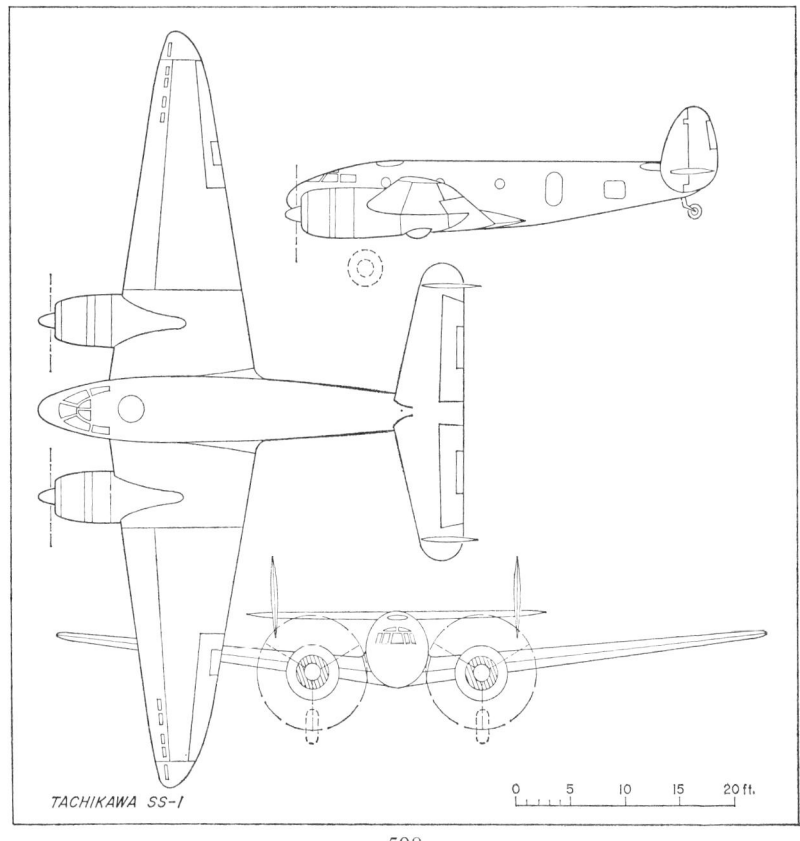

in China, this proposal was favourably received, and in 1939 Tachikawa were instructed to undertake the manufacture of this aircraft to carry military personnel. Powered by two 900 hp Mitsubishi Ha-26-I radials and designated Army Type LO Transport, these aircraft were also built by Kawasaki. As the aircraft's handling characteristics were found somewhat unsatisfactory by Army pilots, Kawasaki were instructed to redesign the aircraft, and eventually this led to the production of the Kawasaki Ki-56 described on page 108. Despite its shortcomings, the Army Type LO Transport, known as THELMA to Allied forces, was operated until the Japanese surrender.

In late 1940, Tachikawa undertook to produce an experimental aircraft specifically for cabin pressurization experiments. To speed up work, the wings, rear fuselage section and tail surfaces of the Army Type LO Transport were retained, and a shorter pressurized forward and centre fuselage section was designed. Of cylindrical cross section, the new forward fuselage had no windscreen step, and other modifications included the replacement of the Type LO powerplants with two 1,080 hp Mitsubishi Ha-102 radials. Designated Tachikawa SS-1, the aircraft was completed in May 1943 and during its brief trials provided valuable data on cabin pressurization.

TECHNICAL DATA

Description: Twin-engined personnel transport (Type LO) or pressurized research aircraft (SS-1). All-metal construction with fabric-covered control surfaces.

Accommodation: Crew of three and twelve passengers (Type LO), crew of six (SS-1).

Powerplant: Two 900 hp Army Type 99 (Mitsubishi Ha-26-I) fourteen-cylinder air-cooled radials, rated at 850 hp for take-off and 875 hp at 3,600 m (11,810 ft), driving three-blade metal propellers (Type LO).

Two Mitsubishi Ha-102 fourteen-cylinder air-cooled radials, rated at 1,080 hp for take-off, 1,055 hp at 2,780 m (9,120 ft) and 955 hp at 5,760 m (18,890 ft), driving three-blade metal propellers (SS-1).

	Type LO	SS-1
Dimensions:		
Span	19·965 m	19·964 m
	(65 ft 6 in)	(65 ft 5 $\frac{31}{32}$ in)
Length	13·42 m	11·76 m
	(49 ft 2 $\frac{9}{16}$ in)	(39 ft 7 in)
Height	3·49 m	3·46 m
	(11 ft 5 $\frac{7}{16}$ in)	(11 ft 4 $\frac{7}{32}$ in)
Wing area	51·3 sq m	51·3 sq m
	(552·193 sq ft)	(552·193 sq ft)
Weights:		
Empty	4,947 kg	5,157 kg
	(10,906 lb)	(11,369 lb)
Loaded	7,100 kg	6,740 kg
	(15,653 lb)	(14,859 lb)
Wing loading	138·4 kg/sq m	131·4 kg/sq m
	(28·4 lb/sq ft)	(26·9 lb/sq ft)
Power loading	4·2 kg/hp	3·1 kg/hp
	(9·2 lb/hp)	(6·9 lb/hp)
Performance:		
Maximum speed	418 km/h at 3,570 m	475 km/h at 5,800 m
	(260 mph at 11,710 ft)	(295 mph at 19,030 ft)
Cruising speed	—	360 km/h at 8,000 m
	—	(224 mph at 26,245 ft)
Climb to	—	8,000 m
	—	(26,245 ft)
in	—	13 min
Service ceiling	—	10,000 m
	—	(32,810 ft)
Range	—	2,200 km
	—	(1,367 st miles)

Production: A total of 119 Type LO Transports were built as follows:

Tachikawa Hikoki K.K.:   Kawasaki Kokuki Kogyo K.K.:
64 aircraft (1940–42)   55 aircraft (1940–41)

One SS-1 was built by Tachikawa Hikoki K.K. in 1943.

APPENDIX D

Aircraft Carriers, Seaplane and Flying-boat Tenders, and Aircraft-carrying Submarines

This appendix provides a quick reference to the aircraft-carrying ships of the Japanese forces during the Pacific War. Only the true aircraft carriers, converted aircraft-carrying battleships (*Ise* and *Hyuga*), seaplane and flying-boat tenders, and aircraft-carrying submarines—of which no less than thirty-six were commissioned by the Japanese Navy—have been included. Listing the many battleships, cruisers and other vessels which carried a limited number of floatplanes was considered as being beyond the scope of this book.

Included among the ships listed in the following tables are the escort carriers operated by the Japanese Army. The use of these ships by the Army can be directly traced to the effectiveness of Allied submarines which disrupted the long military lines of communication between Japan and its far-flung controlled territories. As the Navy kept their carriers for deployment in a strategic role, the Army were forced to commission their own carriers for use in the tactical role of convoy escort.

Imperial Japanese Navy Aircraft Carriers

Name	Description	Completed/Converted	Remarks
AKAGI	Fleet carrier 36,500 tons 31 knots 91 aircraft	25 March, 1927	Sunk off Midway by US aircraft 5 June, 1942.
AMAGI	Light carrier 17,150 tons 34 knots 65 aircraft	10 August, 1944	Heavily damaged by US aircraft 24 July, 1945. Scrapped after the war. *Unryu* class.
ASO	Light carrier 17,150 tons 32 knots 64 aircraft	17 November, 1944 (launched)	Uncompleted. Scrapped after the war. *Unryu* class.
CHITOSE	Light carrier 11,190 tons 29 knots 30 aircraft	1 January, 1944	Converted seaplane tender. Sunk off Leyte Gulf by US aircraft 25 October, 1944. *Chiyoda* class.
CHIYODA	Light carrier 11,190 tons 29 knots 30 aircraft	31 October, 1943	Converted seaplane tender. Sunk off Leyte 25 October, 1944, by US aircraft. *Chiyoda* class.
CHUYO	Escort carrier 17,830 tons 21 knots 27 aircraft	25 November, 1942	Converted liner *Nitta Maru*. Sunk by USS *Sailfish* off Japan 3 December, 1943. *Taiyo* class.
HIRYU	Fleet carrier 17,300 tons 34·5 knots 73 aircraft	5 July, 1939	Sunk off Midway by US aircraft 5 June, 1942. *Soryu* class.
HIYO	Fleet carrier 24,140 tons 25·5 knots 53 aircraft	31 July, 1942	Sunk off the Marianas by US aircraft 20 June, 1944. *Hiyo* class.

Name	Type/Specs	Date	Notes
HOSHO	Light carrier 7,470 tons 25 knots 21 aircraft	27 December, 1922	First Japanese carrier. Scrapped after the war.
HYUGA	Aircraft-carrying battleship 36,000 tons 25·25 knots 22 seaplanes	30 November, 1943	Conversion of battleship *Hyuga* to carry up to 22 E16A1s. Sunk in Kure dockyard by US aircraft 24 July, 1945.
IBUKI	Light carrier 12,500 tons 29 knots 27 aircraft	25 March, 1943 (launched)	Uncompleted at war's end and scrapped in 1947.
IKOMA	Light carrier 17,150 tons 34 knots 53 aircraft	17 November, 1944 (launched)	Sunk by US aircraft in Kure dockyard 24 July, 1945. *Unryu* class.
ISE	Aircraft-carrying battleship 35,800 tons 25·25 knots 22 seaplanes	8 October, 1943	Conversion of battleship *Ise* to carry up to 22 E16A1s. Sunk by US aircraft in Kure dockyard 28 July, 1945.
JUNYO	Fleet carrier 24,140 tons 25·5 knots 53 aircraft	3 May, 1942	Scrapped in 1947. *Hiyo* class.
KAGA	Fleet carrier 38,200 tons 28·3 knots 90 aircraft	31 March, 1928	Sunk off Midway by US aircraft 4 June, 1942.
KAIYO	Escort carrier 13,600 tons 23·75 knots 24 aircraft	23 November, 1943	Converted *Argentina Maru* liner. Sunk by US aircraft in Beppu Bay 24 July, 1945.
KASAGI	Light carrier 17,150 tons 34 knots 64 aircraft	19 October, 1944 (launched)	Uncompleted and scrapped after the war. *Unryu* class.
KATSURAGI	Light carrier 17,150 tons 32 knots 64 aircraft	15 October, 1944 (launched)	Uncompleted and scrapped after the war. *Unryu* class.
OTAKISAN MARU	Escort carrier 11,800 tons 18.5 knots 12 aircraft	14 January, 1945 (launched)	Converted oil tanker. Uncompleted.
RYUHO	Light carrier 13,360 tons 26·5 knots 31 aircraft	28 November, 1942	Converted submarine tender *Taigei*. Scrapped in 1946.
RYUJO	Light carrier 10,600 tons 29 knots 48 aircraft	9 May, 1933	Sunk by US aircraft in battle of Eastern Solomons 24 August, 1942.
SHIMANE MARU	Escort carrier 11,800 tons 18·5 knots 12 aircraft	17 December, 1944	Converted oil tanker. Uncompleted.
SHINANO	Fleet carrier 64,800 tons 27 knots 47 aircraft	19 November, 1944	Sunk by USS *Archerfish* in Inland Sea 29 November, 1944. Converted from battleship hull. Largest wartime carrier.
SHINYO	Light carrier 17,500 tons 22 knots 33 aircraft	15 December, 1943	Converted German liner *Scharnhorst*. Sunk by USS *Spadefish* in Yellow Sea 17 November, 1944.

Navy Aircraft Carriers (contd.)

SHOHO	Light carrier 11,262 tons 28 knots 30 aircraft	26 January, 1942	Converted tanker *Tsurugizaki*. Sunk by US aircraft in Coral Sea 8 May, 1942. *Shoho* class.
SHOKAKU	Fleet carrier 25,675 tons 34 knots 84 aircraft	8 August, 1941	Sunk by USS *Cavalla* during the battle of the Philippine Sea 19 June, 1944. *Shokaku* class.
SORYU	Fleet carrier 15,900 tons 34·5 knots 73 aircraft	29 December, 1937	Sunk by US aircraft off Midway 4 June, 1942. *Soryu* class.
TAIHO	Fleet carrier 29,300 tons 33 knots 53 aircraft	7 May, 1944	Sunk by USS *Albacore* in Philippine Sea 19 June, 1944.
TAIYO	Light carrier 17,830 tons 21 knots 27 aircraft	5 September, 1941	Converted liner *Kasuga Maru*. Sunk by USS *Rasher* off Luzon 18 August, 1944. *Taiyo* class.
UNRYU	Light carrier 17,150 tons 34 knots 65 aircraft	6 August, 1944	Sunk by USS *Redfish* in the East China Sea 19 December, 1944. *Unryu* class.
UNYO	Light carrier 17,830 tons 21 knots 27 aircraft	31 May, 1942	Converted liner *Yawata Maru*. Sunk by USS *Barb* in South China Sea 16 September, 1944. *Taiyo* class.
ZUIHO	Light carrier 11,262 tons 28 knots 30 aircraft	27 December, 1940	Converted tanker *Takasaki*. Sunk by US aircraft off Leyte 25 October, 1944. *Shoho* class.
ZUIKAKU	Fleet carrier 25,675 tons 34 knots 84 aircraft	25 September, 1941	Sunk by US aircraft off Leyte 24 October, 1944. *Shokaku* class.

Imperial Japanese Army Aircraft Carriers

AKITSU MARU	Escort carrier 11,800 tons 20 knots 30 aircraft	1941	Merchant liner converted to carry light aircraft and landing craft. Sunk by US submarine 15 November, 1944.
CHIGUSA MARU	Escort carrier 10,100 tons 15 knots 8 aircraft	29 December, 1944 (launched)	Converted oil tanker. Uncompleted and reconverted for cargo in 1949.
KUMANO MARU	Escort carrier 8,000 tons 19 knots 37 aircraft	28 January, 1945 (launched)	Landing craft carrier. Converted to civilian use in 1947.
NIGITSU MARU	Escort carrier 11,800 tons 20 knots 30 aircraft	1942	Merchant liner converted to carry landing craft and light aircraft. Sunk by US submarine 12 January, 1944. *Akitsu Maru* class.

SHINSHU MARU	Escort carrier 9,000 tons 19 knots 20 aircraft	1935	First ship designed to carry landing craft and light aircraft. Sunk by US aircraft 5 January, 1945.
YAMASHIO MARU	Escort carrier 10,100 tons 15 knots 8 aircraft	1944	Converted oil tanker. Sunk before completion at Yokohama by US aircraft 17 February, 1945.

Imperial Japanese Navy Seaplane Tenders

AKITSUSHIMA	Flying-boat tender 4,650 tons 19 knots 1 large flying-boat	1941	Lost 24 September, 1944.
CHIHAYA	Flying-boat tender 4,650 tons 19 knots 1 large flying-boat		Construction suspended before completion.
CHITOSE	Seaplane tender 11,023 tons 29 knots 24 seaplanes	1938	Converted to escort carrier (q.v.) in 1943.
CHIYODA	Seaplane tender 11,023 tons 29 knots 24 seaplanes	1938	Converted to escort carrier (q.v.) in 1943.
KAMIKA MARU	Seaplane tender 6,863 tons — 8 seaplanes		Converted merchant ship. Lost 28 May, 1943.
KAMOI	Seaplane tender 17,000 tons 15 knots 12 seaplanes	1933	Converted oil tanker. Converted back to oil tanker in 1943.
KIMIKAWA MARU	Seaplane tender 6,863 tons — 8 seaplanes		Converted merchant ship. Converted back to transport in October 1943.
KINAGAWA MARU	Seaplane tender 6,937 tons — 8 seaplanes		Converted merchant ship. Converted back to transport.
KIYOKAWA MARU	Seaplane tender 6,863 tons — 8 seaplanes		Converted merchant ship. Converted back to transport in April 1943.
KUNIKAWA MARU	Seaplane tender 6,863 tons — 8 seaplanes		Converted merchant ship. Converted back to transport in October 1943.
MIZUHO	Seaplane tender 10,929 tons 22 knots 24 seaplanes	1938	Lost 2 May, 1942.
NISSHIN	Seaplane tender 11,317 tons 28 knots 20 seaplanes	1942	Lost 22 July, 1943.

Navy Seaplane Tenders (contd.)

NOTORO	Seaplane tender 14,050 tons 12 knots 8 seaplanes	1924	Converted oil tanker. Converted back to oil tanker in 1942.
SAGARA MARU	Seaplane tender 7,189 tons — 8 seaplanes		Converted merchant ship. Converted back to transport in December 1942.
SANUKI MARU	Seaplane tender 7,158 tons — 8 seaplanes		Converted merchant ship. Converted back to transport in August 1942.
SANYO MARU	Seaplane tender 8,360 tons — 8 seaplanes		Converted merchant ship. Converted back to transport in April 1943.

Imperial Japanese Navy Aircraft-carrying Submarines

I-6	Fleet submarine 2,243/3,061 tons 20/7·5 knots 1 seaplane	1934	Missing 14 July, 1944.
I-7 Class (I-7/I-8)	Fleet submarines 2,525/3,583 tons 23/8 knots 1 seaplane	1935 (I-7) 1938 (I-8)	I-7 lost 22 June, 1943. I-8 lost 31 March, 1945.
I-9 Class (I-9/I-11)	Fleet submarines 2,914/4,150 tons 23·5/8 knots 1 seaplane	1939 (I-9 and I-10) 1940 (I-11)	I-9 lost 11 June, 1943. I-10 lost 4 July, 1944. I-11 lost 11 January, 1944.
I-12	Fleet submarine 2,934/4,172 tons 17·5/6 knots 1 seaplane	1943	Missing in January 1945.
I-15 Class (I-15, I-17, I-19, I-23, I-25/I-27, I-29, I-36, I-37 and I-39)	Fleet submarines 2,584/3,654 tons 23·5/8 knots 1 seaplane	1939/42	All but I-36 were lost during the war.
I-40 Class (I-40/I-45)	Fleet submarines 2,624/3,700 tons 23·5/8 knots 1 seaplane	1942/1943	All lost during the war.
I-54 Class (I-54, I-56 and I-58)	Fleet submarines 2,607/3,688 tons 17·5/6·5 knots 1 seaplane	1943 (I-54 and I-56) 1944 (I-58)	I-54 lost 25 October, 1944. I-56 lost 18 April, 1945. I-58 scuttled by US Navy in 1946.
I-13 Class (I-1, I-13/I-15)	Fleet submarines 3,603/4,762 tons 16·5/5·5 knots 2 M6A1 seaplanes	1944	I-1 uncompleted I-13 lost 16 July, 1945. I-14 and I-15 scrapped by US Navy.
I-400 Class (I-400, I-401, I-402, I-404 and I-405)	Fleet submarines 5,223/6,560 tons 18·5/6·5 knots 3 M6A1 seaplanes	1944	World's largest submarines during the war. I-404 lost 28 July, 1945. Others scuttled by US Navy in 1946.

APPENDIX E

Japanese Aero-engines

This appendix is provided as an aid to understanding the various Japanese engine designation systems and to visualizing the principal powerplants fitted to Japanese Pacific War aircraft. It should not be construed as a study of Japanese aero-engines, which would require considerably more space and is beyond the scope of this book.

Engine designation systems employed by the Imperial Japanese Army

During the early war years the Army designated their engines according to two distinct systems. In the experimental stage, engines were assigned in chronological sequence a Ha—for hatsudoki or engine—number, the Ha numbering system being similar in principle to the Ki numbering system used for aircraft. Once an engine was accepted for quantity production, its Ha designation was complemented by a Type number incorporating the last digits of the Japanese calendar year (e.g. 99 for year 2599 or A.D. 1939) during which the engine was accepted, its maximum rated power, and a description of its class (e.g. radial, liquid-cooled, etc.); a Model number followed the Type number to identify a specific version. Example:

The 900 hp Army Type 99 radial Model 1 was the designation given to the first production version of the Mitsubishi Ha-26-I. This engine was an air-cooled fourteen-cylinder radial.

Engine designation systems employed by the Imperial Japanese Navy

During the same period, the Navy also used two designation systems. One consisted of a combination of three letters and one digit, e.g. NK1C, in which the first letter indicated the name of the company responsible for the design of the engine (N for Nakajima), the second letter was descriptive of the class of engine (K for air-cooled, D for diesel, E for liquid-cooled), the digit was a sequence number within any given class of engines (such as 1 for first air-cooled engine) and the last letter indicated the version of the engine (e.g. C for third version of the NK1 series). The second designation system, applying to production engines, consisted of a name followed by a Model number: for example, the NK1C became known as the Sakae (Prosperity) 12.

Joint Army–Navy engine designation system

As several basic engine types were in production at the same time for the Army and the Navy, such engines were known by no less than four distinct designations (e.g. Mitsubishi Ha-112-II, 1,500 hp Army Type 4 radial—both of these being Army designations; MK8P and Kinsei (Golden Star) 62—these last two being Navy designations) all applying to what was basically the same engine type. Consequently, to simplify the situation, the Ministry of Munitions instigated the use of a joint Army–Navy engine designation system employing the best features of the old systems. Accordingly, the engine in the above example became simply known as the Mitsubishi [Ha-33] 62, the various components of this designation providing specific information as follows:

Ha: abbreviation for hatsudoki (engine).
3: air-cooled, double-row, 14-cylinder radial (see Engine class identification).
3: bore and stroke dimension code (see Bore and stroke identification).
62: model number identifying specific variant in the [Ha-33] series.

515

Engine class identification
 Ha-1: air-cooled inline engine.
 Ha-2: air-cooled single-row radial engine.
 Ha-3: air-cooled 14-cylinder double-row radial engine.
 Ha-4: air-cooled 18-cylinder double-row radial engine.
 Ha-5: air-cooled, more than 18-cylinder, multi-row radial engine.
 Ha-6: liquid-cooled 12-cylinder engine.
 Ha-7: liquid-cooled, more than 12-cylinder, engine.
 Ha-8: diesel engine.
 Ha-9: special engine.

Bore and stroke identification

	Bore/stroke (in millimetres)		Bore/stroke (in millimetres)
..-.1:	140/130	..-.4:	140/160
..-.2:	150/170	..-.5:	130/150
..-.3:	140/150	..-.0:	130/160

Translations of engine names
 Amakaze (Heavenly Wind)
 Atsuta (A Holy Shrine in Aichi Prefecture)
 Hatakaze (Breeze)
 Hatsukaze (Fresh Wind)
 Hikari (Splendour)
 Homare (Honour)
 Jimpu (Encampment Wind)
 Kamikaze (Divine Wind)
 Kasei (Mars)
 Kinsei (Golden Star)
 Kotobuki (Congratulation)
 Mamoru (Protector)
 Sakae (Prosperity)
 Tempu (Heavenly Father)
 Zuisei (Holy Star)

1,150 hp Army Type 1 radial Model 2. This Nakajima fourteen-cylinder engine was initially known as the Ha-115-II but later was redesignated [Ha-35] 25. (*US Navy Department.*)

900 hp Army Type 99 radial Model 2. Designed by Mitsubishi Jukogyo K.K., this fourteen-cylinder engine bore the experimental designation Ha-26-II. (*US Navy Department.*)

1,050 hp Army Type 1 radial. This fourteen-cylinder engine was better known by its experimental designation—Mitsubishi Ha-102—but became known as the [Ha-31] 21 under the joint Army/Navy system. (*US Navy Department.*)

1,450 hp Army Type 2 radial. Bearing the experimental number Ha-109, this Nakajima fourteen-cylinder engine was primarily used in bombers of the Japanese Army and became known as the [Ha-34] 11. (*US Navy Department.*)

1,100 hp Army Type 2 liquid-cooled engine. This twelve-cylinder inverted-vee engine was derived from the German DB 601A. Built by Kawasaki as the Ha-40, it became the [Ha-60] 22 under the joint Army/Navy designation system. (*US Navy Department.*)

Mitsubishi Zuisei (Holy Star) 13 fourteen-cylinder radial. Developing 840 hp for take-off, this engine was generally similar to the Ha-26 and Ha-102 series of the Japanese Army and was redesignated [Ha-31] 13. (*US Navy Department.*)

The Mitsubishi Kasei (Mars) was one of the most important fourteen-cylinder engines used to power Japanese Navy aircraft. Illustrated here is the Kasei 12 (MK4B) or [Ha-32] 12. (*US Navy Department.*)

Fitted with contra-rotating propellers, the Mitsubishi Kasei 14 (MK4D) was redesignated [Ha-32] 14. (*US Navy Department.*)

Developing 1,825 hp for take-off, the Mitsubishi Kasei 25 (MK4T) was one of the major production versions of the Kasei series. It became known as the [Ha-32] 25 under the joint Army/Navy designation system. (*US Navy Department*.)

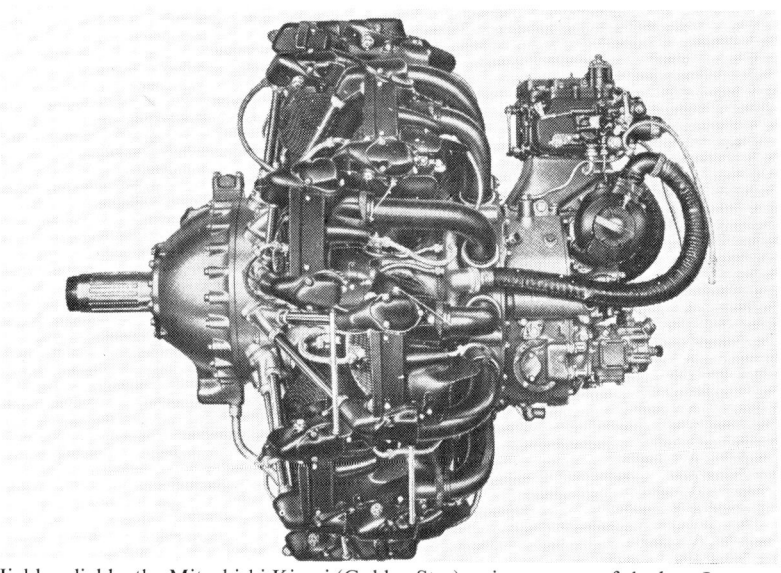

Highly reliable, the Mitsubishi Kinsei (Golden Star) series was one of the best Japanese powerplants. Illustrated here is the Kinsei 51 ([Ha-33] 51) which developed 1,280 hp for take-off. (*US Navy Department*.)

Nakajima Kotobuki (Congratulation) 1 KAI 1 nine-cylinder air-cooled radial. (*US Navy Department.*)

The first prototype of the Nakajima Homare (Honour) 22 NK9K or [Ha-45] 22. The Homare series, in spite of somewhat unreliable performance, became the most important eighteen-cylinder Japanese engine towards the end of the war. (*US Navy Department*.)

The Nakajima Sakae 21 (NK1F), later known as the [Ha-35] 21, powered—among other types—the Mitsubishi A6M5 naval fighter. (*US Navy Department*.)

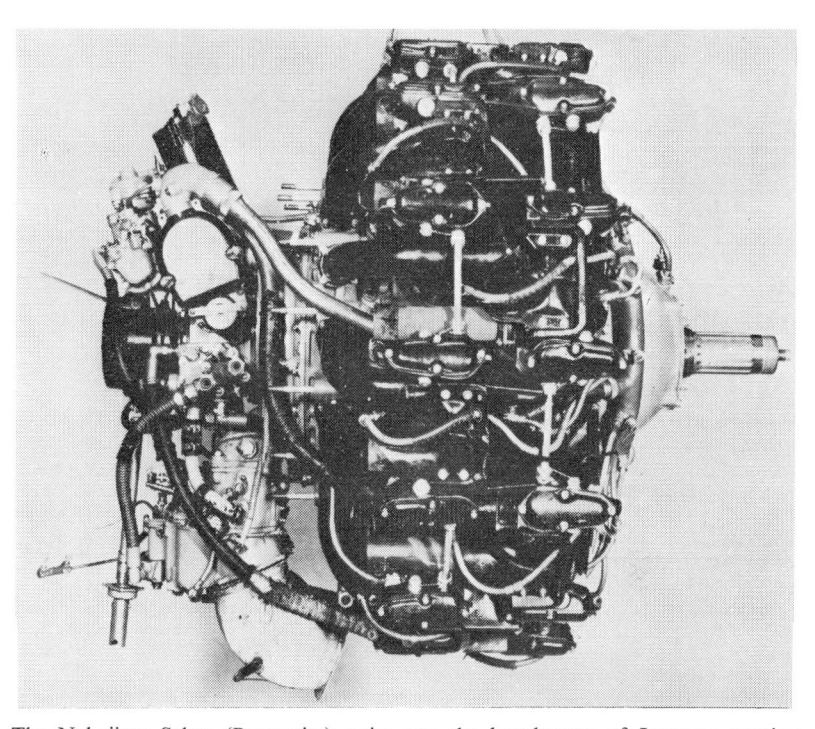

The Nakajima Sakae (Prosperity) series was the best-known of Japanese wartime engines. The one illustrated here is a Sakae 12 (NK1C) which became the [Ha-35] 12 under the joint Army/Navy designation system. (*US Navy Department*.)

The Ne-20 axial-flow turbojet intended to power the Ohka Model 43 Suicide Attacker. (*US Navy Department*).

APPENDIX F

Japanese Aircraft Armament and Guided Missiles

This appendix provides a quick reference to the principal types of machine-guns and cannon fitted to Japanese Pacific War aircraft. Also included are brief data on the embryonic development of guided missiles in Japan.

Machine-guns and cannon fitted to aircraft of the Imperial Japanese Army

7·7 mm Type 89 machine-gun. (*US Navy Department.*)

7·7 mm Type 89 machine-gun
This gas-operated light machine-gun was fitted on flexible mounts on early World War II Japanese aircraft and used flat drum magazines containing 69 rounds. Overall length 42·5 in, weight 20 lb, rate of fire 750 rpm, muzzle velocity 2,450 ft per sec, effective range 600 m (1,970 ft).

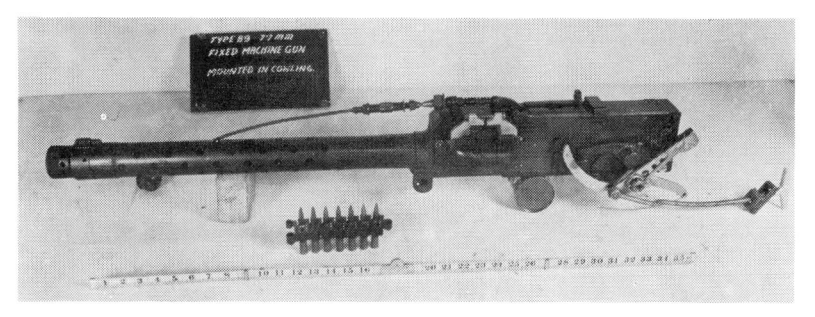

7·7 mm Type 89 Model 2 machine-gun. (*US Navy Department*.)

7·7 mm Type 89 Model 2 machine-gun
This derivative of the British Vickers light machine-gun was one of the standard fixed weapons on Japanese fighter aircraft and used a disintegrating metal link belt. Overall length 40·5 in, weight 26 lb, rate of fire 900 rpm, muzzle velocity 2,660 ft per sec, effective range 600 m (1,970 ft).

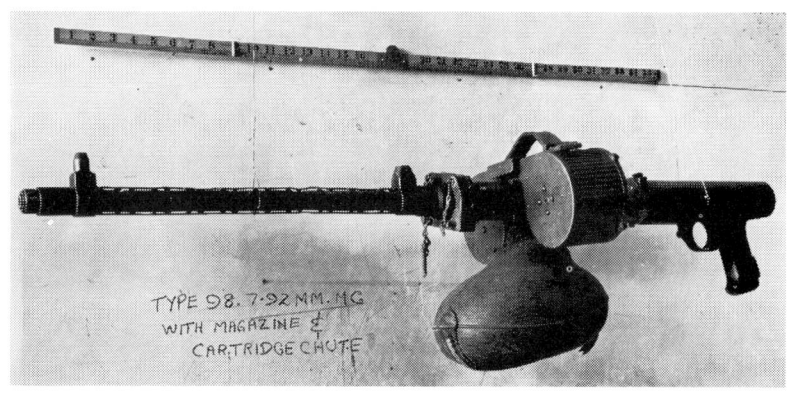

7·92 mm Type 98 machine-gun with magazine and cartridge chute. (*US Navy Department*.)

7·92 mm Type 98 machine-gun
This derivative of the German MG 15 machine-gun was a standard flexible weapon and used saddle drum magazines containing 75 rounds. Overall length 42·5 in, weight 15·5 lb, rate of fire 1,500 rpm, muzzle velocity 2,660 ft per sec, effective range 600 m (1,970 ft).

12·7 mm Type 1 machine-gun. (*US Navy Department.*)

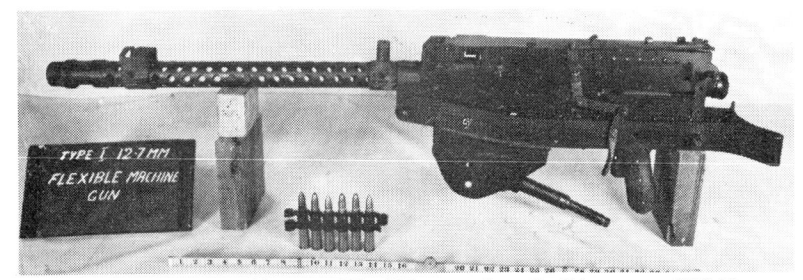

12.7 mm Type 1 machine-gun (Ho-103) as used on flexible mount. (*US Navy Department.*)

12·7 mm Type 1 machine-gun (Ho-103)
Used both on fixed and flexible mounts, this heavy machine-gun was similar to the US Browning 0·50 inch weapon. Disintegrating metal link belt. Overall length 49 in, weight 48 lb, rate of fire 900 rpm, muzzle velocity 2,560 ft per sec, effective range 750 m (2,460 ft).

20 mm Type 97 cannon (Ho-1 and Ho-3)
This gas-operated weapon was derived from an anti-tank cannon and used saddle-type magazines. The Ho-1 was a flexible weapon with 15 rounds per magazine, and the Ho-3 was a fixed weapon with 50 rounds per magazine. Overall length 69·5 in, weight 72 lb (Ho-1) or 95 lb (Ho-3), rate of fire 400 rpm, muzzle velocity 2,690 ft per sec, effective range 900 m (2,950 ft).

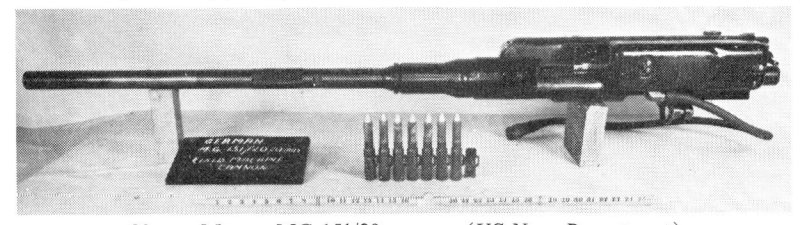

20 mm Mauser MG 151/20 cannon. (*US Navy Department.*)

20 mm Mauser MG 151/20 cannon
Four hundred of these German weapons were imported and used exclusively on specially modified Kawasaki Ki-61-I fighters. Overall length 69·5 in, weight 92 lb, rate of fire 800 rpm, muzzle velocity 2,500 ft per sec, effective range 850 m (2,790 ft).

20 mm Type 1 cannon (Ho-5)

This light-weight cannon, similar in construction to the 12·7 mm Type 1 machine-gun and using disintegrating metal link belt, was one of the best Japanese aircraft weapons. Overall length 58 in, weight 72 lb, rate of fire 850 rpm, muzzle velocity 2,460 ft per sec, effective range 900 m (2,950 ft).

30 mm Ho-105 cannon

Used in limited numbers towards the end of the war, this cannon was intended to see much use had the war lasted longer. Overall length 79·5 in, weight 97 lb, rate of fire 450 rpm, muzzle velocity 2,350 ft per sec, effective range 900 m (2,950 ft).

37 mm Type 98 cannon

Installed in the ventral tunnel of early versions of the Kawasaki Ki-45, this hand-fed cannon was a copy of a French 37 mm field gun. Overall length 54 in, weight 269 lb, rate of fire 15 rpm, muzzle velocity 2,000 ft per sec, effective range 1,000 m (3,280 ft).

37 mm Ho-203 cannon. (*US Navy Department.*)

37 mm Ho-203 cannon

This recoil-operated cannon was fed from a 25-round magazine and was installed on several types of Kawasaki heavy fighters. Overall length 60·3 in, weight 196 lb, rate of fire 120 rpm, muzzle velocity 1,890 ft per sec, effective range 900 m (2,950 ft).

40 mm Ho-301 cannon. (*US Navy Department.*)

40 mm Ho-301 cannon

Installed in the wings of a small number of Nakajima Ki-44-IIc fighters, this weapon was unusual in as much as its ammunition did not use cartridges. Instead, the propelling charge was contained in a cavity in the rear of the projectile. Twelve exhaust ports in the base plate permitted the expanding gases to escape and drive the projectile forward. Overall length 58·5 in, weight 291 lb, rate of fire 450 rpm, muzzle velocity 760 ft per sec, effective range 150 m (490 ft).

40 mm shell used in the Ho-301 cannon. (*US Navy Department*.)

57 mm Ho-401 cannon
Installed, among others, on the Kawasaki Ki-102b heavy fighter, this type of cannon was still under development at war's end. Weight 353 lb, rate of fire 90 rpm, muzzle velocity 1,700 ft per sec.

Machine-guns and cannon fitted to aircraft of the Imperial Japanese Navy

7·7 mm Type 92 machine-gun. (*US Navy Department*.)

7·7 mm Type 92 machine-gun

Derived from the British Lewis machine-gun, this flexible weapon used flat drum magazines with a capacity of either 47 or 97 rounds. Overall length 39 in, weight 18·5 lb, rate of fire 600 rpm, muzzle velocity 2,500 ft per sec, effective range 600 m (1,970 ft).

7·7 mm Type 97 machine-gun

Very similar to the Army's 7·7 mm Type 89 machine-gun, this weapon was the standard fixed light machine-gun on Navy fighters. Overall length 41 in, weight 26 lb, rate of fire 1,000 rpm, muzzle velocity 2,460 ft per sec, effective range 600 m (1,970 ft).

7·92 mm Type 1 machine-gun. (*US Navy Department.*)

7·92 mm Type 1 machine-gun

This flexible weapon, like the Army 7·92 mm Type 98 machine-gun, was a derivative of the German MG 15 and was fed from saddle drum magazines housing 75 rounds. Overall length 42·5 in, weight 15 lb, rate of fire 1,000 rpm, muzzle velocity 2,590 ft per sec, effective range 600 m (1,970 ft).

13 mm Type 2 machine-gun

First belt-fed flexible weapon used on Japanese naval aircraft, this machine-gun was similar to the German MG 131. Overall length 46·2 in, weight 37·5 lb, rate of fire 900 rpm, muzzle velocity 2,460 ft per sec, effective range 900 m (2,950 ft).

13·2 mm Type 3 machine-gun

This belt-fed weapon superseded the 7·7 mm Type 97 machine-gun on Japanese naval fighters and, in particular, was fitted to late versions of the Mitsubishi A6M. Overall length 61 in, weight 66 lb, rate of fire 800 rpm, muzzle velocity 2,590 ft per sec, effective range 900 m (2,950 ft).

20 mm Type 99 cannon

Standard aircraft cannon of the Japanese Navy, this weapon was constantly improved throughout the war and appeared in a variety of versions for use on fixed or flexible mounts. Early version used drum magazines, while the later Type 99 Model 2 Mark 4 was belt-fed. Overall length ranging from 52·5 in (Model 1) to 74·4 in (Model 2 Mark 4), weight ranging from 51 lb (Model 1) to 82·6 lb (Model 2 Mark 4), rate of fire ranging from 490 rpm (Model 2 Mark 3) to 750 rpm (Model 2 Mark 5), muzzle velocity ranging from 1,970 ft per sec (Model 1) to 2,490 ft per sec (Model 2 Mark 5), effective range 800 m (2,625 ft) to 1,000 m (3,280 ft).

20 mm Type 99 Model 1 cannon as used on flexible mounts. (*US Navy Department.*)

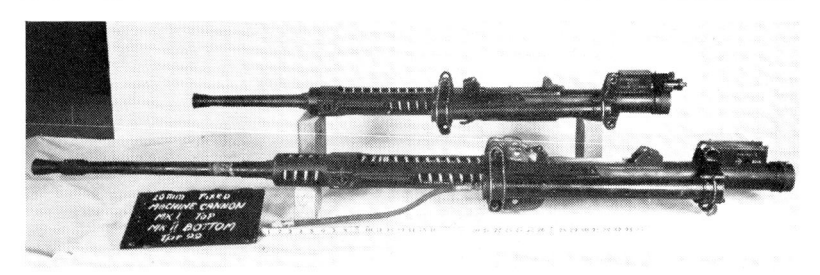

20 mm Type 99 Model 2 Mk 3 cannon (bottom) and 20 mm Type 99 Model 1 Mk 3 cannon. (*US Navy Department.*)

30 mm Type 5 cannon
Basically an enlarged version of the 20 mm Type 99 cannon, this weapon—fed from 42-round magazines—was entering service at war's end. Overall length 82·5 in, weight 154 lb, rate of fire 400 rpm, muzzle velocity 2,460 ft per sec, effective range 900 m (2,950 ft).

Japanese guided missiles

During the mid-war years, the Koku Hombu initiated for the Japanese Army the development of a series of air-to-ground guided missiles.

Igo-1-A: Designed by Mitsubishi and partially built of wood, this missile was of monoplane configuration and was powered by a rocket engine generating 240 kg (529 lb) of thrust for 75 sec. An 800 kg (1,764 lb) warhead was fitted. Intended to be carried beneath the belly of a Mitsubishi Ki-67 bomber, this radio-controlled weapon was first tested during the autumn of 1944 but was too late to be used operationally. Span 3·6 m (11 ft 9$\frac{23}{32}$ in); length 5·77 m (18 ft 11$\frac{5}{32}$ in). Loaded weight 1,400 kg (3,086 lb).

Igo-1-B: Of smaller size than the Igo-1-A, this radio-controlled missile was designed by Kawasaki and was powered by a rocket engine generating 150 kg (331 lb) of thrust for 80 seconds. Test drops were made in late 1944 using a specially modified Kawasaki Ki-48-II bomber, but the intention was that the Kawasaki Ki-102b assault aircraft would be the operational carrier. Even though a total of 180 Igo-1-Bs were built, none was used operationally. Warhead: 300 kg (661 lb). Span 2·6 m (8 ft 6$\frac{3}{8}$ in); length 4·09 m (13 ft 5 in). Loaded weight 680 kg (1,499 lb).

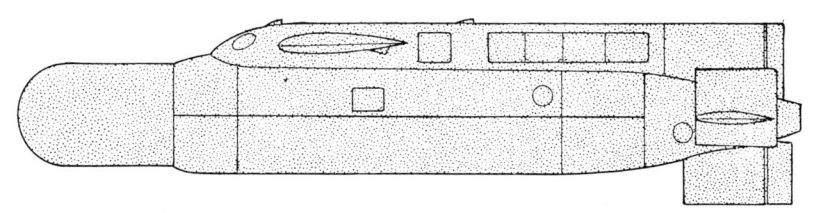

Kawasaki Igo-1-B radio-controlled missile. (*J. Roberts.*)

Igo-1-C: Designed by the staff of Tokyo Imperial University's Aeronautical Research Institute, this missile was intended to home in on the shock waves produced by the guns of the target naval vessels. In spite of promising results obtained during a series of tests made in the spring of 1945, the Igo-1-C could not be placed in production before war's end. Length 3·5 m (11 ft 5$\frac{25}{32}$ in); diameter 0·5 m (1 ft 7$\frac{11}{16}$ in).

Whereas the Army concentrated solely on the development of air-to-surface missiles, the Navy initiated in their Dai-Ichi Kaigun Koku Gijitsusho the development of air-to-surface and surface-to-air guided missiles forming the Funryu (Raging Dragon) series.

Funryu 1: Experimental air-to-surface anti-shipping radio-controlled missile. Not proceeded with.

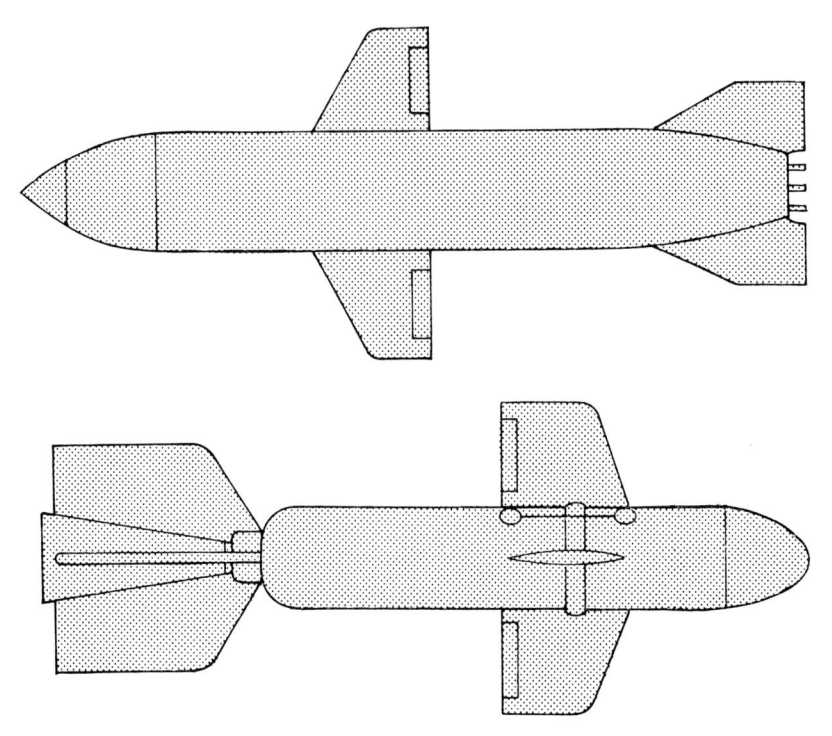

Funryu 2 (bottom) and Funryu 4 air-to-surface missiles. (*J. Roberts.*)

Funryu 2: Experimental gyro-stabilized surface-to-air missile. One solid-propellant rocket generating 2,400 kg (5,300 lb) of thrust for $3\frac{1}{2}$ sec. Warhead: 50 kg (110 lb). Length 2·2 m (7 ft $2\frac{5}{8}$ in); diameter 0·3 m (11$\frac{13}{16}$ in). Loaded weight 370 kg (816 lb). Maximum speed 845 km/h (525 mph); effective ceiling 5,000 m (16,405 ft).

Funryu 3: Experimental development of Funryu 2 with liquid-propellant rocket engine. Not proceeded with.

Funryu 4: Surface-to-air radar-controlled missile intended for quantity production. Ground guidance system included two separate radars for tracking the missile and its target and a computer. Prototype under construction at war's end. Warhead: 200 kg (441 lb). One 1,500 kg (3,307 lb) thrust Toko Ro.2 (KR10) bi-fuel rocket engine. Length 4 m (13 ft $1\frac{15}{32}$ in); diameter 0·6 m (1 ft $11\frac{5}{8}$ in). Loaded weight 1,900 kg (4,189 lb). Maximum speed 1,100 km/h (684 mph); effective ceiling 15,000 m (49,215 ft); range 30 km (19 miles).

Designation Index

This index provides a quick guide to every aircraft designation used during the Pacific War by the Imperial Japanese Army and Navy. As most Japanese designation systems during the war had been introduced prior to 1941, the author has elected to list all designations assigned within each system even though some aircraft types so designated were already out of service when the war began.

References are given in italics to the page(s) in this book where information on a particular aircraft can be found. For those experimental or obsolete types not described in the main body of this work, brief details are given in this index.

The index has been arranged as follows:

    Section I: Japanese Army aircraft designation systems
        A — Kitai (Ki) numbers
        B — Guraida (Ku) numbers
        C — Kazaguruma (Ka) numbers
        D — Sundry designation numbers
        E — Type numbers
        F — Popular names

    Section II: Japanese Navy aircraft designation systems
        A — Shi numbers
        B — Short designation system
        C — Type numbers
        D — Popular names
        E — Service Aeroplane Development Programme (SADP) numbers

    Section III: Allied code name system

Section I: Japanese Army Aircraft Designation Systems

A — Kitai Numbers

Ki-1	Mitsubishi	Army Type 93 Heavy Bomber	Twin-engined monoplane; obsolete in 1941
Ki-2	Mitsubishi	Army Type 93 Twin-engined Light Bomber	Japanese version of Junkers K-37; obsolete in 1941
Ki-3	Kawasaki	Army Type 93 Single-engined Light Bomber	Biplane; obsolete in 1941
Ki-4	Nakajima	Army Type 94 Reconnaissance Plane	Single-engined biplane; obsolete in 1941
Ki-5	Kawasaki	Army Experimental Fighter	Monoplane; not proceeded with
Ki-6	Nakajima	Army Type 95-2 Trainer	Japanese-built Fokker Super Universal; obsolete in 1941
Ki-7	Mitsubishi	Army Experimental Crew Trainer	339
Ki-8	Nakajima	Army Experimental Two-seat Fighter	Single-engined monoplane; five built
Ki-9	Tachikawa	Army Type 95-1 Medium Grade Trainer	246
Ki-10	Kawasaki	Army Type 95 Fighter	86
Ki-11	Nakajima	Army Experimental Fighter	196
Ki-12	Nakajima	Army Experimental Fighter	Monoplane; not proceeded with
Ki-13	Nakajima	Army Experimental Direct Co-operation Plane	Project only
Ki-14	Mitsubishi	Army Experimental Direct Co-operation Plane	Project only
Ki-15	Mitsubishi	Army Type 97 Command Reconnaissance Plane	149
Ki-16	Nakajima	Army Experimental Transport	Project only
Ki-17	Tachikawa	Army Type 95-3 Primary Trainer	248
Ki-18	Mitsubishi	Army Experimental Fighter	343
Ki-19	Nakajima	Army Experimental Heavy Bomber	157, 487
Ki-20	Mitsubishi	Army Type 92 Heavy Bomber	Japanese version of Junkers K-51; obsolete in 1941
Ki-21	Mitsubishi	Army Type 97 Heavy Bomber	155
Ki-22	Kawasaki	Army Experimental Heavy Bomber	Project only
Ki-23	Fukuda	Army Training Sailplane	
Ki-24	Tachikawa	Army Primary Glider	
Ki-25	Tachikawa	Army Experimental Glider	Training glider

535

Ki-26	Tachikawa	Army Experimental Glider	Training glider
Ki-27	Nakajima	Army Type 97 Fighter	*196*
Ki-28	Kawasaki	Army Experimental Fighter	*197*
Ki-29	Tachikawa	Army Experimental Light Bomber	Project only
Ki-30	Mitsubishi	Army Type 97 Light Bomber	*164*
Ki-31	Nakajima	Army Experimental Light Bomber	Project only
Ki-32	Kawasaki	Army Type 98 Light Bomber	*90*
Ki-33	Mitsubishi	Army Experimental Fighter	*197, 343*
Ki-34	Nakajima	Army Type 97 Transport	*204*
Ki-35	Mitsubishi	Army Experimental Direct Co-operation Plane	Project only; *250*
Ki-36	Tachikawa	Army Type 98 Direct Co-operation Plane	*250*
Ki-37	Nakajima	Army Experimental Twin-engined Fighter	*93*
Ki-38	Kawasaki	Army Experimental Twin-engined Fighter	*93*
Ki-39	Mitsubishi	Army Experimental Twin-engined Fighter	*93, 170*
Ki-40	Mitsubishi	Army Experimental Command Reconnaissance Plane	*170*
Ki-41	Nakajima	Army Experimental High-speed Transport	Project only
Ki-42	Mitsubishi	Army Experimental Bomber	Project only
Ki-43	Nakajima	Army Type 1 Fighter Hayabusa	*206*
Ki-44	Nakajima	Army Type 2 Single-seat Fighter Shoki	*215*
Ki-45	Kawasaki	Army Type 2 Twin-engined Fighter Toryu	*93*
Ki-46	Mitsubishi	Army Type 100 Command Reconnaissance Plane	*168*
Ki-47	Mitsubishi	Army Experimental Light Bomber	Project only
Ki-48	Kawasaki	Army Type 99 Twin-engined Light Bomber	*102*
Ki-49	Nakajima	Army Type 100 Heavy Bomber Donryu	*223*
Ki-50	Mitsubishi	Army Experimental Heavy Bomber	Project only
Ki-51	Mitsubishi	Army Type 99 Assault Plane	*178*
Ki-52	Nakajima	Army Experimental Dive Bomber	Project only
Ki-53	Nakajima	Army Experimental Twin-engined Fighter	Project only
Ki-54	Tachikawa	Army Type 1 Advanced Trainer, Operations Trainer and Transport	*254*
Ki-55	Tachikawa	Army Type 99 Advanced Trainer	*250*
Ki-56	Kawasaki	Army Type 1 Freight Transport	*108*

Ki-57	Mitsubishi	Army Type 100 Transport	182
Ki-58	Nakajima	Army Experimental Escort Fighter	225
Ki-59	Kokusai	Army Type 1 Transport	145
Ki-60	Kawasaki	Army Experimental Fighter	110
Ki-61	Kawasaki	Army Type 3 Fighter Hien	112
Ki-62	Nakajima	Army Experimental Fighter	487
Ki-63	Nakajima	Army Experimental Fighter	Project only; 230
Ki-64	Kawasaki	Army Experimental High-speed Fighter	121
Ki-65	Mansyu	Army Experimental Fighter	Several projected versions; none built
Ki-66	Kawasaki	Army Experimental Dive Bomber	123
Ki-67	Mitsubishi	Army Type 4 Heavy Bomber Hiryu	186
Ki-68	Nakajima	Army Experimental Long-range Bomber	425
Ki-69	Mitsubishi	Army Experimental Escort Fighter	190
Ki-70	Tachikawa	Army Experimental High-speed Command Reconnaissance Plane	257
Ki-71	Mansyu	Army Experimental Tactical Reconnaissance Plane	180
Ki-72	Tachikawa	Army Experimental Direct Co-operation Plane	253
Ki-73	Mitsubishi	Army Experimental Fighter	192
Ki-74	Tachikawa	Army Experimental High-altitude Long-range Bomber	259
Ki-75	Nakajima	Army Experimental Twin-engined High-altitude Night Fighter	Project only
Ki-76	Kokusai	Army Type 3 Command Liaison Plane	147
Ki-77	Tachikawa	Army Experimental Long-range Research Plane	262
Ki-78	Kawasaki	Army Experimental High-speed Research Plane	125
Ki-79	Mansyu	Army Type 2 Advanced Trainer	486
Ki-80	Nakajima	Army Experimental Multi-seat Fighter	225
Ki-81	Kawasaki	Army Experimental Multi-seat Fighter	106
Ki-82	Nakajima	Army Experimental Bomber	
Ki-83	Mitsubishi	Army Experimental Long-range Fighter	192
Ki-84	Nakajima	Army Type 4 Fighter Hayate	230
Ki-85	Kawasaki	Army Experimental Long-range Bomber	425

Ki-86	Kokusai	Army Type 4 Primary Trainer	503	
Ki-87	Nakajima	Army Experimental High-altitude Fighter	238	
Ki-88	Kawasaki	Army Experimental Fighter	483	
Ki-89	Kawasaki	Army Experimental Research Plane		Project only
Ki-90	Mitsubishi	Army Experimental Bomber		Project only
Ki-91	Kawasaki	Army Experimental Long-range Bomber	484	
Ki-92	Tachikawa	Army Experimental Transport		Projected (twin-engined)
Ki-93	Rikugun	Army Experimental Heavy Fighter and Assault Plane	244	
Ki-94	Tachikawa	Army Experimental High-altitude Fighter	265	
Ki-95	Mitsubishi	Army Experimental Command Reconnaissance Plane	193	
Ki-96	Kawasaki	Army Experimental Twin-engined Fighter	127	
Ki-97	Mitsubishi	Army Experimental Transport	190	
Ki-98	Mansyu	Army Experimental Assault Plane and Heavy Fighter	486	
Ki-99	Mitsubishi	Army Experimental Short-range Fighter		Project only
Ki-100	Kawasaki	Army Type 5 Fighter	129	
Ki-101	Nakajima	Army Experimental Twin-engined Night Fighter		Project only
Ki-102	Kawasaki	{ Army Type 4 Assault Plane (Ki-102b)	134	
		Army Experimental High-altitude Fighter (Ki-102a)	134	
		Army Experimental Night Fighter (Ki-102c)	134	
Ki-103	Mitsubishi	Army Experimental Fighter	193	
Ki-104	Tachikawa	Army Experimental Fighter		Projected medium-altitude fighter developed from Ki-94
Ki-105	Kokusai	Army Experimental Transport Ohtori	485	
Ki-106	Tachikawa	Army Experimental Fighter	234	
Ki-107	Tokyo Koku	Army Experimental Primary Trainer	488	
Ki-108	Kawasaki	Army Experimental High-altitude Fighter	138	
Ki-109	Mitsubishi	Army Experimental Interceptor Fighter	194	
Ki-110	Tachikawa	Army Experimental Transport	256	
Ki-111	Tachikawa	Army Experimental Transport	256	
Ki-112	Mitsubishi	Army Experimental Multi-seat Fighter	191	
Ki-113	Nakajima	Army Experimental Fighter	235	
Ki-114	Tachikawa	Army Experimental Transport	256	

Ki-115	Nakajima	Army Special Attacker Tsurugi	241
Ki-116	Mansyu	Army Experimental Fighter	235
Ki-117	Nakajima	Army Experimental Fighter	235
Ki-118	Mitsubishi	Army Experimental Fighter	Project only
Ki-119	Kawasaki	Army Experimental Light Bomber	141
Ki-120	not known	Army Experimental Transport	Project only
Ki-128	not known	not known	Possibly experimental fighter or conversion of unspecified existing type for Special Attack
Ki-148	Kawasaki	Army Igo-1-B Guided Missile	532
Ki-167	not known	not known	Possibly Mansyu Intermediate Trainer
Ki-174	Kawasaki	Army Experimental Special Attacker	106
Ki-200	Mitsubishi	Army Experimental Rocket-Powered Interceptor Fighter Shusui	405
Ki-201	Nakajima	Army Experimental Fighter Attacker Karyu	488
Ki-202	Rikugun	Army Experimental Rocket-Powered Interceptor Fighter	406
Ki-230	Nakajima	Army Experimental Special Attacker	243

Details of the following have not been traced: Ki-121–127, Ki-129–147, Ki-149–166, Ki-168–173, Ki-175–199 and Ki-203–229

B — Guraida Numbers

Ku-1	Maeda	Army Type 2 Transport Glider	Light transport; limited production
Ku-2	Kayaba	Army Experimental Tailless Glider	
Ku-3	Kayaba	Army Experimental Tailless Glider	
Ku-4	Kayaba	Army Experimental Tailless Light Aeroplane	
Ku-5	Fukuda	Army Two-seat Training Glider	
Ku-6	Maeda	Army Experimental Vehicle Troop Command Glider	
Ku-7	Kokusai	Army Experimental Transport Glider Manazuru	485
Ku-8	Kokusai	Army Type 4 Large-size Transport Glider	484
Ku-9	Fukuda	Army Experimental Transport Glider	
Ku-10	Maeda	Army Special Training Glider	

Ku-11	Nihon Kogata	Army Experimental Transport Glider
Ku-12	Fukuda	Army Two-seat Secondary Training Glider
Ku-13	Yokoi	Army Experimental Shusui Training Glider
Ku-14	Nihon Kogata	Army Training Glider	406

C — Kazaguruma Numbers

Ka-1	Kayaba	Army Model 1 Observation Autogyro	143
Ka-2	Kayaba	Army Model 2 Observation Autogyro	143

D — Sundry Designation Numbers

Igo-1-A	Mitsubishi	Army Experimental Guided Missile	532
Igo-1-B	Kawasaki	Army Guided Missile (Ki-148)	532
Igo-1-C	Tokyo University	Army Experimental Guided Missile	533
Te-Go	Kobe	Army Experimental Observation Machine	Single-engined monoplane; not proceeded with
SS-1	Tachikawa	Army Experimental Twin-engined Research Plane	508–509

E — Type Numbers

Type 87

Army Type 87 Light Bomber	Mitsubishi (2MB1)	Single-engined biplane; obsolete in 1941
Army Type 87 Heavy Bomber	Kawasaki (Dornier Do N)	Japanese version of Do N; obsolete in 1941

Type 88

Army Type 88 Light Bomber	Kawasaki (KDA-2)	Single-engined biplane; obsolete in 1941
Army Type 88 Reconnaissance Plane	Kawasaki (KDA-2)	Single-engined biplane; obsolete in 1941

Type 91

Army Type 91 Fighter	Nakajima	Parasol monoplane; obsolete in 1941

Type 92

Army Type 92 Heavy Bomber	Mitsubishi Ki-20	Japanese version of Junkers K-51; obsolete in 1941
Army Type 92 Fighter	Kawasaki (KDA-5)	Single-engined biplane; obsolete in 1941
Army Type 92 Reconnaissance Plane	Mitsubishi (2MR8)	Single-engined parasol monoplane; obsolete in 1941

Type 93

Army Type 93 Heavy Bomber	Mitsubishi Ki-1	Twin-engined monoplane; obsolete in 1941
Army Type 93 Twin-engined Light Bomber	Mitsubishi Ki-2	Japanese version of Junkers K-37; obsolete in 1941
Army Type 93 Light Bomber	Kawasaki Ki-3	Single-engined biplane; obsolete in 1941

Type 94

Army Type 94 Reconnaissance Plane	Nakajima Ki-4	Single-engined biplane; obsolete in 1941

Type 95

Army Type 95-1 Medium Grade Trainer	Tachikawa Ki-9	*246*
Army Type 95-2 Trainer	Nakajima Ki-6	Japanese-built Fokker Super Universal; obsolete in 1941
Army Type 95-3 Primary Trainer	Tachikawa Ki-17	*248*
Army Type 95 Fighter	Kawasaki Ki-10	*86*

Type 97

Army Type 97 Command Reconnaissance Plane	Mitsubishi Ki-15	*149*
Army Type 97 Heavy Bomber	Mitsubishi Ki-21	*155*
Army Type 97 Fighter	Nakajima Ki-27	*196*
Army Type 97 Light Bomber	Mitsubishi Ki-30	*164*
Army Type 97 Transport	Nakajima Ki-34	*204*

Type 98

Army Type 98 Light Bomber	Kawasaki Ki-32	*90*
Army Type 98 Direct Co-operation Plane	Tachikawa Ki-36	*250*

Type 99

Army Type 99 Twin-engined Light Bomber	Kawasaki Ki-48	*102*
Army Type 99 Special Attack Plane	Kawasaki Ki-48-II KAI	*106*
Army Type 99 Assault Plane	Mitsubishi Ki-51	*178*
Army Type 99 Advanced Trainer	Tachikawa Ki-55	*250*

Type 100

Army Type 100 Command Reconnaissance Plane	Mitsubishi Ki-46	*168*
Army Type 100 Operations Trainer	Mitsubishi Ki-46-II KAI	*173*
Army Type 100 Air Defence Fighter	Mitsubishi Ki-46-III KAI	*174*
Army Type 100 Assault Plane	Mitsubishi Ki-46-IIIb	*174*
Army Type 100 Heavy Bomber	Nakajima Ki-49 Donryu	*223*
Army Type 100 Transport	Mitsubishi Ki-57	*182*

Type 1

Army Type 1 Fighter	Nakajima Ki-43 Hayabusa	*206*
Army Type 1 Advanced Trainer	Tachikawa Ki-54a	*254*
Army Type 1 Operations Trainer	Tachikawa Ki-54b	*254*
Army Type 1 Transport	Tachikawa Ki-54c	*254*
Army Type 1 Freight Transport	Kawasaki Ki-56	*108*
Army Type 1 Transport	Kokusai Ki-59	*145*

Type 2

Army Type 2 Single-seat Fighter	Nakajima Ki-44 Shoki	*215*
Army Type 2 Two-seat Fighter	Kawasaki Ki-45 KAI Toryu	*93*
Army Type 2 Advanced Trainer	Mansyu Ki-79	*486*
Army Type 2 Transport Glider	Maeda Ku-1	Light transport glider; limited production

Type 3

Army Type 3 Fighter	Kawasaki Ki-61 Hien	*112*
Army Type 3 Command Liaison Plane	Kokusai Ki-76	*147*

Type 4

Army Type 4 Heavy Bomber	Mitsubishi Ki-67 Hiryu	*186*
Army Type 4 Special Attack Plane	Mitsubishi Ki-67-I KAI	*190*
Army Type 4 Fighter	Nakajima Ki-84 Hayate	*230*
Army Type 4 Primary Trainer	Kokusai Ki-86	*503*
Army Type 4 Assault Plane	Kawasaki Ki-102b	*134*
Army Type 4 Large-size Transport Glider	Kokusai Ku-8	*484*

Type 5

Army Type 5 Fighter	Kawasaki Ki-100	*129*

Type LO

Army Type LO Transport	Kawasaki and Tachikawa (Licence-built Lockheed 14)	*507*

Type I

Army Type I Heavy Bomber	Fiat B.R.20	*496*

F — Popular Names

DONRYU (Storm Dragon)	Nakajima Ki-49, Army Type 100 Heavy Bomber	*223*
HAYABUSA (Peregrine Falcon)	Nakajima Ki-43, Army Type 1 Fighter	*206*
HAYATE (Gale)	Nakajima Ki-84, Army Type 4 Fighter	*230*
HIEN (Swallow)	Kawasaki Ki-61, Army Type 3 Fighter	*112*
HIRYU (Flying Dragon)	Mitsubishi Ki-67, Army Type 4 Heavy Bomber	*186*

KARYU (Fire Dragon)	Nakajima Ki-201, Army Experimental Fighter Attacker	*488*
MANAZURU (Crane)	Kokusai Ku-7, Army Experimental Transport Glider	*485*
OHTORI (Phoenix)	Kokusai Ki-105, Army Experimental Transport	*485*
SHOKI (Devil-Queller)	Nakajima Ki-44, Army Type 2 Single-seat Fighter	*215*
SHUSUI (Sword Stroke)	Mitsubishi Ki-200, Army Experimental Rocket-Powered Interceptor Fighter	*404*
TORYU (Dragon Killer)	Kawasaki Ki-45 KAI, Army Type 2 Two-seat Fighter	*93*
TSURUGI (Sabre)	Nakajima Ki-115, Army Special Attacker	*241*

Section II: Japanese Navy Aircraft Designation Systems

A — Shi Numbers

6-Shi

Navy Experimental 6-Shi Carrier Two-seat Fighter	Nakajima NAF-1	Single-engined biplane; not proceeded with
Navy Experimental 6-Shi Carrier Bomber	Yokosuka Ku-Sho	Single-engined biplane; not proceeded with
Navy Experimental 6-Shi Carrier Bomber	Nakajima	Single-engined biplane; not proceeded with
Navy Experimental 6-Shi Night Reconnaissance Flying-Boat	Aichi AB-4	Single-engined biplane; not proceeded with
Navy Experimental 6-Shi Carrier Attack Bomber	Nakajima	Single-engined biplane; not proceeded with

7-Shi

Navy Experimental 7-Shi Carrier Fighter	Nakajima	Single-engined parasol monoplane; not proceeded with
Navy Experimental 7-Shi Carrier Fighter	Mitsubishi 1MF10	Single-engined monoplane; not proceeded with
Navy Experimental 7-Shi Carrier Attack Bomber	Aichi AB-8	Single-engined biplane; not proceeded with
Navy Experimental 7-Shi Carrier Attack Bomber	Mitsubishi 3MT10	Single-engined biplane; not proceeded with
Navy Experimental 7-Shi Carrier Attack Bomber	Nakajima Y3B	Single-engined biplane; not proceeded with
Navy Experimental 7-Shi Carrier Attack Bomber	Yokosuka	Single-engined biplane; not proceeded with
Navy Experimental 7-Shi Carrier Bomber	Nakajima N-35 Tokubaku	Single-engined biplane; not proceeded with

Navy Experimental 7-Shi Reconnaissance Seaplane	Aichi AB-6	Unsuccessful competitor to Kawanishi E7K1
Navy Experimental 7-Shi Reconnaissance Seaplane	Kawanishi E7K1	*297*
Navy Experimental 7-Shi Reconnaissance Seaplane	Nakajima	Unsuccessful competitor to Kawanishi E7K1
Navy Experimental 7-Shi Attack Bomber	Hiro G2H1	Twin-engined monoplane; obsolete in 1941

8-Shi

Navy Experimental 8-Shi Carrier Two-seat Fighter	Mitsubishi Ka-8	Single-engined biplane; not proceeded with
Navy Experimental 8-Shi Carrier Two-seat Fighter	Nakajima NAF-2	Single-engined biplane; not proceeded with
Navy Experimental 8-Shi Carrier Bomber	Aichi D1A1	*268*
Navy Experimental 8-Shi Carrier Bomber	Nakajima D2N1	Unsuccessful competitor to Aichi D1A1
Navy Experimental 8-Shi Carrier Bomber	Yokosuka D2Y1	Unsuccessful competitor to Aichi D1A1
Navy Experimental 8-Shi Reconnaissance Plane	Mitsubishi Ka-9	*350*
Navy Experimental 8-Shi Large-size Flying-Boat	Kawanishi Type Q and R	*301*
Navy Experimental 8-Shi Reconnaissance Seaplane	Aichi AM-7	Single-engined monoplane; not proceeded with
Navy Experimental 8-Shi Reconnaissance Seaplane	Aichi E8A1	*408*
Navy Experimental 8-Shi Reconnaissance Seaplane	Kawanishi E8K1	*408*
Navy Experimental 8-Shi Reconnaissance Seaplane	Nakajima E8N1	*408*

9-Shi

Navy Experimental 9-Shi Single-seat Fighter	Mitsubishi A5M1	*342*
Navy Experimental 9-Shi Single-seat Fighter	Nakajima	Unsuccessful competitor to Mitsubishi A5M1
Navy Experimental 9-Shi Carrier Attack Bomber	Mitsubishi Ka-12	Unsuccessful competitor to Yokosuka B4Y1
Navy Experimental 9-Shi Carrier Attack Bomber	Nakajima B4N1	Unsuccessful competitor to Yokosuka B4Y1
Navy Experimental 9-Shi Carrier Attack Bomber	Yokosuka B4Y1	*449*
Navy Experimental 9-Shi Small Reconnaissance Seaplane	Watanabe E9W1	Single-engined biplane; obsolete in 1941
Navy Experimental 9-Shi Night Reconnaissance Seaplane	Aichi E10A1	Single-engined biplane flying-boat; obsolete in 1941
Navy Experimental 9-Shi Night Reconnaissance Seaplane	Kawanishi E10K1	Single-engined biplane flying-boat; obsolete in 1941
Navy Experimental 9-Shi Medium Attack Bomber	Mitsubishi G3M1	*350*
Navy Experimental 9-Shi Large-size Flying-Boat	Kawanishi H6K1	*301*
Navy Experimental 9-Shi Medium Flying-Boat	Yokosuka H5Y1	*495*

10-Shi

Navy Experimental 10-Shi Carrier Attack Bomber	Nakajima B5N1	*411*
Navy Experimental 10-Shi Carrier Attack Bomber	Mitsubishi B5M1	*491*
Navy Experimental 10-Shi Carrier Reconnaissance Plane	Nakajima C3N1	Single-engined monoplane; not proceeded with
Navy Experimental 10-Shi Observation Seaplane	Aichi F1A1	Unsuccessful competitor to Mitsubishi F1M1
Navy Experimental 10-Shi Observation Seaplane	Kawanishi F1K1	Unsuccessful competitor to Mitsubishi F1M1
Navy Experimental 10-Shi Observation Seaplane	Mitsubishi F1M1	*358*

11-Shi

Navy Experimental 11-Shi Carrier Bomber	Aichi D3A1	*271*
Navy Experimental 11-Shi Carrier Bomber	Mitsubishi D3M1	Unsuccessful competitor to Aichi D3A1
Navy Experimental 11-Shi Carrier Bomber	Nakajima D3N1	Unsuccessful competitor to Aichi D3A1
Navy Experimental 11-Shi Night Reconnaissance Seaplane	Aichi E11A1	*489*
Navy Experimental 11-Shi Night Reconnaissance Seaplane	Kawanishi E11K1	Unsuccessful competitor to Aichi E11A1
Navy Experimental 11-Shi Advanced Trainer Seaplane	Kawanishi K6K1	Single-engined biplane; not proceeded with
Navy Experimental 11-Shi Advanced Trainer Seaplane	Mitsubishi K6M1	Single-engined biplane; not proceeded with
Navy Experimental 11-Shi Advanced Trainer Seaplane	Watanabe K6W1	Single-engined biplane; not proceeded with
Navy Experimental 11-Shi Crew Trainer	Mitsubishi K7M1	Twin-engined monoplane; not proceeded with

12-Shi

Navy Experimental 12-Shi Carrier Fighter	Mitsubishi A6M1	*362*
Navy Experimental 12-Shi Two-seat Reconnaissance Seaplane	Aichi E12A1	*277*
Navy Experimental 12-Shi Two-seat Reconnaissance Seaplane	Kawanishi E12K1	*277*
Navy Experimental 12-Shi Two-seat Reconnaissance Seaplane	Nakajima E12N1	*277*
Navy Experimental 12-Shi Three-seat Reconnaissance Seaplane	Aichi E13A1	*277*
Navy Experimental 12-Shi Three-seat Reconnaissance Seaplane	Kawanishi E13K1	*277*

Navy Experimental 12-Shi Small Reconnaissance Seaplane	Watanabe E14W1	*451*
Navy Experimental 12-Shi Small Reconnaissance Seaplane	Yokosuka E14Y1	*451*
Navy Experimental 12-Shi Attack Bomber	Mitsubishi G4M1	*378*
Navy Experimental 12-Shi Special Flying-Boat	Yokosuka H7Y1	Project only
Navy Experimental 12-Shi Primary Trainer Seaplane	Kawanishi K8K1	Single-engined biplane; fifteen built
Navy Experimental 12-Shi Primary Trainer Seaplane	Nihon K8P1	Single-engined biplane; not proceeded with
Navy Experimental 12-Shi Primary Trainer Seaplane	Watanabe K8W1	Single-engined biplane; not proceeded with

13-Shi

Navy Experimental 13-Shi High-speed Reconnaissance Plane	Aichi C4A1	Project only
Navy Experimental 13-Shi Carrier Bomber	Yokosuka D4Y1	*454*
Navy Experimental 13-Shi Attack Bomber	Nakajima G5N1	*423*
Navy Experimental 13-Shi Large-size Flying-Boat	Kawanishi H8K1	*307*
Navy Experimental 13-Shi Training Flying-Boat	Aichi H9A1	*281*
Navy Experimental 13-Shi Three-seat Escort Fighter	Mitsubishi	Project only
Navy Experimental 13-Shi Three-seat Escort Fighter	Nakajima J1N1	*417*
Navy Experimental 13-Shi Small Amphibious Transport Plane	Nihon L7P1	Single-engined monoplane; not proceeded with

14-Shi

Navy Experimental 14-Shi Carrier Attack Bomber	Nakajima B6N1	*429*
Navy Experimental 14-Shi High-speed Reconnaissance Seaplane	Kawanishi E15K1	*314*
Navy Experimental 14-Shi Reconnaissance Seaplane	Aichi AM-22	*284*
Navy Experimental 14-Shi Medium Flying-Boat	Hiro H10H1	Project only
Navy Experimental 14-Shi Interceptor Fighter	Mitsubishi J2M1	*388*
Navy Experimental 14-Shi Primary Trainer	Hitachi	Unsuccessful competitor to Kyushu K9W1
Navy Experimental 14-Shi Primary Trainer	Watanabe	*503*
Navy Experimental 14-Shi Intermediate Trainer	Kyushu K10W1	*506*

15-Shi

Navy Experimental 15-Shi Interceptor Fighter	Mitsubishi	Project only
Navy Experimental 15-Shi Operations Trainer	Kyushu K11W1	330
Navy Experimental 15-Shi Fighter Seaplane	Kawanishi N1K1	317
Navy Experimental 15-Shi Twin-engined Bomber	Yokosuka P1Y1	462
Navy Experimental 15-Shi Training Fighter	Mitsubishi A5M4-K	346

16-Shi

Navy Experimental 16-Shi Fighter Seaplane	Nakajima A6M2-N	426
Navy Experimental 16-Shi Carrier Attack Bomber	Aichi B7A1	288
Navy Experimental 16-Shi Reconnaissance Seaplane	Aichi E16A1	284
Navy Experimental 16-Shi Attack Bomber	Mitsubishi G7M1	Projected twin-engined heavy bomber; not realized

17-Shi

Navy Experimental 17-Shi Ko (A) Type Carrier Fighter	Mitsubishi A7M1	399
Navy Experimental 17-Shi Carrier Reconnaissance Seaplane	Nakajima C6N1	434
Navy Experimental 17-Shi Otsu (B) Type Interceptor Fighter	Kawanishi J3K1	490
Navy Experimental 17-Shi Otsu (B) Type Interceptor Fighter	Mitsubishi J4M1	491
Navy Experimental 17-Shi Otsu (B) Type Interceptor Fighter	Mitsubishi A7M3-J	402
Navy Experimental 17-Shi Attack Bomber	Kawanishi G9K1	Project only
Navy Experimental 17-Shi Special Attack Bomber	Aichi M6A1	291
Navy Experimental 17-Shi Patrol Plane	Kyushu Q1W1	332
Navy Experimental 17-Shi Reconnaissance Plane	Yokosuka R1Y1	472
Navy Experimental 17-Shi Training Fighter	Mitsubishi A6M2-K	397
Navy Experimental 17-Shi Training Glider	Mizuno	Two-seat light glider

18-Shi

Navy Experimental 18-Shi Attack Bomber	Nakajima G8N1	*440*
Navy Experimental 18-Shi Otsu (B) Type Interceptor Fighter	Kawanishi J6K1	*490*
Navy Experimental 18-Shi Otsu (B) Type Interceptor Fighter	Kyushu J7W1	*335*
Navy Experimental 18-Shi Otsu (B) Type Interceptor Fighter	Nakajima J5N1	*492*
Navy Experimental 18-Shi Reconnaissance Plane	Yokosuka R2Y1	*472*
Navy Experimental 18-Shi Hei (C) Type Night Fighter	Aichi S1A1	*295*

19-Shi

Navy Experimental 19-Shi Rocket-Powered Interceptor Fighter	Mitsubishi J8M1	*404*
Navy Experimental 19-Shi Patrol Bomber	Mitsubishi Q2M1	Projected twin-engined ASW patrol bomber

20-Shi

Navy Experimental 20-Shi Ko (A) Type Carrier Fighter	Kawanishi	Project only
Navy Experimental 20-Shi Ko (A) Type Carrier Fighter	Mitsubishi Rifuku	*403*

B — Short Designation System

A — Carrier Fighter

A1N1/A1N2	Nakajima—Navy Type 3 Carrier Fighter	Single-engined biplane; obsolete in 1941
A2N1/A2N3	Nakajima—Navy Type 90 Carrier Fighter	Single-engined biplane; obsolete in 1941
A3N1	Nakajima—Navy Type 90 Training Fighter	Single-engined two-seat biplane; obsolete in 1941
A4N1	Nakajima—Navy Type 95 Carrier Fighter	Single-engined biplane; obsolete in 1941
A5M1/A5M4	Mitsubishi—Navy Type 96 Carrier Fighter	*342*
A5M4-K	Mitsubishi—Navy Type 2 Training Fighter	*346*
A6M1/A6M8	Mitsubishi—Navy Type 0 Carrier Fighter	*362*
A6M2-K/A6M5-K	Mitsubishi—Navy Training Fighter	*397*

A6M2-N	Nakajima—Navy Type 2 Fighter Seaplane	*426*
A7M1/A7M3	Mitsubishi—Navy Experimental 17-Shi Ko (A) Type Carrier Fighter Reppu	*399*
A7M3-J	Mitsubishi—Navy Experimental 17-Shi Otsu (B) Type Interceptor Fighter Reppu Kai	*402*
A7He1	Heinkel—Navy Type He Air Defence Fighter (Heinkel He 112B-0)	*496*
A8V1	Seversky—Navy Type S Two-seat Fighter (Seversky 2PA-B3)	*496–497*
AXB1	Boeing—Navy Experimental Type B Carrier Fighter (Boeing Model 100)	One aircraft tested
AXG1	Canadian Car and Foundry—Navy Experimental Type G Carrier Fighter (Grumman FF-1)	One aircraft tested
AXH1	Hawker—Navy Experimental Type H Carrier Fighter (Hawker Nimrod)	One aircraft tested
AXHe1	Heinkel—Navy Experimental Type He Interceptor Fighter (Heinkel He 100D-0)	Three aircraft tested; projected production in Japan by Hitachi not realized
AXV1	Vought—Navy Experimental Type V Interceptor Fighter (Vought V-143)	One aircraft tested

B — Carrier Attack Bomber

B1M1/B1M3	Mitsubishi—Navy Type 13 Carrier Attack Bomber	Single-engined biplane; obsolete in 1941
B2M1/B2M2	Mitsubishi—Navy Type 89 Carrier Attack Bomber	Single-engined biplane; obsolete in 1941
B3Y1	Yokosuka—Navy Type 92 Carrier Attack Bomber	Single-engined biplane; obsolete in 1941
B4N1	Nakajima—Navy Experimental 9-Shi Carrier Attack Bomber	Unsuccessful competitor to Yokosuka B4Y1
B4Y1	Yokosuka—Navy Type 96 Carrier Attack Bomber	449
B5M1	Mitsubishi—Navy Type 97-2 Carrier Attack Bomber	491
B5N1/B5N2	Nakajima—Navy Type 97-1 and 97-3 Carrier Attack Bomber	411
B6N1/B6N3	Nakajima—Navy Carrier Attack Bomber Tenzan	429
B7A1/B7A3	Aichi—Navy Carrier Attack Bomber Ryusei	288

C — Reconnaissance Plane

C1M1/C1M2	Mitsubishi—Navy Type 10 Carrier Reconnaissance Plane	Single-engined biplane; obsolete in 1941
C2N1/C2N2	Nakajima—Navy Fokker Reconnaissance Plane	Japanese-built Fokker Super Universal; obsolete in 1941
C3N1	Nakajima—Navy Type 97 Carrier Reconnaissance Plane	
C4A1	Aichi—Navy Experimental 13-Shi High-speed Reconnaissance Plane	Single-engined monoplane; not proceeded with
C5M1/C5M2	Mitsubishi—Navy Type 98 Reconnaissance Plane	Project only
		149
C6N1/C6N3	Nakajima—Navy Carrier Reconnaissance Plane Saiun	*434*

D — Carrier Bomber

D1A1	Aichi—Navy Type 94 Carrier Bomber	*268*
D1A2	Aichi—Navy Type 96 Carrier Bomber	*268*
D2N1/D2N3	Nakajima—Navy Experimental 8-Shi Carrier Bomber	Unsuccessful competitor to Aichi D1A1
D2Y1	Yokosuka—Navy Experimental 8-Shi Carrier Bomber	Unsuccessful competitor to Aichi D1A1
D3A1/D3A2	Aichi—Navy Type 99 Carrier Bomber	*271*
D3M1	Mitsubishi—Navy Experimental 11-Shi Carrier Bomber	Unsuccessful competitor to Aichi D3A1
D3N1	Nakajima—Navy Experimental 11-Shi Carrier Bomber	Unsuccessful competitor to Aichi D3A1
D3Y1-K/D3Y2-K	Yokosuka—Navy Training Bomber Myojo	*469*
D4Y1/D4Y5	Yokosuka—Navy Carrier Bomber Suisei	*454*
D4Y1-C/D4Y2-Ca	Yokosuka—Navy Type 2 Carrier Reconnaissance Plane	*454*
D5Y1	Yokosuka—Navy Special Attacker Myojo Kai	*470*
DXD1	Douglas—Navy Experimental Type D Attack Plane (Douglas DB-19)	One aircraft tested
DXHe1	Heinkel—Navy Experimental Type He Attack Plane (Heinkel He 118V4)	One aircraft tested

E — Reconnaissance Seaplane

E1Y1/E1Y3	Yokosuka—Navy Type 14-1 Reconnaissance Seaplane	Single-engined biplane; obsolete in 1941
E2N1/E2N2	Nakajima—Navy Type 15 Reconnaissance Seaplane	Single-engined biplane; obsolete in 1941
E3A1	Aichi—Navy Type 90-1 Reconnaissance Seaplane	Single-engined biplane; obsolete in 1941
E4N1/E4N3	Nakajima—Navy Type 90-2 Reconnaissance Seaplane	Single-engined biplane; obsolete in 1941

E4N2-C	Nakajima—Navy Type 90-2-3 Reconnaissance Plane	Single-engined biplane; obsolete in 1941	
E5K1	Kawanishi—Navy Type 90-3 Reconnaissance Seaplane	Single-engined biplane; obsolete in 1941	
E5Y1	Yokosuka—Navy Experimental Type 14-2 Kai-1 Reconnaissance Seaplane	Single-engined biplane; obsolete in 1941	
E6Y1	Yokosuka—Navy Type 91 Reconnaissance Seaplane	Single-engined monoplane; obsolete in 1941	
E7K1/E7K2	Kawanishi—Navy Type 94 Reconnaissance Seaplane		297
E8A1	Aichi—Navy Experimental 8-Shi Reconnaissance Seaplane	Unsuccessful competitor to Nakajima E8N1	
E8K1	Kawanishi—Navy Experimental 8-Shi Reconnaissance Seaplane	Unsuccessful competitor to Nakajima E8N1	
E8N1/E8N2	Nakajima—Navy Type 95 Reconnaissance Seaplane		408
E9W1	Watanabe—Navy Type 96 Small Reconnaissance Seaplane	Single-engined biplane; obsolete in 1941	
E10A1	Aichi—Navy Type 96 Night Reconnaissance Seaplane	Single-engined biplane flying-boat; obsolete in 1941	
E10K1	Kawanishi—Navy Type 94 Transport Seaplane	Single-engined biplane flying-boat; obsolete in 1941	
E11A1	Aichi—Navy Type 98 Night Reconnaissance Seaplane		489
E11K1	Kawanishi—Navy Type 96 Transport Seaplane	Unsuccessful competitor to Aichi E11A1; three prototypes modified for transport duties	
E12A1	Aichi—Navy Experimental 12-Shi Two-seat Reconnaissance Seaplane		277
E12K1	Kawanishi—Navy Experimental 12-Shi Two-seat Reconnaissance Seaplane		277
E12N1	Nakajima—Navy Experimental 12-Shi Two-seat Reconnaissance Seaplane		277
E13A1	Aichi—Navy Type 0 Reconnaissance Seaplane		277
E13K1	Kawanishi—Navy Experimental 12-Shi Three-seat Reconnaissance Seaplane		277
E14W1	Watanabe—Navy Experimental 12-Shi Small Reconnaissance Seaplane		
E14Y1	Yokosuka—Navy Type 0 Small Reconnaissance Seaplane		451
E15K1	Kawanishi—Navy Type 2 High-speed Reconnaissance Seaplane Shiun		451
			314
E16A1/E16A2	Aichi—Navy Reconnaissance Seaplane Zuiun		284

F — Observation Seaplane

F1A1	Aichi—Navy Experimental 10-Shi Observation Seaplane	Unsuccessful competitor to Mitsubishi F1M1
F1K1	Kawanishi—Navy Experimental 10-Shi Observation Seaplane	Unsuccessful competitor to Mitsubishi F1M1
F1M1/F1M2	Mitsubishi—Navy Type 0 Observation Seaplane	358

G — Attack Bomber

G1M1	Mitsubishi—Navy Type 93 Attack Bomber	Twin-engined biplane; obsolete in 1941
G2H1	Hiro—Navy Type 95 Attack Bomber	Twin-engined monoplane; obsolete in 1941
G3M1/G3M3	Mitsubishi—Navy Type 96 Attack Bomber	350
G4M1/G4M3	Mitsubishi—Navy Type 1 Attack Bomber	378
G5N1/G5N2	Nakajima—Navy Experimental 13-Shi Attack Bomber Shinzan	423
G6M1	Mitsubishi—Navy Type 1 Wingtip Convoy Fighter	380
G6M1-K	Mitsubishi—Navy Type 1 Large Land Trainer	380
G6M1-L2	Mitsubishi—Navy Type 1 Transport	380
G7M1	Mitsubishi—Navy Experimental 16-Shi Attack Bomber Taizan	Projected twin-engined heavy bomber
G8N1/G8N3	Nakajima—Navy Experimental 18-Shi Attack Bomber Renzan	440
G9K1	Kawanishi—Navy Experimental 17-Shi Attack Bomber	Project only
G10N1	Nakajima—Navy Experimental Super Heavy Bomber Fugaku	493

H — Flying-Boat

H1H1/H1H3	Hiro—Navy Type 15 Flying-Boat	Twin-engined biplane; obsolete in 1941
H2H1	Hiro—Navy Type 89 Flying-Boat	Twin-engined biplane; obsolete in 1941
H3H1	Hiro—Navy Type 90-1 Flying-Boat	Three-engined monoplane; obsolete in 1941
H3K1/H3K2	Kawanishi—Navy Type 90-2 Flying-Boat	Three-engined biplane; obsolete in 1941
H4H1/H4H2	Hiro—Navy Type 91 Flying-Boat	Twin-engined monoplane; obsolete in 1941
H5Y1/H5Y2	Yokosuka—Navy Type 99 Flying-Boat	495
H6K1/H6K5	Kawanishi—Navy Type 97 Flying-Boat	301
H6K2-L/H6K4-L	Kawanishi—Navy Type 97 Transport Flying-Boat	304
H7Y1	Yokosuka—Navy Experimental 12-Shi Special Flying-Boat	Project only
H8K1/H8K4	Kawanishi—Navy Type 2 Flying-Boat	307
H8K2-L	Kawanishi—Navy Transport Flying-Boat Seiku	310

H9A1	Aichi—Navy Type 2 Training Flying-Boat	281
H10H1	Hiro—Navy Experimental 14-Shi Medium Flying-Boat	Project only
H11K1-L	Kawanishi—Navy Experimental Large-size Transport Flying-Boat Soku	Projected four-engined transport flying-boat with clamshell loading doors in the nose
HXC1	Consolidated—Navy Experimental Type C Flying-Boat (Consolidated P2Y-1)	One aircraft tested
HXD1	Douglas—Navy Experimental Type D Flying-Boat (Douglas DF)	Two aircraft tested; 496–497

J — Land-based Fighter

J1N1	Nakajima—Navy Experimental 13-Shi Three-seat Fighter	417
J1N1-C/J1N1-R	Nakajima—Navy Type 2 Reconnaissance Plane	418–419
J1N1-S	Nakajima—Navy Night Fighter Gekko	421
J2M1/J2M7	Mitsubishi—Navy Interceptor Fighter-Raiden	388
J3K1	Kawanishi—Navy Experimental 17-Shi Otsu (B) Type Interceptor Fighter	490
J4M1	Mitsubishi—Navy Experimental 17-Shi Otsu (B) Type Interceptor Fighter Senden	491
J5N1	Nakajima—Navy Experimental 18-Shi Otsu (B) Type Interceptor Fighter Tenrai	492
J6K1	Kawanishi—Navy Experimental 18-Shi Otsu (B) Type Interceptor Fighter Jinpu	490
J7W1/J7W2	Kyushu—Navy Experimental 18-Shi Otsu (B) Type Interceptor Fighter Shinden	335
J8M1/J8M2	Mitsubishi—Navy Experimental 19-Shi Rocket-Powered Interceptor Fighter Shusui	404

K — Trainer

K1Y1/K1Y2	Yokosuka—Navy Type 13 Training Seaplane	Single-engined biplane; obsolete in 1941
K2Y1/K2Y2	Yokosuka—Navy Type 3 Primary Trainer	493
K3M1/K3M3	Mitsubishi—Navy Type 90 Operations Trainer	339
K4Y1	Yokosuka—Navy Type 90 Training Seaplane	494
K5Y1/K5Y5	Yokosuka—Navy Type 93 Advanced Trainer	446

K6K1	Kawanishi—Navy Experimental 11-Shi Advanced Trainer Seaplane	Single-engined biplane; not proceeded with
K6M1	Mitsubishi—Navy Experimental 11-Shi Advanced Trainer Seaplane	Single-engined biplane; not proceeded with
K6W1	Watanabe—Navy Experimental 11-Shi Advanced Trainer Seaplane	Single-engined biplane; not proceeded with
K7M1	Mitsubishi—Navy Experimental 11-Shi Crew Trainer	Twin-engined monoplane; not proceeded with
K8K1	Kawanishi—Navy Type 0 Primary Trainer Seaplane	Single-engined biplane; fifteen built
K8P1	Nihon—Navy Experimental 12-Shi Primary Trainer Seaplane	Single-engined biplane; not proceeded with
K8W1	Watanabe—Navy Experimental 12-Shi Primary Trainer Seaplane	Single-engined biplane; not proceeded with
K9W1	Kyushu—Navy Type 2 Primary Trainer Momiji	*503*
K10W1	Kyushu—Navy Type 2 Intermediate Trainer	*506*
K11W1	Kyushu—Navy Operations Trainer Shigariku	*330*
KXA1/KXA2	North American—Navy Experimental Type A Intermediate Trainer (North American NA-16)	*506*
KXBu1	Bücker—Navy Experimental Type Bu Primary Trainer (Bü 131)	*503*
KXC1	Caudron—Navy Experimental Type C Trainer (Caudron C-600)	One aircraft tested
KXHe1	Heinkel—Navy Experimental Type He Trainer (Heinkel He 72)	One aircraft tested
KXJ1	Junkers—Navy Experimental Type J Trainer (Junkers-A 50)	One aircraft tested

L — Transport

L1N1	Nakajima—Navy Type 97 Transport	*204*
L2D1	Douglas—Navy Type D Transport (Douglas DC-3)	*499*
L2D2/L2D5	Douglas—Navy Type 0 Transport	*499*
L3Y1/L3Y2	Yokosuka—Navy Type 96 Transport	*356*
L4M1	Mitsubishi—Navy Type 0 Transport	*183*
L5?	Unidentified transport	No details available
L6?	Unidentified transport	No details available
L7P1	Nihon—Navy Experimental 13-Shi Small Amphibious Transport	Single-engined monoplane; not proceeded with
LXC1	Curtiss Wright—Navy Experimental Type C Amphibious Transport (Curtiss Courtney)	One aircraft tested
LXD1	Douglas—Navy Experimental Type D Transport (DC-4E)	*423*

LXF1	Fairchild Navy Experimental Type F Amphibious Transport (Fairchild A942)	One aircraft tested; *496–497*
LXHe1	Heinkel—Navy Experimental Type He Transport (Heinkel He 70)	One aircraft tested
LXK1	Kinner—Navy Experimental Type K Transport (Kinner Envoy)	One aircraft tested

M — Special Floatplane

M6A1	Aichi—Navy Special Attack Bomber Seiran	*291*
M6A1-K	Aichi—Navy Special Attack Training Bomber Nanzan	*292*

MX — Special Purpose Aircraft

MXJ1	Nihon Kogata—Navy Primary Training Glider Wakakusa	Two-seat glider
MXY1/MXY2	Yokosuka—Navy Experimental Test Plane	Single-engined research aircraft
MXY3	Yokosuka—Navy Experimental Target Glider	Radio-controlled target drone
MXY4	Yokosuka—Navy Type 1 Target Plane	Radio-controlled target drone
MXY5	Yokosuka—Navy Experimental Transport Glider	Assault glider; twelve built
MXY6	Yokosuka—Navy Experimental Ente-type Glider	*335*
MXY7	Yokosuka—Navy Suicide Attacker Ohka	*476*
MXY8	Yokosuka—Navy Experimental Training Glider Akigusa	*405*
MXY9	Yokosuka—Navy Experimental Trainer Shuka	*406*
MXY10	Yokosuka—Navy Bomber Ginga Ground Decoy	Non-flying replica of Yokosuka P1Y1
MXY11	Yokosuka—Navy Type 1 Attack Bomber Ground Decoy	Non-flying replica of Mitsubishi G4M2

N — Fighter Seaplane

N1K1/N1K2	Kawanishi—Navy Fighter Seaplane Kyofu	*317*
N1K1-J	Kawanishi—Navy Interceptor Fighter Shiden	Landplane development of Kyofu; *320*
N1K2-J/N1K5-J	Kawanishi—Navy Interceptor Fighter Shiden Kai	Landplanes; *324*
N1K2-K	Kawanishi—Navy Training Fighter Shiden Kai Rensen	Landplane; *325*

P — Bomber

P1Y1/P1Y6	Yokosuka—Navy Bomber Ginga	*462*
P1Y1-S	Yokosuka—Navy Night Fighter Byakko	*465*
P1Y2-S	Yokosuka—Navy Night Fighter Kyokko	*465*

Q — Patrol Plane

Q1W1/Q1W2	Kyushu—Navy Patrol Plane Tokai	332
Q2M1	Mitsubishi—Navy Experimental 19-Shi Patrol Plane Taiyo	Projected twin-engined ASW patrol bomber
Q3W1	Kyushu—Navy Patrol Plane Nankai	332

R — Land-based Reconnaissance

R1Y1	Yokosuka—Navy Experimental 17-Shi Reconnaissance Plane Seiun	472
R2Y1/R2Y2	Yokosuka—Navy Experimental 18-Shi Reconnaissance Plane Keiun	472

S — Night Fighter

S1A1	Aichi—Navy Experimental 18-Shi Hei (C) Type Night Fighter Denko	295

Note: Modifications of service aircraft to fit them for different missions received the symbol letter of their new use. Most of these modifications were the responsibility of field units and/or Navy Arsenals. Aircraft which were so modified are numerous, e.g. B5N2-K, G3M1-L, etc., and no attempt has been made to list them in this index. Only similar modifications effected at the time of original manufacture (e.g. D4Y1-C) or later on a large scale basis (A5M4-K) have been recorded here.

C — Type Numbers

Type 89

Navy Type 89 Carrier Attack Bomber	Mitsubishi B2M1/B2M2
Navy Type 89 Flying-Boat	Hiro H2H1

Single-engined biplane; obsolete in 1941
Twin-engined biplane; obsolete in 1941

Type 90

Navy Type 90 Carrier Fighter	Nakajima A2N1/A2N3
Navy Type 90 Training Fighter	Nakajima A3N1
Navy Type 90-1 Reconnaissance Seaplane	Aichi E3A1

Single-engined biplane; obsolete in 1941
Single-engined two-seat biplane; obsolete in 1941
Single-engined biplane; obsolete in 1941

Navy Type 90-2 Reconnaissance Seaplane	Nakajima E4N1/E4N3	Single-engined biplane; obsolete in 1941
Navy Type 90-3 Reconnaissance Seaplane	Yokosuka E5Y1	Single-engined biplane; obsolete in 1941
	Kawanishi E5K1	Single-engined biplane; obsolete in 1941
Navy Type 90-1 Flying-Boat	Hiro H3H1	Three-engined monoplane; obsolete in 1941
Navy Type 90-2 Flying-Boat	Kawanishi H3K1/H3K2	Three-engined biplane; obsolete in 1941
Navy Type 90 Operations Trainer	Mitsubishi K3M1/K3M3	339
Navy Type 90 Training Seaplane	Yokosuka K4Y1	494

Type 91

Navy Type 91 Advanced Trainer	Yokosuka	446
Navy Type 91 Reconnaissance Seaplane	Yokosuka E6Y1	Single-engined monoplane; obsolete in 1941
Navy Type 91 Flying-Boat	Hiro H4H1/H4H2	Twin-engined monoplane; obsolete in 1941

Type 92

Navy Type 92 Carrier Attack Bomber	Yokosuka B3Y1	Single-engined biplane; obsolete in 1941

Type 93

Navy Type 93 Attack Bomber	Mitsubishi G1M1	Twin-engined biplane; obsolete in 1941
Navy Type 93 Advanced Trainer	Yokosuka K5Y1/K5Y5	446

Type 94

Navy Type 94 Carrier Bomber	Aichi D1A1	268
Navy Type 94 Reconnaissance Seaplane	Kawanishi E7K1/E7K2	297
Navy Type 94 Transport Seaplane	Kawanishi E10K1	Single-engined biplane flying-boat; obsolete in 1941

Type 95

Navy Type 95 Carrier Fighter	Nakajima A4N1	Single-engined biplane; obsolete in 1941
Navy Type 95 Reconnaissance Seaplane	Nakajima E8N1	408
Navy Type 95 Attack Bomber	Hiro G2H1	Twin-engined monoplane; obsolete in 1941

Type 96

Navy Type 96 Carrier Fighter	Mitsubishi A5M1/A5M4	*342*
Navy Type 96 Carrier Attack Bomber	Yokosuka B4Y1	*449*
Navy Type 96 Carrier Bomber	Aichi D1A2	*268*
Navy Type 96 Small Reconnaissance Seaplane	Watanabe E9W1	Single-engined biplane; obsolete in 1941
Navy Type 96 Night Reconnaissance Seaplane	Aichi E10A1	Single-engined biplane flying-boat; obsolete in 1941
Navy Type 96 Transport Seaplane	Kawanishi E11K1	Unsuccessful competitor to Aichi E11A1; three prototypes modified for transport
Navy Type 96 Attack Bomber	Mitsubishi G3M1/G3M3	*350*
Navy Type 96 Transport	Yokosuka L3Y1/L3Y2	*356*

Type 97

Navy Type 97-1 and 97-3 Carrier Attack Bomber	Nakajima B5N1/B5N2	*411*
Navy Type 97-2 Carrier Attack Bomber	Mitsubishi B5M1	*491*
Navy Type 97 Carrier Reconnaissance Plane	Nakajima C3N1	Single-engined monoplane; not proceeded with
Navy Type 97 Flying-Boat	Kawanishi H6K1/H6K5	*301*
Navy Type 97 Transport Flying-Boat	Kawanishi H6K2-L/H6K4-L	*304*
Navy Type 97 Transport	Nakajima L1N1	*204*

Type 98

Navy Type 98 Reconnaissance Plane	Mitsubishi C5M1/C5M2	*149*
Navy Type 98 Night Reconnaissance Seaplane	Aichi E11A1	*489*

Type 99

Navy Type 99 Carrier Bomber	Aichi D3A1/D3A2	*271*
Navy Type 99 Flying-Boat	Yokosuka H5Y1/H5Y2	*495*

Type 0

Navy Type 0 Carrier Fighter	Mitsubishi A6M1/A6M8	*362*
Navy Type 0 Reconnaissance Seaplane	Aichi E13A1	*277*

Navy Type 0 Small Reconnaissance Seaplane	Yokosuka E14Y1	*451*
Navy Type 0 Observation Seaplane	Mitsubishi F1M1/F1M2	*358*
Navy Type 0 Primary Trainer Seaplane	Kawanishi K8K1	Single-engined biplane; fifteen built
Navy Type 0 Transport	Douglas L2D1/L2D5	*499*
Navy Type 0 Transport	Mitsubishi L4M1	*183*

Type 1

Navy Type 1 Attack Bomber	Mitsubishi G4M1/G4M3	*378*
Navy Type 1 Wingtip Convoy Fighter	Mitsubishi G6M1	*380*
Navy Type 1 Large Land Trainer	Mitsubishi G6M1-K	*380*
Navy Type 1 Transport	Mitsubishi G6M1-L2	*380*
Navy Type 1 Target Plane	Yokosuka MXY4	Radio-controlled target drone

Type 2

Navy Type 2 Training Fighter	Mitsubishi A5M4-K	*346*
Navy Type 2 Fighter Seaplane	Nakajima A6M2-N	*426*
Navy Type 2 Carrier Reconnaissance Plane	Yokosuka D4Y1-C/D4Y2-Ca	*454*
Navy Type 2 High-speed Reconnaissance Seaplane	Kawanishi E15K1	*314*
Navy Type 2 Flying-Boat	Kawanishi H8K1/H8K4	*307*
Navy Type 2 Transport Flying-Boat	Kawanishi H8K2-L	*310*
Navy Type 2 Training Flying-Boat	Aichi H9A1	*281*
Navy Type 2 Reconnaissance Plane	Nakajima J1N1-C/J1N1-R	*417*
Navy Type 2 Primary Trainer	Kyushu K9W1	*503*
Navy Type 2 Intermediate Trainer	Kyushu K10W1	*506*

Foreign Aircraft

Navy Experimental Type A Intermediate Trainer	North American KXA1/KXA2 (NA-16-4R and NA-16-4RW)	*506*
Navy Experimental Type B Carrier Fighter	Boeing AXB1 (Model 100)	One aircraft tested
Navy Experimental Type Bu Primary Trainer	Bücker KXBu1 (Bü 131)	*503*
Navy Experimental Type C Flying-Boat	Consolidated HXC1 (P2Y-1)	One aircraft tested

Navy Experimental Type C Trainer	Caudron KXC1 (C-600)	One aircraft tested
Navy Experimental Type C Amphibious Transport	Curtiss Wright LXC1 (Curtiss Courtney)	One aircraft tested
Navy Experimental Type D Attack Aircraft	Douglas DXD1 (DB-19)	One aircraft tested
Navy Experimental Type D Flying-Boat	Douglas HXD1/HXD2 (DF)	Two aircraft tested; *496–497*
Navy Experimental Type D Transport	Douglas LXD1 (DC-4E)	*423*
Navy Experimental Type F Amphibious Transport	Fairchild LXF1 (A942)	One aircraft tested; *496–497*
Navy Experimental Type G Carrier Fighter	Grumman AXG1 (FF-1)	One aircraft tested
Navy Experimental Type H Carrier Fighter	Hawker AXH1 (Nimrod)	One aircraft tested
Navy Experimental Type He Interceptor Fighter	Heinkel AXHe1 (He 100D-0)	Three aircraft tested
Navy Experimental Type He Attack Aircraft	Heinkel DXHe1 (He 118V4)	One aircraft tested
Navy Experimental Type He Trainer	Heinkel KXHe1 (He 72)	One aircraft tested
Navy Experimental Type He Transport	Heinkel LXHe1 (He 70)	One aircraft tested
Navy Experimental Type K Transport	Kinner LXK1 (Envoy)	One aircraft tested
Navy Experimental Type V Interceptor Fighter	Vought AXV1 (V-143)	One aircraft tested
Navy Type He Air Defence Fighter	Heinkel A7He1 (He 112B-0)	*496*
Navy Type S Two-seat Fighter	Seversky A8V1 (2PA-B3)	*496–497*

D — Popular Names

Blossom — Special Attack (Suicide) Plane

BAIKA (Plum Blossom)	Kawanishi, Navy Experimental Special Attacker	*490*
KIKKA (Orange Blossom)	Nakajima, Navy Experimental Special Attacker	*443*
OHKA (Cherry Blossom)	Yokosuka MXY7, Navy Suicide Attacker	*476*
TOKA (Wistaria)	Showa, Navy Experimental Special Attacker	*243*

Cloud — Reconnaissance Plane and Seaplane

KEIUN (Beautiful Cloud)	Yokosuka R2Y1/R2Y2, Navy Experimental 18-Shi Reconnaissance Plane	*472*
RAIUN (Thunder Cloud)	Aichi E13A1, Navy Type 0 Reconnaissance Seaplane (name not confirmed)	*277*

SAIUN (Painted Cloud)	Nakajima C6N1/C6N3, Navy Carrier Reconnaissance Plane	*434*
SEIUN (Blue Cloud)	Yokosuka R1Y1, Navy Experimental 17-Shi Reconnaissance Plane	*472*
SHIUN (Violet Cloud)	Kawanishi E15K1, Navy Type 2 High-speed Reconnaissance Seaplane	*314*
ZUIUN (Auspicious Cloud)	Aichi E16A1/E16A2, Navy Reconnaissance Seaplane	*284*

Grass or Tree — Trainer

AKIGUSA (Autumn Grass)	Yokosuka MXY8, Navy Experimental Glider	*405*
MOMIJI (Maple)	Kyushu K9W1, Navy Type 2 Primary Trainer	*503*
SHIRAGIKU (White Chrysanthemum)	Kyushu K11W1, Navy Operations Trainer	*330*
WAKAKUSA (Young Grass)	Nihon Kogata MXJ1, Navy Primary Training Glider	
WAKAZAKURA (Young Cherry)	Yokosuka, Navy Experimental Special Attack Trainer Ohka Model 43 K-1 KAI	*481*

Light — Night Fighter

BYAKKO (White Light)	Yokosuka P1Y1-S, Navy Night Fighter	*465*
DENKO (Bolt of Light)	Aichi S1A1, Navy Experimental 18-Shi Hei (C) Type Night Fighter	*295*
GEKKO (Moonlight)	Nakajima J1N1-S, Navy Night Fighter	*421*
KYOKKO (Aurora)	Yokosuka P1Y2-S, Navy Night Fighter	*465*

Mountain — Attack Plane

FUGAKU (Mount Fuji)	Nakajima G10N1, Navy Super Heavy Bomber	*493*
NANZAN (Southern Mountain)	Aichi M6A1-K, Navy Experimental 17-Shi Training Special Attack Bomber	*292*
RENZAN (Mountain Range)	Nakajima G8N1/G8N3, Navy Experimental 18-Shi Attack Bomber	*440*
SEIRAN (Mountain Haze)	Aichi M6A1, Navy Experimental 17-Shi Special Attack Bomber	*291*

SHINZAN (Mountain Recess)	Nakajima G5N1/G5N2, Navy Experimental 13-Shi Attack Bomber	423
TAIZAN (Great Mountain)	Mitsubishi G7M1, Navy Experimental 16-Shi Attack Bomber	Projected twin-engined heavy bomber; not realized
TENZAN (Heavenly Mountain)	Nakajima B6N1/B6N3, Navy Carrier Attack Bomber	429
TOZAN (Eastern Mountain)	Mitsubishi, Navy Experimental Attack Plane	Project only

Sea — Land-based Patrol Plane

NANKAI (South Sea)	Kyushu Q3W1, Navy Patrol Plane	332
TAIYO (Ocean)	Mitsubishi Q2M1, Navy Experimental 19-Shi Patrol Bomber	Projected twin-engined ASW patrol bomber
TOKAI (Eastern Sea)	Kyushu Q1W1/Q1W2, Navy Patrol Plane	332

Sky — Transport

SEIKU (Clear Sky)	Kawanishi H8K2-L, Navy Type 2 Transport Flying-Boat	310
SOKU (Blue Sky)	Kawanishi H11K1-L, Navy Experimental Large Transport Flying-Boat	Projected four-engined transport flying-boat with clamshell loading doors in the nose

Star — Bomber

GINGA (Milky Way)	Yokosuka P1Y1/P1Y6, Navy Bomber	462
MOKUSEI (Jupiter)	Aichi, Navy Experimental Carrier Bomber	291
MYOJO (Venus)	Yokosuka D3Y1-K/D3Y2-K, Navy Experimental Training Bomber	469
MYOJO KAI (Venus Modified)	Yokosuka D5Y1, Navy Special Attacker	470
RYUSEI (Shooting Star)	Aichi B7A1/B7A3, Navy Carrier Attack Bomber	288
SUISEI (Comet)	Yokosuka D4Y1/D4Y5, Navy Carrier Bomber	454

Thunder and Lightning — Land-based Interceptor Fighter

JINPU (Squall)	Kawanishi J6K1, Navy Experimental 18-Shi Otsu (B) Type Interceptor Fighter	490
RAIDEN (Thunderbolt)	Mitsubishi J2M1/J2M7, Navy Interceptor Fighter	388

SENDEN (Flashing Lightning)	Mitsubishi J4M1, Navy Experimental 17-Shi Otsu (B) Type Interceptor Fighter	491
SHIDEN (Violet Lightning)	Kawanishi N1K1-J, Navy Interceptor Fighter	320
SHIDEN KAI (Violet Lightning Modified)	Kawanishi N1K2-J/N1K5-J, Navy Interceptor Fighter	324
SHINDEN (Magnificent Lightning)	Kyushu J7W1, Navy Experimental 18-Shi Otsu (B) Type Interceptor Fighter	335
TENRAI (Heavenly Thunder)	Nakajima J5N1, Navy Experimental 18-Shi Otsu (B) Type Interceptor Fighter	492

Wind — Carrier Fighter and Fighter Seaplane

KYOFU (Mighty Wind)	Kawanishi N1K1/N1K2, Navy Fighter Seaplane	317
REPPU (Hurricane)	Mitsubishi A7M1/A7M3, Navy Experimental 17-Shi Ko (A) Type Carrier Fighter	399
REPPU KAI (Hurricane Modified)	Mitsubishi A7M3-J, Navy Experimental 17-Shi Otsu (B) Type Interceptor Fighter	402
RIFUKU (Land Wind)	Mitsubishi, Navy Experimental 20-Shi Ko (A) Type Carrier Fighter	403

Miscellaneous and Unofficial Names

CHIDORI II (Plover II)	Tokyo Gasu Denki LXG1, Navy Light Transport	
CHIKARA (Strength)	Yokosuka, Navy Special Training Glider	Impressed single-engined biplane
FUNRYU (Raging Dragon)	Yokosuka, Air-to-surface (Funryu 1), and Surface-to-air (Funryu 2, 3 and 4)	Under development at war's end
HAMAKI (Cigar)	Mitsubishi G4M1/G4M3, Navy Type 1 Attack Bomber (Unofficial nickname)	533–534
HIKARI 6-2 (Ray of Light 6-2)	Fukuda, Navy Two-seat Training Glider	378
KIRIGAMINE (Summit in the Mist)	Nihon Kogata K-14, Navy Primary Training Glider	High-performance sailplane
SHINRYU (Divine Dragon)	Mizumo, Navy Special Attack Glider	Two-seat glider trainer
SHUKA (Autumn Fire)	Yokosuka MXY9, Navy Experimental Trainer	Explosive-carrying
SHUSUI (Sword Stroke)	Mitsuoishi J8M1/J8M2, Navy Experimental 19-Shi Rocket-Powered Interceptor Fighter	406
		404

Note: Names such as Reisen or Reisui are often confused with popular names. Actually they were contractions of Type numbers and duty descriptions, such as:

REISEN = REI SENTOKI or Zero Fighter: Mitsubishi A6M2/A6M8, Navy Type 0 Carrier Fighter
REIKAN = Zero Observation: Mitsubishi F1M2, Navy Type 0 Observation Seaplane
REISUI = Zero Reconnaissance: Aichi E13A1, Navy Type 0 Reconnaissance Seaplane

E — Service Aeroplane Development Programme (SADP) Numbers

K-10	Kawanishi E15K1, Navy Experimental 14-Shi High-speed Reconnaissance Seaplane	*314*
K-20	Kawanishi N1K1, Navy Experimental 15-Shi Fighter Seaplane	*317*
K-30	Kawanishi H8K2-L, Navy Experimental Transport Flying-Boat	*310*
K-60	Kawanishi, Navy Experimental Large Flying-Boat	Projected four-engined flying-boat; not realized
K-90	Kawanishi J3K1, Navy Experimental 17-Shi Otsu (B) Type Interceptor Fighter	*490*
K-100	Kawanishi KX-1, Navy Experimental 17-Shi Attack Bomber	Projected twin-engined light bomber; not realized
M-20	Mitsubishi J2M1, Navy Experimental 14-Shi Interceptor Fighter	*388*
M-50	Mitsubishi A7M1, Navy Experimental 17-Shi Ko (A) Type Carrier Fighter	*399*
M-60	Mitsubishi G7M1, Navy Experimental 16-Shi Attack Bomber	Projected twin-engined heavy bomber; not realized
M-70	Mitsubishi J4M1, Navy Experimental 17-Shi Otsu (B) Type Interceptor Fighter	*491*
N-10	Nakajima B6N1, Navy Experimental 14-Shi Carrier Attack Bomber	*429*
N-20	Nakajima J5N1, Navy Experimental 18-Shi Otsu (B) Type Interceptor Fighter	*492*
N-40	Nakajima G8N1, Navy Experimental 18-Shi Attack Bomber	*440*
N-50	Nakajima C6N1, Navy Experimental 17-Shi Carrier Reconnaissance Plane	*434*
Y-20	Yokosuka P1Y1, Navy Experimental 15-Shi Twin-engined Bomber	*462*
Y-30	Yokosuka R1Y1, Navy Experimental 17-Shi Reconnaissance Plane	*472*
Y-40	Yokosuka R2Y1, Navy Experimental 18-Shi Reconnaissance Plane	*472*
Y-50	Yokosuka D3Y1-K, Navy Experimental Training Bomber	*469*

Section III: Allied Code Name System

Code	Aircraft	Page	Notes
ABDUL	Nakajima Ki-27, Army Type 97 Fighter (duplication for NATE)	196	
ADAM	Nakajima SKT-97, Navy Type 97 Fighter Seaplane		Fictional type
ALF	Kawanishi E7K, Navy Type 94 Reconnaissance Seaplane	297	
ANN	Mitsubishi Ki-30, Army Type 97 Light Bomber	164	
BABS	Mitsubishi Ki-15, Army Type 97 Command Reconnaissance Plane	149	
	Mitsubishi C5M, Navy Type 98 Reconnaissance Plane	149	
BAKA	Yokosuka MXY7, Navy Special Attacker Ohka	476	
BELLE	Kawanishi H3K1, Navy Type 90-2 Flying-Boat		Three-engined biplane; obsolete in 1941
BEN	Nagoya-Sento KI-001, Navy Carrier Fighter		Fictional type
BESS	Heinkel He 111		Erroneously believed to be licence-built by Aichi as a Type 98 Medium Bomber
BETTY	Mitsubishi G4M1/G4M3, Navy Type 1 Attack Bomber	378	
	Mitsubishi G6M1, Navy Type 1 Wingtip Convoy Fighter	380	
	Mitsubishi G6M1-K, Navy Type 1 Large Land Trainer	380	
	Mitsubishi G6M1-L2, Navy Type 1 Transport	380	
	Aichi, Navy Type 97 Reconnaissance Seaplane		Fictional type
BOB	Kawasaki Ki-28, Army Experimental Fighter		Erroneously believed to be in production as an Army Type 97 Fighter
BUZZARD	Kokusai Ku-7, Army Experimental Transport Glider Manazuru	485	
CEDAR	Tachikawa Ki-17, Army Type 95-3 Primary Trainer	248	
CHERRY	Yokosuka H5Y, Navy Type 99 Flying-Boat	495	
CLARA	Tachikawa Ki-70, Army Experimental Command Reconnaissance Plane	257	
CLAUDE	Mitsubishi A5M, Navy Type 96 Carrier Fighter	342	
CYPRESS	Kyushu K9W, Navy Type 2 Primary Trainer Momiji	503	
	Kokusai Ki-86, Army Type 4 Primary Trainer	503	
DAVE	Nakajima E8N, Navy Type 95 Reconnaissance Seaplane	408	
DICK	Seversky A8V1, Navy Type S Two-seat Fighter	496–497	
DINAH	Mitsubishi Ki-46, Army Type 100 Command Reconnaissance Plane	168	
DOC	Messerschmitt Bf 110		Erroneously believed used by JNAF
DORIS	Mitsubishi B-97 Darai Medium Bomber		Fictional type

566

Code	Aircraft	Page
DOT	Yokosuka D4Y, Navy Carrier Bomber Suisei (Duplication for JUDY)	454
EDNA	Mansyu Ki-71, Army Experimental Tactical Reconnaissance Plane	180
EMILY	Kawanishi H8K, Navy Type 2 Flying-Boat	307
EVA (EVE)	Mitsubishi Ohtori, Civil Long-range Communication Plane	Erroneously believed to be a bomber
FRANCES	Yokosuka P1Y, Navy Bomber Ginga	462
	Yokosuka P1Y1-S, Navy Night Fighter Byakko	465
	Yokosuka P1Y2-S, Navy Night Fighter Kyokko	465
FRANK	Mitsubishi TK-4, Army Type 0 Special Twin-engined Fighter	Fictional type also called HARRY
	Nakajima Ki-84, Army Type 4 Fighter Hayate	Second allocation of name; 230
FRED	Focke-Wulf Fw 190A-5	Erroneously believed used by JAAF
GANDER	Kokusai Ku-8, Army Type 4 Large Transport Glider (formerly GOOSE)	484
GEORGE	Kawanishi N1K1-J/N1K5-J, Navy Interceptor Fighter Shiden and Shiden Kai	320
GLEN	Yokosuka E14Y, Navy Type 0 Small Reconnaissance Seaplane	451
GOOSE	Kokusai Ku-8, Army Type 4 Large Transport Glider (later GANDER)	484
GRACE	Aichi B7A, Navy Carrier Attack Bomber Ryusei	288
GUS	Nakajima AT-27, Twin-engined Fighter	Fictional type
GWEN	Mitsubishi Ki-21-IIb, Army Type 97 Heavy Bomber Model 2B (later SALLY III)	160
HAMP	Mitsubishi A6M3, Navy Type 0 Carrier Fighter Model 32 (this aircraft was first coded HAP, then HAMP, and finally ZEKE 32)	
HANK	Aichi E10A, Navy Type 96 Night Reconnaissance Seaplane	369
HAP	See HAMP	
HARRY	Mitsubishi TK-4, Type 0 Special Twin-engined Fighter	Fictional type, originally coded FRANK
HELEN	Nakajima Ki-49, Army Type 100 Heavy Bomber Donryu	223
HICKORY	Tachikawa Ki-54, Army Type 1 Advanced Trainer, Operations Trainer and Transport	
IDA	Tachikawa Ki-36, Army Type 98 Direct Co-operation Plane	254
	Tachikawa Ki-55, Army Type 99 Advanced Trainer	250
IONE	Aichi AI-104, Navy Type 98 Reconnaissance Seaplane	252
IRENE	Junkers-Ju 87A	Single-engined biplane flying-boat; obsolete in 1941
IRVING	Nakajima J1N1-C and -R, Navy Type 2 Reconnaissance Plane	418–420
	Nakajima J1N1-S, Navy Night Fighter Gekko	421

Code	Aircraft	Page
JACK	Mitsubishi J2M, Navy Interceptor Fighter Raiden	388
JAKE	Aichi E13A, Navy Type 0 Reconnaissance Seaplane	277
JANE	Mitsubishi Ki-21, Army Type 97 Heavy Bomber (later changed to SALLY)	155
JANICE	Junkers-Ju 88A-5	Erroneously believed used by JAAF
JEAN	Yokosuka B4Y, Navy Type 96 Carrier Attack Bomber	449
JERRY	Heinkel A7He1, Navy Type He Air Defence Fighter (Heinkel He 112B-0)	496
JILL	Nakajima B6N, Navy Carrier Attack Bomber Tenzan	429
JIM	Nakajima Ki-43, Army Type 1 Fighter Hayabusa (duplication for OSCAR)	206
JOE	TK-19, Single-seat Fighter	Fictional type
JOYCE	Misidentified HICKORY believed to be a Type 1 Light Bomber	254
JUDY	{Yokosuka D4Y1-C/D4Y2-Ca, Navy Type 2 Carrier Reconnaissance Plane	454
	{Yokosuka D4Y, Navy Carrier Bomber Suisei	454
JULIA	Misidentified LILY believed to be a Type 97 Heavy Bomber	102
JUNE	Misidentified JAKE believed to be a floatplane version of VAL	277
KATE	Nakajima B5N, Navy Type 97 Carrier Attack Bomber	411
KATE 61	Mitsubishi B5M, Navy Type 97 Carrier Attack Bomber (formerly MABEL)	491
LAURA	Aichi E11A, Navy Type 98 Night Reconnaissance Seaplane	489
LILY	Kawasaki Ki-48, Army Type 99 Twin-engined Light Bomber	102
LIZ	Nakajima G5N, Navy Experimental 13-Shi Attack Bomber Shinzan	423
LORNA	Kyushu Q1W, Navy Patrol Plane Tokai	332
LOISE/LOUISE	Mitsubishi Ki-2, Army Type 93 Twin-engined Light Bomber	56
LUKE	Mitsubishi J4M, Navy Experimental 17-Shi Otsu (B) Type Interceptor Fighter Senden	491
MABEL	Mitsubishi B5M, Navy Type 97 Carrier Attack Bomber (later KATE 61)	491
MARY	Kawasaki Ki-32, Army Type 98 Light Bomber	90
MAVIS	Kawanishi H6K, Navy Type 97 Flying-Boat	301
MIKE	Messerschmitt Bf 109E	Erroneously believed used by JAAF; 498
MILLIE	Vultee V-11GB	Erroneously believed to be built by Showa as a Type 98 Light Bomber
MYRT	Nakajima C6N, Navy Carrier Reconnaissance Plane Saiun	434
NATE	Nakajima Ki-27, Army Type 97 Fighter	196

Code	Aircraft	Page
NELL	{ Mitsubishi G3M, Navy Type 96 Attack Bomber	350
	{ Yokosuka L3Y, Navy Type 96 Transport	356
NICK	Kawasaki Ki-45 KAI, Army Type 2 Two-seat Fighter Toryu	93
NORM	Kawanishi E15K, Navy Type 2 High-speed Reconnaissance Seaplane Shiun	314
NORMA	Misidentified BABS believed to be a Type 97 Light Bomber	149
OAK	Kyushu K10W, Navy Type 2 Intermediate Trainer	506
OMAR	Suzukaze 20, Twin-engined Fighter	Fictional type
OSCAR	Nakajima Ki-43, Army Type 1 Fighter Hayabusa	Known for a time in China–Burma–India theatre as JIM; 206
PAT	Tachikawa Ki-74 (initially reported as being a fighter aircraft)	259
PATSY	Tachikawa Ki-74, Army Experimental Long-range Bomber	259
PAUL	Aichi E16A, Navy Reconnaissance Seaplane Zuiun	284
PEGGY	Mitsubishi Ki-67, Army Type 4 Heavy Bomber Hiryu	186
PERRY	Kawasaki Ki-10, Army Type 95 Fighter	86
PETE	Mitsubishi F1M, Navy Type 0 Observation Seaplane	358
PINE	Mitsubishi K3M, Navy Type 90 Crew Trainer	339
RANDY	Kawasaki Ki-102b, Army Type 4 Assault Plane	134
RAY	Misidentified ZEKE believed to be a Mitsubishi Type 1 Fighter	362
REX	Kawanishi N1K, Navy Fighter Seaplane Kyofu	317
RITA	Nakajima G8N, Navy Experimental 18-Shi Attack Bomber Renzan	440
ROB	Kawasaki Ki-64, Army Experimental High-speed Fighter	121
RUFE	Nakajima A6M2-N, Navy Type 2 Fighter Seaplane	426
RUTH	Fiat B.R.20, Army Type I Heavy Bomber	496
SALLY	Mitsubishi Ki-21, Army Type 97 Heavy Bomber (formerly JANE)	155
SAM	Mitsubishi A7M, Navy Experimental 17-Shi Ko (A) Type Carrier Fighter Reppu	399
SANDY	Mitsubishi A5M, Navy Type 96 Carrier Fighter (duplication of CLAUDE)	342
SLIM	Watanabe E9W, Navy Type 96 Reconnaissance Seaplane	Single-engined biplane; obsolete in 1941
SONIA	Mitsubishi Ki-51, Army Type 99 Assault Plane	178
SPRUCE	Tachikawa Ki-9, Army Type 95-1 Medium Grade Trainer	246
STELLA	Kokusai Ki-76, Army Type 3 Command Liaison Plane	147

569

STEVE	Mitsubishi Ki-73, Army Experimental Fighter	192
SUSIE	Aichi D1A1, Navy Type 94 Carrier Bomber	268
	Aichi D1A2, Navy Type 96 Carrier Bomber	268
TABBY	Douglas L2D, Navy Type 0 Transport	499
TESS	Douglas DC-2	498
THALIA	Kawasaki Ki-56, Army Type 1 Freight Transport	108
THELMA	Lockheed 14, Army Type LO Transport	507
THERESA	Kokusai Ki-59, Army Type 1 Transport	145
THORA	Nakajima Ki-34, Army Type 97 Transport	204
	Nakajima L1N, Navy Type 97 Transport	204
TINA	Mitsubishi Ki-33, Army Type 96 Transport (misidentified Yokosuka L3Y)	356
TILLIE	Yokosuka H7Y, Navy Experimental 12-Shi Flying-Boat	Project only
TOBY	Lockheed 14 (commercial version)	507
TOJO	Nakajima Ki-44, Army Type 2 Single-seat Fighter Shoki	215
TONY	Kawasaki Ki-61, Army Type 3 Fighter Hien	112
TOPSY	Mitsubishi Ki-57, Army Type 100 Transport	182
	Mitsubishi L4M, Navy Type 0 Transport	183
TRIXIE	Junkers-Ju 52/3m	Erroneously believed used by JAAF
TRUDY	Focke-Wulf Fw 200	Erroneously believed used by JNAF
VAL	Aichi D3A, Navy Type 99 Carrier Bomber	271
WILLOW	Yokosuka K5Y, Navy Type 95 Intermediate Trainer	446
ZEKE	Mitsubishi A6M, Navy Type 0 Carrier Fighter	362